SharePoint Online from Scratch

Peter and Kate Kalmström

Copyright © 2022 Peter Kalmström

All rights reserved

ISBN: 9798408067589

SHAREPOINT ONLINE FROM SCRATCH

Welcome to *SharePoint Online from Scratch*! This book is intended for SharePoint administrators, content creators and other power users. In my work as a SharePoint consultant and trainer for IT professionals, I have come to understand what areas are the most important to SharePoint power users. This book focuses on those areas.

The questions I get are most often concrete – "How do I ...? or "Can SharePoint ...?" – and I hope this book will give the answers to the most common of them. Therefore, *SharePoint Online from Scratch* has many images and step by step instructions, and to be even clearer, I sometimes refer to my online video demonstrations.

SharePoint Online from Scratch is not intended to be a full description of everything in SharePoint Online. The topic is huge, and Microsoft has a lot of detailed information on their websites. Instead, I want this book to give hands-on instructions on how to practically make use of a SharePoint tenant for an organization, or parts thereof.

I will start with an overview of the very basics of SharePoint Online. I describe the Microsoft 365 and SharePoint Admin centers, and after that I explain in detail how to manage and use the SharePoint building blocks: site, app and page. The later part of the book has more advanced information.

SharePoint Online from Scratch includes descriptions of both the modern and the classic experience, but the modern experience has a more prominent place. Microsoft is constantly developing the modern experience, so a lot that earlier required the classic experience can now be achieved in an easier way with the modern experience.

Even if *SharePoint Online from Scratch* primarily is a handbook, explanations on how SharePoint works are mixed into the instructions. I hope they will give you a good understanding and help you to further explore SharePoint Online.

I sometimes give links to articles with video demonstrations on the kalmstrom.com website. Many of these have been recorded with earlier versions of SharePoint Online than the one described in this book, but I have still decided to keep the links. Even if the interface looks different, I hope you will find it interesting to hear my reasoning about different features and their use.

I will of course update the demos eventually, but I did not want to delay the publishing of this version of *SharePoint Online from Scratch* until that has been done. Readers and buyers deserve a book that is as up to date as possible, even if the free online demos are not!

Microsoft has developed SharePoint so that it is possible to get substantial benefit from a SharePoint system without coding experience, and I have made *SharePoint Online from Scratch* as much no-code as possible. None of my instructions and suggestions require knowledge of how to write code, but in a few cases, I have given samples of code that you can use.

I often give several suggestions on how something can be done, so that you can choose the method that suits you and your organization best. When I give recommendations, they are mainly based on user friendliness and scalability.

Your SharePoint becomes what the users make of it, and believe me, it will grow! You and your colleagues will discover more areas where SharePoint is the best option, and Microsoft will continue to give us new features that expand SharePoint further.

The main part of *SharePoint Online from Scratch* is a manual: how to do various things in SharePoint Online and why you should do it. I also give some examples on SharePoint solutions for different information sharing situations, where you can take advantage of what you have learned and see how it can be used in practical applications.

For even more hands-on exercises, I recommend that you study my book *SharePoint Online Exercises* together with this book. *SharePoint Online Exercises* contains 10 chapters with step-by-step instructions on how to build common business solutions in SharePoint Online.

SharePoint Online Exercises has some explanations, but not at all as much as this book. If you are new to SharePoint, you should therefore study at least the first 13 chapters in *SharePoint Online from Scratch*, before you try the first exercises. Then you can work with both books in parallel.

Primarily, I am a developer and systems designer, not an author. Therefore, my mother Kate has helped me get the content of *SharePoint Online from Scratch* together, so that it is introduced to you in a way that we hope is easy to read and understand.

Kate is a former teacher and author of textbooks, so she knows how to explain things in a pedagogic way. She has worked with SharePoint Online in our family business for many years and has seen the product develop.

I have had the last word and approved of all the final text in the book, and it is my "voice" you hear. And of course, I take the full responsibility for the technical content and for the correctness of everything said about SharePoint Online in this book.

Good luck with your studies!

Borgholm, Sweden, January 2022

Peter Kalmström

TABLE OF CONTENTS

1	**INTRODUCTION**	**21**
2	**MICROSOFT 365**	**22**
2.1	Office 365 and Microsoft 365	22
2.2	Apps	22
2.3	Set up a 365 Trial	23
2.3.1	*Tenant*	*23*
2.3.2	*Setup Steps*	*23*
2.4	Sign in to 365	25
2.4.1	*Stay Signed In*	*26*
2.4.2	*Connect Windows 10 to 365*	*26*
2.4.3	*Single Sign-On*	*27*
2.5	The Office.com Homepage	27
2.6	The 365 navigation bar	28
2.6.1	*The Left Navigation Bar*	*28*
2.6.1.1	The App Launcher	28
2.6.2	*The Search Box*	*29*
2.6.3	*The Right Navigation Bar*	*29*
2.6.3.1	Settings Icon	30
2.6.3.2	Question Mark	30
2.6.3.3	Profile Picture	31
2.7	Summary	32
3	**THE MICROSOFT 365 ADMIN CENTER**	**33**
3.1	Settings	34
3.1.1	*Search & Intelligence*	*34*
3.1.2	*Org Settings*	*34*
3.1.2.1	Release Options	35
3.2	Users	36
3.2.1	*Add Users*	*36*
3.2.1.1	Create a Single User Account	36
3.2.1.2	User Templates	37
3.2.1.3	Import Multiple Users	38
3.2.1.4	Add Users with a PowerShell Script	39
3.2.1.5	User Actions	40
3.2.2	*Administrator Roles*	*40*
3.2.2.1	Assign Admin Role	40
3.3	Setup	41
3.4	Admin Centers	42
3.4.1	*Security and Compliance Centers*	*42*
3.4.1.1	Audit	42
3.4.1.2	Policies	42
3.4.1.3	Retention Policies	42
3.4.1.4	Records Management	43
3.4.2	*Azure AD*	*46*
3.4.2.1	LinkedIn Connection	47
3.5	Summary	48
4	**GET STARTED WITH SHAREPOINT ONLINE**	**49**
4.1	Architecture	49
4.1.1	*Sites Introduction*	*49*

  4.1.2 *Apps Introduction* 50
  4.1.3 *Pages Introduction* 50
 4.2 MODERN AND CLASSIC EXPERIENCES 51
  4.2.1 *Experience = Type* 51
  4.2.2 *Experience = Interface* 52
 4.3 SEARCH 52
  4.3.1 *The Search Crawler* 52
  4.3.2 *Modern Search* 52
  4.3.3 *Classic Search* 54
 4.4 ADD CONTENT 54
  4.4.1 *Naming New Content* 55
   4.4.1.1 Make Camel Case Names User Friendly 55
 4.5 SUMMARY 56

5 THE SHAREPOINT ADMIN CENTER 57

 5.1 EXPERIENCES 57
 5.2 LEFT NAVIGATION MENU 58
  5.2.1 *Homepage* 58
  5.2.2 *Sites* 59
  5.2.3 *Policies* 59
   5.2.3.1 Access Control 59
  5.2.4 *Settings* 59
  5.2.5 *Content Services* 60
  5.2.6 *Migration* 60
  5.2.7 *More Features* 60
   5.2.7.1 Apps – App Catalog 60
   5.2.7.2 Search 62
  5.2.8 *OneDrive Admin Center* 62
 5.3 SUMMARY 63

6 SHAREPOINT SITES 64

 6.1 SITE TERMS 65
  6.1.1 *Root Site and Homepage* 65
  6.1.2 *Site and Site Collection* 65
 6.2 SITES IN THE SHAREPOINT ADMIN CENTER 65
  6.2.1 *Sites* 66
   6.2.1.1 Edit an Active Site 67
 6.3 COMMON SITE FEATURES 69
  6.3.1 *Site Contents* 69
   6.3.1.1 The Recycle Bins 70
   6.3.1.2 The Modern Site Contents 70
   6.3.1.3 The Classic Site Contents 72
  6.3.2 *Site Settings* 72
   6.3.2.1 Change the Look 74
   6.3.2.2 Site Collection Administration 75
   6.3.2.3 Site Actions 75
  6.3.3 *Site Usage* 75
  6.3.4 *Site Permissions* 76
 6.4 MODERN SITES 76
  6.4.1 *Command Bar* 76
  6.4.2 *'Change the Look' Pane* 77
   6.4.2.1 Mega Menu 77

6.4.3　　*App Bar* *78*
　　6.4.4　　*Templates* *78*
　　6.4.5　　*Communication Site* *79*
　　　6.4.5.1　Classic Compatibility 79
　　　6.4.5.2　Footer 80
　　　6.4.5.3　Page Translations 80
　　　6.4.5.4　Schedule Site Launch 81
　　6.4.6　　*Modern Team Site* *84*
　　　6.4.6.1　Classic Compatibility 84
　　　6.4.6.2　Group Team Site 84
　　　6.4.6.3　Team Site without a Group 86
　6.5　Classic Team Site 86
　　6.5.1　　*Modern Compatibility* *88*
　　6.5.2　　*Save Site as a Template* *88*
　　6.5.3　　*Web Designer Galleries* *89*
　6.6　Add Microsoft 365 Group 89
　6.7　OneNote 91
　　6.7.1　　*OneNote in SharePoint Libraries* *91*
　6.8　Site Comparison 92
　6.9　Tenant Root Site 92
　　6.9.1　　*Make Home Site* *93*
　　　6.9.1.1　Global Navigation 93
　　　6.9.1.2　Viva Connections 94
　　　6.9.1.3　News Site 94
　6.10　Create a Site 94
　　6.10.1　　*Auto-Created Apps* *95*
　　6.10.2　　*User Site Creation* *95*
　　　6.10.2.1　Communication site 96
　　　6.10.2.2　Group Team Site 96
　　　6.10.2.3　Create Group Team Site from OneDrive 97
　　6.10.3　　*Admin Site Creation* *98*
　　　6.10.3.1　Modern Sites 99
　　　6.10.3.2　Classic Team Site 100
　6.11　Site Access 101
　6.12　Hub Families 101
　　6.12.1　　*Register as Hub Site* *102*
　　　6.12.1.1　Changes in the Hub Site 103
　　6.12.2　　*Associate with a Hub Site* *103*
　　　6.12.2.1　Associate in the SharePoint Admin Center 103
　　　6.12.2.2　Associate from a Site 104
　　　6.12.2.3　Create Associated Sites from a Hub Site 104
　　6.12.3　　*Hub Visitor Permission* *104*
　　6.12.4　　*Connect Hub Sites* *105*
　6.13　Create a Subsite 106
　　6.13.1　　*Create a Subsite* *107*
　　6.13.2　　*Disallow Subsites* *108*
　6.14　Delete and Restore Sites 108
　　6.14.1　　*Delete a Site* *108*
　　6.14.2　　*Restore a Root Site* *109*
　　6.14.3　　*Restore a Subsite* *109*
　6.15　Summary 109

7　SHAREPOINT APPS 111

7.1	Benefits	111
7.2	Row = Item	112
7.2.1	Item Limit	113
7.3	Modern and Classic App Interface	113
7.3.1	Differences	114
7.3.1.1	Modern Command Bar Controls	114
7.3.2	Switch Interface	115
7.3.2.1	Admin control	116
7.4	App Settings	116
7.5	Create an App	118
7.5.1	Add an App	118
7.5.1.1	Apps in Communication Sites	120
7.5.1.2	Custom Apps	121
7.6	Display Modes	121
7.6.1	Standard	121
7.6.2	Grid	122
7.6.2.1	Switch Mode	123
7.7	Columns	123
7.7.1	List Columns and Site Columns	124
7.7.2	Create List Columns	124
7.7.2.1	The Modern Location List Column	127
7.7.3	Create Site Columns	128
7.7.4	Column Types	129
7.7.4.1	Calculated Column	129
7.7.4.2	Choice Column	130
7.7.4.3	Date and Time Column	131
7.7.4.4	Lookup column	132
7.7.4.5	Character Limits in Text Columns	132
7.7.5	Filter, Sort and Group	133
7.7.5.1	Links	134
7.7.6	Edit List Columns	135
7.7.6.1	Edit via the List Settings	135
7.7.6.2	Edit in the Modern Interface	135
7.7.6.3	Format a Modern Column	136
7.7.6.4	Rename a Column	137
7.7.7	Edit Site Columns	137
7.7.8	Edit Column Values	138
7.7.8.1	Edit Values in Grid Mode	138
7.7.8.2	Edit Values in Standard Mode	138
7.8	Edit the Form	140
7.9	Views	140
7.9.1	Modern App Views	141
7.9.2	Classic App Views	142
7.9.3	Edit a View	143
7.9.4	Modern "New View" Options	144
7.9.5	Classic "New View" Options	146
7.9.5.1	Calendar and Gantt Views	147
7.9.6	Default View	148
7.9.7	Grouped View	148
7.9.8	Totals	149
7.10	Alerts	151
7.11	Delete and Restore Content	152
7.11.1	Delete Item	152

7.11.1.1	Modern Experience	153
7.11.1.2	Classic Experience	153
7.11.2	*Delete Columns*	*153*
7.11.2.1	Delete a List Column	154
7.11.2.2	Delete a Site Column	154
7.11.3	*Delete a View*	*154*
7.11.4	*Delete an App*	*155*
7.11.5	*Restore Deleted Content*	*155*
7.12	VERSION HISTORY	155
7.12.1	*See Version History*	*155*
7.12.2	*Version History in Library Apps*	*157*
7.12.3	*Version History in List Apps*	*157*
7.13	INTERNAL NAME	158
7.14	TEMPLATE OPTIONS	158
7.14.1	*Create from Existing List*	*158*
7.14.2	*Save as Template*	*158*
7.14.2.1	Use a Template in Another Site	159
7.15	APPLY LABELS	160
7.16	DECLARE RECORD	160
7.16.1	*Declare Record Indication*	*161*
7.16.2	*Activate the In Place Records Management*	*162*
7.16.2.1	Allow Record Declaration for a Single App	163
7.17	SUMMARY	163

8 LIST APPS 165

8.1	THE MODERN LIST EXPERIENCE	165
8.1.1	*No Item Selected*	*165*
8.1.1.1	Integrate	166
8.1.2	*One Item Selected*	*166*
8.1.3	*Multiple Items Selected*	*166*
8.2	CLASSIC LIST EXPERIENCE	166
8.3	MICROSOFT LISTS	167
8.3.1	*Tile Options*	*168*
8.3.2	*Create a List from MS Lists*	*169*
8.3.2.1	Blank list	169
8.3.2.2	From Excel	170
8.3.2.3	From Existing List	171
8.3.2.4	From Template	171
8.3.3	*Lists Desktop App*	*172*
8.3.3.1	Download the app	173
8.3.3.2	Resolve Sync Issues	173
8.3.4	*Create a List from SharePoint*	*173*
8.4	CREATE A NEW LIST ITEM	174
8.4.1	*Standard Mode*	*174*
8.4.2	*Quick Edit Mode*	*174*
8.4.3	*Mandatory Title*	*175*
8.5	OPEN LIST ITEMS	175
8.6	EDIT LIST ITEM	175
8.7	THE MODERN ITEM COMMENTS	176
8.8	THE MULTI-LINE COLUMN	177
8.8.1	*Enhanced Rich Text*	*178*
8.8.1.1	Enable Rich Text	179

    8.8.2   Append Changes to Existing Text 179
        8.8.2.1   Enable Append 180
  8.9   TASKS AND ISSUE TRACKING 180
    8.9.1   Tasks and Issues Alerts 181
  8.10   CALENDAR APP 182
    8.10.1   Views in the Calendar App 182
    8.10.2   Create a New Event 183
    8.10.3   Edit an Event 183
    8.10.4   See Multiple Calendars in One 183
  8.11   SUMMARY 185

9 LIBRARY APPS 186

  9.1   WHY DOCUMENT LIBRARIES? 186
  9.2   DOCUMENT LIBRARY UNIQUE FEATURES 187
    9.2.1   No Item Selected 187
    9.2.2   One Item Selected 188
    9.2.3   Multiple Items Selected 189
    9.2.4   Other Unique Features 189
  9.3   CREATE A DOCUMENT LIBRARY 191
    9.3.1   Auto-Created Columns 191
  9.4   CREATE OTHER LIBRARY APPS 191
  9.5   ADD CONTENT TO DOCUMENT LIBRARIES 192
    9.5.1   Create a File 192
        9.5.1.1   Naming 193
    9.5.2   Upload Files or Folders 194
        9.5.2.1   Select Multiple Files 194
        9.5.2.2   Upload Button 194
        9.5.2.3   Save a File to SharePoint 195
        9.5.2.4   Drag and Drop 196
        9.5.2.5   Other Methods 197
  9.6   EDIT PROPERTIES 197
  9.7   RENAME A FILE OR FOLDER 197
  9.8   OPEN BEHAVIOR FOR OFFICE FILES 198
  9.9   EDIT OFFICE FILES 199
    9.9.1   Editing by Multiple Users 199
  9.10   THE TITLE COLUMN 200
    9.10.1   Add to View and Change the Display Name 200
    9.10.2   Auto-fill the Title Field 201
    9.10.3   Hide the Title Field 201
  9.11   LIBRARY FOLDERS 201
    9.11.1   Create a New Folder 201
    9.11.2   Move Files Into and Out of Folders 201
    9.11.3   Hide the Folder Option 202
  9.12   CHECK OUT / CHECK IN 202
    9.12.1   Check Out / Check In Commands 202
    9.12.2   Require Check Out 203
  9.13   COPY ITEMS 203
    9.13.1   Modern Copy Method 204
    9.13.2   Classic Copy Method 204
  9.14   MODERN '+NEW' MENU OPTIONS 205
    9.14.1   Edit the '+ New' Menu 205
    9.14.2   Upload an Office Template 205

9.15 Summary 206

10 SHAREPOINT DESIGNER 207

10.1 Install SharePoint Designer 2013 207
10.2 Open a Site in SharePoint Designer 208
10.3 Create an App in SharePoint Designer 209
10.4 Import Files or Folders with SharePoint Designer 209
10.5 Summary 210

11 SHAREPOINT NAVIGATION 211

11.1 Site Navigation/Quick Launch 211
   11.1.1 *Add an App to the Site navigation* *211*
   11.1.2 *Add a Subsite to the Site Navigation* *212*
11.2 Classic Top Link Bar 213
   11.2.1 *Inherit links* *213*
11.3 Hub Navigation 213
11.4 Edit Navigation 214
   11.4.1 *Navigation Settings* *214*
   11.4.2 *Modern Experience* *215*
      11.4.2.1 Edit Hub Navigation 217
   11.4.3 *Classic Experience* *218*
   11.4.4 *Site Navigation Hierarchy* *218*
11.5 Focus Mode 219
11.6 Summary 220

12 PERSONAL CONTENT 221

12.1 The SharePoint Online Start Page 221
   12.1.1 *Follow Sites* *222*
      12.1.1.1 Stop Following 222
   12.1.2 *Save for Later* *222*
12.2 OneDrive for Business 222
   12.2.1 *The "My Files" Library* *223*
   12.2.2 *Sharing from OneDrive* *224*
   12.2.3 *OneDrive for Business Sync* *225*
      12.2.3.1 First Library Sync 226
      12.2.3.2 Sync Issues 227
      12.2.3.3 Sync Settings 227
      12.2.3.4 Files On-Demand 227
   12.2.4 *OneDrive User Settings* *228*
      12.2.4.1 Create Apps and Sites within OneDrive 229
      12.2.4.2 Restore OneDrive 230
   12.2.5 *OneDrive in Admin Centers* *231*
      12.2.5.1 OneDrive Settings 232
      12.2.5.2 Sharing 232
      12.2.5.3 Control OneDrive Usage for Specific Users 232
12.3 Summary 233

13 SHAREPOINT SITE PAGES 234

13.1 The Site Pages Library 235
   13.1.1 *Site Type Differences* *236*
   13.1.2 *Experience Differences* *236*
   13.1.3 *Check Out* *236*

- 13.1.3.1 Modern Check Out 237
- 13.1.3.2 Classic Check Out 237
- 13.1.4 *Version History for Pages* *238*
- 13.1.5 *Scheduled Page Publishing* *238*
- 13.1.6 *Copy a Page*... *239*
- 13.1.7 *Set a Page as Homepage* *239*
- 13.2 WEB PARTS INTRODUCTION 239
  - 13.2.1 *App Parts*... *240*
- 13.3 CREATE A PAGE 240
  - 13.3.1 *Create a Page from Site Pages* *240*
  - 13.3.2 *Create a Modern Page from '+ New' or 'Add a Page'* *241*
- 13.4 CUSTOMIZE A MODERN PAGE 241
  - 13.4.1 *Page Templates* *242*
    - 13.4.1.1 Save a Page as a Template 243
  - 13.4.2 *Edit and Publish a Modern Page*... *244*
  - 13.4.3 *Title Area*... *245*
  - 13.4.4 *Comments* *246*
  - 13.4.5 *Sections* *246*
    - 13.4.5.1 Edit Sections and Web Parts.. 247
  - 13.4.6 *Add Web Parts*... *247*
  - 13.4.7 *Add Content to Web Parts* *248*
    - 13.4.7.1 Add an Image or File... 249
  - 13.4.8 *Web Part Examples* *249*
    - 13.4.8.1 365 Apps.. 249
    - 13.4.8.2 Button and Call to action 249
    - 13.4.8.3 Divider 249
    - 13.4.8.4 Document Library and List 250
    - 13.4.8.5 Events... 250
    - 13.4.8.6 Hero 251
    - 13.4.8.7 Highlighted Content 252
    - 13.4.8.8 My Feed 253
    - 13.4.8.9 Organization Chart.. 253
    - 13.4.8.10 Spacer... 254
    - 13.4.8.11 Text 254
  - 13.4.9 *Page Details* *255*
  - 13.4.10 *Promote a Page* *256*
  - 13.4.11 *The News Web Part* *257*
    - 13.4.11.1 Create a News Post 258
    - 13.4.11.2 Create a News Link 259
  - 13.4.12 *Space*.. *259*
- 13.5 CUSTOMIZE A WIKI PAGE 261
    - 13.5.1.1 Enter and Format Text 262
    - 13.5.1.2 Add a Table 263
    - 13.5.1.3 Edit Source 263
    - 13.5.1.4 Insert a Web Part 264
    - 13.5.1.5 Save 264
    - 13.5.1.6 The Get Started Web Part 264
  - 13.5.2 *Edit a Web Part Page*.. *264*
    - 13.5.2.1 Add a Web Part to a Web Part Page 265
  - 13.5.3 *Edit Classic Web Parts* *265*
    - 13.5.3.1 The Content Editor Web Part 266
    - 13.5.3.2 Add a Web Part to a Form 267
    - 13.5.3.3 The Calendar App Part.. 267

12

13.6	PAGE DIAGNOSTICS	268
13.7	ADD FILES TO PAGES	269
13.7.1	*Add One File to a Page*	*269*
13.7.1.1	File Viewer	269
13.7.1.2	Modern Embed	271
13.7.1.3	Classic Embed	271
13.7.1.4	The No Access Issue	271
13.7.2	*Add Multiple Files to a Page*	*271*
13.7.2.1	Modern Highlighted Content Method	272
13.7.2.2	Classic Content Search Method	272
13.8	PAGES INSTEAD OF DOCUMENTS	272
13.9	SUMMARY	273
14	**PERMISSIONS**	**274**
14.1	SITE PERMISSIONS AND INHERITANCE	274
14.1.1	*Default Site Permissions*	*274*
14.1.2	*SharePoint Groups*	*275*
14.2	PERMISSION LEVEL CONSIDERATIONS	277
14.3	SECURITY GROUPS	277
14.3.1	*Create a New Security Group*	*278*
14.4	CLASSIC PERMISSIONS SETTINGS	280
14.4.1	*Permissions Levels*	*281*
14.4.1.1	Custom Permission Level	281
14.4.2	*Modify Permissions*	*282*
14.4.2.1	Remove Users	283
14.4.3	*Create a Custom SharePoint Group*	*283*
14.5	BREAK THE INHERITANCE	284
14.5.1	*Break App Inheritance*	*284*
14.5.2	*Break Item Inheritance*	*285*
14.5.3	*Break Inheritance at Subsite Creation*	*285*
14.6	SUMMARY	286
15	**SHARING**	**287**
15.1	ADMIN CENTER SHARING SETTINGS	287
15.2	SHARE A SITE	289
15.2.1	*Share a Site with the Share Button*	*290*
15.2.1.1	Modern Share Button	290
15.2.1.2	Classic Share Button	290
15.2.2	*Share a Site from the Modern Permissions Pane*	*291*
15.2.3	*Share a Group Team Site with an External Guest*	*292*
15.2.4	*Site Sharing Settings*	*293*
15.2.4.1	Access Request	294
15.2.5	*Manage Site Members in the Modern Experience*	*295*
15.2.5.1	Manage Members in Sites without a Group	295
15.2.5.2	Manage Members in Group Team Sites	295
15.2.6	*Manage Site Members in the Classic Experience*	*296*
15.3	SHARE SITE CONTENT	296
15.3.1	*Manage Access*	*297*
15.3.2	*Share with "Share" Buttons*	*298*
15.3.2.1	Sharing with the Modern 'Share' Command	298
15.3.2.2	Sharing with the Classic 'Shared With' Command	300
15.3.3	*Share with a Link*	*302*

15.3.4	Cancel a Link	303
15.3.5	E-mail Attachments	304
15.3.6	Modern Page Sharing Options	305
15.4	EXTERNAL USERS	306
15.4.1	Authenticated and Anonymous Users	307
15.4.2	External Guest Access to Group Team Site	307
15.5	AUDIENCE TARGETING	309
15.5.1	Target Links	309
15.5.2	Target Items	310
15.5.2.1	Target Modern Web Parts	311
15.5.2.2	Target Classic Web Parts	311
15.6	SUMMARY	312

16 CATEGORIZATION 313

16.1	COLUMNS	313
16.1.1	Mandatory Column Values	314
16.1.1.1	Mandatory List Columns	314
16.1.1.2	Mandatory Library Columns	314
16.1.2	Default Column Values	315
16.1.2.1	Set Static Default Value	315
16.1.2.2	Set Calculated Default Value	316
16.2	RATING	316
16.2.1	Enable Rating	316
16.2.2	Rate with Stars	317
16.2.3	Rate with Likes	317
16.3	MULTIPLE APPS	317
16.4	TERM STORE AND TAGGING	318
16.4.1	Add Terms in the Term Store	319
16.4.2	Term Store Settings	320
16.4.3	Permissions	322
16.4.4	Local Term Groups	322
16.4.5	Enterprise Keywords	323
16.4.5.1	Add an Enterprise Keywords Column	323
16.4.5.2	Tag with Enterprise Keywords	324
16.4.5.3	Remove the Enterprise Keywords column.	324
16.4.6	Custom Managed Metadata Column	324
16.4.6.1	Connect to a Term Set	325
16.4.6.2	Tag a Custom Managed Metadata Field	325
16.5	PAGE CATEGORIZATION	326
16.5.1	Add Property Column	326
16.5.1.1	Properties in Modern Pages	326
16.5.2	Edit Page Properties	327
16.6	MANAGED PROPERTIES	328
16.6.1	Automatic Managed Properties Creation	328
16.6.2	Find Managed Properties	328
16.7	SUMMARY	329

17 LINKS 330

17.1	GET THE URL	330
17.1.1	Item Link	330
17.1.2	Site Link	330
17.2	ADD LINKS TO A PAGE	331

17.2.1	*Add Links to a Modern Page*	*331*
17.2.1.1	The Link Web Part	331
17.2.1.2	The Quick Links Web Part	331
17.2.1.3	The Highlighted Content Web Part	332
17.2.1.4	The Sites Web Part	332
17.2.2	*Add Links to a Classic Page*	*333*
17.2.2.1	Link Options	333
17.3	ADD LINKS IN APPS	334
17.3.1	*The Hyperlink Column*	*334*
17.3.2	*The Multi-Line Column*	*334*
17.4	LINK AN IMAGE IN A PAGE	335
17.5	VIEWS LANDING PAGE	336
17.5.1	*Modern Views Landing Page*	*337*
17.5.2	*Classic Views Landing Page*	*337*
17.6	WIKI LINKING	338
17.6.1	*Wiki Link and Create a Wiki Page*	*338*
17.6.2	*Wiki Link to an App*	*339*
17.6.3	*Wiki Link to a View*	*339*
17.6.4	*Wiki Link to an Item*	*340*
17.6.5	*Manipulate Display Text*	*340*
17.7	CREATE A LINKS APP	341
17.7.1	*Add a Links App to a Page*	*342*
17.8	PROMOTED LINKS	342
17.8.1	*Create a Promoted Links App*	*343*
17.8.1.1	Promoted Links Images	344
17.8.2	*Add Promoted Links to a Page*	*344*
17.9	SUMMARY	344

18 PICTURES **345**

18.1	THE MODERN IMAGE COLUMN	345
18.2	LIBRARY IMAGE OPTIONS	346
18.2.1	*Image Tags*	*346*
18.2.2	*Image Filters*	*346*
18.3	PICTURE LIBRARY	346
18.4	ADD IMAGES TO PAGES	347
18.4.1	*Modern Page Picture Options*	*347*
18.4.1.1	The Image Web Part	347
18.4.1.2	The Image Gallery Web Part	348
18.4.1.3	Picture Library in Document Library Web Part	349
18.4.2	*Classic Page Picture Options*	*349*
18.4.2.1	Picture Display	350
18.4.3	*Classic Picture Web Parts*	*350*
18.4.3.1	The Picture Library Slideshow Web Part	350
18.4.3.2	The Image Viewer Web Part	351
18.5	HOTSPOT IMAGE	352
18.5.1	*Add a PowerPoint File to a Page*	*352*
18.5.2	*Add an Excel image to a Classic Page*	*352*
18.6	SUMMARY	353

19 CONNECT WEB PARTS **354**

19.1	WEB PART CONNECTION IN MODERN PAGES	354
19.1.1	*Dynamic Filtering*	*354*

19.1.2 Connect to Source.. *355*
    19.1.2.1 File Viewer Example *356*
    19.1.2.2 Embed Examples *356*
19.2 WEB PART CONNECTION IN CLASSIC PAGES............................... *358*
    19.2.1 Choice Filter Web Part *359*
    19.2.2 Click to Filter with Connected List Web Parts *360*
    19.2.3 Show Connected List Data in Display Form *361*
19.3 SUMMARY.. *362*

20 SURVEYS **363**

20.1 FORMS FOR EXCEL... *363*
    20.1.1 Create a Form *364*
        20.1.1.1 Edit.. *364*
        20.1.1.2 Branching *365*
    20.1.2 Share the Form *365*
    20.1.3 Check Form Results... *366*
    20.1.4 Form Options *367*
        20.1.4.1 Settings... *367*
        20.1.4.2 Multilingual *368*
        20.1.4.3 Print... *368*
    20.1.5 Forms Admin Settings.. *368*
20.2 EXCEL SURVEY *369*
    20.2.1 Create an Excel Survey *370*
    20.2.2 Share an Excel Survey.. *371*
    20.2.3 See Excel Survey Results *372*
20.3 SURVEY APP *373*
    20.3.1 Create a Survey App *373*
        20.3.1.1 Survey Branching Logic *374*
    20.3.2 Respond to a Survey App *374*
    20.3.3 See Survey Results *374*
20.4 SUMMARY.. *375*

21 POWER APPS **376**

21.1 POWER APPS IN SHAREPOINT *377*
21.2 THE POWER APPS STUDIO *377*
    21.2.1 Preview, Save and Publish.. *379*
21.3 CUSTOMIZE A LIST FORM IN POWER APPS *380*
    21.3.1 Why Customize a Form?... *380*
    21.3.2 Example Form *380*
    21.3.3 Modifications *382*
        21.3.3.1 Edit the Form *382*
        21.3.3.2 Edit Fields.. *383*
21.4 CREATE A POWERAPP FROM A SHAREPOINT LIST *384*
    21.4.1 Change the General Layout *385*
        21.4.1.1 Hide a Field... *385*
        21.4.1.2 Change what is Displayed *386*
    21.4.2 Add a Field... *387*
    21.4.3 Change Text Color *387*
        21.4.3.1 Conditional Formatting *388*
    21.4.4 Share a PowerApp... *388*
        21.4.4.1 Publish Changes *390*
    21.4.5 Use a Powerapp *390*

          21.4.5.1   Power Apps Mobile 390
          21.4.5.2   Add to a Page 390
    21.5 POWER APPS ADMIN CENTER 390
    21.6 SUMMARY 391

22 **CONNECT AND EXPORT SHAREPOINT DATA** 392
    22.1 CONNECT SHAREPOINT AND OUTLOOK 392
      22.1.1   *Synch Calendar, Contacts and Tasks with Outlook* 393
          22.1.1.1   Calendar Benefits in Outlook 393
      22.1.2   *Remove a Synchronized List from Outlook* 394
      22.1.3   *Import an Outlook Calendar to SharePoint* 394
    22.2 CONNECT SHAREPOINT AND EXCEL 395
      22.2.1   *Export a SharePoint App to Excel* 396
          22.2.1.1   Analyze SharePoint Data in Excel 397
      22.2.2   *Direct Export from Excel to SharePoint* 398
          22.2.2.1   Enhance a SharePoint List Created from Excel Export 399
      22.2.3   *Display Excel Data in a Web Part* 400
          22.2.3.1   Show Excel Data in a Modern Page 400
          22.2.3.2   Show Excel Data in a Classic Page 400
    22.3 CONNECT SHAREPOINT AND ACCESS 401
      22.3.1   *SharePoint-Access Synchronization* 401
      22.3.2   *Open a SharePoint App in Access* 402
          22.3.2.1   User Info 403
      22.3.3   *Edit Multiple List Items* 404
      22.3.4   *Export an Excel Table to a SharePoint List via Access* 405
      22.3.5   *Recurring Tasks* 407
          22.3.5.1   Export to SharePoint 408
          22.3.5.2   Create a To Do List 408
          22.3.5.3   Update the To Do list with an Access Query 408
      22.3.6   *Import Data from SQL to SharePoint* 411
          22.3.6.1   Update Imported SQL Data 413
    22.4 SUMMARY 416

23 **ISSUE TRACKING TIPS** 417
    23.1 LIST TEMPLATES 417
      23.1.1   *Multiple Assignees* 419
    23.2 CREATE A HELPDESK LIST 419
      23.2.1   *Data Entry View* 419
          23.2.1.1   Hide Previous Items 420
    23.3 MY TASKS VIEW 421
      23.3.1   *Embed My Tasks/My Issues* 422
          23.3.1.1   Single List 422
          23.3.1.2   Multiple Lists 422
    23.4 LANDING PAGES 425
      23.4.1   *Landing Page with Tasks* 425
      23.4.2   *Landing Page with Chart* 426
          23.4.2.1   Refresh an Excel Chart on a SharePoint Page 427
          23.4.2.2   VBS Script that Updates an Excel Chart on a SharePoint Page 427
    23.5 SUMMARY 429

24 **SHAREPOINT AUTOMATION** 430

24.1	Why automate?	430
24.2	Components	430
24.3	Flow versus Workflow	431
24.3.1	Storage	431
24.3.2	Changes in SharePoint	432
24.4	Power Automate Built-In Flows	432
24.4.1	Create a Rule	432
24.4.2	Reminder	433
24.4.3	Require Association Approval	434
24.4.4	Approve/Reject App Items	435
24.4.4.1	Request Sign-off	435
24.4.4.2	Content Approval	436
24.4.5	Approve/Reject Pages	437
24.4.5.1	Configure the Flow	437
24.4.5.2	Process	438
24.4.5.3	Turn Off Page Approval	439
24.4.5.4	Edit a Page Approval Flow	439
24.5	Power Automate Custom Flows	440
24.5.1	Flow Editor	440
24.5.2	Create a Flow from SharePoint	441
24.5.3	Create a Flow from Blank	441
24.5.4	Finalize the Flow	443
24.5.5	Flow Activity	443
24.5.6	Dynamic Content	444
24.5.7	Custom Value	444
24.6	Export and Import Flows	445
24.6.1	Export a Flow	445
24.6.2	Import a Flow	445
24.7	Workflows	447
24.7.1	Start Creating a List Workflow	447
24.7.2	Dynamic Content	448
24.7.3	Finalize the Workflow	449
24.7.4	The Workflows Page	449
24.8	Exercise: Set Titles	450
24.8.1	Set Titles Flow	450
24.8.1.1	Actions	450
24.8.1.2	Condition	451
24.8.1.3	Steps	452
24.8.2	Set Titles Workflow	453
24.8.2.1	Steps	454
24.9	Summary	455

25 CONTENT TYPES 456

25.1	Content Type Example	456
25.2	Site and List Content Types	456
25.2.1	Use Custom Columns with a Content Type	457
25.3	The Content Type Gallery/Hub	457
25.4	Create a Content Type for the Tenant	458
25.4.1	Add Site Columns to a Content Type	459
25.4.2	Edit Site Column	459
25.5	Edit Content Type Settings	461
25.5.1	Associate a Template with a Content Type	461

25.5.2	*Policy Settings*	*461*
25.5.2.1	Retention Settings	462
25.6	TEST A CONTENT TYPE	463
25.7	PUBLISH AND UNPUBLISH A CONTENT TYPE	463
25.8	ADD A CONTENT TYPE TO AN APP	464
25.8.1	*Allow Management of Content Types*	*464*
25.8.2	*Classic Method*	*464*
25.8.3	*Modern Option*	*465*
25.8.4	*Delete Default Content Type*	*466*
25.9	CREATE A CONTENT TYPE FOR A SITE	466
25.10	DOCUMENT TEMPLATE WITH METADATA COLUMNS	467
25.11	THE DOCUMENT SET CONTENT TYPE	468
25.11.1	*Use A Document Set in a Library*	*468*
25.11.2	*The Document Set Files*	*469*
25.11.3	*Create a Document Set Content Type*	*470*
25.11.3.1	Add Files to the Document Set	470
25.12	CONTENT TYPES IN THE HIGHLIGHTED CONTENT WEB PART	471
25.13	DATA ENTRY CONTENT TYPE	471
25.13.1	*Create a Data Entry Content Type*	*472*
25.13.2	*Workflow that Switches Content Type*	*472*
25.14	SUMMARY	473

26 CSS, JAVASCRIPT AND RSS IN CLASSIC PAGES 474

26.1.1	*Script Editor*	*474*
26.1.2	*Content Editor Source*	*474*
26.1.2.1	Content Editor Link	475
26.1.3	*The RSS Viewer Web Part*	*475*
26.2	SUMMARY	476

27 SHAREPOINT SERVER PUBLISHING INFRASTRUCTURE 477

27.1	ACTIVATE THE PUBLISHING INFRASTRUCTURE	477
27.2	NAVIGATION CHANGES WITH PUBLISHING INFRASTRUCTURE	477
27.3	SHAREPOINT SERVER PUBLISHING	479
27.4	THE CONTENT QUERY WEB PART	480
27.4.1	*Link to an Alternate CSS File*	*481*
27.4.2	*Publishing Pages*	*482*
27.4.2.1	Image Renditions	482
27.5	SUMMARY	485

28 CREATE EXAMPLE DATA 486

28.1	COPY AND PASTE EXAMPLE DATA FROM EXCEL	486
28.2	CREATE EXAMPLE DATA IN ACCESS	486
28.3	SUMMARY	489

29 MEETING NOTES AND ACTION POINTS 490

29.1	CONSIDERATIONS	490
29.2	CREATE CONTENT TYPES	491
29.2.1	*Meeting Content Type*	*491*
29.2.1.1	Set Retention on the Meeting Content Type	492
29.2.2	*Action Point Content Type*	*492*
29.3	CREATE APPS AND ADD CONTENT TYPES	492

29.3.1	*Meetings List*	*492*
29.3.2	*Action Points List*	*493*
29.3.2.1	Use "Action Points" as a Template	493
29.4	CREATE A MEETINGS OVERVIEW PAGE	494
29.5	SUMMARY	494

30 RENTAL AGREEMENTS 495

30.1	CREATE A CONTENT TYPE	495
30.2	"RENTAL AGREEMENTS" TEMPLATE	496
30.3	SCHEDULED REVIEW ALERT FLOW	496
30.3.1	*Steps*	*497*
30.4	SUMMARY	500

31 ABOUT THE AUTHORS 501
32 INDEX 502

1 INTRODUCTION

SharePoint is Microsoft's platform for enterprise content management and sharing. It is also a place for social networking within organizations. The cloud edition of SharePoint is called SharePoint Online. It is included in most Microsoft 365 and Office 365 subscriptions, and you need such a subscription to fully use SharePoint Online. Therefore, this book begins with some general information on how to set up Microsoft/Office 365.

After that, I go through the general build and use of SharePoint, before I describe the different parts and usage possibilities more in detail. The chapters about the SharePoint Online Start page and OneDrive for Business, describe parts of SharePoint that are especially designed for standard users, but the rest of the book is intended for administrators and site owners.

In the first chapters, I describe in detail how to perform certain actions. When these steps are included in other descriptions later, I don't repeat the steps. That would make the book unreasonably long and boring for everyone who has studied the book from the beginning – which I strongly recommend! – and learned the steps. For example, I only explain once how to open the Site settings. If there is no reference, please use the index to find instructions! There I give the page number for the most detailed explanation.

For the same reason, to save space, I don't explain each time that you must save your changes or click OK when you are done with a modification or have filled out a form. Where possible, I have also cut the screenshots horizontally or vertically inside the image, where SharePoint only shows blank space.

The screenshots are taken from various SharePoint Online sites in different browsers on a computer with the Windows 10 operating system.

SharePoint Online is an ever-changing platform, so some things will change and no longer work as described in this book. That is part of the charm of the product! I would recommend that you not learn by heart how to do things step by step, but instead look at the instructions as a way of getting to know SharePoint better.

I also recommend that you study the book with a computer at hand, so that you can really try everything I describe, not just read about it.

The steps will change, but if you understand why things are done the way they are, you will be able to figure out how to do what I describe in this book anyway. Even more important is that the knowledge I hope you will acquire by studying *SharePoint Online from Scratch* will help you explore SharePoint far beyond the limitations of this book!

2 MICROSOFT 365

Microsoft 365 and Office 365 are Microsoft's brand names for a group of software and services. Most of them are cloud based, but several subscription plans also include desktop editions of common software like Word, Excel, PowerPoint and Outlook.

In this chapter, you will learn how to set up and configure Microsoft/Office 365 in general. After a short introduction, you will see how you can set up a tenant (an "office in the cloud") for an organization, add users to it and assign them roles. All this is needed before you can start working with SharePoint Online.

I have also included some general information about navigation and given an overview of the Microsoft 365 Admin center, which is the place where you manage your tenant.

If your organization already has a functioning Microsoft/Office 365 system, you probably don't need this chapter. Instead, you can go directly to chapter 4, where we will start studying SharePoint.

For information about all the 365 apps and services and more details on how to get started with the platform, *refer to* my book *Office 365 from Scratch*.

2.1 OFFICE 365 AND MICROSOFT 365

Office 365 and Microsoft 365 are two brand names that are often confused. Strictly speaking, the Microsoft 365 platform includes Microsoft Azure and Windows 10 together with Office 365.

However, the Office 365 Business plans have been renamed Microsoft 365 Business, and when it comes to the Enterprise plans there are currently both Microsoft 365 Enterprise plans and Office 365 Enterprise plans.

Except for the Trial section below, it does not matter for the understanding of this book which of the product packages your organization uses, or plan to start using. I will refer to them as "Microsoft 365" or just "365".

SharePoint is included in all 365 Business and Enterprise plans.

2.2 APPS

The word "app" is used widely and with different meanings, but in Microsoft 365, an app is generally a web based application that is run in a web browser (most often Edge, Google Chrome or Firefox).

365 comes with various apps, and many third-party apps can be used together with the apps in a tenant – like my own products, the kalmstrom.com SharePoint solutions. When you build your SharePoint platform, you will use templates to create your own apps for various purposes.

There are also apps that must be downloaded and installed by each user:

- Desktop apps – special editions of the cloud-based apps that are run in each user's computer.
- Mobile apps – apps that run in smart phones and tablets.

2.3 SET UP A 365 TRIAL

Microsoft/Office 365 has several different subscription plans for various kinds of businesses and organizations. In Kalmstrom Enterprises we use the Enterprise E3 plan. This plan includes some of my favorite features, like unlimited mailbox archiving in Exchange and unlimited file storage in OneDrive for Business. It also includes several useful apps such as Teams and Power Automate.

For organizations who need advanced voice, analytics, security and compliance services, the E5 plan is a better choice.

It is currently possible to try the Microsoft 365 Business Basic, Standard and Premium plans and the Office 365 E3 and E5 plans for one month without any costs.

Note: When you set up a new 365 tenant, the tenant language is set automatically according to the location of the person who sets up the tenant. Even if each user can set a preferred language, this can create problems for an international company and should be considered. When this is written, there is no way to change the global language after the setup.

2.3.1   *Tenant*

When you start a trial of one of the 365 plans, your organization is assigned a tenant, "an office in the cloud". You can keep the same tenant and all the work you have done, if you decide to go from a trial to a paid subscription.

When you set up your 365 trial you need to specify a name for the tenant, and it should have the form NAME.onmicrosoft.com. The tenant name cannot be changed after you have started your trial, and it must be unique.

2.3.2   *Setup Steps*

The setup steps below refer to the Office 365 E3 plan. The process is similar for other plans, but if you want to try a Business package you need to start at https://www.microsoft.com/microsoft-365/business/compare-all-microsoft-365-business-products instead.

1. In the web browser, type the web address https://www.microsoft.com/en-us/microsoft-365/enterprise/compare-office-365-plans. The Compare plans page will open.
2. Click on 'Try for free' under the Office 365 E3 option.

Microsoft 365 Apps for enterprise	Office 365 E1	Office 365 E3	Office 365 E5
The enterprise edition of the Office apps plus cloud-based file storage and sharing. Business email not included[1].	Business services such as email, file storage and sharing, Office for the web, meetings and IM, and more. Office apps not included[1].	All the features included in Microsoft 365 Apps for enterprise and Office 365 E1 plus security and compliance[1].	All the features of Office 365 E3 plus advanced security, analytics, and voice capabilities[1].
$12.00 user/month (annual commitment)	$8.00 user/month (annual commitment)	$20.00 user/month (annual commitment)	$35.00 user/month (annual commitment)
Buy now	Buy now	Buy now	Buy now
Learn more >	Learn more >	Try for free > Learn more >	Try for free > Contact sales > Learn more >

3. Enter your work or school e-mail address. This is to check if you need to create a new account for Microsoft 365. If you already have an account, you will be offered to either sign in or create another account.
4. Fill out your name, phone number and company name.
5. Select how many employees your company has. This does not affect which features you will have access to, because that was decided when you selected your subscription plan.
6. Select your country.
7. Now Microsoft wants to verify your identity. Choose if you want to have an automatic call or a text message.
8. Enter the verification code you received in the call or message.
9. Enter a user name and a tenant name (= "Yourcompany"). Note that the tenant name cannot be changed later. All users will have the tenant name you decide on here – unless you create another 365 account with a new tenant name, of course.

Create your user ID

You need a user ID and password to sign in to your account.

| User name | @ | Yourcompany | .onmicrosoft.com |

username@Yourcompany.onmicrosoft.com

10. Enter a password.
11. Check or uncheck boxes to decide if and how you want to be contacted by Microsoft.

Now the trial account will be created, and you will be asked to add users to the new tenant and install the included desktop apps. This can also be done later. When you are finished, you will be directed to the Microsoft 365 Admin center.

Now you can use 365 for free and try it as a Global Administrator. When the evaluation period is finished, you need to subscribe to 365 to continue using the platform. This is done in the Microsoft Admin settings under 'Billing', *refer to* chapter 3.

Demo:

https://www.kalmstrom.com/Tips/Office-365-Course/Setting-up-Office-365.htm

2.4 SIGN IN TO 365

When you have created an account, you need to sign in to 365. These are the steps:

1. Open a web browser and type the web address office.com in the address bar.
2. Click on the 'Sign in' button in the middle of the page, or at the top right corner. A Sign in wizard will open.
3. Type the e-mail address of your 365 account.
4. Click on 'Next'. Now your e-mail address will be analyzed. If the service can decide if it is a work or school account or a personal Microsoft account, you will be taken directly to step 6.
5. (If you are asked to select account type, select "Work or school account".)
6. Type your password.
7. Click on 'Log in'.
8. The 365 homepage will open. It will now look as described in 2.5, The Office.com Homepage below.

2.4.1 Stay Signed In

When you are on a secure computer, that is locked with a password or PIN, it is convenient to not have to log in each time you want to use Microsoft 365.

The most obvious method is to let the browser save the password.

You should also answer Yes when 365 asks if you want to stay signed in, as this reduces the number of login occasions.

Below I describe more ways to avoid the log in procedure.

2.4.2 Connect Windows 10 to 365

Each user can set Windows 10 to handle the 365 login details. This way the user doesn't have to log in so often.

1. In the computer, click on the Windows icon to open the start menu.
2. Click on the Settings icon and then on 'Accounts'.
3. Click on 'Access work or school'.
4. Click on the 'Connect' button and log in to your 365 account.

When the connection has been established, you will see the Windows icon and the account username below the 'Connect' button, as in the image below.

If you no longer want Windows to manage your 365 login, click on the account under the 'Connect' button. Now you can either manage the account or click on the 'Disconnect' button.

Demo:

https://www.kalmstrom.com/Tips/Office-365-Course/Signing-into-Office-365.htm

2.4.3 Single Sign-On

Another way to log into 365 is to use the 365 credentials as log-in for the computer. This feature only works with Windows 10 Pro and the Edge browser, but if you have that, the browser will pick up the log-in details, so that you have access to 365 without further log-in as soon as you are logged in to the computer.

2.5 THE OFFICE.COM HOMEPAGE

When you are signed in to 365, you will be met by a different office.com homepage, compared to when you started the trial. Now you can reach all your 365 apps, content that you have used recently, shared or marked as a favorite. You can also create new content here, take recommended actions and download desktop apps.

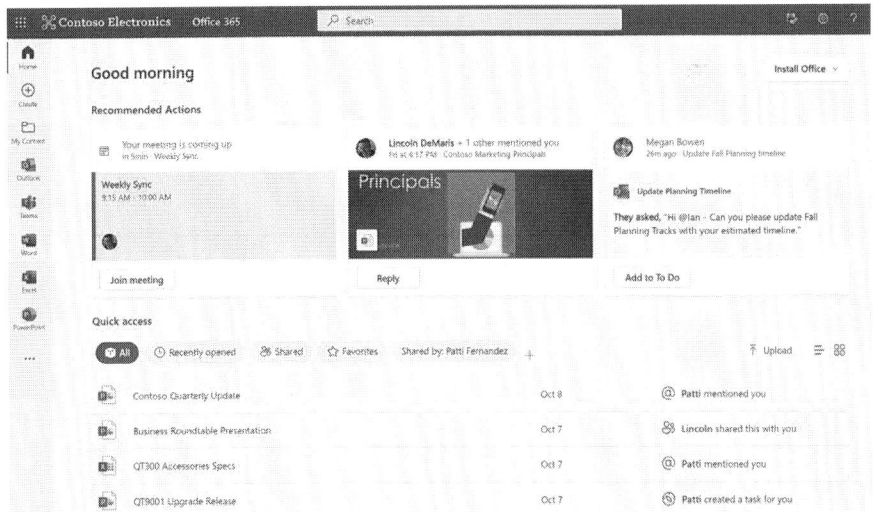

When you click on the All apps icon in the bottom left corner, the main area will instead show all 365 apps, Business apps and tips and tricks.

2.6　THE 365 NAVIGATION BAR

In this section, we will look at how you find your way around Microsoft 365. The navigation is managed in the navigation bar, which is present in all 365 apps.

2.6.1　*The Left Navigation Bar*

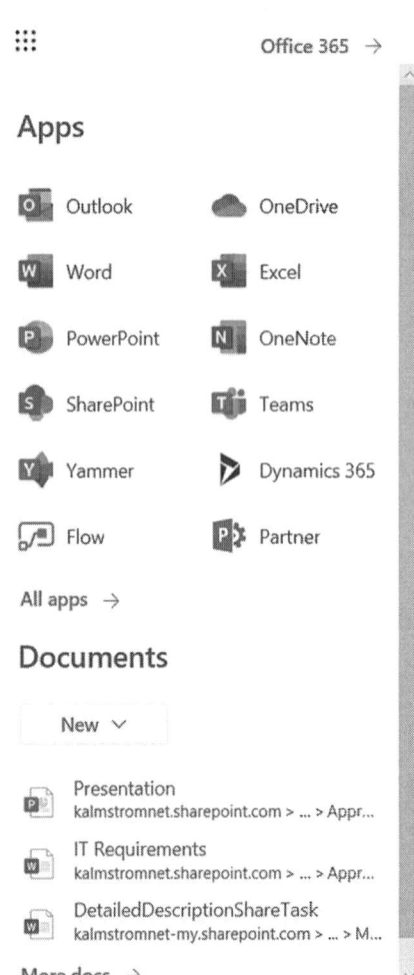

The left 365 navigation bar has two parts: the App launcher or start menu and the name of the current app or service.

2.6.1.1　The App Launcher

You can reach all 365 apps you have access to by clicking on the App launcher in the left corner of the navigation bar.

Apps that are relevant to users and much used across 365 are shown with tiles in the launcher.

Only administrators will see the Admin tile. When you click on it, you will be directed to the Microsoft 365 Admin center, where you can manage the tenant, *refer to* chapter 3.

Below the app tiles, there is a link to all apps, a button for document creation and links to the current user's recent documents.

At the bottom of the App launcher, there is an 'Explore all your apps' link that opens the same page as when you click on the apps icon on the Office.com page.

When you click on a tile in the App launcher, the corresponding app will open in a new tab.

28

When you hover the mouse over an app tile, three dots, a so called ellipsis, will be visible.

Click on the ellipsis at an app icon, if you want to open the app in a new tab, unpin the app from the launcher (so that it is not visible there anymore) or if you want to learn more about the app.

2.6.2 The Search Box

There is often a search box in the middle of the 365 navigation bar. If you have a low resolution screen, the search box is replaced with a magnifying icon that opens a search box over the whole navigation bar.

In section 4.3, I will describe how the search is used to find content in SharePoint.

2.6.3 The Right Navigation Bar

On the right side of the 365 navigation bar, all apps have the profile picture of the current user. Most apps also have a Settings icon and a question mark. On  small screens, the settings and help icons are placed under an ellipsis.

Some apps also have app specific icons to the left of the Settings icon. For example, modern SharePoint pages have a megaphone icon that gives users suggestions on next steps, such as add team members and post news. You can see this icon in the image below.

2.6.3.1 Settings Icon

The Settings icon on the right side of the 365 navigation bar opens a right pane with different content in different apps. There are always some personal 365 settings and some app specific settings or commands.

In SharePoint, the 365 Settings icon often shows links to add a new app or page, to see site information and content and more.

There are also personal settings for theme, language, time zone (by default, 365 gets the same regional settings as your computer), password and contact preferences.

If you change your 365 theme, your selected theme will only be visible to you, even if you are the admin of the tenant.

(A default theme for the whole tenant can be set in the Microsoft 365 Admin settings, under Settings >Org settings. Each site can also have its own theme.)

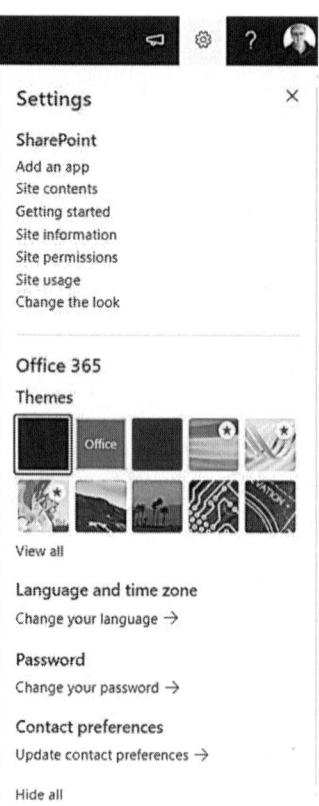

2.6.3.2 Question Mark

Under the question mark icon in the 365 navigation bar, you can find Help on app specific topics. In SharePoint, the topics are gathered under headings.

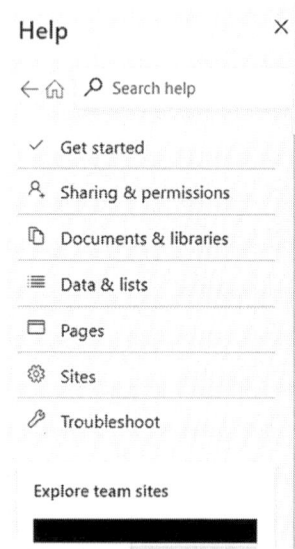

2.6.3.3 Profile Picture

When users are new to Microsoft 365, the icon far to the right in the navigation bar has the initials of the current user's name. They are meant to be replaced with the user's photo. The photo (or initials) will be show in many apps and in various contexts within the tenant.

Click on the icon to have more options. It is also under your profile picture that you should sign out when you want to leave Microsoft 365.

In SharePoint, the options under the profile picture are View account and My Office profile, but some other apps have additional options.

- Click in the icon to add your photo, or to change it.
- Click on 'View account' to find details about your account.

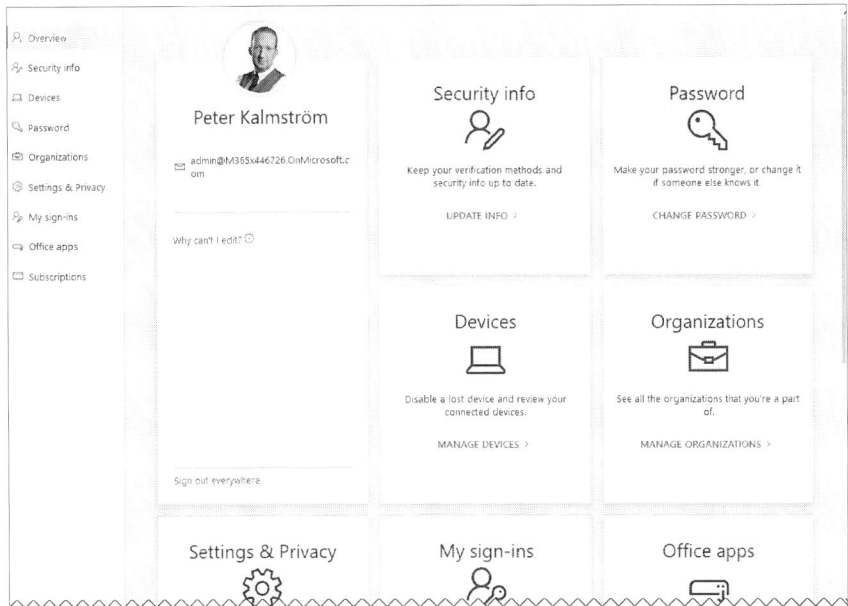

31

- 'My Office profile', opens the Delve site, where you should add and edit information about yourself that is useful and relevant to your colleagues.

  Here you can also find links to your recent work and to people in the organization that you have cooperated with.

2.7 SUMMARY

Now you have set up your tenant, and you know how you can sign in and navigate in Microsoft/Office 365. Next step is to learn where you can manage the tenant and how you can add user accounts and assign user roles. This is done in the Microsoft 365 Admin center.

If you have created the new tenant, you have automatically become its Global Admin and have full access to the Microsoft 365 Admin center. If you instead are a SharePoint admin or have another admin role, it is still useful to know some about what can be handled in the Microsoft 365 Admin center.

3   THE MICROSOFT 365 ADMIN CENTER

When you click on the Admin tile in the 365 App Launcher or on office.com, you will be directed to the Microsoft 365 Admin center. Here, administrators can manage and monitor applications, services, data, devices and users across the organization's tenant.

Only Global Admins can change *all* settings in the Microsoft 365 Admin center. Other admins can change some of them.

To go through everything in the Microsoft 365 Admin center would require its own book, so I will not do that here. However, I strongly recommend that you explore the Admin center if you have permission to use it, because it is here you find almost everything needed for the management of your organization's tenant.

In this chapter, we will only have a look at how to add users to the tenant and assign administrator roles. I will also explain how to find more Admin centers and point at some other settings in the Microsoft 365 Admin center that might be interesting for your use of SharePoint.

The Microsoft 365 Admin center has a menu to the left and a dashboard to the right. The dashboard content depends on what has been selected in the menu.

The Home dashboard has some default cards with links to often used features. It can however be customized. Above the cards, there is a plus sign for addition of more cards, and under the ellipsis on each card you can remove it from the homepage.

When the tenant is new or on trial, you will see a link to a guided setup above the cards, like in the image below.

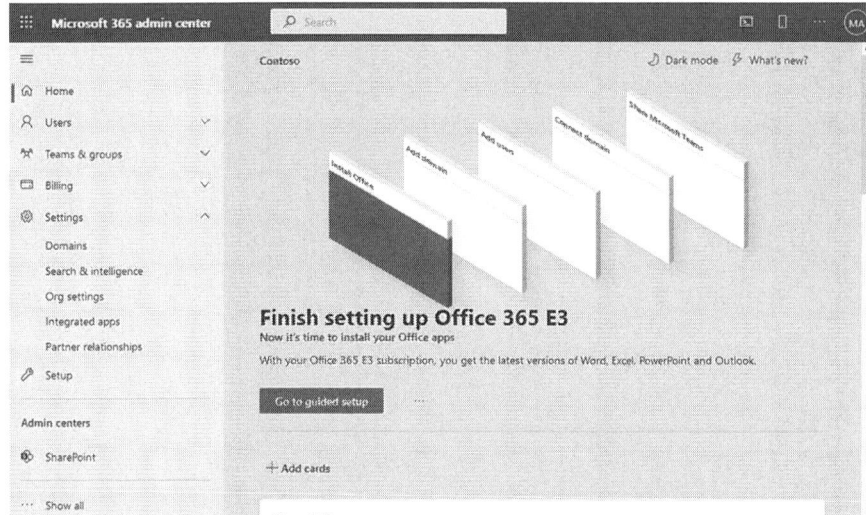

There is a choice between showing pinned entries, as in the image above, or showing all of them. When you click on 'Show all' at the bottom of the left menu, more entries and links to more admin centers will be visible.

Most of the SharePoint management is performed in the SharePoint Admin center, which I will describe in chapter 5, and not in the Microsoft 365 Admin center. The link to the SharePoint Admin center is always visible in the left menu.

Via the menu icon on top of the left menu, you can collapse the navigation menu to get more space in the main area to the right.

There is an admin mobile app for iOS and Android. With this app, admins can receive critical notifications, add users, reset passwords, manage devices, create support requests and more.

3.1 SETTINGS

Under Settings in the Microsoft 365 Admin center left menu, there are multiple tabs for various tenant settings.

3.1.1 Search & Intelligence

Search & intelligence has five tabs. General Search & intelligence settings are configured under the Configurations tab.

Under Insights, you can see how people have used Microsoft Search during the last 7, 30 or 90 days. You can also add answers to specific search terms.

Search & intelligence

Insights   Answers   Data sources   Customizations   Configurations

Under the Data sources tab, you can connect third party data sources to have results from them included under the default All tab in search results. There are more than 100 connectors to choose from: https://www.microsoft.com/microsoft-search/connectors/.

Under Customizations >Verticals, you can decide how search results should be displayed in the tenant.

3.1.2 Org Settings

Under Org settings , you can configure many apps and services for the organization.

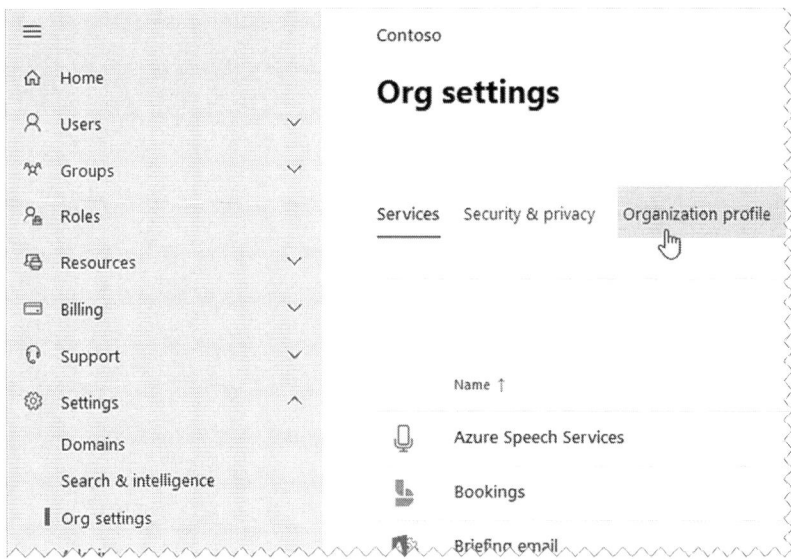

3.1.2.1 Release Options

Microsoft/Office 365 is continuously updated, and under Org settings >Organization you can manage how your tenant receives these updates.

1. Select the Organization profile tab and click on 'Release preferences'.
2. A right pane will open where you can make your choices. The image shows the default setting.

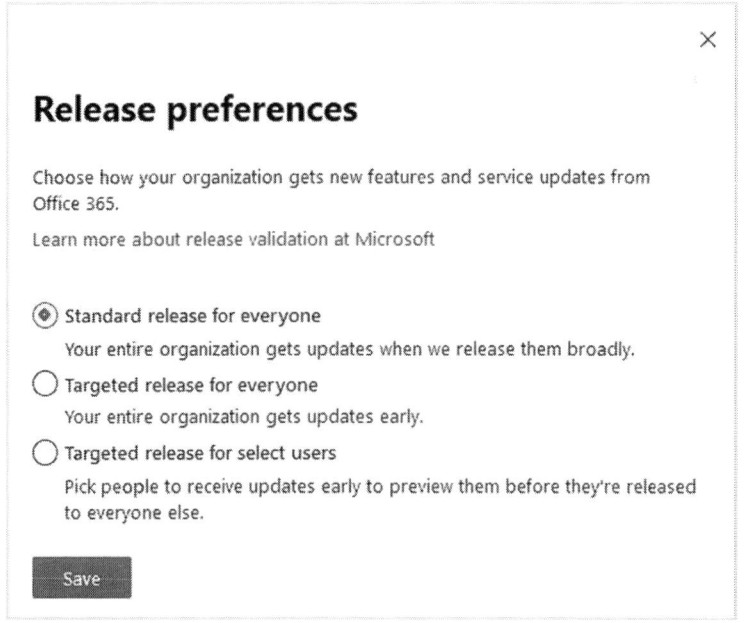

Targeted release means that you get the updates earlier than with the standard release. That way, you can help shaping the product by providing feedback on new features.

A good option for a bigger organization is to give only certain people the early updates. These people should be in a position where they can see what each update would mean to the other users and take any actions needed.

When you choose 'Targeted release for select users', you currently need to click on 'Save' to get a possibility to pick the select users. You can also upload a text file with the relevant e-mail addresses.

3.2 USERS

Most user management can be handled in the Microsoft 365 Admin center, under Users >Active users.

Here, you can add new users and manage their roles, and you can also delete users, reset passwords, manage product licenses and more.

3.2.1 *Add Users*

Each 365 user must have his/her own account in the organization's tenant. These accounts are created the Microsoft 365 Admin center >Users >Active Users, and here is also where most of the tenant's user management is handled.

To create user accounts, you need to be Global, License or User administrator. The accounts can be added one by one or in a bulk.

    👤 Add a user   📋 User templates   👥 Add multiple users

3.2.1.1 Create a Single User Account

These are the steps to add a single user to Microsoft 365:

1. In the Microsoft 365 Admin center >Active users, click on the 'Add a user' button.
2. Enter name, display name, username and password settings.

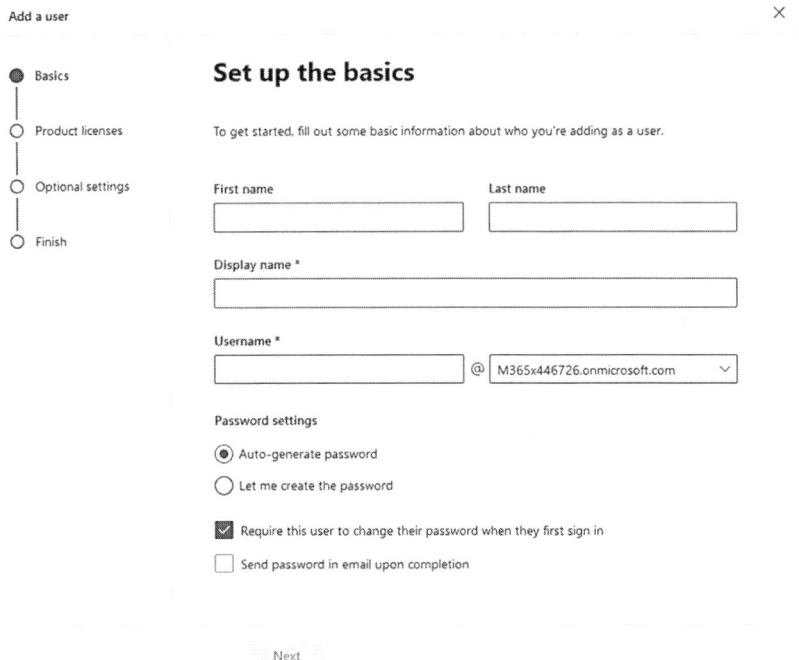

3. Click on 'Next'.
4. Select country and assign licenses and apps.
5. Click on 'Next' .
6. If you want to give the user administrator permissions, this is done in the third step, Optional settings.

   Below the list of permission levels sorted by category, you can fill out additional information about the new user.
7. Click on Next.
8. Review the settings and modify them if necessary.
9. Click on the 'Finish adding' button to add the new user to the tenant.

3.2.1.2 User Templates

To quickly add new users, you can create one or more user templates with a saved configuration. When you have created a template, it will be visible in the dropdown so that you can select it to add a user. Then you only need to enter the name, display name and username for each user in a right pane.

In the image to the right, a template called "Standard User" has been created and can be selected for new users.

37

The template creation process reminds of the process to add a single user to the tenant.

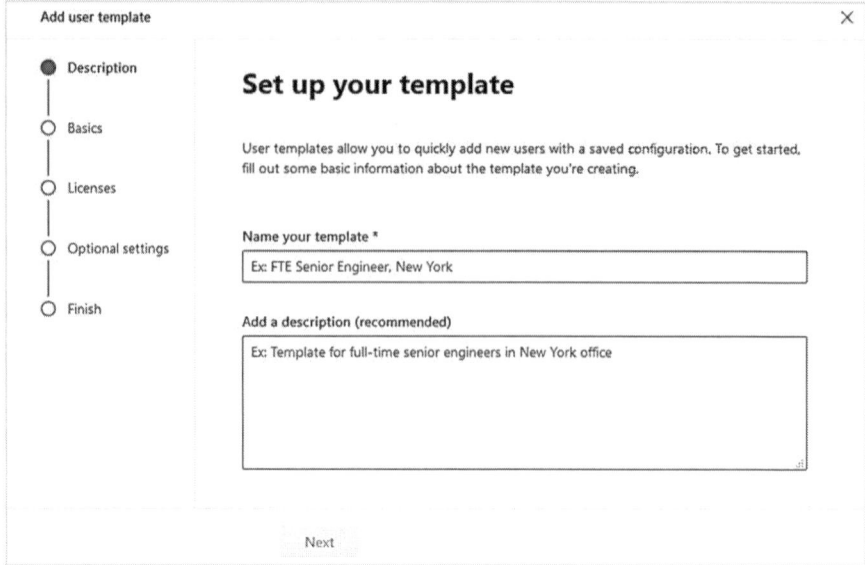

3.2.1.3 Import Multiple Users

Instead of adding the users one by one, from scratch or with a template, you can add a group of users or all users at the same time with a CSV file. This is a file with comma separated values that you can create or edit in any text editor or spreadsheet program, for example Excel.

I recommend that you download a CSV file from the 'Import multiple users' pane and enter your user information to it. You may also use another CSV file with the user data, but it must have the same column headings as the downloadable file.

1. In the Microsoft 365 Admin center >Users >Active users, click on 'Add multiple users'.
2. The right pane that opens has two download choices:
   - Download a CSV file with headers.
   - Download a CSV file with headers and sample data.
3. Download one of the CSV files, open it and enter your user information. (Remove the sample data if you use that file.)
4. Click on 'Browse' to upload the CSV file to Office 365.
5. Verify the file.

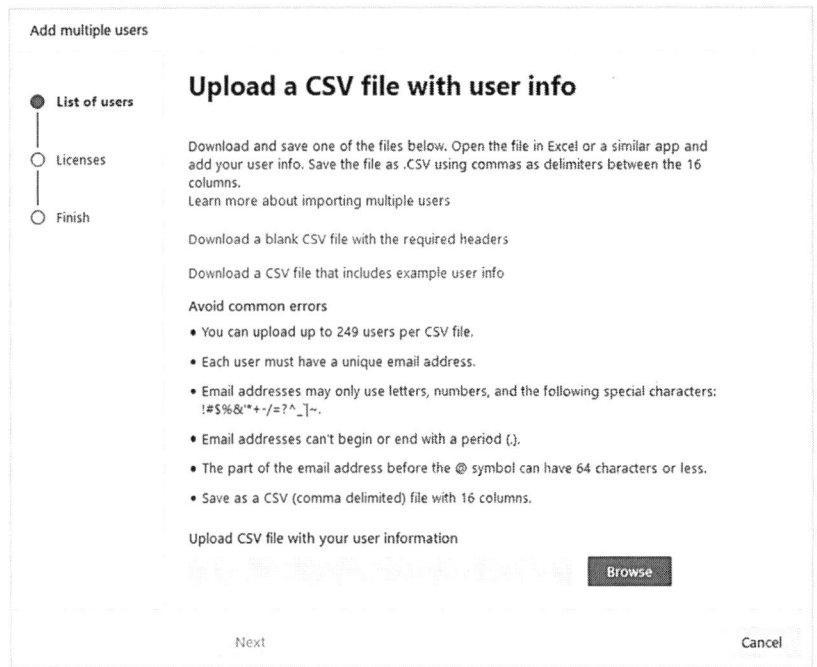

6. Click on Next.
7. Set log-in status and assign product licenses. As this is a bulk creation, all users must be given the same status and licenses.
8. Click on Next to create the user accounts.
9. Now you can download a CSV file with all the usernames, names and temporary passwords. By default, e-mails with login details, in plain text, are sent out to the users.
10. Click on 'Send and close' to finish.

3.2.1.4 Add Users with a PowerShell Script

It is possible to add users to Microsoft 365 with a PowerShell script. Scripts are re-usable and give consistency, but to fully describe the user import PowerShell script is out of scope for this book. Therefore, I will just give a few hints to readers who already know PowerShell and want to try this method.

(If you are new to PowerShell but interested in learning how you can use it with SharePoint, I recommend my book *PowerShell with SharePoint from Scratch*.)

1. Download and install the Azure AD Module, if you don't already have it on your computer.
2. Run PowerShell ISE as an administrator.

3. Run the cmdlet Connect-MsolService to connect to the Azure AD which has the Office 365 user accounts.
4. Create a new user, assign license and add location and user properties.

   Start with the cmdlet New-MsolUser and select the parameter LicenseAssignment and its value. Then select the rest of the required parameters and give their values.
5. Run the script to add the user. The temporary password will be shown in the object.

Demo:

https://www.kalmstrom.com/Tips/PowerShell/Add-Users-PowerShell-Azure-Ad.htm

3.2.1.5   User Actions

When a user has received the account information, he/she can log in (and change the password if that is required), install the Office desktop apps and start using the sites, apps and pages that he/she has access to.

3.2.2   *Administrator Roles*

Microsoft 365 comes with a set of administrator roles that can be assigned to users. Each admin role gives permission to perform specific tasks.

The person who signs up for a Microsoft/Office 365 subscription gets the role Global administrator, and he or she is at first the only person who can assign other admin roles. However, one of the roles that can be assigned is Global admin, so there can still be more than one Global administrator for a tenant.

Global admins can modify the settings all over Microsoft 365, so to minimize security risks I recommend that you have more than one Global admin but not more than five.

Instead of Global administrator, you can give the role Global reader to people who need to read settings and administrative information across Microsoft 365 but who not necessarily need to take management actions.

The Global reader role can be combined with a more limited admin role, like SharePoint administrator, to make it easier to get work done without using the Global administrator role.

Make sure that all administrators give a mobile number and an alternate e-mail address in their contact information.

3.2.2.1   Assign Admin Role

By default, new users have no administrator permissions. Global administrators can give administrator permissions when the new user account is created, *see* above, or at any time after creation. People who are License or User administrators are also allowed to set and change permissions for standard users.

To change a user's role, select the user and click on 'Manage roles' above the list of account names to open the right pane. You can also click on the user's name in the list of active users and then select 'Manage roles' in the right pane.

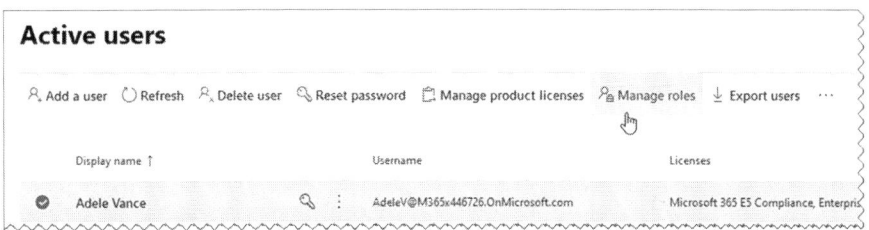

In the 'Manage roles' pane, you can assign one or several admin roles. Each permission level has an information icon that opens a pop-up explanation on what the level allows.

Only the most common permission levels are displayed when the pane opens, but you can find them all sorted by category in the collapsed section at the bottom of the pane.

3.3 SETUP

The Setup tab in the left menu of the Microsoft 365 Admin center is important for organizations that are new to 365, as it gives help with setting everything up.

41

3.4 ADMIN CENTERS

Under 'Show' more' in the Microsoft 365 Admin center left menu, you can find specific Admin centers for apps and features. Here I will just mention a few of them that are especially interesting for SharePoint usage.

Only Global admins and Global readers can see all Admin center entries. If you, for example, is a SharePoint admin, you will only see the SharePoint and OneDrive Admin centers in the left menu. I will introduce OneDrive in chapter 12, Personal Content.

3.4.1 Security and Compliance Centers

The Security entry opens the Microsoft 365 Defender center with a lot of different settings to keep the organization secure.

The Compliance entry also opens a center with many options. Here I will just mention two options that are available in both centers and two features that are special for the Compliance center.

3.4.1.1 Audit

Under the Audit tabs in the Security and Compliance centers, you can search and view activity in the whole organization. The only users you cannot monitor here are unauthenticated external users, *refer to* 15.4.1, Authenticated and Anonymous Users.

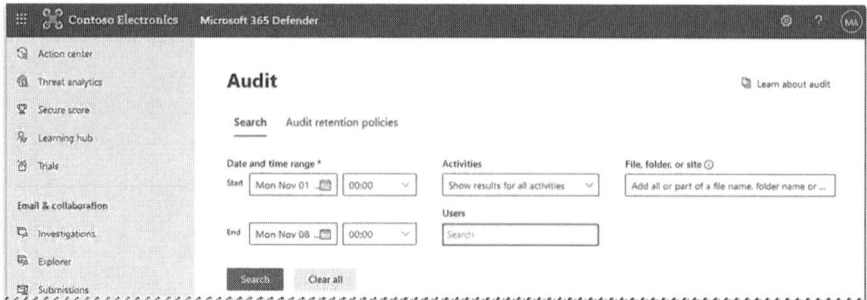

3.4.1.2 Policies

Under Security >Policies & rules and Compliance >Policies, you can find wizards for various policies that protect your organization and its content.

3.4.1.3 Retention Policies

In the Compliance center >Policies >Retention, Global and Compliance admins can create retention policies that apply to specific locations or users.

You can configure how long content should be retained and if the period should be calculated from the Created date or Last Modified date. You should also specify whether you want to keep or delete the content after the retention period expires.

When you define where to apply the policy, the default option, Adaptive, is to specify a location or group where the policy should be used. This policy will be updated automatically, but the option is still in preview, and I have found that it does not work very well yet. There is also a static option that I would prefer so far:

Choose locations to apply the policy

The policy will apply to content that's stored in the locations you choose.

Status	Location	Included	Excluded
On	Exchange email	All recipients Edit	None Edit
On	SharePoint sites	All sites Edit	None Edit
On	OneDrive accounts	All accounts Edit	None Edit
On	Microsoft 365 Groups	All groups Edit	None Edit
Off	Skype for Business		
Off	Exchange public folders		

After setting your preferred logics, you can click on Next and create the policy.

To add a retention period for items that use a specific content type, *refer to* 25.5.2.1, Retention Settings.

3.4.1.4 Records Management

In the Compliance center, Solutions >Records management >File plan, Global and Compliance admins can create and configure labels that mark content with retention and sensitivity information. The labels can be applied either manually, for example on SharePoint documents, or automatically based on content.

Labels are mainly used for items, as opposed to retention policies, but users can set the same label to all items in an app via the List settings.

The labels give more options than the retention policies, and retention can be combined with record declaration.

Records management

Overview **File plan** Label policies Adaptive scopes (preview) Policy lookup (preview) Events Disposition

Whether starting from scratch or an existing file plan, Microsoft 365 file plan uses advanced analytics and insights to help automate your retention plan so you can collaborate with stakeholders on your retention label strategy. When ready, simply upload the completed plan to Microsoft 365.

+ Create a label   Publish labels   ↑ Import   ↓ Export   ↻ Refresh

Name	Status	Based on	Is record	Retention duration	Disposition type
Private	Inactive	When created	No	5 years	Auto-delete
PII Retention Policy	Active	When created	No	7 years	No action

You can import data from a spreadsheet and bulk-create labels, and you can also export the whole file plan.

Click on the '+ Create a label' button above the list of file plans to create a label in four steps. First, you are asked to name and describe the label, and then you can categorize it in several ways.

The third step has multiple options for retention and what should be done with a marked item after the retention period. When you use the default option for what should be allowed during the retention period, users can edit and delete the item, and most often they don't even notice that the item has a retention label.

When users delete or change an item that has a retention label, a copy of the original is moved to the site's Preservation Hold library. The content in this library is included in the site's storage quota, so you might need to increase it when you use retention settings for SharePoint sites.

When you use the other option for what is allowed during the retention period, to mark the item as a record, the item cannot be edited or deleted during the retention period.

Note: When you apply a retention label to a list item that has an attachment, it does not inherit the retention setting. If the same list item instead is declared a record with a retention label, the document attachment will inherit the retention settings and cannot be deleted.

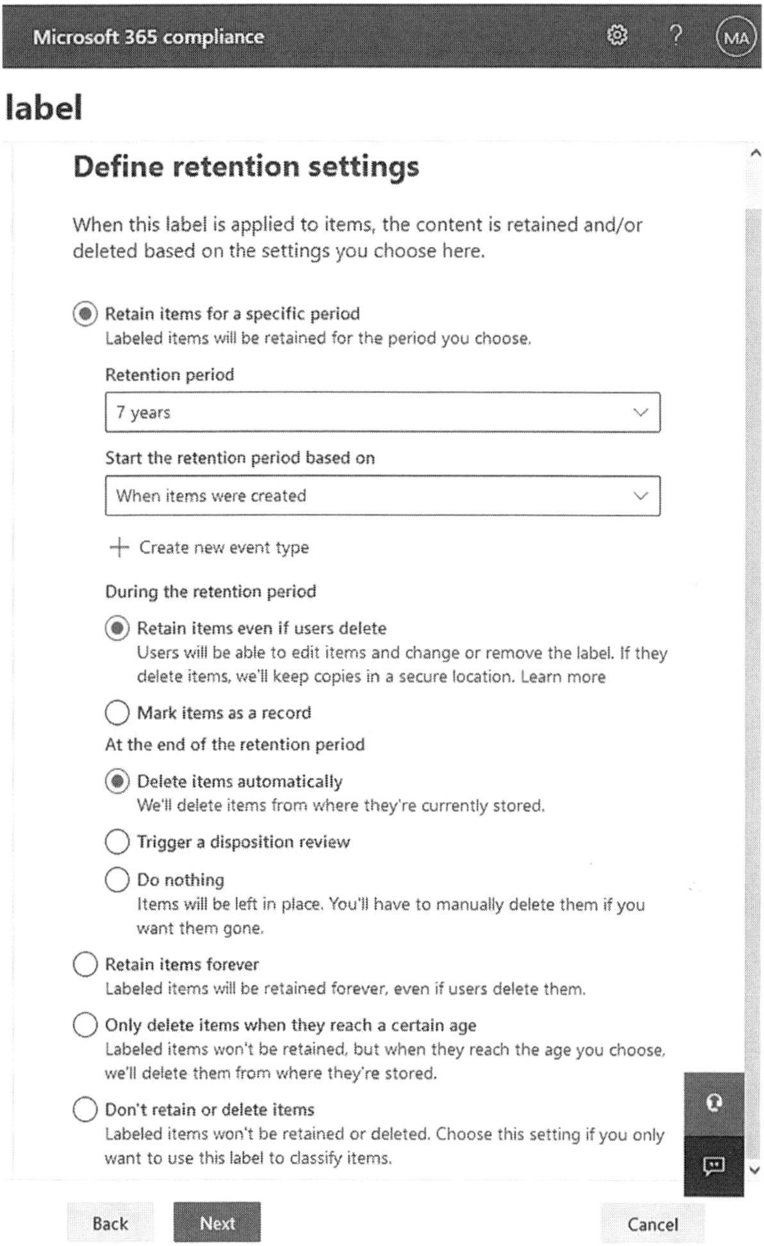

label

Define retention settings

When this label is applied to items, the content is retained and/or deleted based on the settings you choose here.

◉ Retain items for a specific period
  Labeled items will be retained for the period you choose.

  Retention period

  [7 years ⌄]

  Start the retention period based on

  [When items were created ⌄]

  + Create new event type

  During the retention period

  ◉ Retain items even if users delete
    Users will be able to edit items and change or remove the label. If they delete items, we'll keep copies in a secure location. Learn more

  ○ Mark items as a record

  At the end of the retention period

  ◉ Delete items automatically
    We'll delete items from where they're currently stored.

  ○ Trigger a disposition review

  ○ Do nothing
    Items will be left in place. You'll have to manually delete them if you want them gone.

○ Retain items forever
  Labeled items will be retained forever, even if users delete them.

○ Only delete items when they reach a certain age
  Labeled items won't be retained, but when they reach the age you choose, we'll delete them from where they're stored.

○ Don't retain or delete items
  Labeled items won't be retained or deleted. Choose this setting if you only want to use this label to classify items.

[Back] [Next]   [Cancel]

The fourth step is to review the information, and after that you can either publish the label, auto-apply the label for a specific content or choose to select one of these options later. There is an adaptive and a static option, just like for Retention policies.

45

Publish labels so users can apply them to their content

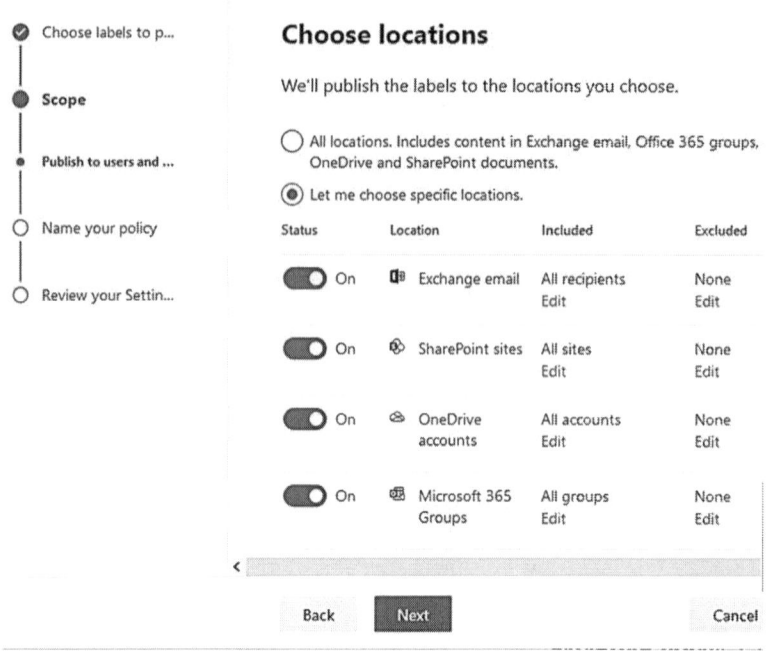

Note that it may take a day or even more before the labels are displayed in all places and for all people that you have defined in the policy.

Refer to 7.15. Apply Labels to learn how these labels are set manually in apps.

When you auto-apply the label for a specific content, you can choose between applying the label to sensitive info or to content that has specific words, properties or classifiers. In all cases, you will continue by selecting or adding the type of content that the auto-apply should look for.

3.4.2   *Azure AD*

Microsoft 365 uses the cloud-based user authentication service Azure Active Directory, or Azure AD, to hold its account information.

Azure AD does not have its own tile in the App Launcher, but Azure AD is one of the specific Admin centers that you can reach from the Microsoft 365 Admin center.

The 365 user accounts are stored in the Azure AD, but normally administrators create and manage users in the Microsoft 365 Admin center, as described above. However, users can be managed in Azure Active Directory too, and Azure AD also gives other possibilities that are out of scope for this book.

In this section, we will just have a look at the LinkedIn Connection, that can be disabled from Azure AD. We will also come back to Azure AD in section 14.10.2, External Guest Access to Group Team Site.

3.4.2.1 LinkedIn Connection

By default, users can share SharePoint content with their first level LinkedIn contacts. This setting can be disabled in the Azure AD User settings, or only specific groups can be given this sharing possibility.

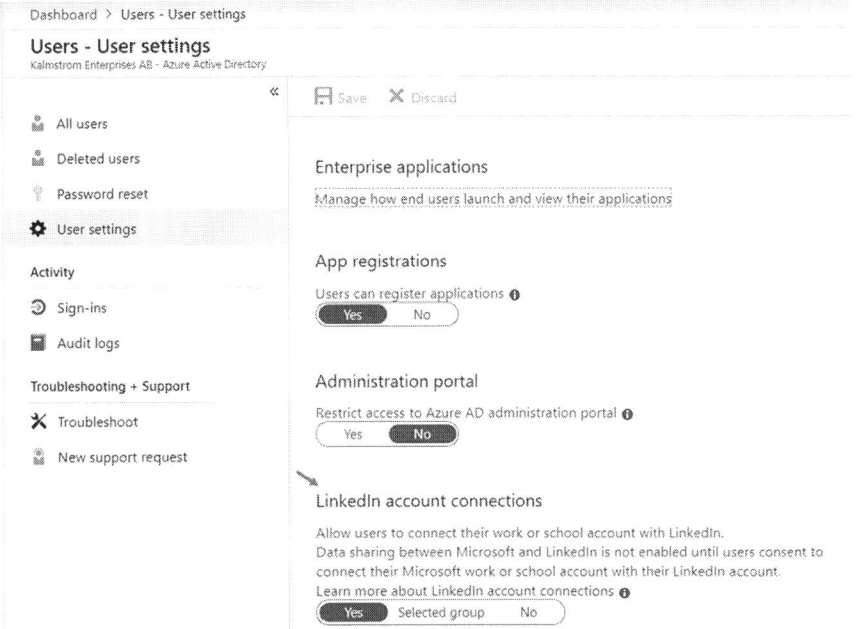

When LinkedIn connection is allowed, users will be prompted to connect their accounts the first time they click to see someone's LinkedIn information on a profile card in Outlook, OneDrive or SharePoint Online. The LinkedIn connection is not fully enabled for each user until the user has agreed to the connection.

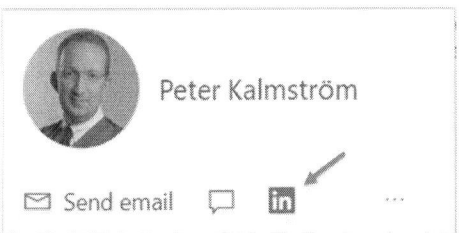

3.5 Summary

In this chapter, we have looked at some important parts of the Microsoft 365 Admin center. You now understand how to add user accounts and assign user roles for the tenant, and you know where to find the SharePoint Admin center and many other Admin centers. I have also explained how you can set retention policies and create labels that users can apply to their SharePoint content.

It is time to start using SharePoint!

4 GET STARTED WITH SHAREPOINT ONLINE

In this chapter, we will look at how SharePoint is built and describe the two SharePoint Online experiences: modern and classic. I will also give an overview over the search features and give a few tips about content and naming.

4.1 ARCHITECTURE

SharePoint is built as a hierarchy, where the highest level consists of multiple sites. The lowest level contains column values in list and library items.

Each site can have all the lower levels, and things like permissions, navigation and themes can be inherited from higher to lower levels.

Multiple sites can be connected with a hub site, and this is what Microsoft recommends.

There is also a possibility to create subsites to a site – which is then called "root site". Root sites and subsites used to be very popular when SharePoint was younger. I have seen examples of deep hierarchical site structures with hundreds of subsites. Such hierarchies quickly become very difficult to manage, and even if they are technically possible and fully supported, they are not recommended. Instead, Microsoft now recommends that we create hub families, *refer to* 6.12.

4.1.1 Sites Introduction

The SharePoint sites are the core of the SharePoint tenant. All content is added, and all work is done, within the context of a site. A site can contain apps, pages and subsites. A site and its subsites form a site collection. Often the word "site" refers to a whole site collection.

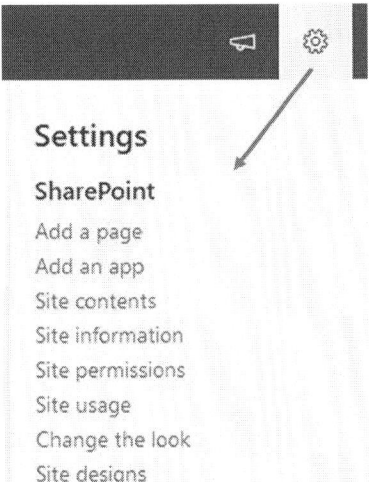

Each site has a huge number of settings that control how the site works and looks. These settings can be reached from the 365 Settings icon. Sometimes, you must first select 'Site information' and then 'Site settings'.

All the contents of a site can be seen and reached in the Site contents. There is a 'Site contents' link under the 365 Settings icon, *see* the image above.

When you need to create a new site that is connected to another site, you can create it as a subsite to an existing site. However, Microsoft now recommends that you instead connect sites via a hub site. I will describe how to do all that later in this book.

4.1.2 Apps Introduction

SharePoint apps can do various things, but here we will focus on lists and libraries. These apps are intended for content creation, sharing and storage.

Apps can be of three different types:

- Lists. A list is very much like a database or an Excel table. It contains items such as appointments in a Calendar list, contacts in a Contact list or tasks in a Tasks list.

    You can also create your own custom lists, for example a Cost Center list. Each list has many settings that for example decide which columns, views and permissions should be used in the list. *Refer to* chapter 8, List Apps.

- Libraries. A library can do almost everything that a list can do, and it has most of the same settings and features. The main difference between a list and a library is what they contain.

    You use list apps to store and share data, while libraries are used to store and share files. Each item in a library contains a file. List items can have attached files, but when the file is the most important content, you should use a library.

    There are several types of SharePoint libraries, but when nothing else is said, I am referring to document libraries when I mention libraries in this book. *Refer to* chapter 9, Library Apps.

- Other apps. These can look and behave in many ways. Your organization can purchase or build them, and they are out of scope for this book. When I talk about apps here, I refer to SharePoint lists or libraries and not to other apps.

Apps always exist within a site. Each app has its own URL, typically

https://TENANT.sharepoint.com/sites/SITE/Lists/LIST/

or https://TENANT.sharepoint.com/sites/ SITE/LIBRARY/

Lists and libraries use columns to characterize the content with metadata and keywords. The columns can be filtered, and the apps themselves can have views that display the content in various ways. You will find much more information about this in chapter 7, SharePoint Apps.

4.1.3 Pages Introduction

A SharePoint page has a big area in the middle of the SharePoint interface, often delimited by a navigation bar. Each page has its own URL, such as https://TENANT.sharepoint.com/sites/SITE/SitePages/PAGE.aspx

A page can be automatically created and contain settings or an app, but SharePoint also gives a possibility to create custom pages. Such pages can contain text, images, videos, content from apps and much more.

In chapter 13, SharePoint Site Pages, I will describe how pages can be created and customized.

4.2 Modern and Classic Experiences

In 2016, Microsoft started to roll out a new experience for SharePoint Online. It is called the modern, or new, experience, and it changes the look and also some features for sites, apps, pages and admin centers.

There are important differences between the experiences, and one such difference lies in the interface. The modern interface is better adapted to smart devices and more touch friendly than the classic one. It is also more intuitive to use, so it is easier to manage for the average user.

Microsoft is not deprecating the classic experience. Instead, the classic and modern experiences will coexist. The two experiences complement each other. Some things can only be done with the classic experience, as you will notice later in this book.

There are also several features that only exist in the modern experience. Therefore, SharePoint admins and power users should learn to manage both experiences, to be able to judge which experience is best for each purpose. I will describe both in this book.

You can often switch between the experiences as you prefer when you use a SharePoint Online app. The interface is different, but the app content and settings are the same. Modern SharePoint pages, on the other hand, are different from classic pages, and you cannot switch interface. Modern sites are also different from classic sites.

Even if the two experiences complement each other, they can be confusing – and they do complicate things for authors of SharePoint books! I still hope that I have managed to clarify the differences in this book, so that you will always understand which experience I am referring to in various parts of the book.

In this book, I have often used a smaller font for the classic experience – not because the classic experience is less important to power users, but because you often want to start with learning the modern experience when you are new to SharePoint Online. Using a smaller font for the classic experience makes it easier for readers to separate the experiences. For the same reason, I have also sometimes used bold text when I mention the words "modern" and "classic".

4.2.1 *Experience = Type*

The modern and classic SharePoint sites and pages are different types of sites and pages.

- Pages. New pages are by default modern, while settings pages have the classic experience.

    Modern and classic pages are different kinds of pages with different features, and they are built and managed in different ways. You cannot make a classic page modern – or vice versa.

- Sites. Modern and classic sites give different options, and you cannot make a classic site modern – or vice versa.

4.2.2 Experience = Interface

In all kinds of Team sites, most apps can be viewed in either the modern or the classic experience. It is the same app, just with two different interfaces.

If you make a change in the app contents or settings and then switch experience, you will see the change in the other interface too.

4.3 SEARCH

SharePoint Online has two search experiences, Microsoft Search and SharePoint Search. Both are active, and administrators cannot enable or disable one of them. The experience used depends on where you search from.

- Microsoft Search is used in the modern experience.
- SharePoint Search is used in the classic experience.

The search results are always trimmed by permissions. Therefore, each user will only see results that he or she has permission to open.

4.3.1 The Search Crawler

SharePoint content is automatically crawled based on a schedule. The crawler picks up content that has changed since the last crawl and updates an index. A search schema helps the crawler decide what content and metadata to pick up. In Microsoft 365, we have limited control over that process.

Content will not be included in search results until it has been crawled and added to the index. Therefore, it may take a few minutes before new additions to SharePoint show up in searches. Both search experiences use the same search index to find the results.

An important advantage of search in SharePoint is that the file content is also indexed, not only the file name. This means that you can search for files that have certain words the document text just as quickly and easily as you search file names.

4.3.2 Modern Search

The Microsoft Search box in the middle of the 365 navigation bar is present in all 365 apps, not only in SharePoint. It is however not present in the classic SharePoint interface.

The modern search box suggests results even before you start typing, based on your recent activity, and it updates the suggestions as you type.

When you start the search from an app and there are hits in that app, the app content is filtered to show only items that matches the search.

If there are no hits, or if you don't select one of the suggestions, the process continues in several steps:

1. There is a suggestion to show more results. Press Enter or click on the "Show more results" link to continue the search.

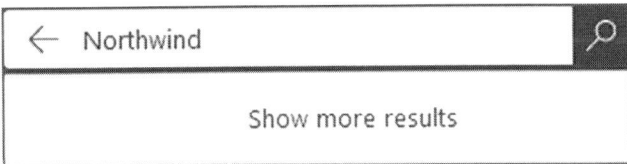

2. The expanded search takes you to a Search center. By default, it has the verticals All, Files, Sites, News and Images.

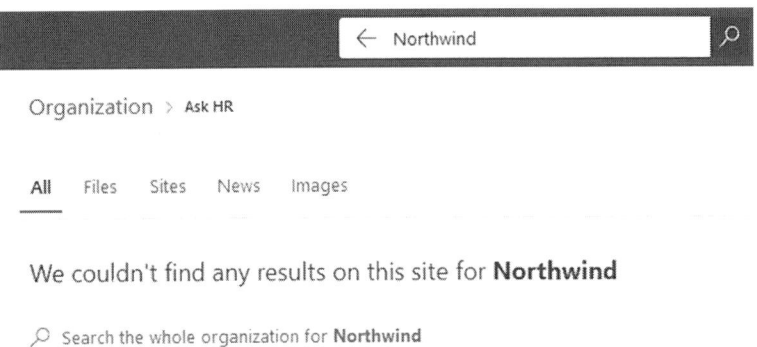

3. You get a chance to search the whole tenant.
4. Now the Search center also gets verticals for People and Power BI.

All search verticals give the possibility to filter by latest modified time, and the Files vertical can also be filtered by file type.

Each hit in the Search center has an ellipsis with options. How many options there are depends on the type of search hit.

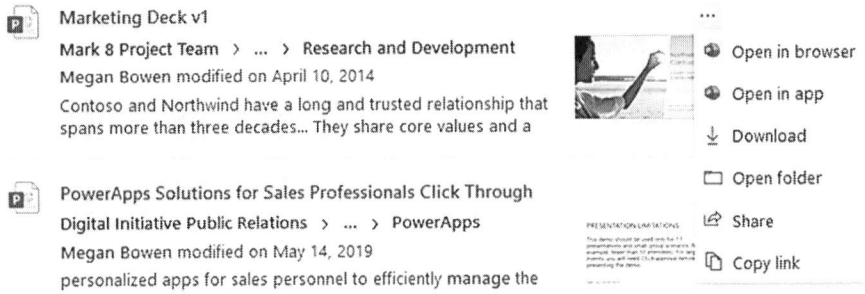

Click on the arrow to the left of the search term to finish the search and return to the page where you started the search.

Microsoft plans to expand the search possibilities for the modern search, so that users can search among Teams and Outlook conversations that they were part of or took place in Microsoft 365 Groups and teams they have access to. The search results will be displayed in a 'Conversations' vertical.

4.3.3 Classic Search

The SharePoint **classic** interface has a global search in the top right corner. When you use the global search with the default option, This Site, the search results will be shown on a search results page for the current site.

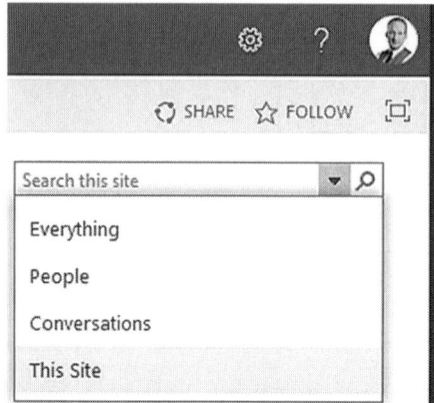

When you use the global search with the options Everything, People and Conversations, the search engine goes through the whole tenant, and the results are shown in a Search Center page for the tenant.

Most apps with the classic interface also have a local search field to the right of the view selector. When you enter something in the local search box and press Enter, SharePoint searches only the current app, and the app content is filtered to show only items that matches the search.

4.4 ADD CONTENT

One of the most important reasons for using SharePoint is that you want to share information and documents within a company or organization. Generally, you share the content with either a group of people within the tenant or with everyone in the tenant.

These are the most common methods to add content that should be shared among colleagues within the same tenant:

- Create a new document directly in SharePoint or upload an existing document to a SharePoint library.
- Add info to a SharePoint list, for example a team tasks list or a team calendar.

- Add a comments to list items, files or to a modern page.
- Use the Newsfeed on a SharePoint page. Create a new entry or reply to an existing entry or upload an image or even tag someone.
- Create SharePoint pages. You can fill your pages with text, images, links or videos and insert tables, app parts and web parts.

There will be a lot more information and examples of these ways to share information throughout the book.

Demo:

https://kalmstrom.com/Tips/SharePoint-Online-Course/Share-Info-In-SharePoint.htm

4.4.1 Naming New Content

When you create a new site, app, column or page, you need to give it a name. This name can be changed later, but the first name will always be kept as what is called the internal name.

Internal SharePoint names should not have spaces. When the name has a space, you will sometimes see irritating extra characters in URLs. These characters are added automatically by SharePoint to avoid a space.

kalmstromnet.sharepoi site/Kick%20Off%20Menus/I

Ideally, internal names should consist of one word or be written in CamelCase style. CamelCase naming is when you write two separate words together without a space and use capital first letters in both words. *SharePoint* is a good example.

 Using CamelCase naming give better URLs when a name consists of multiple words:

kalmstromnet.sharepoir site/KickOffMenus/I

When you create content from the classic interface, for example from the List settings, you should be extra careful to name the content you create with a good internal name – one word or CamelCase writing.

When you use the modern experience, SharePoint removes spaces in the internal names for apps and columns and thus in automatically created URLs. In other URLs the spaces can be visible. Spaces might however still create problems, for example when you use SharePoint names in programming. We will see an example on that in the last chapter of this book, when we need to use a column name in a flow query.

4.4.1.1 Make Camel Case Names User Friendly

Even if CamelCase naming has advantages and sometimes is necessary, it can make names more difficult to read for users. If you want to have a more user friendly name in the user interface, you can rename the content after creation. The internal name will be kept as it was from the beginning when you rename your content.

Demo:

https://www.kalmstrom.com/Tips/SharePoint-Online-Course/CamelCase-Naming.htm

4.5 SUMMARY

In this chapter, I have given an overview of the SharePoint building blocks that we will look at in more detail later in the book: sites, apps and pages. I have also introduced the two experiences for these building blocks.

I hope that you now have an idea on how the search features in SharePoint work and how you can create new content in SharePoint.

In the next chapter, you will learn how SharePoint, and also some parts of your 365 tenant, can be controlled from the SharePoint Admin center.

5 THE SHAREPOINT ADMIN CENTER

Most administrator settings for SharePoint are handled through the SharePoint Admin center, which you can reach from the left navigation menu in the Microsoft 365 Admin center.

Note that the settings in the SharePoint Admin center are for the tenant, not for a site. An exception is when one site is selected under Sites >Active sites, for example when changing sharing options for that specific site.

Once you have found your way to the SharePoint Admin center, it is a good idea to bookmark it in your web browser. If you have permission to use the SharePoint Admin center, you will probably want to come back here often.

5.1 EXPERIENCES

The SharePoint Admin center has two experiences, just like apps, and you can control which interface should be displayed for all admins that have access to the SharePoint Admin center. The new experience is default.

Select 'Settings' in the left menu of the SharePoint Admin center, and then 'Default admin experience'. A right pane will open, where you can select if the new (= modern) or classic experience of the Admin center should open by default.

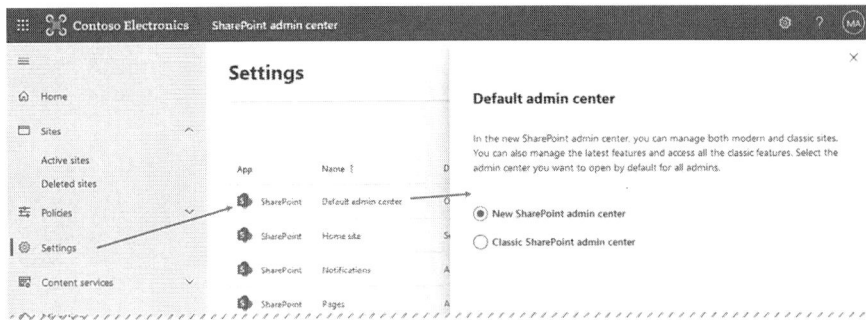

Everything can be managed from the new SharePoint Admin center, both classic and modern sites and features. The new experience is also what Microsoft recommends, so in this chapter I will focus on the new SharePoint Admin center.

For a few settings in classic pages, you need to use the classic settings page, which you can reach from the new SharePoint Admin center via a link at the bottom of the Settings page. I will come back to a few such settings later.

> Can't find the setting you're looking for? Go to the classic settings page.

The classic Admin center has no setting for experience selection. Instead, there is a banner on top of each page, where users are urged to open the new Admin center. Some sections that have been moved and only exist in the new experience gives information about that and redirects automatically after a few seconds.

5.2 LEFT NAVIGATION MENU

Below, I will shortly go through the entries in the left navigation menu of the new SharePoint Admin center in the order they are displayed by default. I will go deeper into several of the settings in the SharePoint Admin center later in the book, in contexts where the different tabs belong.

Via the 'Customize navigation' link at the bottom of the left menu, each admin who has access to the SharePoint Admin center can hide items they don't use without disturbing the navigation for other admins. You can always find the hidden items by selecting 'Show all' in the menu.

When you have learned to find your way around the SharePoint Admin center, you can click on the menu icon in the top left corner of the left menu to collapse the navigation and only see the icons, not the text. That way, you will get more space in the main area to the right.

5.2.1 *Homepage*

The homepage of the new SharePoint Admin center has the same card design on the dashboard as the Microsoft 365 Admin center. By default, it shows site search, service health, messages from Microsoft and statistics on file activity, site usage, storage and users.

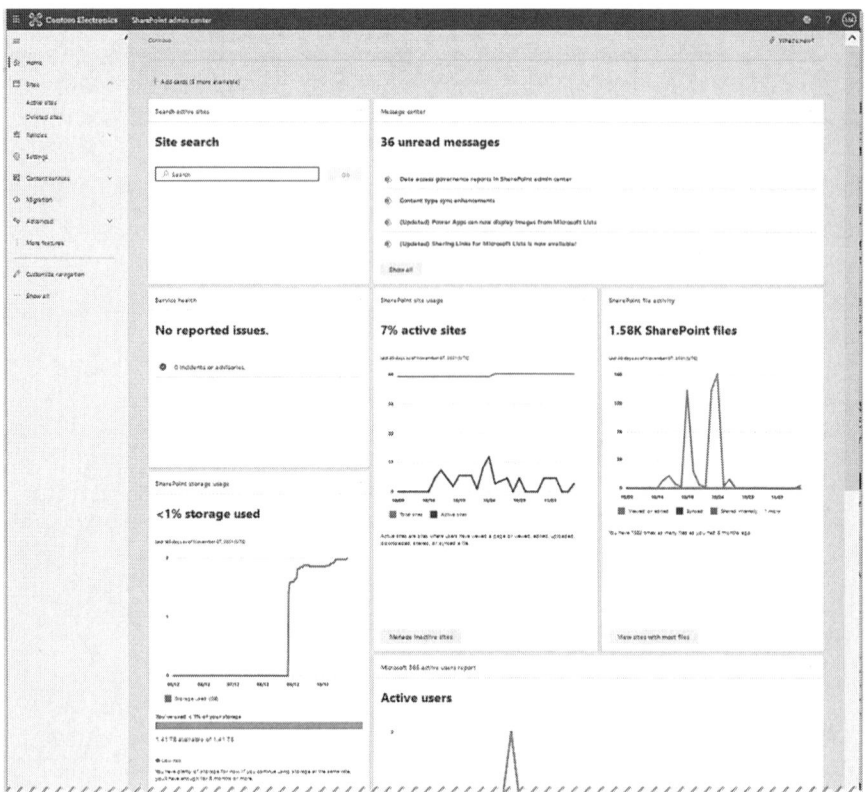

58

5.2.2 Sites

Under the Sites entry, you can see and edit all active sites, delete and restore sites and create new sites. This subject is expanded in 6.6, Sites in the SharePoint Admin Center.

5.2.3 Policies

Under the Policies entry, you can make some setting that increases the security for the organization's data. You can for example set tenant wide limits for sharing, *refer to* 15.1, Admin Center Sharing Settings.

5.2.3.1 Access Control

The Access control entry under 'Polices' lets admins restrict how users can access SharePoint content. You can for example only allow access from certain IP addresses or sign out users automatically from inactive browser sessions.

5.2.4 Settings

As we have already seen, it is on the Settings dashboard that you can decide the default experience for the Admin center. It is also here you can set a Home site for the tenant, *refer to* 6.9.1, Make Home Site.

Under Settings, you can also disable some default permissions. You can, for example remove the permission for users to create sites or modern pages, and you can set storage limits, change the tenant's landing page and more.

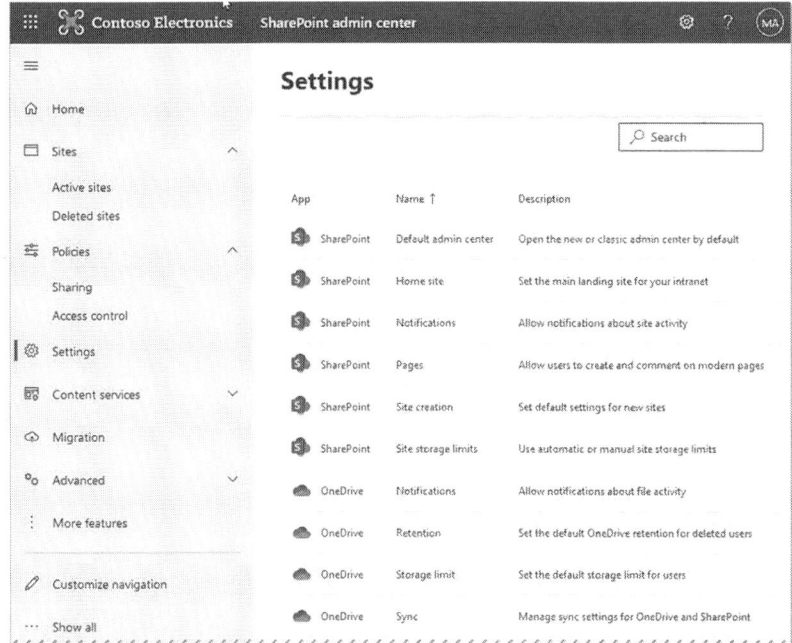

Note that even if you disable creation of modern sites, all users by default are allowed to create Microsoft 365 Group s. When such a group is created, a SharePoint Group Team site will be created automatically, even if site creation is disabled in the SharePoint Admin center.

5.2.5 Content Services

Under 'Content services' in the SharePoint Admin center, you can find the Term store and the Content type gallery. These are meant for more advanced use of SharePoint Online, and we will come back to both later in this book.

5.2.6 Migration

The Migration entry is useful when you need to migrate content from another cloud platform or from SharePoint on-premises to SharePoint Online.

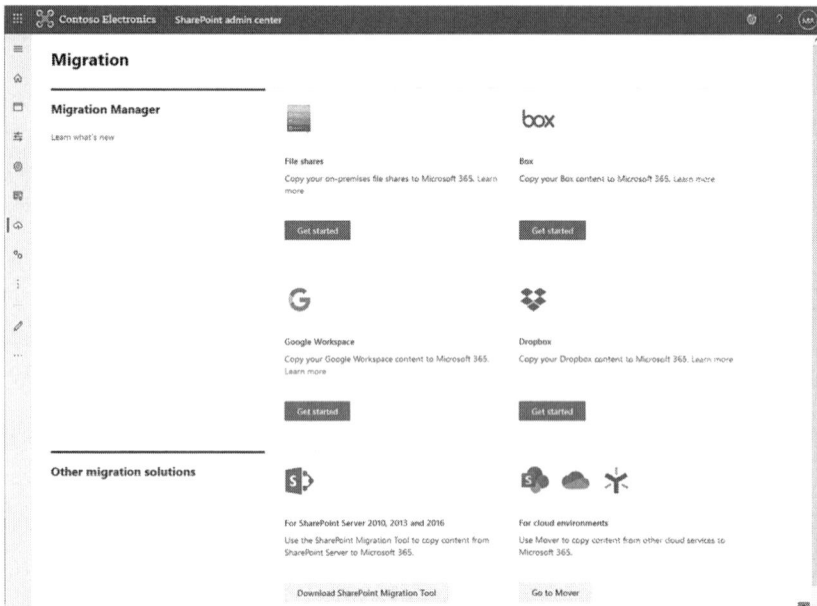

5.2.7 More Features

Under 'More features', you can find settings from the classic experience. Some of these features are interesting even if you use the modern experience.

5.2.7.1 Apps – App Catalog

Under 'Apps' in the SharePoint Admin center >More features, you can configure the SharePoint App Store and manage app licenses in various ways.

Here is also where you create an App Catalog site for the tenant. When you add and update custom or third-party APP and SPPKG files, for example SharePoint products from kalmstrom.com, to the App Catalog, users can easily install them in sites or embed them in pages.

1. Under Apps, click on 'App Catalog'.
2. Keep the default option, 'Create a new app catalog site' and click OK.
3. Fill out the details.
4. Click on the address book icon at 'Administrator' and search for an administrator name. Select a name and click OK.

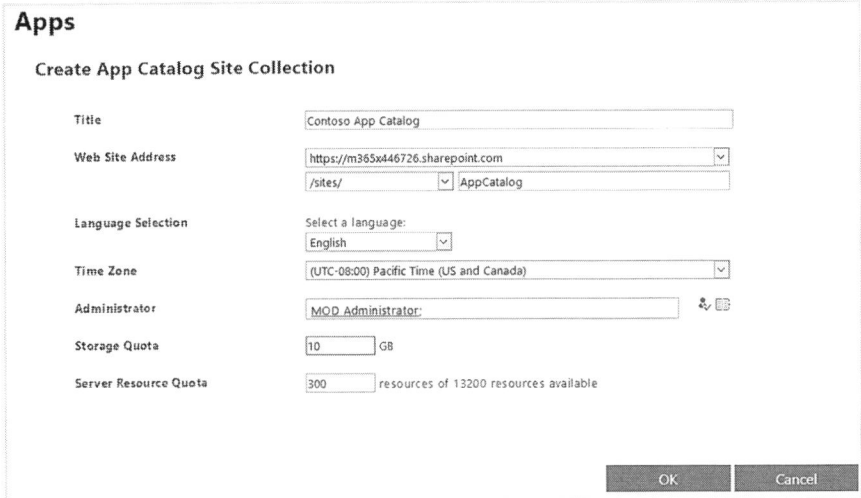

Now you can find the App Catalog under 'Active sites' in the SharePoint Admin center.

The App Catalog is a special kind of site, but it reminds of the classic Team site that I will describe later in this book.

61

Click on 'Apps for SharePoint' to get to a library where you can upload APP or SPPKG files that you want to have available in the tenant. You can also drag files from your computer to the Apps for SharePoint library.

Be careful when you upload files to the App Catalog. Only add files from trusted sites and suppliers.

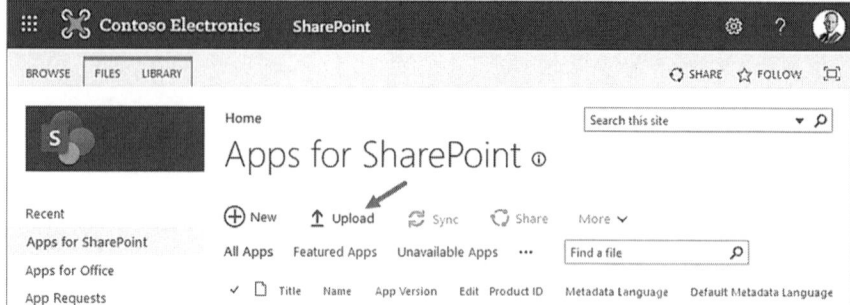

Uploaded APP files will be displayed under 'From Your Organization' when users use the command 'Add an app'. SPPKG files will show up among the available web parts in modern pages.

Demo:

https://kalmstrom.com/Tips/SharePoint-Online-Course/App-Catalog.htm

5.2.7.2   Search

As we saw in section 4.3, Search, SharePoint has two search experiences that work on different content. Under More features >Search, in the SharePoint Admin center, you can find many settings for the classic search. (The modern search is managed in the Microsoft 365 Admin center, *refer to* 3.1.1, Search and Intelligence.)

As both search experiences use the same index, most customizations in the classic experience affect the modern search, but there is an important exception:

Some Microsoft Search features might not work if the classic global Search Center URL is set to something else than "yourcompanyname.sharepoint.com/search/pages". Therefore, I recommend that you don't make any changes to the Search Center URL here.

5.2.8   *OneDrive Admin Center*

OneDrive for Business is each users personal SharePoint site. We will have a closer look at OneDrive for Business in chapter 12, Personal Content, and in that chapter, I have also included a section about how to control OneDrive from the Microsoft 365 and SharePoint Admin centers.

5.3 Summary

We have now had a first look at the SharePoint Admin center, but we will have reason to come back here later in this book. This chapter has just given an overview of the SharePoint Admin center.

In the next chapter, I will describe the most important SharePoint building block: the site. I will explain what is common for all sites and what is the difference between the most used SharePoint site templates.

6 SHAREPOINT SITES

The sites are the core of SharePoint. All content is added, and all work is done, within the context of a site. A site nearly always contains apps and pages that users have created, and the site might also have subsites with its own apps and pages.

One tenant can have from a few up to two million sites. I would recommend that you have many, instead of gathering too much data in the same site.

SharePoint Online has several different kinds of sites, and in this chapter, I will describe the commonly used site types. These are the sites that you most likely want to create when you are new to SharePoint, and as they can be highly customized for different needs, they are sufficient for most businesses and organizations.

In addition to the classic Team site, which I will describe below, there are, some other classic site types. Should your organization need to use one of these sites, I am sure that you can explore them on your own when you have been used to working with the common site types. The differences are not that extensive.

SharePoint sites can be customized in many ways. You can modify the site's homepage and add different kinds of apps, pages and subsites to it. And all these additions can in turn be customized, so how a SharePoint site looks and how it is used is very flexible.

Three of the site types I will describe here are called modern sites, and one is a classic site. The site types are:

- The modern Communication site
- The modern Group Team site
- The modern Team site without a group
- The classic Team site

The three Team site types are all intended for collaboration. Therefore, they have common features that are not present in the Communication site. On the other hand, the Communication site has some features that are not present in any of the other site types.

Team sites and Communication sites also look different. All SharePoint Team sites by default have a navigation pane to the left on the page. It is called Site navigation, as it usually shows links to content within the current site. Communication sites instead have the navigation on top of the page. You will learn more about navigation in chapter 11.

I will start with clarifying a few terms before I describe the site types and explain how they are created and how they can be managed.

At the end of the chapter, I will go through two ways of connecting sites, and I will also explain how to delete and restore sites.

6.1 Site Terms

Before we go into the different site types, there are some terms that you need to understand.

6.1.1 Root Site and Homepage

Each site has its own URL, and by default sites that users can create have the URL https://[tenant name].sharepoint.com/sites/[site name].

https://m365x446726.sharepoint.com/sites/ContosoNews

(The 'sites' part can be changed, *refer to* 5.2.4, Settings, but if you are new to SharePoint, I recommend that you keep the default.)

The site is called "root site", as opposed to any potential subsites, and the landing page of the root site is called the site's "homepage".

When you add content to the site, the name and storage place of that content will be added to the root site URL.

Modern sites get a modern homepage that is customized with dedicated web parts, which you can add, remove or reorder as needed. Classic sites get another kind of homepage, which also can be highly customized. I describe all page customization in chapter 13, SharePoint Site Pages.

6.1.2 Site and Site Collection

A root site, its subsites, and all their content, can be called a "site collection", but often the word "site" is also used to indicate a root site *and* any subsites and all content.

Microsoft has recently announced that the usage of the label "site collection" will go away. Instead, the word site will always be used for a root site and all its content. I will use "site" in that meaning here, but you will meet the word "site collection" in many of the SharePoint settings and in documentation online.

In retrospect, it would perhaps have been better to never have introduced the concept of subsites, but that design choice was made by Microsoft more than 20 years ago. Subsite creation is still supported, and I will explain how to create subsites below – but I will also explain how to create the currently recommended hub families!

6.2 Sites in the SharePoint Admin Center

There are settings for sites in two places in the SharePoint Admin center. Some general settings for all sites are found under 'Settings', *refer to* 5.2.4, Settings.

If your organization just started to use SharePoint, you might want to disable the standard users' possibility to create sites here, until you all feel more comfortable with SharePoint.

Most of the site management is however handled under 'Sites' in the SharePoint Admin center.

6.2.1   Sites

Under 'Sites' in the SharePoint Admin center, you can select to show either active or deleted sites. Under 'Deleted sites' you can see and restore deleted sites, *refer to* 6.14, Delete and Restore Sites.

In the 'Active sites' page, you can reach information about all active sites, create new sites, register hub sites and associate sites with a hub site. Note that only root sites are displayed under 'Active sites', not subsites. Sites that are used by a team in Microsoft Teams are marked with the Teams icon in a separate column.

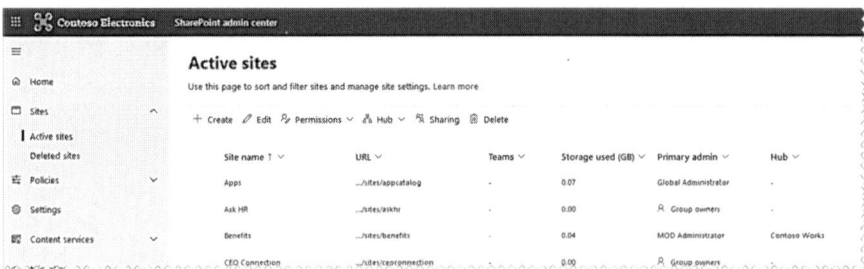

You can select multiple sites and edit or delete them in bulk, and you can also bulk edit the external sharing and hub site association settings.

The list of sites under 'Active sites' gives a lot of information in the many columns, but the presentation can be customized. The dropdown at each column has a 'Customize columns' command that opens a right pane where you can decide which columns to show and in what order. The dropdowns also have sort or filter options.

There are multiple built-in views for Active sites, in addition to the default "All sites". Create custom views by combining the built-in views with filter options for the columns in the site list. There is a 'Save view as' command in the View selector to the right, so that you can keep the custom view.

With the 'Track view' command, you can add information from all sites in a view to your SharePoint Admin center homepage. As the cards on the homepage dashboard are personal, each admin can customize the homepage to suit themselves.

Select a view in the View selector, click on 'Track view' in the command bar and then click on 'Add card'. The 'All sites' view cannot be tracked.

Active sites

Use this pa Add a card to your homepage to track these sites tings. Learn more

When no site is selected, the command bar above the list of sites gives the options to create a new site, export the site information to a CSV file, track the current view, search the sites and select another view.

When one site is selected under Active sites, the command bar gives multiple options for how to manage that site.

When multiple sites are selected, there is a Bulk edit option.

6.2.1.1 Edit an Active Site

Under 'Active sites', you can manage administrators for the site, set rules for sharing and storage and delete the site. When you click on a site name in the list, or if you select a site and click on the information icon to the right in the command bar, an Information pane for the site will open to the right.

Green restaurant	
General Activity Permissions Policies	
Site name	**URL**
Green restaurant	.../sites/Greenrestaurant
Edit	Edit
Hub association	**Storage limit**
Restaurants	1.00 TB
Edit	Edit
Template	**Microsoft 365 Group connected**
Team site	Yes
Domain	**Description**
kalmstromnet.sharepoint.com	None

The first tab gives general information and a link to open the site. (You can also open the site directly by clicking on the URL in the list of sites.)

As you see in the image above, it is possible to edit the site name part of the URL. For example, if you have a site named https://contoso.sharepoint.com/sites/Develpment, you can rename the site to correct the incorrect spelling of "development".

A redirect will be generated automatically, to ensure that links do not break, but an URL change can still create problems so you should not change a site URL unless it is necessary.

Note that this change only modifies the URL, not the site name that is visible on the site itself. To rename the site, *refer to* 6.3.2, Site Settings.

Depending on the size of the site, it can take up to ten minutes to change the site address. During this time, the site will be read-only, so if you need to change a site URL you should do it when site usage is low.

Under the Activity tab, you can see statistics for the site.

General	**Activity**	Permissions	Policies

As of October 4, 2020 (UTC)

Last site activity	**Files stored**
October 4, 2020 (UTC)	45 files
Page views in the last 30 days	**Page visits in the last 30 days**
46 page views	14 page visits
Files viewed/edited in the last 30 days	**Storage usage**
11 files	1017.38 MB
	10% (1017.38 MB of 10.00 GB)

Under the Permissions tab, you can set the permissions for the site.

Under the 'Policies' tab, you can edit the site's settings for external sharing and sensitivity. It is here you may restrict external sharing for the site when it is allowed in the tenant.

General	Activity	Permissions	**Policies**

External sharing	**Sensitivity**
Files and folders on this site can be shared with anyone	None
Edit	Edit

6.3 COMMON SITE FEATURES

All sites have some common features that are reached from the Settings icon in the 365 navigation bar. Some of these features can also be reached in other ways, as described below.

6.3.1 *Site Contents*

To see all the contents of a site, click on the 'Site contents' link in the site's navigation, or open the 365 Settings icon and select 'Site contents'.

A page with links to all content in the site will open. In all Team sites, this page can be viewed in both the modern and the classic experience (as opposed to other SharePoint pages). There is a switch link under the Site navigation to the left.

Return to classic SharePoint

Exit classic experience

The Communication site can only show the Site contents modern experience.

Both interfaces have links to the site's workflows, settings and recycle bin above the actual contents of the site.

Modern pages also have site statistics, and if Access requests are enabled in the site's sharing settings, *refer to* 15.2.4.1, there is an 'Access requests' button.

6.3.1.1 The Recycle Bins

In the site's Recycle bin library, deleted content is retained for 93 days. Here, you can either restore selected content or delete it.

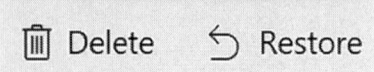

When no item is selected, there is instead a button to empty the recycle bin of all content.

Content that is deleted from the recycle bin, and content that has been in the Recycle bin for 93 days, is not permanently deleted. Instead, will be moved to the Second-stage recycle bin, where it is kept for another 93 days.

The link to the Second-stage bin is found below the items in in the Recycle bin library, but only the Site admin can see the link and restore or permanently delete content from the Second-stage bin.

> Can't find what you're looking for? Check the Second-stage recycle bin

6.3.1.2 The Modern Site Contents

The modern Site contents interface has two tabs: one for subsites and one for other content.

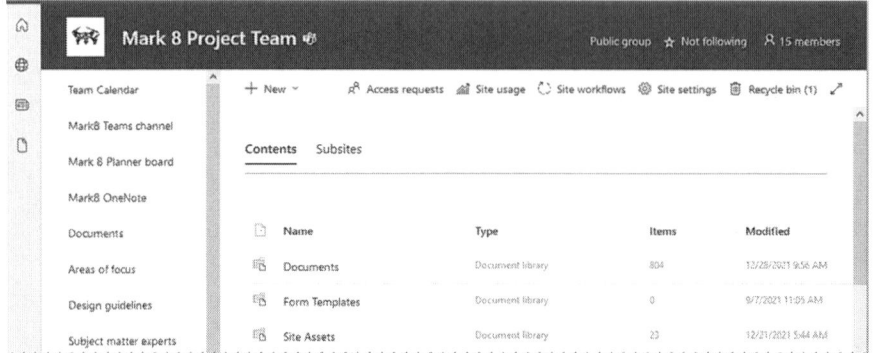

To the right of each app name in the Site contents, an ellipsis becomes visible when you hover the mouse over the item.

Click on the ellipsis to reach more information about the app.

Under the Contents tab, the app ellipses let you delete the app, reach the app settings and see details.

When you select the 'Details' option under the ellipsis, you will have a description of the app. You can also create another app of the same type by clicking on the ADD IT button.

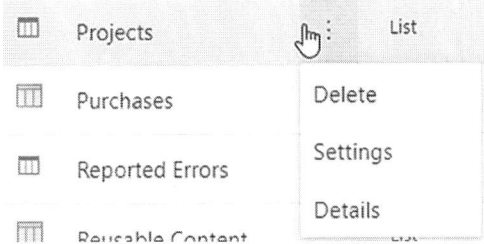

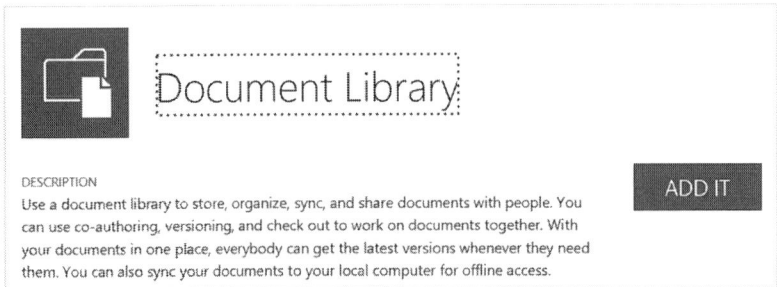

Under the Subsites tab, the ellipsis gives a link to the Site contents of the subsite. The subsite Site contents is built in the same way as the Site contents of the root site.

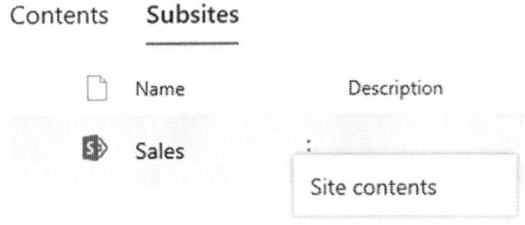

In the Site contents command bar, there is a 'New' button to create new apps, pages and subsites. We will come back to this dropdown many times in later chapters.

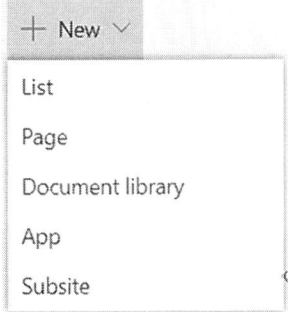

6.3.1.3 The Classic Site Contents

The **classic** Site contents interface shows the items as tiles and gives a possibility to add an app. Any subsites are placed below the other content.

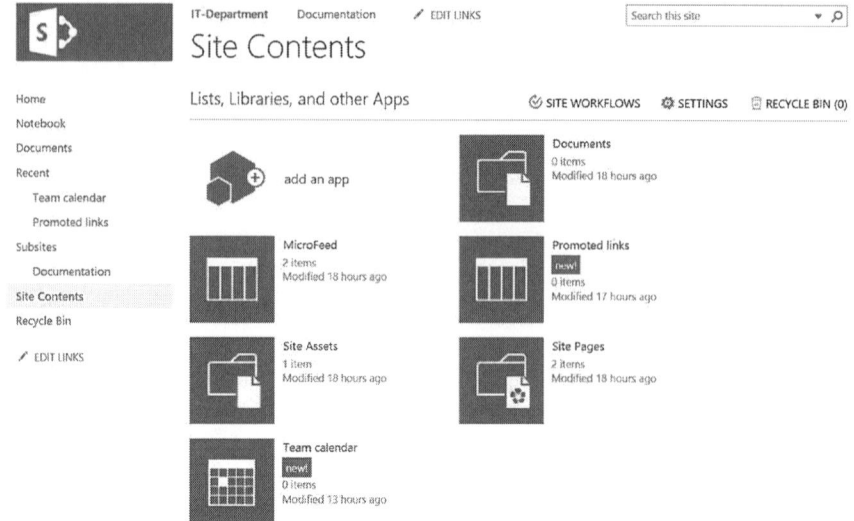

Click on the ellipsis in the top right corner of a tile to reach the same three options as under the ellipsis in the modern experience, here called Settings, About and Remove.

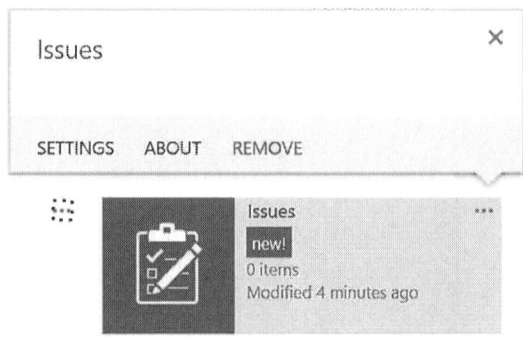

6.3.2 Site Settings

The administration of a site is most often done in the Site settings. You can reach the settings for the current site via the settings button in the Site contents, *see* above, and from the 365 Settings icon.

The classic experience has a 'Site settings' link directly under the Settings icon.

The image to the right comes from a page with the modern interface. Here, the 365 Settings icon has a 'Site information' link.

When you click on 'Site information', some basic site settings are displayed in a right pane. Here, you can for example upload a site logo and rename the site. (In the classic experience, this is done under the Look and Feel heading in the Site settings.)

At the bottom of that pane, click on 'View all site settings' to reach the full site settings page.

Settings

SharePoint
Add a page
Add an app
Site contents
Site information
Site permissions
Apply a site template
Site usage
Site performance
Schedule site launch
Change the look

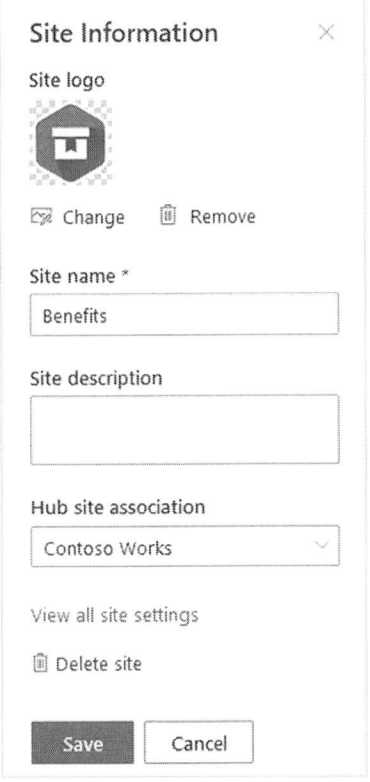

The Site settings page has links to site control pages, grouped under headings to be easier to find. Which controls you can find depend on the site type and on your permission level.

Root sites have more controls than subsites, and settings that are only available in the root site apply to the subsites too. The image below comes from a root site built on the classic team site, which is the one that gives most options.

Home   Sales   Development   ✏ EDIT LINKS

Site Settings

Users and Permissions
People and groups
Site permissions
Access requests and invitations
Site collection administrators
Site app permissions

Web Designer Galleries
Site columns
Site content types
Web parts
List templates
Master pages
Themes
Solutions
Composed looks

Site Administration
Regional settings
Language settings
Site libraries and lists
User alerts
RSS
Sites and workspaces
Workflow settings
Site Closure and Deletion
Term store management
Popularity Trends
Translation Status

Search
Result Sources
Result Types
Query Rules
Schema
Search Settings
Search and offline availability
Configuration Import
Configuration Export

Look and Feel
Title, description, and logo
Quick launch
Top link bar
Navigation Elements
Change the look

Site Actions
Manage site features
Enable search configuration export
Reset to site definition
Delete this site

Site Collection Administration
Recycle bin
Search Result Sources
Search Result Types
Search Query Rules
Search Schema
Search Settings
Search Configuration Import
Search Configuration Export
Site collection features
Site hierarchy
Site collection audit settings
Audit log reports
Portal site connection
Content Type Policy Templates
Storage Metrics
Site collection app permissions
Record declaration settings
Site Policies
Content type publishing
Popularity and Search Reports
Translatable columns
HTML Field Security
SharePoint Designer Settings
Site collection health checks
Site collection upgrade

We will come back to the Site settings many times in this book. Here I will just mention a few of the controls, while others will be introduced later.

6.3.2.1   Change the Look

Under the Site settings 'Look and Feel' heading, see the image above, you can change the name and description of the site and replace the default SharePoint logo with a custom image.

You can also change the site's colors and fonts under 'Change the look'. The default theme is called Office, but there are various other themes to choose from.

The default Team site layout, 'Seattle', has the Site navigation pane to the left. Communication sites use the 'Oslo' layout, which has the Site navigation on top of each page.

The modern experience has additional 'Change the look' settings, *see* below.

6.3.2.2 Site Collection Administration

The links under the Site Collection Administration heading can only be reached from the root site of the site collection, and the group can only be seen and used by Site admins.

One of the links under Site Collection Administration is 'Site collection features'. Here, site admins can activate features that are not enabled by default, for example the 'SharePoint Server Enterprise Site Collection features' for the Enterprise subscriptions. It gives classic web parts for InfoPath Forms Services, Visio Services, Access Services, and Excel Services.

Another site collection feature is 'SharePoint Server Publishing Infrastructure', which we will come back to in chapter 27.

6.3.2.3 Site Actions

The 'Manage site features' link under the Site Actions heading, takes you to a page where site owners can activate various extra SharePoint features for the current site.

Site owners can also deactivate features that are activated by default, such as users' possibility to create site pages or follow sites and documents.

Classic sites can be saved as a template under the Site Actions heading. (Modern sites cannot easily be saved as a template.)

6.3.3 *Site Usage*

The Site usage page shows various statistics on the site usage and sharing of site contents. Pages with the **modern** interface have a link to the Site usage page under the 365 Settings icon, and the modern Site contents experience has a 'Site usage' button in the command bar.

Pages with the **classic** interface do not have a Site usage link under the Settings icon, but if you open the Site contents with the modern interface, you will see site usage for classic sites too.

At the bottom of the Site usage page, site owners can generate a CSV file that shows how the site's content has been shared inside and (if external sharing is allowed) outside the organization.

The report is saved to a new or existing folder in the default document library, and an e-mail with a link is sent to the person who generated the file.

6.3.4   Site Permissions

By default, there are four permission levels on a site:

- Admin. In bigger organizations, the Site admins are the link to the IT department. Site admins are the only people who can manage the search, the recycle bin, the web designer galleries and the site collection features.
- Owner. The Site owners have full control over all the site's content, but they are not allowed to view or modify the more technical aspects of the site management.
- Members have edit permissions on the SharePoint site and can add, change and remove apps and items and create pages.
- Visitors can only view content, not change or add anything on the site, but they can download files.

The person who creates a site automatically becomes Site admin as well as Site owner, but Global and SharePoint administrators can edit these permissions under 'Active Sites' in the SharePoint Admin center.

Refer to chapter 14, Permissions, for more information about site permissions.

6.4   MODERN SITES

By default, all SharePoint users can create modern sites from their SharePoint start page. We will come back to site creation in section 6.10, but first we will have a look at the commonly used site types.

We will start with the modern site types, as they are the most common. They have some shared features in addition to the fact that they use a modern interface in most pages.

The homepage of a modern site is always a modern page that can – and should – be customized. Dedicated web parts are used for the customization, *refer to* 13.4, Customize a Modern Page.

6.4.1   Command Bar

The homepage of a modern site has a command bar above the actual page content. It has controls for new content, page information and analytics, but there may also be other controls, like Immersive reading. Other modern pages also have this command bar.

To the right, the command bar has information about the page publication, a possibility to open the page in Edit mode and a control that hides the navigation so that you get a bigger workspace.

Published 11/14/2021   ✏ Edit   ↗

The Site contents has a similar command bar in the modern interface, but only a '+New' button is displayed to the left. As you have seen above in 6.3.1, Site Contents, other options are displayed to the right. The Site contents '+New' button gives less options than the '+New' button on the homepage, but the options are also different for different site types.

Apps with the modern interface also has a command bad, but it has other controls. These are described in the chapters about apps below.

6.4.2 'Change the Look' Pane

In addition to the settings under 'Look and Feel', in the Site settings, the modern experience has a 'Change the look' setting under the 365 Settings icon. It gives additional options that are only available to modern sites.

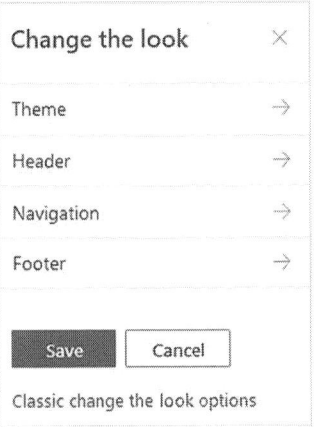

When you click on the modern 'Change the look' link, a pane will open where you can select a theme and customize the site's header with an image, background color and more.

There are also options for the navigation. Site owners can choose to show or hide the site navigation, and in modern Team sites, they can choose between vertical or horizontal orientation.

The image to the right comes from a Communication site. This site type also gives a possibility to customize the footer.

At the bottom of the right pane, there is a link to the classic 'Change the look' page that also can be reached from the Site settings.

Note that there are templates for modern sites that also change the look, *refer to* 6.4.4.

6.4.2.1 Mega Menu

Instead of the traditional cascading menu where links come in a row, you can use a mega menu, where the links are placed in a hierarchy. It is possible to create mega menus in all site types, but in modern sites Microsoft has made it easy to arrange the links in three levels.

In the mega menu in the image below, 'Events' and 'Join the conversation' are labels under 'Happenings', and the third level has links to the different happenings.

The mega menu is default in Communication sites. In Team sites, a mega menu can be used if you change the navigation orientation from vertical to horizontal.

The mega menu is edited just like other navigation, as described in chapter 11, SharePoint Navigation.

6.4.3   App Bar

To the left in all modern sites, below the App launcher, an app bar gives each user access to his/her SharePoint start page, sites, news and recently used files and lists.

The Home icon can be customized to point to other content, for example to the top SharePoint landing page for the organization's tenant.

List apps are fetched from and open in Microsoft Lists, *refer to* 8.3. Only shared lists that can have the modern interface are included.

The app bar will not be visible to external or guest users from outside of the tenant.

Microsoft plans to make it possible for admins to add an app bar to classic sites manually.

6.4.4   Templates

When you have created a modern site, you can apply a template to it. The template creates a new homepage with pre-populated content and web parts. It also adds pre-built pages, apps and news post templates to the site.

The site's existing content will be kept and can be reached from the Site content, but the default homepage will be the one that the template created.

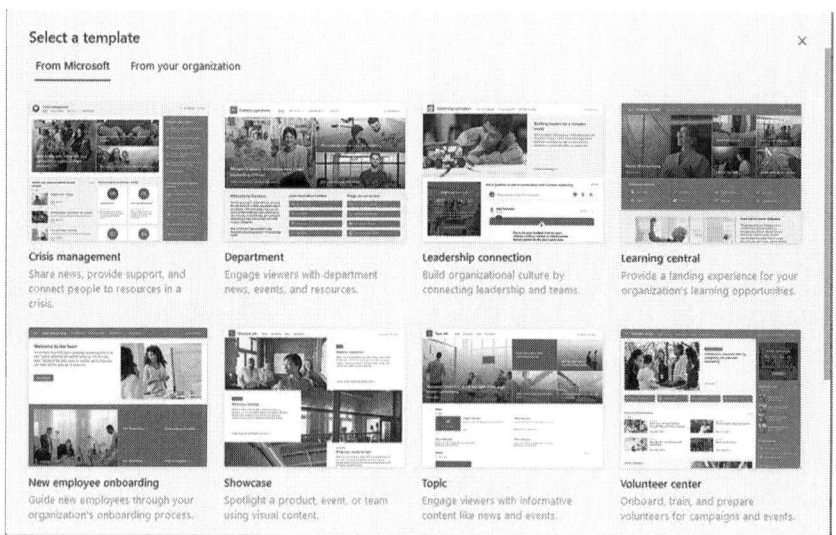

When you click on 'Apply a site template' under the 365 Settings icon, a dialog with multiple template options will open. The image above comes from a Communication site. Team sites have different options.

The templates may be provided by either Microsoft or the organization/a third party. (Template creation for the 'From your organization' tab requires PowerShell knowledge, so it is out of scope for this book.)

When a template has been applied, the site should of course be customized to fit the needs of your organization. The customization is performed in the same way whether you use a template or not, and it is described in detail later in this book.

Each template also has its own customization guide to help site owners and editors to get started.

6.4.5   Communication Site

Just as the name suggests, a Communication site is used to communicate information, not primarily for collaboration. Usually, a Communication site has only a few authors but a larger number of readers. A high-traffic Communication site is also called a "portal".

A new Communication site has web parts for News, Events, Documents, Quick links and Comments.

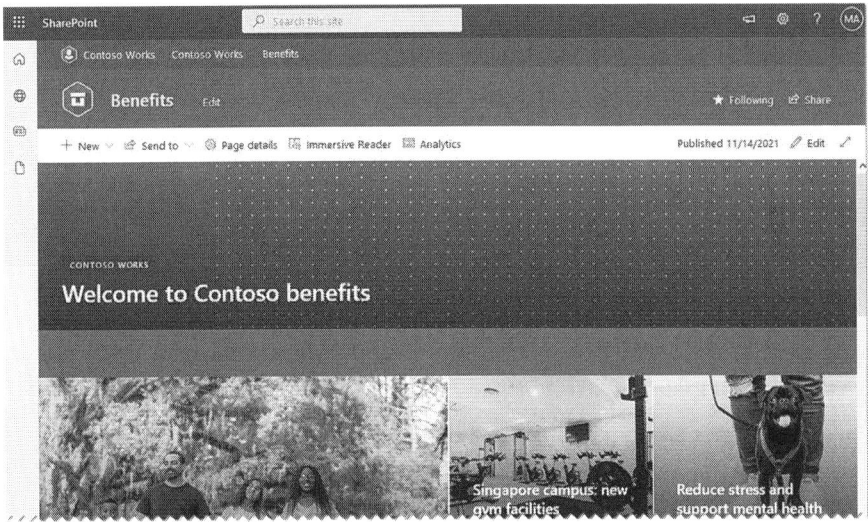

The Communication site has a navigation bar on top of each page except settings pages.

6.4.5.1   Classic Compatibility

Communication sites are meant to be modern. The only content with the classic experience in Communication sites are settings pages and other automatically created pages.

It is not possible to add a classic page to a Communication site, and apps only have the modern interface. There is no possibility to switch to the classic interface.

Compared to Team sites, only a few apps can be created in a Communication site. By default, it is only possible to add one app that solely has the classic interface: the Calendar app. The commonly used Tasks list, that only has the classic interface, cannot be added to a Communication site.

There is a setting that gives more app options, among them the Tasks list, *refer to* 7.5.1.1, Apps in Communication Sites. You should however be aware that the Communication site is primarily intended for information, not for cooperation.

6.4.5.2 Footer

By default, the Communication site has a footer that can be customized with links, text and a logo. You can however disable the footer.

The footer is edited in the 'Change the look', right pane, which you can reach from the 365 Settings icon, *see* above.

Note that the footer is only shown in the homepage and modern pages. It is not displayed if you switch to an app.

If you want to use the footer and enhance it further, click on 'Edit' in the bottom right corner of the footer and add links or text in the left menu that opens.

Text will automatically be placed to the left and links to the right in the footer.

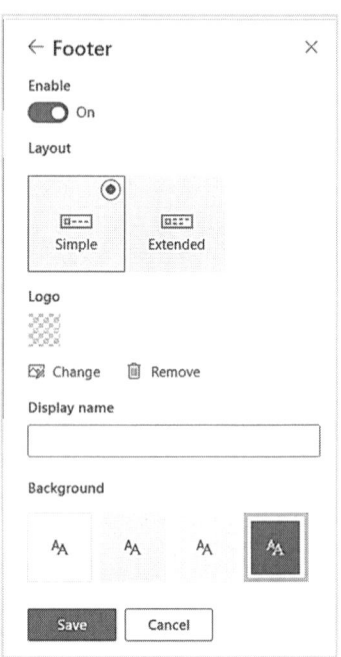

6.4.5.3 Page Translations

Organizations with staff in different countries will benefit from having their intranet sites available in multiple languages. Communication sites take this into regard in Site settings > Site Administration >Language settings.

Here, site owners can enable translation of pages and news and assign translators for each language. The translators will be notified by e-mail when a page has been created or updated in the default language, so that they can translate the content.

Site languages

The default language for this site is English. You can choose options for using multiple languages on this site.

Enable pages and news to be translated into multiple languages
On

Add or remove site languages

Language	Translators	
English	Not applicable for site default language	
Swedish	kate@kalmstrom.com × Select or type a translator	Remove language
Spanish	MOD Administrator × Select or type a translator	Remove language

Select or type a language

When the translation has been enabled, there will be two new links under the Site Administration heading, to export and import translation files. These files are in the .resx format, and translators can for example work with them in Visual Studio.

Site visitors will automatically see pages and news in their preferred user language, if it is available. Otherwise, the default language will be used.

Site Administration
Regional settings
Language settings
Export Translations
Import Translations

6.4.5.4   Schedule Site Launch

Communication sites give a possibility to schedule the launching of new or updated sites. This feature is primarily intended for portals with many visitors, such as a tenant's Home site.

When you use the scheduling tool, the launch is done in at least two waves. This way, you can let groups of users give feedback, and you will have a chance to make changes and monitor performance before the site is launched to all users.

It is suitable to use Security groups, *refer to* 14.3, Security Groups, to add people that should be included in the waves. Other groups can also be used, but Microsoft 365 Groups are currently not supported.

The first times you edit and republish changes to the tenant's start page, you will be prompted to use the scheduler tool. Select 'Republish if you don't want to use the tool.

After that, and in other Communication sites, you can open the 365 Settings icon and select 'Schedule site launch'. You need to be at least Site owner to use the scheduling tool.

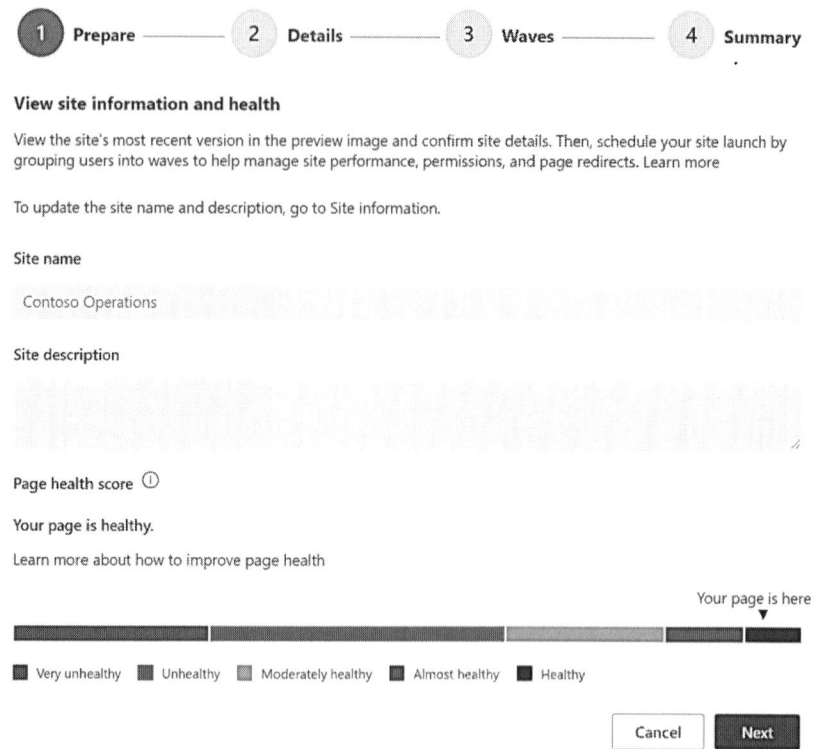

These are the steps in the scheduled site launch:

1. Give each user or group that needs access to the site permission as Site owner, Site member, or Visitor.
2. Check the portal's health score. If needed, use the Page Diagnostics tool, *refer to* 13.6, Page Diagnostics, to achieve the score Healthy. (This can be achieved even if the diagnostics tool points to minor issues.)
3. Select the number of expected users who will need access to the site, and the scheduler will automatically determine the ideal number of waves. Two waves are recommended for less than 10 000 users.
4. Determine the redirect needed. In the image below, the default option is selected, so users in the wave will reach the new portal while other users will be sent to the old site.

   The other options are to send users in the wave to a temporary or external page.

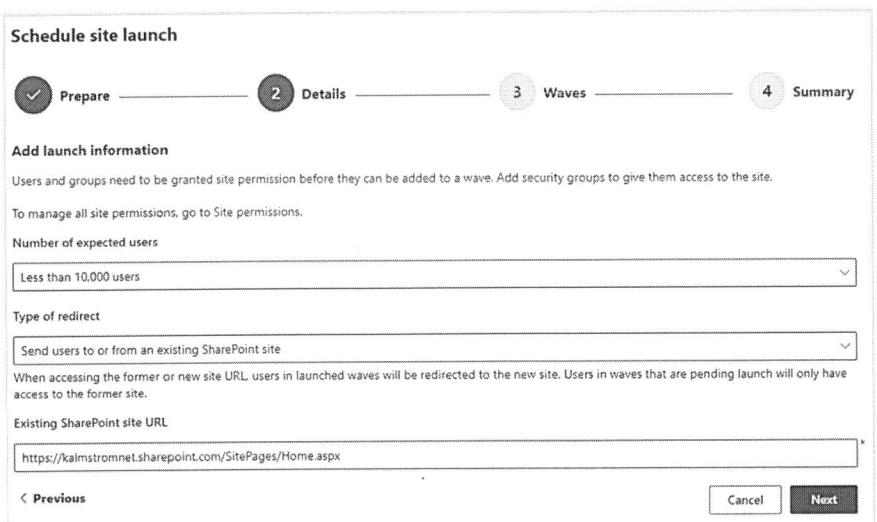

5. Enter the groups that should be included in the waves and set the times for when the wave should start. Each wave can last between 24 hours and seven days before the next wave gets access to the site.

   At 'Users exempt from waves' you can add users who need to view the site right away. These users will not be redirected.

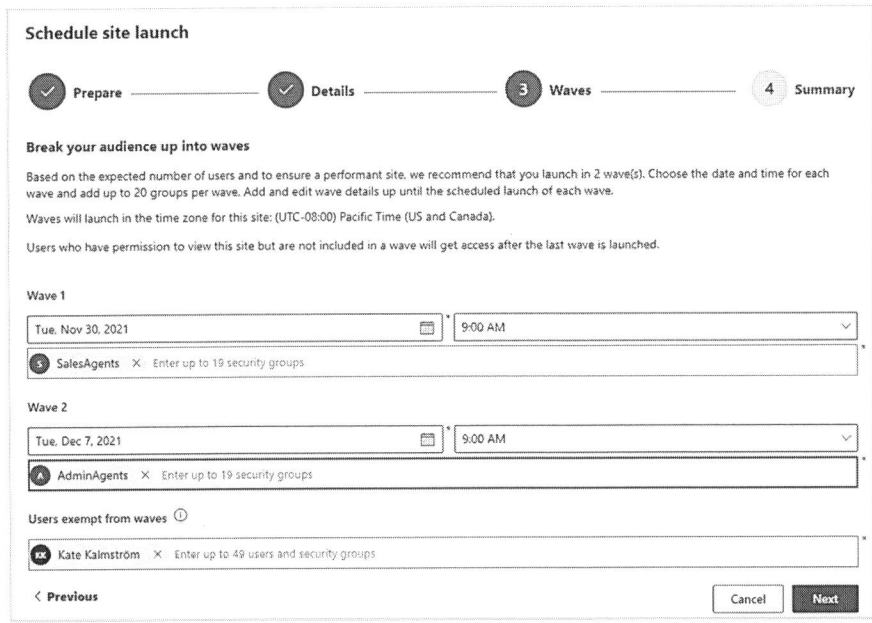

6. Review the summary and submit the launch details.

6.4.6 Modern Team Site

A Team site is a place for collaboration, so it is a site where many people both add content and view it.

By default, the homepage of the modern Team site has web parts for News, Activity, Quick links, Documents and Comments. Above these web parts, there is a command bar of the same kind as in the Communication site, but the Site navigation is placed to the left, not on top.

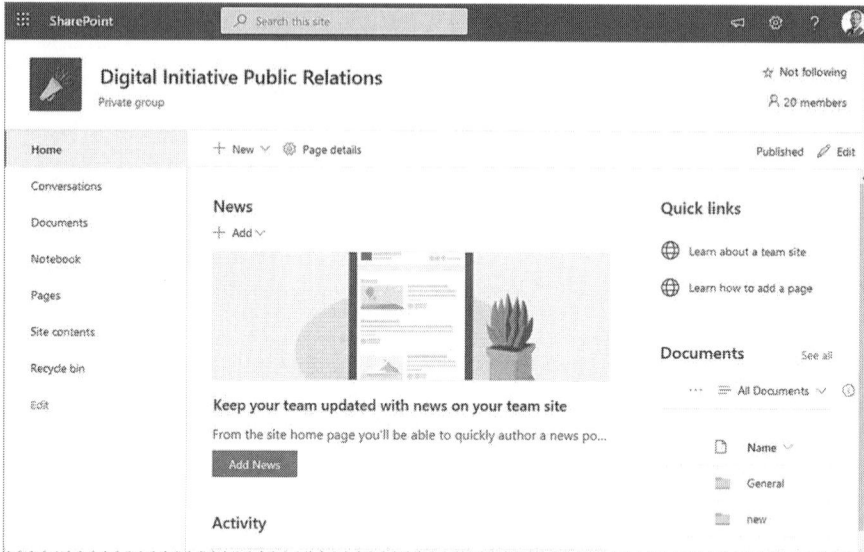

The modern Team site is often connected to a Microsoft 365 Group. In those cases, it is called a Group Team site.

6.4.6.1 Classic Compatibility

The modern Team site is fully compatible with the classic experience. You can create classic pages in modern Team sites, and you can switch to the classic interface and use apps that only have the classic interface without problems.

The only issue is that a few classic web parts do not work well in classic pages that are contained in modern Team sites. The examples I give in this book are not among those!

6.4.6.2 Group Team Site

When a modern Team site is created from the SharePoint start page, it will always be a Group Team site, and a Microsoft 365 Group will be created automatically together with the site.

A Microsoft 365 Group is a group of people that share resources. The site owner will also be the group owner, and all users that are added as site members in the site creation process will be members of the group.

In addition to the Group Team site, the Microsoft 365 Group also has other shared apps and services. Some of them can be reached from the group's SharePoint site:

- There is always a shared e-mail inbox, and the group e-mail name is by default the same as the Group Team site name.

  The Group's inbox, settings and other shared resources can be reached via the 'Conversations' link in the Group Team site's Site navigation.

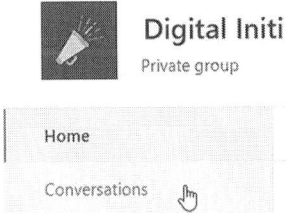

- Planner is a planning app connected to Microsoft 365 groups. The Planner icon is visible to all users in the 365 App launcher.

  A Planner "plan" is a goal that you want to achieve or a project you are working on, and in Planner, you can see and manage the various tasks and steps that you and your colleagues must perform to reach the goal or finish the project.

  When you click on the Planner tile in the App launcher, you will be directed to the Planner hub at https://tasks.office.com,

  When you select 'Plan' from the '+ New' button on the homepage of a Group Team site, you can work with the plans directly in SharePoint.

  A right pane will open, where you can either create a new plan or open an existing plan.

  The new or existing plan will open on the Group Team site homepage, and all changes are synchronized with the Planner site.

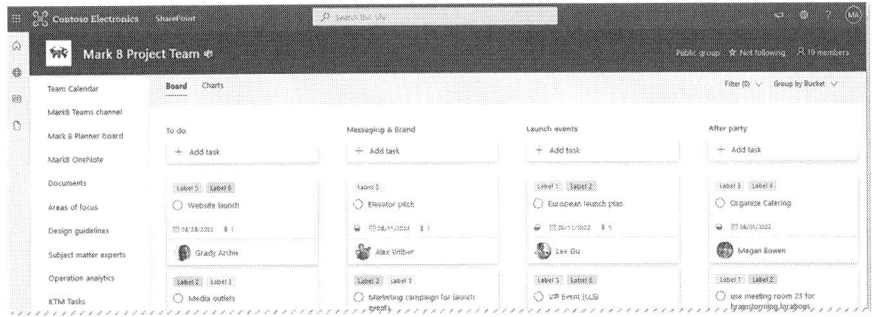

85

- Microsoft 365 Groups often cooperate via Microsoft Teams. When the group is not connected to Teams, a team can easily be created via a prompt below the Site navigation in the Group Team site.

    When the Microsoft 365 Group is connected to Teams, the group can also be managed in Teams. The apps and pages in the Group Team site can easily be added to Teams, so that people can work with the SharePoint content in Teams instead of going to the SharePoint site.

    Add real-time chat

    Add Microsoft Teams to collaborate in real-time and share resources across Microsoft 365 with your team.

    Add Microsoft Teams

    A Group Team site that is used by a Teams team, has an icon at the site name in SharePoint. Click on the icon to open Teams.

    Refer to my book *Office 365 from Scratch* for more info about Microsoft 365 Groups and to *Microsoft Teams from Scratch* for information about Teams.

6.4.6.3 Team Site without a Group

A modern Team site can also be created without being connected to a Microsoft 365 Group. This is suitable when the collaboration is broader and involves people who should not form a Microsoft 365 Group.

While all users with Edit permission can create Group Team sites, they can only create a modern Team site without a group as a subsite. Admins can however create a new Team site without a group in the SharePoint Admin center.

It is possible to add a group to a modern Team sites without a group, *refer to* 6.6, Add Microsoft 365 Group below.

6.5 CLASSIC TEAM SITE

The classic Team site is intended for collaboration, just as the modern Team site. It is not connected to a Microsoft 365 Group by default, but after the site has been created, you can add such a group to a classic Team site, *see* below,

The classic Team site has a classic homepage, a so called wiki page. It can be customized in many ways and not only with web parts. The image below shows the default homepage of a classic Team site.

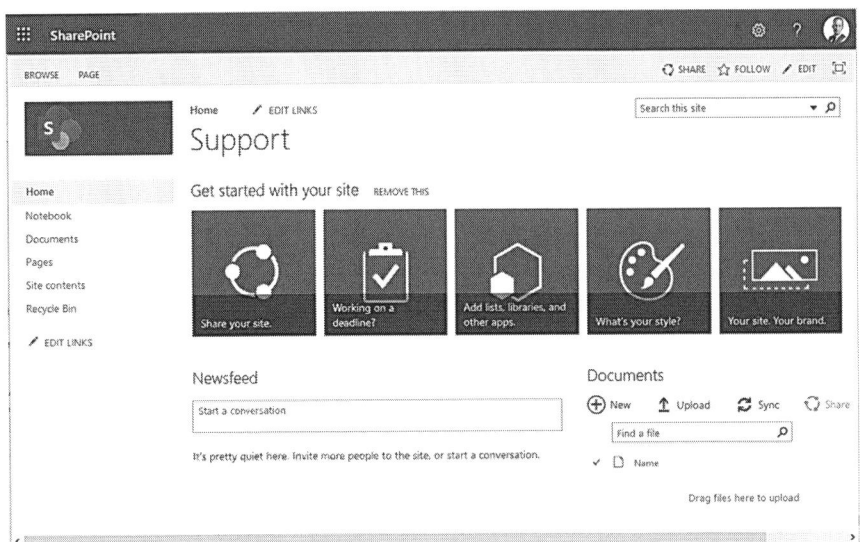

The default homepage does not have the Microsoft Search, but apps with the modern interface and modern pages added to a classic site have that search feature. You can create a modern page and make it homepage in the classic site if you so prefer, *refer to* 13.1.7, Set a Page as Homepage.

The default classic homepage has three web parts:

- The Get Started tiles are so called Promoted links. They give links that may be important when you are new to SharePoint. These tiles are often removed after a while, when the team site is customized. Remove the tiles by clicking on REMOVE THIS.

- The Newsfeed is intended for sharing information and ideas among the people who use the site. The content is stored in an automatically created "MicroFeed" list in the site.

- The default Documents web part displays the files in the automatically created "Documents" library, so that users can work with the files directly on the homepage.

Just like the other Team sites, the classic Team site has a Site navigation pane to the left. It also has a Top link bar, sometimes called Global navigation.

The Top link bar usually shows links to other sites within the same collection, but you can add any links you want, also links to external content, outside your SharePoint tenant. The current site is displayed with a distinct color, depending on theme.

kalmstrom.com demos   Sales   Development   ✏ EDIT LINKS

The classic Team site has no command bar. Instead, it has a ribbon with two or three tabs, similar to the ribbon you can find in Office apps. Which buttons are active depend on what you have selected in the page and which object you are working with.

The image below shows the PAGE tab in the ribbon on the homepage above.

87

On the page, below the ribbon, you can find various commands that we will come back to later.

6.5.1 Modern Compatibility

Apps that are added to a classic team site can be viewed in the modern experience as well as in the classic, and you can add modern pages to a classic team site.

You can add a modern Team site without a Microsoft 365 Group as a subsite to a classic Team site.

6.5.2 Save Site as a Template

Classic Team sites have the possibility to save the site as a template. That feature is also missing in Communication sites and modern Team sites.

Under the Site Actions heading in the Site settings, you can save a **classic** site as a template, to be used when you create subsites in the same or another site.

The template will be saved to the Solutions gallery in the site where you created the template. From there, it can be downloaded and then uploaded to Solutions galleries in other sites.

Site Settings › Save as Template ⓘ

File Name
Enter the name for this template file.

File name:
KTMDevTemplate

Name and Description
The name and description of this template will be displayed on the Web site template picker page when users create new Web sites.

Template name:
KTM Development

Template description:

Include Content
Include content in your template if you want new Web sites created from this template to include the contents of all lists and document libraries in this Web site. Some customizations, such as custom workflows, are present in the template only if you choose to include content. Including content can increase the size of your template.

☐ Include Content

Caution: Item security is not maintained in a template. If you have private content in this Web site, enabling this option is not recommended.

To create a new subsite from the template, open the 'Custom' tab when you create a new site and select the template.

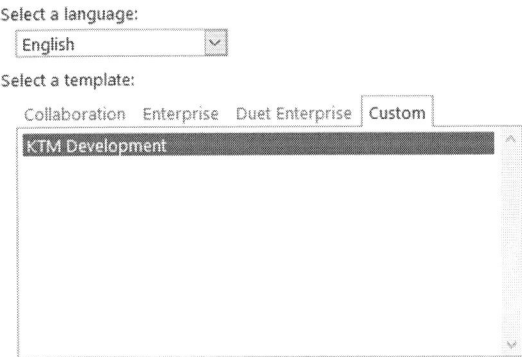

Classic sites also give a possibility to save an app as a template, *refer to* 7.14.2. Both these template options are lost if you add a Microsoft 365 Group to the site.

6.5.3   *Web Designer Galleries*

In classic Team sites, the Web Designer Galleries section in the Site settings have some features that are not available in Communication and modern Team sites, like the possibility to upload sandboxed solutions. These sites, by default only have the two first features in the image from a classic site to the right.

Web Designer Galleries
Site columns
Site content types
Web parts
List templates
Master pages
Themes
Solutions
Composed looks

If you need a Group Team site with the full Web Designer Galleries, there is solution: add a Microsoft 365 Group to a classic Team site, *see* below.

When you do that, you will have a Team site connected to a Microsoft 365 Group but with more options in the site settings that the modern Group Team site! If you are a SharePoint or Global administrator this might be a good workaround to get both the extra features and a group.

SharePoint site pages are customized with web parts, and some classic web parts are only available in classic sites. This might be another reason why you should use a classic site with a Microsoft 365 Group instead of a modern Group Team site. We will come back to page customization in chapter 13.

6.6   ADD MICROSOFT 365 GROUP

Site administrators can use the 'Connect to new Microsoft 365 Group' link under the 365 Settings icon, to add a new Microsoft 365 Group to a modern Team site without a group or a classic Team site. It is not possible to connect a Microsoft 365 Group to a Communication site.

When you add a Microsoft 365 Group to a classic site, the full Web Designer Galleries and all classic web parts will be kept but, as mentioned above, the possibility to save a site or an app as a template will be lost.

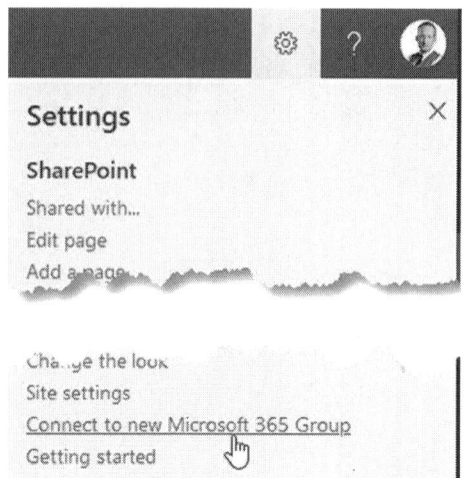

When you use the 'Connect to new Microsoft 365 Group' command, a new modern homepage will be created for the site. A new Microsoft 365 Group with some shared resources will also be created and associated with the site.

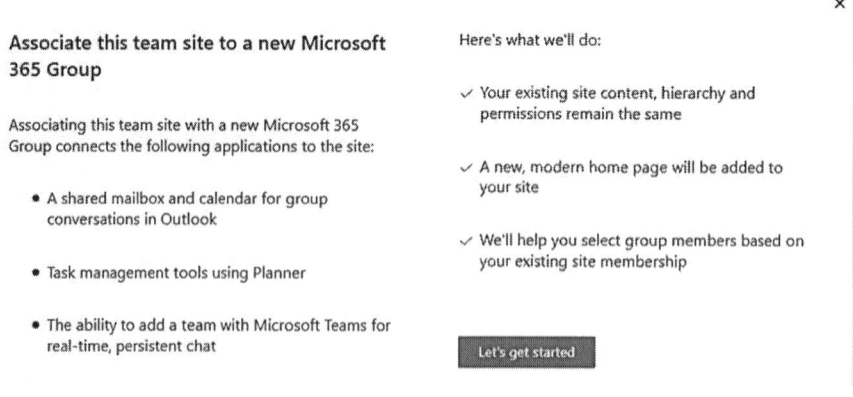

The name of the Microsoft 365 Group will by default be the same as the name of the site, but when you click on the 'Let's get started' button you can change the name. You can also decide if the group should be private or public (for the whole organization).

Now you only need to add members to the group and click on 'Finish'. Members can also be added later.

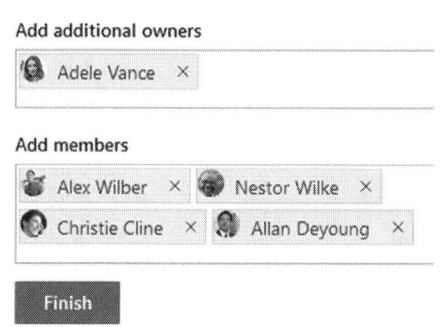

6.7 ONENOTE

Each SharePoint Team site comes with a Notebook link in the Site navigation. It opens the Online version of OneNote, Microsoft's note-taking tool that is part of the Office package.

OneNote Online works well in the browser, and by having it in SharePoint you can easily share it with other team members. The default OneNote notebook, and all other notebooks you create, are stored in each team site's Site Assets library.

When you open OneNote Online via the Notebook link in the Site navigation, you will have various options to insert text, images and links.

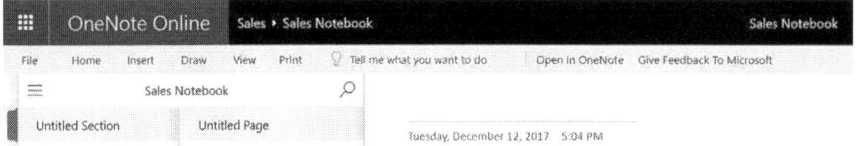

You can reach all the Team site's notebooks by clicking on the menu icon at the top left in the current notebook.

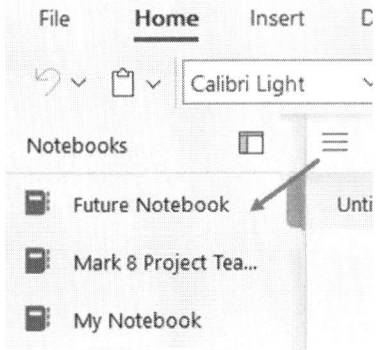

The notebooks are stored in the Site Assets library and can be deleted there.

6.7.1 *OneNote in SharePoint Libraries*

The notebook file type is one of the file types you are offered when you create a new file in a document library that has the default content type.

If you don't want users to have access to OneNote, you can edit the '+New' menu in the **modern** interface and uncheck the box for OneNote, *refer to* 9.14.1, Edit the '+ New' Menu.

You should also remove the link in the Site navigation, *refer to* 11.4, Edit Navigation.

Demo:

https://www.kalmstrom.com/Tips/SharePoint-Online-Course/OneNote.htm

6.8 SITE COMPARISON

The table below gives a summary of the differences between the commonly used SharePoint sites.

Feature	Commu-nication	Group Team	Team, no Group	Team, no Group with Group added	Classic	Classic with Group added
Full gallery					X	X
Save site as template					X	
Save app as template					X	
Oslo layout	X					
Seattle layout		X	X	X	X	X
Modern homepage	X	X	X	X		X
MS 365 Group		X		X		X
Admin created			X	X	X	X
Compatible classic/ modern		X	X	X	X	X

6.9 TENANT ROOT SITE

When you create a subsite to a site, the higher level site is called the "root site" of that site collection. There is also a Root site for the whole tenant.

When you open the SharePoint Admin center >Active sites for the first time, you will notice that a site has been created automatically during the 365 setup: the tenant's Root site. This site cannot be deleted, unless it is replaced with another site, *see* below.

The homepage of the tenant's Root site is the top SharePoint landing page for your organization's tenant. It usually has links to all Hub sites and other important information, and news that concerns the whole organization should be published here.

The Root site is based on the Communication site template. The title of the site is "Communication site", but I recommend that you rename it into something more descriptive.

The Root site has certain specific characteristics:

- The URL of the root site is the tenant domain + .sharepoint.com (for example https://kalmstromnet.sharepoint.com). All other sites by default have the addition of "/sites/[site name]".
- All the tenant's users are by default added to the Root site.
- All the tenant's users have Edit permission on the Root site. (Note that this is a very high permission level for everyone to have. Most SharePoint administrators want to change that, *refer to* chapter 14, Permissions.)
- External sharing is enabled. (Again, this is something that most SharePoint administrators want to change, *refer to* chapter 15.)
- Microsoft Search always searches the whole tenant when you search from the Root site.
- The Home button in the SharePoint Online mobile app directs the user to the Root site.

It is possible to create a new Communication site and make it the tenant's Root site. Select the current Root site under Active sites in the SharePoint Admin center and click on 'Replace site' in the command bar.

6.9.1 *Make Home Site*

I recommend that you set the tenant's Root site as Home site. This is done in the SharePoint Admin center >Settings >Home site. This will give a possibility to facilitate access to important resources, as described below. .

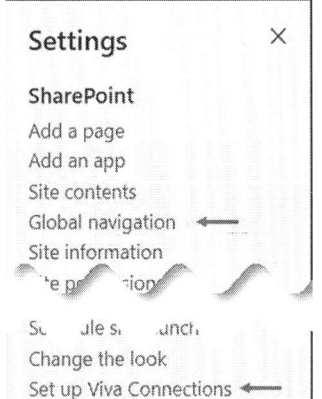

When you have made a site Home site in the SharePoint Admin center, you will have two new links under the settings icon in the 365 navigation bar: for Global navigation and Viva Connections.

It might take a few minutes before you can see the change.

6.9.1.1   Global Navigation

By default, the Home icon in the SharePoint app bar directs users to their SharePoint start page, but it is often more useful to direct them to the Home site and let them see the Home site navigation when they click on the Home icon.

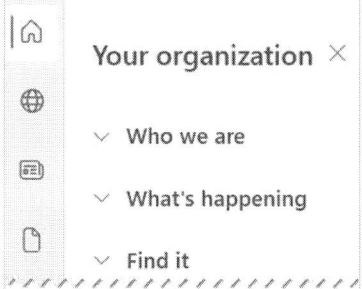

To make that change, click on the Global navigation link under the settings icon in the Home site. A right pane will open, where you can enable global navigation.

93

Here, you can also add an icon that will replace the default Home icon. For best result, it should be a 20x20 pixels PNG file with transparent background.

There are two options for which navigation should be displayed: the Home site navigation or the Hub or global navigation. Both can be edited.

6.9.1.2 Viva Connections

Viva Connections integrates tailored news, resources and conversations from the whole tenant into a branded app in Microsoft Teams. It is out of scope for this book, but please refer to https://docs.microsoft.com/en-us/SharePoint/viva-connections-overview to learn more.

6.9.1.3 News Site

If you set the Root site or another Communication site as the Home site for the tenant, the site is automatically configured as an organization News site. This means that news posts here get special visual treatment and are displayed on each user's SharePoint start page, *refer to* 12.1, The SharePoint Online Start Page.

(SharePoint admins can specify up to 250 news sites for the organization, but that is done with PowerShell and out of scope for this book.)

People with Edit permission on a News site can boost up to 10 posts per site, so that it gets more extended visibility throughout the tenant.

Refer to 13.4.11, The News Web Part for more info about news and news posts.

6.10 CREATE A SITE

By default, all users are allowed to create Group Team sites and Communication sites. Global and SharePoint admins can also create the other site types.

All sites except the root site of the tenant will have a URL that consists of the root site URL + sites + the site name.

When the site has been created, you can create apps, pages and subsites within that site. They will all belong to the same site, and their URLs will all begin with the site URL. For example, if the site name is https://kalmstromnet.sharepoint.com/sites/RetailOperations/, all content in the Retail Operations site will have URLs that begin this way.

By default, everything in a site will have the same permissions, because lower levels, like apps and items, inherit the same permissions as the higher level. It is possible, but seldom recommended, to break the inheritance. *Refer to* chapter 14, Permissions, for more info.

Microsoft plans to modify the graphics in the site creation, so there might be some differences from the images below when you read this.

6.10.1 *Auto-Created Apps*

When you create a new site, SharePoint also creates the default document libraries. Your choice of site type decides which default apps are included and which features are enabled by default.

When you create one of the common site types, these libraries will be created automatically with the site:

- A document library called "Documents".
- A "Form" document library for forms used in the site.
- A "Styles" document library for styles used in the site.
- A "Site Pages" page library for pages that users create in the site.
- A "Site Assets" document library for other content that is used in the site, for example images that are added to pages. (In Communication sites, this library is not created until you actually add some content that needs to be saved there.)

In Communication sites an "Events" calendar app is also created automatically, and classic Team sites gets a "MicroFeed" list app for news comments.

6.10.2 *User Site Creation*

By default, all users can create Communication and Group Team sites from their SharePoint Online start page. This is the page that users land on when they click on 'SharePoint' in the 365 navigation bar or on the SharePoint icon under the 365 App launcher.

As mentioned above in 5.2.4, Settings, Administrators can disable the users' possibility to create sites in the SharePoint Admin center >Settings >Site creation.

The site creator will automatically follow the new site, so it will appear among the user's followed sites on the SharePoint Online start page, *refer to* 12.1, The SharePoint Online Start Page.

The first creation steps are the same for the two site types.

1. Click on the 'Create site' button in the top left corner of the SharePoint Online start page.
2. Select the site type you want to use.

95

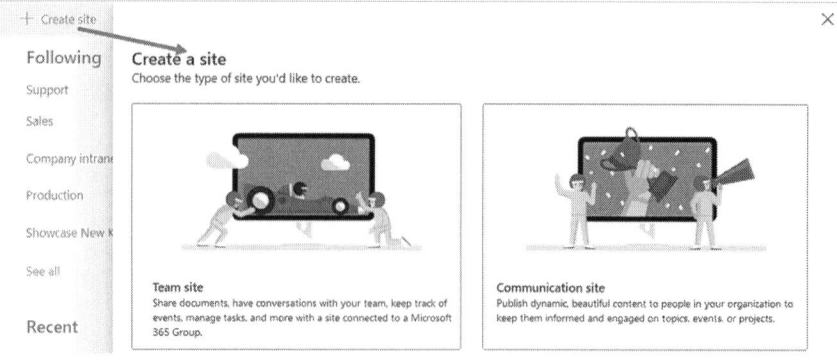

6.10.2.1 Communication site

When you select to create a Communication site, you only need to give the site a name and a description and click on 'Finish' to create the new site.

6.10.2.2 Group Team Site

When you create a Group Team site, fill out the site name and description. The group e-mail address and the site address will be added automatically when you have entered the name. Any spaces in the name will be removed.

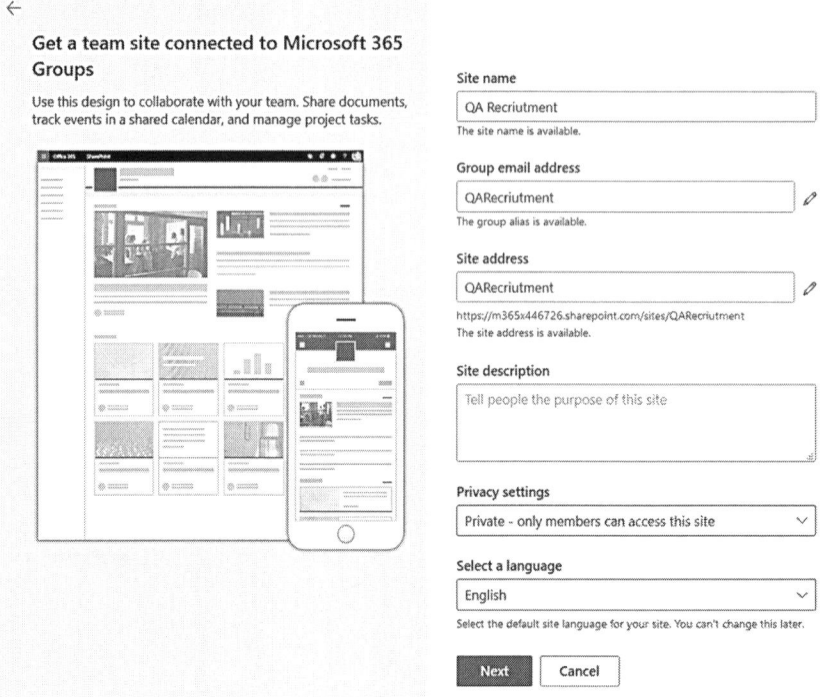

By default, the Group Team site is private, and if you keep that setting you must add the group members manually.

When you select the other option, public, all users in the tenant will have access to the new Group Team site. Depending on your company culture, this might be exactly what you want or totally wrong, so consider this choice carefully.

When you create a Group Team site, you will automatically be its Owner and Administrator, but you can add additional Owners.

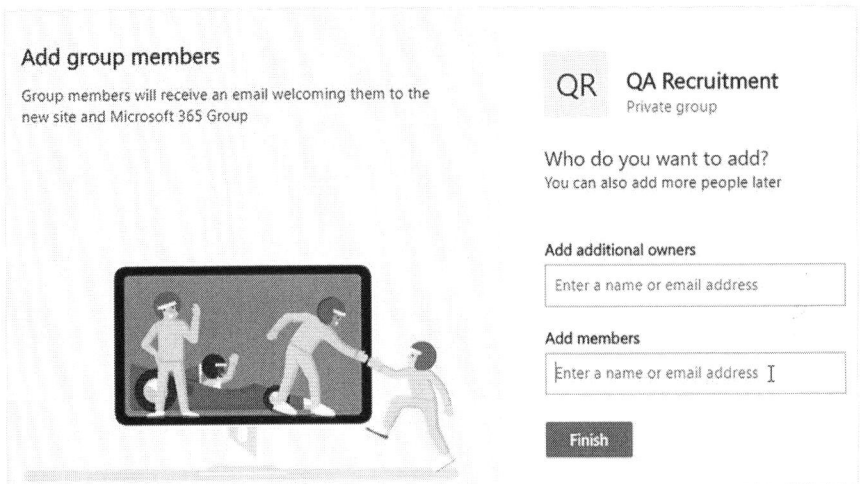

The new site will open automatically, and members will receive an e-mail where they are welcomed to the site.

6.10.2.3 Create Group Team Site from OneDrive

The 365 account gives each user a limited SharePoint site for personal use. It is called OneDrive for Business and is described in chapter 12, Personal Content. Users can create Group Team sites from their OneDrive for Business library.

When you click on "Create shared library" in the OneDrive left menu, you will get a simplified experience for creating a Group Team site. (This experience respects all existing admin settings and behaviors around Team site creation.)

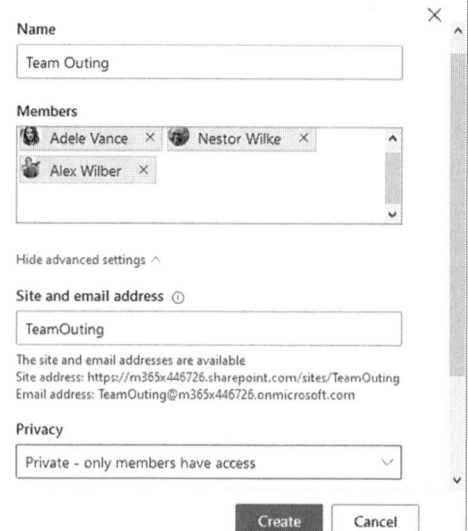

When the site has been created, the document library of the new Group Team site will open in the OneDrive for Business main area. In the top right corner of the page, there is a link to the site's home page.

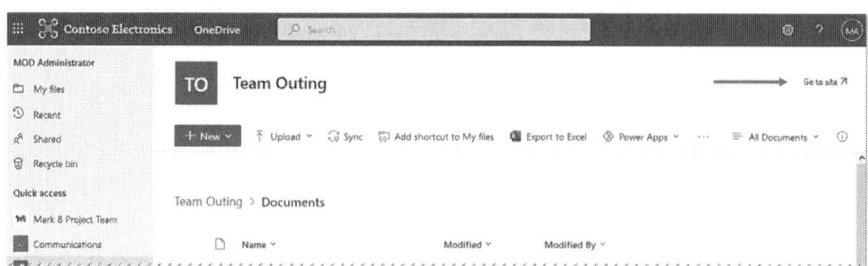

6.10.3   Admin Site Creation

The SharePoint Admin center >Active sites has a '+ Create' button in the command bar.

The 'Create' button opens a right pane that has some more options than what is given to standard users.

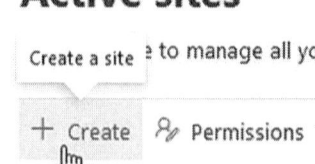

When a modern site has been created in the SharePoint Admin center, it will show up at once under 'Active sites'.

For classic sites, it may take a few minutes before the site has been created and can be reached from 'Active sites'.

6.10.3.1   Modern Sites

When administrators start creating a site from the SharePoint Admin center, they will have the options Group Team and Communication site, just like standard users.

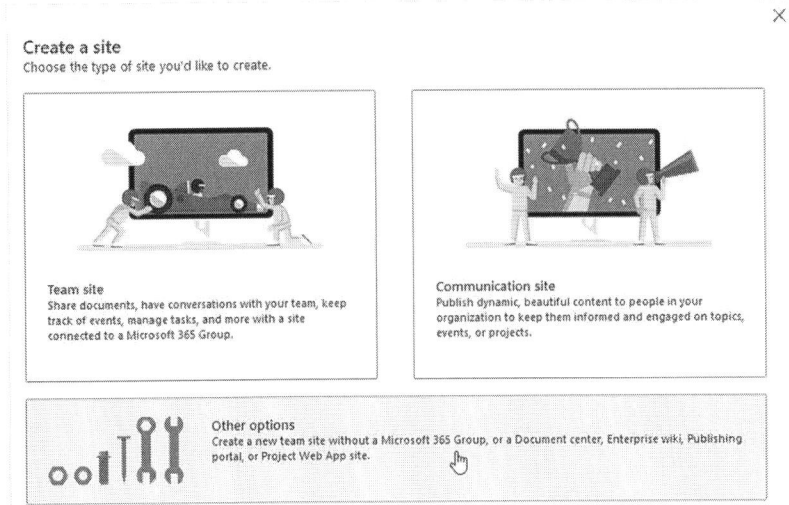

Admins however have some more options for these site types. Under the Advanced settings, they can set the time zone and storage limit.

Admins do not automatically become Site owners and Site administrators for the site they create from the SharePoint Admin center. Instead, they must assign one or more Site owners, who will also become Site administrators.

If you want to assign another Site administrator, that can be done when the site has been created, *refer to* 6.2.1.1, Edit an Active Site.

The 'Other options' tile below the Group Team and Communication tiles gives a choice of other site types. The default option is a modern Team site without a Microsoft 365 Group.

It is also from here you can create the Classic Team site.

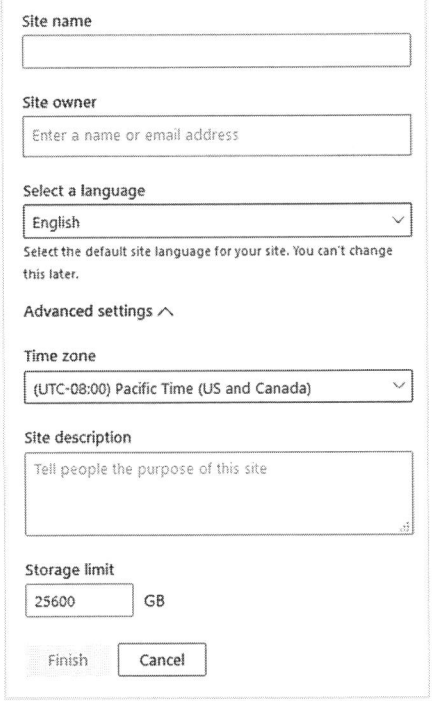

6.10.3.2 Classic Team Site

Classic Team sites can only be created from the SharePoint Admin center.

1. Click on '+Create' and select 'Other options' in the right pane.
2. Select the option 'More templates' at the bottom of the dropdown. Do *not* fill out anything in the fields to the right.

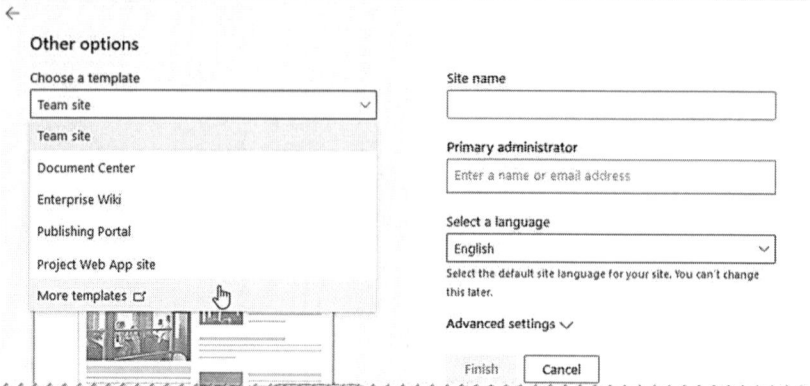

3. Select the default option, 'Team site (classic experience)', and specify the details of the classic site. Click on the book icon to search for a Site admin.
4. The Site admin does not become the Site owner automatically, so if you want another person for that role, you can set it under 'Permissions' in the site's Information pane under 'Active sites', when the site has been created.

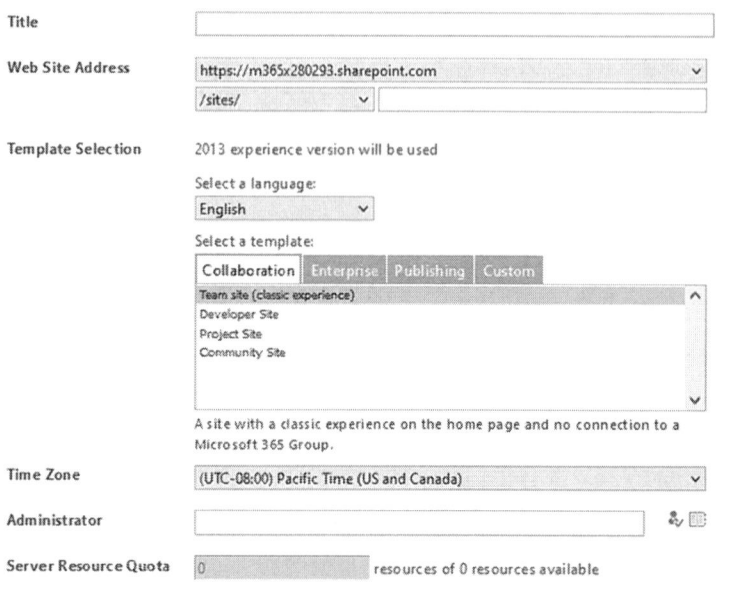

6.11 SITE ACCESS

When a site is created from the SharePoint Online start page, it is only accessible by the creator = owner.

When a site is created from the SharePoint Admin center, a Site owner/admin is appointed at creation, and it can very well be another person than the site creator, *see* above.

If you have created a Group Team site, you can add Site members in the creation process. In other cases, you must share the site manually, so that other people get access to it. *Refer to* chapter 15, Sharing.

6.12 HUB FAMILIES

As mentioned before, SharePoint sites have no connection with each other. Each site is a separate unit with its own permissions and management. You can link to other sites but that is all – unless you register a hub site and create a hub family.

A hub family consists of a hub site and several other sites that are associated with the hub site. This way, related sites can be connected based on project, department, division, region or anything else.

Within a hub family, it is easy for users to discover related content, news and site activity across all associated sites. When you search from the hub site, content from the hub family will be prioritized.

Only Global and SharePoint admins can register sites as hub sites, but site owners can associate their sites with a hub site.

When you associate a site with a hub site, this will happen to the associated site:

- Content like news and activity from your site will be visible on the hub site homepage.
- You can no longer edit the theme of your site, as it will use the hub site theme.
- Your site will inherit the specific Hub navigation from the hub site.
- You can choose to sync site permissions with hub permissions to increase site access for viewers.

The relationship between the sites in a hub family is not hierarchical. Therefore, each site is governed independently. If you stop associating a site with a hub site, it does not affect any of the other sites in the hub family.

Hub families is something that Microsoft recommends that we use instead of subsites, at least with modern sites. In classic sites, the hub navigation and hub settings are only visible in modern pages.

In a small business, you might want to use the Home Site as a hub and associate all or most of the other sites to it. In a bigger organization, you need to have more hub sites.

In a hub site, you can display content that is common to a larger group, while the associated sites can be intended for smaller sections of that group. You can for example have hub sites for HR, Finance, Marketing, Legal and IT. Big organizations should of course have many more hub sites, and there can be up to 2000 hub sites in a tenant.

Global and SharePoint admins can convert any site to a hub site, but I recommend that you first plan how your organization's intranet should be organized.

I also recommend that you create new Communication sites to use as hub sites. The Communication site type is best suited for these kinds of informative sites.

6.12.1 Register as Hub Site

Any site that is not already a hub site, or associated with a hub site, can be registered as a hub site. This is done in the SharePoint Admin center >Active sites.

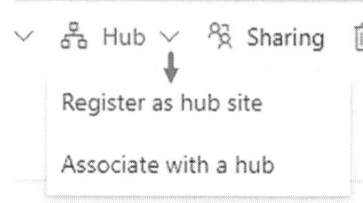

Select a site and register it as a hub site via the 'Hub' button in the command bar.

When you choose the option 'Register as hub site', a right pane will open, where you can give the site a hub name. This name will show up in a dropdown when people associate sites, so choose a name that explains what kind of sites should be associated with this hub.

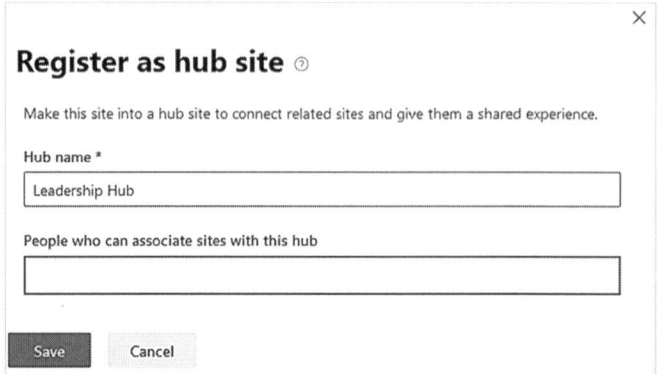

You can also enter people who should have permission to associate sites with the hub site. If you leave the 'People who can associate sites with this hub' box empty, all site owner who have access to the hub site can associate their site with the hub.

When a hub site is selected, the dropdown under the 'Hub' button gives the options to edit the hub site settings or unregister the site as hub site.

If you want to change the hub site display name or the list of people who can associate sites with the hub, you can do that in the hub site settings.

6.12.1.1 Changes in the Hub Site

When a modern site has been registered as a hub site, it gets a new navigation bar on top, below the 365 navigation bar.

At first, the hub navigation only has the hub site name and an 'Add link' command, but when sites are associated, you should add them here. The same hub navigation bar will be displayed on modern pages in all the associated sites.

The hub site also gets a new link under the 365 Settings icon: 'Hub site settings'. Here you can upload an image to be used as a hub site icon and create an approval flow. *Refer to* chapter 24, SharePoint Automation.

Finally, there will be a new 'Hub' tab in the 'Site permissions' pane when a site is registered as hub site, *refer to* 6.12.3. below.

6.12.2 Associate with a Hub Site

There is no limit to the number of sites that can be associated with a hub site, but you can only associate a site with one hub site.

(Hub sites can however be associated with a Parent hub for extended search options, see 6.12.4. below.)

6.12.2.1 Associate in the SharePoint Admin Center

Global and SharePoint administrators can associate sites with a hub site from the SharePoint Admin center >Active sites. Select the site, click on the 'Hub' button in the command bar and select 'Associate with a hub'.

In the right pane that opens, you can select the hub you want to associate the site with.

Edit hub association

When you associate this site with a hub, it inherits the hub site's theme and navigation. Content from the site will roll up to the hub site and be included in searches on the hub site.

Select a hub

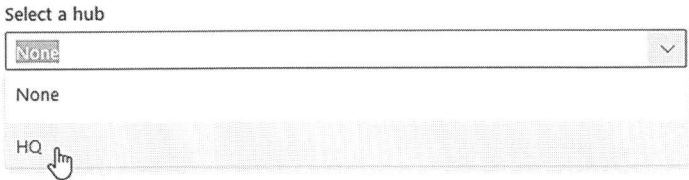

The association can be performed in bulk if you select multiple sites under 'Active sites'.

All hub sites and associations are shown in the 'Hub' column in the SharePoint Admin center >Active sites.

6.12.2.2 Associate from a Site

By default, all site owners can associate their sites with a hub site, but as we have seen above, that permission can be restricted in the SharePoint Admin center to only allow specific people.

To associate a site with a hub site from inside the site, open the 365 Settings icon and select 'Site information'. There, you can select a hub site from a dropdown.

When you have selected the hub site and clicked on 'Save', the site will be associated, either immediately or after approval.

When you see the hub site navigation bar in the top right corner of the site, your will know that the site has been (approved and) associated.

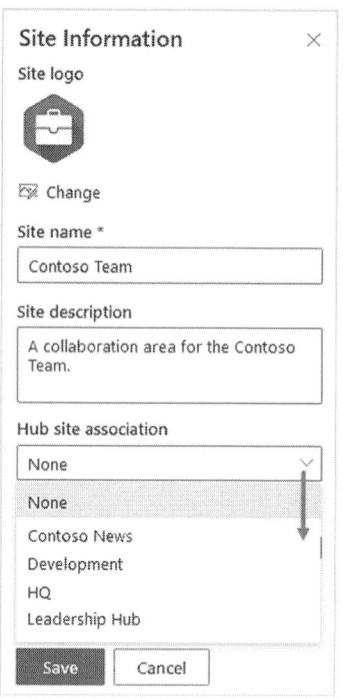

6.12.2.3 Create Associated Sites from a Hub Site

The hub site owner can create a new site from the hub site. This site will then be automatically associated with that hub site.

When you click on 'Create site', a right pane with the options Group Team site and Communication site will be displayed, in the same way as when users create sites from the SharePoint Online start page.

6.12.3 Hub Visitor Permission

In a hub family, each associated site has its own permissions, just as the hub site has. Hub site owners can however give Visitor permission to people and groups, and this permission can be synchronized with the associated sites.

This will increase access for viewers across all sites in the hub, but it will not override or change any site permissions.

The hub permission setting is Off by default, both in the hub site and in the associated sites, and it must be activated in both places to work.

1. When a site is registered as hub site, there will be a new 'Hub' tab in the 'Site permissions' pane, which you can reach via the 365 Settings icon. Here you can enable hub permissions and enter visitor names.
2. When 'Sync hub permissions' has been turned on in the hub site, the associated sites will also have a 'Hub' tab under 'Site permissions', and if needed, the site owners can set the synchronization to On.

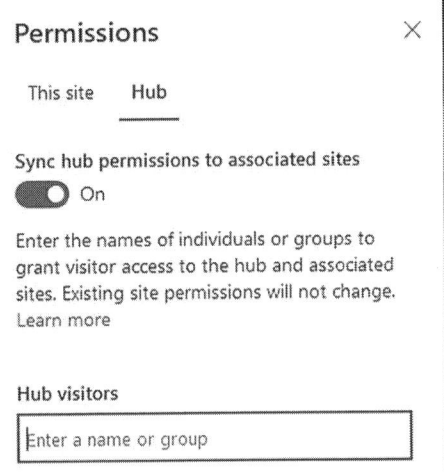

The synchronization can be turned off anytime, and you should not sync the hub permissions if your site contains sensitive information.

6.12.4 Connect Hub Sites

It is possible to associate a hub site to another hub site. This expands search results across multiple hubs and enables users to discover relevant content when searching on any sites related to the associated hubs.

When you associate hub sites to each other, the only visual change to the user is when search results are viewed. Then the breadcrumb path at the top of the page will display the name of the hub where the content can be found.

The hub association can only be performed in the SharePoint Admin center >Active sites. Select the hub site you want to connect to another hub site. The site you connect is called Child hub.

Then select 'Hub site settings' under 'Hub' in the command bar. A right pane will open, where you can select the hub site you want to connect to - the Parent hub.

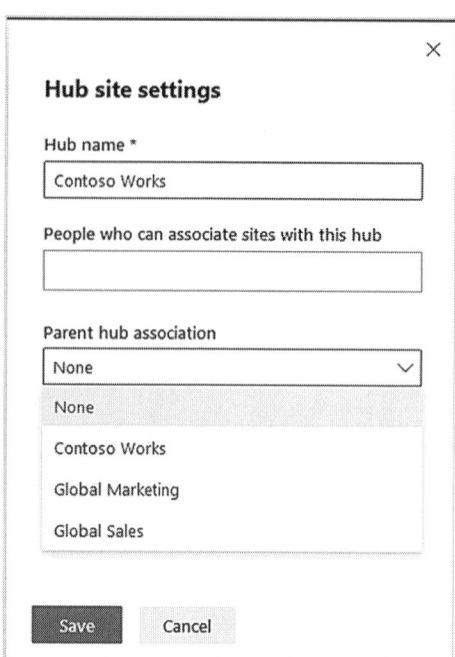

The Parent hub can be seen, but not edited, in the Hub site settings right pane of the Child hub.

The Parent hub instead has a link, 'View hubs associated to this hub' in its Hub site settings.

6.13 CREATE A SUBSITE

The hub family is one way of linking sites together. Another way is to create subsites and use shared navigation for all sites in the collection. This is the best way if you prefer the classic experience, because the hub navigation and settings will only appear in the modern experience.

It is possible to create subsites in sites that belong to a hub family, but Microsoft recommends that you instead create a new site.

The subsite method to link sites creates a hierarchy, and that gives some drawbacks:

- Subsite URLs reflect that they are subsites to another site, so if you reorganize relationships, you will break the links.

- Some features, like policies, apply to the root site and all subsites in a collection, whether you want it or not.

6.13.1 *Create a Subsite*

Some site types have a possibility to nest sites within sites by creating subsites to the root site or even to another subsite. Communication sites and Group Team sites cannot be created as subsites.

To create a new SharePoint subsite, open the Site contents of an existing site, click on 'New' and select 'Subsite'.

When you create a new subsite, there are different kinds of site templates to select from. The default option is a modern Team site without a group, but you can also create a classic Team site and a Project site.

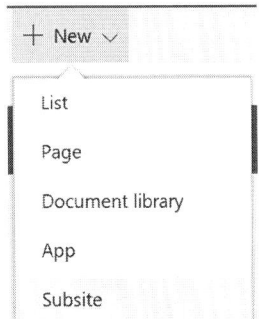

The image below comes from a Group Team site, and here it is also possible to create a Community site, where group members can discuss topics of common interest.

The Enterprise tabs have options for more rarely used site types.

By default, subsites inherit the parent permissions, but you can also create unique permissions for the subsite. The image below shows the default option.

Permissions

You can give permission to access your new site to the same users who have access to this parent site, or you can give permission to a unique set of users.

User Permissions:
◉ Use same permissions as parent site
◯ Use unique permissions

When you select unique permissions, a new page will open when you have clicked on 'Create'. Here you can add people or groups to the main groups Owner, Member and Visitor. Also refer to chapter 14, Permissions.

There are also choices for the navigation when you create a subsite but remember that only classic Team sites have a Top navigation. If you select to display the subsite in the Top link bar of a modern parent, the link will be there, but on the place for the Hub navigation. *Refer to* chapter 11, SharePoint Navigation, for more info.

6.13.2 Disallow Subsites

Amins can select to allow subsites only in classic sites or decide to not allow subsite creation at all. This is done in the SharePoint Admin center >Settings >classic settings page >Subsite Creation. The image below shows the default setting, where subsite creation is allowed for all sites.

Subsite Creation
Control subsite creation for people who have permission to create sites.
This controls visibility of the Subsite option on the Site contents page and enables new subsite creation.

○ Disable subsite creation for all sites
○ Enable sub site creation for classic sites only
● Enable subsite creation for all sites

When subsite creation is disabled, the subsite option will be hidden from the command bar in the Site contents.

6.14 DELETE AND RESTORE SITES

The tenant's automatically created Root site cannot be deleted, unless it is first replaced, but all other sites can be deleted – and restored within a certain time. The removal is performed in the same way for all sites, but the restoration process is different for root sites and subsites.

6.14.1 Delete a Site

To delete a **modern** site, click on the 365 Settings icon and then on 'Site information'. Now you can delete the site directly from the right pane.

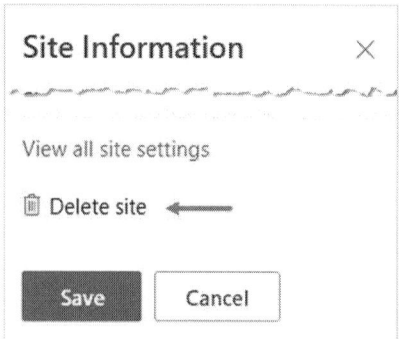

Classic sites are deleted under the site's Site settings >Site Actions >Delete this site. When you delete a site, any subsites will be deleted too.

> Site Actions
> Manage site features
> Reset to site definition
> Delete this site ←

If you want to delete a subsite, you can follow the same steps but from within the subsite.

Global and SharePoint admins can delete sites in the SharePoint Admin center >Active sites. Select the site you want to remove and click on 'Delete' in the command bar. To just delete a subsite is not possible here, as the Admin center does not show subsites.

In all cases, you will be asked to confirm the removal.

6.14.2 *Restore a Root Site*

If the site you are deleting is a root site, you are in fact deleting all the site's content. In that case, the site can be restored from the SharePoint Admin center >Deleted sites. Here, sites are retained for 93 days before they are permanently deleted.

> ↶ Restore   🗑 Permanently delete

When you restore a modern Group Team site, the group and all its resources are also restored. The group resources are however only retained for 30 days.

If you want to permanently delete a site before the 93 days have passed, you can do that too under 'Deleted sites'.

6.14.3 *Restore a Subsite*

Subsites that have been deleted separately go directly to the Second-stage recycle bin, where they are kept for 93 days. The site admin can either restore or permanently delete the subsite from the Second-stage bin.

6.15 SUMMARY

In this long chapter, you have learned about the main building block of SharePoint: the site. Now you should know what is common for all sites and what is the difference between the commonly used site types.

You understand how to create different types of sites, and you can connect them in a hub family or by creating subsites.

SharePoint has several kinds of groups, and in this chapter, we have met the Microsoft 365 Group. This is a group that shares resources, among them a

SharePoint Group Team site. You will encounter other groups later in this book.

We will of course come back to sites many times in this book, as it is in the sites everything is contained. In chapter 12, you will learn about each user's personal SharePoint site, OneDrive for Business, and in chapter 14 and 15 we will go through site permissions and sharing.

Before that, I will however explain how you can build and customize SharePoint apps. In the next chapter, I will describe features that are the same in both list and library apps, and after that, the lists and the libraries will have their own chapters where their specific features are described.

7 SHAREPOINT APPS

Within SharePoint sites, content can be stored and shared in apps. Document and picture libraries, contact lists and calendars are all examples of apps.

SharePoint apps can be either lists or libraries. Libraries are used when the most important content is a file. In other cases, we use list apps. These app types have common features, and in this chapter, we will look at them.

Currently, apps do not have their own icon in the SharePoint user interface. Instead, they are represented by the folder icon. The word "folder" is also sometimes used instead of "app" in the SharePoint settings, and as SharePoint library apps can contain folders, this might be a bit confusing.

In this chapter, I will explain what is common for both app types:

- The app settings page
- The Standard and Grid/Quick Edit view modes
- Columns, filter and sort
- Views
- Alerts
- Version history
- Apply labels and declare record

I will also describe the two interfaces, how to create apps, the template options and the permission settings.

In the next two chapters, we will have a closer look at first list apps and then library apps.

I strongly recommend that you create your own apps to test the features I describe in this chapter. I advise you to create blank list apps or libraries or custom list apps via the 'Add an app' command, as described in section 7.5. These have all the features described in this chapter but no other features that might disturb your learning process. It will be time to create other apps later in this book.

Apps can be embedded in SharePoint pages, and that is something I will describe later in the book.

Note that SharePoint apps are normally shared within a group of people – that is the main point of SharePoint, after all! – so use them for information that should be shared, not for personal data. An exception to that is apps in your personal OneDrive for Business site, which is described in chapter 12, Personal Content.

7.1 BENEFITS

SharePoint apps have many benefits:

- SharePoint apps give a good overview over data.

- Use the powerful Search engine to find information. You can start with searching just the current app, and if there are hits, the app content will be filtered to show only the hits.
- The version history feature lets you see earlier versions of each item and what exactly was changed in each version. If needed, you can also restore an earlier version.
- You can filter and sort items to study the information in different ways.
- You can create different views to permanently filter or display items in a preferred way.
- With the Totals feature you can summarize values with sum, average etc.
- You can export SharePoint data to Excel and open an app in Access. In the classic experience you can also connect and export to Outlook and Project.
- You can set permissions on a singular item or folder, so that only specific people can view or edit it.
- You can let SharePoint send alerts when items have been added, changed or deleted.

7.2　Row = Item

A SharePoint app is like a database table or spreadsheet. Data is distributed in rows, and each row is known as an item. The image below shows part of a list app, where you can see four items.

Department Name ⌄	Manager ⌄	Staff ⌄
South	Peter Kalmström	15
North	Peter Kalmström	200
East	Kate Kalmström	50
West	Kate Kalmström	4

Each row, or item, has various columns where you can enter metadata, called values or properties, that describes the item. This information is used by the search crawler to update the search index, so metadata plays an important role to make content easy to find.

The value in one of the columns, usually the first column from the left, becomes underlined when you hover the mouse over it. Click on this value to open the item in a list app and to open the file in a library app. The image below comes from a library.

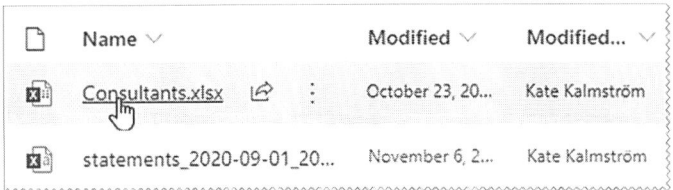

When you create a new item in an app, the metadata is filled out in a form. Item creation and editing is done a bit differently for list apps and library apps, so I will describe that in the two chapters that follow this one.

7.2.1 Item Limit

I recommend that you create many apps instead of trying to get too much data into one app. You should not have more than 5000 items in any app, as that is the limit for what SharePoint can display.

Microsoft is working on removing this limit, but it is no doubt still there when this is written. You will be able to add much more than 5000 items in an app, but it will create many different problems. Therefore, I strongly recommend that you avoid pushing that limit.

7.3 MODERN AND CLASSIC APP INTERFACE

Most apps can be viewed in both the classic and the modern interface. Below are images from the upper part of a document library app, and I hope they will give an idea about the differences between the two experiences.

The modern experience:

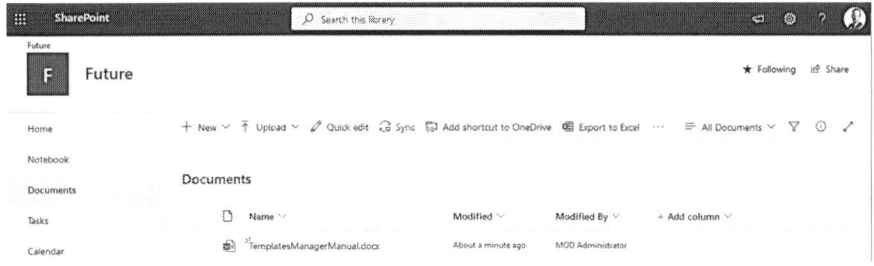

The classic experience:

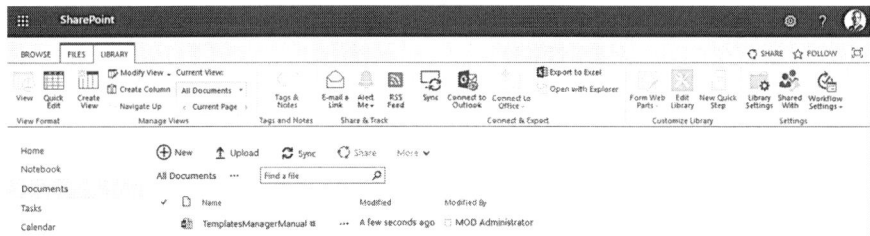

113

7.3.1 Differences

The most obvious difference between the modern and classic interface is that the classic interface has a ribbon, with the commands grouped under tabs. The modern app interface, instead have a command bar, also called "quick actions pane".

Generally, both interfaces have the same commands. However, while the classic ribbon shows all commands all the time, even if some may be greyed out, the modern command bar shows different controls depending on what has been selected in the list of items below. The command bar looks different when no item is selected, compared to when one item or multiple items have been selected.

Another difference between the app interfaces is that much of the settings and editing in the modern interface is performed in a right pane, like the Information pane in the image below. The classic interface opens a dialog or a new page in these situations.

When you can switch between the interfaces, which is possible in almost all apps, you can use all features by switching to the interface that is most suitable for each occasion.

7.3.1.1 Modern Command Bar Controls

The command bar in the modern app interface has three features that are not available in the classic ribbon:

- The 'Power Apps' command lets you create a powerapp from the app and also customize the app form in an advanced manner. This is described in chapter 21. (To just decide which columns should be visible in the form, *refer to* 7.8, Edit the Form.) The 'Power Apps' option does not exist at all in the classic interface.

- The 'Automate' command lets you create a flow connected to the app and reach all flows saved in the current user account. *Refer to* chapter 24, SharePoint Automation. The 'Automate' option does not exist at all in the classic interface.

- The information icon in the right part of the command bar opens a right Information pane. 'Details', under the item ellipsis, opens the same Information pane. (Except for recent activity, the classic interface gives the same information, but it is not gathered together in one place.)

When no item has been selected in the app, the Information pane for list apps shows who has access to the list. The Information pane for library apps shows the latest activity in the library.

When one item is selected in the app, you can see and edit details about the item, such as the item properties and who has access to the item. You can also see recent activity for the item and more.

In library apps, there is a preview of the file in the selected item on top of the Information pane, like in the image to the right.

When multiple items are selected, you can bulk edit properties when the selected items need the same value in one or more fields.

Click on the X in the top right corner of the pane to close it.

We will come back to the Information pane several times in this book.

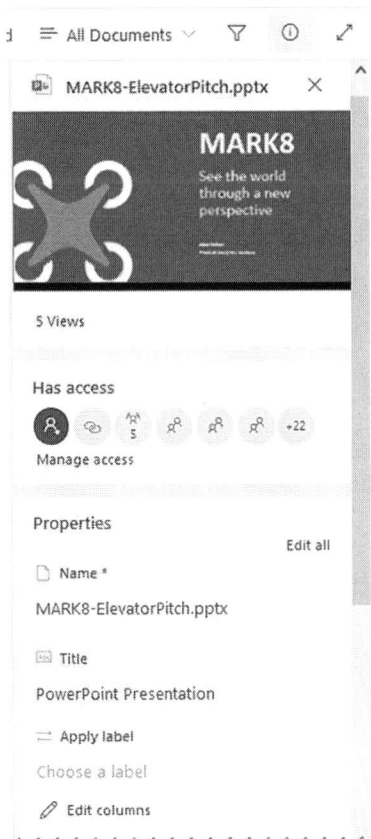

7.3.2 Switch Interface

Almost all apps give a possibility to use either the modern or the classic interface. When that is possible, there is a switch link under the Site navigation.

Modern interface link:

Return to classic SharePoint

Classic interface link:

Exit classic experience

App owners and administrators can set the default experience for each app in the app's List/Library settings:

1. Open the settings, *see* the section below, and click on the link 'Advanced settings' under the General Settings heading.
2. Set the 'List experience' at the bottom of the page to the interface that should be default.

115

List experience

Select the experience you want to use for this list. The new experience is faster, has more features, and works better across different devices.

Display this list using the new or classic experience?
○ Default experience set by my administrator
● New experience
○ Classic experience

Note that this setting only decides which experience the app should open with. Individual users can always switch app interface by clicking on the links 'Return to classic SharePoint' in the modern experience and 'Exit classic experience' in the classic interface, in apps where such links exist.

As mentioned in chapter 6, you cannot switch between the interfaces in Communication sites. Here, apps can only have the modern interface, except the Events app, which only has the classic interface.

Demo:

https://www.kalmstrom.com/Tips/SharePoint-Online-Course/Library-Interface.htm

7.3.2.1 Admin control

Global and Tenant admins can use PowerShell to control whether the "Return to classic SharePoint" and "Exit classic experience" links are shown in apps.

To remove the experience switch links use the PowerShell cmdlet: Set-SPOTenant -DisableBackToClassic $true

To show the links again, run the following PowerShell cmdlet: Set-SPOTenant -DisableBackToClassic $false

7.4 APP SETTINGS

Each app has a settings page where you can find many kinds of settings, including settings for permissions, columns and views.

You can reach the settings for all app types from the Site contents. Click on the ellipsis to the right of the app name or title and select Settings.

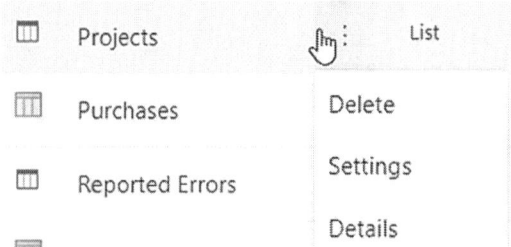

When you have the app open, the **modern** interface has a List settings link in the right pane that opens when you click on the 365 Settings icon.

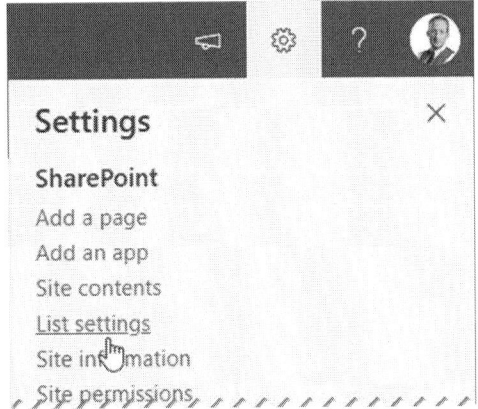

In library apps, the link is instead 'Library settings'.

The **classic** interface has the settings link in the ribbon:

- In most lists, the List Settings button is found under the LIST tab in the ribbon.
- In calendars, the List Settings button is found under the CALENDAR tab in the ribbon.
- In document libraries, you can find the Library Settings button under the LIBRARY tab in the ribbon.

In the continuation, I will use the word "List settings" also for library and calendar settings, when the text is applicable to all kinds of apps.

The settings pages are a bit different depending on app type, but all app settings show the app's columns and views and give a possibility to open and customize them.

List Information

Name: Documents
Web Address: https://m365x446726.sharepoint.com/sites/DigitalInitiativePublicRelations/Shared Documents/Forms/AllItems.asp:
Description:

General Settings
- List name, description and navigation
- Versioning settings
- Advanced settings
- Validation settings
- Column default value settings
- Audience targeting settings
- Rating settings
- Form settings

Permissions and Management
- Permissions for this document library
- Manage files which have no checked in version
- Information Rights Management
- Workflow Settings
- Apply label to items in this list or library
- Enterprise Metadata and Keywords Settings

Communications
- RSS settings

Columns

A column stores information about each document in the document library. The following columns are currently available in this document library:

Column (click to edit)	Type	Required
Title	Single line of text	
Modified	Date and Time	
Created	Date and Time	
Created By	Person or Group	
Modified By	Person or Group	
Checked Out To	Person or Group	

- Create column
- Add from existing site columns
- Column ordering
- Indexed columns

Views

A view of a document library allows you to see a particular selection of items or to see the items sorted in a particular order. Views currently configured for this document library:

View (click to edit)	Default View	Mobile View	Default Mobile View
All Documents	✓	✓	✓

- Create view

7.5 CREATE AN APP

Microsoft has made it easy to create new apps in SharePoint Online, because you can use a template and modify it to suit your needs. Each new app will be stored and reachable inside the SharePoint site where you created it.

Below, I will describe general app creation. There are also specific creation options for lists and libraries, and I will come back to them in the chapters about specific features for these apps.

7.5.1 Add an App

SharePoint Online offers many templates that you can build a new app on. Many of them can be reached via the command 'Add an app'. This is a classic method to create a list or library, but nearly all the app templates can be used with the modern as well as the classic experience. We will come back to apps created via "Add an app" many times in this book.

1. Open the 365 Settings icon and select 'Add an app'.

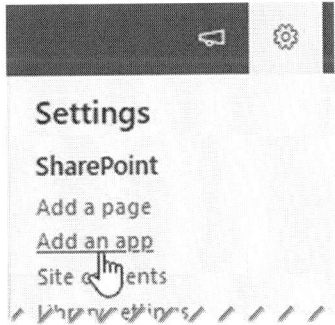

You can also click on '+ New' and then 'App' on a **modern** homepage or in a Site contents with the modern interface.

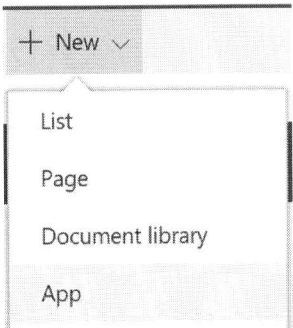

2. The "My apps" page will open. Here, you can see apps that your organization has added to the tenant, and you can also reach the SharePoint Store.
3. To reach the classic app templates, click on the 'classic experience' link.

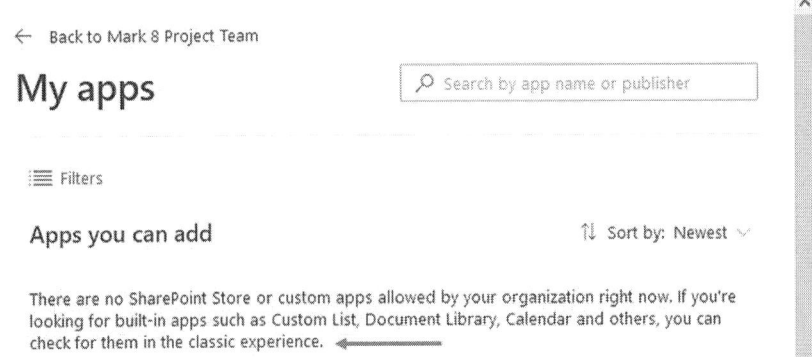

119

4. The "Your Apps" page will open. Search for a template that is similar to the app you want to create. Click on the icon to create the new app.

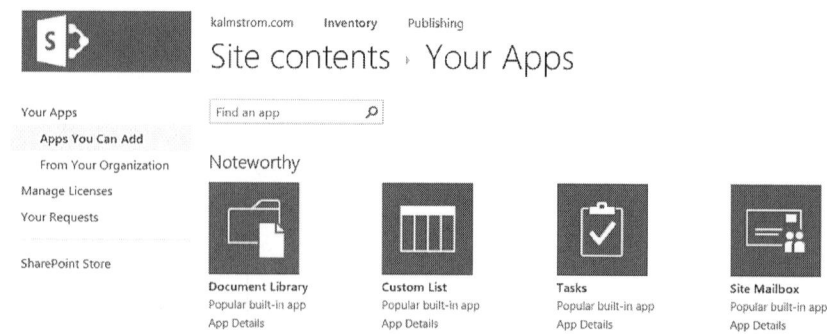

5. Give the app a name and click on 'Create'. If you click on the 'Advanced Options' link, you can give a description of the new app. Some app templates also have a few settings under 'Advanced Options'.

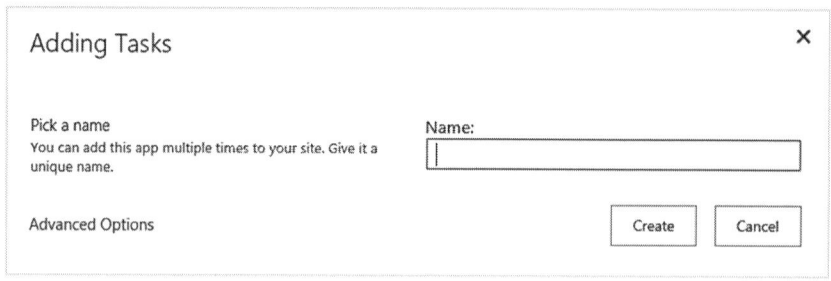

When the new app has been created in this way, it will not be opened automatically. Instead, you will be directed to the Site contents, where you can open the app or its settings.

To display the app in the Site navigation, open its settings >General Settings >List name, description and navigation, and select the 'Yes' radio button for display in the Site navigation – here called with its classic name "Quick launch.

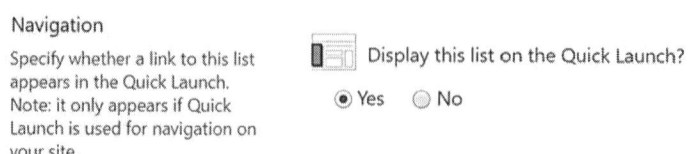

7.5.1.1 Apps in Communication Sites

Communication sites are primarily intended for information, and not for collaboration, so by default they only give a few options in the "Your Apps" page.

To have the same app options in a Communication site as in Team sites, open the Site settings and click on 'Manage site features' under the Site

Actions heading. When a new page opens, scroll down to the Team Collaboration Lists feature and activate it.

Team Collaboration Lists
Provides team collaboration capabilities for a site by making standard lists, such as document libraries and issues, available.   Activate

In Team sites, this feature is activated by default.

7.5.1.2 Custom Apps

Custom apps only have a few columns from start. In list apps, only the "Title" column is visible the default "All items" view. In custom library apps, the columns "Name", "Modified" and "Modified by" are visible in the default view.

There are also "Created" and "Created by" columns in both app types, but they are not displayed in the default view. The rest of the columns must be added by the creator.

You can create a custom app by following the 'Add an app' steps above and selecting the 'Custom List' or 'Document Library' template.

7.6 DISPLAY MODES

Apps can be displayed in Standard or Grid view mode. You can create new items and edit items in both modes.

7.6.1 *Standard*

The Standard view mode is displayed by default when you open an app. You cannot edit the items directly on the page when an app is displayed in Standard view mode. Instead, you need to open the item in edit mode. (How to do that, will be described later.)

In the Standard view mode, each item has an ellipsis (…) to the right of the Title column in lists and to the right of the Name column in libraries. That is normally the first column from the left. In the modern interface, the ellipsis is only visible when you hover over the item.

When you click on the ellipsis, you can see options for what to do with the item and information about it.

The options are different, depending on what kind of app it is. The image to below comes from a list app in the modern interface.

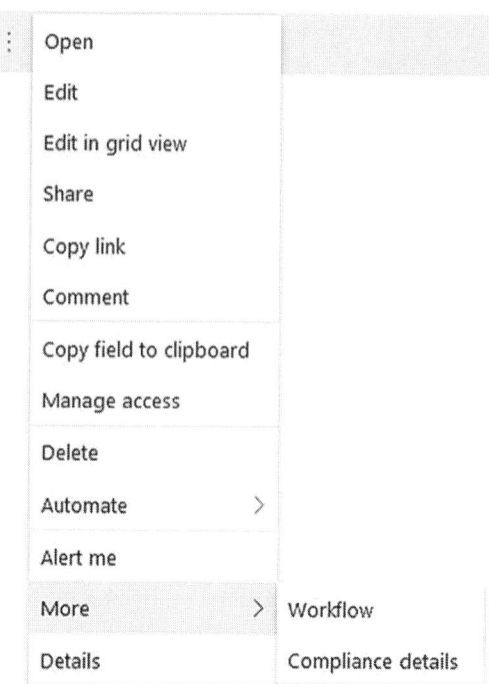

7.6.2 Grid

When an app is displayed in the Grid (modern) or Quick Edit (classic) view mode, it looks like a spreadsheet, and you can edit items directly in the cells. You can navigate across the rows and columns with the tab key or navigation keys.

Select a cell and press Enter or click in the cell to start typing in it. Your changes will be saved when you move to the next row or when you leave the Grid view.

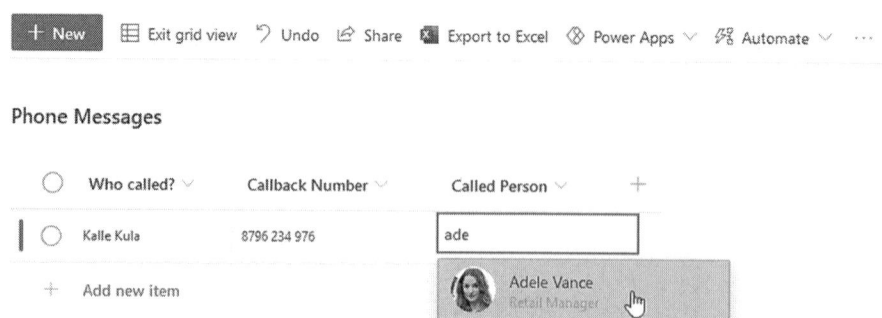

The Grid view mode is very popular and powerful for all who know how to use Excel lists. Copy and paste as well as some fill commands work in this view. With the little handle in the bottom right corner of the cell, you can drag values down, just like you can do in Excel.

The modern Grid view shows 100 items on each page, while the classic only shows 30 by default. If the app has more items, there is a "next page" arrow below the last item on the page in both interfaces.

< 401 - 500 >

The item limit can be modified in the Edit view page, *refer to* 7.9.3, Edit a View.

The **modern** Grid interface has 'Undo' and 'Redo' buttons. Ctrl + Z and Ctrl + Y (Windows) and Command + Z and Command + Shift + Z (Mac OS) will work as well.

⊞ Exit grid view ✏ Edit ↶ Undo

7.6.2.1 Switch Mode

To change the mode in **modern** apps, use the 'Edit in grid view' button in the command bar to open the Grid.

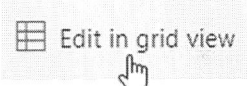

In the Grid mode, modern apps instead have an 'Exit grid view' button in the command bar. Click on that button when you are finished with the editing, and the list will go back to the Standard view mode.

In apps with the **classic** interface, the 'Quick Edit' button is found under the LIST or LIBRARY tab. Lists also have an 'edit this list' button that opens the Quick Edit mode.

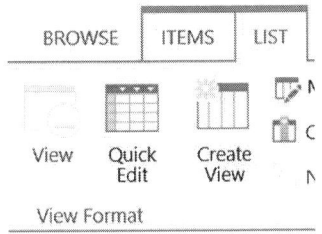

Click on the "Stop editing" command above the grid to go back to the Standard view mode.

Stop editing this list

7.7 COLUMNS

Information about each app item is kept in columns. The column content is often referred to as values, metadata or properties. Another popular name for column is field, and that term is used when automating SharePoint with programming languages.

When users add a new item to an app, they fill out the metadata in a form where each column is represented by a field. In this book, I will therefore use the term "column" when I refer to the app interface and the different types of metadata and "field" when I refer to the form where the metadata is filled out.

The columns are generally the same for each item in the app, even if each field does not have to be filled out for each item. (An exception to this is when you use several content types in an app; *refer to* 25.10.1, Create a Data Entry Content Type.)

When you create a column, you must select column type depending on what kind of metadata the column should contain, like names, dates or hyperlinks. The default column type is 'Single line of text', but there are many other options.

7.7.1 List Columns and Site Columns

Columns can be created for just an app or for the whole tenant.

In the List settings, below the names of the existing columns, there are three options for adding a new column: create a list column, add from existing site columns and indexed columns.

- Create column
- Add from existing site columns
- Indexed columns

List columns, created with the 'Create column' command, are the easiest column type to create. They can only be used in the app where they were created.

Even if list columns are a bit easier to create the first time, I recommend that you for the long run use site columns as much as possible. They are reusable and more available to the Search engine. From the app settings, you can only add existing site columns to the app, but below I will describe how you can create new site columns.

Indexed columns can be valuable for very large lists, with more than 5000 items, but I recommend that you instead archive items or split lists and don't let them grow that big. Therefore, I will not go into indexed columns in this book.

7.7.2 Create List Columns

The 'Create column' option in the List settings, opens a "Create Column" page. The column you create here, will only be available for the current app.

Give the column a name and select column type. Then you will have different options depending on what type of column you selected.

The image below shows the options for the default column type, Single line of text.

Settings ▸ Create Column ⓘ

Name and Type

Type a name for this column, and select the type of information you want to store in the column.

Column name:

[   ]

The type of information in this column is:

- ⦿ Single line of text
- ○ Multiple lines of text
- ○ Choice (menu to choose from)
- ○ Number (1, 1.0, 100)
- ○ Currency ($, ¥, €)
- ○ Date and Time
- ○ Lookup (information already on this site)
- ○ Yes/No (check box)
- ○ Person or Group
- ○ Hyperlink or Picture
- ○ Calculated (calculation based on other columns)
- ○ Task Outcome
- ○ External Data
- ○ Managed Metadata

Additional Column Settings

Specify detailed options for the type of information you selected.

Description:

[   ]

Require that this column contains information:

○ Yes ⦿ No

Enforce unique values:

○ Yes ⦿ No

Maximum number of characters:

[255]

Default value:

⦿ Text ○ Calculated Value

[   ]

☑ Add to all content types
☑ Add to default view

List columns can also be created in other ways:

- In the **modern** interface, click on '+ Add column' in the Standard or Grid view, *see* the image to the right.

    When you click on one of the options, a right pane will open where you find many of the settings that also exist in the Create Column page.

    'More Column Types...' directs you to the Create Column page.

- In the modern interface, Standard view mode, open the dropdown at one of the existing columns and select 'Column settings' >'Add a column'.

- In the **classic** experience, Quick Edit mode, click on the plus sign to the right of the existing columns.

Now you will have a choice of column types, but the classic interface has less options than the modern, before you need to click on "More ..."

A new cell will be created, where you can add the column name. You can also add values for the existing items in the cells below the column name, but you must go to the List settings and edit the column to make any column settings.

You can also click on the Create column button under the LIST/LIBRARY/CALENDAR tab. It will take you to the Create Column page.

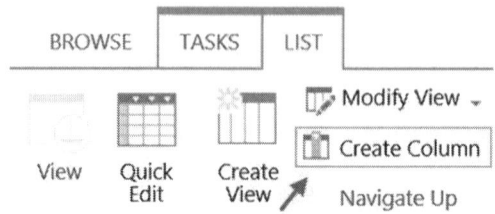

Demo:

https://www.kalmstrom.com//Tips/SharePoint-Online-Course/Categorization-Columns.htm

7.7.2.1 The Modern Location List Column

The Location list column type makes it possible to have location data from Bing Maps, or from your organization's directory, filled out automatically when a new item is created.

This column is currently only possible to create from the '+ Add column' command in the **modern** interface, Standard view mode.

When you create a Location column, you can select which other location data columns should be filled out automatically. (By default, no boxes are checked.)

Think twice when you choose a name for the column, because if you change the column name, the connected location data columns will still have the original name.

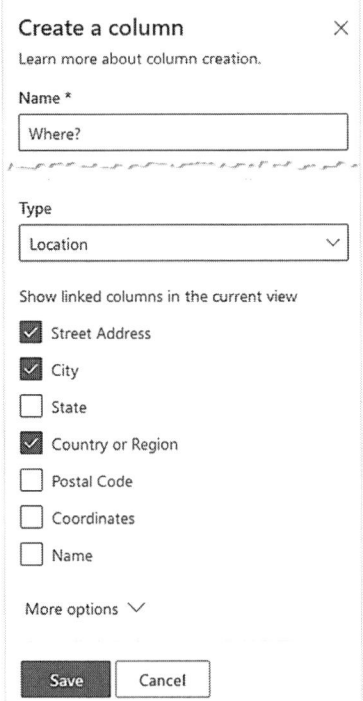

When a new item is created, users only need to select the location.

The other location details will be filled out automatically according to the column settings.

Note: The Location column type is a *list* column. If you select the "Location" *site* column, it will not be of the Location type. Instead, it will be a single line of text column with no extra features.

127

7.7.3 Create Site Columns

A site column is a reusable column that you can assign to multiple apps in a site or even in the whole tenant. Site columns are useful for establishing consistency across lists and libraries, and their values are automatically indexed by the Search engine.

You can use the settings for a site column in multiple apps, so that you don't have to recreate them each time you create a new app. For example, if you create a site column named Consultants, users can add that column to other apps, and it will have the same settings in the whole site collection or tenant. Only the column values will be different in each case.

Site columns are always used in the reusable sets of columns and settings called content types. You can use site columns without creating a content type, and you can create a site column for the site, but when you want the site column to be available for the whole tenant you need to use it in a content type. We will come back to content types in chapter 25.

When you select the second option for adding a column in the List settings, 'Add from existing site columns', you will have many different columns to choose from.

Microsoft gives a huge number of built-in site columns, but any site columns that you create will also show up here and can be selected.

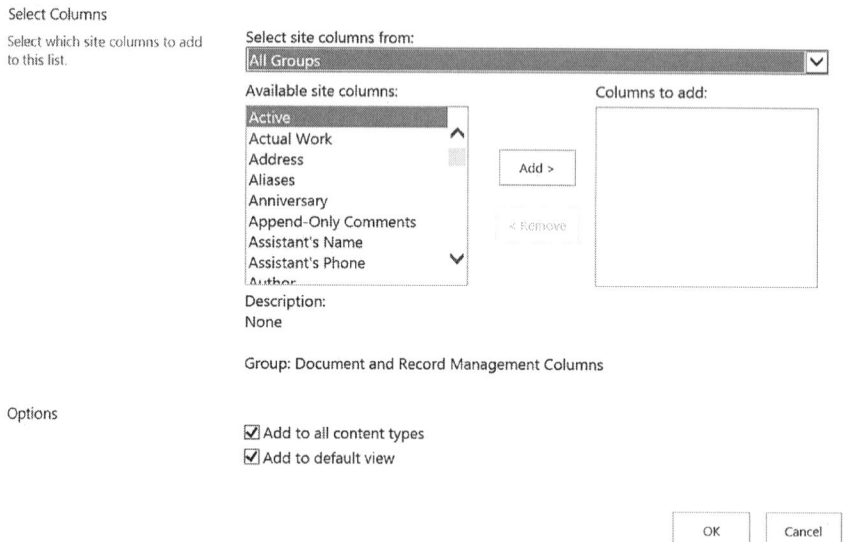

You can create custom site columns for apps in the site from the Site Settings >Site columns.

When you open the Site columns page and click on the 'Create' button, a "Create Column" page will open with the same kind of choices as when you create a list column, *see* above.

Web Designer Galleries
Site columns ←
Site content types
Web parts

7.7.4 *Column Types*

As you have seen in the images above, there are many column types. Here, I will just mention some of them that I think might need some extra explanations. These column types can be created as list columns as well as site columns.

The images below in this section mainly come from Create Column pages, but in the modern app interface most of these settings can be found in the right pane also.

7.7.4.1 Calculated Column

When you create a column of the type Calculated, you can set the values of that column to be a calculation of the item's values in other columns in the app. The calculated values are filled out automatically.

In the image below, I am setting the Total cost column value to be the value in the Hardware Cost column plus the value in the Setup Cost column in the same item.

Name and Type	Column name:
Type a name for this column.	Total Cost
	The type of information in this column is:
	Calculated (calculation based on other columns)
Additional Column Settings	Description:
Specify detailed options for the type of information you selected.	
	Formula: Insert Column:
	=[Hardware Cost]+ Location: Country/Re... Location: Name Modified Position **Setup Cost** Title Year
	Add to formula
	The data type returned from this formula is:
	○ Single line of text
	○ Number (1, 1.0, 100)
	◉ Currency ($, ¥, €)
	○ Date and Time

129

The Calculated column type is not visible in the dropdown when you create a new column from the **modern** interface. When you select 'More', you will be directed to the "Create Column" page, where you can select the Calculated column and create the formula for it.

Note: The modern Column settings pane gives the option 'Calculated value' for some column types, but this is a validation feature. You can find the same feature in the 'Column Validation' section of the "Create Column" page.

7.7.4.2 Choice Column

When a column is of the Choice type, users are asked to make a choice among several alternatives.

In the right pane, or at the bottom of the "Create Column" page, you should fill out the choices in the order you want them to be shown and select display method for the choices. If you choose to have a default value, it will be filled out if no other value is selected.

It is usually recommended to enter the choices alphabetically, but another option is to add figures before the options, to indicate a proper order.

When there are only a few options, it is nice to have radio buttons for the choice.

Require that this column contains information:
○ Yes ● No

Enforce unique values:
○ Yes ● No

Type each choice on a separate line:
```
1. Undecided
2. Yes
3. No
```

Display choices using:
○ Drop-Down Menu
● Radio Buttons
○ Checkboxes (allow multiple selections)

Allow 'Fill-in' choices:
○ Yes ● No

Default value:
● Choice ○ Calculated Value
```
1. Undecided
```

In the **modern** right pane, you can give different colors to the options.

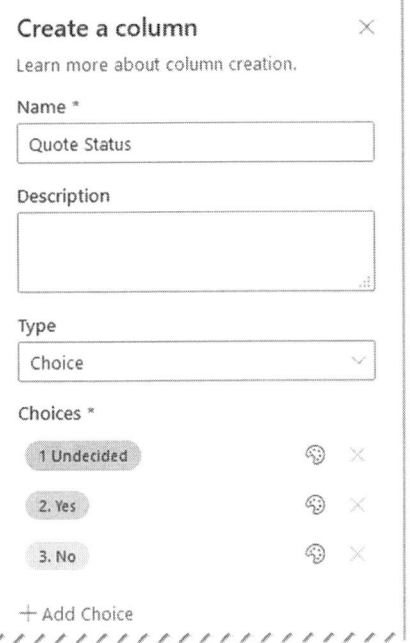

7.7.4.3 Date and Time Column

Columns of the type Date and Time have a DateTimePicker at the Date field.

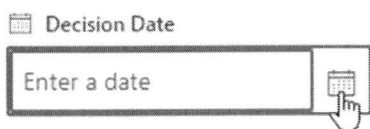

When you create a column of the type Date and Time, you will have some options that are only available for this column type.

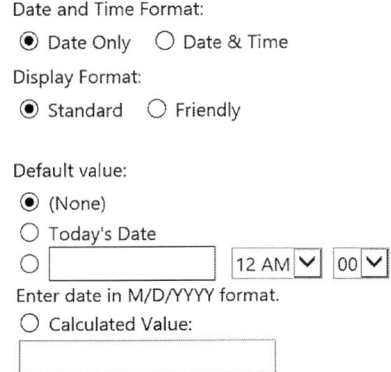

131

If you change the Display Format from Standard to Friendly, the selected date will be shown like this:

Quote Date

Tomorrow

Thursday

7.7.4.4 Lookup column

The Lookup column lets you connect an app to a column from another app in the same site. Select first app and then column, and the app with the Lookup column will get its value from the selected app and column.

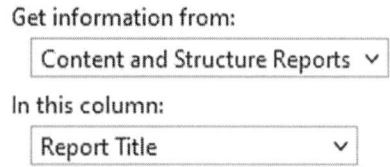

7.7.4.5 Character Limits in Text Columns

SharePoint apps have two text columns: Single line of text and Multiple lines of text. One line can only have 255 characters, so the Single line of text column is limited to that.

For the 'Multiple lines of text' there are two ways to give more space.

- When the column is created in the List settings 'Create column' dialog, there is a setting for number of rows. The default number is 6.

  Number of lines for editing:

  6

  This option is available for all apps, experiences and modes.

- When then column is created with the '+ Add column' command in the **modern** interface, Standard view mode, **document libraries** have a setting for unlimited length in the right pane. This option is disabled by default.

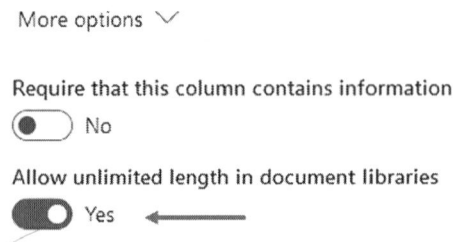

7.7.5 Filter, Sort and Group

SharePoint app items can be filtered by the various column values they contain. The column values can also be sorted ascending or descending, and you can combine filtering and sorting of several columns.

In general, app filtering works in the same way as in Excel and Access. A funnel icon to the right of the column name shows that a column has been filtered, so that it does not show all items.

In the **modern** experience, the options to filter on are selected with check boxes in a right pane. It works in the same way in Standard and Grid view. In the image below, the Department column is ready to be filtered.

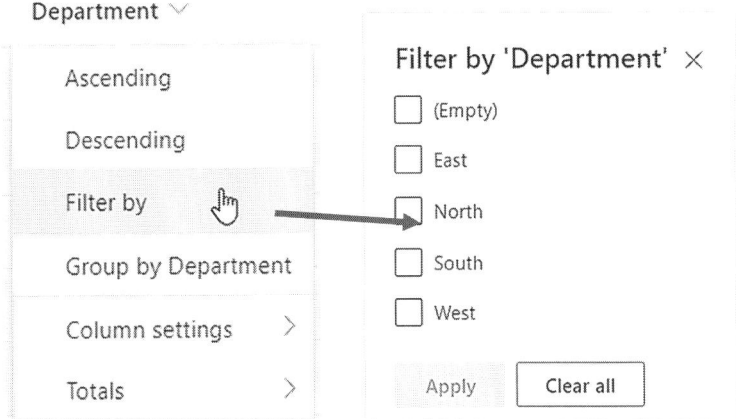

Check the boxes for the values you want to show and click on 'Apply'.

Uncheck boxes or click on 'Clear all' and then 'Apply' to remove the filter.

The **modern** experience also gives a possibility to filter multiple columns in an app at the same time, via the funnel icon in the right part of the command bar.

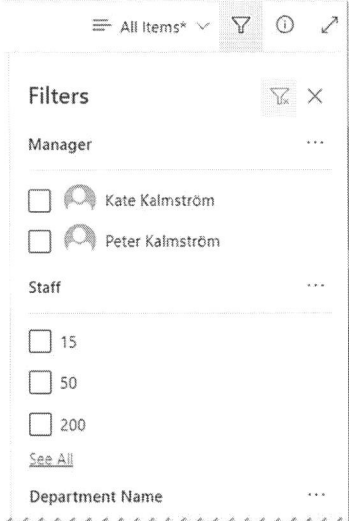

The images below show the **classic** experience. To the left is a Product column in the Quick Edit mode. Here you can select one of the values and sort the column by it. 'Clear Filter' will be active when the column is filtered.

The image to the right is from the Standard view mode. Here you can filter by more than one value, just as in the modern interface.

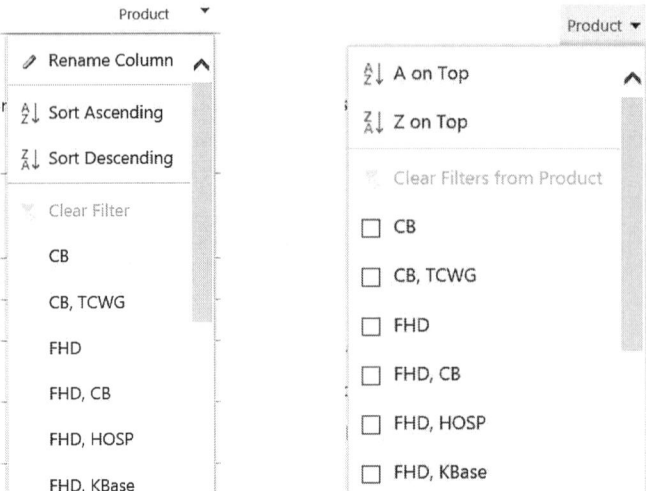

The **modern** Standard view mode also lets you group items. In the image to the right, the "Manager" column has been grouped, so there is an icon to the right of the column name. Click on the 'Group by' entry in the dropdown to remove the grouping.

(It is possible to group items in the classic interface too, but then you need to create a grouped view in the List settings, *refer to* 7.9.7, Grouped View below.)

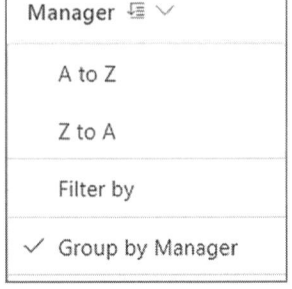

Note that there is no Grid view mode when you have grouped items, either you have done it in the modern interface or via the List settings.

7.7.5.1 Links

The filter, sorting or grouping is dynamically added to the URL, so you can link directly to a specific filter or sort option. You can see this at the end of the URL. For example, "FilterField1%3D**Country**-FilterValue1%3D**Canada**" at the end of a URL shows that the Country column is filtered to only show items with the value Canada.

Demo:

https://www.kalmstrom.com//Tips/SharePoint-Online-Course/Categorization-Column-Filtering.htm

7.7.6 *Edit List Columns*

Columns can be edited in different ways, depending on if they are list columns or site columns. For list columns and for site columns that you want to use as list columns, you can use the methods described in the sections below.

7.7.6.1 Edit via the List Settings

To edit a list column, open the List settings and find the Columns group.

Click on the column you want to edit, and the 'Edit Column' page for that column will open. Here you will have the same options as in the "Create Column" page, except for the full column type selection. Only the column types that are possible to switch to are displayed.

Columns

A column stores information

Column (click to edit)

Title

Created

Modified

Created By

Modified By

Checked Out To

Switch of column type can only be done under certain circumstances. For some column types it is not possible to switch type at all. Other column types give such a possibility, but you cannot switch to any other type. For example, you can switch from a Single line of text to a Choice column type, but not to a Person or Group-column type.

You cannot change column type for the "Title" column. It must always be a Single line of text column. You can however rename this column and in many cases, it is highly recommended. Often the name "Title" is too generic.

7.7.6.2 Edit in the Modern Interface

In apps with the **modern** interface in Standard view mode, columns can be moved, hidden and edited directly from the dropdown at the column. Select first 'Column settings' and then the modification you want to perform.

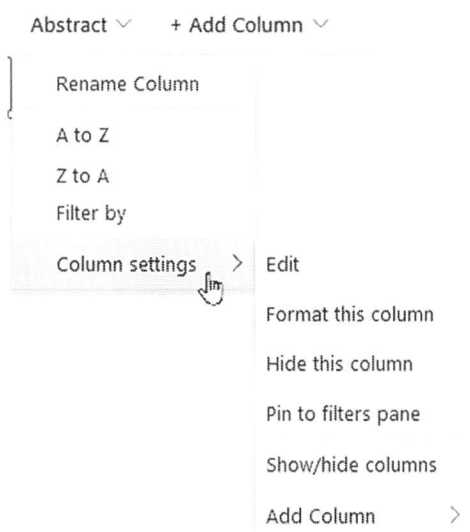

Some options open an Edit column right pane, where you can make your changes. Options like 'Move' and 'Hide' are performed immediately.

Note that 'Hide this column' does not remove the column from the form. It a view setting that removes the column from the interface of the current view, *refer to* 7.9, Views.

135

7.7.6.3 Format a Modern Column

Apps with the **modern** interface have a possibility to format columns with data bars and conditional formatting via Column settings >Format this column, *see* the image above. You can also reach the column formatting options from the View selector, *refer to* 7.9.1, Modern App Views.

- Number columns have the two options you can see in the image below, Data bars and Conditional formatting.
- Date and Time columns have Format dates and Conditional formatting.
- Other column types only have the Conditional formatting option.

The column formatting will not be visible if you switch to the classic interface.

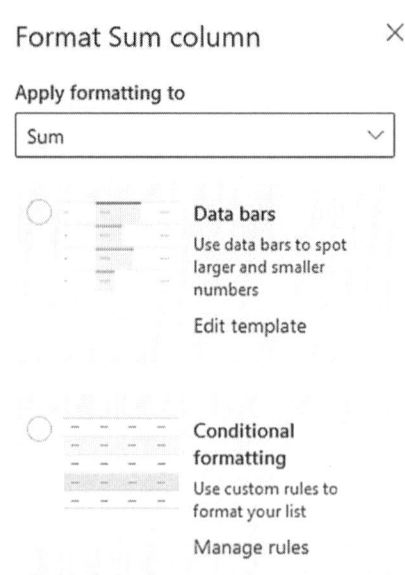

The Data bars option can show different colors for positive and negative numbers, and the bar size adapts to the number value. You can also set a minimum and maximum number to format.

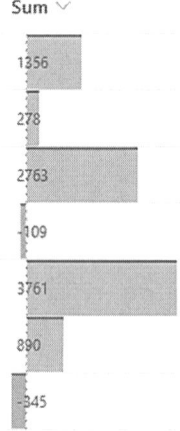

The Conditional formatting option lets you create a rule – or a combination of rules. In the image below I have selected to mark all values greater than 1000 with green color.

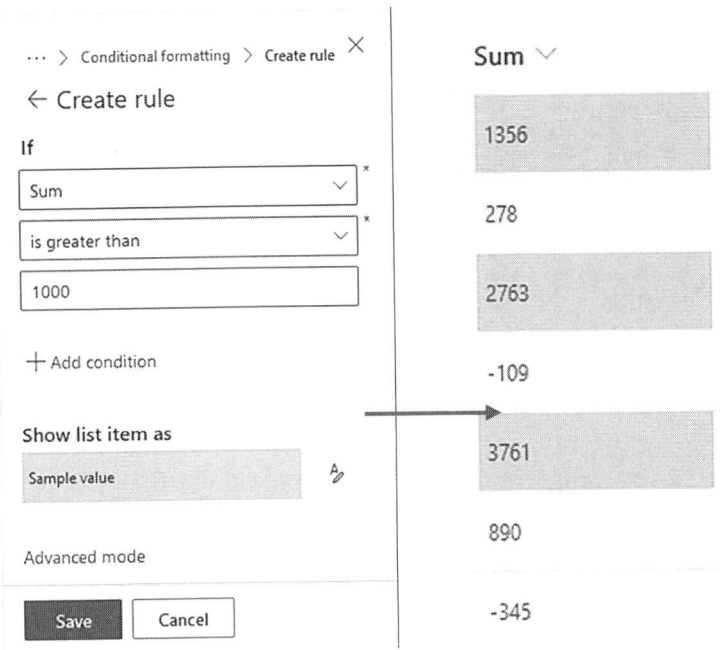

In the Advanced mode, you can use JSON code for the formatting. That is out of scope for this book, but you can see some examples at https://docs.microsoft.com/en-us/sharepoint/dev/declarative-customization/column-formatting.

7.7.6.4 Rename a Column

You can rename all columns via the List settings. Just click on the column name to open the 'Edit Column' page and write another name in the 'Column name' field. Note that the internal name for the column will not be changed.

In **modern** apps, it is possible to rename columns directly in the app interface, via the column settings dropdown or in the Edit column right pane. I have however found that when I use Power Automate to create flows for a SharePoint app, new column names are only displayed in the flow's dynamic content if I rename the column in the List settings.

7.7.7 Edit Site Columns

Site columns can be edited as described above, that is, just like list columns. Site columns can also be edited at Site Settings >Site columns.

Which method you choose, depends on if you want to continue using the column as a site column or not:

- When a site column is added to an app, a copy is made of the column settings. When those column settings are edited as described in 'Edit the Column' sections above, the link to the site column is broken, and the edited column will become a list column instead.
- If you want to keep the column as a site column, you should go to Site Settings >Site columns and edit the column there. Now the changes will be propagated to all apps that use this column.

7.7.8 Edit Column Values

Most editing methods are available for all apps, such as the Grid editing. If you are used to working in datasheet, this is a quick way to edit column values.

7.7.8.1 Edit Values in Grid Mode

In the Grid/Quick edit view mode, you can edit the metadata of all app items by simply changing the values in the cells.

In the Grid/Quick edit view mode, you can also drag a value in a cell down to the cells below, like you can do in Excel. This is convenient when you want to give multiple items the same value in one or more columns.

7.7.8.2 Edit Values in Standard Mode

In the **modern** app interface, the metadata of any selected item can be edited in the Information pane. Click on 'Edit all' at 'Properties' to open the item in edit mode.

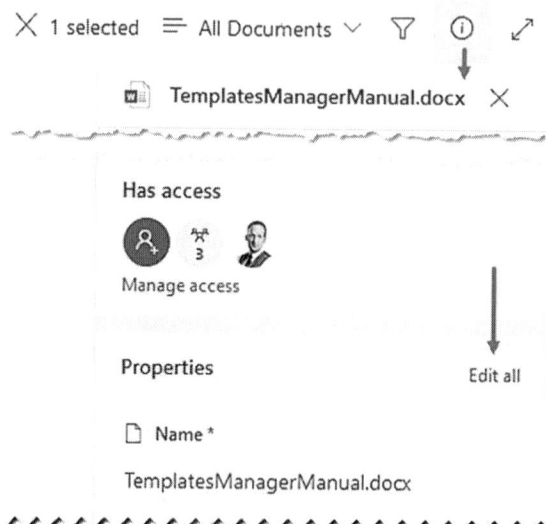

In the modern interface, you can edit multiple items at the same time, which is convenient when you want to give multiple items the same value in one or more columns. The values you enter in the right pane will be applied to all selected items.

When you select multiple items, all columns that can be edited are displayed in the Information pane. You can also click on 'Edit' (in lists) or 'Properties' (in libraries) to have a wider pane to edit.

Of course, you only need to add a value in one of them – or in those columns that you want to change. The other columns will keep their current values.

The bulk edit feature is especially useful if you cannot sort the items in a way that makes it possible to drag down a value in the Grid view mode.

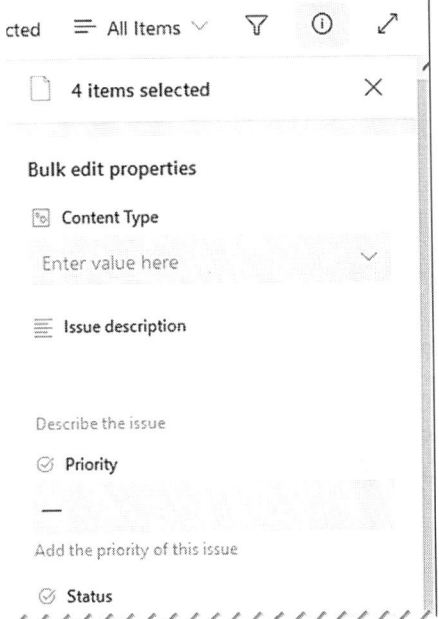

In the **classic** library interface, you must go to the ribbon if you want to edit an item from the Standard view mode. Library apps have an 'Edit Properties' button under the FILES tab, and list apps have an 'Edit Item' button under the ITEMS tab.

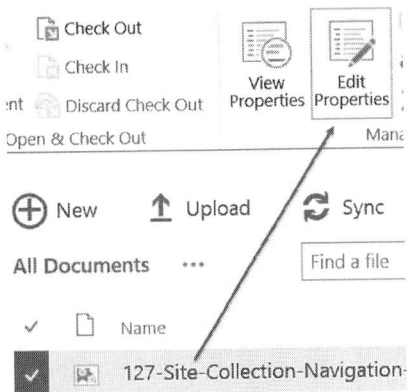

The Grid view is the only option if you want to edit multiple items in the classic interface.

139

7.8 Edit the Form

The **modern** interface gives a possibility to decide which columns should be displayed in the app form – that is, which fields users see when they fill out the properties of an item.

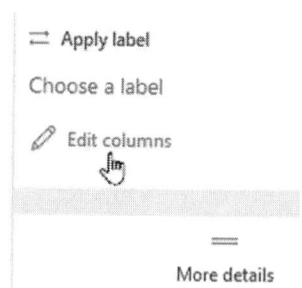

1. Select an item and click on 'Edit columns' in the Information pane.
2. Uncheck the boxes for the columns that you don't want to show in the item form, *see* the image below.
3. Move columns if needed, so that you get the fields in the preferred order.
4. Click on 'Save'.

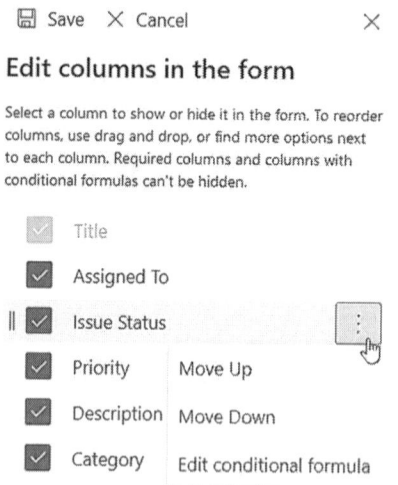

5. Close the Information/New item pane.

Now all new and existing items will show only the checked columns as fields in the form, in the modern as well as in the classic interface.

Use views instead, *see* below, if you want to change how the columns are shown in the app interface.

7.9 Views

All apps can show the data stored in the app in different views. A view is a permanent way to display app items and properties, as opposed to a temporary ad-hoc filtering or grouping.

Each view is a separate .aspx page that can be shared, opened in a new tab, customized and so on.

There are two kinds of views: personal and public. The personal view is only shown to the person who created the view, while public views are shown to all users. The public view is the one I am referring to below.

The default view, created by SharePoint, is called "All Items" in lists, "All Documents" in libraries and "Calendar" in calendars. These are basic views that show all items in the app.

I would recommend that you create new views and arrange data in ways that suit your organization. When doing so, you should combine meaningful views with the use of columns for relevant metadata. This way the information can be sliced and diced in many ways, and your SharePoint apps will be very informative.

A view should not show more columns than necessary, but you can still use the columns you select to hide from the users in each view.

When you have many views for a list or library, you can create a Views landing page, *refer to* 17.5.

7.9.1   *Modern App Views*

In modern apps, you can find all views in the View selector to the right in the command bar. Only the name of the current view is displayed in the command bar. To see the other views, you must open the dropdown at the View selector. This dropdown also has options for layout and for work with the views.

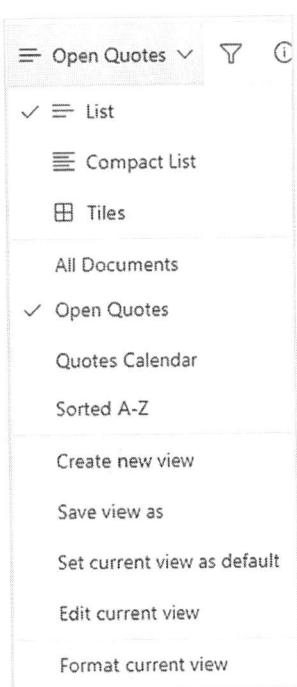

Layout options:
Above the views in the View selector, there are layout options. The 'List' option is default, but both list and library apps also have a 'Compact List' layout.

The third layout option is 'Gallery' in lists and 'Tiles' in libraries.

In Grid view mode, the default option is 'Autofit height', but there is also a 'Fixed height' option.

Create view:
Below the existing views, the 'Create new view' link opens a dialog with a choice to show the data in the default list view or in a calendar or gallery view, *see* 7.9.4, Modern "New View" Options" below.

To create a new view, you can also use the 'Save view as' option. This saves the current configuration of the page (for example the filter options) as a new view.

Set default view:
The command, 'Set current view as default', is displayed when another view than the default

view is selected. When you make a view default, all users will reach that view first, regardless of how they open the app.

Edit view:
In the View dropdown, you can also find a link to editing of the current view.

Format view:
The last option 'Format current view' gives options that remind of the column formatting I described above, and columns can also be formatted here.

In views, the formatting options are conditional formatting and different colors on even and odd rows.

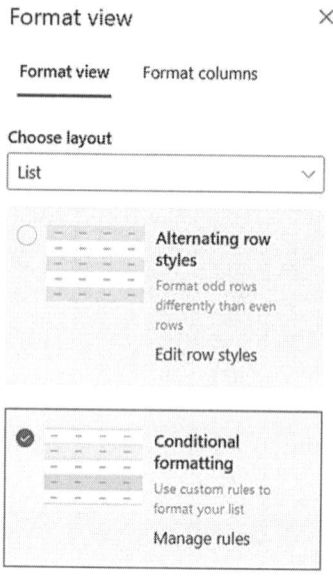

7.9.2 Classic App Views

In the classic experience, you can see a maximum of three views above the items in a list or library. The other views are hidden under an ellipsis, where you also can find the links to modify the view and create a new view.

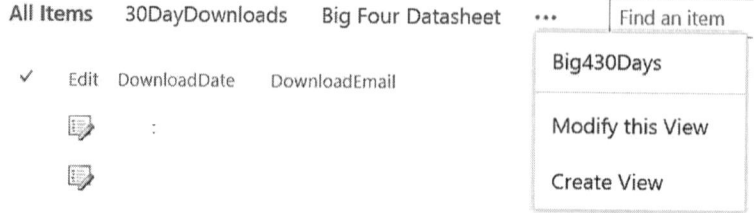

There are also a View selector and buttons for view creation and modification in the ribbon, under the LIST/LIBRARY tab.

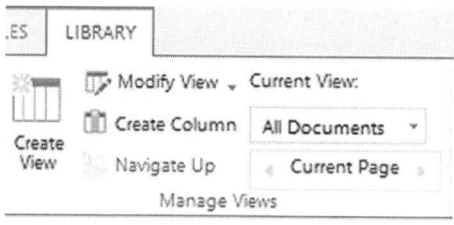

Demo:

https://www.kalmstrom.com/Tips/SharePoint-Online-Course/View-Intro.htm

142

7.9.3 Edit a View

These are the ways to start modifying an existing view:

- In the List settings, click on the view name under 'Views'.

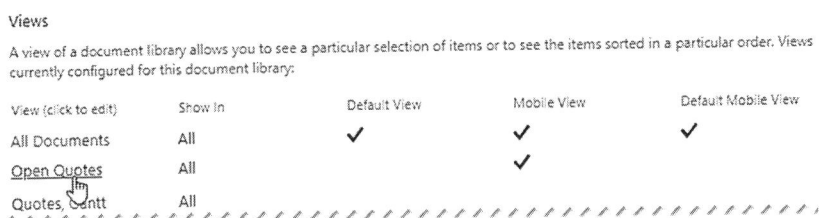

- In a **modern** app, select 'Edit current view' in the View selector.
- In a **classic** app, click on the ellipsis after the view name(s) and select 'Modify this View', or click on the 'Modify View' button under the LIBRARY/LIST tab.

In all three cases, an Edit View page will open where you can include/exclude and order columns, sort, filter and group the content and much more. (By default, the 'Columns', 'Sort' and 'Filter' sections are expanded when the page opens.)

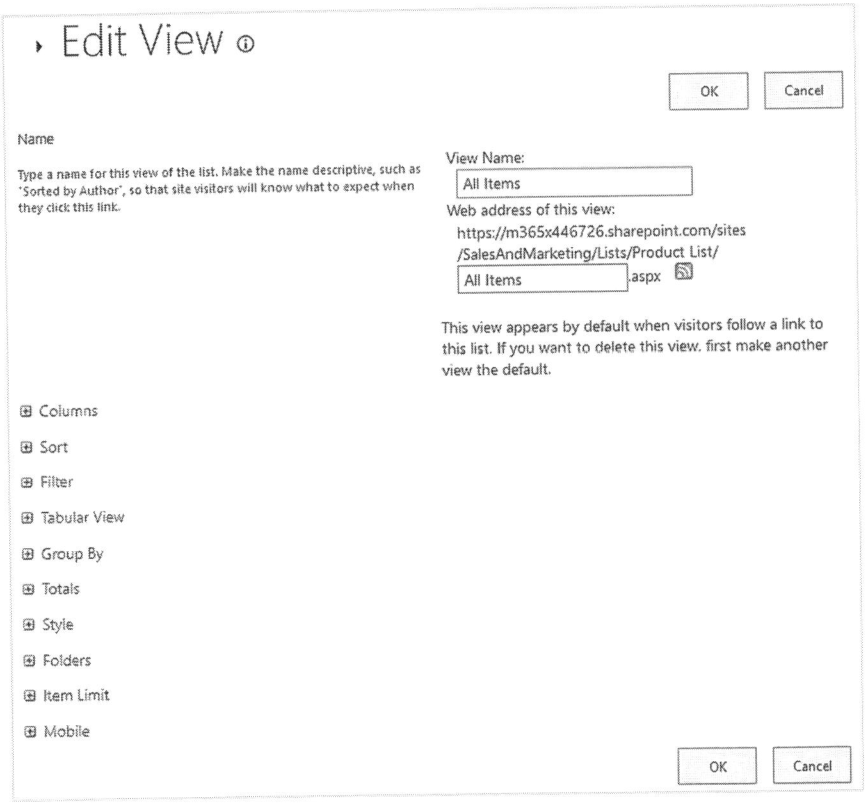

143

The image below shows the upper part of the 'Columns' section. Of course, the column names are different in each app, depending on app type and how the columns have been created and modified.

Check the box for the columns you wish to show in the view and put them in the preferred order. When you change the order number of one column, the others will adapt automatically.

Display	Column Name	Position from Left
☑	Title (linked to item with edit menu)	1
☑	Code Name	2
☑	Product Line	3
☑	Product Type	4
☑	Color	5
☑	Notes	6
☑	Enterprise Keywords	7
☐	App Created By	8
☐	App Modified By	9
☐	Attachments	10

The **modern** interface has 'Hide' and 'Move' settings under Column settings that changes the current view, *refer to* 7.7.6.2, Edit in the Modern Interface.

7.9.4 Modern "New View" Options

In an app with the modern interface, you can create a new view by filtering and/or grouping any view and then opening the View selector and selecting 'Save view as'. Give the view a new name, and it will be added as a new view in the View selector dropdown.

Another modern option is to use the 'Create new view' link in the View selector. This opens a dialog with a choice to show the data in the default list view, a Calendar view or a Gallery view. Microsoft plans to also add a Board view option.

The 'List' option, works well in the classic experience too, and it can be edited from under 'Views' in the List settings, as described above.

When you select to show the view as a calendar, you will have some options to fill out. SharePoint needs to know which dates should be the start and end dates of the calendar and which column name should be displayed on the calendar "event".

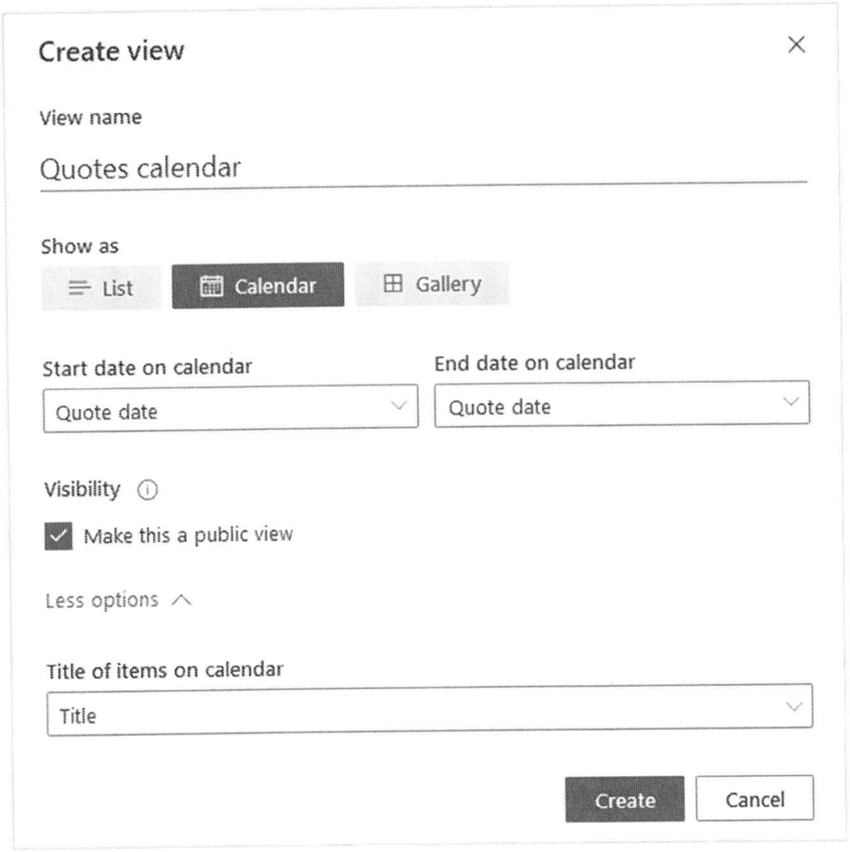

Create view

View name

Quotes calendar

Show as

≡ List | 📅 Calendar | ⊞ Gallery

Start date on calendar

Quote date

End date on calendar

Quote date

Visibility ⓘ

☑ Make this a public view

Less options ∧

Title of items on calendar

Title

Create | Cancel

The Calendar view is of course most suitable for lists where you want to show dates, but it is possible to use it for all apps.

The Calendar view might be a modern alternative to the classic Calendar app, *refer to* 8.10, even if the classic Calendar app has more features adapted for a calendar.

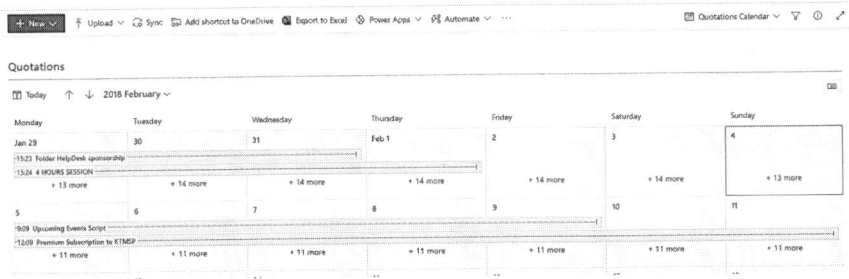

The Gallery view shows items as tiles. List items show metadata from the columns in the tiles. In document libraries, the files are shown on the tile, and if the file is a Word file there is a preview to the right when you hover the mouse cursor over the tile.

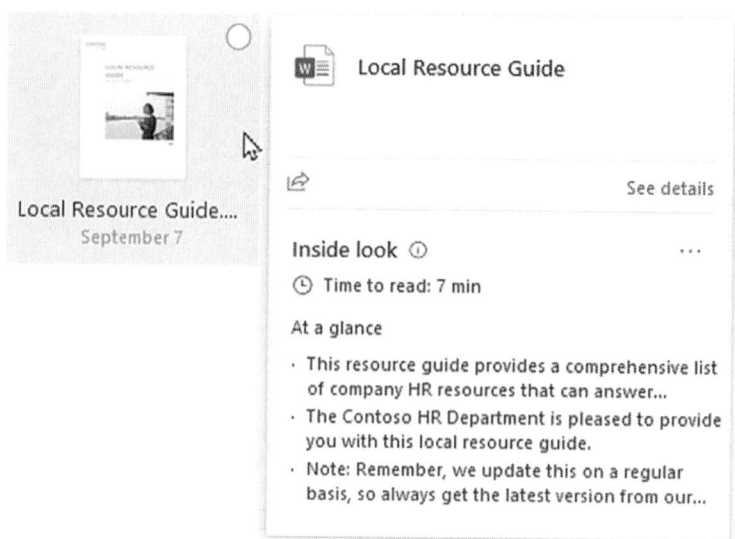

Note that the app data is only shown in a Calendar or Gallery view if you use the modern interface. If you switch to the classic experience, the items will be shown in a list.

7.9.5   Classic "New View" Options

Click on the 'Create View' link under the list of existing views in the List settings, to create a classic view from scratch. That will direct you to a 'View Type' Page with some view options.

The "Create View'" button in the ribbon, under the LIBRARY/LIST/CALENDAR tab will also directed you to the View Type page.

In the View Type page, you can select what kind of view you want to create. You can also start from a view that already exists for the app and modify it.

Choose a view type

Standard View
View data on a Web page. You can choose from a list of display styles.

Datasheet View
View data in an editable spreadsheet format that is convenient for bulk editing and quick customization.

Calendar View
View data as a daily, weekly, or monthly calendar.

Gantt View
View list items in a Gantt chart to see a graphical representation of how a team's tasks relate over time.

Start from an existing view

- All Items
- Entry
- Grouped

When you choose one of the four view type options, a Create View page will open. It has similar options as in the Edit View page shown above, but it is a bit different for each view type.

When you modify an existing view by clicking on one of the views under 'Start from an existing view', the Create View page will also open, but with the settings from the selected view. The original view will be kept.

Classic sites also give an option to open SharePoint Designer and create a view there.

7.9.5.1   Calendar and Gantt Views

When an app has columns with dates that form a period of time, it is often easier to overview it in a Calendar or Gantt view.

The Calendar view:

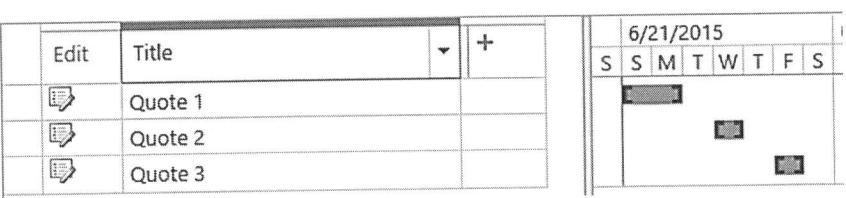

The Gantt view is a type of bar chart that illustrates start and end dates:

These two views look like they do above only in the **classic** experience, and that will create a problem when you open the Calendar or Gantt view from a view with the modern interface.

To avoid this problem, you can set the app to use only the classic experience, under List settings >Advanced settings.

As you see in the image above, the Gantt view has links to the other views. That is not the case with the Calendar view. Even if you get a link to the Calendar view in the other app views, there are no links to the other views in the Calendar view itself.

To leave the Calendar view, you must either click on the app link in the Site navigation, use the browser's back arrow or open the ribbon and switch view in the view selector there.

For both views, you need to specify which columns should be used for the dates and which column should be used as title. In library apps, I have found that the Gantt view works better with the Title column than with the Name. This is an issue when the Title field is not filled out, *refer to* 9.10, The Title column.

147

⊟ Gantt Columns

Specify columns to be represented in the Gantt chart. Start Date and Due Date are required date fields. Title is a required text field. Percent Complete is an optional number field. If no fields appear in a list, they must be created to support this view.

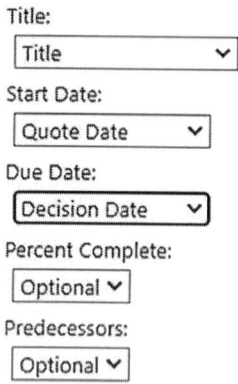

Demos:

https://kalmstrom.com/Tips/SharePoint-Online-Course/Quotes-Calendar.htm

https://kalmstrom.com/Tips/SharePoint-Online-Course/Quotes-Gantt.htm

7.9.6   Default View

When you make a custom view default, all users will reach that view first, regardless of how they open the app. Make a view default by checking the default box in the Create View/Edit View page.

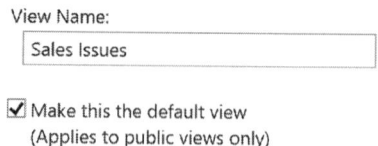

If you check the default box for another view, that view will become default instead. If you just uncheck the box in the default view, the 'All documents' or 'All items' view will become default, as it was from the beginning.

In **modern** apps, you can also set the default view in the View Selector, as described above.

Demo:

https://www.kalmstrom.com/Tips/SharePoint-Online-Course/View-Default.htm

7.9.7   Grouped View

As we have seen above, the modern interface has a possibility to group items directly from the column dropdown. If you use the classic experience, or if you want a more advanced grouping, you should open the List settings and use the 'Group By' section in the Create View/Edit View page.

Click on the plus sign to expand the Group by accordion. Here you can select what columns to group by on a first and second level and how data in them should be displayed.

The image below shows the default, before any grouping has been made. Not all types of columns can be used for grouping, so only columns suitable for grouping are shown in the dropdowns.

The Grid view mode does not work in grouped views. This might be a reason for not making a grouped view default.

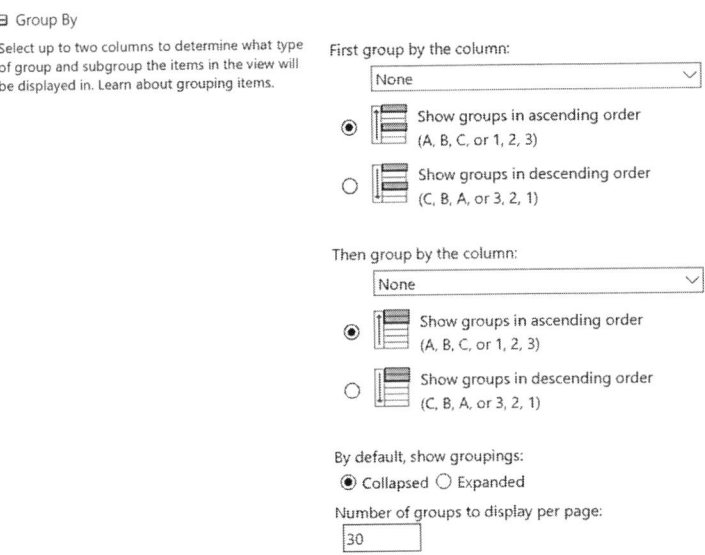

Demo:

https://www.kalmstrom.com/Tips/SharePoint-Online-Course/View-Grouped.htm

7.9.8 Totals

The 'Totals' section in the Create View/Edit View page can be used to summarize the values in an app column. The feature works best on number and currency columns, somewhat less on text-based columns and not at all on Calculated and Multiple lines of text columns.

Computers

Title ∨	Hardware Cost ∨	Setup Cost ∨
Kalle's laptop	$500	$100
Stina's tablet	$400	$50
Bert's desktop	$800	$200
	Sum $1,700	Sum $350

149

In Number and Currency columns, the SharePoint 'Totals' can calculate sum and other numeric values, like average, maximum and minimum. In columns of other types, the 'Totals' feature can be used to count the number of items in a column.

The result of the calculation is shown below (modern) or above (classic) the column that is calculated.

Totals can only be displayed in the Standard view mode. When this is written, the Total is not visible in the Grid view mode.

In the **modern** app interface, Totals can be added to a column directly from the column dropdown. The image below shows the dropdown for a Currency column.

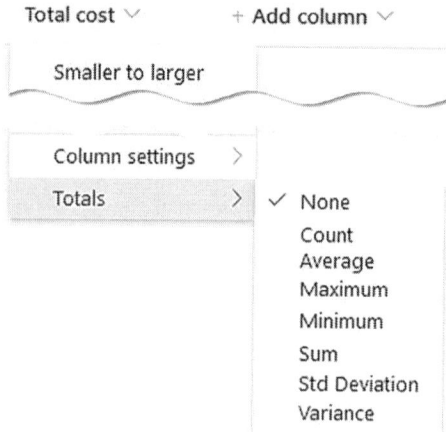

Totals can also be applied from the Create View/Edit View page. Select the preferred option from the dropdown to the right of the column that should have the Total – the "Cost" column in the image below.

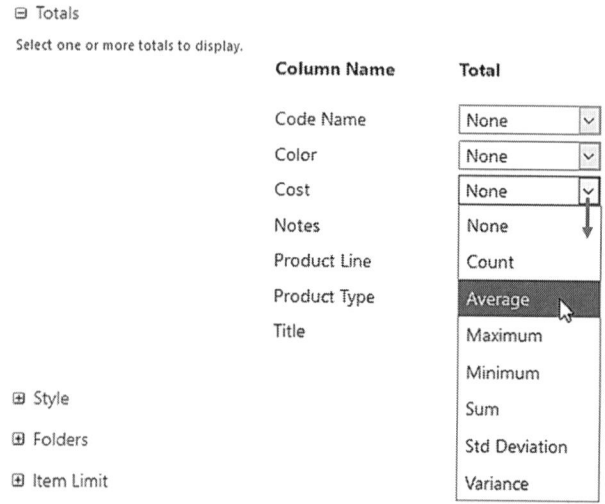

Demo:

https://www.kalmstrom.com//Tips/SharePoint-Online-Course/View-Total.htm

7.10 ALERTS

SharePoint apps have an alert feature that sends e-mail notifications on changes in the app. It is possible to have alerts for changes in single items and files. You can also set an alert for changes in a whole list or library.

The 'Alert Me' link can be found under the ellipsis in the modern command bar. The classic experience has buttons under the ITEMS and LIST tabs in the ribbon.

Both buttons have a 'Manage my alerts' option. Here, you can edit or stop the alert, and via an 'Add Alert' link you can reach other apps in the same site and set alerts for them.

Both interfaces also have 'Alert me' links for single items under the item ellipsis.

Each user can set and manage his/her own alerts. Site admins can also set alerts to be sent to other users. These alerts are managed in the Site Settings >Site Administration >User alerts.

The alerts can be somewhat customized, because you can decide at what time they should be sent and for what changes.

Only send me alerts when:
- ⦿ All changes
- ◯ New items are added
- ◯ Existing items are modified
- ◯ Items are deleted

Send me an alert when:
- ◯ Anything changes
- ◯ Someone else changes an item
- ◯ Someone else changes an item created by me
- ◯ Someone else changes an item last modified by me

- ⦿ Send notification immediately
- ◯ Send a daily summary
- ◯ Send a weekly summary

Time:

151

1. Change the title (= e-mail subject) if you don't want to use the default: app name (+ item).
2. If you are a Site administrator, add people who should get the alert.
3. If you have text messaging service set up, you can choose between having the alert by SMS or by e-mail. (This is not possible in all countries.) Otherwise e-mail is the only option.
4. Select at what changes you want to receive alerts.
5. Select when you want to receive alerts.
6. Click OK.

You will now receive an e-mail confirming that your alert has been set up.

Demo:

https://kalmstrom.com/Tips/SharePoint-Online-Course/HelpDesk-Alerts.htm

To have customized notifications, you should create a flow or workflow, *refer to* chapter 24, SharePoint Automation.

7.11 DELETE AND RESTORE CONTENT

Users can delete and restore content that they have created. Site admins and owners can delete and restore other content too. Only apps (lists and libraries) and items (including files) can be restored – not columns and views. The user who deletes content will be asked to confirm each deletion.

Deleted content is moved to the site's recycle bin, *refer to* 6.3.1.1, The Recycle Bins.

7.11.1 Delete Item

In both experiences, you can delete one item at a time via the item ellipsis when the app is in Standard view mode.

In the Grid mode of both experiences, you can select several rows and delete multiple items:

In the modern interface, click in the rings to the left of the items you want to delete.

In the classic interface, hold down the Ctrl or Shift key and click in the first cell to the left at each item you want to delete.

Now you can either right-click and select 'Delete' or press the delete button on your keyboard.

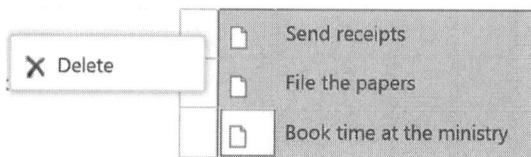

7.11.1.1 Modern Experience

In apps with the modern interface, you can use the 'Delete' button in the command bar, in both Standard and Grid view. This option can be used for several multiple items at the same time.

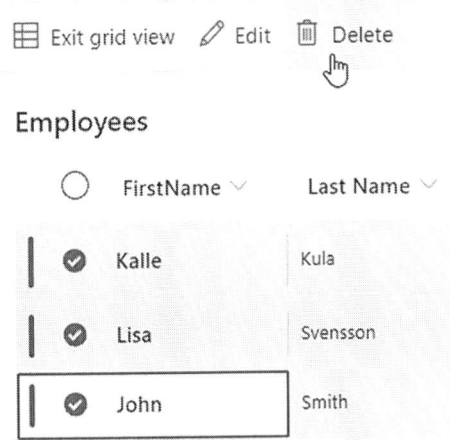

7.11.1.2 Classic Experience

The classic experience has a delete button under the ITEMS/FILES/EVENTS tab. Hold down the Shift or Ctrl key when you select the items, to select and delete multiple items at the same time.

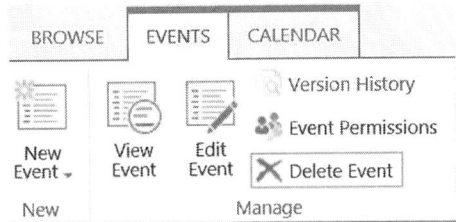

7.11.2 *Delete Columns*

When a column is deleted, it will be removed from all interfaces and forms, and all data in the column is lost. If you are unsure of this, a better option might be to hide the column from the form and views.

Some automatically created columns are required and cannot be deleted, for example the "Title" column. If you don't need such a column, you can rename it and use it for something else that requires the same column type. (The "Title" column is a Single line of text column.)

7.11.2.1 Delete a List Column

To delete a list column, open the List settings and find the list of columns. Click on the column you want to delete to open the 'Edit Column' page. Then click on the 'Delete' button at the bottom of the page.

In the **modern** interface, you can also open the column settings, *refer to* 7.7.6, Edit List Columns, and select 'Edit'. A right pane will open, and it has a 'Delete' button at the bottom.

7.11.2.2 Delete a Site Column

It is usually difficult to remove site columns that have been used in a content type or in a list.

Site admins can delete site columns at Site Settings>Site Columns. Click on the site column that you want to remove to open its Edit column page. It has a Delete button at the bottom, but when you try it, you might very well get a message that the site column has been used and thus cannot be removed.

You need to first remove all existing references to the site column before it can be removed, both in lists and in content types. This includes any items in the recycle bin!

A better way is to go via the SharePoint Admin center >Content type gallery. Here, you can remove a column without interfering with existing items. The deleted column will not be visible in the new item form, but existing items will not be affected.

The Admin center deletion is however not without issues. If the content type has been used and the column has been added to a view, it will still be visible, and properties can be added in the Grid view mode. Therefore, you need to make sure that the column is either deleted or hidden from all views in apps where the content type is used.

7.11.3 Delete a View

The Delete button for views is found in the "Edit View'" page for views that are not default. If the view is default, you cannot delete it until you have set another view as default.

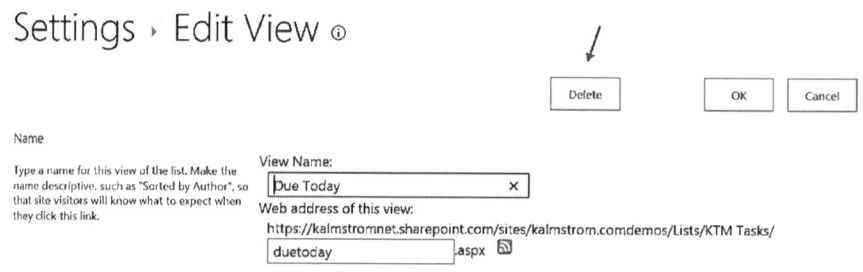

154

7.11.4 Delete an App

To delete an app, open the List settings and click on the link 'Delete this list' or 'Delete this document library' under the 'Permissions and Management' heading.

Permissions and Management

- Delete this list

You can also open the Site contents, click on the ellipsis at the app you want to delete and select Delete.

7.11.5 Restore Deleted Content

Deleted apps and items are stored in the site's Recycle bin for 93 days. All users can see and restore content they have deleted themselves, and the Site admin can see and restore all deleted content.

If a larger number of files than usual are deleted from a document library within one hour, SharePoint will send an e-mail to the user who deleted them, with an option to restore the files.

Content that is deleted from the Recycle bin, and content that has been in the Recycle bin for 93 days, is moved to the Second-stage recycle bin, where it is kept for another 93 days.

7.12 VERSION HISTORY

The SharePoint Version history feature, also called versioning, makes it possible to see and restore earlier versions of items in a list app and files in a library app. Version history is always set for the whole app, so that it applies to all the items contained in the app.

Version history is enabled by default when a new SharePoint app is created, and I recommend that you keep it that way.

The versions do not have any effect on the number of items in the app, so you don't have to worry that you increase the number of items by using Version history.

The Version history settings are managed in the List settings >Versioning settings.

General Settings

- List name, description and navigation
- Versioning settings ←
- Advanced settings

7.12.1 See Version History

To see the version history, select the item, click on the item ellipsis and select 'Version history'.

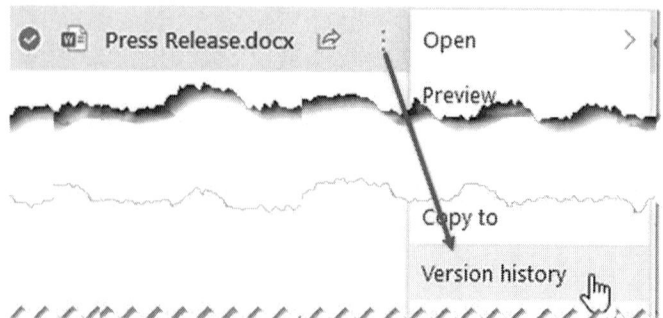

Apps with the **modern** interface also have a Version history command under the command bar ellipsis.

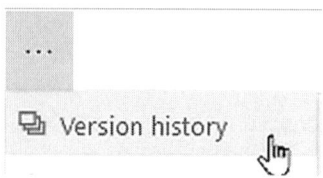

In **classic** calendars, select or open an event and click on the 'Version History' button under the EVENTS tab.

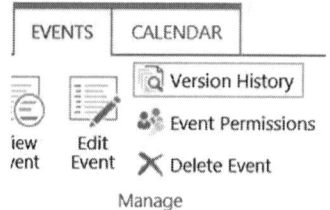

Other apps with the classic interface also have a 'Version History' button in the ribbon.

The 'Version history' commands open a dialog that looks the same for library files and list items. Here, each version has a number and a date and time when the item was modified.

Click on a Modified date to open a dropdown, where you can view the item properties, restore the item or delete it. (The current version cannot be deleted here.)

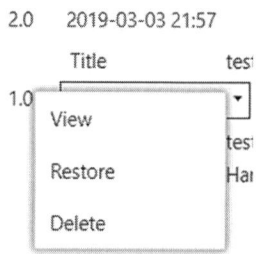

The image below shows the version history for an item that has six versions. When the item comes from a document library, as in this image, changes in the file as well as in the metadata are recorded.

No. ↓	Modified		Modified By	Size	Comments
6.0	11/20/2021 6:44 AM		MOD Administrator	32.4 MB	
	Status	Finished			
5.0	11/20/2021 6:43 AM		MOD Administrator	32.4 MB	
4.0	11/20/2021 6:42 AM		MOD Administrator	32.5 MB	
	Title	Build an Approval Process with Microsoft Power Au			
3.0	11/20/2021 6:30 AM		MOD Administrator	32.5 MB	
	Status	Under review			
2.0	9/7/2021 12:23 PM		Megan Bowen	32.5 MB	
1.0	9/4/2021 12:23 PM		Megan Bowen	32.5 MB	

7.12.2 Version History in Library Apps

When you click on a modified date on the Version History page in a document library, Office, image and PDF files are opened in that version. Files of other types are instead downloaded.

To see the properties of an earlier version, click on the arrow at the date and select 'View'. From the dialog that opens, you can also edit the properties.

When you open an earlier version of an Office file, it has a Restore button below the ribbon.

Word files can be both restored and compared to other versions.

7.12.3 Version History in List Apps

When you click on the date and time on the Version History page in a list app, or if you select 'View' under the dropdown, the item properties are displayed, and the item can be directly restored or deleted.

157

Demo:

https://www.kalmstrom.com/Tips/SharePoint-Online-Course/Version-History.htm

7.13 INTERNAL NAME

As mentioned in 4.4.1. Naming New Content, SharePoint content can have different internal and user interface names. You can see the internal name in the URL for an open app, for libraries after the site name and for list apps after /Lists/.

🔒 kalmstromnet.sharepoint.com/sites/ /Lists/Employees/

To see the internal name for a column, open the app settings and then the column. The internal column name comes after Field=, last in the URL.

kalmstromnet.sharepoint.com/ &Field=Department

7.14 TEMPLATE OPTIONS

Sometimes you want to use an existing app as a template for a new app, instead of creating the new app from scratch. This can be done in different ways depending on what kind of site the original app is stored in and if the app is a list or a library.

Before you start using a new app that you have created from a template, remember to change any default column values that are set to suit the original app but maybe not is suitable for the new one.

7.14.1 *Create from Existing List*

In homepages and Site contents with the **modern** interface, you can use existing list apps as templates for new apps via Microsoft Lists, *refer to* 8.3.

This option has both advantages and drawbacks:

- You can create new lists from existing lists in any site in the tenant.
- You can only create new lists from existing lists that you have access too.
- You cannot create a document library from an existing library.
- You cannot create a new list from a list that only has the classic interface, for example a Tasks list.

7.14.2 *Save as Template*

When you want to use a custom app several times, you can save it as a template. Then it will be available to select when you use the 'Add an app' command.

Apps can only be saved as templates in **classic** Team sites where no Microsoft 365 Group has been added, but in those sites, both list and library apps can be saved as templates.

When you add a Microsoft 365 Group to the classic site, the 'Save list as template' option will be removed, but it is still possible to upload a template from another site.

In the List settings, click on the link 'Save list as template' or 'Save document library as template' under the 'Permissions and Management' heading.

Give the template a file name, a template name and a description and save it. Most often you want to save the template without content, which is default.

A page with a success message and a link to the Templates gallery will be displayed. Click OK.

The template is stored as an STP file in the List Templates gallery of the site where you created it, and it will show up among the classic app templates and be available for the site.

To create a new list from the template, just add an app as described in section 7.5.1, Add an App, and select your template.

Demo:

https://kalmstrom.com/Tips/SharePoint-Online-Course/Content-Types-Library-Template.htm

7.14.2.1 Use a Template in Another Site

To make the app template available in another site, save the STP file to your computer and then upload it to the other site's List Templates gallery.

You can find the List Templates gallery under the Web Designer Galleries heading in the Site settings of classic sites.

The List Templates gallery is a kind of classic library, and under the FILES tab in the ribbon there are buttons for upload and download of template files. This gallery will be there even if you add a Microsoft 365 Group to a classic Team site, so that you can use templates from other classic sites.

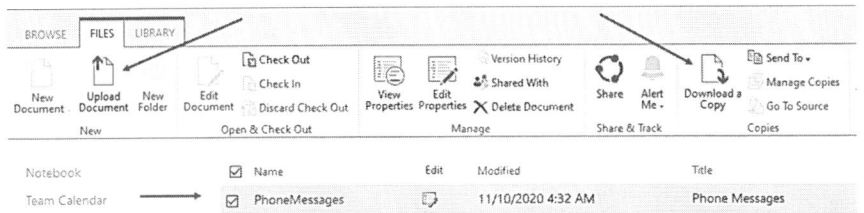

Demo:

https://kalmstrom.com/Tips/SharePoint-Online-Course/SharePoint-Meetings-Upload-Templates.htm

7.15 Apply Labels

Labels are created in the Microsoft 365 Admin center, *refer to* 3.4.1.4, Records Management. These labels marks sensibility or sets limits on how long the item should be kept in the app and what users can do with them.

In the **modern** interface, select the item and choose a label at **Error! Reference source not found.**the bottom of the Properties section in the right Information pane. When you hover over a label name, you will see a description of how the label affects the item.

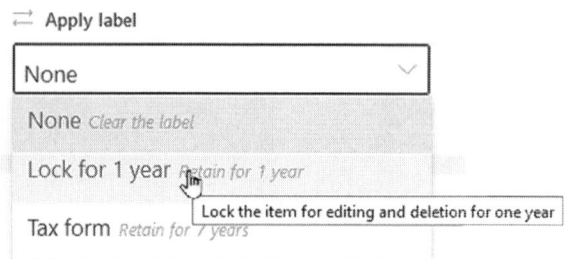

In the **classic** interface, open the item ellipsis and select Advanced >Compliance Details. A dialog will open.

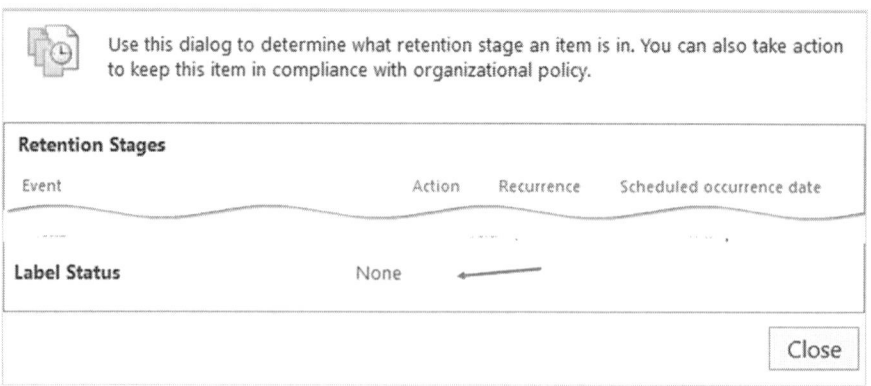

Click on 'None', and a new page will open where you can select among the available labels.

When labels are created in the Microsoft 365 Admin center, the List settings get a new entry under the Permissions and Management heading: 'Apply label to items in this list or library'. Here, you can apply the same label to all items in the app.

7.16 Declare Record

When you want to protect an item in a SharePoint app, you can declare it as a "record". Declare record means that you put certain restrictions on an item, restrictions that are not tied to permissions.

Most often you want to protect items from being edited or deleted when you declare them record. When people try to edit or delete metadata or file content in such items, the changes to column values or file content cannot be saved.

You can declare record with a label, if such a label is created in the SharePoint Admin center. In that case, there is always a connection to a retention period.

Record can also be declared without a label, if that feature is activated for the site. *See* below how to do that. When you declare record from an app, there is no connection to a retention period.

In both interfaces, you can declare record via the item ellipsis >More/Advanced >Compliance details.

A dialog will open, where you can declare the item as an in place record. (If the feature has not been activated in the site, there is a message that the item cannot be declared record.) This is the dialog that is also used for retention labels in the classic interface.

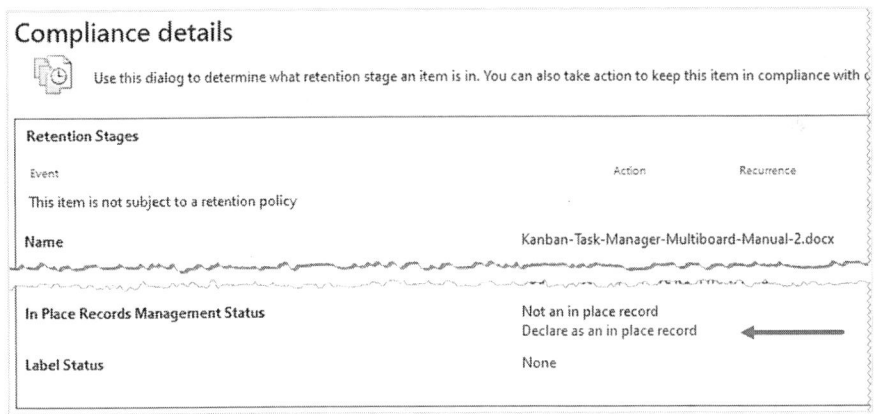

When you have declared the item as an in place record, the link text will be changed into 'Undeclare in place record', and the text above the link will give the date when the item was declared as a record.

7.16.1 *Declare Record Indication*

In library apps, you can see in the app interface if an item has been declared record:

- In the **modern** interface, an item that has been declared record via the Compliance details dialog will have an arrow icon to right of the file name.

    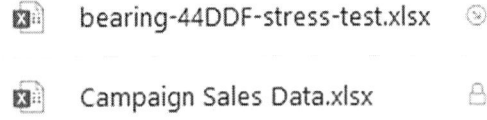

When the item has been declared record with a label, it will instead have a lock icon to the right of the file name.

161

- In the **classic** interface, the file type icon will have a lock in both cases.

List items that have been declared record are not marked in any way, but when you try to edit or delete it you will have a message that the changes cannot be saved.

7.16.2   Activate the In Place Records Management

In Place Records Management can only be activated by Site admins, as it is done under the Site collection Administration heading.

When 'In Place Records Management' has been activated, you can define which restrictions should be set on files that are declared record. If you don't do this, the default settings will be applied.

1. Open the Site settings.
2. Under Site Collection Administration, click on 'Site collection features'.
3. Activate 'In Place Records Management'.

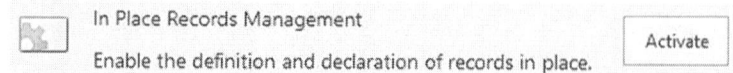

4. When an 'Active' button appears to the right and the 'Activate' button text is changed into 'Deactivate', go back to the Site settings.
5. Click on the new link 'Record declaration settings' under the Site Collection Administration heading.
6. Make the settings you prefer.

   ○ No Additional Restrictions
   Records are no more restricted than non-records.

   ○ Block Delete
   Records can be edited but not deleted.

   ⦿ Block Edit and Delete
   Records cannot be edited or deleted. Any changes will declaration to be revoked.

   Manual record declaration in lists and libraries should be:

   ○ Available in all locations by default

   ⦿ Not available in all locations by default

   The declaration of records can be performed by:

   ⦿ All list contributors and administrators

   ○ Only list administrators

   ○ Only policy actions

   Undeclaring a record can be performed by:

   ○ All list contributors and administrators

   ⦿ Only list administrators

   ○ Only policy actions

7.16.2.1 Allow Record Declaration for a Single App

As you see in the image from the 'Record declaration settings' above, you can decide whether manual records declaration should be available for all apps. The default option is 'Not available in all locations by default', and I would recommend that you keep it that way.

Instead of giving a general possibility to declare record, you can allow record declaration for each app where you want to use the feature. This way, you will have more control over how record declaration is used.

Here I will give the necessary settings for a document library that should have the possibility to declare record. The principle is the same for other SharePoint apps.

1. Open the Library settings.
2. Click on the link 'Record declaration settings' under the Permissions and Management heading. A new page will open, which is called 'Library Record Declaration Settings' even if you open it from a list.
3. The default record declaration setting is to use the same setting as for the site. If you have kept 'Not available in all locations by default' checked, you must change the setting in the Library settings to "Always allow" for this library.

Library Record Declaration Settings ⓘ

Manual Record Declaration Availability

Specify whether this list should allow the manual declaration of records. When manual record declaration is unavailable, records can only be declared through a policy or workflow.

- ⦿ Use the site collection default setting: Allow the manual declaration of records
- ◯ Always allow the manual declaration of records
- ◯ Never allow the manual declaration of records

Automatic Declaration

Specify whether all items should become records when added to this list.

☐ Automatically declare items as records when they are added to this list.

[OK] [Cancel]

Another option in the 'Library Record Declaration Settings' is to automatically declare files as records when they are added to this app. If you check that box, you don't have to manually declare items as records. Instead, you can place items that should be declared records in this app.

Demo:

https://kalmstrom.com/Tips/SharePoint-Online-Course/Declare-Record.htm

7.17 SUMMARY

With this chapter, I wanted to give an overview over how you can create and edit SharePoint apps and use them to share information in an efficient and user-friendly way. We have looked at features that are common for all apps, and you have also learned how to use existing apps as templates.

I hope that you now understand how important it is to create suitable columns for metadata in apps and that you know how to filter and sort data in various ways and create different views. You should also understand how to use versioning and alerts, how to delete and restore SharePoint apps and how to set labels and declare items as in place record.

There is more to learn about SharePoint apps. In this chapter, I have not included the 'Automate' button and the Approvals feature that is only available in the modern experience. It is described in chapter 24, SharePoint Automation.

Another SharePoint feature that will be explained later in the book is the content type, which I have only mentioned briefly in this chapter. With content types, you can help users create library and list items with a consistent look and valuable metadata.

In the next chapter, we will take a closer look at features that are specific for list apps. I will also describe two app types that are a bit different: the Tasks list and the Calendar.

8 LIST APPS

In the previous chapter, we looked at features that are common for all SharePoint Online apps. Now, we will go into features that only exist in list apps, and in the next chapter, we will do the same with library apps.

The main difference between list apps and library apps is that you use library apps to store and share files. List apps are used to store and share other data (even if you can attach files to them), for example data about departments, issues, staff or tasks.

When new list items are created, metadata info is added to fields in a form. Each field represent a column. When the form is saved, the values added to the form fields are displayed under the column headings in the app interface.

As you already know, most apps can have two interfaces, modern and classic. In this chapter, I will start with describing how the upper part of a list app can look and work in the two experiences.

After that, I will introduce the Microsoft Lists platform and show how to create list apps and use list items. Finally, I will describe two classic lists that have special features: the Tasks list and the Calendar.

8.1 THE MODERN LIST EXPERIENCE

The buttons in the modern experience command bar varies depending on the selection in the list of items below the command bar. Only relevant buttons are shown to the users.

The images in the two sections below show the modern command bar in Standard view mode. The Grid view looks the same, except that 'Edit in grid view' is replaced by 'Exit grid view'.

8.1.1 No Item Selected

When no item has been selected in the list, the command bar shows buttons to create new items, edit the list in grid view, share the list, export the list, create simple flows for the list and integrate the list in Power Apps, Power Automate or Power BI.

Under the ellipsis, you can find the controls for alerts, *refer to* 7.10, Alerts.

The '+ New' button opens a right pane where you can fill out metadata, or values, in the different column fields of a new item.

For Windows, the 'Export' button gives two options for the export: Excel Workbook and CSV. On Macs, only the Export to CSV option is available.

I will come back to the 'Share' and 'Automate' commands in later chapters.

165

8.1.1.1 Integrate

The Integrate dropdown lets you connect the list to Microsoft's three Power apps:

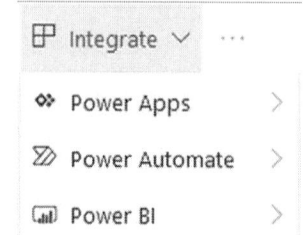

- Power Apps is described in chapter 21.
- Power Automate is described in chapter 24.
- Power BI lets you autogenerate a Power BI report that visualizes list data in supported columns. Complex column types as Lookup, Image, Location and Person or Group are currently not supported here.

To edit and publish the report you need a separate license, but all users can see the report. Once a report is saved and published, it will appear under Integrate >Power BI.

Microsoft plans to add the same Integrate functionality to SharePoint Online libraries, but when this is written, that feature has not yet been launched.

8.1.2   One Item Selected

When one item has been selected, the command bar has no 'Export to Excel' or 'Integrate' commands. Instead, there are commands to Edit the selected item, Copy a link to the item, Comment on the item and see other comments and Delete the item.

Under the ellipsis we can now also find a command for Version history.

The 'Edit' command opens the same form as when you click on 'Edit all' in the Information pane, *refer to* 7.7.8, Edit Column Values. In the Standard view mode, you can also click on the item's "Title" value to open the item and then click on 'Edit item' above the form.

8.1.3   Multiple Items Selected

When multiple items have been selected, there are only commands for New, Edit, Edit in grid view and Delete.

8.2   CLASSIC LIST EXPERIENCE

The classic list experience has a ribbon with three tabs: BROWSE, ITEMS and LIST. The 'BROWSE' tab shows no ribbon buttons, but 'ITEMS' and 'LIST' show all available commands even if some of them are greyed out.

When the 'ITEMS' tab is selected, you can recognize some of the commands from the modern interface.

Declare Record, Workflows and Approve/Reject can be found under the item ellipsis in the modern interface, while attachments are added in the right Edit pane in the modern lists.

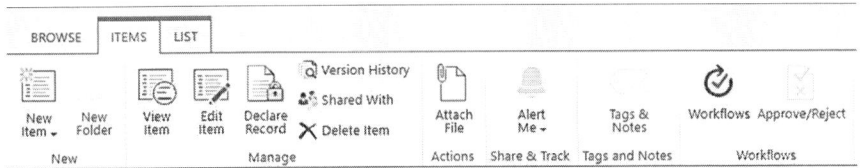

Under the LISTS tab, most of the other commands are displayed, among them the List settings.

Here you can find 'Export to Excel' but also some other features that cannot be found at all in the modern interface. I will come back to these features later in the book.

Below the ribbon, the classic interface has commands for new item and edit this list, which opens the Quick Edit/Grid view mode.

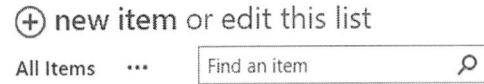

Here you can also find the views and a search box for the list. Up to three views can be displayed to the left of the search box. If there are more views, they are found under the ellipsis, from where you also can modify the view and create a new view.

8.3 Microsoft Lists

The Microsoft Lists app is part of the SharePoint based OneDrive for Business service, that each 365 user has access to for personal use.

You can open Lists via the App Launcher in the top right corner of all Microsoft 365 apps. There are also a desktop app and mobile apps for Android and iOS.

In Microsoft Lists, each user can find all lists in the tenant that he/she has access to and has used recently, including lists that the user has created – except for lists that only can have the classic interface.

167

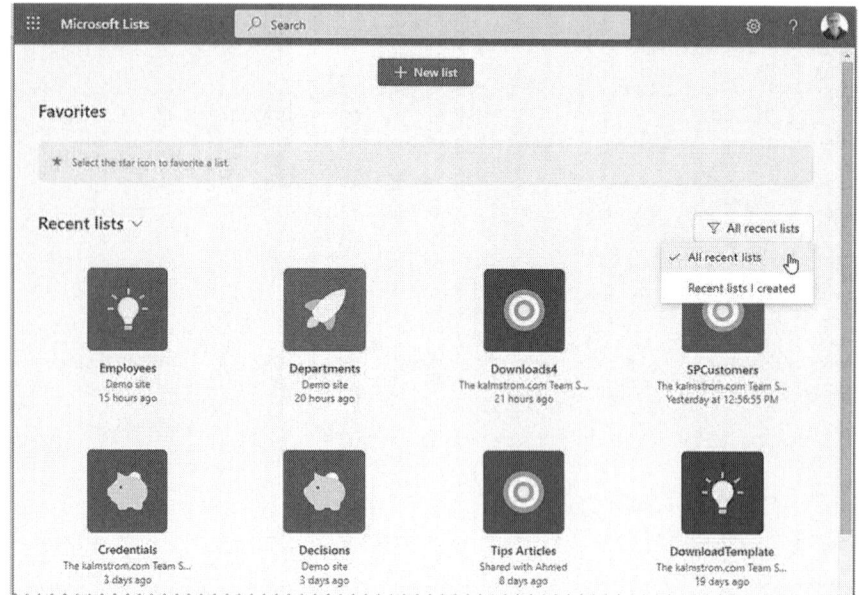

The lists can be opened directly in Microsoft Lists, where they have the same functionality as in SharePoint – except that they cannot show the classic interface.

By default, the Microsoft Lists homepage shows Recent lists, with the filter options 'All recent lists' and 'Recent lists I created'.

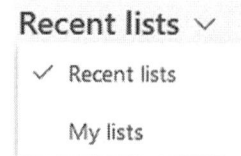

The other option in the dropdown is 'My lists'. Here, the lists can be sorted alphabetically or by creation date.

There is a limit on 100 lists, and I have found that "recent" can be six months back if that limit is not exceeded.

8.3.1   Tile Options

When you hover the mouse cursor over a list icon in Microsoft Lists, a star and an ellipsis become visible on the tile. Click on the star to add the list to the Favorites section on top of Microsoft Lists.

Via the ellipsis, you can modify the list's color and icon and change the list name, and you can also share the list.

In the 'Recent list' view, the ellipsis on each tile also gives the option to remove the list from the recent lists. In the 'My lists' view, the option is instead to delete the list.

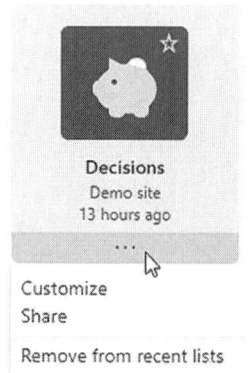

8.3.2 Create a List from MS Lists

With the '+ New list' button below the Search field in Microsoft Lists, users can create new list apps and add them to any site they have access to. There are four options for the creation: a blank list, a list from an Excel file, a list created from an existing list and a list created from a template.

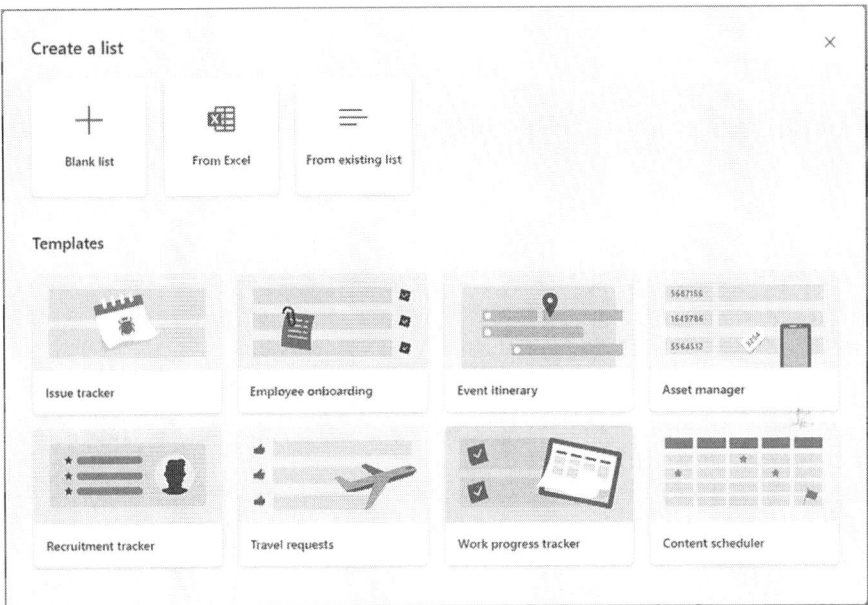

The default option when you create a new list from inside Microsoft Lists, is to save the new list in Microsoft Lists. There, you can reach the list from "My lists" and use it as a personal app. These personal lists are stored in the user's OneDrive for Business, and they are only displayed in Microsoft Lists.

You can however save the list to any SharePoint site that you have access to – included classic sites – and thereby you can use the list as any other shared SharePoint list app. When you save the list to a Team site, you can use the classic as well as the modern app interface.

The new list will open after creation. When you have added the list to a SharePoint site, the list will have a link to the site above the list name.

8.3.2.1 Blank list

When you select the 'Blank list' option, a custom (also called generic) list with only a "Title" column will be created in the site you select, or in the default 'My lists'.

You will have a possibility to select a theme color and icon for the list, in addition to giving it a name and a description.

Note that when the list app is added to a site in a hub family, the hub theme will override the list theme.

169

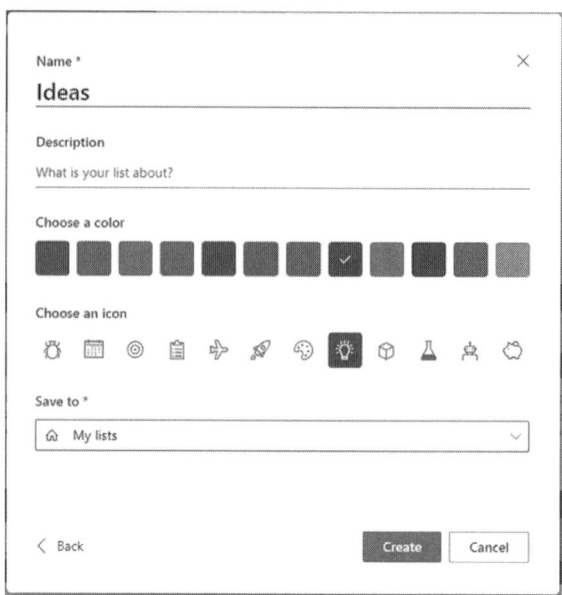

8.3.2.2 From Excel

Creating a list directly from an Excel workbook is often a good way to migrate data into SharePoint. Before you do that, make sure that the data you want to include is formatted as a table with no empty rows or columns.

The Excel file can be uploaded from your computer or selected from OneDrive for Business. After upload/selection of the file, you will have a possibility to change table – in case the file has multiple tables – and column types. You can also select to not include a column.

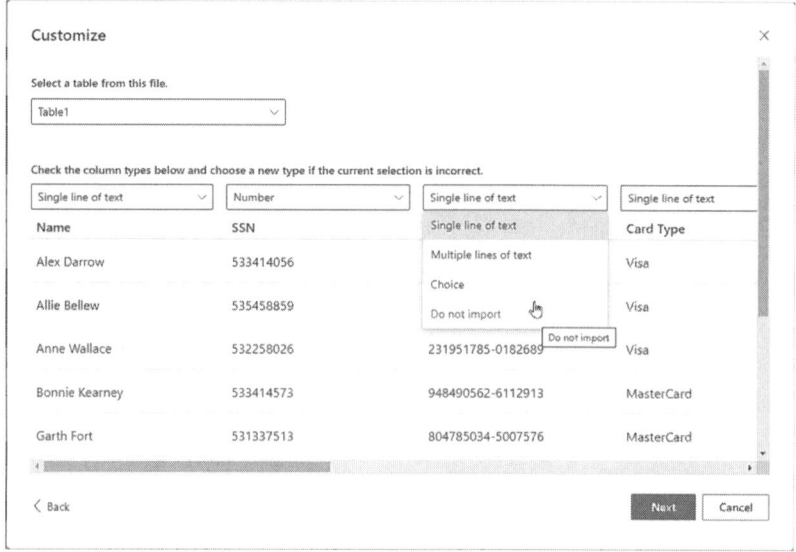

When you click on 'Next' you will have the same options as when you create a list from blank.

Note that the new list is independent from Excel. There is no synchronization, so changes in Excel are not reflected in the list app or vice versa. *Refer to* 22.2, Connect SharePoint and Excel, if you need updates to be displayed in both apps. In that section, you can also find a comparison between SharePoint and Excel.

8.3.2.3   From Existing List

When you create a list from an existing list, you can create a new list from any list that can have the modern interface and that you have access to. The new list will have the same columns, views and formatting as the original list. Content cannot be included.

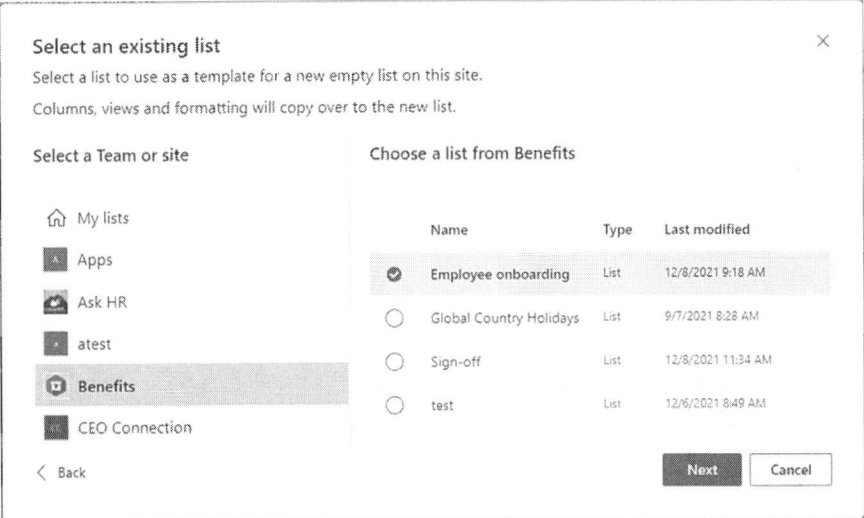

Select first site and then list app. When you have selected a list to create a new list from, you will have the same options as when you create a blank list.

8.3.2.4   From Template

Microsoft Lists gives some templates that you can create new lists from, but not at all as many templates as the "Your Apps" page, *refer to* 7.5.1, Add an app. However, all the Lists templates take advantage of the 'Format this column' feature, which is not the case with the templates you can create from the "Your Apps" page.

When you click on a template, a preview will open. If you change your mind after seeing the preview, you can select another template in the menu to the left.

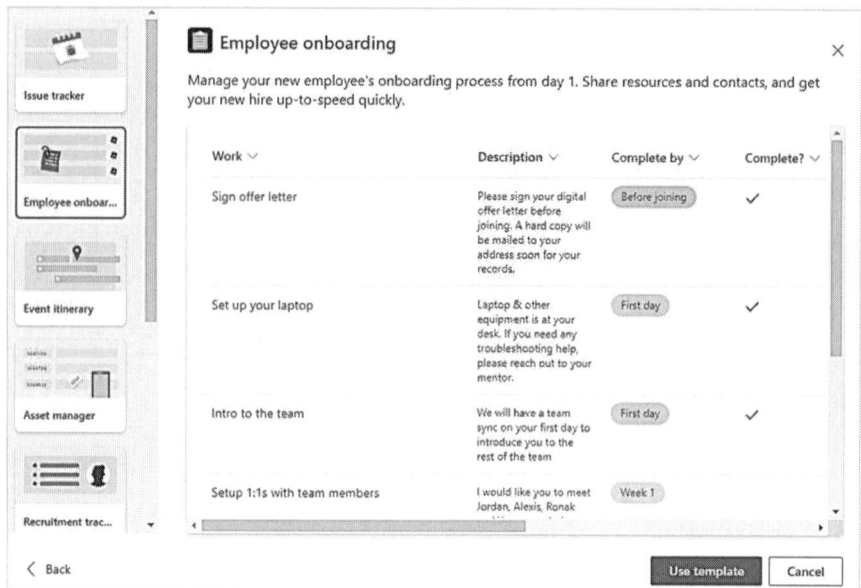

When you click on 'Use template', you will have the same options as when you create a blank list, but the new list will of course have all the columns, views and formatting of the template.

8.3.3 Lists Desktop App

Microsoft Lists has a desktop app that can be downloaded when the web app is open in the browser. You can work in the app when you are offline and perform common list operations, for example change view and sort, filter and group the content. All changes will be synchronized to the cloud once you are online again.

The list data is stored in a local database in your profile directory, and the sync runs as a separate background process.

If you delete a list, or lose access to it, that list will be automatically removed from the Lists app. You can also stop synching any list manually, by clicking on the ellipsis on the list tile and selecting 'Stop syncing'.

When this is written, the Lists app is new and has some rather serious limitations concerning which lists can be opened in the app. Among them are lists that have:

- a Lookup or a Calculated column
- a column with a default value
- the default experience set to classic
- only the classic interface
- a custom content type
- content approval set to required

- append changes to existing text set to 'Yes' in a multiline column.

Lists that cannot be synched have a "no sync" icon.

All these "no sync" features are described in this book, because I find that they are important, so I hope Microsoft soon will enhance the Lists app to support them.

8.3.3.1 Download the app

When you open Microsoft Lists in the browser, you might get a message that prompts you to download the app. If that does not happen, Edge and Google Chrome have an 'Apps' entry under the ellipsis in the top right corner. If you open this entry from the browser edition of Microsoft Lists, it shows an installation link to Lists app.

8.3.3.2 Resolve Sync Issues

When you use the Microsoft Lists app in an organization, it is possible that two people change the same item at the same time in different ways. The app tries to resolve the conflict automatically, but if that is not possible, a red dot at the list's View selector indicates that there is a conflict.

Open the View selector and click on the 'Items with sync issues+' to see the conflict and either dismiss it or correct it.

8.3.4 Create a List from SharePoint

You can always create a new list app with the 'Add an app' command that I described in the previous chapter. I also mentioned that you can click on the 'New' button in a modern SharePoint homepage or Site contents and select 'App', to be directed to the same "Your Apps" page as when you select 'Add an app' under the 365 Settings icon.

Here, we will have a look at another option to create a list, that makes use of Microsoft Lists.

The '+ New' button in a **modern** SharePoint homepage or Site contents gives the option 'List'. When you click on the 'List' link, you will be directed to a limited version of Microsoft Lists.

You cannot see all your other lists here, but you will have the same four list creation options as in the full version:

- a blank list
- a list from an Excel file

- a list created from an existing SharePoint list
- a list created from a template.

The new list will be created in the current site, and it will open after creation. By default, a link to the app is added to the site's Site navigation.

The 'From blank' dialog, which you also meet after 'Next' in the other options, gives less possibilities than if you create the list from within Microsoft Lists. Otherwise, the creation processes are the same.

8.4 CREATE A NEW LIST ITEM

There are several ways to create a new item in a list app, depending on which interface and mode you are using.

8.4.1 Standard Mode

To create a new item in Standard view mode, click on the '+ New' button in the command bar (modern) or above the list of items (classic).

When you create a new item in the standard mode, a form will be displayed, where you can fill out the item's metadata. The modern interface opens the form in a right pane and classic interface in a new page.

8.4.2 Quick Edit Mode

Lists in Grid/Quick Edit mode have a blank row at the bottom. Here, you can create a new item by entering or selecting values for each column.

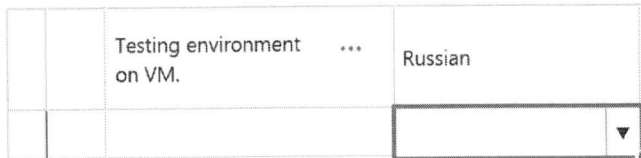

In the **modern** interface, this last row is marked with '+ Add new item', and when you click in it, the cells become visible.

The modern Grid also has a '+New' button in the command bar, just like in the Standard view mode.

The **classic** SharePoint interface has a "New" button in the left corner of the 'Items' tab in both view modes.

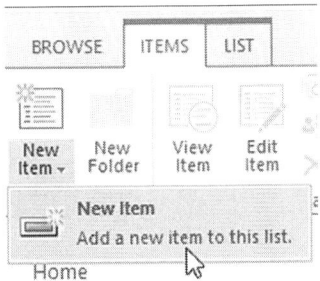

8.4.3 Mandatory Title

The "Title" field is mandatory to fill out in list apps, so you cannot save a new list item until you have entered a value in the "Title" field. This column is created automatically when you create any list app, and it cannot be deleted.

You can very well rename the "Title" column to give it a more descriptive name, but you cannot change its column type. It must be a Single line of text column.

Even if the Title column is renamed, the internal name is always "Title".

8.5 OPEN LIST ITEMS

To open a list item, click on the value in the "Title" column in Standard view mode. This value gets underlined when you hover the mouse cursor over it, and normally it is found in the column far to the left.

In the **modern** interface, you can also open a list item by clicking on the comment icon in the command bar, *see* below. A right pane will open in both cases.

8.6 EDIT LIST ITEM

In addition to the editing methods mentioned in 7.7.8, Edit Column Values, both interfaces have an 'Edit' button in the command bar/ribbon, and an Edit command under the item ellipsis. It opens the selected list item in edit mode, so that you can modify the column values.

8.7 THE MODERN ITEM COMMENTS

The modern interface opens the item in a right pane, where you can add comments to the item.

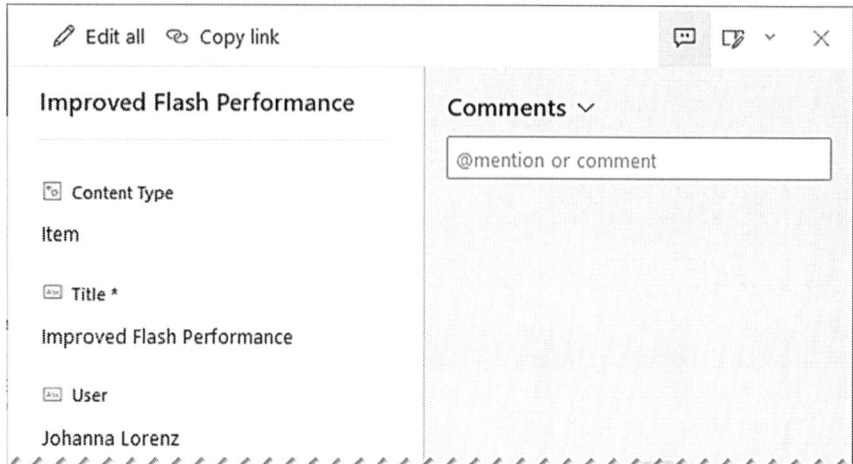

Instead of comments, you can open the dropdown at 'Comments' and select to show all activity for the item.

The 'Comments' pane is open by default, but you can hide it by clicking on the comment icon above the 'Comments' field. Comments can be turned off in the List settings >Advanced settings.

A Comment icon is displayed to the right of the first column in a selected item. If there is a comment on the item, the icon has three dots.
If there is no comment, the icon is empty and has a plus sign.

When you click on the Comment icon or the Comment button in the command bar, the selected item will open in view mode in the right pane.

Comments can be added in view mode as well as in edit mode. Type your text and click on the arrow to submit the comment.

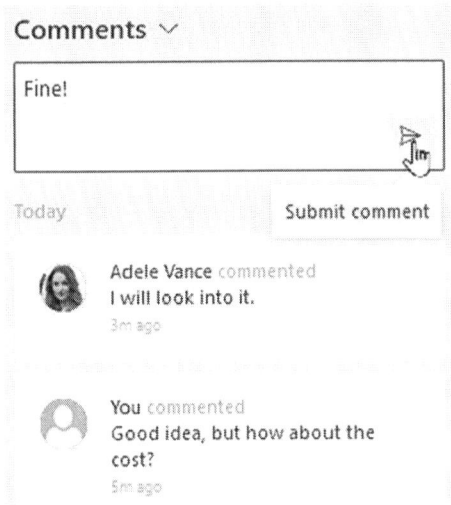

You can mention colleagues with @ before the name, just like in social media. People who are mentioned will get an e-mail that contains the comment and a link to the item.

If you need formatting, you can instead use a Multiple lines of text "Comment" column with the feature 'Append changes to existing text' *see below*. With that option, you can however not see from an icon if the item has a comment, and @mention does not work.

In view mode, list apps have an additional possibility to edit the form and to customize the form in Power Apps, via the icon on top of the Comments pane.

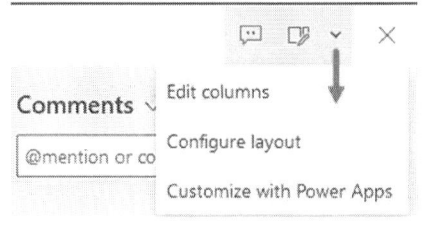

'Edit columns' opens the same right pane as the same command in the Information pane, *refer to* 7.8, Edit the form.

'Customize with Power Apps' opens the form in Power Apps for more advanced customization, *refer to* chapter 21.

'Configure layout' requires addition of JSON code and is out of scope for this book.

8.8 THE MULTI-LINE COLUMN

The column type Multiple lines of text (also called "multi-line column") has some features that are only available in list apps: rich text and append changes to existing text.

When you combine these two features, you can have a comments field with formatting that you can use instead of the 'Comment' feature described above. It gives you formatting, but you cannot see in the app interface if the item has a comment or not, and the @mention notification does not work.

A multi-line column with the append feature enabled is especially useful for discussions and issue tracking.

8.8.1 Enhanced Rich Text

When rich text is enabled in the 'Multiple lines of text' column, it is possible to add formatting, tables, hyperlinks and images to the field when you create or edit the item.

In the **modern** interface, a pen icon to the right of the column name in the edit pane shows that rich text is enabled.

When you click on the pen icon, a new right pane will open where you can format the text.

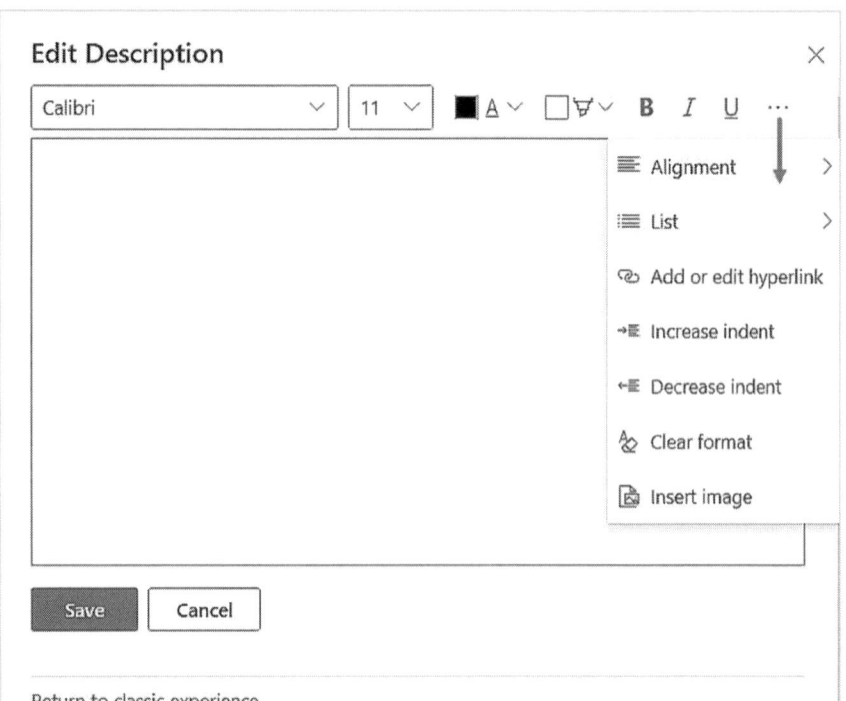

Should you need more options, click on the link to the classic experience. That opens yet another right pane, and when you click in the text field more options will open in the ribbon.

In the **classic** interface, a ribbon with rich text controls opens when you click in a rich text field.

8.8.1.1 Enable Rich Text

If the enhanced rich text feature is enabled by default or not, depends on how you create the column:

- When you create a multi-line column from the '+ Add column' command in the modern interface, rich text is not enabled by default, but you can enable it under 'More options'.

  More options ∨

  Use enhanced rich text (Rich text with pictures, tables, and hyperlinks)
   No

- When you create a multi-line column from the List settings 'Create column' dialog, rich text is enabled by default. If you only want users to add plain text, you must change the setting.

    Specify the type of text to allow:
    ○ Plain text
    ⦿ Enhanced rich text (Rich text with pictures, tables, and hyperlinks)

8.8.2 *Append Changes to Existing Text*

In list apps, columns of the type 'Multiple lines of text' have a feature called 'Append changes to existing text'. It reminds of the Version history feature described in 7.11.

There is however an important difference between Version history and Append changes: you cannot see the version history when you open an item – you must open the Version history to see it.

If you want to see the history for a 'Multiple lines of text' column as soon as you open the item, you should enable the 'Append changes to existing text' for that column. When you do that, all changes are shown as a thread in the 'Multiple lines of text' field.

The earlier text cannot be modified, but new text is shown above the earlier text in the field. The image below shows a "Comments" field where comments from different versions are shown as a part of the open item.

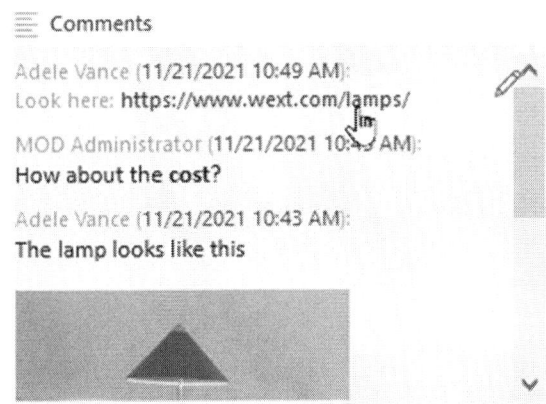

When the append feature is enabled, the multi-line column gets links that open the item.

Comment ⌄

View Entries

View Entries

View Entries

8.8.2.1 Enable Append

To enable the append feature, you need to edit the column where you want to append changes.

In the List settings, open the column and select the 'Yes' radio button for 'Append changes to existing text'.

Append Changes to Existing Text
● Yes   ○ No

In the **modern** app interface, you can also edit the column directly from the list interface and set the toggler to 'Yes' under 'More options' in the right pane.

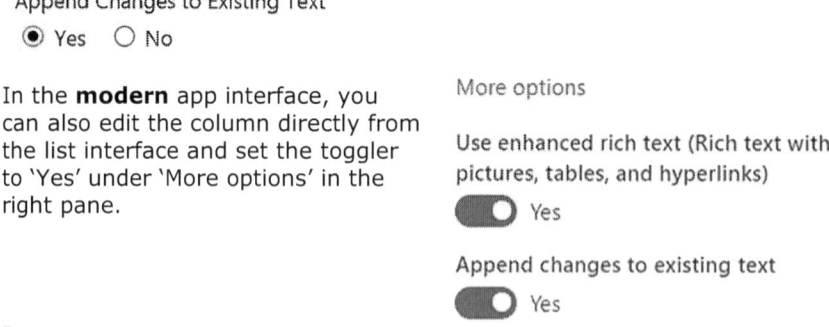

Demo:

https://www.kalmstrom.com/Tips/SharePoint-Online-Course/Append-Changes-to-Existing-Text.htm

8.9 TASKS AND ISSUE TRACKING

When you create a list that builds on the Tasks list template, the new list has some special features:

- A timeline above the list of tasks.

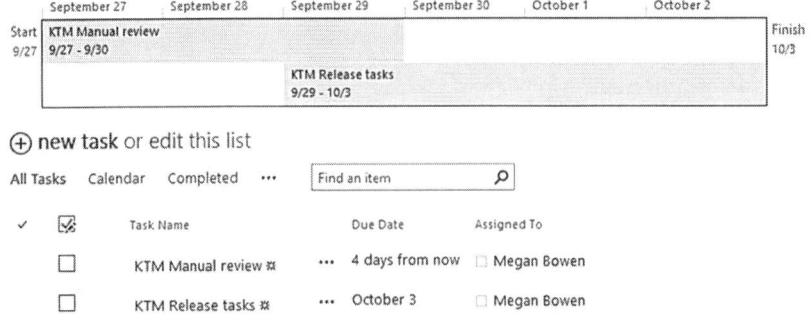

- Time related commands in a TIMELINE tab in the ribbon. Click on the timeline to show this tab.

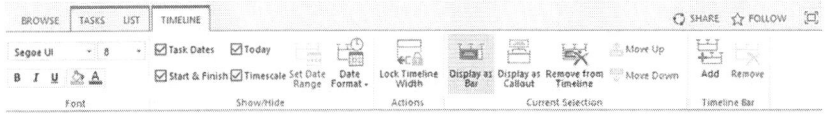

- A TASKS tab instead of the ITEMS tab.
- The default view is called 'All tasks'.

When this is written, the Tasks list can only be used with the classic experience, and because of that, it can only be created from the "Your Apps" page.

If you want to use the modern interface, I recommend one of these:

- The Issue Tracking list, also created from the "Your Apps" page.
- The Issue tracker list created from Microsoft Lists.
- The Work progress tracker list, also created from Microsoft Lists.

All three of these list apps can use the modern as well as the classic interface, but they don't have a timeline or as many other task tracking features as the Tasks list.

8.9.1 *Tasks and Issues Alerts*

SharePoint lists that build on the Tasks, Issue Tracking and Issue tracker templates have a view selector under "Send me an alert when'.

⦿ Someone changes an item that appears in the following view:

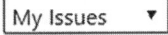

The Tasks and Issue Tracking lists have an additional option under 'Advanced settings' in the List settings: a possibility to send an automatic e-mail to the person to whom a task is assigned. The default value is 'No'.

181

E-Mail Notification

Send e-mail when ownership is assigned or when an item has been changed.

Send e-mail when ownership is assigned?

◯ Yes ◉ No

Demo:

https://kalmstrom.com/Tips/SharePoint-Online-Course/HelpDesk-Email-Notification.htm

8.10   CALENDAR APP

The calendar is a list type that has its own, classic interface. Use a SharePoint calendar to share event information like holidays, leaves, delivery dates and other information that is of common interest to the users who have access to the calendar.

A very common question is how SharePoint calendars relate/connect/interact with Outlook calendars. The short answer is that they do not. They are stored in totally different places, and SharePoint calendars lack a range of important features that Outlook calendars have, such as invites, reminders and integration with Microsoft Teams.

On the other hand, the SharePoint Calendar app has more features than the calendar list view that I described in section 7.9.4.1, Modern "New View" Options.

To create a SharePoint calendar, add an app built on the Calendar template from the "Your Apps" page.

8.10.1   Views in the Calendar App

By default, a calendar list displays a "Calendar" view that shows all events in a calendar-like interface. The "Calendar" view can display the events for a Day, Week or Month via buttons under the CALENDAR tab.

In the "Calendar" view, you can switch between periods with arrows.

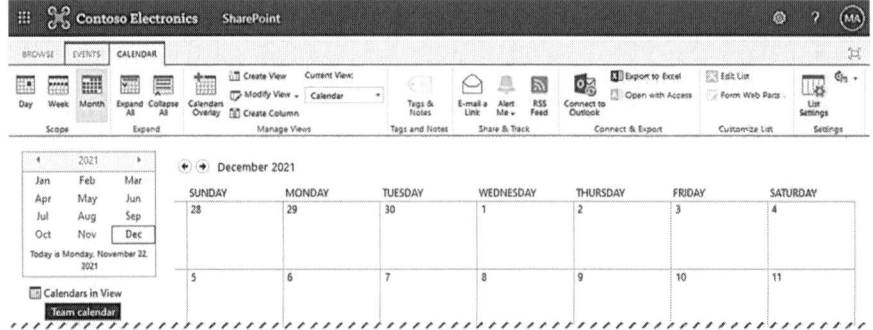

There are two more built-in views, "All Events" and "Current Events". Both these views show the events in the classic SharePoint list interface. These views are suitable for editing of many events at the same time, as they have the 'Quick Edit' button that is missing in the "Calendar" view.

You can create more views in the same way as for other apps.

8.10.2 Create a New Event

In the default "Calendar" view, new events are created with a '+ Add' link that is displayed when you hover the mouse cursor over a calendar date in the Month view or over an hour section in the Week and Day views.

You can also use the 'New Event' button under the EVENTS tab in the ribbon.

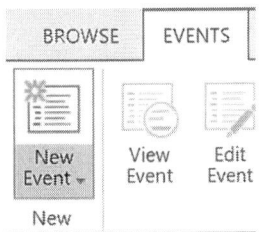

In other views than the calendar views, new items are created like in other classic lists.

8.10.3 Edit an Event

Use the 'Edit Event' button in the ribbon to open a selected event in edit mode.

You can also double-click on the event to open it and then click on the 'Edit Item' in the ribbon of the open event.

8.10.4 See Multiple Calendars in One

With the Calendars overlay feature, you can merge multiple calendars and display all their events in one single view. All calendars must be in the same site, except if you use the Exchange option and add your own Outlook calendar to a calendars overlay.

183

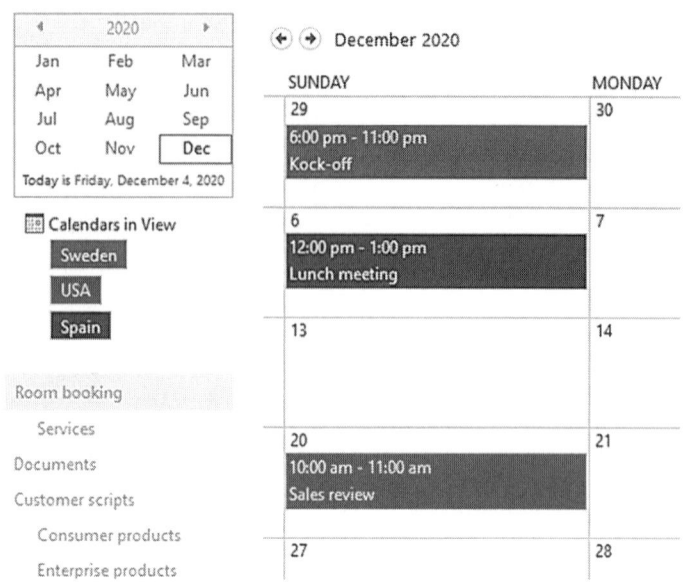

Create a calendar overlay in this way:

1. Open one of the calendars.
2. Click on 'Calendars Overlay' under the CALENDAR tab.
3. Add another calendar to the Calendars Overlay:
   a. Click on 'New Calendar'.

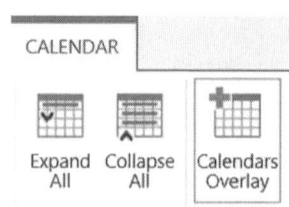

   b. Fill out the Calendar name.
   c. In this example, we keep the SharePoint option.
   d. Select color.
   e. The site URL should be filled out automatically. Click on 'Resolve'.
   f. Select the calendar and the calendar view from the dropdowns.
   g. Check 'Always show' if you want the overlay calendar to always be shown. If you not check the box, you will be able to turn different overlay calendars on and off.
   h. Click OK.

Calendar Overlay Settings

Name and Type
Type a name for this calendar, and select the type of calendar you want to store in the view.

Calendar Name: USA

The type of calendar is:
- ◉ SharePoint
- ○ Exchange

Calendar Overlay Settings
Specify detailed options for the type of information you selected.

Description:

Color: Red, #ed0033

Web URL: https://m365x446726.sharepoint.com/sites/   [Resolve]

List: USA

List View: Calendar

☑ Always show

[Delete] [OK] [Cancel]

4. Repeat step 3 until you have merged all the calendars.

When you select to overlay your personal Exchange calendar, you need to give the Outlook Web Access URL and the Exchange Web Service URL.

8.11 SUMMARY

In this chapter, we have studied some features that are specific for list apps. You have been introduced to Microsoft Lists, and you know how to create a list app with the 'List' command.

SharePoint lists also can be created with a PowerShell script. How to do that is described in my book *PowerShell with SharePoint from Scratch*, but it is out of scope for this book.

On the kalmstrom.com website there is a tool that helps you create a list using PowerShell. You can use this tool even if you don't know how to write PowerShell scripts. Please *refer to*:
https://www.kalmstrom.com/Tips/PowerShell/PnP-SharePoint-List-Generator-Intro.htm.

In this chapter, I have also described how to create and manage list items, and I have introduced the list features Comment, Rich text and Append. Finally, we looked at a few lists with special features.

We will come back to list for tasks and issue tracking in chapter 23, but now it is time to have a look at the library apps.

9 LIBRARY APPS

A SharePoint library is an app with some unique qualities and features, and in this chapter, we will have a look at these.

What distinguishes libraries from other apps, is that each item consists of a file or a folder plus metadata for that file or folder.

The files/folders are placed in a "Name" column. In the modern interface this column can be renamed, and there are some limited customization possibilities. The column is however not displayed under Columns in the Library settings, and from the classic interface it cannot be customized at all.

The other columns in the library contain metadata related to the file or folder in the same item. Some of the columns are built-in, such as 'Created' and 'Modified By', and their metadata is filled out automatically. You can also create your own, custom columns.

As we saw in section 6.10.1, Auto-Created Apps, a document library called "Documents" is created automatically when a new site is created, along with some other libraries.

There are several types of SharePoint libraries, but here, I will focus on SharePoint document libraries. When I write "library" in this book, I refer to a document library if nothing else is mentioned.

In this chapter, I will explain why using SharePoint document libraries is a good way to store and share files. You will also learn how to:

- Create content directly in document libraries
- Upload files to document libraries in various ways
- Use – or rather not use! – folders
- Check out and check in documents
- Manage file properties
- Copy and move files
- Use Word Online and OneNote
- Create a Word template for a document library

Finally, I will describe some features that only exist in the modern interface.

9.1 WHY DOCUMENT LIBRARIES?

Document libraries are often the best way to share files within an organization, and it is certainly much better than sending e-mail attachments.

When you use SharePoint document libraries for file sharing you have everything in one place, and all who have been given permission can reach the files.

A SharePoint document library is however more than a place for file storage and sharing – it is also a place where you can create and work with Office files.

I would recommend that you use many document libraries, as a way of categorizing files. For example, if your site is made for sharing information about a new product, you could have these libraries:

- Suggested Specifications
- Supplier Contracts
- Design Sketches
- Radio Commercials

In these libraries you would of course have files. Those files are sometimes referred to as documents in the SharePoint user interface. You can download files from a document library to your computer and vice versa, and you can also automatically synchronize a library with a folder on your computer.

9.2 DOCUMENT LIBRARY UNIQUE FEATURES

When you click on the ellipsis to the right of the file name in a document library in Standard view mode, you will have many options for what to do with the file.

You can work with the file online or open it in a desktop application. You can also download the file, share it, rename it and much more. The most used of these options are also displayed in the modern command bar and in the classic ribbon.

SharePoint document libraries have most of the features that are also found in list apps, like alerts, Version history and filtering, but document libraries also have some additional features that I will describe below.

Document libraries can be used with both the modern and the classic interface. I will show the library unique features with images from the modern experience, because some of the features are only available there. I will mention which ones they are.

Most of the library specific commands affect the file that is stored in the library item – not the whole item.

9.2.1 *No Item Selected*

When no item is selected in the library, the command bar has three specific buttons, in addition to the buttons that are available in all apps:

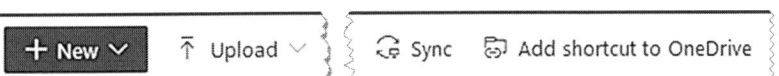

- Upload – for uploading content to the library. A new item for the content and its metadata will be created automatically. The modern interface gives three upload options: file, folder and template. The classic interface only allows upload of files.

- Sync – to synchronize the library with a folder on your computer *refer to* 12.2.3, OneDrive for Business Sync.
- Add shortcut to OneDrive – to add a shortcut to this library in the left menu of your default OneDrive for Business library, *refer to* 12.2.1, The "My Files" Library. This command is only available in the modern experience.

9.2.2   One Item Selected

When one item is selected, there are more library specific features. We will come back to most of them later.

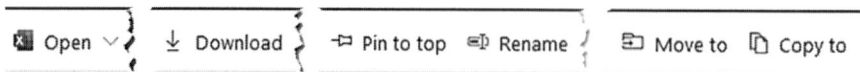

- Open the file. Office files have two options: open in the desktop app or open in the browser. Word files may also be opened in Immersive Reader, just like text files.

The 'Open' button is not visible for all file types, and neither for folders, but you can also click on the name to open a file/folder. By default, Office files open in the browser when you click on the file name.

- Download the file to your computer. Folders can also be downloaded in the modern interface, but as compressed files. Folders cannot be downloaded with the classic 'Download a Copy' button.
- Pin a thumbnail of the file or folder above the list of items. This feature is only available in the modern experience.

188

When an item has been pinned, the command is changed into 'Edit pin' when the same item is selected again. Now you can unpin or change the position of the pin.

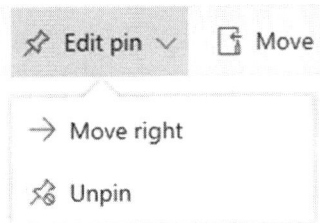

- Rename, opens a dialog where you can give the file or folder a new name. This feature is only found under the item ellipsis in the classic experience.
- Move to, moves the item into or out of a subfolder in the current library, to another library that you have access to or to your OneDrive for Business. This feature is only available in the modern experience.
- Copy to, copies the item to a subfolder in the current library, to another library that you have access to or to your OneDrive for Business. This feature is only available in the modern experience.

There are more library specific commands under the command bar ellipsis:

- Properties, opens a right pane that shows the selected item's metadata and gives a possibility to edit them.
- Check out a file when you don't want other users to see your changes, or you don't want the changes to be visible in the version history yet, *refer to* 9.12, Check Out / Check In.

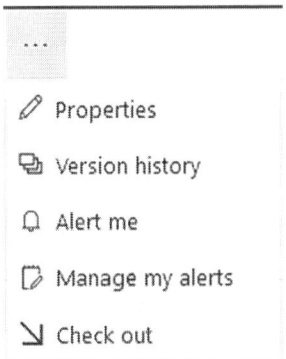

9.2.3 Multiple Items Selected

The image below shows the full command bar when multiple library items have been selected. There are no new library specific commands here, but as you see, it is possible to use several of the commands for multiple items.

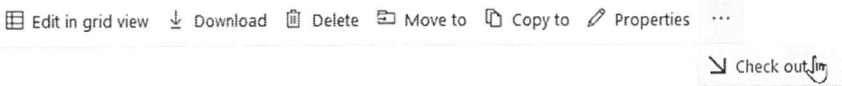

9.2.4 Other Unique Features

When you hover the mouse cursor over the file name in a document library with the **modern** interface, a tile will be visible. It shows the share icon and a 'See details' link that opens the file's Information pane. Office files also have views information.

When the file is a Word file, there is an 'Inside look' section with information about average reading time for the document and a part of the text.

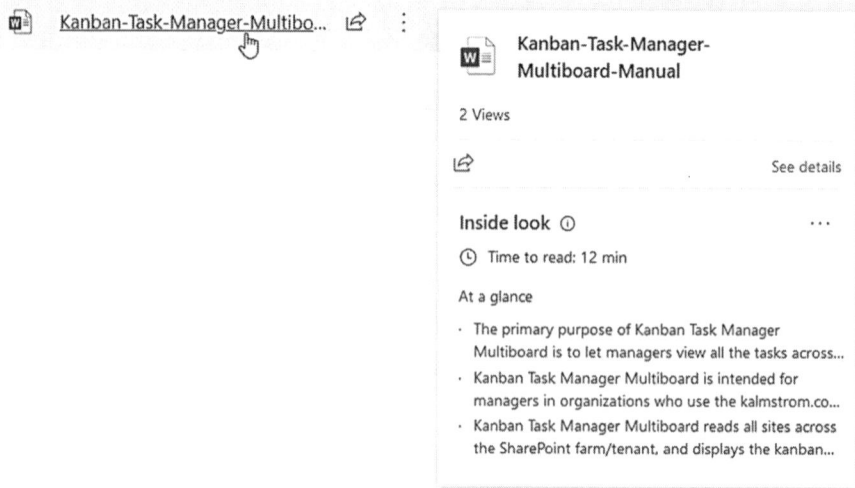

The **classic** library interface gives different results depending how you click on the ellipsis at a selected item.

Right-click gives a dropdown similar to the one in lists and in the modern interface.

Left-click gives dialog with the options open and share the item and with an ellipsis at the bottom. The ellipsis gives the same dropdown as right-click on the item ellipsis.

The dialog also has a preview of the file, and PowerPoint and Word files have a menu where you can print to PDF and get the embed code to the file.

(The modern interface has a preview in the Information pane, but no easy possibility to print to PDF or get the embed code.)

(The FOLLOW command in this dialog is a classic feature that does not work in the modern interface. It adds a copy of an Office file in your OneDrive, *refer to* 12.2, OneDrive for Business, and you can see the file in the classic OneDrive interface if you click on the 'Followed' link in the Quick launch. The modern OneDrive interface has no such link.)

9.3 CREATE A DOCUMENT LIBRARY

You can create a new library app with the "Add an app" command under the 365 Settings icon or with the 'App' command under the 'New' button in a modern SharePoint homepage or Site contents. This was described in chapter 7.

The '+ New' button in a modern SharePoint homepage or Site contents also gives the option 'Document library'.

When you use this option to create a document library, you will not be directed to the "Your Apps" page. Instead, a right pane will open, where you can enter a name and a description for the new document library.

A document library created with the 'Document library' option from the homepage or Site contents, will open when you have filled out the details and clicked on 'Create'.

9.3.1 *Auto-Created Columns*

When you create a new document library, several columns will be added automatically. You can see all of them except the "Name" column in the Library settings.

The automatically created columns "Name", "Modified" and "Modified by" are visible in the default "All Documents" view.

The "Name" column shows the file or folder name, so it should of course always be visible, but you can very well create a view where you hide the other two columns. They are filled out automatically.

The columns "Created", "Created by", "Title" and "Checked out to" are also created automatically, but they are not displayed in the "All Documents" view. These columns are also filled out automatically.

Only the "Name" and the "Title" columns are by default visible in the item form.

9.4 CREATE OTHER LIBRARY APPS

As mentioned above, you can create a document library from the "Your Apps" page. You can also create other types of library apps from the "Your Apps" page. Team sites have more options than Communication sites.

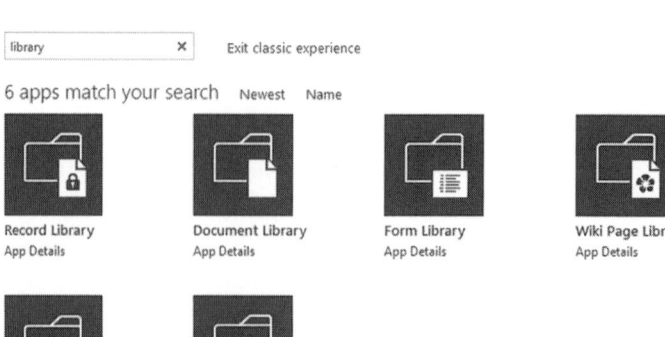

9.5 Add Content to Document Libraries

You can add content to a SharePoint document library either by creating a new Office document directly in the library or by uploading any existing file (or folder) to the library.

The upload of existing content can be done in several different ways, and I will mention them below. Another way, to synchronize SharePoint libraries with folders in the File Explorer, is described in section 12.5, Synchronize with Local Folder.

9.5.1 Create a File

A good way to get content into a SharePoint library, is to create a new Office file from the library. Click on the '+ New' button in the command bar (modern) or above the list of items (classic), to start the creation.

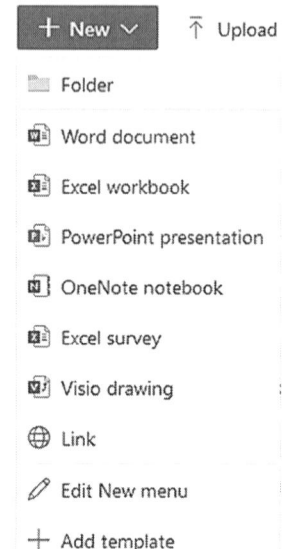

By default, the '+ New´ menu gives a choice of Office file templates and a folder option, but the menu can be customized. Many organizations choose to have some libraries with only one, custom template for specific content.

(Classic libraries also have a 'New Document' button under the FILES tab. This button by default only gives the Word document option.)

The **modern** interface also gives an option to create an item with a link. The link itself will be clickable and placed in the "Name" column.

As you see from the image to the right, the modern interface gives more options. I will describe them at the end of this chapter.

Additionally, Group Team sites have an option to

create a Forms survey, and when external sharing is enabled for other sites, the 'New' button in the modern interface gives an Excel survey option. *Refer to* chapter 20 to learn more about the different kinds of surveys available in SharePoint.

These are the steps to create a new Office file in a SharePoint library:

1. Open the library where you want to create the new file and click on the '+ New' button.
2. Click on one of the template options.
3. Click 'Yes' to the warning message.

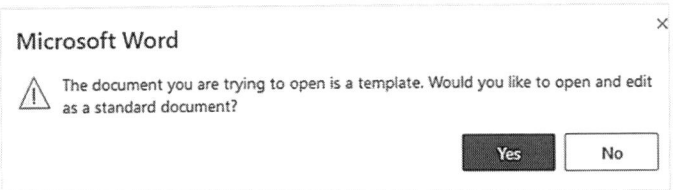

4. A new document will open, by default in the online version of the document type you selected. If you create the file from the modern interface, it opens in a new tab. (When you create a OneNote file, you will be asked to give it a name before it opens.)
5. Now you can start working with the document. Changes are saved automatically.

To switch to the desktop version, click on 'Open in …' under the 'Editing' button in the document.

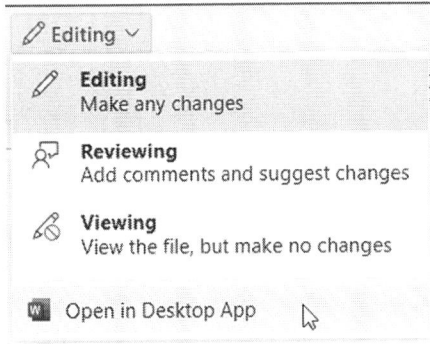

9.5.1.1 Naming

When new files are created inside a SharePoint library, they get a default name: Document, Book or Presentation, depending on file type.

If the creator does not change the default name, the library will eventually contain many documents with different content but with the same, non-descriptive names. That will of course make it difficult to find the correct file on each occasion. Therefore, users should be taught to name their files consistently and well.

Click in the default name – 'Book, 'Document' or 'Presentation' – above the ribbon. Now you can give the file a new name.

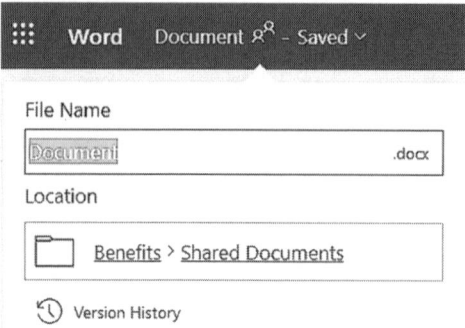

Here, you can also see links to the site, to the document library and to the Version history (which of course only is interesting for older files, not for new ones).

See 9.9, Edit Office files, below to learn more about how you can work with Office files in a SharePoint library.

9.5.2   Upload Files or Folders

All file types can be uploaded to SharePoint libraries. When you add files or folders to SharePoint by the methods described below, they will be copied to items in the library. They will not be removed from your computer.

When you copy files/folders to a SharePoint library as described below, the file name is always kept. But you should be aware that the file creator, creation and modified dates, security settings and most other metadata is NOT copied to SharePoint. Instead, the addition of such metadata will start from scratch after the upload. The only way to include metadata like Date modified and Permissions is to write code or use third-party software.

9.5.2.1   Select Multiple Files

Use one of these methods to select multiple files in your File Explorer:

- To select any files, hold down the Ctrl key and click on the files you want to add.
- To select files that are sorted together, hold down the Shift key while you click on the first file and then on the last file.
- To select all files in a folder, hold down the Ctrl key and press the A key.

(Folders can only be uploaded one at a time and in the modern interface.)

9.5.2.2   Upload Button

In the **modern** experience, click on the 'Upload' button in the command bar to upload one or several files, or a folder, to a SharePoint library.

Select 'Files' or 'Folder'. Then you can browse to the item(s) on your computer that you want to upload and click OK. Now the file(s) or folder will be uploaded.

Here, you can also upload a file that should be used as a template, *refer to* 9.14.2, Upload Office Template.

When you upload a file or folder that has the same name as an existing file/folder in a modern library, you will get a question about replacing the file, but the modern interface has no field for a version comment. If you choose to not replace, the new file or folder name gets a (1) after the name.

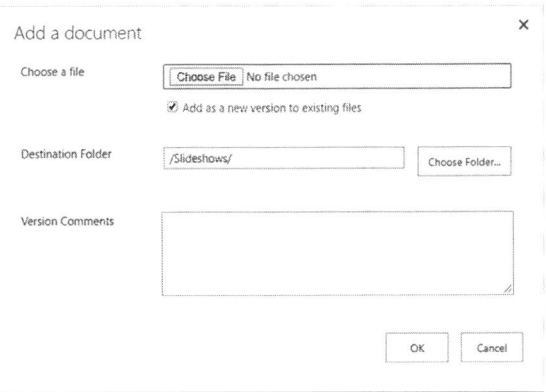

In the **classic** experience, you can either click on the 'Upload' button above the existing items or on the 'Upload Document' button under the FILES tab in the ribbon. Here you can only upload files, not a folder.

On the other hand, in the classic interface, you can add a file as a new version to an existing file and give a version comment, and you can also select to place the file in a folder. (With the modern interface, you must open the folder and upload the file there or move the file to the folder after upload.)

9.5.2.3 Save a File to SharePoint

There are two ways to save an open Office file from a computer to a SharePoint library. In both cases, start by opening the Files tab in Excel, PowerPoint or Word and selecting 'Save as'.

- Use the Sites button.

This will open a choice of sites that you have access to, and you can select first the site and then the document library.

- Use the Browse button.

195

a. Copy the path to the SharePoint library where you want to save the file. Leave out the last part, which should look like this: Forms/AllItems.aspx.
b. Click on 'Browse'.
c. Paste the path you copied into the address field.

d. Click on 'Save. You will now also have a chance to rename the file.
e. (You must log in to SharePoint, if you have not saved your log in information.)

Demo:

https://kalmstrom.com/Tips/SharePoint-Online-Course/Upload-File.htm

9.5.2.4 Drag and Drop

It is possible to drag and drop files from a computer to a SharePoint Online library. This can be done with one or multiple files at the same time, so drag and drop is a fast and convenient way to add files to SharePoint document libraries.

You can also drag one or multiple folders to a SharePoint library, if you use the modern interface.

1. Open the File Explorer on your computer in a small window over the SharePoint library window or put the two windows side by side using the Windows button + the left/right keys.
2. Select the file(s) you want to copy to the library.

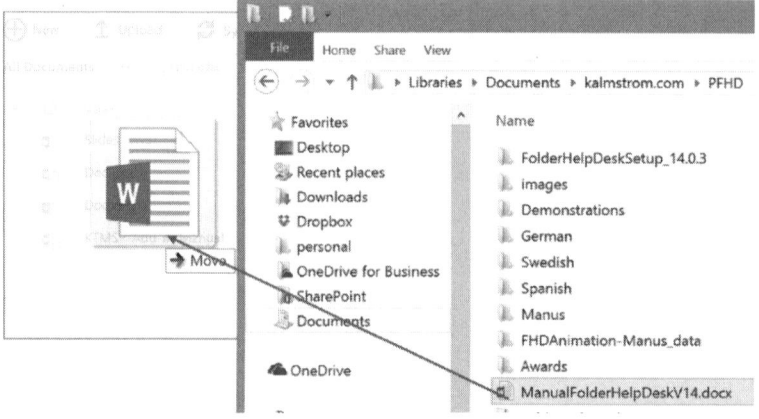

3. Drag the files to the the library and drop them in the box that appears.

You may also drag the files to the browser icon. The browser will then open in the latest visited window, and if that is the SharePoint library you can drop the file as described in point 3 above.

9.5.2.5 Other Methods

In section 12.3, I describe another way to move files to a SharePoint library: synchronize a SharePoint or OneDrive document library with a folder in your File Explorer.

When you want to move a lot of files and folders into SharePoint, I would recommend using SharePoint Designer, as described in chapter 10. This is the most stable no-code method.

To move many files on one occasion, or move files automatically on regular basis, you can use a PowerShell script. In my book *PowerShell with SharePoint from Scratch*, I have described how to write a script that copies all files in a local folder to a SharePoint library and then moves the copied files to a subfolder.

Demo:

https://www.kalmstrom.com/Tips/SharePoint-Online-Course/Upload-Multiple-Files-Drag.htm

9.6 EDIT PROPERTIES

In addition to the editing methods mentioned in 7.7.8, Edit Column Values, you can add or edit metadata in a library item by selecting the item and clicking on 'Properties' in the command bar. There is also a 'Properties' link under the item ellipsis >More. A right pane with the property fields will open, and you can click on 'Edit all' to modify the values.

9.7 RENAME A FILE OR FOLDER

If you want to rename a file or folder in a document library, you can change the name in already saved or uploaded files by editing the properties, as described above.

You can also click on 'Rename' under the item ellipsis. The modern interface also has a 'Rename' command in the command bar.

When an Office document is open, you can rename it in two ways:
- Click on the name to change it, as described in 9.4.1.1, Naming, above.
- Click on 'Save as' under the File tab and then on 'Rename'.

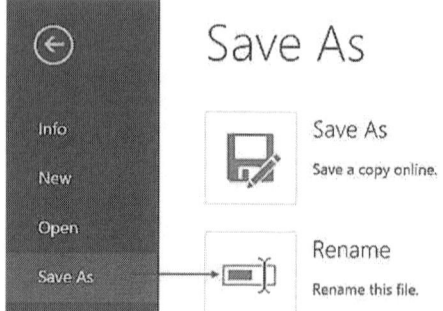

Demo:

https://kalmstrom.com/Tips/SharePoint-Online-Course/Create-Content-in-SharePoint.htm

To have documents created and named automatically based on specified templates; *refer to* 25.8, The Document Set Content Type.

9.8 OPEN BEHAVIOR FOR OFFICE FILES

When you want to view or edit an Office file, you can just click on the file name to open the file in edit mode. By default, it will open in the browser edition. Word documents are for example opened in Word Online.

Administrators can change the default behavior in the Library settings >Advanced settings. In the image below, documents are instead set to open in the client application when you click on the name.

Default open behavior for browser-enabled documents:

- ⦿ Open in the client application
- ◯ Open in the browser
- ◯ Use the server default (Open in the browser)

If the user's client application is unavailable, the document will open in the browser even if you have set documents to open in the client application.

If you use the 'Open' command in the **modern** command bar or under the item ellipsis, you will have a choice where to open the file.

In the **classic** interface, the item ellipsis gives the same opening options.

9.9 EDIT OFFICE FILES

When you select an item in a library app Standard view mode, you either want to edit the file or the metadata. We have already seen how you can edit the metadata via 'Properties' or in the Grid/Quick edit mode. Here, we will have a look at how Office files can be edited directly in the SharePoint library.

The Online editions of the Office apps run in the browser, and they automatically save your files to the document library where they were created or opened. These online editions are similar to the desktop/client editions, but some client features are missing.

On the other hand, the browser editions have some features that facilitates cooperation: different kinds of editing and a possibility to have a Comments thread in a right pane. The PowerPoint browser edition also has options for presenting the slideshow.

9.9.1 *Editing by Multiple Users*

Several people can work on the same Word Online, Excel Online or PowerPoint Online file at the same time in a SharePoint library. You can also use a shared OneDrive for Business folder, *refer to* 12.2.2, Sharing from OneDrive.

If you select to edit a Word, Excel or PowerPoint file in the Online edition, and another person is editing the same document, you will have a message about it:

&& Antonio Moreno is editing this document.

You can also see where in the document the other user is working.

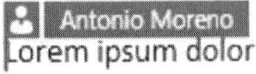
Lorem ipsum dolor

You may continue with your editing, because all changes will be visible in the document, no matter which one of the users who made them.

In some scenarios this multiple editing is a fantastic benefit. You can be more than two users on the same document. I have seen around 15 people collaborating on a document in Word Online!

Demo:

https://www.kalmstrom.com/Tips/SharePoint-Online-Course/Word-Offline-Overview.htm

9.10 THE TITLE COLUMN

When you create a new item in a list app, you cannot save it until the "Title" field is filled out. Therefore, most users learn to add values that give relevant information in that field.

When you create a new file in a SharePoint library, on the other hand, there is no such compulsion. On the contrary, the "Title" field is rather hidden, because by default it is not visible in the "All documents" view. To enter something in the "Title" field, users must therefore edit the file properties.

This means that the 'Title' field is often left empty in library items, which is a pity as it is important for the SharePoint search engine. In SharePoint searches, the "Title" field has the highest rank of all, so the title is where SharePoint begins the search after you have written a search word or phrase.

Hits in the title also comes first among the results. For the search to work well, it is therefore important that "Title" columns are filled out with words that give relevant information.

When the "Title" column in a SharePoint library is empty, the file name becomes prominent. Imagine how the search will work if users leave the title field empty and don't change the default file name, 'Document', 'Book' or 'Presentation'!

On the other hand, if people don't use the "Title" field, why have it there at all? It is possible to hide it, but before we come to that, I will give a few suggestions on how to get data into the field.

9.10.1 Add to View and Change the Display Name

If you add the "Title" column to the default view, users will hopefully consider it more than if it is hidden. It is a good idea to combine this with changing "Title" into something that is more explanatory. Renaming the "Title" column can also be an alternative to adding a new column.

Sometimes people avoid filling out "Title" fields, or fill them out badly, because they don't understand the meaning of the field. For example, if the documents in a library have IDs, changing the display name of the "Title" column to "DocumentID", would make it very easy for users to understand the meaning of the column and also to search and sort library items.

This method works well in SharePoint list apps, where something must be entered anyway, and a relevant name gives relevant input. In libraries, users might be more inclined to actually fill out a visible field called "Keywords", or something else that they understand, but showing and renaming the "Title" field does not force them to do it.

When you change the column name, only the name displayed to the users will be changed. The internal column name, which is used in queries and some other contexts, will still be "Title".

9.10.2 Auto-fill the Title Field

If we assume that users change the default file names when they create new files in SharePoint libraries, it is possible to let a flow or workflow add the same value as in the file name to the "Title" field.

This solution is not optimal, but it is better to have the file name in the title field than having it blank. This flow/workflow is also useful if you want to add titles to a lot of files where the field is empty. At the end of chapter 24, SharePoint Automation, I have suggested a flow and a workflow that gives the "Title" field the same value as the "Name" field.

9.10.3 Hide the Title Field

As a last resort, you can hide the "Title" field in a library. I would only do this when it is not used or repeatedly is filled out in the wrong way. You can do this in the **modern** interface, by editing the form, *refer to* 7.8, Edit the form.

9.11 LIBRARY FOLDERS

The old and tried folder is the most popular but least recommended way of categorization in SharePoint. It has some benefits, though, especially when used with OneDrive for Business, *refer to* chapter 12.

The main argument for folders is that users will feel at home, and you will not have to change the way information is stored compared to the file server. However, you will quickly experience that folders have some major drawbacks. SharePoint is not built for handling folders in a good way, and it has some serious folder-related annoyances.

If you don't want to allow user to create new library folders, you can hide that option, *refer to* 9.11.3, Hide the Folder Option, below.

9.11.1 Create a New Folder

To create a new folder in a SharePoint library, click on '+ New' and select the folder option.

Give the folder a name that tells what kind of items it contains and click on 'Create'.

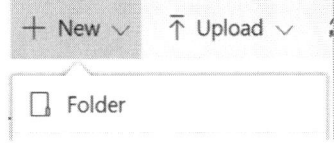

In the **classic** experience, you can also select 'New Folder' under the 'FILES' tab.

9.11.2 Move Files Into and Out of Folders

To move a document **into** a folder in a SharePoint library, click on the file and drag and drop it on the folder. This works in the same way in both experiences.

To move a document **out of** a folder in the **modern** experience, select the file and drag and drop it on the upper level heading.

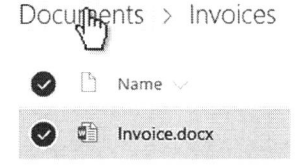

201

In the **classic** experience, you should instead drag the file to the document library link in the Site navigation to move it out of the folder.

The drag and drop method does not always work well, but in the **modern** experience, you can instead use the 'Move to' command in the command bar and under the item ellipsis, to move files into and out of a folder.

The best method is probably to move the files in the File Explorer by synchronizing, *refer to* 12.2.3, OneDrive for Business Sync. When you use that method the drag and drop works better, and you can also cut and paste.

Demo:

https://www.kalmstrom.com//Tips/SharePoint-Online-Course/Categorization-Folders.htm

9.11.3   *Hide the Folder Option*

When you click on '+ New' in a SharePoint library, you may by default also create a folder. As mentioned above, I generally don't recommend the use of library folders.

If you agree and don't want users to be able to create folders, you can hide the option to create new folders from the library interface. This is done in the Library settings >Advanced settings.

(It is also possible to hide the Folder option by editing the '+ New' menu in the modern interface, but when you do that, users can still create folders from the classic interface. *Refer to* 9.14.1, Edit the '+ New' Menu, below.)

9.12   CHECK OUT / CHECK IN

When you work with an Office file that is stored in a SharePoint document library and you don't want other users to see your changes, or you don't want them to be visible in the version history quite yet, you can check out the file.

A check out also prevents that several people edit the same file simultaneously. When a file is checked out, you can edit and save it as many times as you wish. No other user will be able to see your changes until you check in the file again.

When a file is checked out, it has a red icon to the right of the file name in the **modern** interface.

In the **classic** experience, the file type icon has a green arrow on checked out files.

9.12.1   *Check Out / Check In Commands*

Both library experiences have a 'Check out' option under the ellipsis at the file name.

202

Modern document libraries also have a 'Check out' command under the ellipsis in the command bar when a file is selected.

When you have checked out a file, the 'Check out' command is replaced with two other commands: 'Check in' and 'Discard check out'.

Check in the file when you want other users to see your changes.

Discard the check out if you don't want to keep your changes. When you do that, the Version history of the file will not be affected.

The **classic** interface, instead has 'Check Out', 'Check in' and 'Discard Check Out' buttons under the FILES tab in the ribbon.

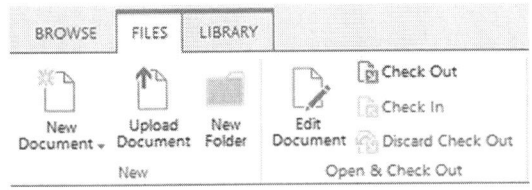

9.12.2 Require Check Out

Check out can be set to mandatory in the Library settings >Versioning settings. The default setting is No.

Require documents to be checked out before they can be edited?
○ Yes   ◉ No

If you set check out to be required before editing, you will overcome the issue with several people editing the same document incidentally, when the document has not been checked out.

On the other hand, you will probably have issues because people forget to check in the edited file again! In my experience, the Require Check Out feature creates more problems than it solves.

Demo:

https://www.kalmstrom.com/Tips/SharePoint-Online-Course/Check-Out.htm

9.13 COPY ITEMS

It is possible to copy one or more items from one document library in the tenant to another, by selecting or entering the destination library in the source library.

The item in the destination document library will always contain the file, but metadata is only added to the new library when there are columns for it.

When the source library and the destination library have columns of the same type with the same name, the copied item's values in these fields will be copied too.

9.13.1 Modern Copy Method

Libraries with the modern interface have a 'Copy to' link in the command bar and under the item ellipsis.

Select one or multiple items, click on 'Copy to' and a right pane will open. Here you can select first site and then library (and folder) to copy to.

Both files and folders can be copied in the modern interface.

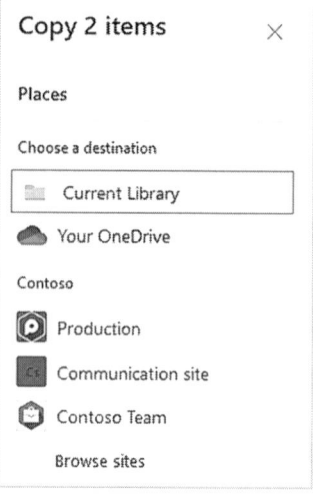

9.13.2 Classic Copy Method

You will find a 'Copy' link if you right-click on the ellipsis at a selected item in the classic library experience. Here you can only copy one file at a time, and folders cannot be copied this way. Furthermore, you must enter the path to the destination library yourself.

On the other hand, the dialog that opens in the classic interface gives a possibility to rename the file and to have alerts when the original file is changed.

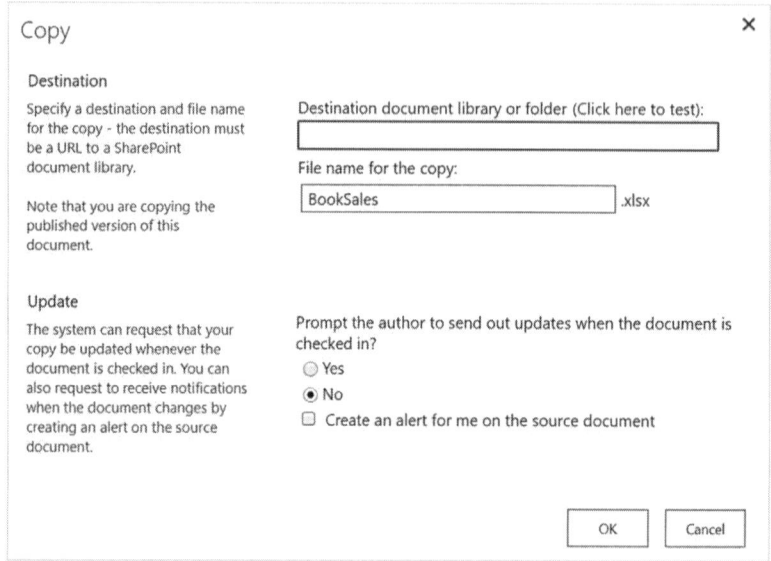

9.14 Modern '+New' Menu Options

The modern library interface makes it easy to upload a template to use with the '+ New' command and to edit the '+ New' menu.

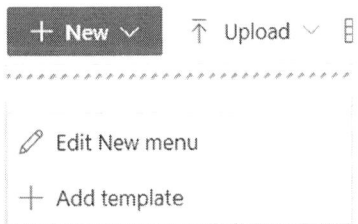

Note that changes in the '+ New' menu made from this command will *not* reflect to the classic interface. Neither can a template that is uploaded here in the way described below be selected in the classic interface.

9.14.1 Edit the '+ New' Menu

When you want users to only use custom templates when they create new documents in a modern SharePoint library, or when you want to limit their choices, you can edit the menu to only show the template(s) that should be used.

The image to the right shows an example.

1. Click on the '+ New' button and select 'Edit New menu'.

2. A right pane with all templates will open, and you can uncheck the templates you want to hide.

3. To reorder the templates, select any template in the right pane, open its ellipsis and move it up or down.

   You can also just drag the templates to your preferred order.

4. Save your changes.

9.14.2 Upload an Office Template

You can upload any Office document and use it as a template in the modern interface. Create the template in your desktop application and save it with a suitable name. You don't have to use a specific template format, .docx, .pptx and .xlsx will do fine.

1. Click on the '+ New' button in the command bar and select '+ Add template', or click on the 'Upload' button and select 'Template'.

2. Select the template you have created. It will now be uploaded and added to the templates in the '+ New' dropdown.

205

The template option is only suitable for simple templates that should be used with the modern library interface. If users switch to the classic interface, the template you want them to use will not be displayed!

In general, I would recommend that you instead use content types for more advanced template options, *refer to* chapter 25. A custom content type is the only option for the classic interface. When you use content types, you can also add and remove them from the '+ New' menu as you like.

9.15 SUMMARY

This chapter about SharePoint libraries has shown how to create content inside a document library and how to upload files and folders. I have also explained how you can check out documents to keep your changes to yourself and how several people can work with the same Excel, PowerPoint or Word Online file.

Discussions about using folders and about the "Title" field in library items have also been included in this chapter, and I have described how to edit, copy and move files in the modern as well as the classic experience.

Finally, I have pointed out some new features in the modern library interface that makes it easier to manage the templates used in a document library.

In chapter 25, Content Types, I describe how an administrator can make it easy for users to fill out metadata right in a document, instead of going into the item properties.

In the next chapter, I will introduce a tool that is helpful when you work with SharePoint: SharePoint Designer.

10 SharePoint Designer

If you want to be a SharePoint power user, it is a good idea to have SharePoint Designer 2013 installed on your computer. SharePoint Designer is mostly known as a workflow creation tool, but it is also useful for managing SharePoint sites and apps.

In this chapter, you will learn how to find and install SharePoint Designer and how to open a SharePoint Online site in SharePoint Designer. I will also explain how to create a list and how to import files to a library with SharePoint Designer.

All kinds of SharePoint sites can be managed in SharePoint Designer, but Microsoft is regretfully not continuing to develop this useful tool. There is no "SharePoint Designer 2016" or later, and each time you install a later Office version on a computer that has SharePoint Designer 2013 installed, it will be removed. You can continue using SharePoint Designer 2013, but you will have to download it and install it again.

10.1 Install SharePoint Designer 2013

SharePoint Designer 2013 is a free Office application, but it is not included in any Office package installation. You will have to install it separately.

1. Click on your profile picture in the right part of the 365 navigation bar and then on 'View account' to open your 365 account page.
5. Click on 'Office apps' in the left menu and then on 'Tools & add-ins'.

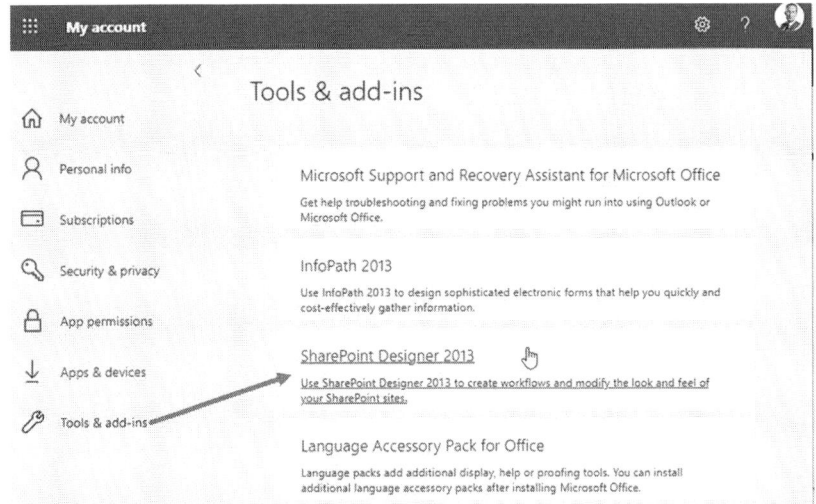

2. Click on SharePoint Designer 2013. You will now be directed to a Microsoft download page.
3. Select language if you want another language than the default one.

4. Click on the 'Download' button.
5. Select the 32- or 64-bit version. It should be the same as your installed Office version.
6. Click on 'Next' and save the file to your computer.
7. Run the file.

10.2 OPEN A SITE IN SHAREPOINT DESIGNER

You should always first open the *site* in SharePoint Designer, even if you want to work with an app. Then you can select the app you want to work with.

1. In SharePoint Designer, click on the 'Open Site' button.

2. Paste or type in the URL of the site you want to open. Note that only the first part of the URL you see when you open the site should be entered, like this: https://kalmstromdemo.sharepoint.com/sites/Example/.

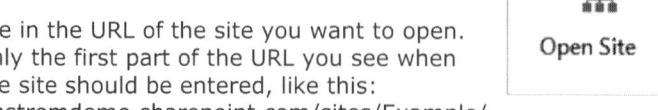

3. Click on Open.

When a SharePoint site is open in SharePoint Designer, you can see the site contents in the menu to the left. To the right, there is a summary page with information about the item you have selected in the left menu. This is what you work with in SharePoint Designer: one site and its contents, design and settings.

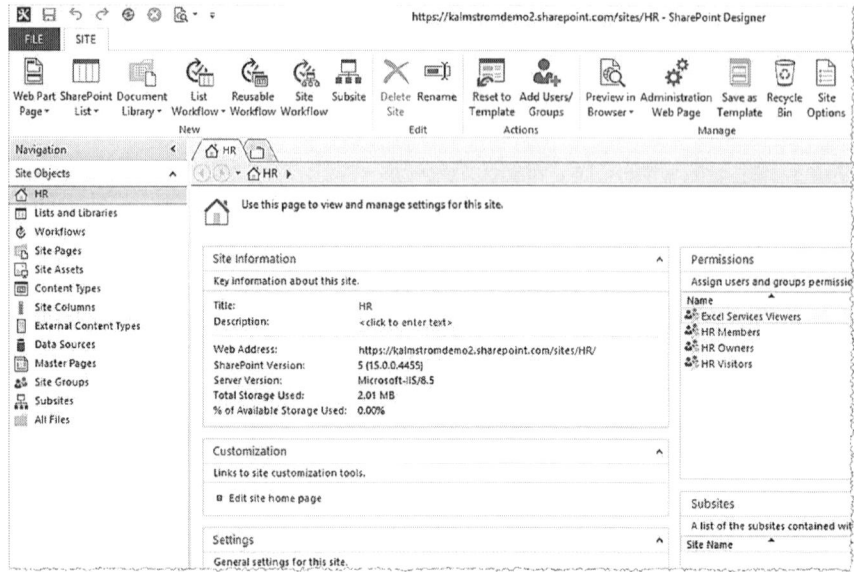

Above the site contents and summary page there is a ribbon with various controls. Which controls are displayed, depends on what has been selected.

Demo:

https://kalmstrom.com/Tips/SharePoint-Online-Course/SharePoint-Designer.htm

10.3 CREATE AN APP IN SHAREPOINT DESIGNER

Instead of creating a new app in the web browser interface, you can use SharePoint Designer 2013. It is quicker and saves you some clicks and loading of new pages.

1. Open the site in SharePoint Designer.
2. Click on either the 'SharePoint List' or the 'Document Library' button in the ribbon.
3. Select the list or library type you want to use.
4. Give the app a name (and a description) and click OK.

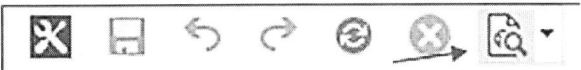

Now the list or library options are shown on the SharePoint Designer summary page, and you can customize your app more quickly than in the browser. You can select settings options and add, remove and edit columns, views and forms.

When you have the app open in SharePoint Designer, you can preview it in the browser with the preview button above the ribbon.

Demo:

https://kalmstrom.com/Tips/SharePoint-Online-Course/SharePoint-Designer-2013-Create-List.htm

10.4 IMPORT FILES OR FOLDERS WITH SHAREPOINT DESIGNER

This is the process to add files and folders to a SharePoint library with SharePoint Designer 2013.

1. Open the site in SharePoint Designer.
2. In SharePoint Designer, open the 'All Files' folder in the left menu.
3. In the main area, select the document library that you want to add files or folders to.
4. The 'Forms' folder will be selected automatically when the library opens. Make sure that you de-select that folder, because you probably do not want to add files in that hidden folder.

5. Click on the 'Import Files' button in the ribbon.

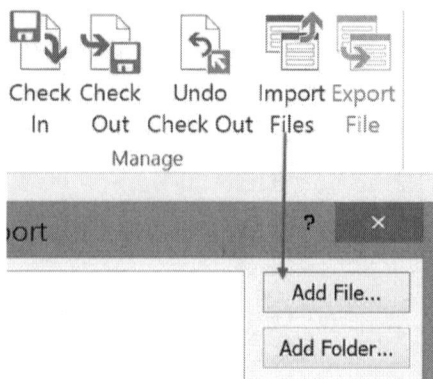

6. Click on the 'Add File...'" or "'Add Folder...' button in the dialog that opens.
7. Select the files or folder from your computer that you want to add to the document library.
8. Click on Open and then OK, and the upload begins.

Demo:

https://www.kalmstrom.com/Tips/SharePoint-Online-Course/Import-Files-SPD.htm

10.5 Summary

This chapter has introduced SharePoint Designer. You have learned how to find and install SharePoint Designer 2013 and how to open a site in SharePoint Designer.

Now you also know how to create a SharePoint list or library in SharePoint Designer, but you can do much more, for example automate SharePoint processes. We will come back to that in chapter 24, SharePoint Automation.

11 SHAREPOINT NAVIGATION

SharePoint administrators need to understand how the SharePoint navigation is built and can be manipulated, so that users can easily find content they are looking for, not only by search but also by using the navigation.

11.1 SITE NAVIGATION/QUICK LAUNCH

| Home |
| Conversations |
| Documents |
| Notebook |
| Pages |
| Site contents |
| Recycle bin |
| Edit |

All SharePoint Team sites have a navigation pane to the left on each page. It is called Site navigation, as it usually shows links to content within the current site. Other names are Quick launch and Current navigation. Quick launch is the classic name that is often used in settings pages.

By default, the Site navigation has links to content in that a team might need for collaboration, like a Notebook and a document library.

The Site navigation also has links to the Site Pages library and to the Site contents. All default links point to content in the same site.

The left pane Site navigation can be hidden via the Site settings >Navigation Elements. This can be suitable in certain contexts when you don't want users to be able to easily reach other content on the site.

Microsoft has recently added a possibility for Site owners to put the modern Team site navigation on top instead of to the left. When top navigation is selected, there it will also be possible to use the Mega menu style in modern Team sites.

Communication sites have the Site navigation on top of the page, not to the left, and the default navigation includes Documents, Pages, and Site contents. These links are helpful when you are building the site, but they might not be the best for people who visit the Communication site to get information. Therefore, you should plan to replace these links with more relevant links when you are ready to launch the Communication site.

The links in the Site navigation are same on every page in the site, so when you change anything in the Site navigation on one page, it will be changed for the whole site.

11.1.1 Add an App to the Site navigation

Often, and especially in Team sites, you want to make it easy for users to find apps that are commonly used in the site. When that is the case, you should add links to the apps to the Site navigation.

A link in the Site navigation is added by default when you create an app from a **modern** homepage or a modern Site contents interface. Select List or Document library in the '+

☑ Show in site navigation

New' button dropdown and keep the box checked.

For other app creation methods, you can add the app to the Site navigation at List settings >List name, description and navigation.

Select the radio button 'Yes' for 'Display this list/library on the Quick launch'.

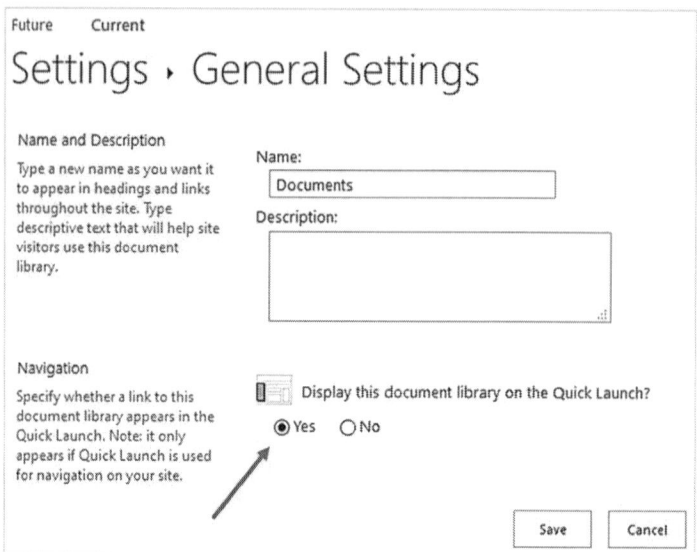

11.1.2   Add a Subsite to the Site Navigation

When you create a subsite, you can decide to show a subsite link in the parent site's Site navigation. The default option is No.

There are also top link options when you create a subsite, but they are only valid for classic sites, *see* below.

In Communication sites, where the Site navigation is placed on top of the page, the link to the subsite will be placed under a 'Subsites' heading, if you select 'Yes' to display the site on the Quick launch of the parent site.

The "Development" site in the image below has two subsites: Current and Future.

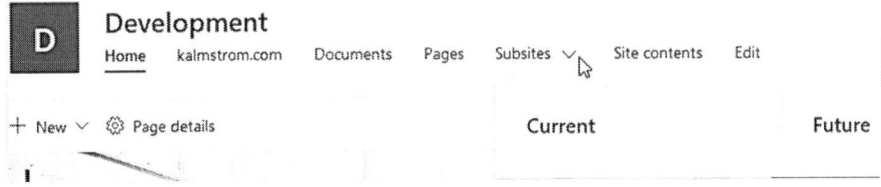

11.2 Classic Top Link Bar

The navigation bar on top of SharePoint pages in classic Team sites is called the Top link bar or Global navigation. The Site navigation – or Quick launch – is to the left, as in all Team sites.

You can add any links to both navigations, but I would recommend that you use them differently. It is easier for users to learn that content in the same site is found to the left, while other links, that they might use more seldom, are found at the top of the page.

11.2.1   Inherit links

When you create a subsite, you can decide if the subsite should inherit the top link bar from the parent site. I often find it useful to change the default setting into 'Yes' for classic Team sites, to have a connection to the root site.

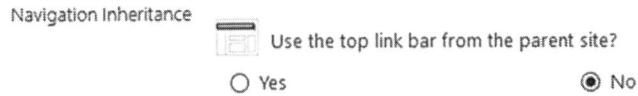

You can stop inheriting the navigation under the Site settings >Top Link Bar.

11.3   Hub Navigation

When a site is registered as a Hub site, it gets an extra hub navigation bar on top of the page. This hub navigation can only be edited in the Hub site, and it is inherited by all the associated sites. In classic sites, the hub navigation will only appear on modern pages.

The image below shows the Hub navigation on the Development hub site. As you see, this is a Communication site with its Site navigation just below the site name.

Hub site owners should customize the Hub navigation to include resources that might be of interest to users in all the associated sites. It is often suitable to add links to the associated sites in the Hub navigation, so that users can easily reach the other sites in the hub family.

The hub site navigation can have up to three levels, so site owners don't need to add all links in a long row on top of the page. Instead, the links can be organized under labels, in a way that helps users discover and find relevant content.

11.4 EDIT NAVIGATION

The navigation can be edited in several ways, and I recommend that you consider which navigation options are the best for each site. Bad or lacking navigation can be very frustrating to users, while good navigation will make work smoother and more efficient.

When working with navigation, it is also important not to over-engineer it. Current usability recommendations are to always push users to search for content instead of trying to figure out where it would logically fit within a hierarchical structure. For example, does the "Vacation rules" document exist in the HR site "Documents" library or in the HQ site "Company policies" library or even in both? Searching is usually the best way to find content.

11.4.1 Navigation Settings

The navigation for all sites can be edited from the Site settings, via links under the Look and Feel heading. Only classic Team sites and modern Team sites without a group have all the links shown in the image to the right.

Look and Feel
Title, description, and logo
Quick launch
Top link bar
Navigation Elements
Change the look

Communication sites have no 'Top link bar' or 'Navigation Elements' links and Group Team sites have no 'Top link bar' or 'Title, description and logo'.

Modern Team sites without a group have the 'Top link bar' control, even if they don't have a Top link bar, so by adding links there you can get a Top link bar in these sites. It will however be placed in the same space as the Hub navigation.

The Hub navigation cannot be edited at all under the Look and Feel heading.

The 'Quick launch' control gives most options. On the Quick launch page, you can create new links in the Site navigation and change their order. You can also create headings, to group the navigation links, and change the order of links and headings.

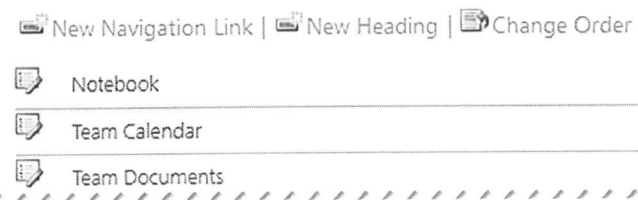

New Navigation Link | New Heading | Change Order

- Notebook
- Team Calendar
- Team Documents

You can edit or delete each link by clicking on the edit icon to the left of the link display text.

The 'Top link bar' page, only has the 'New Navigation Link' option.

The 'Navigation Elements' page gives two options: to hide the Site navigation and to show a tree view. Unfortunately, the tree view only works in the classic experience.

11.4.2   Modern Experience

When you use the modern interface, the navigation can be easily edited via the 'Edit' link. You can find this link at the bottom of the Site navigation in Team sites and to the right in the Site navigation in Communication sites.

The 'Edit' command opens a left pane with the Site navigation in edit mode.

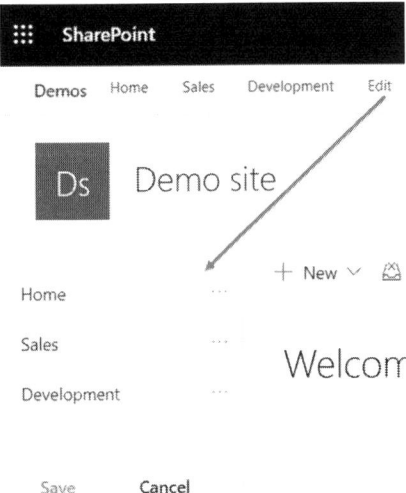

When the navigation is in edit mode, each link will have an ellipsis with various options, see the image below.

To add a new link, move the cursor to where you want to place the link and click on the plus sign that appears when it is possible to insert a new link (above 'Documents' in the image below).

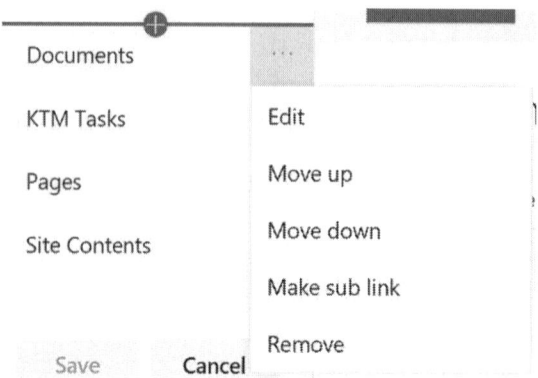

When you add a new link, the Hub navigation and Site navigation in Communication sites give an extra option: a choice between Link and Label. When Label is selected, the Address field is greyed out.

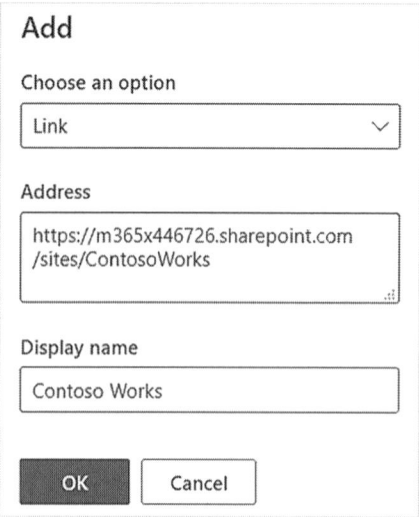

The Group Team site navigation pane instead has suggestions on links to shared group resources above the 'Address' and 'Display name' fields.

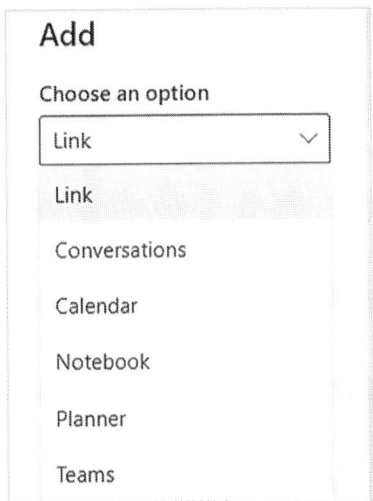

When you select one of the resources instead of the Link option, the link and the display name will be added automatically. Conversations give a link to the group's shared e-mail inbox.

Modern Team sites without a group, only have the option to add a link and a display text.

11.4.2.1 Edit Hub Navigation

Select 'Edit' in the hub navigation bar to edit the hub navigation. In addition to standard links, you can link to associated hub sites, if there are any.

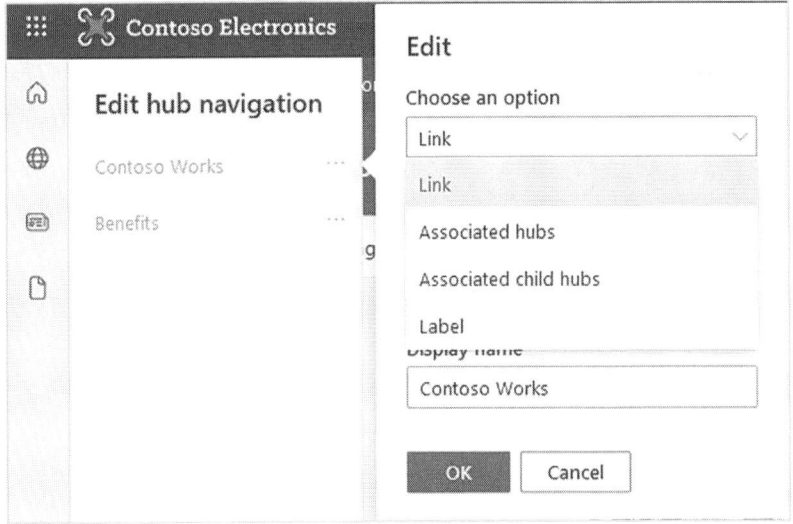

Note that links to associated hubs are not automatically updated when there are changes to hub associations in the SharePoint admin center. That must be done manually.

11.4.3 Classic Experience

Click on 'EDIT LINKS' to open the navigation in edit mode when the page has the classic experience interface. The image below shows the Top link bar, but the Site navigation can be edited in a similar way.

kalmstrom.com demos   ×   Sales   ×   Development   × | Drag and drop link here   ⊕ link   Save   Cancel

- Use the X icon to delete a link.
- Use the eye icon to hide a link.
- Change the order of links by drag and drop.
- Add new links by clicking on the '+link' icon. Give the new link a display text and paste or type in the path in the dialog that opens.

11.4.4 Site Navigation Hierarchy

When you have many navigation links, it is useful to arrange them in groups with headings and sub links.

In the **modern** experience, you can arrange the links in a hierarchy by using the 'Make sub link' command in the modern Site navigation.

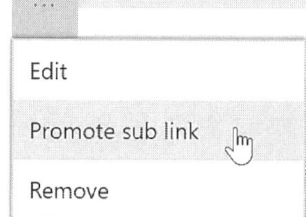

The command moves the selected link a little bit to the right, and the command changes into 'Promote sub link' – which moves the link back again.

In the **classic** experience, you can drag the links in the Site navigation, but that is more difficult. If you have a possibility to use the modern experience just when you arrange the links, for example by switching interface in an app, that is a quicker method.

In classic Team sites, you can also use the Site settings >Quick launch.

📧 New Navigation Link | 📧 New Heading | 📑 Change Order

'New Heading' puts a heading to the far left in the Site navigation. You must link this heading – it cannot remain unlinked, like the modern labels.

When you click on 'New Navigation Link' you can enter a URL and its description and select under which heading the link new link should be placed.

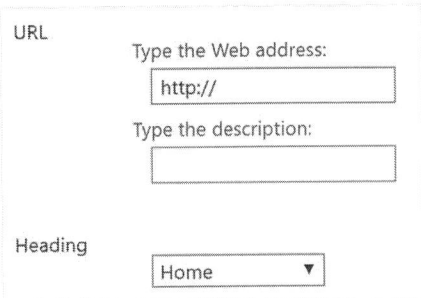

In the classic Top link bar, it is possible to create a hierarchy. When you need a heading, create a link without a path and drag other links under it. In the image to the right, the 'Departments' caption is not linked.

If you want to try this, be aware that you might need to try several times before you get the dropped link to stay under the heading.

It is easier to create headings in the top navigation when you use the Navigation Settings page. This page is available when the SharePoint Server Publishing Infrastructure has been activated for the site collection; *refer to* 27.2, Navigation Changes with Publishing Infrastructure.

Demo:

https://www.kalmstrom.com/Tips/SharePoint-Online-Course/SharePoint-Navigation.htm

11.5 FOCUS MODE

Each user can temporarily hide the header and navigation to see more of the content on the screen.

Modern apps have an 'Expand content' icon to the right in the command bar.

All **classic** pages have a 'Focus on content' icon to the right under the 365 navigation bar.

219

In both experiences, click on the icon to enter focus mode and click again to exit focus mode.

All Team sites have a 'Navigation Elements' control in the Site settings, *see* 11.4.1 above. Here, Site owners can permanently hide the Site navigation in the **classic** experience by unchecking the 'Enable Quick Launch' box.

11.6 SUMMARY

In this chapter, you have learned how to edit the different kinds of navigation found in SharePoint sites. You have now seen the extra possibilities given by Hub and Communication site navigation, and you also know the specifics of the navigation in other sites.

As the navigation is the same for the whole site, you also understand that you sometimes can switch between app interfaces to have the best possibilities for your Site navigation.

In the next chapter, I will introduce SharePoint content that is personal to each user. You have already met Microsoft Lists, that can be used for personal lists and not only for shared data. Now it is time to look at the options on the SharePoint Online start page and to learn to take advantage of OneDrive for Business.

12 PERSONAL CONTENT

SharePoint has a few parts that are not primarily intended for collaboration but instead for personal use. On the SharePoint Online start page, users can find important content and create sites and news, and in OneDrive for Business each user has a personal site for content storage.

12.1 THE SHAREPOINT ONLINE START PAGE

When a user clicks on the SharePoint tile in the 365 App Launcher, or on 'SharePoint' in the left part of the 365 navigation bar, he/she is directed to the SharePoint Online start page.

The SharePoint Online start page is a kind of SharePoint Favorites page. Here each SharePoint user can find links to SharePoint sites he or she has decided to follow, to recent or frequently used sites, to saved news and to sites promoted by the organization.

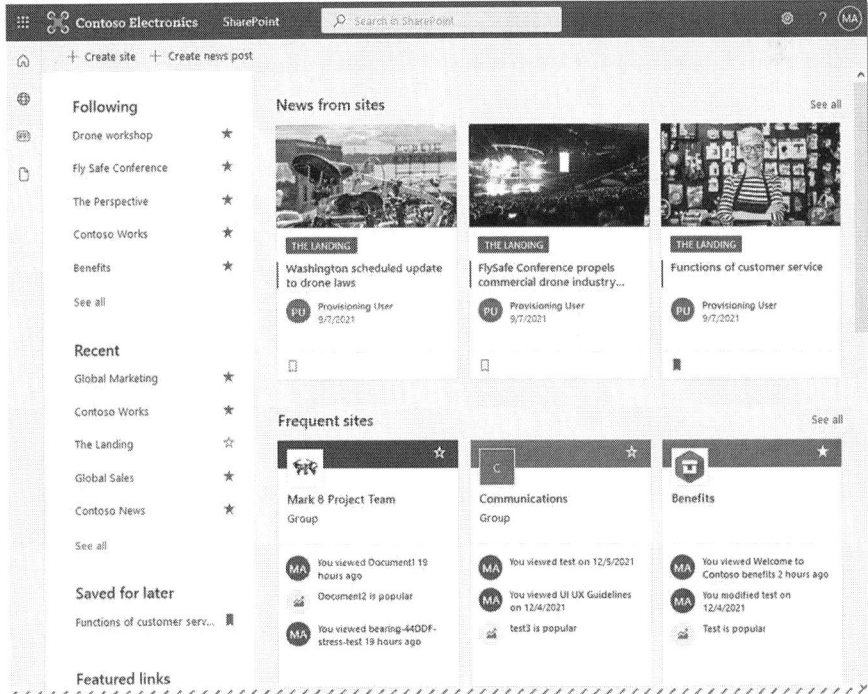

In this section I will explain how to follow and unfollow sites and how to save items for later. For site creation, *refer to* chapter 6, SharePoint Sites, and for News creation *refer to* section 13.4.11, The News Web Part.

12.1.1 Follow Sites

To follow an open site, each user can click on 'Not following' (modern) or 'FOLLOW' (classic) to the right above the site's command bar/ribbon:

☆ Not following

To follow a site from the SharePoint Online start page, click on the star to the right of the site icon. (Click again to stop follow the site.)

Followed sites will be displayed in the left menu of the SharePoint start page.

12.1.1.1 Stop Following

When you follow a site in the **modern** experience, the text will be changed into 'Following'. Click on 'Following' to stop following the site, and the text will be changed into 'Not following' again.

In the **classic** interface, the text will not change. Instead, you must go to the SharePoint Online start page and click on the star to the right of the site icon to stop following.

12.1.2 Save for Later

The news displayed in the main area of the SharePoint start page can be bookmarked, so that you can read them later.

When you click on the "Save for later" icon, the notation will change to "Saved for later", and the news item will be visible under its own heading in the left menu. If you click on the icon again, the entry will be removed from the left menu.

12.2 ONEDRIVE FOR BUSINESS

OneDrive for Business, also called OneDrive for work and school, contains a personal site that gives each SharePoint Online user a 1 TB storage space. In the E3 and E5 Office 365 subscriptions, the storage space is even unlimited. The files stored in that site are private – unless the owner decides to share them.

In this section, I will describe the OneDrive for Business document library and explain how sharing files in that library works. I will also show how you can use OneDrive for Business to synchronize the OneDrive for Business library and any other SharePoint library that you have access to, with your computer.

Finally, I will explain how users can create a site that has many more of the useful SharePoint features than the default OneDrive for Business site, providing that the default Admin settings are kept.

The path to the OneDrive site collection looks like this:

https://TENANTNAME-my.sharepoint.com/personal/LOGINNAME/

(Note that there is also a "OneDrive" included in Windows 8.1 and 10. It is connected to a Microsoft account – not to an organizational 365 account. It has less storage space and does not build on SharePoint, and that "OneDrive" is *not* what we are talking about here.)

Demo:

https://www.kalmstrom.com/Tips/SharePoint-Online-Course/OneDrive-Intro.htm

12.2.1   The "My Files" Library

When you click on the OneDrive for Business icon under the 365 App Launcher or at office.com, you will reach your OneDrive for Business document library, "My files".

As you see from the image below, the 'My files" library resembles other SharePoint document libraries, but some of the features you can find in other document libraries are missing.

You can share files and folders in the "My files" library, and you can add new content to it in the same way as with all SharePoint libraries. But the "My files" library lacks many of the other library features.

For example, you cannot create more columns for metadata or edit the existing columns, and there is no possibility to create different views.

Moreover, you cannot create new apps, pages or subsites from the "My files" library.

The left menu cannot be edited. It has the following entries below 'My files':

- Recently used files
- Shared files
- Recycle bin for OneDrive, where deleted content can be restored or permanently deleted.
- Quick Access has the site names in the list, but the links open the default document library in that site. Libraries you have added a shortcut to are prominent here.
- More places: sites with libraries you have access too, grouped by Frequent and Followed in the main area. On top of the main area, there is a link to "SharePoint Home", which is the SharePoint start page.
- Create shared library: create a modern Group Team site, for collaboration or for your own use.

- Get the OneDrive apps: get a download link to the Android or iOS OneDrive for Business mobile app.
- Return to classic OneDrive: show the library in the classic interface

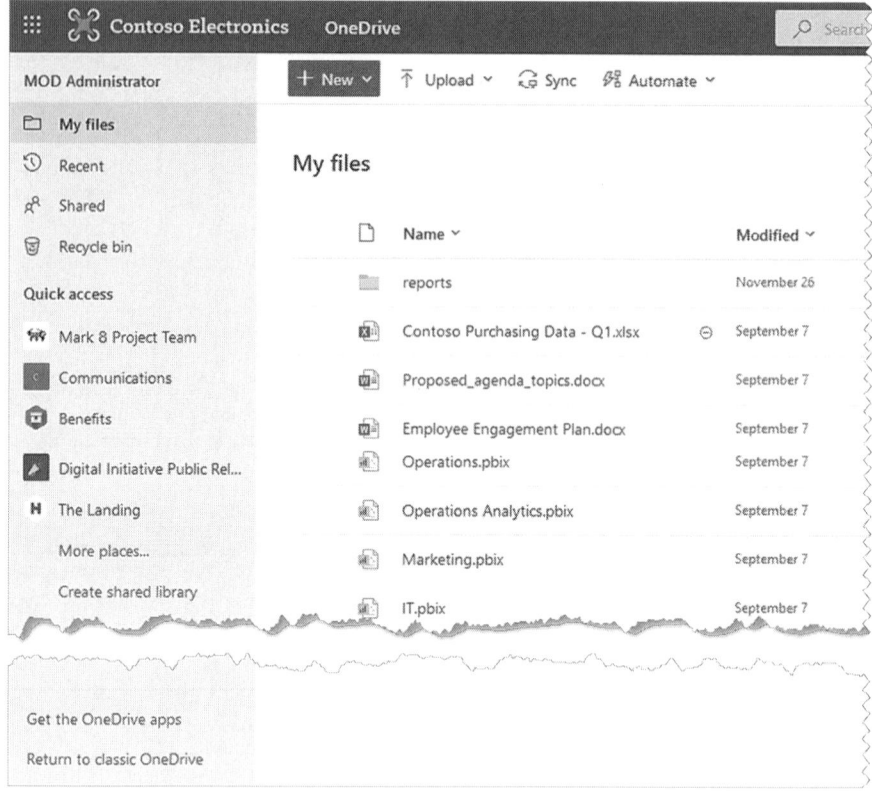

12.2.2 Sharing from OneDrive

All files and folders that you store in OneDrive for Business are private until you decide to share them. The sharing is done with the 'Share' button or by sending a link, and it works in the same way as sharing a file from a SharePoint document library, *refer to* 15.3, Share Site Content.

To easily share files with different groups of people in your organization, you can place files that should be shared with the same people in folders in the "My files" library and then share each folder.

You can manage the access to your files in the same way as in a SharePoint document library too, but the "My files" library also has an automatically filled out "Sharing" column in the library interface. It has the value 'Private' or 'Shared', and when you click on 'Shared' or 'Private' in the Sharing column, you can see and modify access to the file.

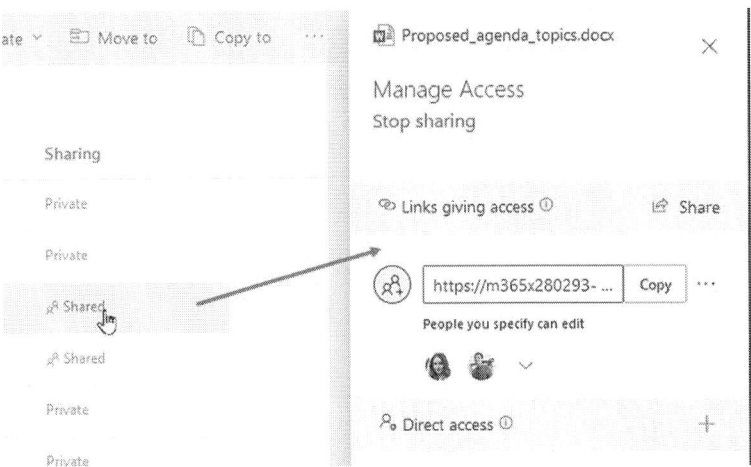

If you hover over the file name, you will see a card that shows information about the file and who has viewed it.

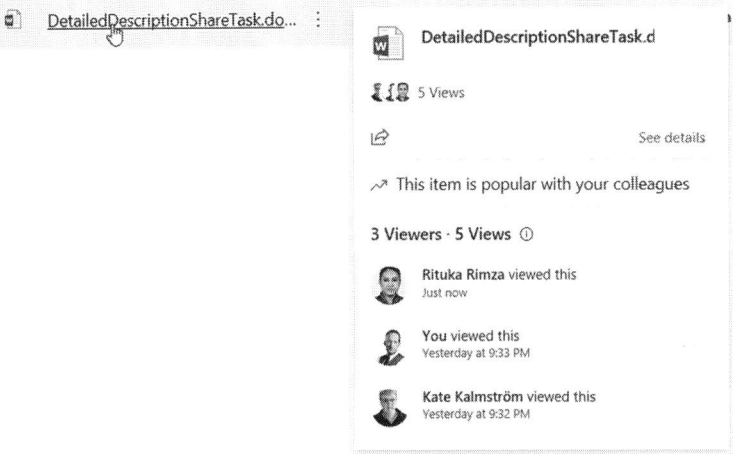

In your OneDrive settings, you can download a CSV file with sharing data. You can open this file in Excel. The first time you generate a report, you must create a folder in your "My Files" library for it.

12.2.3   OneDrive for Business Sync

As we have seen earlier, it is possible to synchronize list apps between SharePoint lists and the Microsoft Lists desktop app, *refer to* 8.3.3, Lists Desktop App. OneDrive for Business manages this synchronization, and OneDrive can also synchronize files in SharePoint libraries and a local File Explorer.

The library synchronization means that you can add SharePoint and OneDrive document libraries (or library folders) as folders in your personal computer or smart device and edit them there. You can also add new files to these library folders, and they will be uploaded to the SharePoint or OneDrive library when you are signed in to SharePoint.

In this section I will describe how the synchronization between libraries and the File Explorer folders should be set up.

12.2.3.1 First Library Sync

Once you have set up the synchronization between a library and your device, OneDrive for Business will keep track of changes and synchronize this library and folder automatically.

However, the first time you must do it manually. You can also perform the steps below anytime you need to make a manual sync.

1. Open any SharePoint document library.
2. Click on the 'Sync' button in the command bar or under the ribbon LIBRARY tab.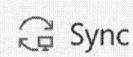
3. A 'Getting ready to sync' dialog will open. It has a link to download OneDrive for Business, but as it is included in the Office 365 subscription, you should not have to use that link.
4. You might be asked to open OneDrive for Business and/or to log in with your Office 365 account. Then you will see the location and name of the library folder that will be created on your computer. You now have a possibility to change the location.

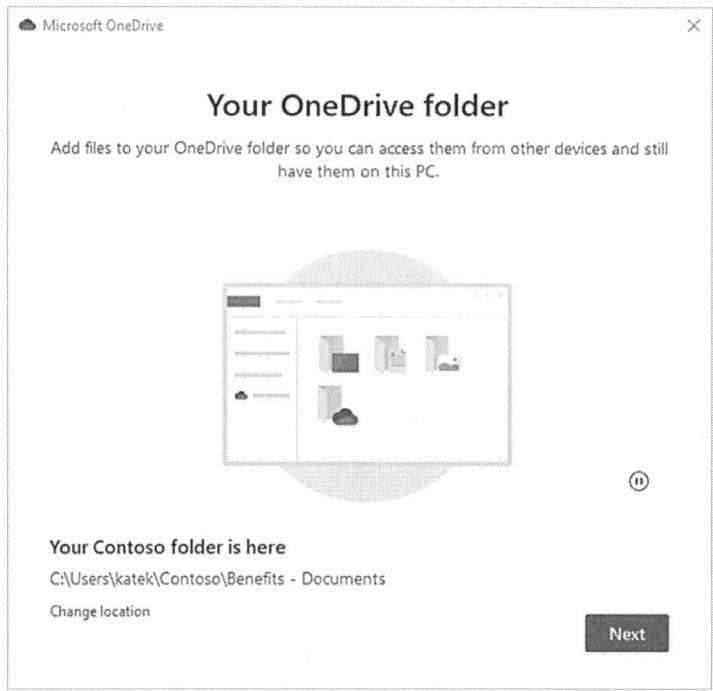

226

5. When you click on 'Next', you will get a presentation of OneDrive for Business. You will also have a possibility to download the OneDrive for Business mobile app.

If you add the new library folder to your Favorites/Quick access, it will be smooth to move files between that folder and your other folders. When you drag or copy/cut and paste items to the synchronized library folder, they will be automatically uploaded to the library when you are online and logged in to Microsoft/Office 365.

When you synchronize the OneDrive for Business "My files" library, the folder name will be OneDrive - COMPANY.

When you synchronize other SharePoint document libraries, they will be gathered as subfolders under a COMPANY folder. The subfolders have the names SITE - LIBRARY

Kalmstrom Enterprises AB   Sales - Sales Documents

Demo:

https://www.kalmstrom.com/Tips/SharePoint-Online-Course/OneDrive-Sync.htm

12.2.3.2   Sync Issues

If the synchronization does not work, make sure that the not synchronized file is closed. There are also characters and other points to consider, please refer to https://support.microsoft.com/en-us/office/restrictions-and-limitations-in-onedrive-and-sharepoint-64883a5d-228e-48f5-b3d2-eb39e07630fa.

12.2.3.3   Sync Settings

Click on the OneDrive icon in the task bar on your computer to reach the library synchronization settings. (You might need to click on the 'Show hidden icons' arrow to see the OneDrive icon.)

12.2.3.4   Files On-Demand

OneDrive Files On-Demand is a feature that saves storage space on the computer, as it helps users to access synchronized files without downloading all of them. The Files On-Demand setting is found under the Settings tab in the synchronization settings, and it is enabled by default.

When Files On-Demand is enabled, you can access your files without having to download them and take up storage space on your device:

New files created online or on another device appear as online-only files, so they don't take up space on your device. When you are connected to the internet, you can use the online files like every other file on your device.

In your File Explorer, each synchronized file has a status icon that shows how the file is available. These are the icons, from top to bottom in the image to the right:

- Online-only: These files don't download to your device until you open them. You can only open these files when the device is connected to the internet.

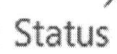

- Locally available: When you open an online-only file, it downloads to your device and becomes a locally available file. Now you can open it anytime, even if you don't have internet access.

These local files are cached, and if the drive gets low on space, some of the oldest files that have not been accessed in a while may be moved back to a cloud state to free up space. You can set this in Windows 10 under Storage >Change how we free up space automatically.

- Always keep: Files marked "Always Keep On Device" will always stay on the device and will not be moved back to cloud state automatically, even if drive space is low.

If you want to change the setting for a file or folder, right-click on the item on your device and select either 'Always keep on this device' or 'Free up space'.

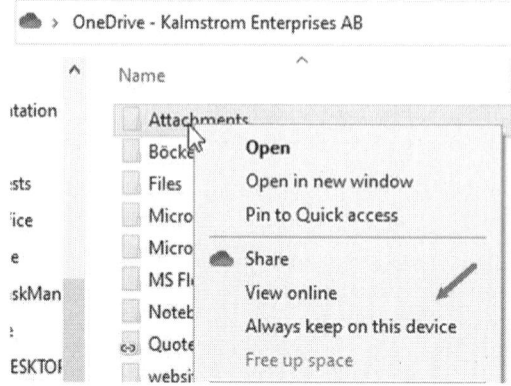

12.2.4 OneDrive User Settings

Each user can reach his or her personal OneDrive settings from the 365 Settings icon of the "My files" library.

The Settings dropdown also gives a possibility to restore the OneDrive library.

228

In the OneDrive settings, each user can turn off notifications. 'More settings' opens a page with links to some other settings that are available under the Site settings in standard SharePoint sites.

MOD Administrator	More Settings
⌁ Notifications	
⚙ More Settings	Manage access
	Site collection administrators
	Manage guest expiration
	Run sharing report
	Region and Language
	Regional settings
	Language settings
	Features and storage
	Site collection features
	Storage Metrics
	Can't find what you are looking for?
	Return to the old Site settings page

12.2.4.1 Create Apps and Sites within OneDrive

If you click on 'Return to the old Site settings page', you will have a possibility to create new sites and apps within OneDrive.

In the old Site settings page, open the 365 Settings icon. Now you can either select 'Add an app' or open the Site contents and create new apps or even subsites from there. These apps and sites have the full SharePoint functionality.

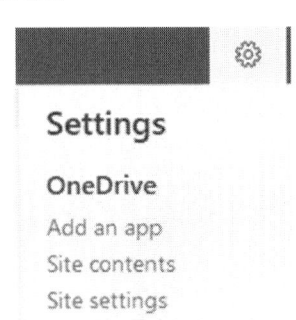

When SharePoint administrators want to control site creation, this is a work-around those limitations if an admin has placed them on you.

Are you an admin and want to stop others from using this loophole? As far as I know, there is no simple way to block it.

Even if site creation is allowed, users benefit from using OneDrive to create sites and apps for their personal use, as it gives the unlimited space and full admin rights. Sites created as subsites via the OneDrive Site contents will show up in the user's Followed sites on the SharePoint Start page, but they will not be visible in the SharePoint Admin center.

One way of taking advantage of this possibility is to create multiple libraries. This gives important advantages and lets you share and synchronize in a more controlled way than if you use only the default OneDrive for Business library:

- SharePoint does not work well when you have more than 5000 items in a library. If you create more libraries in your site, you will overcome that problem.
- You can share different libraries with different groups of people.
- When you create multiple libraries, you can choose to not synchronize all of them to your device, *see* below. The libraries you don't synchronize, can be used for storage of files that you don't need to access very often. You can also sync different libraries with different devices.

12.2.4.2 Restore OneDrive

Each user can restore his/her OneDrive to an earlier time 30 days back, to undo unwanted changes:

1. In the OneDrive "My files" library, open the 365 Settings icon and select 'Restore your OneDrive'.
2. Select 'Custom date and time'.
3. Move the slider to the left and study the changes. The activity chart shows the volume of activities each day, so that you can see when an unusual activity, like when your OneDrive was infected by malware, has happened.
4. Select an activity. All activities that occurred after that will be selected automatically.
5. Click on the Restore button, and your OneDrive will be restored to the selected activity. All activities after that will be undone.

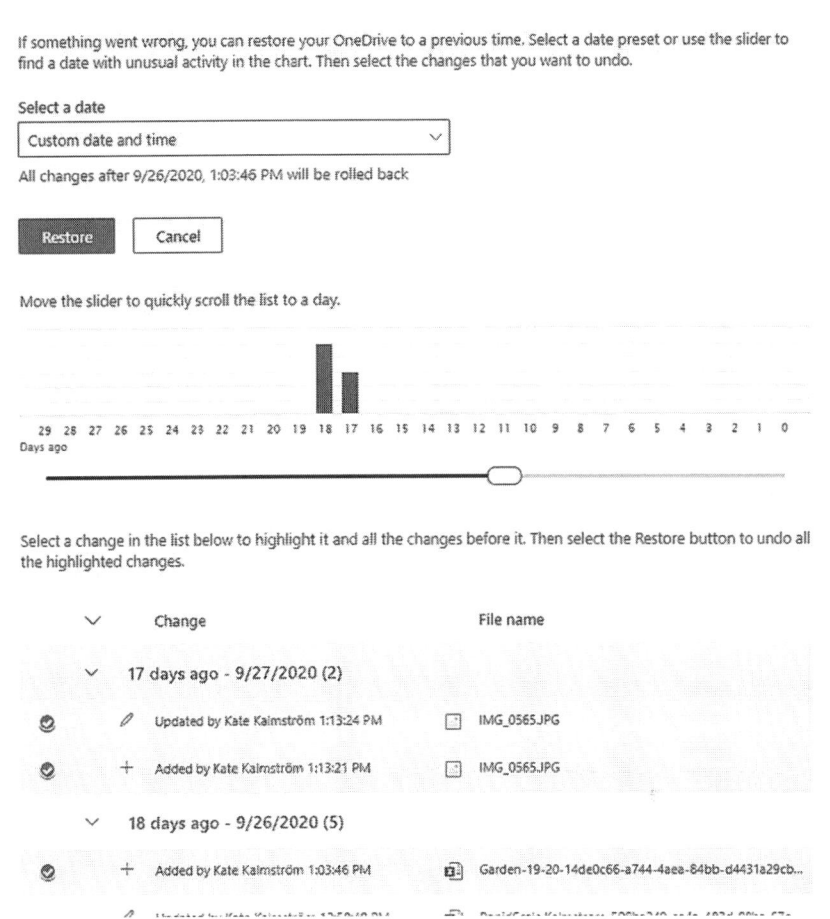

12.2.5 OneDrive in Admin Centers

In the Microsoft 365 and SharePoint Admin centers, Global and SharePoint administrators can control OneDrive users' sharing, synchronizing, storage, devices and more.

The default settings for sharing and synchronization are generous. For example, 'Anyone with the link' is default for sharing, and synchronization can be made to folders belonging to other organizations.

These generous permissions can of course be beneficial for business cooperation, but I strongly recommend that you study the default OneDrive settings and policies and restrict them if necessary.

12.2.5.1 OneDrive Settings

Under Settings in the SharePoint Admin center, you can find multiple settings for OneDrive. A description and the current value are visible to the right of the entries. The four entries open a right pane, as the Sync pane in the image below.

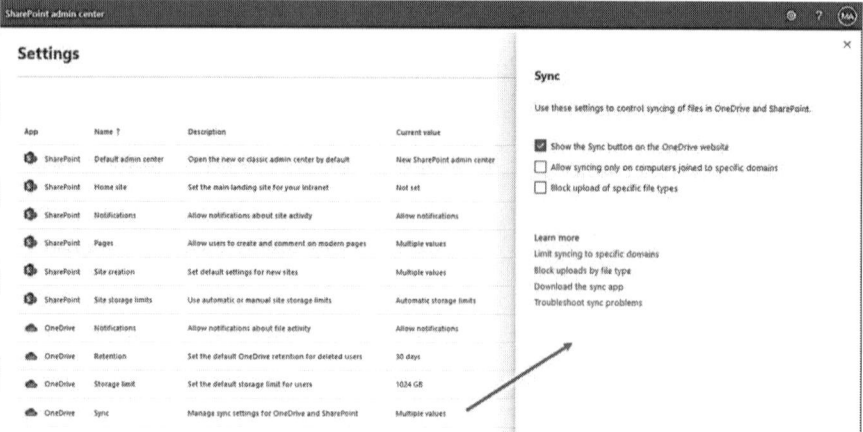

12.2.5.2 Sharing

Under Policies in the SharePoint Admin center, you can find the sharing settings, together with the SharePoint sharing. The OneDrive settings are synchronized with the corresponding SharePoint settings. The OneDrive settings can be more restrictive than the SharePoint settings, but never more allowing.

12.2.5.3 Control OneDrive Usage for Specific Users

Administrators can control each user's OneDrive for Business usage from the Microsoft 365 Admin center >Active users. Click on the account name you want to manage to open the right pane. Then select the OneDrive tab. Now you can for example get a link to access the user's "My files" library and manage external sharing and OneDrive storage.

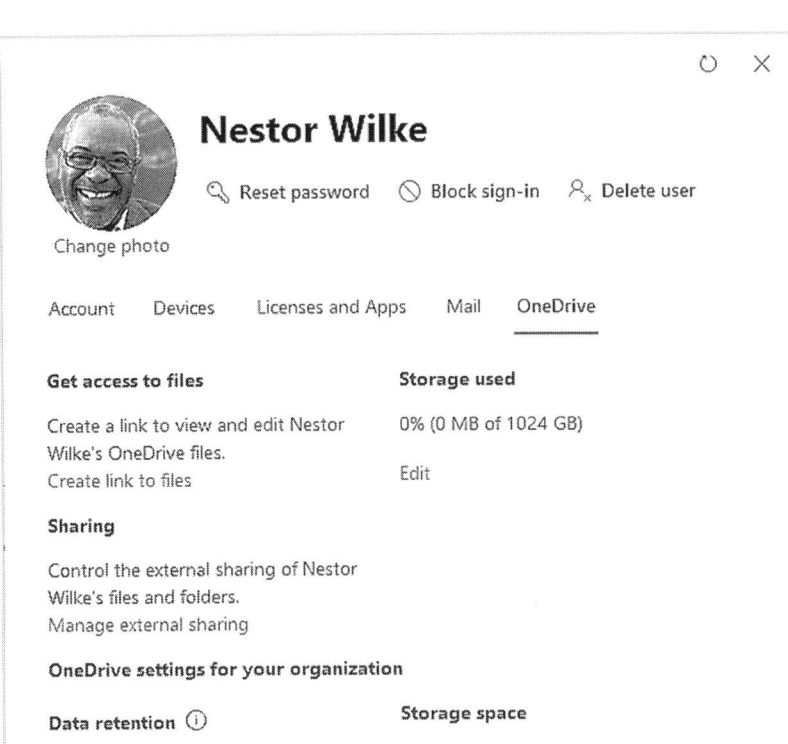

12.3 SUMMARY

In this chapter, you have learned how to reach your personal SharePoint Online start page and how you can use it to find content that you access often.

I have also introduced OneDrive for Business. I have explained the limitations of the "My files" library and described how to create a site that can give many more options.

After reading this chapter, you should also know how OneDrive for Business manages synchronization with folders on your computer, of both the 'My files' library and any other SharePoint document library.

As an admin, it is important that you now understand how you can control OneDrive for Business via the Microsoft 365 and SharePoint Admin centers.

Security and permissions are important all over Microsoft 365, and we will come back to that. But before we do that, we will have a look at the SharePoint building block that we have not gone into yet: the page.

In the next chapter you will learn about the different kinds of SharePoint site pages, and I will explain how you can create and customize them.

13 SHAREPOINT SITE PAGES

As we have seen earlier, SharePoint sites can store a lot of various content. All content that should be visible to users is displayed on pages inside a site.

Each page is an ASPX file, which you can see on the URL. We have already talked about the homepage of a site. Its URL ends with Home.aspx, and each page that you create yourself ends with the page name + .aspx.

Some pages, like settings pages, are created by SharePoint and cannot be customized. These pages are called application pages, and they usually have a classic interface. An exception is the Site contents page. As we have seen earlier, the Site contents can have both experiences and often works better with the modern interface.

Apps are contained in automatically created pages, and even if you can customize the app these pages cannot be customized.

This chapter is about so called site pages – pages that users can create and customize. The automatically created homepages are also site pages and can be customized. All users with Edit or Contribute permission or higher can create and customize the pages described here.

The most common reason for creating a new page is probably that users need to have an additional space for some specific content. Instead of adding that content to an existing page, it is often better to create a new page for it. If you give the page a good name, the content will be easier to find than if you add it to a page that already has other content.

By default, site pages inherit the permissions from the site.

SharePoint Online offers three types of pages that can be customized: the modern page and the classic wiki and web part pages.

Today, the **modern** page is the most used site page in SharePoint Online. Even if modern pages give less customization possibilities than the wiki pages, the options are easy to understand and use. In some contexts, the term "site page" only refers to the modern page.

Modern pages have a command bar with various controls above the actual page content. They are customized with specific web parts that are added to the page and modified. These web parts cannot be used in classic pages.

Classic pages give other options and can look very different, but they are often a more complex to customize and use.

In wiki pages, you can either use various web parts and add the content in them or add text or links or insert images, videos etc. directly in the content area of the page.

Web part pages can only be customized with web parts. These web parts are the same as in wiki pages. The classic web part pages are by default stored in the site's "Site Assets" library.

I hope this chapter will explain the differences between the three types of site pages clearly. You will learn how to:

- Create pages and open them in edit mode.

- Add and edit modern and classic web parts.
- Edit modern pages.
- Publish news to modern pages.
- Edit wiki pages and use the commands in the ribbon.
- Edit web part pages.
- Save and publish page modifications.
- Add files to page
- Use pages instead of files
- Manage files in the "Site pages" library

If you want to have more layout options than given by the default three page types, *refer to* chapter 27. There, I describe how to make a site use Publishing pages instead.

Demo:

https://kalmstrom.com/Tips/SharePoint-Online-Course/Site-Pages-and-Application-Pages.htm

13.1   THE SITE PAGES LIBRARY

SharePoint pages are files, and all modern pages and the classic wiki pages are stored in the site's "Site Pages" library. You can reach this library from the Site contents, and often also via a 'Pages' link in the Site navigation.

The "Site Pages" library is created automatically by SharePoint when a new site is created. Generally, it works in the same way as a document library, but there are no buttons for upload or download.

You can add extra columns to the "Site Pages" library, to categorize the pages with metadata, and you can make columns mandatory to fill out. If a mandatory property is missing at publishing, the page author will have a message about it, and the page cannot be published until the mandatory property has been filled out.

The page properties can be managed in the "Site Pages" library in the same way as file properties in a document library.

Page properties can also be seen and edited directly in **modern** pages, via the 'Page details' button in the command bar, *refer to* 13.4.9.

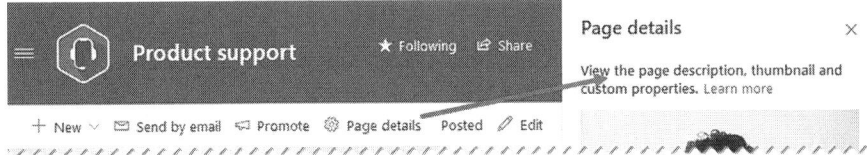

13.1.1 Site Type Differences

Team sites have more features in the "Site Pages" library than Communication sites.

Experience:

- In modern and classic Team sites, you can use both experiences in the "Site Pages" library, and you can switch interface with a link under the Site navigation, just like in other libraries.
- In Communication sites, the "Site Pages" library can only have the modern interface.

New pages:

- In Team sites, you can create both modern and classic pages from the "Site pages" library.
- In Communication sites, you can only create modern pages.

13.1.2 Experience Differences

The classic "Site Pages" interface gives less features than the modern, so I recommend that you use the modern interface in all "Site Pages" libraries, also in classic sites.

- When you use the modern interface in a "Site Pages" library, you can create approval flows and other flows for new pages, *refer to* chapter 24, SharePoint Automation.
- When you use the modern interface, you can schedule the publication of modern pages.
- The modern interface lets you make a page, modern as well as classic, homepage of the site.
- The modern interface has icons that show if the page is unpublished or checked out.

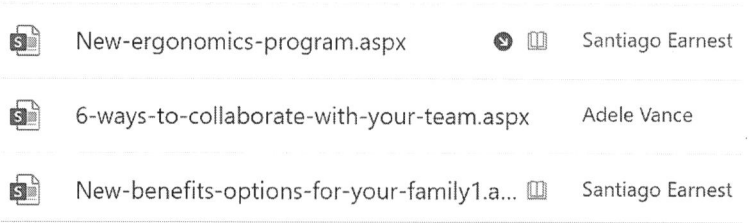

13.1.3 Check Out

Conflicting situations, where several people edit the same page, cannot occur in modern pages. For classic pages a setting is available to avoid such conflicts.

13.1.3.1 Modern Check Out

Modern pages are checked out automatically when someone opens the page in edit mode, whether check out is set to be required or not. Therefore, conflicting situations can never occur in modern pages.

Users who start editing a modern page, can see if someone else is already editing the same page, who that person is and how to contact him/her.

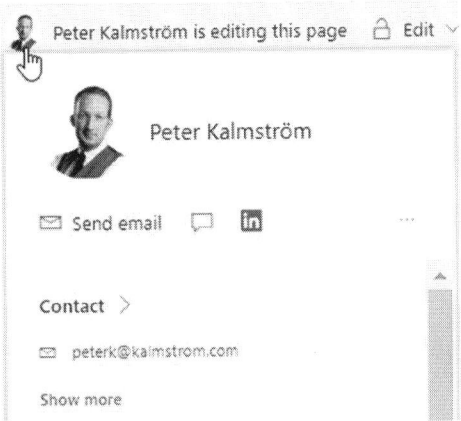

The page cannot be edited, but the site owner can discard the other person's changes.

13.1.3.2 Classic Check Out

If you are concerned about editing conflicts in classic pages, you can set the "Site Pages" library to always require check out of pages that go into edit mode. That is done under Library settings >Versioning Settings and applies to all pages in the "Site Pages" library.

1. In the Library settings, open the Versioning settings under the General Settings heading.
2. Select Yes at "Require documents to be checked out before they can be edited". (Pages are documents, remember?)

   Require documents to be checked out before they can be edited?
   ◉ Yes   ○ No

When a user tries to edit a classic page after the mandatory check out setting has been activated in the "Site Pages" library, a warning message is displayed.

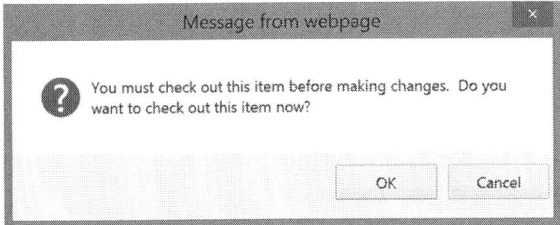

237

Even if check out is not set to mandatory in the "Site Pages" library, users can check out a classic page while editing it. Click on the 'Check Out' button under the ribbon PAGE tab to check out.

The 'Check Out' button will now be replaced with a 'Check In' button, which you can use when you are finished editing. The page will also have a status message.

 Status: Checked out and editable.

If you save the page without checking in, it will remain checked out. You must check in the page to give other users access to the edited version and to let other users edit the page.

If you check in the page without saving first, it will be saved automatically.

13.1.4   Version History for Pages

Just as document libraries, the "Site Pages" library has Version history enabled by default. It gives a possibility to restore earlier page versions and works just as it does for apps, *refer to* 7.12, Version History.

You can see the version history for all pages via the ellipsis at each page item and via the command bar/ribbon. Modern pages also have a link to the page's Version history in the 'Page details' pane, *see* 13.4.9.

13.1.5   Scheduled Page Publishing

The command bar in the "Site Pages" library **modern** interface has a 'Scheduling' button. It opens a right pane where you can enable scheduling for the site.

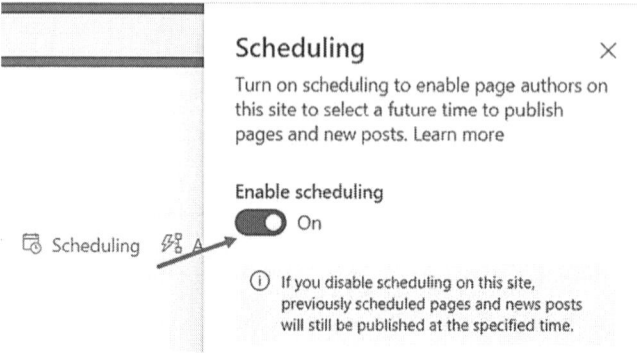

When scheduling has been enabled in the "Site Pages" library, page creators can schedule the publishing of new or modified pages if needed. This is done in the page's "Page details" pane, *refer to* 13.4.9. below.

This also applies to modern news posts, as each news post is a page, *see* 13.4.11, The News Web Part, below.

238

13.1.6 Copy a Page

In the "Site Pages" **modern** interface, you can use the 'Copy to' command that I earlier described for libraries to copy a page with all its content and layout. (That is not possible with the classic 'Copy' command.)

The page will be copied to the same "Site Pages" library, so that you can use the page as a template for another page in the site.

1. Select the page file you want to copy.
2. Click on 'Copy to' in the command bar or under the item ellipsis.
3. Click on 'Copy here' in the right pane (it is not possible to change the destination.)
4. The page will be copied and named with the suffix "1" after the original page name.
5. Rename the page.

13.1.7 Set a Page as Homepage

From the "Site Pages" library, you can easily replace a site's homepage with another page from the same site.

When you use the **modern** "Site Pages" interface, select the page you want to set as the site's homepage and click on the ellipsis in the command bar or at the item. Select 'Make homepage'.

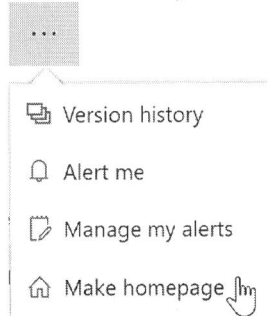

This command can make a homepage from both modern and classic pages, even if the command itself is only available in the modern interface.

In the **classic** "Site Pages" interface, you can only make a classic page homepage. Open the page and click on the 'Make Homepage' button under the PAGE tab in the ribbon. There is no command to make a modern page homepage from the classic "Site Pages" interface.

13.2 WEB PARTS INTRODUCTION

All three types of pages can be customized with web parts. A SharePoint web part is a building block that you can add to a SharePoint page. Most often, you also need to fill the web part with content, and there are different web parts for different kinds of content.

Modern pages have their own web parts that cannot be used with other page types. The modern web parts are very easy to use, but they have limited customization possibilities compared to classic web parts.

As the modern page is prioritized by Microsoft, new useful web parts are published continuously, and modern pages now have many web parts that don't have a corresponding web part in classic pages.

The **classic** web parts are used in wiki and web part pages. They cannot be used in modern pages, but I would recommend that you explore the classic web parts too. They give some possibilities that are not present in the modern web parts, as you will see later in this book.

13.2.1 App Parts

App parts are **classic** SharePoint web parts connected to apps that exist within the current site. When app data is displayed in app parts, they can be added to wiki and web part pages in that site in the same way as the other web parts.

From a user perspective app parts and web parts are the same, and some parts are found under both Web Parts and App Parts when the classic page is in edit mode. Therefore, I don't go into the differences here. You can use app parts in the same way as web parts.

Modern pages also have web parts that display app content, but here they are called web parts!

13.3 CREATE A PAGE

Modern pages can be created in several ways, but Classic pages can only be created from the "Site Pages" library in Team sites.

13.3.1 Create a Page from Site Pages

In Team sites, all kinds of pages can be created from the "Site Pages" library with the **modern** interface. When you click on '+ New' to create a new page, you can create all three types of site pages. Here, the modern page is called Site Page.

In Communication sites, only the 'Site Page' and 'Link' options are given under '+ New' in the "Site Pages" library. This means that you only can create modern pages in Communication sites.

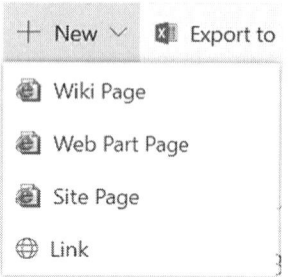

When modern pages are created from the "Site Pages" library, a new blank page will open without any choice of template.

If the "Site Pages" library has the **classic** interface, you can only create a wiki page from the '+new' button.

Under the FILES tab you can create all three page types.

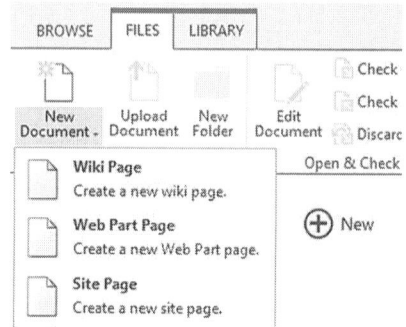

240

13.3.2 Create a Modern Page from '+ New' or 'Add a Page'

You can create modern pages outside the "Site Pages" library in three ways:

- Click on the 365 Settings icon and select 'Add a page'.

  This will give you a modern page even if you create the page in a classic site or from a page with the classic interface.

  A right pane with a choice of templates will open.

- In a modern homepage, click on '+ New' and select 'Page'. A right pane with a choice of templates will open.

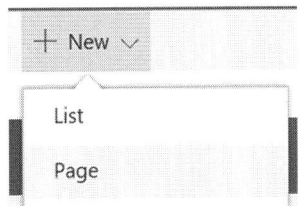

- In an existing modern page that is not a homepage, click on '+ New' and select 'Page' or 'Copy of this page'. A right pane with a choice of templates will open when you select 'Page'.

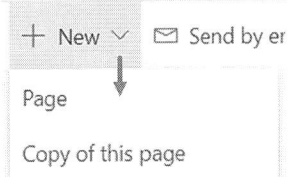

- Click on '+ New' in the modern 'Site contents' interface and select 'Page'. A new blank page will open without any choice of template.

13.4 CUSTOMIZE A MODERN PAGE

Modern pages have their own web parts that cannot be used in other types of pages. These web parts can be combined on the page to make it interesting and useful.

By default, all users with Edit permission are allowed to create modern pages, also called site pages, in modern as well as classic sites. This possibility can be disabled in two places:

- In the SharePoint Admin center >Settings >Pages, the possibility to create modern pages can be turned off for the whole organization.
- Site owners can deactivate the possibility to create modern pages for the site, under Site settings >Manage site features >Site pages.

When the possibility to create modern pages is disabled, you can still create classic pages in all Team sites, but no pages can be created in Communication sites.

News on modern pages are their own modern pages contained in a special News web part, so most of what is said below also applies to news creation. *Refer to* 13.4.11 for info about unique characteristics for news pages and the News web part.

Microsoft offers a tour the first time a user creates a new page or news post. It shows how to pick a template, add and edit sections and web parts, title the page, and choose a title image.

During the first months of 2022, Microsoft plans to roll out some changes to the editing experience for modern site pages. As they are not yet launched even to targeted users, I cannot test and show the features, but below is the information given from Microsoft. When you read this book, the features are hopefully implemented!

- It will be possible to name sections and set the default display to collapsed instead of the default expanded.
- The webpart toolbars will be placed horizontally instead of vertically and actions will be consolidated into that single web part toolbar.

13.4.1 *Page Templates*

When you begin creating a modern page from the '+ New' button on a page or via the 'Add a page' link under the 365 Settings icon, a right pane will open where you will have a choice of templates. Select the template you want to use and click on 'Create page'.

By default, a blank page is pre-selected, but site owners can make another template pre-selected via the ellipsis on the template card.

From the template card ellipsis, you can also open the template, and custom templates can be edited or deleted from the site.

The custom templates are only displayed on the site where the page was saved as a template, and they can only be used there.

The Built-in templates are displayed in all sites. They cannot be edited or removed, so the ellipsis dropdown only shows the option 'Set default selection'.

Page templates are draft copies of pages. The custom templates are stored in an automatically created "Templates" folder in the "Site Pages" library.

When you have selected your template, click on the 'Create' button at the bottom of the pane, and the new page will open in edit mode.

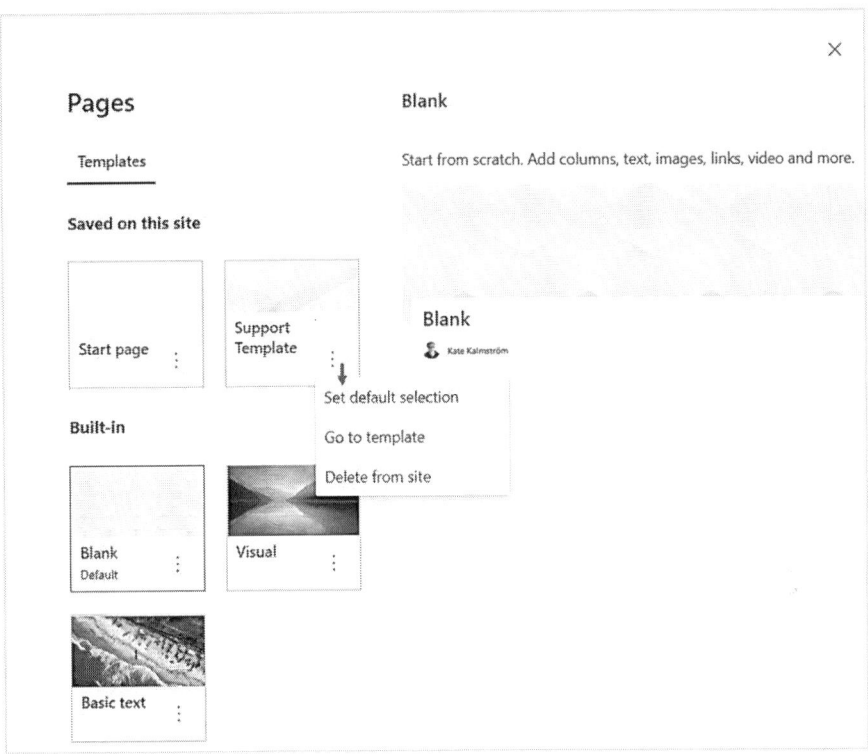

Microsoft is planning to add a new feature to the templates pane that will let authors create private drafts for pages and news posts. This draft will only be visible to site admins, the author and people who the author chooses to share the page with.

13.4.1.1   Save a Page as a Template

When you have created a page, you can let other people who have access to the site use your page as a template. When you do that, the template will show up among the other templates when users create new modern pages.

To save a page as a template, click on the 'Promote' button in the command bar when the page is in view mode and select the template option.

The 'Promote' right pane also opens automatically when you publish a page.

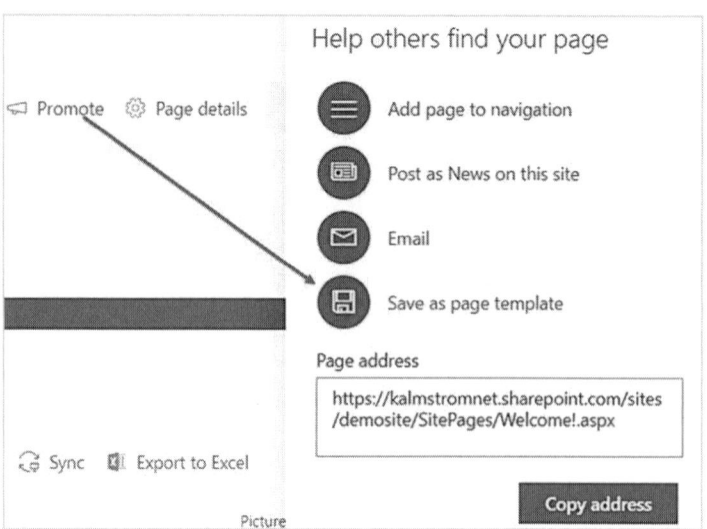
Picture

13.4.2 Edit and Publish a Modern Page

To open an existing modern page in edit mode, click on the Edit button to the right in the command bar. Pages will automatically get focus mode when they are edited, so that the header and navigation is not visible. Click on the focus icon if you want to exit focus mode.

When the page is open in edit mode, there will instead be a 'Publish' button to the right in the command bar. Use it to publish your modifications, so that other users can see them.

After the first publication, the button text is 'Republish' when you edit the page again.

The page in edit mode has a title area on top, a canvas for the web parts below the title area and a pane for web part editing that opens to the right. The command bar has an option to undo or redo recent modifications.

When the page has been published before, you can also select to discard all changes and go back to the earlier version of the page.

Use the 'Save as draft' button to see how the page looks for users or to continue working with the page on another occasion.

13.4.3 Title Area

There is no name giving when you create a modern page. Instead, you should change the text "Add a name" in the title area of the new page. That text will be used for automatic naming.

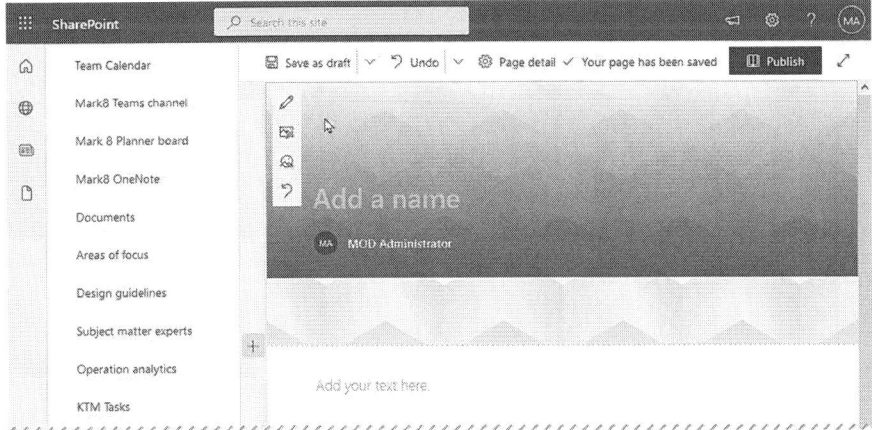

No styles can be applied in the title area, but there are some customization options.

A toolbar appears when you hover the mouse cursor over the top left corner of the title area, see the image above. Here, you can change the background image, set its focal point and reset the default image.

When you click on the edit icon in the title area toolbar, a right pane will open where you can make some modifications to the area.

Use the 'Plain' option if you don't want to use a background image at all.

The image to the right shows the options that are common for all the layout alternatives. Some of the layouts give more options: alternative text and background gradient.

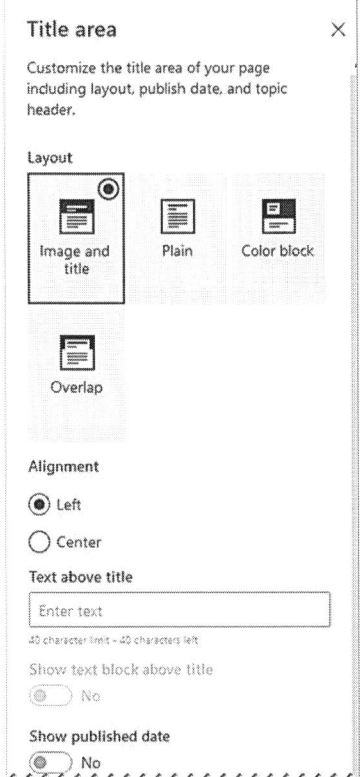

13.4.4 Comments

By default, modern pages that are not homepages have a Comments area at the bottom. You can hide it with the toggle to the right of the text 'Comments' when the page is in edit mode.   Comments 🔘 On

When a modern page is made into a homepage, the comments section will be disabled automatically on that page.

Administrators can disable the comments section for all modern pages. This is done in the SharePoint Admin center >Settings >Pages.

13.4.5 Sections

To organize the content on a modern page, you should use the sections feature to compose a nice-looking page. A page often has multiple sections, and each section can have its own color and layout.

To show the layout options, click on the plus sign to the left under the title area or under an existing section. The "One column" section is default.

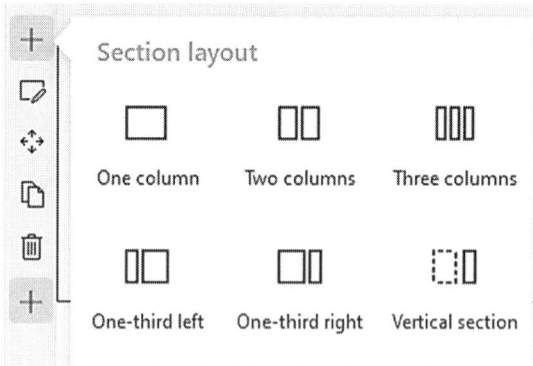

A section can have one, two or three columns. The web parts are placed inside the columns. When you put one web part in each column, a section can have one, two or three web parts. It is also possible to stack multiple web parts inside one column.

With the option 'Vertical section', you can add a new column to the right that will run along all the other sections.

The image above comes from a Team site. Communication sites have an additional option: a full-width column, where the layout expands to the full width of the page.

When you create a new page, SharePoint automatically adds a one column section with a text web part below the title area, but if no text is entered, the text web part will not be visible on the published page.

13.4.5.1 Edit Sections and Web Parts

When you have added a section, some icons will appear under the section plus sign to the left, *see* the image above.

- The Edit icon in the Section command bar opens a right pane with options for layout and background color. There are currently four colors to choose from.
- With the Move icon, you can drag the whole section up and down on the page.
- The Duplicate icon adds a section of the same kind below the original section.
- The waste basked icon deletes the section.

When you add web parts to the section columns, the same kind of icons will appear to the left of the web part when you select it. Here, the commands apply to the web part and not to the section. The content in the right Edit pane is different for each web part.

13.4.6 *Add Web Parts*

The modern page gives a choice of dedicated web parts that can be added to the page. Some modern web parts allow extensive customization, but many of them only have a few options.

When you have added a section to the page, it is time to start adding web parts to the section. Click on the plus sign in the middle of a column to show the web part selection dialog.

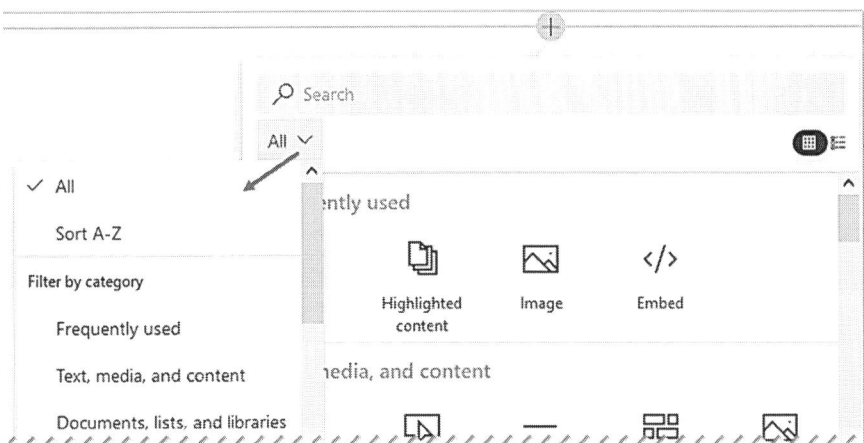

Start typing in the Search box to easily find the web part you are looking for. You can also search for web parts by category, and there is a toggle to switch between grid view and a list view with web part descriptions. Your most frequently used web parts will be shown on top.

Add the web part you prefer to the page by clicking on its icon in the grid view and the description in list view.

When you have added and edited the web part, you can add more web parts in the same section or add a new section to add more web parts below or above the first section.

You can also anytime add new sections and web parts between existing sections and web parts.

13.4.7 Add Content to Web Parts

Most web parts are empty until you fill them with a specified kind of content. This content is linked to the web part, not added directly on the page. All content is governed by permissions, so users will only see what they have access to.

When you upload content from your computer to a web part, everyone who has access to the page will also get access to the content from your computer. Uploaded content will be added to a "SitePages" folder in the site's "Site Assets" library. Each page will have its own folder inside the "SitePages" folder.

Most often, your changes to the web part will be saved automatically, but if you see an 'Apply' button at the bottom of the right Edit pane you should click on it!

In many web parts, the content is added in one of these ways:

- The web part opens with a field where the content, for example text or a link, can be added directly into the web part.
- The web part and the right Edit pane opens at the same time, so that you can customize the web part in the Edit pane.
- When you have clicked on the web part to add it to the page, a wide, right pane for location selection opens. Here you can find a menu to the left and content options to the right.

  Select a link in the left hand menu and then select the content you want to add from the main area to the right (except for the Upload option, which opens your File Explorer).

  The left Location menu is the same in most web parts. This means that you might get options that are not suitable for the web part you have chosen.

  - Recent
  - Stock images
  - Web search
  - OneDrive
  - Site
  - Upload
  - From a link

- The web part opens on the page, and you can add content by clicking on a button in the web part. When you do that, either the Location menu or the right Edit pane opens, so that you can make your choices.

You can always select the web part to display the left command bar, *see* above in 13.4.5.1, Edit Sections and Web Parts. Click on the pen icon to edit the web part or replace the content.

Some web parts can collect data from multiple sites or the whole tenant. In that case, it might take a while before all content is displayed in the web part, as it picks the data from the Search index.

13.4.7.1 Add an Image or File

When you want to add just one image to a page, you should use the Image web part, and for just one file you should use the File Viewer web part.

When you use these web parts, you don't need to add the web part to the page first. You can just drag the image or file to the canvas area when the page is in edit mode.

Drop the file when you see a line on the page. Now the Image or File viewer web part will be added automatically, filled with the image or file that you dragged to the page.

13.4.8 Web Part Examples

When this is written, Microsoft supplies 53 web parts to use with modern pages, and new web parts are published continuously. In addition to that, each tenant can have third party apps/add-ins that have been added to the organization's App Catalog and are available for the whole tenant.

Most web parts have names that tell what they can display, and they are not difficult to figure out. Therefore, I will not go into each of them here but just give some examples on how you can use modern web parts. I will also mention and describe several modern web parts in other chapters of this book.

Should you need assistance, Microsoft has a good online guide where most modern web parts are described in detail: https://support.office.com/en-us/article/Using-web-parts-on-SharePoint-Online-pages-336e8e92-3e2d-4298-ae01-d404bbe751e0

The web part setting options I describe in the sections below are set in the right pane that opens when you edit the web part.

13.4.8.1 365 Apps

Several 365 apps and services have their own modern web parts, where you can display content that has been created with the apps. Such web parts are Group calendar, Microsoft Forms, Microsoft Stream, Power BI and Yammer.

13.4.8.2 Button and Call to action

The Button and Call to action web parts let you create a button that loads the content you specify with a link.

13.4.8.3 Divider

The Divider web part is simply a vertical line that divides web parts. Its color follows the theme of the site, but you can control the length and to some extent also the thickness.

13.4.8.4 Document Library and List

The Document library and List web parts show the library or list you select (only from within the site and only the modern interface). These web parts don't have all the features that are present in the apps, but for many purposes the existing features are enough to work with the app.

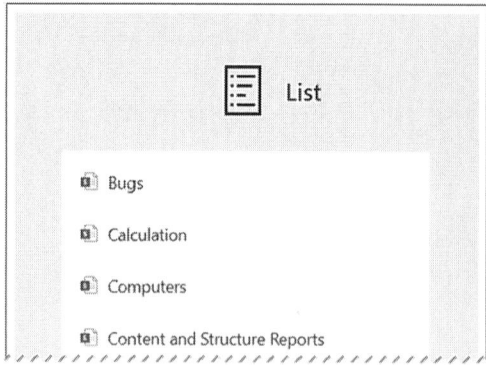

When you have added the web part to the page, the libraries or lists in the site will be displayed in the web part, so that you can select one of them to display.

In the Document library web part, all libraries in the site will show up for selection, not only document libraries. Therefore, you can add other kinds of libraries to this web part too, for example a Picture library, *refer to* 18.3.

With list apps, it is the other way around. As the modern web parts cannot display the classic app interface, you cannot add list apps built on the classic Tasks and Calendar templates. These apps only have the classic interface.

When you add a Document library or List web part to a page, files and items can be opened directly from the page. You can also do much other work without leaving the page. You can switch view and open the grid, and when you select an item and click on the Information icon, the right pane will open in edit mode so that you can edit the metadata.

New items can be created, and in the library web part, files can be uploaded or downloaded.

13.4.8.5 Events

The Events web part can show the contents of a calendar, also the classic calendar, from the site, from selected sites or from the whole tenant. When you use the site option, you can select a calendar to show. The other options give you a possibility to filter the calendars by category and/or date range. Recurring events are however not supported.

Events can be added to the calendar when the page has been published. When you click on '+ Add event' a new page will open where you can create the actual event. It will be placed in the current site's Events list.

The Title area in this page gets the date you select in the date picker below, and you can also add an image for the event. The page author can however disable images in the Events web part right pane.

If your location is recognized, you have the option to add a map, and you can add a link to an online meeting. If you don't enter anything in a field, it will not be visible in the saved event.

All events created this way will be visible in the calendar, and when users click on an event in the page, they can add that event to their personal Outlook calendar

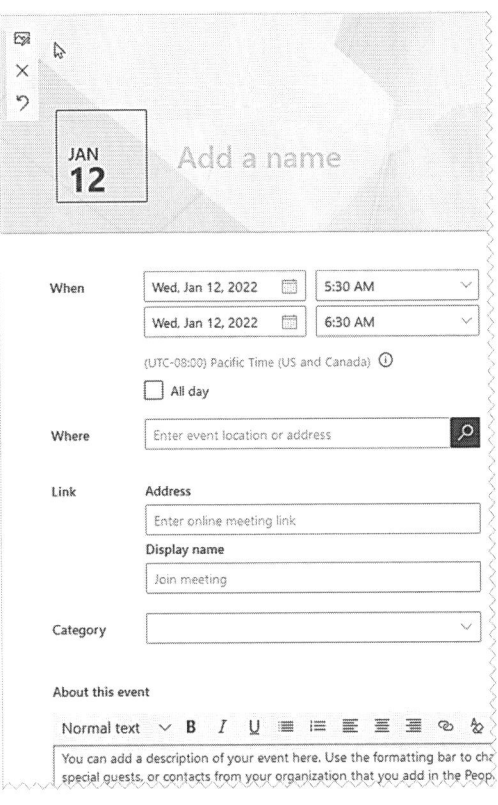

13.4.8.6 Hero

The Hero web part is especially striking in a Communication site with the full-width column, but you can add it to other modern pages too. In the Hero web part, you can add up to five items in tiles or layers and use images and text to draw attention to them.

Videos can also be added, but they are not played on the page. Instead, users are taken to the video player or link source when they click on the video tile.

The image above shows the Tiles layout, which lets you add a title on each item. In the Tiles layout, the height of the web part is scaled to follow an aspect ratio of 8:3, and images inside the web part scale to an aspect ratio of 4:3.

The Layers layout give room for a title and description beside each item. In the Layers layout, an individual layer scales to an aspect ratio of 8:3, and images inside each layer scale to an aspect ratio near 9:16.

In the right Edit pane for the Hero web part, you can select several layout options for both tiles and layers.

When you have chosen layout, add the items by clicking on the 'Select link' buttons. Then you can edit each item with the icons you see when you hover over a tile.

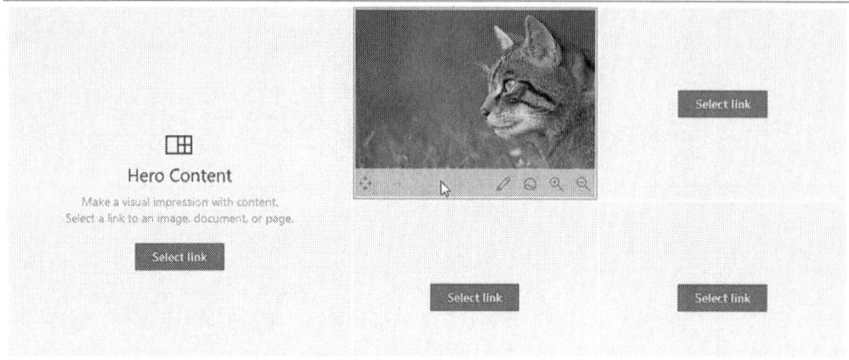

From left to right, the icons on the tiles let you:

- Open a right pane to edit the tile.
- Move the item. Select with the icon and then use Ctrl + left or right arrow to move.
- Set the focal point of the tile.
- Enlarge or decrease what is shown in the tile.

13.4.8.7 Highlighted Content

By default, the Highlighted content web part displays each user's most recently used content in the site, but in the right Edit pane you can customize what the web part should search for and display.

The Highlighted content web part can also filter and sort the items, and you can select layout and decide how many items should be displayed.

With the Highlighted Content web part, you are invited to specify source, content type (*refer to* chapter 25) and metadata, and the web part will show items according to that.

This means that if you don't want to show the default content, you must in some way narrow the search to display exactly the content you want to show. You can, for example:

- keep the content you wish to display in a specific document library
- select to show a certain kind of content type, for example videos or documents
- give a specific keyword to each item you want to include
- filter by a managed metadata, refer to 16.4, Term Store and Tagging.

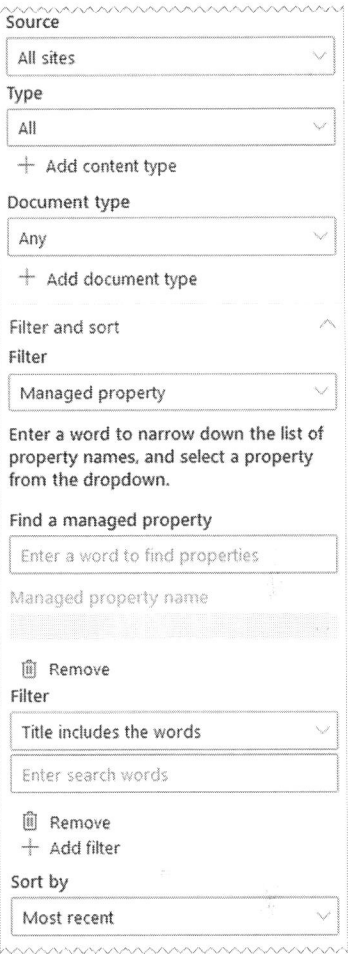

13.4.8.8   My Feed

The My feed web part shows relevant content from the whole tenant to each user. The feed is personal to each user, so each users sees different content.

In the My feed web part, you can for example see documents that are shared with you, a link that someone sent you by e-mail, Teams meetings (that you can join directly from the web part), suggested tasks or information about people that you work with.

The feed is populated with content as soon as you add it to a page. The only settings are the number of items to be shown and if news should be included.

13.4.8.9   Organization Chart

With the Organization chart web part, you can generate an organization chart centered on an individual.

253

When you have added the web part, enter any user and then select in the Edit pane how many levels to display.

Here, I show an image of how the chart looks when I add Miriam Graham to the web part. After publication, users can select any of the people in the chart, to see the people who report to that person.

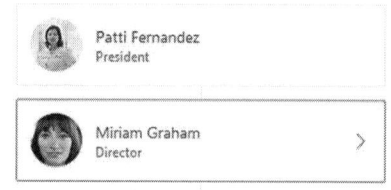

13.4.8.10   Spacer

The Spacer web part gives a horizontal space that divides sections or web parts. It is possible to change the size by dragging the bottom line up and down. You can also use the arrow keys.

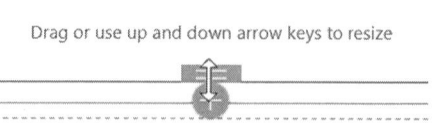

13.4.8.11   Text

The Text web part lets you add text, images, links and a simple 3x3 table. The text is automatically checked for spelling and grammar errors, and the images can be aligned to the left, right or center with text wrapping.

The Text web part has a toolbar above the text field. The image below shows the text web part in a one column section. If you choose another section layout, the text field and toolbar will resize dynamically to match the width. Then some of the tools will be found under an ellipsis to the right.

The Property pane icon far to the right in the toolbar, opens a right pane for text and table formatting. Here you can find some options that are not included in the toolbar, for example addition and removal of rows and columns in the table.

Under the 'Normal text' dropdown you can find various styles. When the page is published, the Heading 1 style gets a page anchor that becomes visible when you hover over the heading. If you right-click a page anchor, you can copy the page link with the addition of the hash sign (#) + the Heading 1 text.

You can add # + the Heading 1 text to any hyperlink in a modern page, to jump to a Heading 1 in a text web part in the same or another page.

https://m365x280293.sharepoint.com/SitePages/The-importance-of-branding-at-Contoso.aspx#branding

Demos:

https://www.kalmstrom.com/Tips/SharePoint-Online-Course/New-Page-Model-Intro.htm

https://www.kalmstrom.com/Tips/SharePoint-Online-Course/New-Page-Model-Highlighted.htm

13.4.9   *Page Details*

When you click on the Page details button in the command bar in a page in Edit mode, you can add a description and a custom thumbnail for the page. These will be shown in the SharePoint search results and news. You can also modify and copy the page URL, apply a label and delete the page.

Custom columns that have been added in the Site Pages library will be visible in the Page details, and you can add or modify the metadata here. Page owners can also delete the page.

When Audience Targeting has been enabled in the "Site Pages" library, *refer to* 15.5, you can enter an audience in the Page details right pane.

If scheduling has been enabled, *refer to* 13.1.5, the Site details pane has a scheduling option. Set the Scheduling toggle to On and click in the field to select a date and a time for the publishing.

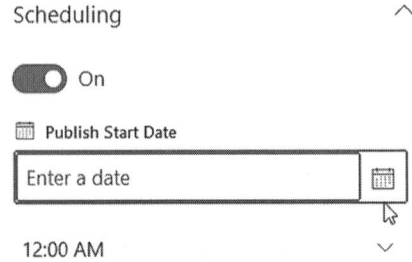

When the page has been published and is not in Edit mode, the Page details show the same information, and the label and the delete link are still active for the author.

Now you can also find a link to the Version history for the page. It opens the version history in the same pane, and here you can compare versions and restore or delete earlier versions of the page.

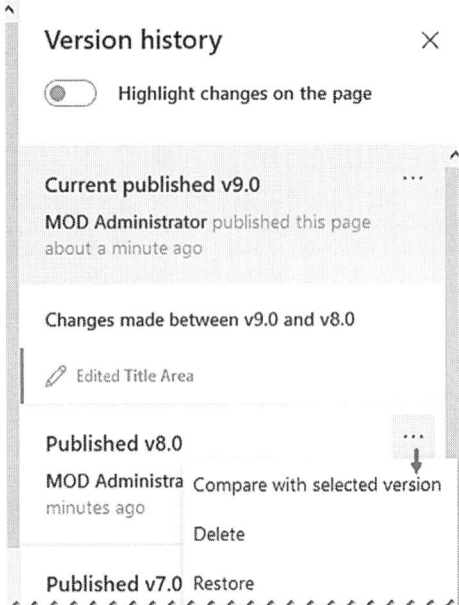

13.4.10 Promote a Page

The Promote right pane, gives several options for sharing information about the page. This pane opens when you publish a page and when you click on the 'Promote' button in the modern page command bar.

You can also promote the page via the e-mail button in the command bar. Also *refer to* 15.3.6, Modern Page Sharing Options.

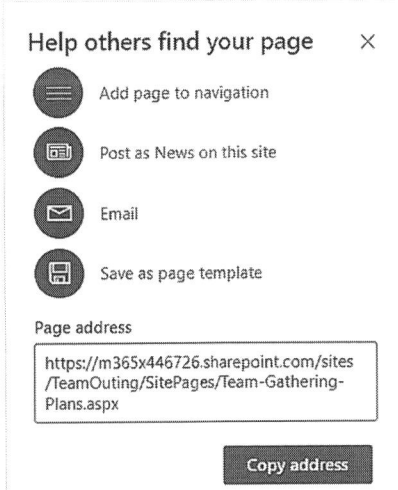

13.4.11   *The News Web Part*

When you add a News web part to a page, you only select the source(s) for the news and decide the layout. The actual content in the News web part comes when you and other users start creating news posts.

News posts can come from the site, from all sites in the hub or from one or more individual sites.

You can also choose the option 'Recommended for current user', which displays different posts for each user: from people the user works with, managers and connections and followed and frequently visited sites.

You can select from multiple layouts for the News web part. The default layout depends on what kind of modern site the page is created in.

By default, the News web part shows the news posts in the order they are published, with the most recent on the prominent place, but you can reorder them by drag and drop under 'News Order' in the right Edit pane. The News web part also has many other settings in the right pane.

A News web part is added to the site's homepage when you create a modern Group Team or Communication site.

13.4.11.1 Create a News Post

News posts are modern SharePoint pages. They are shown and can be managed in the "Site Pages" library, and they are created in the same way as other modern pages. The only difference is how you start creating them.

- News posts can be created from the SharePoint Online start page.

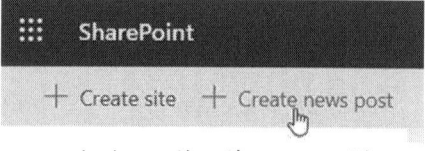

  A right pane will open, where you must select site where the news post should be posted. Then a blank modern page will open, and you can start creating the page with any web parts you wish to use.

  When you are done with creating your new post, click on 'Post news' to the right in the command bar to publish it.

  The news post will now be published to the site you selected and to other pages with a News web part that fetches news posts from that site.

- News posts can also be created from the '+ New' button in modern homepages and from the '+ Add' dropdown in pages with a News web part.

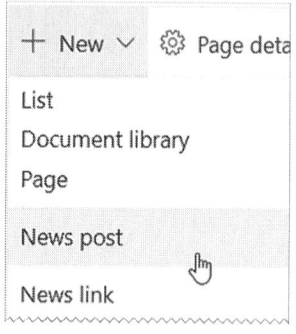

In these cases, you will have a possibility to select template before you start editing the page, but there is no site selection. The post will be published in the News web part on the current site and in other pages with a News web part that fetches news posts from that site.

Demo:

https://www.kalmstrom.com/Tips/SharePoint-Online-Course/New-Page-Model-News.htm

13.4.11.2 Create a News Link

As you see from the images above, it is also possible to add a news post via a link to content inside or outside the tenant. The content you link to will be displayed as a news post.

In this case, you don't have to create a new page. All the editing is performed in a right pane, which also has a 'Post' button.

When the link has been added, a preview of the content is loaded, and a title and a description are suggested. You can of course change the preview image and edit the title and description before you post the news.

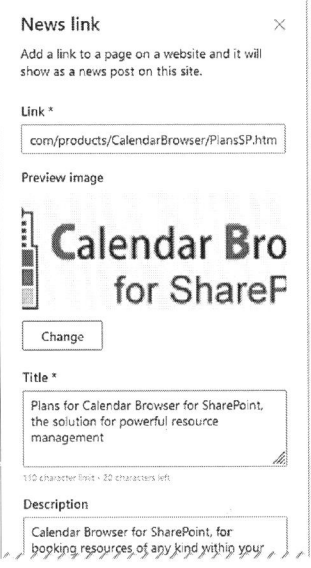

13.4.12 *Space*

Microsoft has recently introduced a new kind of modern page called Space. A Space page is very graphic, with a possibility to add 2D and 3D web parts and to rotate the page 360°.

When you understand how to create modern pages, the space pages are not difficult to figure out. Therefore, I will not go into spaces more deeply here.

Creation of space pages is enabled by default, but Site owners can disable Spaces under Site settings >Site Actions >Manage site features.

A space is created from the 'Space' command under the '+ New' button in modern homepages and "Site Pages" libraries. A right pane opens where you can give the space a name and description and select a structure.

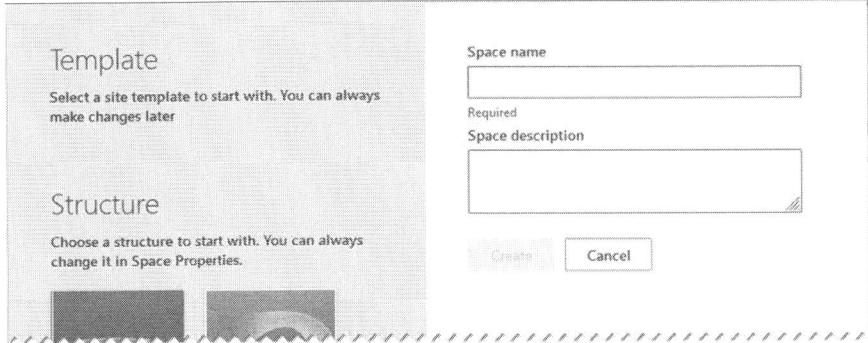

259

Now the space page opens in focus mode.

Click on 'Space design' in the command bar to continue the creation in a right pane. Here, you can add a background image, an ambient sound and an audio file with a recorded welcoming message.

Click on the plus sign in the top left corner of the page to select web parts. They are few, and some of them remind of the other modern web parts – but when you add them to the page, you will see a difference.

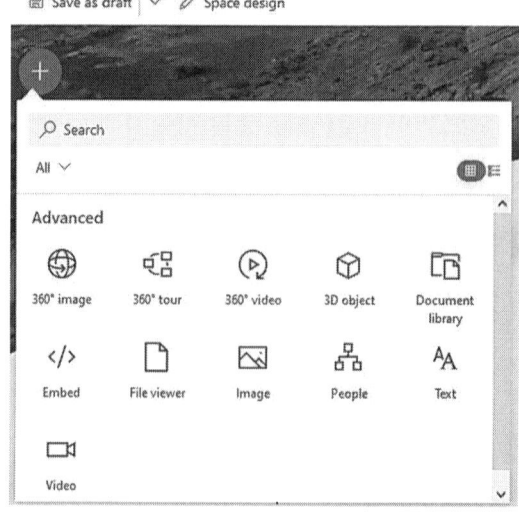

You can add the web parts anywhere around the 360° area, and they are minimized until you click on one of them to bring it to the front – as I have done with a document in the image below.

13.5 Customize a Wiki Page

The wiki page is the site page that gives the most customization possibilities. Here you can add text or links or insert images, videos etc. directly into the page or insert various kinds of web parts and customize them. Wiki pages can however only be created from the "Site pages" library in Team sites.

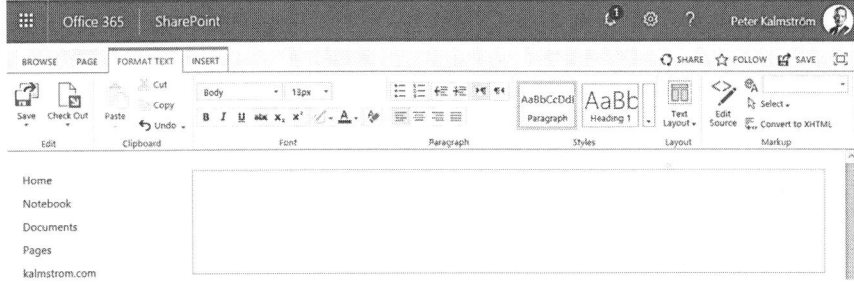

New wiki pages will open in edit mode. There are three ways to open an existing wiki page in edit mode:

- Click on the 'EDIT' button in the top right corner of the page.
- Click on the 'Edit' button under the ribbon 'PAGE' tab.
- Click on the 365 Settings icon and select 'Edit page'.

When the page opens in edit mode, the 'EDIT' button will be replaced with a 'SAVE' button. There is also a 'SAVE' button to the left under the 'PAGE' tab.

Wiki pages are coded in HTML, but various tools in the SharePoint ribbon make it easy to modify the pages and insert items. It is also easy to undo changes.

If you want to use HTML code, you should be aware that there are some restrictions in the use of CSS and JavaScript. Here I will only show how to reach the HTML code and instead focus on no-code customization with the SharePoint tools.

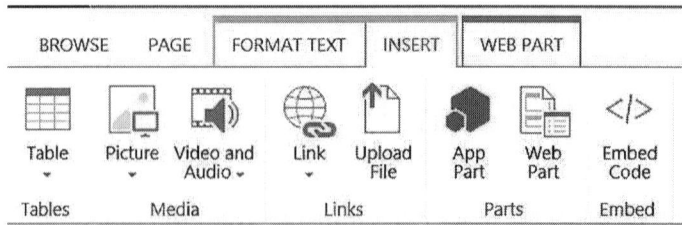

Besides customizing the wiki page directly, you can add web parts to the page and customize them.

13.5.1.1 Enter and Format Text

You can enter and format text in a wiki page just like you do in Word and other Office apps. Place the mouse cursor where you want to start typing or where you want to paste. Under the ribbon FORMAT TEXT tab, there are many options for text formatting.

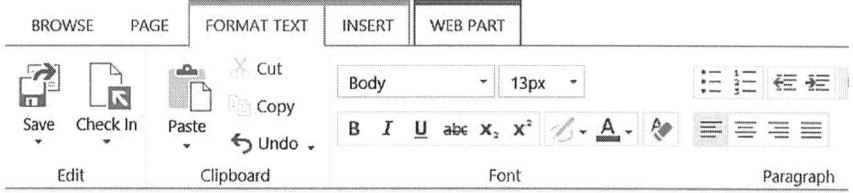

You can easily undo changes with the Undo button or with the Ctrl key + the Z key. Use Ctrl + Y to repeat.

Instead of using the controls in the 'Font' ribbon group, I would recommend that you use styles. The 'Styles' ribbon group is found further to the right under the FORMAT TEXT tab.

The styles are stored in a "Styles" library that is common for a site and all its subsites. It is a bit of work to edit the styles so that they become as you want them, but when the work is done the styles are there and can be used in other pages too.

The styles will give your SharePoint site a consistent look, and if you want to change something, you can just change the style. Then the change will be applied on all pages where that style is used.

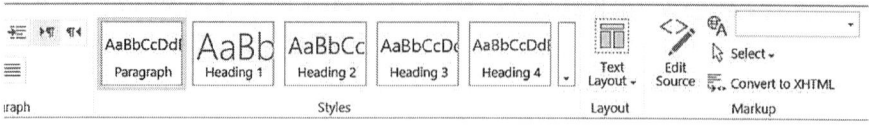

Demo:

https://www.kalmstrom.com/Tips/SharePoint-Online-Course/Start-Edit-Webpart.htm

262

13.5.1.2 Add a Table

It is not as easy as in Word, and there are not as many features, but it is quite possible and not very difficult to add a table to a SharePoint wiki page.

1. Under the INSERT tab, click on the Table button.
2. Select Insert Table to open a dialog OR use the grid below the button.

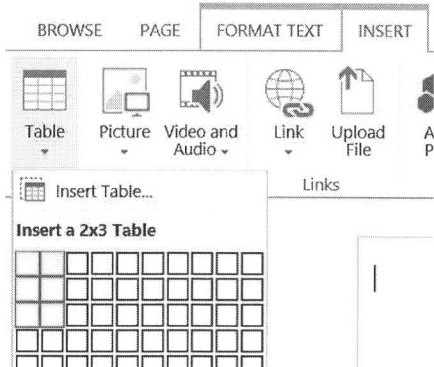

3. In the Insert Table dialog, enter the number of columns and rows you want the table to include, or drag the mouse over the preferred number of columns and rows in the grid.
4. When you click OK in the dialog or let go of the mouse, the table will be inserted into the page.

When you place the mouse cursor inside the table, two table tool tabs will be displayed: TABLE LAYOUT and DESIGN. Here you can edit the table.

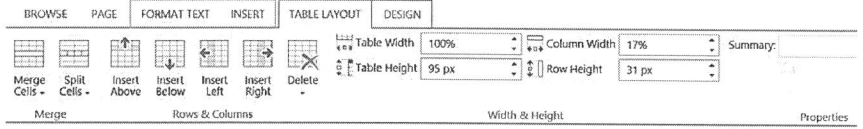

If you prefer to create the table in Word or another Office application, you can copy that table and paste it into the SharePoint wiki page.

Demo:

https://www.kalmstrom.com/Tips/SharePoint-Online-Course/Table.htm

13.5.1.3 Edit Source

Far to the right in the ribbon, under the FORMAT TEXT tab, you can find the 'Edit Source' button. This control opens the web part in HTML so that you can edit the code or paste code from another editor.

Note that only the code of the body is displayed, and there are some limitations when it comes to JavaScript and CSS. Also *refer to* chapter 26, CSS, JavaScript and RSS in Classic Pages.

263

13.5.1.4 Insert a Web Part

The classic web parts and app parts are found under the INSERT tab. Click on the button and select a category. Then select a web/app part and click on the Add button.

To edit the web part; *refer to* 13.5.3, Edit Classic Web Parts, below.

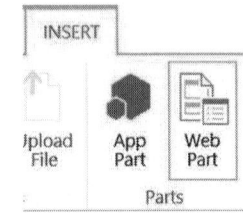

Modern sites have a more limited selection of classic web parts than the classic Team site. All web parts are kept when you add a Microsoft 365 group to a classic page.

13.5.1.5 Save

When you have finished editing the page, you must save it to keep the changes.

Click on the SAVE link on the top right of the page. You can also click on the Save button under the ribbon PAGE and FORMAT TEXT tabs.

The Save button has more options. Use the Stop Editing option when you want to discard your changes.

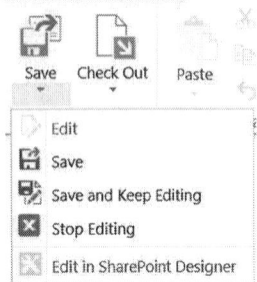

13.5.1.6 The Get Started Web Part

When you create a classic team site, the home page is a wiki page. It has a "Get started with your site" web part with five links displayed as tiles, so called promoted links.

The "Get started with your site" web part is the only web part you can delete without first opening the page in edit mode, and that is because Microsoft has given a "REMOVE THIS" link for removal of the Get Started web part.

If you want to have the Get Started web part back again, you need to add it like you add other web parts to a wiki page.

Demo:

https://kalmstrom.com/Tips/SharePoint-Online-Course/Get-Started-Web-Part.htm

13.5.2 *Edit a Web Part Page*

In web part pages the customization is not done freely, as in the wiki pages, because it is not possible to simply type directly into a web part page. Instead, the customization is structured with web part zones.

Web part pages can only be created from the "Site pages" library in Team sites. When you create a web part page, you will have a choice of layouts, with different options for header, footer, columns and body.

Choose a Layout Template:

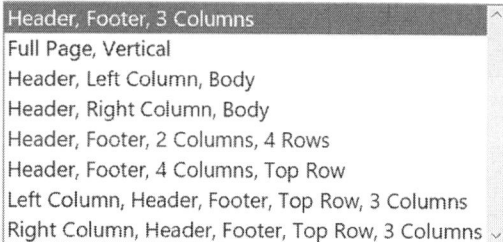

To open a web part page in edit mode, click on the 365 Settings icon and select 'Edit page'. This is the same as the third option for opening wiki pages in edit mode, see above.

The page will open in edit mode. It will now have a 'Stop Editing' button under the ribbon 'PAGE' tab, and the page will be saved automatically when you click on that button.

13.5.2.1 Add a Web Part to a Web Part Page

Web part pages have an 'Add a Web Part' link on top of each web part zone, and the web part page is often published instead of saved. Otherwise, the steps to add web parts in a web part page are like the steps for the wiki page.

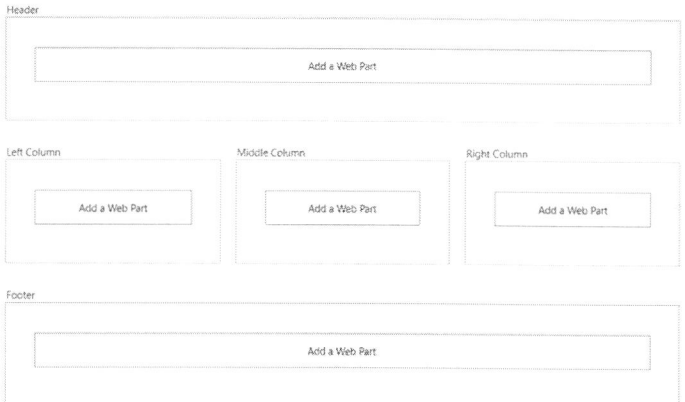

13.5.3 Edit Classic Web Parts

Wiki and web part pages use the same kind of web parts, and those can be edited and highly customized.

Modify the classic web part properties by clicking on the arrow in the top right corner of the web part and selecting 'Edit Web Part'.

Here you can also delete and minimize the web part, and some web parts can be exported to your computer.

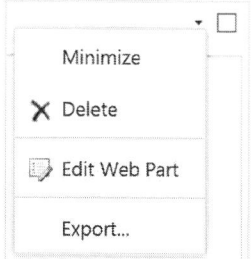

265

Another way to reach the Edit Web Part command is to open the WEB PART tab in the ribbon and click on the 'Web Part Properties' button.

The 'Edit Web Part' pane is shown to the right of the web part and has the name of the web part in the top banner. These panes look different for each web part, but all of them have multiple options. The image to the right shows the pane for a "Documents" web part.

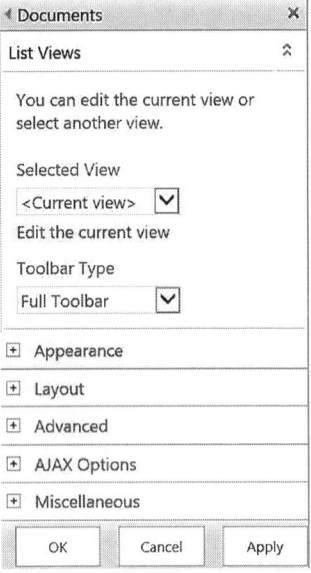

Most web parts require that you press OK or Apply to save the web part property modifications. Otherwise, the changes will not be saved when you save the page.

Below, I will give one example of an app part and one example of a web part, but later in this book you will find more examples.

13.5.3.1 The Content Editor Web Part

In SharePoint 2007 and earlier, the Content Editor web part was the only way to insert text, images and so on in a web page, and it still works in the same way.

The most common reason for using the Content Editor web part in a web part page, is to give a web part page the same features as a wiki page. That is because the Content Editor ribbon gives the same options as you get in wiki pages without adding a web part.

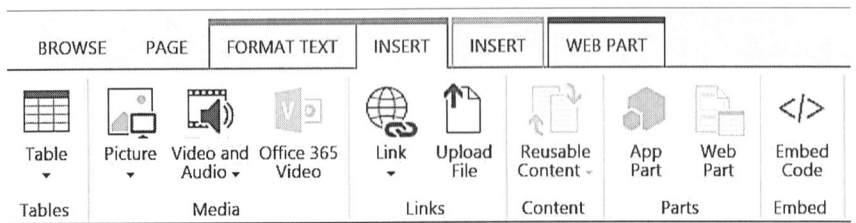

Therefore, if nothing else is mentioned, when I just say classic pages in this book, I refer to wiki pages as well as web part pages where the Content Editor web part has been added.

There are however reasons to use the Content Editor web part in wiki pages too. You can for example add JavaScript and CSS to a page with the Content Editor, something that cannot be done directly in a wiki page.

The Content Editor web part is only available in classic Team sites, with or without a Microsoft 365 group.

Demo:

https://kalmstrom.com/Tips/SharePoint-Online-Course/Content-Editor-Intro.htm

13.5.3.2 Add a Web Part to a Form

Maybe you want to add something on the new item form page that is not part of the form itself, for example information on how the form should be filled out? That can be done by adding a web part to the list form page. This method is only possible with the **classic** app interface, and only with list apps. Libraries do not open a form page when you click on 'new'.

Note: If you use the classic interface to edit the form in the way described below it will not be possible to switch to the modern interface.

The classic SharePoint list forms are contained in web part pages, and the existing web parts cannot be customized without extensive coding. You can however add other web parts on top of the web part that contains the app, and I would recommend the Content Editor web part.

In the Content Editor web part, you can embed code and add tables, links, pictures, videos or even another web part, so this is the only no-code way to show for example an instruction or a video above the new item form.

The classic experience has three item forms: New, Display and Edit. In the steps below, I will describe how to add a web part to the New form. That web part will only be visible in the new item form, not in the Display or Edit forms.

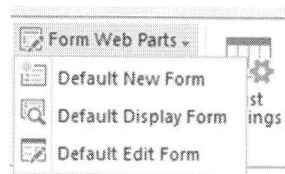

You can either select the form under the LIST tab in the ribbon or just open the form you want to edit.

1. When the page is in Edit mode, add the Content Editor web part from the Media & Content category.

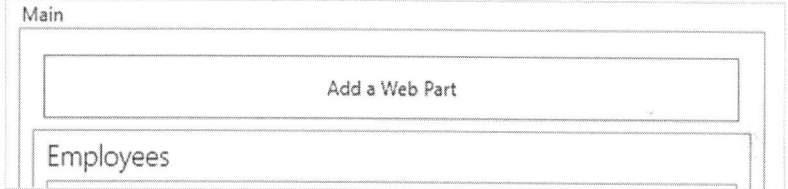

2. Add the content you wish to add from the options under the ribbon tabs.
3. Edit the web part and set the Chrome Type to None to avoid having the Content Editor caption on the web part.
4. Click on the 'Stop Editing' button.

Demo:

https://kalmstrom.com/Tips/SharePoint-Online-Course/SharePoint-Forms-Browser.htm

13.5.3.3 The Calendar App Part

When you have created a team calendar, you probably want to display it on a page, maybe on the homepage of the Team site, instead of having it as a separate list. To do that, you can insert a calendar app part in a classic page.

(Modern pages have a Group Calendar web part, but it can only be used for calendars belonging to a Microsoft 365 Group. There is currently no other possibility to add a calendar app to a modern page. However, the modern calendar view, *refer to* 7.9.4, Modern "New View" Options, can be selected when you add a List web part to a modern page.)

Demo:

https://www.kalmstrom.com/Tips/SharePoint-Online-Course/Calendar-App.htm

13.6   PAGE DIAGNOSTICS

At https://docs.microsoft.com/en-us/microsoft-365/enterprise/page-diagnostics-for-spo you can find information about and download links to a tool that helps you run a diagnostic check before you publish a SharePoint Online site page.

The tool is available for the browser Microsoft Edge and Google Chrome, and it can be used on both modern and classic site pages. It gives information about possible issues and loading speed.

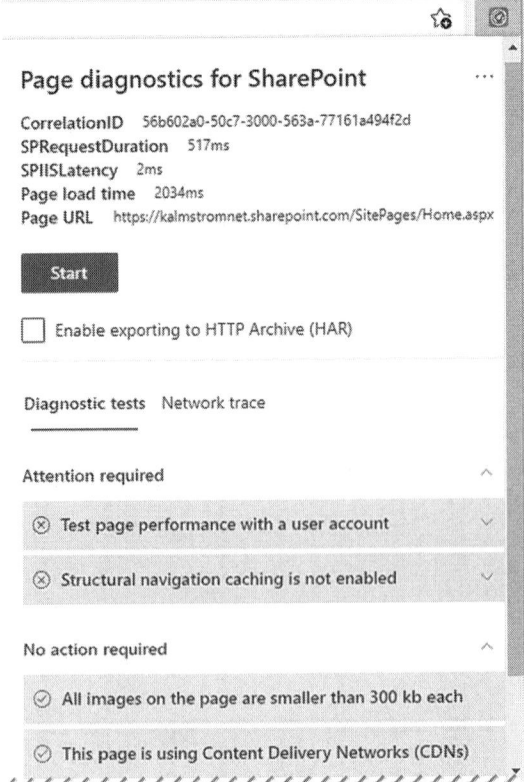

If you use the site scheduler, *refer to* 6.4.5.4, Schedule Site Launch, you need to first run the diagnostics tool on the site's homepage.

268

13.7 ADD FILES TO PAGES

Shared documents should be kept in one place, so that you don't need to change in several places when a document must be edited.

Therefore, it is a bad idea to upload the same document to multiple libraries. It is better to add the file to pages in those sites, because when you do that, they will be updated automatically when the file is updated in the library.

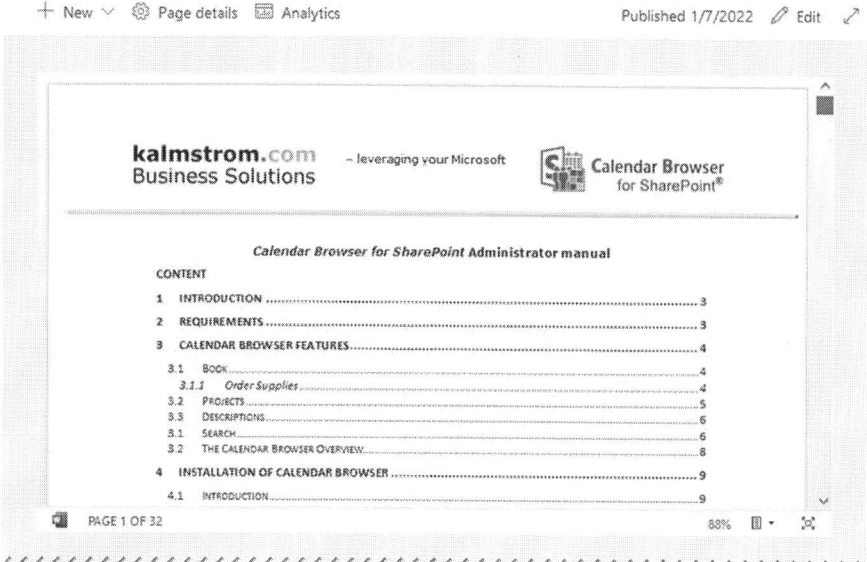

I would recommend that you add an Enterprise Keywords column, *refer to* 16.4.5, to SharePoint libraries that contain files you want to share between sites. This makes the files easy to find in filtering and search.

13.7.1   Add One File to a Page

Modern pages have two web parts that are suitable for showing one specific file embedding: File viewer and Embed.

- The File viewer web part can only show content from inside the tenant.
- The Embed web part can show content from a range of common sites. Site administrators can however control this embedding under Site settings >HTML Field Security.

In **classic** pages, a file can be embedded with its embed code.

13.7.1.1   File Viewer

The **modern** File viewer web part lets you add files from sources within the tenant that you have access to without using an embed code. You can add the File viewer web part to a page in two ways.

- Drag the file to the page. It will be automatically contained in a File viewer web part.
- Add the File viewer web part to the page. Now you can select a file from your recently used files, from your OneDrive, from the current site or from your computer. You can also link to a file anywhere in OneDrive or SharePoint Online.

  Use the link option when you want to display a file from another site. When you have the link to the file, you can add any file that you have access to from the SharePoint tenant, and as we have seen in 9.4, Find a File Link, you can easily get these links in the library where the file is stored.

The File viewer web part can only display a file that is stored in SharePoint Online or OneDrive for Business. When you select to upload a file to the File viewer web part, it will be saved in the site's Site Assets library.

Excel, Word, PowerPoint, Visio, PDFs, video files and 3D models are among the supported files. Images embedded in other files, like in a slideshow, are displayed, but image files are currently not supported by the File Viewer web part.

If you update an Office file that is displayed in the File viewer web part, it will be updated on the modern page automatically.

When you add Office files to a File viewer web part, they get a small toolbar when you hover the mouse over the bottom right corner of the web part, *see* the image to the right. Click on the menu icon to view the options.

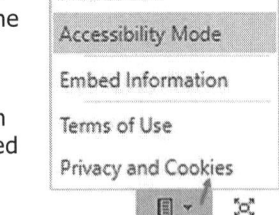

PFD files get another toolbar, and here the "Open in new window" icon to the right is important. You need to use it to be able to print the file.

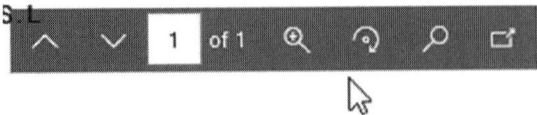

In the Edge browser, Word files have an additional toolbar above the file. If the toolbar is not pinned, you can click inside the file on the page to show it.

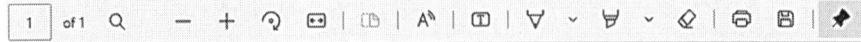

This toolbar gives multiple options for work with the file directly on the page. Each icon has a tooltip that explains its function.

The Save icon saves the file in PDF format to your computer. You can save any drawings or highlights that you make on the file to your computer, but not back to the file's online storage place.

13.7.1.2 Modern Embed

Sometimes the modern Embed web part accepts a link, but I have found that an embed code that starts with <iframe>works best. Many sites give such code snippets, so look for "Embed code" or the "</>" icon if you want to embed content from a website.

Refer to section 9.2.4, Other Unique Features, for information on how to get the embed code for Word and PowerPoint files.

13.7.1.3 Classic Embed

To embed a file in a wiki page you need the embed code. Open the page in edit mode and click on the 'Embed Code' button under the INSERT tab. Paste the embed code into the form (and modify it if needed) and click on 'Insert'.

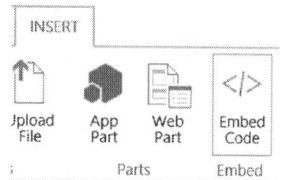

13.7.1.4 The No Access Issue

When you add files to SharePoint pages to share them, you need to consider how a file is displayed to users who don't have access to it.

SharePoint only shows content to those who have permissions to see it. Normally, all site members have access to all files in the site, but if the file is stored in another site, there might be a problem. Therefore, you should always consider how the page will look for people who have access to the page but not to all the shared files.

All the methods for adding one file to a page will show the web part even to users who don't have access to the file. Instead of the file, users without permission to view it will have an Access Denied message and a possibility to request access.

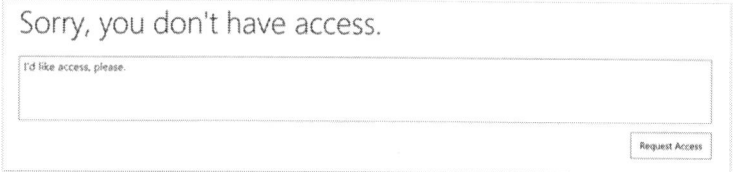

13.7.2 *Add Multiple Files to a Page*

You can add a library in a web part in both modern and classic pages, and this is a good solution if you have relevant files there and want users to be able to work with them directly from the page.

When you want to add selected files from different libraries to a page, some additional planning is necessary, because the files need to have some common categorization to be able to search. You can for example set the web part to pick files that are tagged with certain keywords, *refer to* 16.4, Term Store and Tagging.

271

An advantage with showing multiple files in a web part, is that there are no "access denied" messages. Users will only see the files they have access to, and the web part adapts better in size than the one file web parts.

13.7.2.1 Modern Highlighted Content Method

We have already met the Highlighted content web part in section 13.4.8.7, and if you combine it with Managed Metadata columns in the libraries that contain the files you want to display, you can make this web part show relevant documents.

13.7.2.2 Classic Content Search Method

With the Content Search web part, you can quickly gather files from several sites to one classic page. In this example, the web part gives links to all files that are tagged with a certain keyword. Note that this is a **classic** web part that only can be used in classic sites.

1. Edit the web part and set the query in the Query Builder to show only documents that are tagged in a certain way.
   a. Select the query 'Items matching a tag (System)'.
   b. Select to not restrict the results by app if you want to have files from the whole tenant.
   c. Restrict the results by tag and enter the tag you wish to use.
   d. Click OK.
2. Define the other settings for the web part and click on Apply.
3. Publish or Save the page.

Demo:

https://kalmstrom.com/Tips/SharePoint-Online-Course/Share-Docs-Between-Collections.htm

13.8 PAGES INSTEAD OF DOCUMENTS

The easiest way to share documents is of course to just upload them to a document library, but there is a more elegant way: pages. I will give an example of how pages can be used instead of documents. Pages are easier to read than documents, and pages load much quicker than documents and can be more interactive, containing videos etc.

To use this method, add the content of each document on a separate page and link to those pages from the Site navigation. This can be done with modern pages as well as with wiki pages.

Most organizations have documents for company guidelines that should be shared among users. Therefore, I have used company guidelines as document examples here, but the method can of course be used for all kinds of content.

1. Create a new site for the guidelines.

2. Create a new page and give it the same name as one of the guideline documents.
3. Add the document, or the content of the document, to the page.
4. (Add additional content if needed.)
5. Repeat step 2-4 for all documents.
6. Remove all links from the Site navigation.
7. Add links to the guideline pages in the Site navigation instead.
   a. Open the Site contents and then the "Site Pages" library.
   b. Click on 'Edit' at the bottom of the Site navigation and then on 'Edit Links'.
      o When the "Site Pages" library has the modern interface, select one of the pages and click on 'Add to navigation' in the command bar. That page will now get a link in the Site navigation.
      o In the **classic** experience, click on 'Edit links' at the bottom of the Site navigation and drag and drop a page file to the navigation.
   c. Repeat the addition to the navigation for each page.

The site should have a suitable homepage, and for that you can either customize the default homepage or make one of the guidelines pages the homepage, *refer to* 13.1.7, Set a Page as Homepage.

Demo:

https://www.kalmstrom.com/Tips/SharePoint-Online-Course/Company-Guidelines.htm

13.9 SUMMARY

This chapter has explained the difference between the three types of site pages, and now you should be able to recognize and start customizing all three of them. You should also be able to judge which kind of page will be best in each case, when you need to create a new page.

You have also learned how to find the "Site Pages" library, where you can manage the settings for all pages in a site.

We have looked at both classic and modern web parts, and I have described how to set a page as homepage. Finally, I have given examples on how files can be shared via pages and how pages can be used instead of documents.

For more information about web parts, *refer to* chapter 19, Connect Web Parts. I will also give examples on page customization in other chapters later in this book.

Now it is high time to look at the SharePoint permissions. When you share content, it is important to consider the permissions you give, so after the chapter with general permission information follows a chapter about sharing.

14 PERMISSIONS

All SharePoint content is governed by permissions. If the permissions are set correctly, users will never see anything that they don't have access to, and they can never do anything they should not be allowed to do.

For this ideal situation to come true, it is important that SharePoint administrators and site owners understand how permissions are set and inherited.

SharePoint permissions are very easy to use when you accept the default settings. That can work for a small team, but if you want to have more control over what users can see and do, SharePoint permissions get more complex.

However, when you understand how the SharePoint permissions work, you can also take advantage of the benefits they give. That is what we will study in this chapter.

We will start with the basic site permission settings. These are more easily accessed and used, especially in the modern experience, and for many organizations, these basic permissions are quite enough. After that, I will introduce some more advanced features that mostly are valid for classic sites.

14.1 SITE PERMISSIONS AND INHERITANCE

SharePoint pages, apps, subsites and items, by default inherit the same permissions as the higher level. This means that subsites inherit the same permissions as the root site, apps inherit the site permissions – and pages and other items inherit the app permissions.

- Site collections
  - Sites
    - Lists and Libraries
      - Items

Therefore, users who have Edit permission on a site, by default also have Edit permission on all apps in that site, and they even have Edit permission on all items in each app – if you don't break the inheritance, *refer to* 14.5.

For permissions on apps and app items, also *refer to* the next chapter, Sharing.

14.1.1 Default Site Permissions

As permissions are inherited within a site if you don't do something to change that, it is important to understand the default permission level for different site types:

- For Communication sites and modern Team sites without a group, the default permission option is Read.

- For classic Team sites and modern Group Team sites, the default option is Edit. The default tenant Root site also has Edit permission for all users.

As you see, the default permissions are extensive for Team sites, but site owners can restrict the options, and Global and SharePoint administrators can restrict the options for the tenant in the SharePoint Admin center >Policies. Site settings can never allow more than what is set in the tenant settings.

Global and SharePoint administrators can also restrict permissions for single sites under Active sites in the SharePoint Admin center.

14.1.2   *SharePoint Groups*

The permission levels in SharePoint are packages of connected permissions. Users who have the same permission *on a site* belong to the same permission group, also called SharePoint group. When you create a site, SharePoint automatically creates a set of SharePoint groups for that site.

Note that a SharePoint group is not the same as a Microsoft 365 Group. In a Microsoft 365 Group, colleagues share several resources and work together on them.

A SharePoint Group has no other purpose or features then being a container for users with the same permission. The SharePoint group can very well have Edit permission on one site and Read permission on another site, but this applies to everyone in the group.

These are some of the more common SharePoint groups:

- Site owners have Full control over the site's content and can do anything with it – except perform actions that have been forbidden in the SharePoint or Microsoft Admin centers.

  By default, Site admins and Site owners are the same people, but that can be changed in the SharePoint Admin center >Site actions. If a separate Site admin is appointed, the Site owner still has full control over all content in the site, but there are some technical limitations.

- Site members have Edit permission, which means that they can view, add, update and delete apps, items and folders in a site.

- Site visitors have Read permission. They can only view pages and items, but they can download files.

In **modern** sites, you can set and change site permission for people directly on a site or in an app. When you do that, you normally use one of the pre-defined SharePoint groups.

People or groups who have access to a modern site can have either Full control (Owners), Edit (Members) or Read (Visitors) permission over the site's content. (Classic sites can have more levels.)

In the modern experience, you can see the SharePoint groups and their members under the Settings icon >Site permissions.

When you expand a SharePoint group in Communication sites and Team sites without a group, you can see all members of that group.

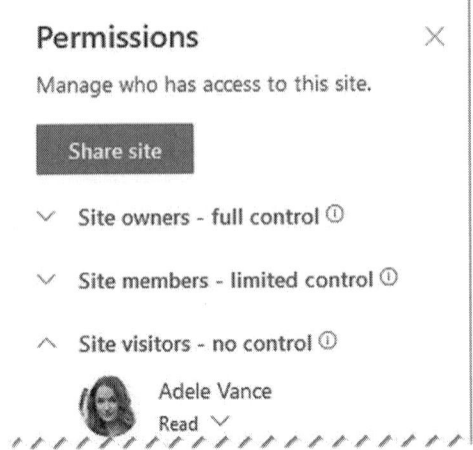

In Group Team sites, you will at first only see the Microsoft 365 group, not the individual members. This way, you can change the permission level for the whole group.

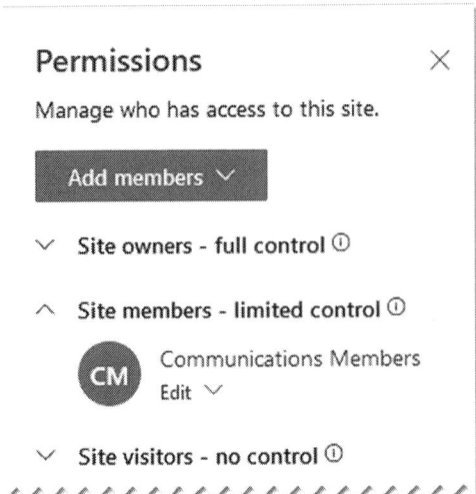

When you click on the group icon, a dialog with member information will open.

Refer to 15.2.5, Manage Site Members in the Modern Experience, for detailed information on how to change site user permissions.

In the classic interface, you need to use the Site settings page to change the permissions, *refer to* 14.4.2, Modify Permissions.

14.2 Permission Level Considerations

As we saw in chapter 3, the tenant's administrator roles are defined in the Microsoft 365 Admin center.

Permissions for other users are set in the sites, and as mentioned above, the default permission is Edit in some site types.

The Edit permission allows users to do a lot in SharePoint even if they don't have access to admin centers. They can view, add, update and delete items, and they can also add, edit and delete whole apps, as well as create, edit and delete columns and public views. It is important that you are aware of this, so that you can decide if you should keep the default permission or change it.

In my opinion, Edit is a high default permission level. It gives users the ability to do a lot of damage to the site. They can for example delete an entire app, maliciously or by accident. The app can be restored, but it still means extra trouble.

I recommend that you always consider permission levels and give users the lowest permission required for them to do their jobs.

In contradiction to the above, I would also urge that you consider what users will do if they do *not* have enough permissions in SharePoint. Instead of creating a new document library, they will create a new file folder, instead of creating a new view they will export the data to Excel to make summaries, instead of using external sharing they will e-mail a copy of a file etc.

To do the correct thing, users must have both the right knowledge and the right permissions. Your goal as a SharePoint administrator should be to make it easy for users to do the right thing.

14.3 Security Groups

For easier permission management, I would recommend that you create Security groups of people who should have the same permission level.

As we saw above, a SharePoint group is a group of people who have the same permissions on a specific site. A security group, on the other hand, can be used in multiple sites and have different permission levels on different sites – but everyone in the group has the same permission.

Security groups are created in the Microsoft 365 Admin center and can be used in the whole tenant. This simplifies the management, for example when you want to give people access to several sites.

Technically a Security Group is not stored in SharePoint but in Azure (AD) Active Directory.

Security groups show up among the user accounts when you start typing a name and when you give permissions, so it is much quicker to add a security group to a SharePoint group in a site than to add each user separately.

14.3.1 Create a New Security Group

Security groups are created in the Microsoft 365 Admin center >Teams & groups >Active teams & groups. Here you can see and manage all the tenant's different groups, and you can also create new groups.

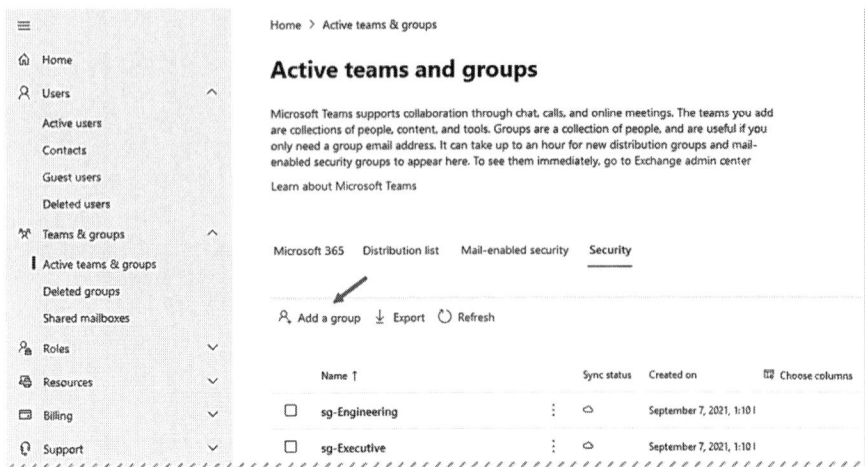

1. Click on the '+ Add a group' button.
2. Select the Security group and click on 'Next'.
3. Give the group a name and a description and click on 'Next'.
4. Review the details and click on 'Create group' when everything is good.
5. To add group members, select the new security group in the list of active groups. (It might take a few minutes from creation until the group is displayed in the list.) A right pane will open, and here you can add owners and members to the group.
6. At first the group has no owners, so there is a 'Add group owners' button under the General tab.
7. When you have added at least one group owner, you can add members of the security group under the Members tab. It is also here you can manage both owners and members.

Sales Agents

Security group • 2 owners • 4 members

General   Members

Owners (2)

Allan Deyoung
AllanD@M365x446726.OnMicrosoft.com

Christie Cline
ChristieC@M365x446726.OnMicrosoft.com

View all and manage owners

Members (4)

Allan Deyoung
AllanD@M365x446726.OnMicrosoft.com

Cameron White
CameronW@M365x446726.OnMicrosoft.com

Chris Green
chris@M365x446726.onmicrosoft.com

Ben Andrews
ben@M365x446726.onmicrosoft.com

View all and manage members

The new Security group will show up among other groups when you add members to a site.

Add users, Microsoft 365 Groups, or security groups to give them access to the site.

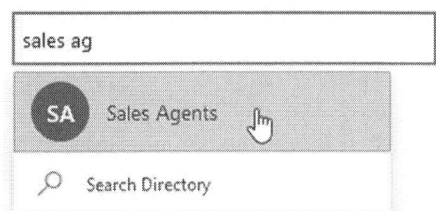

Set the permission level for the Security group in the same way as you do with single users. That will give all owners and members of the security group the selected permission level on that site.

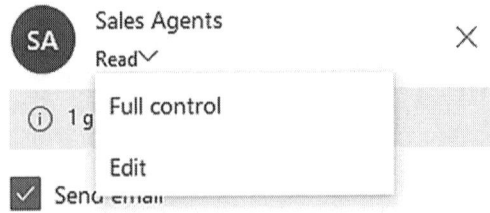

You can add new users to a Security group anytime. They will then have all permissions given to that group on different sites.

Accordingly, when you remove a user from a security group, that user will lose all permissions connected to the group.

Demo:

https://kalmstrom.com/Tips/SharePoint-Online-Course/SharePoint-Permissions.htm

14.4 CLASSIC PERMISSIONS SETTINGS

Advanced permissions management for a site, app, page or item is performed in the Site settings. You can reach these settings in several ways:

- For a site, open the Site settings and select 'Site permissions' under the Users and Permissions heading.
- The permission settings can also be reached from the link 'Advanced permission settings' in the right Permissions pane in **modern** sites. (This link is the only option for modern Group Team sites, as these sites do not have the link in the Site settings page.)
- Finally, the ADVANCED link in the **classic** Share dialog, *see* next chapter, Sharing, points to the advanced permission settings.

The image below shows the Permissions page for a site. The permissions pages for other content looks the same, but they don't have as many commands in the ribbon.

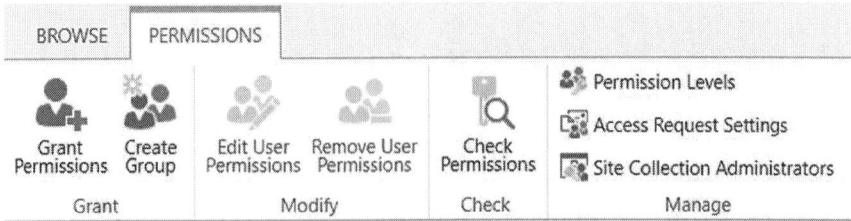

In all permissions pages, you can check the permission for each team member or group by clicking on the 'Check Permission' button in the ribbon and enter the name of the person or group.

Instead of adding and removing members from the site interface, you can manage SharePoint group memberships from the Site settings >People and

Groups in all sites except Group Team sites. The Microsoft 365 Group is instead managed from Outlook.

Modern sites are designed to work with the three default SharePoint groups and their default permission levels, but if you use anything but Full control, Edit and Read, the modern site permissions pane and Share buttons will not work well.

Therefore, what I suggest below is primarily intended for **classic sites and the classic interface**.

14.4.1 Permissions Levels

When you click on the 'Permission Levels' button under the 'PERMISSIONS' tab in the Permissions page for a site, you can see what the different levels give users permission to do.

It is possible to edit the permission levels, but I would recommend that you don't do that even for classic sites. It is safer to create your own custom permission levels, see below.

You can also remove levels on this page, but think twice before you do that, and test three times in a non-production site!

Permissions › Permission Levels ⓘ

Add a Permission Level | ✗ Delete Selected Permission Levels

Permission Level	Description
Full Control	Has full control.
Design	Can view, add, update, delete, approve, and customize.
Edit	Can add, edit and delete lists; can view, add, update and delete list items and documents.
Contribute	Can view, add, update, and delete list items and documents.
Read	Can view pages and list items and download documents.
Limited Access	Can view specific lists, document libraries, list items, folders, or documents when given permissions.
View Only	Can view pages, list items, and documents. Document types with server-side file handlers can be viewed in the browser but not downloaded.
Approve	Can edit and approve pages, list items, and documents.
Manage Hierarchy	Can create sites and edit pages, list items, and documents.
Restricted Read	Can view pages and documents, but cannot view historical versions or user permissions.
Restricted Interfaces for Translation	Can open lists and folders, and use remote interfaces.

14.4.1.1 Custom Permission Level

If none of the pre-defined levels fit, you can easily create your own permission level, but once again this does not work well with modern sites.

In a classic site, click on 'Add a Permission Level' in the Permission Levels page, and a new page will open where you can select what the new permission level should allow. One such commonly requested permission level is "Add but not delete".

List Permissions
- ☐ Manage Lists - Create and delete lists, add or remove columns in a list, and add or remove public views of a list.
- ☐ Override List Behaviors - Discard or check in a document which is checked out to another user, and change or override settings which allow users to read/edit only their own items
- ☐ Add Items - Add items to lists and add documents to document libraries.
- ☐ Edit Items - Edit items in lists, edit documents in document libraries, and customize Web Part Pages in document libraries.
- ☐ Delete Items - Delete items from a list and documents from a document library.

When you have created the new permission level, you should assign that permission level to a SharePoint group.

If you add a person to a custom SharePoint group on a modern site without a Microsoft 365 Group, via Site settings >People and Groups, that person will be invited and get access to the site. The person will however not show up in the Permissions right pane among the other users.

14.4.2 Modify Permissions

In classic sites, it is not difficult to change the default permission. When you modify the permission level for a group, the new level will be reflected in the sharing dialog.

You can for example set the default permission level for the Members group to be Contribute instead of Edit, to restrict users from creating and deleting apps:

1. In Site settings >Site permissions, select the Members group.
2. Click on 'Edit User Permissions' in the ribbon.

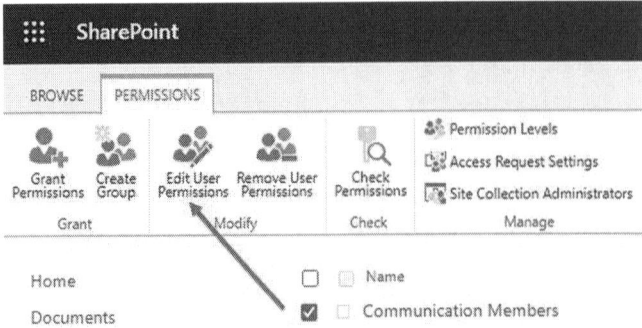

3. In the new page that opens, uncheck the Edit box and check the box for Contribute.
4. Click OK.

Unfortunately, the modern pages are not adapted to such modifications.

282

In Communication sites and Team sites without a group, the 'Edit User Permissions' button is active, and the modification can be made, but the result does not affect the Permissions right pane and the Share button in a good way. In Group Team sites, the button is greyed out.

14.4.2.1 Remove Users

To stop sharing a site with a user, go into the Site settings >People and Groups. Here you can see everyone that is sharing the site and take actions. External sharers will show up here after they have accepted the sharing invitation.

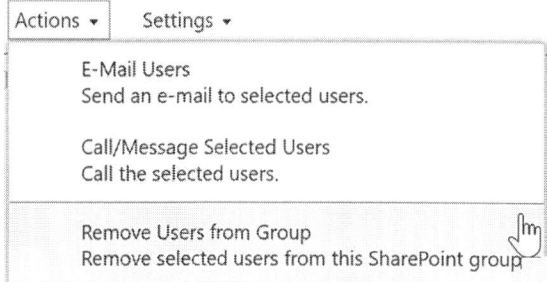

14.4.3 *Create a Custom SharePoint Group*

Administrators can create a custom SharePoint group by pressing the 'Create Group' button in the ribbon of the Site Permissions page.

At the bottom of the creation page, you can specify what permission level should be used for this group. Any custom permission levels you have created will also show up here.

Choose the permission level group members get on this site:
https://m365x446726.sharepoint.com/sites/SupportCases

- ☐ Full Control - Has full control.
- ☐ Design - Can view, add, update, delete, approve, and customize.
- ☐ Edit - Can add, edit and delete lists; can view, add, update and delete list items and documents.
- ☐ Contribute - Can view, add, update, and delete list items and documents.
- ☐ Read - Can view pages and list items and download documents.
- ☐ View Only - Can view pages, list items, and documents. Document types with server-side file handlers can be viewed in the browser but not downloaded.

When you have created the SharePoint group, the group page opens so that you can add users.

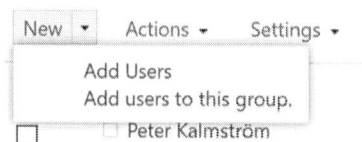

Under 'Actions', you can e-mail and remove users.

Under 'Settings', you can see the permissions that this group has in the site and make the group default.

283

14.5 BREAK THE INHERITANCE

By default, permissions are inherited from the upper level, but you can break this inheritance. Breaking the inheritance can be done for all levels down to item level, but not on column level.

Note that an alternative to breaking the inheritance is to create more sites, with different permissions. This is especially interesting for modern sites, that can be connected to a hub site.

For classic sites, subsites with broken inheritance might be a better option in some cases, but breaking inheritance should be an *exception* on all levels. It complicates management and might be confusing for users.

Also, consider if the goal achieved by breaking inheritance is convenience or security. I often encounter a confusion between these two in requirement documents.

- Convenience: "Users should be shown only their own tasks". This can very easily be achieved by a filtered view.
- Security: "Users should never be allowed to see the tasks assigned to others". This requires breaking the inheritance (or creating more sites).

14.5.1 *Break App Inheritance*

To break the permission inheritance for an app, go to List settings > Permissions and Management >'Permissions for this list' or 'Permissions for this document library'.

Click on 'Stop Inheriting Permissions' in the ribbon to stop the inheritance.

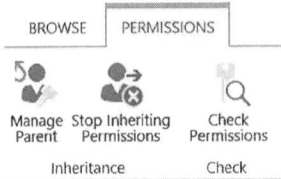

Now the ribbon will change, so that you can grant new permissions and/or remove users or groups.

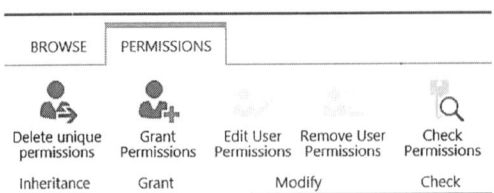

Click on 'Delete unique permissions' if you want to go back to the inherited permission levels.

14.5.2 *Break Item Inheritance*

To set permissions on site content that should not inherit the site permission:

- To set specific permissions on a file, folder or list item in an app with the **modern** interface, open the ellipsis at the item and select 'Manage access'. Set the basic permission directly in the right pane that opens, or click on the 'Advanced' link at the bottom.
- In the "Site Pages" library, you can set specific permissions for page files. For example, you might not want users to be able to change the homepage of a site, after you have spent a lot of time on making it appealing. Open the page's Information pane and click on 'Manage Access', to set the permission level to View for all or selected users.
- For a file, folder or list item in an app with the classic interface, open the ellipsis at the item and select 'Share'. Set the basic permission directly in the dialog that opens, or click on the 'ADVANCED' link or under 'Shared with'.

Also *refer to* 15.3, Share Site Content.

14.5.3 *Break Inheritance at Subsite Creation*

When you create a new subsite, you can just select another radio button than the default one.

When you check the radio button for unique permissions, a permissions page will be displayed where you can define the SharePoint groups for the site and add people to them if needed.

User Permissions:

○ Use same permissions as parent site

◉ Use unique permissions

People and Groups ▸ Set Up Groups for this Site

Visitors to this Site
Visitors can **read** content in the Web site. Create a group of visitors or re-use an existing SharePoint group.

◉ Create a new group   ○ Use an existing group

Permission Visitors

Members of this Site
Members can **contribute** content to the Web site. Create a group of site members or re-use an existing SharePoint group.

◉ Create a new group   ○ Use an existing group

Permission Members

Kate Kalmström

Owners of this Site
Owners have **full control** over the Web site. Create a group of owners or re-use an existing SharePoint group.

◉ Create a new group   ○ Use an existing group

Permission Owners

Kate Kalmström

OK

14.6 SUMMARY

SharePoint Online is a place in the cloud where teams and organizations can share content, but the sharing can get out of hand if administrators don't understand how the permission and sharing processes work.

We will go into the sharing processes in the next chapter, but in this chapter, we have seen how the permissions work. I have described the modern and classic permission settings, and you have learned how to manage them.

You now also understand how the SharePoint permission inheritance works, and you know the difference between Microsoft 365 Groups, SharePoint groups and Security groups.

In the next chapter, you will learn how users can share SharePoint content in a secure manner.

15 SHARING

One of the strengths of SharePoint Online is that it is easy to share and collaborate on content, not only within an organization but also with people outside the organization (so called "guests").

It is easy to share content in SharePoint, and in this chapter, we will have a look at how it is done and how you can set permissions when you share something that is contained in a SharePoint Online tenant.

It is important to understand that SharePoint sites cannot be made totally public. You cannot host a regular website on SharePoint. The kind of sharing we are talking about here is specific sites or specific site content.

15.1 ADMIN CENTER SHARING SETTINGS

The organization's policies for external and internal sharing are set in the SharePoint Admin center under Policies >Sharing. These settings apply to the whole tenant.

In most sites, SharePoint gives users a possibility to share items via 'Share' buttons, and sharing with these buttons breaks the item's default, inherited permissions. This may lead to a situation where you have a lot of broken permissions and no real control over how SharePoint content is distributed. Administrators should be aware of this problem.

In the SharePoint Admin center, you can restrict the sharing options in various ways, both for SharePoint and for each user's OneDrive for Business site. If you want to allow unauthenticated sharing of files and folders, choose the default 'Anyone'. (Sites can never be shared with unauthenticated people.)

If you want to ensure that all people outside your organization have to authenticate, choose 'New and existing guests'. You can also disallow external sharing completely.

On the Sharing page, you can change the default permission for shared contents and links and make other settings that might be necessary for your organization's security.

Sharing

Use these settings to control sharing at the organization level in SharePoint and OneDrive. Learn more

External sharing

Content can be shared with:

SharePoint   OneDrive

Most permissive		**Anyone** Users can share files and folders using links that don't require sign-in.
		New and existing guests Guests must sign in or provide a verification code.
		Existing guests Only guests already in your organization's directory.
Least permissive		**Only people in your organization** No external sharing allowed.

You can further restrict sharing for each individual site and OneDrive. Learn how

More external sharing settings ∨

File and folder links

When you expand "More external sharing settings", you will have a possibility to limit the general sharing for the tenant in more ways. The image shows the default settings. As you see, there is a possibility to let access expire.

More external sharing settings ∨

☐ Limit external sharing by domain

☐ Allow only users in specific security groups to share externally

☐ Guests must sign in using the same account to which sharing invitations are sent

☑ Allow guests to share items they don't own

☐ Guest access to a site or OneDrive will expire automatically after this many days `60`

☐ People who use a verification code must reauthenticate after this many days ⓘ `29`

When you revoke guest user access, the guest loses access to all content in the site after the specified number of days after the day when the guest was granted access to the site.

288

Site admins will receive an e-mail notification when a guest user access is near expiration. The site admin can then extend the access when needed, but only up to the limit of the tenant policy. The access can be extended an unlimited number of times.

Note that the guest expiration policy has no effect on guests that have been added to a Microsoft 365 Group. It only affects links that give guest access to apps and app items, changes in site memberships and direct permission changes.

I recommend that you consider carefully which sharing permissions would work best for your organization. The sharing permissions of a single site can never go beyond the maximum allowed level for the tenant. Therefore, in the SharePoint Admin center, you must choose the most permissive setting that is needed by any site in the tenant.

The sharing setting can always be restricted at a lower level:

- Administrators can set the external sharing policy for a single site under the Active sites tab in the SharePoint Admin center, *refer to* 6.2.1.1, Edit an Active Site.
- Site owners can limit the sharing from the site's permission settings, *refer to* 15.2.4, Site Sharing Settings.

This is useful when the organization has confidential information that should never be shared externally but external sharing still needs to be allowed for the tenant. In those cases, the sensitive information can be stored in one or more sites that have external sharing turned off.

As mentioned above, you can never make it the other way around – allow external sharing in some sites when it is disabled for the tenant. Sharing settings for individual sites can never be more allowing than the policy set for the tenant in the SharePoint Admin center. They can only be more restrictive.

15.2   SHARE A SITE

As we have seen earlier, the settings for how much sharing should be allowed are made in the SharePoint Admin center for the whole tenant. Global and SharePoint administrators can also limit sharing options for individual sites.

If allowed in the SharePoint Admin center, site owners can give other people access to the site by adding them as owners, members or visitors. The site owner can also allow site members to invite people to the site, *see* below.

You can share a site in different ways, but in all cases, you must start typing a name or an e-mail address. Then you will get suggestions on people and groups in the tenant to select from. You can either keep the default permission level for the invited person or group or change it.

In the same right pane or dialog where you add new people to the site, you can also see who are already sharing the site, and in modern sites you can also see their permission level.

Note that the people you invite also will get access to other content that have shared permissions with this site. For example, if subsites have inherited the parent permissions, you will share all the subsites by sharing the parent site.

When you share a site from the modern experience, you can select Read, Edit or Full Control permission for each user or group that you share the site with. When you share from the classic experience, you can select among more levels.

15.2.1 Share a Site with the Share Button

Sites without a group have a 'Share' button in the top right corner of all pages. When you use that button, you will share the whole site with the people you invite.

15.2.1.1 Modern Share Button

In the modern experience, the 'Share' command will open a right pane where you can add people and groups and select permission level.

Start writing a name or e-mail address to get suggestions. Select one of the suggestions, and the person or group will be added below the field.

The default permission for the site type is assigned automatically, *refer to* 14.1.1, Default Site Permissions, but you can change it before you share the site. This is done with the little arrow at the permission information below the name of the added person or group.

An e-mail invitation will be sent by default, and you can also add a message.

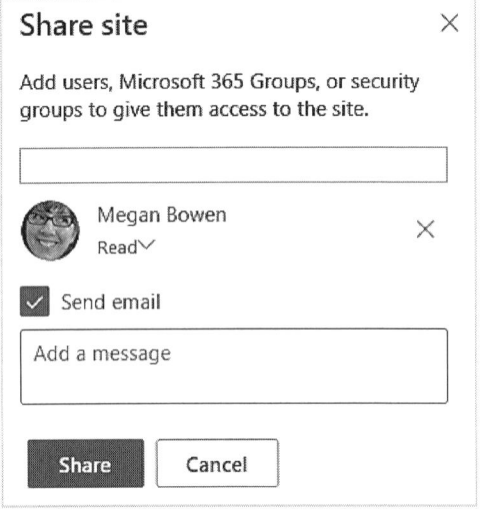

15.2.1.2 Classic Share Button

In the classic interface, a dialog will open when you click on the 'Share' button. Here, you will have the option to enter 'Everyone' if you want to include all people in the organization.

290

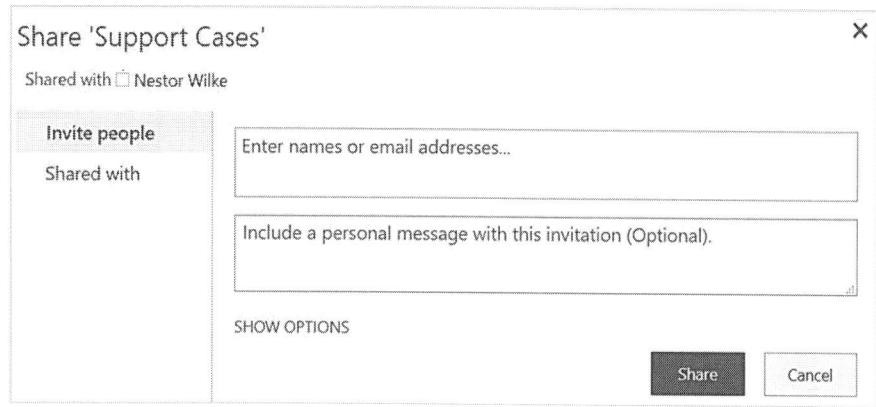

Under 'SHOW OPTIONS' you can send an e-mail invitation (default) and set another permission level than the default 'Edit'.

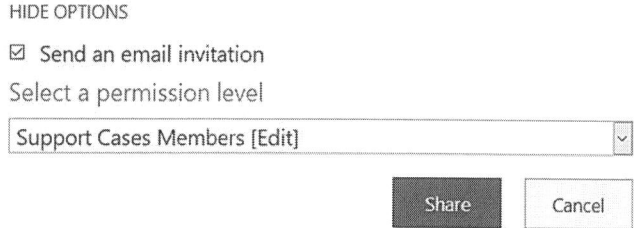

Under the Shared with tab in this dialog, you can see who is already sharing the site. You can e-mail everyone, and via the 'ADVANCED' link you can reach the site's permissions page in the Site settings.

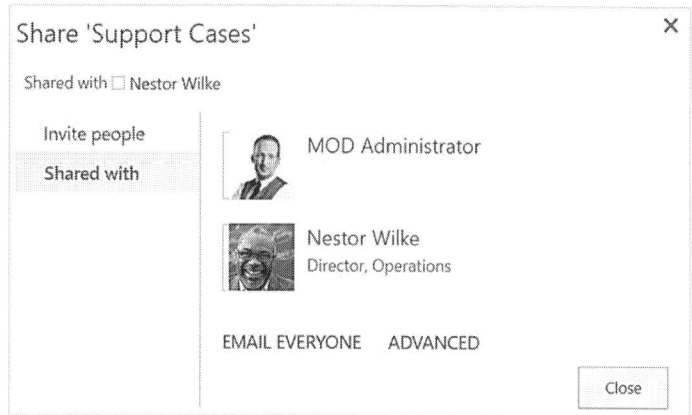

15.2.2 Share a Site from the Modern Permissions Pane

The modern experience has a 'Site permissions' link under the 365 Settings icon. It opens a right pane where you can invite users and manage permissions and sharing settings. All modern sites can be shared from the Site permissions pane.

In Communication sites and modern Team sites without a group, the Permissions right pane has a 'Share site' button on top. When you click on the 'Share site' button, the same invitation pane opens as when you use the modern 'Share' button, *see* above

Group Team sites instead have an 'Add members' button in the Permissions right pane. It has a dropdown with two options: to add members to the Microsoft 365 group connected to the site or to just share the site and not the other shared group resources.

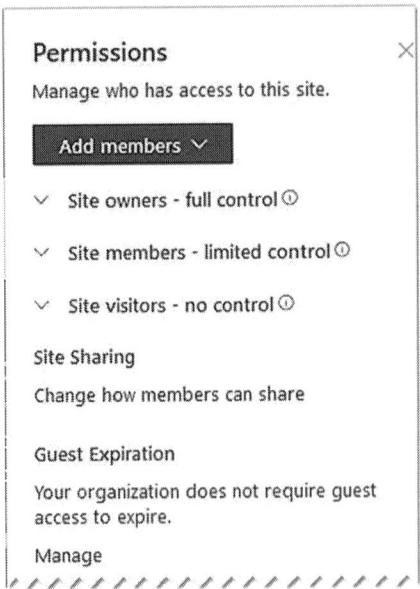

In the Permissions right pane, there is also a link that open the pane for site sharing settings, *see* below, and a link to a pane where you can clear expirations for the site sharing that were set in the SharePoint Admin center >Policies >Sharing.

15.2.3   *Share a Group Team Site with an External Guest*

When external guest access is allowed for the Group Team site, the guests are invited from Outlook on the web, not from SharePoint. (*Refer to* 15.4.2, External Guest Access to Group Team Site, for information on how guest access is allowed.)

1. Under Groups in Outlook on the web, click on the group to which you want to invite guests.
2. Open the group contact card and click on the Members link.

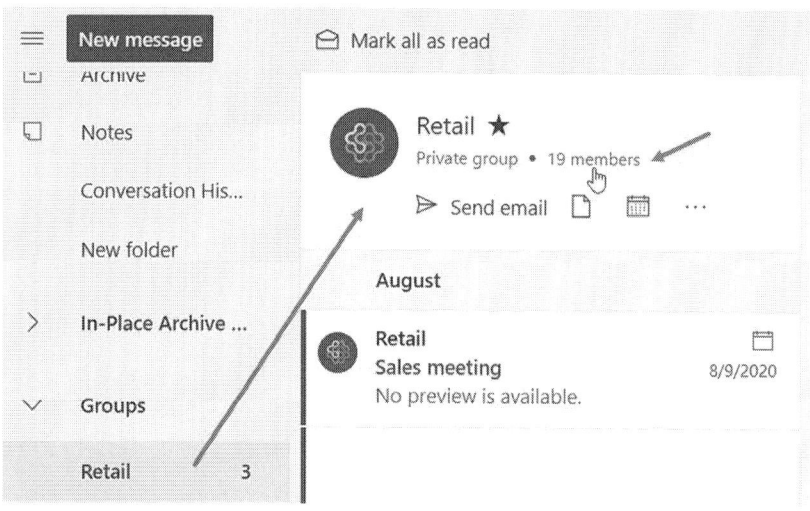

3. Click on 'Add members' in the dialog that opens.
4. Type the guest's e-mail address and then click on 'Add'.
5. Click on Close when you have finished adding guests.

15.2.4 *Site Sharing Settings*

In the **modern** experience, site owners can click on the "Change how members can share" link in the 'Permissions' pane, to modify who can share the site and its files and folders. You can, for example, decide that only owners can share files, folders and the site.

To manage the sharing from the **classic** experience, open the Site settings and select 'Site permissions' under the Users and Permissions heading. This page can also be reached from the ADVANCED link in the classic 'Share' dialog.

15.2.4.1 Access Request

If someone who is not a site owner uses the 'Share' command to invite other people to a site, an access request for the site can be sent to site owners or to a specified e-mail address. If the invitation is accepted, the approver can specify the permission level for the user.

The access request also allows people to request access to content that they do not have permission to see.

When 'Allow access requests' is enabled, an e-mail with an access request will be sent to the specified e-mail address. Requests can also be seen and acted on from the 'Access requests' button in the modern Site contents command bar and under Site settings >Users and Groups >Access requests and invitations.

From the **modern** experience, you can reach the Access request settings from the Permissions right pane >Site sharing settings. Access requests are enabled by default.

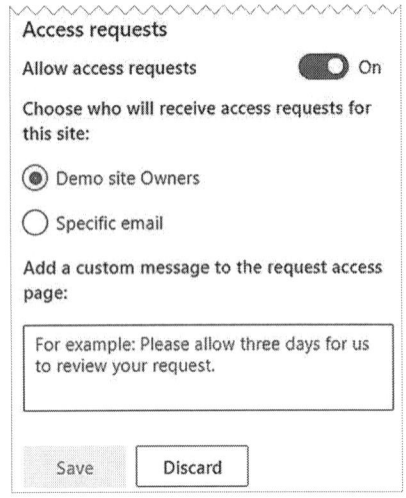

From the **classic** interface, you need to go into Site settings >Site permissions >Access Request Settings.

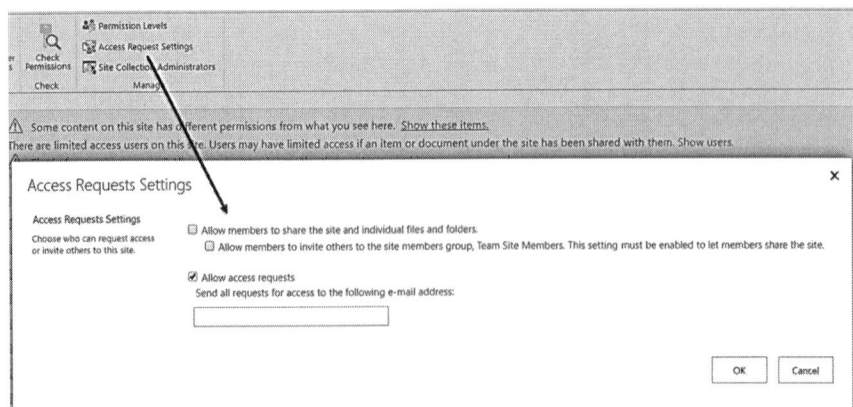

The first two boxes, that allow sharing, are checked by default.

☑ Allow members to share the site and individual files and folders.
　☑ Allow members to invite others to the site members group, c

If you uncheck these two boxes, the sharing will be blocked for all users but the site owner.

Note that the 'Share' buttons will be displayed to the users even if sharing is disabled. If "access requests" has not been activated, the user will receive an error message when trying to use a 'Share' button.

If you uncheck the two sharing boxes in the 'Access Request Settings' dialog and instead activate the third box, 'Allow access requests', all users can share the site or site contents, but the site owner has the ultimate authority over who gets access to the site and what level of permission users are assigned.

If a subsite has inherited permissions from an upper level, the Access Request settings link will not be visible in the ribbon. You must first stop inheriting or change the sharing in the parent site instead.

15.2.5   Manage Site Members in the Modern Experience

As you know by now, the modern experience has a Permission pane, where you can invite users and manage permissions and sharing settings.

15.2.5.1   Manage Members in Sites without a Group

In Communication sites and Team sites without a group, the Permissions right pane shows the three SharePoint groups below the share button. Here, Site owners can change member permissions and remove people from the site.

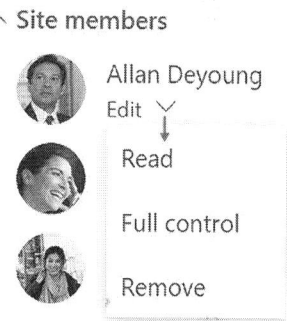

When you select another permission level, the person will automatically be moved to that SharePoint group.

If you, for example, change Allan Deyoung's permission (see the image to the right) from Edit to Full control, he will be moved from the Site members to the Site owners SharePoint group.

15.2.5.2   Manage Members in Group Team Sites

In Group Team sites and classic Team sites where a Microsoft 365 Group has been added, only the group name is displayed under the SharePoint groups in the Permissions pane. Here, only the permissions for the whole SharePoint group can be edited but not the permission level for an individual member.

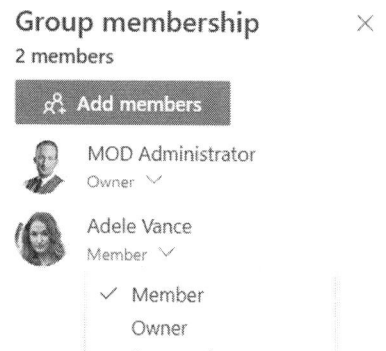

If you want to manage individual members, you can click on 'Add members' in the Permissions pane and then select to add members to the Microsoft 365 Group.

Now all members are displayed, and you can change their status with the little arrow to the right of the current status.

295

You can also manage the Microsoft 365 Group in Outlook on the web:

1. Under Groups in the Outlook left menu, select the Microsoft 365 Group you want to manage.
2. Click on the Members link in the group's contact card.
3. A dialog will open, where you can change permission level or remove users from the Microsoft 365 Group – and thereby also from the site – with the x icon.

15.2.6 Manage Site Members in the Classic Experience

In the classic experience, you can see the people and groups who have access to the site in the 'Share' dialog, *see* above, but you cannot change a permission level or remove a user there. If you want to do that, you must go into the Site settings, *refer to* 14.4.2, Modify Permissions.

15.3 SHARE SITE CONTENT

Sometimes you need to share site content with people who don't have access to it. Users with Edit permission can by default share lists and items (=files, folders, pages and list items). When you use the classic interface, library apps can also be shared, *see* below.

In the "Site Pages" library, all site pages can be shared in the same way as other files. Pages can also be shared from the page's command bar, *refer to* 13.4.10, Promote a Page.

By default, an invitation is sent by e-mail to the people who are given access to an app or item. You can also get a link to the shared content and share it in another way.

When you share a file with an e-mail link, the link in the e-mail will become a so-called short link, showing the document name and the file type icon.

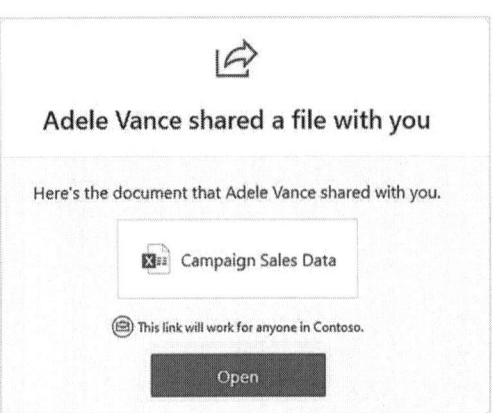

15.3.1 Manage Access

In both app interfaces, you can see with whom a list or item has been shared, but the modern interface is easier to work with.

In the **modern** interface, you can see the sharing information in the list's or the selected item's Information pane. Click on 'Manage access' to have details on the sharing and permissions and modify them. Here, you can also invite more people to share.

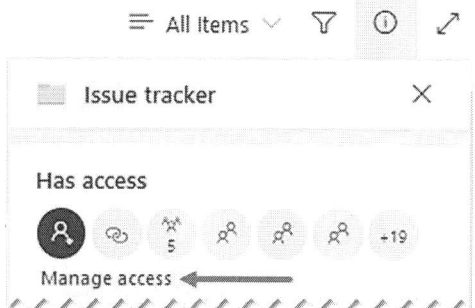

You can also find links to the 'Manage access' pane under the ellipses at the item and in the Sharing dialog.

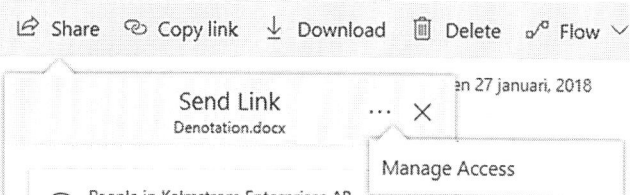

To grant access to people who have access to the site but not to the specific list or item, you can click on the icon with a plus above 'Manage access' in the Information pane.

You can also open the 'Manage access' right pane and click on the plus sign at 'Direct access' to invite site members.

(Use the link or 'Share' button option when you want to share an item with people who don't have access to the site, see below.)

To stop sharing an item with everyone, click on the 'Stop sharing' link on top of the 'Manage Access' pane.

To stop sharing a list with everyone, you need to cancel the link, see below.

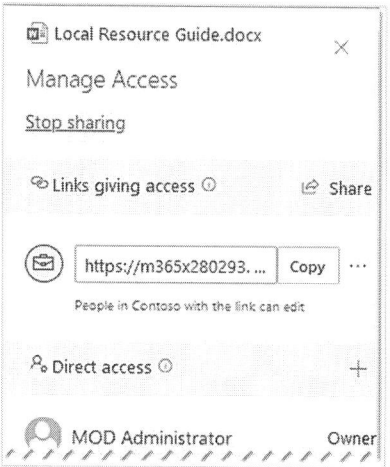

In the 'Manage Access' right pane, you can easily edit the permissions from the dropdown at each user or group. Here, you can also stop sharing the list or item with specific people.

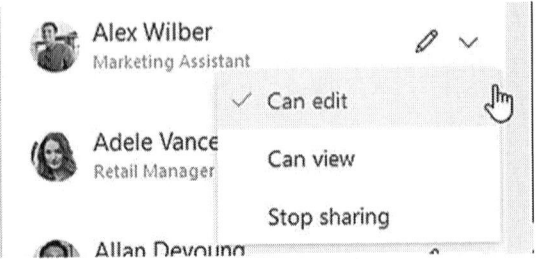

In the **classic** interface, you can see the sharing under 'Shared with' in the sharing dialog, but it is more complicated to edit the permission for an already shared item. I suggest that you switch to the modern *experience*, when you want to edit item permissions. If that is not possible, refer to 14.4.2, Modify Permissions.

15.3.2   Share with "Share" Buttons

Both app interfaces have commands that let you share site content to people who don't have access to the site.

15.3.2.1   Sharing with the Modern 'Share' Command

The modern app interface has a 'Share' button in the command bar.

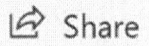

When you select an item, it also has a 'Share' icon to the right of the item ellipsis and a 'Share' command under the ellipsis.

All these commands work in the same way:

- If no list item has been selected, the 'Share' button applies to the whole list app, and the whole list will be shared.
- If a library item has been selected, only the file will be shared.
- If a folder or a list item has been selected, all columns in the item will be shared.

The 'Share' command opens a dialog where you can give names or e-mail addresses to specific people or groups with whom you want to share the list or item. Above that field, there is a Permission selector.

At the bottom of the dialog, you can see who is already sharing this list or item. Click on a profile picture to open another dialog where that person's access can be revoked.

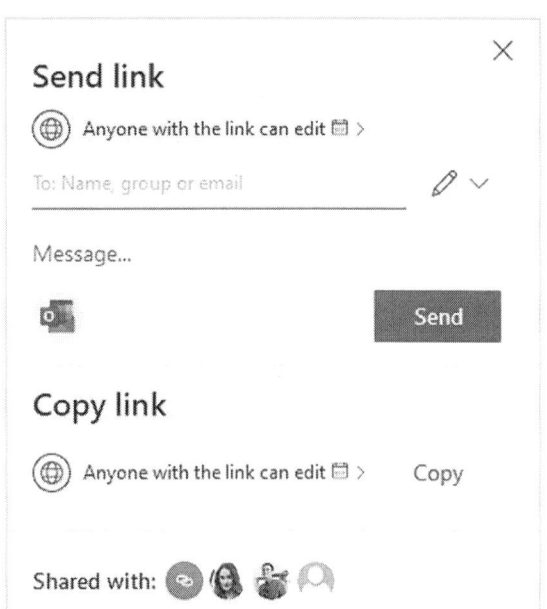

You can – and should! – decide which people should be able to use the sharing link and if the link should give edit permission or not. The default permission when sharing is Edit.

You must click on the permission selector above the field where you enter the person/group you want to share with, before you can see and change the permission you are giving.

The permission options are: Anyone with the link, People in the organization with the link, People with existing access and Specific people. The number of options can be limited in the SharePoint Admin center, so 'Anyone with the link' might not be active.

When you share the same list or item with different permission options, multiple links will be created. You can see, use and revoke all links under 'Manage access', *see* above.

I recommend that you think twice before you use the option 'Anyone with the link', even if it is available, because this option allows even people outside the organization to access the shared list or item. They don't have to

299

log in, so their access cannot be audited, and you cannot see which people have used what you have shared.

File options:
Most sharing links give the option to disallow editing, but for some file types you can also block download. When you uncheck the 'Allow editing' box, the 'Block download' option will be active, so that you can enable it if you want the recipient to be able to view the shared file but not download it.

Currently, users can create such SharePoint and OneDrive read-only sharing links that block download for Office files, PDF files, images, audio files and video files.

When you share a Word file, there is one more option: 'Open in review mode only' lets a receiver without edit permission comment on the file but not edit it.

Anyone options:
If you select the 'Anyone with the link' option, you will get the option to set an expiration date and a password for the link. (If you set a password, you must distribute it yourself.)

In the SharePoint Admin center >Policies >Sharing, administrators can set such links to always expire after a certain time, and in that case, users can only make the time before expiration shorter, not longer.

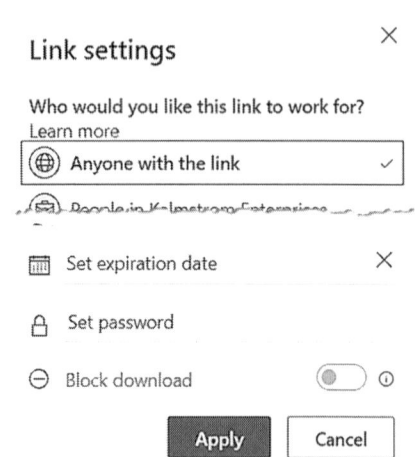

15.3.2.2 Sharing with the Classic 'Shared With' Command

List and library apps with the classic interface have a 'Shared With' button under the LIST/LIBRARY tab in the ribbon. It opens a dialog where you can invite people to share a library, list or item.

In addition to the ribbon buttons, list and library items have a 'Share' command under the item ellipsis.

In the classic sharing dialog, you can set the permission directly after adding the people or group you want to share with. The options are 'Can edit' and 'Can view'. To have options corresponding to the modern usage options, you need to share a link instead, *see* below.

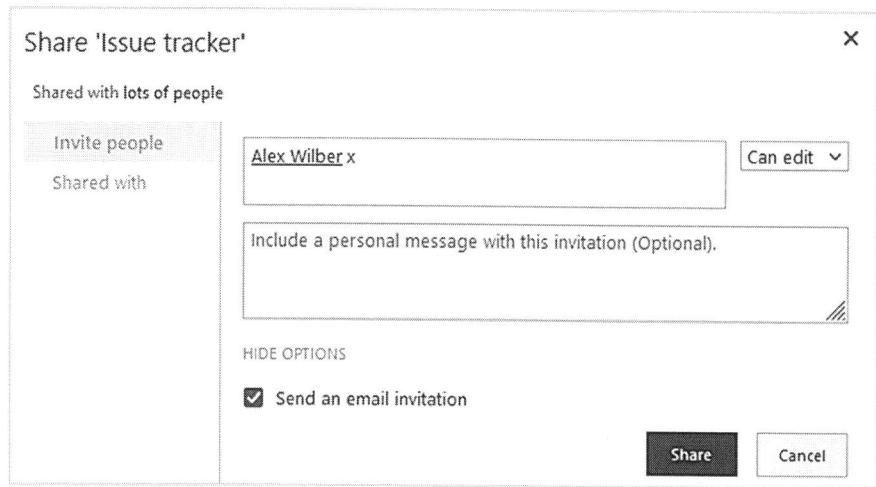

Lists and libraries is **classic sites** can also be shared via the advanced permission settings:

1. Open the Library/List settings and click on "Permissions for this library/list" under the Permissions and Management heading.

2. Click on the 'Grant permission' button in the ribbon. (You might need to first click on the 'Stop Inheriting Permissions' button to see 'Grant Permissions'.)

3. Now you can invite people and set the permission level you want them to have. Uncheck the box for "share everything" if you want to exclude items with unique permissions from the sharing.

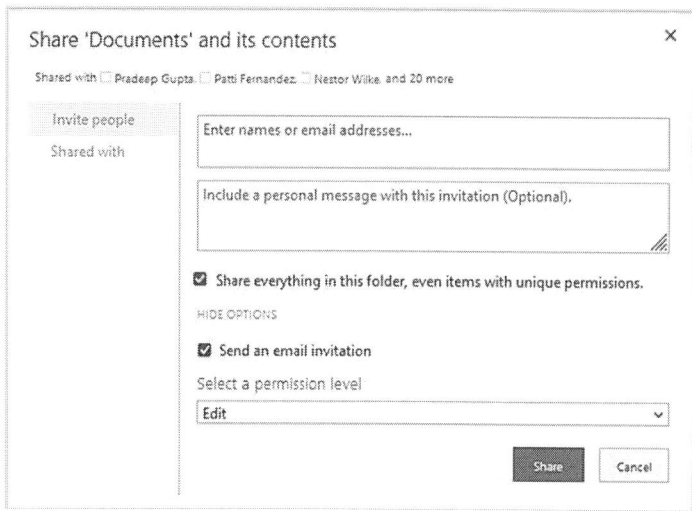

(I do *not* recommend that you use this option for modern sites, even if it is possible to reach the advanced permission settings. They are not created for modern site, and the combination can create problems.)

301

15.3.3 Share with a Link

Instead of sharing with the 'Share' command, you can send a link to the SharePoint content that you want to share in another way. By default, only the people you have specified can use the link.

To have the correct link, select an item and use the command 'Copy link', which you can find in the command bar and under the item ellipsis in **modern** apps.

When you click on 'Edit all' in the 'Properties' section of the Information pane, a new right pane with a small command bar will open. In this command bar, you can also copy a link to the item.

Use the 'Copy link' command when you need the link to an item. You will then have a possibility to set permissions on the item before you share it. The link opens the document from the selected item.

If you use the 'Copy link' command for a list item or a folder, the link will point to the item or to the open folder with all its items.

When you use the 'Copy link' command for an item in a library app, the link will point to the file, not to the whole item.

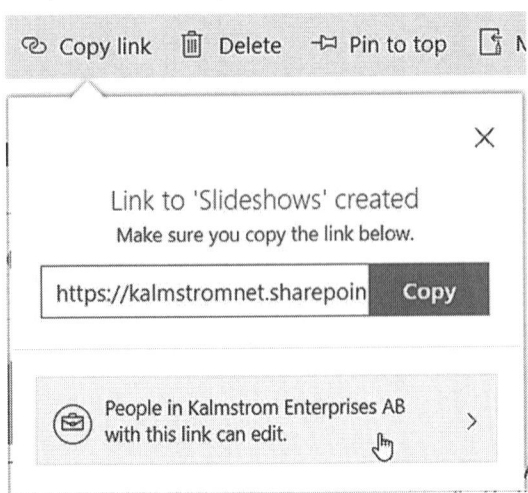

Lists have no 'Copy link' in the command bar when no item has been selected, but you can find a link to the whole list in the 'Manage Access' pane if the list has earlier been shared with the 'Share' command.

Note that the default permission when sharing with a link is very generous. It allows every person that gets access to the link to edit your item. Click on the default option if you want to change what people can do, just like when you use the 'Share' command.

To avoid mistakes, Microsoft plans to change the Copy link feature, so that users more easily can change the link type and permissions before the sharing link is generated.

In the **classic** experience, you cannot share a whole app with a link. For items, you can go via the 'Shared with' button in the ribbon or 'Share' under the item ellipsis to get a link.

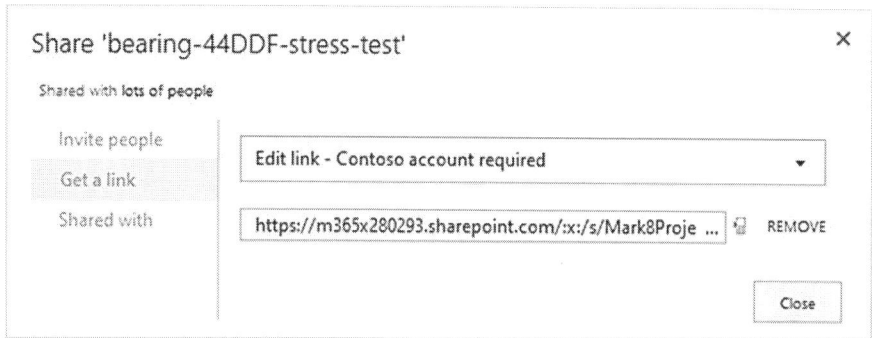

In libraries, you can also find a 'Get a link' command under the ellipsis at the selected file or folder. The classic 'Get a link' dialog is similar to the modern 'Share' dialog. The classic dialog also has an icon that opens the item in a mobile device.

15.3.4   Cancel a Link

When you share the same list or item with different permission options, multiple links will be created. You can see and use all links under 'Manage access'.

It is possible to revoke the link to a list or item, so that it no longer can be used:

A new link will be created automatically next time anyone use the Share command for the same list or item.

This is the process in the **modern** interface:

1. Open the Information pane and click on 'Manage access'.
2. Click on the ellipsis to the right of the sharing link.

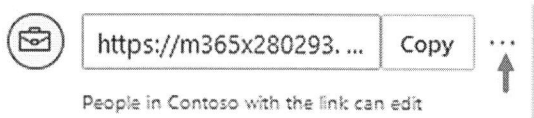

3. Click on the X to the right of the sharing link.

In the **classic** interface, use the REMOVE command in the sharing dialog, *see* the image in 15.3.3, above. It is only available for library folders and files (including pages).

303

15.3.5 E-mail Attachments

When you click on the 'Attach' button in an e-mail that is open in Outlook on the web, you will have several options:

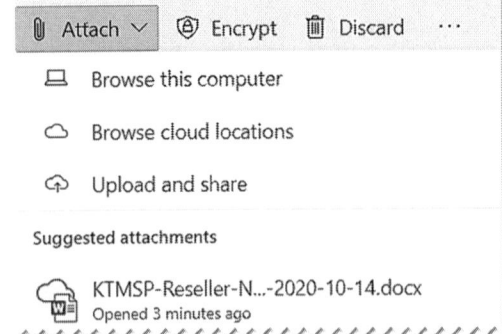

- Browse the computer and upload a file.
- Browse libraries in OneDrive and SharePoint Online.
- Upload a file from the computer to OneDrive and share it from there.
- Attach a recently used OneDrive or SharePoint file.

When you send an attachment from OneDrive or SharePoint, you can select to share a link to the file. This gives some benefits, compared to uploading a file from the computer or sending a copy of the file:

- You will have a possibility to set permissions on the file.
- To share a link instead of the actual file saves mailbox space, both for the sender and the recipient(s).
- You are not creating a duplicate of the file. When users access the file, they will always see the latest version.

By default, the receiver will get edit permission on the file if it is an Office file, but in all options where the file is stored in the cloud, you will have a possibility to change the permission when the file has been attached.

How many options you have, depends on the sharing settings in the SharePoint Admin center.

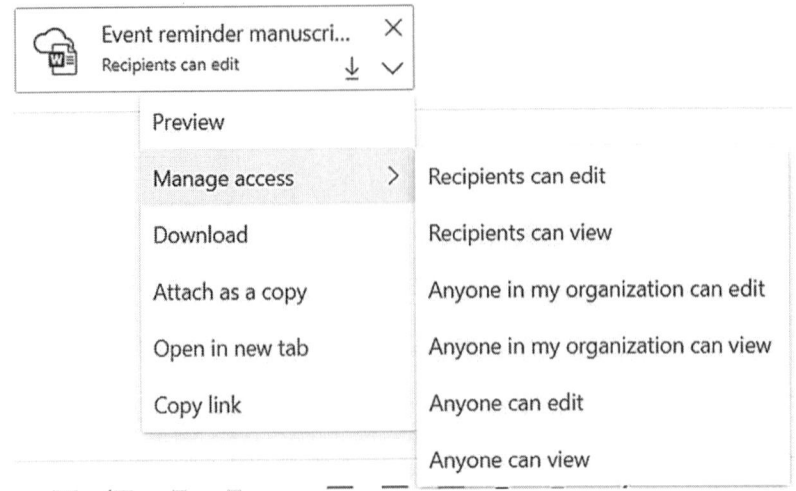

When you upload the file from your computer, there is no possibility to modify the permission. But when the file has been attached, you can upload it to OneDrive and then you will have the same options as in the image above. (It is of course quicker to use the 'Upload and share' option directly.)

Sometimes it is necessary to give the receiver(s) permission to edit the file, so that several people can edit the same copy of a file, *refer to* 9.9.1, Editing by Multiple Users. In other cases, it is more secure to limit the permission.

15.3.6   *Modern Page Sharing Options*

Modern site pages have a 'Promote' button in the command bar. It opens a right pane with six options for sharing.

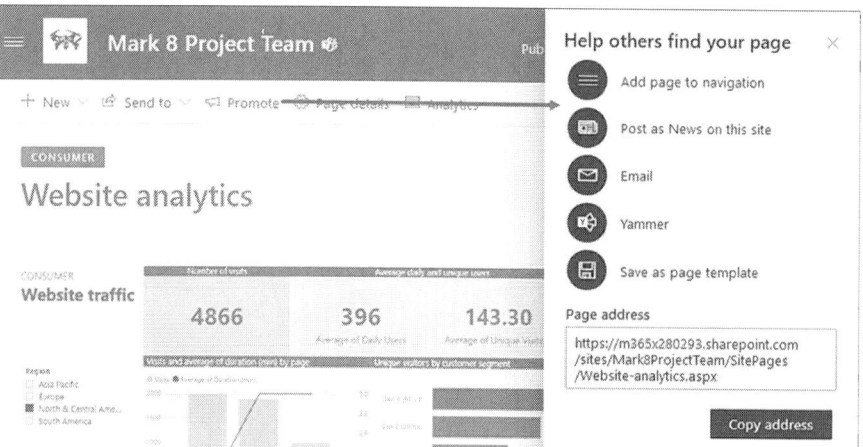

- When you click on 'Add page to navigation' and 'Post as News on this site', the action is taken immediately, and you don't need to do anything more.
- The 'Email' link opens a dialog where you can enter an e-mail address and a message to send a link to the page.
- Click on Yammer to share the page with a Yammer community. When you click on 'Add community', a selection of all communities that you are a member of will be displayed in a dropdown.

305

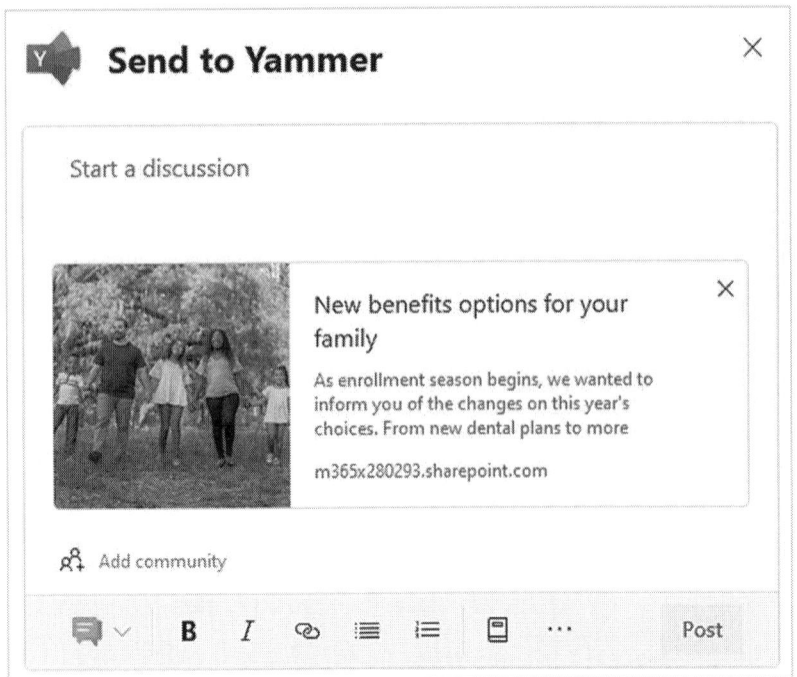

- When you save the page as a template, it will show up among the templates when users create another page on the same site.
- The URL to the page can be used to share the page in other ways.

The Email and Yammer options are also available under the 'Send to' button in the command bar of pages that are not homepages.

15.4 External Users

If allowed in the SharePoint Admin center and in the site, it is possible to share sites and site content with people outside the tenant and not only with internal users. The external users will have an e-mail invitation with a link when something is shared with them.

As we have seen earlier, external sharing is allowed by default for the tenant. This setting in the SharePoint Admin center can of course be changed, but external sharing can also be restricted for single sites by SharePoint admins, under 'Active sites' in the SharePoint Admin center.

In addition to the direct sharing described in the sections above, Microsoft 365 Group owners can invite guests to Group Team sites and give them access to all the shared content.

These guests can be from inside the organization, but if it is allowed, people from outside the tenant can also be invited to the Group Team site.

In all cases, you must be aware that there are different types of external users, as described below.

15.4.1 Authenticated and Anonymous Users

There are two kinds of external users:

- **Authenticated** users have a Microsoft account or a work or school account in Azure AD from another organization, and they are asked to log in when they click on the link. You can share sites and site content with these users, and permissions and groups work as they do for internal users.

  When authenticated users log in for the first time, they are added to the tenant's as well as the site's users lists. They can do many of the things internal users can do, but they don't have access to more advanced features.

  For example, authenticated external users cannot create Power Automate flows for the content they have access to, and they have no OneDrive for Business storage. For those things, they will need a license in the tenant.

- **Anonymous** users can view or edit SharePoint content without having to log in. Only files and folders can be shared with anonymous users, and you can set an expiration date for the sharing link as described above.

This is important to consider if you use the 'Share' or 'Link' command:

- By default, all users get Edit permission, even if they are external.
- When you share with authenticated users, you can see which user has made any modifications.
- When a file has been changed by an anonymous user, you can only see that it is modified by a 'Guest Contributor', Therefore, you have no control over who is changing your content when you give the default Edit permission!

Demo:

https://www.kalmstrom.com/Tips//SharePoint-Online-Course/External-Sharing.htm

15.4.2 External Guest Access to Group Team Site

A Microsoft 365 Group might need to share their Group Team site with people outside the organization, but external access to Group Team sites must be granted on several levels.

Guest access must also always be authenticated, and it must be allowed on the higher level to be possible to enable on a lower level.

1. Guest sharing must be allowed in in the Azure Active Directory >All services >External Identities > External collaboration settings. The image below shows the default settings.

   Here, you can change settings for which permissions guests should have, who should be allowed to invite guests and to which domains these invitations can be sent.

Guest user access

Guest user access restrictions ⓘ
Learn more

○ Guest users have the same access as members (most inclusive)
◉ Guest users have limited access to properties and memberships of directory objects
○ Guest user access is restricted to properties and memberships of their own directory objects (most restrictive)

Guest invite settings

Guest invite restrictions ⓘ
Learn more

◉ Anyone in the organization can invite guest users including guests and non-admins (most inclusive)
○ Member users and users assigned to specific admin roles can invite guest users including guests with member permissions
○ Only users assigned to specific admin roles can invite guest users
○ No one in the organization can invite guest users including admins (most restrictive)

Enable guest self-service sign up via user flows ⓘ
Learn more

(Yes **No**)

Collaboration restrictions

◉ Allow invitations to be sent to any domain (most inclusive)
○ Deny invitations to the specified domains
○ Allow invitations only to the specified domains (most restrictive)

2. Guest invitation must be allowed in the Microsoft 365 Admin center >Settings >Org settings >Microsoft 365 Groups.

   Make sure that the 'Let group owners add people outside your organization to Microsoft 365 Groups as guests' and 'Let guest group members access group content' are enabled. These are the default settings.

   ## Microsoft 365 Groups

   Choose how guests from outside your organization can collaborate with your users in Microsoft 365 Groups. Learn more about guest access to Microsoft 365 Groups

   ☑ Let group owners add people outside your organization to Microsoft 365 Groups as guests

   ☑ Let guest group members access group content
   If you don't select this, guests will still be listed as members of the group, but they won't receive group emails or be able to access any group content. They'll only be able to access files that were directly shared with them.

3. The sharing option must be at least 'New and existing guests' in the SharePoint Admin center >Policies >Sharing, *refer to* 15.1, Admin Center Sharing Settings.
4. In the SharePoint Admin center >Sites >Active sites, the sharing level for the site must be set to at least 'New and existing guests' under the 'Policies' tab, *refer to* 6.2.1.1, Edit an Active Site.

   Here you can also set several other options for the external site sharing.

Now, people who are allowed to invite guests can do so. The guest will have an e-mail invitation with links to the group's e-mail inbox, SharePoint site and Notebook.

15.5 Audience Targeting

Audience targeting gives users a possibility to promote content to specific audiences. This feature is off by default, but when audience targeting is enabled, certain content is shown only to the specified audience.

Audience targeting can be enabled for:

- navigation links
- list items
- library files and folders
- pages
- the modern Events, High-lighted content, News and Quick links web parts
- the classic Content Query web part.

It is possible to add users directly in the audience, but I recommend that you use Microsoft 365 or Security groups. It is often more convenient to have people who need the same kind of information in a group.

Note that audience targeting is a way to *direct* relevant content to users. It is not a way to hide content from users. Audience targeted content can still be reached by other users than the audience, for example if they search for it or have a link to it.

To hide content from users, you should use permissions, as described above. When a user lacks permission to see content, that content is hidden from the user, and the user cannot reach it.

15.5.1 *Target Links*

Open the Site navigation in edit mode to enable audience targeting of links. At the bottom of the menu, you can find the toggle for audience targeting.

Once the audience targeting has been enabled in the Site navigation, all links in all menus in the site, including hub and footer menus can be directed to specific audiences.

When you open the ellipsis at a link in the navigation and select 'Edit', you can add groups that this link should be displayed to.

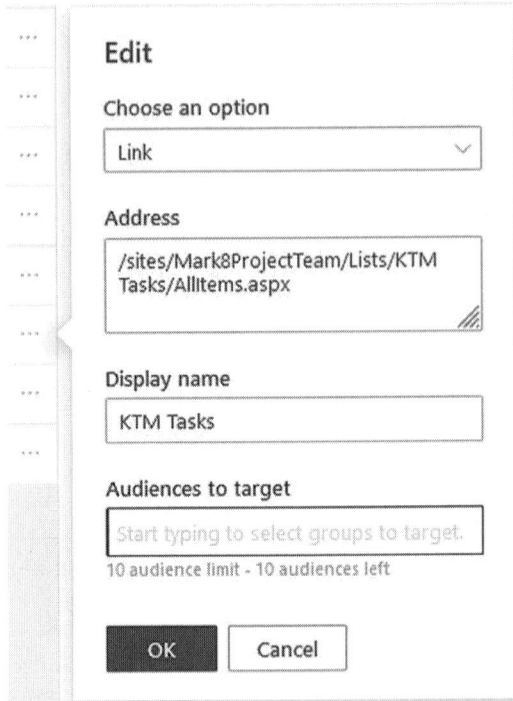

Audience targeting for navigation must be enabled by a Site owner, but when that is done, all users with Edit permission can target menu links.

15.5.2 Target Items

To direct certain list items, files, folders or pages to certain audiences, you must first enable the audience targeting in the settings of the list or library that has the content you want to target.

1. In the settings click on click on 'Audience targeting settings' under the General settings heading.
2. Enable audience targeting.

Enable Audience Targeting

Promote content to specific audiences. An audience can include Office 365 groups and Azure Active Directory groups.

☑ Enable audience targeting

☑ Enable classic audience targeting

Select Enable audience targeting for use with modern web parts such as News, Highlighted content, and others.

Select Enable classic audience targeting for use with classic web parts such as the Content Query web part.

3. A new "Audience" column will be added to the library.

Now, you can select an item and open its Information pane to specify an audience.

There may be a delay before the audience targeting take effect.

15.5.2.1 Target Modern Web Parts

When you have enabled targeting in the "Site Pages" library, you can enable targeting for the modern web parts Events, High-lighted content, News and Quick links in pages in that site. That will direct the content in the web part to users who are members of the audience you specified in the "Site Pages" library.

1. Open the page in edit mode.
2. Add the web part, or use an existing web part.
3. Edit the web part and enable targeting in the right pane.

Enable audience targeting ⓘ
⬤) Off

15.5.2.2 Target Classic Web Parts

When classic audience targeting is enabled in the "Site pages" settings, you should specify the audience in the properties of the classic page in the same way as described above.

Then you can specify under 'Query' in the web part that content should be fetched from the list or document library.

Audience Targeting:
☑ Apply audience filtering

Note: All classic web parts also have a 'Target Audiences' in the Edit web part pane. This setting determines whether the web part is visible to the current user or not.

311

15.6 Summary

I the previous chapter, I described the SharePoint Online permission management. In this chapter, we have looked at how these permissions are used when SharePoint content is shared.

You have learned how to manage the sharing of sites and Site contents via the 'Share' command and by link, and we have seen how both administrators and site owners can restrict the default permissions when sharing.

I have also described the two kinds of external users and explained what must be in place before you can share content to people outside the tenant. To control external sharing is of course an important security measure.

At the end of the chapter, I introduced Audience targeting, which is not permission setting but a way to help users find relevant content.

After this chapter, we will go back to the more hands-on work with the SharePoint content. I will first give some tips on how you can categorize the content, and after that we will have a closer look at how you can use links and pictures in SharePoint.

16   CATEGORIZATION

When you add more and more documents and list items to SharePoint, it becomes increasingly important to have them categorized in a good way, so that users quickly can find the data they need.

In this chapter, we will look at various ways to categorize items in SharePoint apps. I will point out how you, as a content creator or administrator, can make it easier for users to categorize content. I will discuss benefits and drawbacks of each method, so that you can use and combine the different methods in a way that suits your organization.

I will also describe how you can manage keywords centrally for the whole organization. That gives users suggestions when they start writing a keyword, so that the categorization becomes more consistent.

I will recommend several categorization methods in this chapter, but using folders is *not* one of them. SharePoint gives us much better options. These are the categorization methods I discuss in this chapter:

- Create columns. Items can be sorted and filtered based on the values in the columns, so columns are very useful for categorization. The filtered options can be saved in views, as described in section 7.8.
- Required Column Values. Make it mandatory to enter a column value.
- Default column value. Use a static or calculated value that is added by default.
- Create multiple apps. You should for example use different document libraries for different content instead of adding new folders to the default library. Adding content to a specific app is a type of categorization that most users are familiar with.
- Let users rate app items.
- Tag items with Enterprise Keywords. Such keywords can be used by the whole organization, and they are synchronized between all apps and managed centrally in the Term Store.
- Use dedicated term sets. These can be shared across the organization or within specific site collections.

16.1   COLUMNS

Imagine if a hotel booking site was organized into folders. Folders rely on information being categorized in one dimension only, and it would start out rather well. I could click my way into the Europe folder and then into the London folder – but then I would quickly realize that once I get into deeper categories it gets complex. Where will I find the hotels that have both "Free breakfast" and "Free Wi-Fi"? In one of those folders or both?

As you see, at a certain level of complexity the folder way of storing information breaks down. Most likely your information is that complex too. A good way of categorization is to create columns and combine them with views.

If we continue using the hotels example from above, I would create a country column based on the Choice, Managed Metadata or Lookup column type, and then I would create two Yes/No Choice columns for the breakfast and the Wi-Fi.

If I fill out the column values for my hotel descriptions correctly, it would be very easy for anyone to find hotels with free Wi-Fi and breakfast in London by filtering the list for those three values.

Title	Town ▼	Rating	Price level	Free Wifi in room ▼	Breakfast included ▼	Pets	Room Service
Elite ✱	··· London	5 stars	High	Yes	Yes	No	Yes
Star ✱	··· London	3 stars	Low	Yes	Yes	No	No
Johnson's ✱	··· London	4 stars	Middle	Yes	Yes	No	Yes
More ✱	··· London	3 stars	Middle	Yes	Yes	Yes	No

16.1.1 Mandatory Column Values

With mandatory, or required, column values, you can be sure that all new files and list items will be categorized.

To make a column value mandatory, click on the 'Yes' radio button under "Require that this column contains information" in the Edit Column dialog.

Require that this column contains information:
◉ Yes   ○ No

16.1.1.1 Mandatory List Columns

In list apps, some columns may very well be set to required, because when you do that, a new list item cannot be saved until a value is entered in the mandatory field. Users will have more work, but you can feel that sure the categorization will be done.

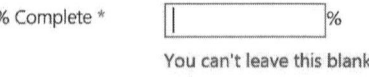

16.1.1.2 Mandatory Library Columns

With libraries there is more to consider before you set a column to be mandatory. When there is a required column in a library, a file can still be uploaded or created.

In the **modern** interface, there is a message in the column where a value is missing.

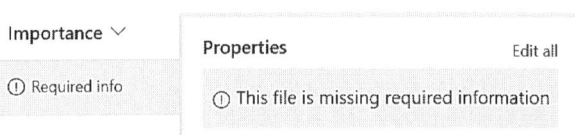

The **classic** interface instead checks out the file and shows a Check in dialog. The file cannot be accessed by other users until the required field has been filled out and the file has been checked in.

When a new file is created in the library, or when a file is added to a synchronized library folder in File Explorer, no dialog will be shown. Instead, both experiences mark the file will with the checked out icon, *refer to* 9.12, Check Out / Check In. The modern interface also has the message in the column.

Demo:

https://www.kalmstrom.com/Tips/SharePoint-Online-Course/Categorization-Required-Values.htm

16.1.2 *Default Column Values*

If you want to avoid mandatory columns and still want to have items categorized, you can use a static or calculated value that is added by default to each new item. Default values increase the risk of wrong categorization, but on the other hand, default values can help users get started with categorization.

The default value is set automatically when the item is created, but it can be changed by the item creator.

All column types cannot have default values. SharePoint shows the option when it is possible to apply.

16.1.2.1 Set Static Default Value

The default value for a column can be set in the Edit Column dialog or in the modern right pane. Enter or select the value that should be default. The default setting looks a bit different in different column types.

Default value:

● Choice ○ Calculated Value

(2) Normal

When a default value has been added to a column, it can be seen and changed in the App Settings, 'Column default value settings' under the General Settings heading.

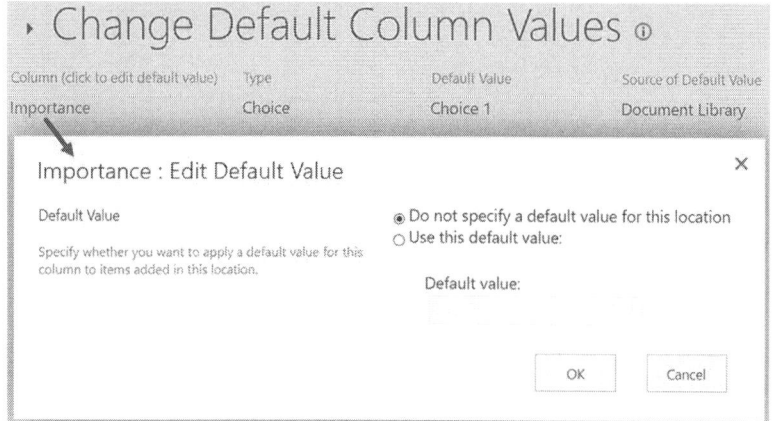

315

16.1.2.2 Set Calculated Default Value

When a column has a default value, it is nice if you can calculate that value for each item instead of setting a static value.

If you, for example, want to register the year when an order was placed, you can use a single line of text column with the calculated default value of the current year (when the item was added to the app).

1. Create a Single line of text column and call it "Year". (It will not work with a Date & Time column.)
2. Under default value, in the right pane or in the Create column page, check the box for 'Use calculated value'.
3. Add the formula =Text([TODAY],"YYYY") in the formula box.

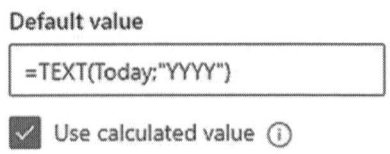

Demo:

https://www.kalmstrom.com/Tips/SharePoint-Online-Course/Categorization-Default-Values.htm

16.2 RATING

SharePoint apps have two options for rating: stars and likes. When this is written, rating is not available in Communication sites.

Rating has several benefits:

- You can filter the column by rating.
- You can create views based on the rating.
- Search results are shown in rating order. By default, the highest rated/most liked hits are shown first.
- SharePoint shows how many users have rated the item.

Rating columns can be used for other than strict rating also. You can for example use rating to indicate urgency or importance.

16.2.1 *Enable Rating*

To allow rating in an app, go into the List settings and click on the 'Rating settings' link under General Settings.

Now you can allow rating and decide which kind of rating, likes or stars, should be used.

Rating Settings
◉ Yes   ○ No

Which voting/rating experience you would like to enable for this list?
○ Likes   ◉ Star Ratings

A new rating column will be created and displayed in the default view. You may of course also include the column in any other view.

16.2.2 Rate with Stars

The star rating column has five empty stars, and you can rate each item by clicking on a star. When you do that, all stars to the left of the star you clicked on will be filled, so if you want to rate an item with three stars you should click on the third star.

16.2.3 Rate with Likes

The **modern** interface shows the likes with hearts. Click on the heart again to unlike.

In the **classic** interface, the like rating has a 'Like' link, and when you click on it, a smiley emoticon is shown at the item. It is possible to remove the linking by clicking on 'Unlike'.

☺ 1   Unlike

Demo:

https://www.kalmstrom.com//Tips/SharePoint-Online-Course/Categorization-Ratings.htm

16.3 MULTIPLE APPS

The categorization methods mentioned in the sections above work well for all apps, and what I say in this section also applies to all kinds of apps – it is better to have more! In my discussion below, though, I focus on libraries.

When you share documents in SharePoint, it is possible to put all your files directly into a big document library with lots of folders within folders. Most things will work as they do in a file server, and you will have the additional features of version history, full text search, flows and workflows, views and alerts. But there are better ways!

Once you start building a library with views and columns, it quickly becomes apparent which files fit into your document library and which don't. To continue with the hotels example I started above, it would be silly to fill out the "Swimming Pool" column value on an excursion and the "Mode of transportation" value for a hotel building.

Instead of trying to fit both excursions and hotels in one document library, it makes sense to create one document library for each of those information types. Using multiple libraries for different kinds of files is generally a good idea. These four features work better if you use multiple libraries, instead of one library with folders:

- Permissions
- Search
- Navigation
- Scaling. A SharePoint app cannot display more than 5000 items, so if you put all your documents in one library you will sooner or later have to move files to new libraries anyway.

To further facilitate switches between multiple libraries in a site, Microsoft plans to add a possibility to select a different document library via a dropdown in the modern library interface.

Demo:

https://www.kalmstrom.com//Tips/SharePoint-Online-Course/Categorization-Create-Libraries.htm

16.4 TERM STORE AND TAGGING

The concept of tagging with keywords is well-known from social media, and it usually works well in SharePoint too. SharePoint has a special column type for such tags that should be used either in the whole tenant or in a site. This column type is called Managed Metadata.

When values are added to a Managed Metadata column in any app, they are synchronized between apps, either in a site or in the whole tenant, and can be managed centrally.

The Managed Metadata column type can be used in two ways:

- Use the Enterprise Keywords column for a free addition of keywords. The Enterprise Keywords column is a special kind of Manage Metadata column.
- Use a custom Manage Metadata column for a more controlled tagging.

In both cases, the values added to these columns in the whole tenant can be seen and managed in the SharePoint Admin center >Term store.

It is also possible to create a collection of metadata terms just for a site, but we will start with the tenant-wide option.

You can find the tenant's Term store under 'Content services' in the SharePoint Admin center left menu. In this Term store, you can manage the terms used in Managed Metadata columns in the whole tenant.

In the Term store, you can find all terms that users have added in Managed Metadata columns, but you can also create a taxonomy for the organization.

A taxonomy is a collection of terms that should be used in tagging. In SharePoint, the terms are organized based on similarities in a hierarchy with three levels: Term group >Term set >Term. The 'Term' level can however have multiple sublevels, so in practice you can have more levels than three.

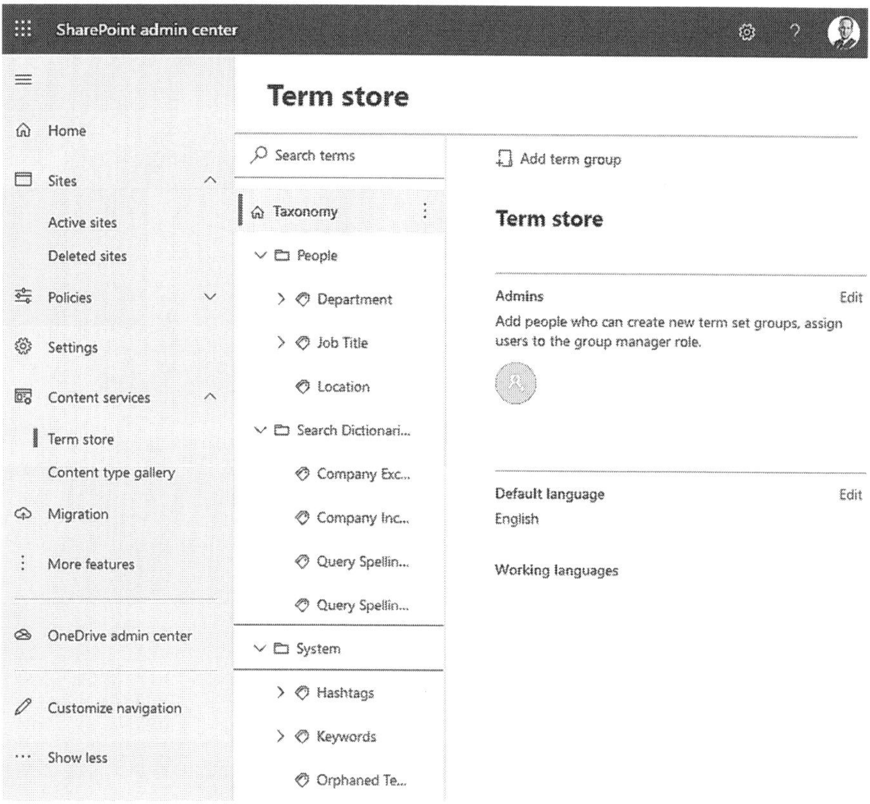

16.4.1 Add Terms in the Term Store

Here, I will describe how you can add a new term group and term set in the Term store, but you can of course also add terms to existing term sets and term sets to existing groups in the same way as described below.

1. In the Term store, click on the ellipsis at the top level, Taxonomy, and select 'Add term group'.

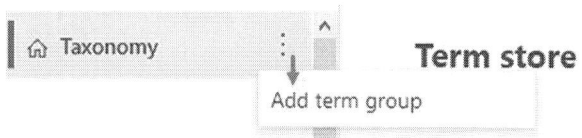

2. Enter a name for the new group.

319

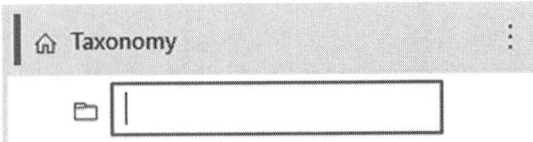

3. Click on the ellipsis at the new Term group to add a new Term set, or select 'Import term set' to import data from a CSV file.

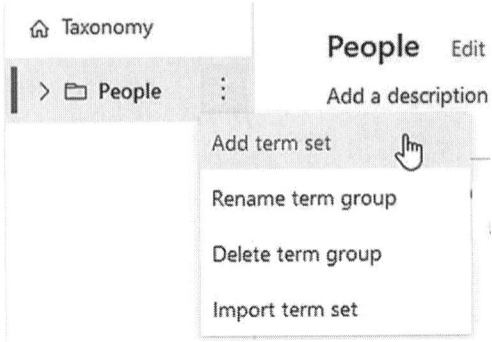

4. Enter a name for the new Term set.
5. In the same way, click on the ellipsis at the Term set heading to add a Term.
6. Enter the term.
7. (Click on the ellipsis at the term and add another term if you want to add a sublevel of terms).
8. Click on the ellipsis at the Term set heading again to add another term.

As you see, there is first a click on the Term set each time you want to add a new term, so even if you don't already have the terms in a CSV file, it might be quicker to enter the keywords in an Excel file, save it as .cvs and import it to the Term store.

16.4.2   Term Store Settings

In the main area to the right of the left menu and taxonomy hierarchy, there are settings for Term groups, Term sets and Terms. The commands on top are the same as under the ellipses, and further down you can find various other settings.

The Term sets have most settings. Under the 'General' tab you can manage the people who are responsible for the Term set.

Term store

Search terms	Add term Rename term set ...
Taxonomy	**Department** Edit
∨ People	Add a description to help users understand the purpose of this term set.
> Department	
> Job Title	General Usage settings Navigation Advanced

The 'Usage settings' tab lets you decide how the terms should be sorted, and if the Term set should be open or closed.

By default, Term sets are open – that is, users can add terms by tagging with terms that do not exist in the Term set. When the Term set is closed, only terms from the Term set can be selected for tagging.

General **Usage settings** Navigation Advanced

Submission policy   Edit
◉ Open policy: Users can add terms from a tagging application.

Available for tagging   Edit
This term set will be available to end users and content editors of sites consuming this term set.
◉ Enabled

Sort order   Edit
Terms can be sorted alphabetically or in a custom order.
◉ Alphabetical

Each term can be managed with translation and synonyms. Select the term and click on '+ Add' under the term's General tab.

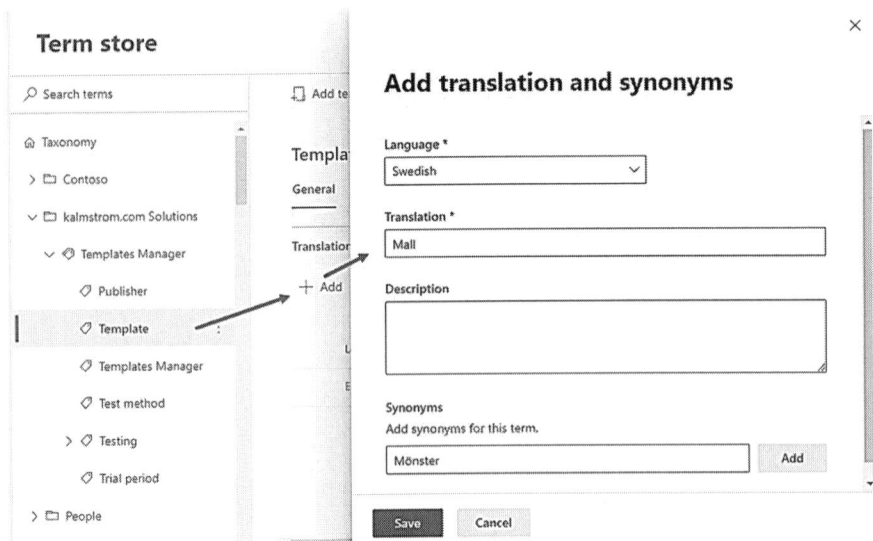

16.4.3 Permissions

A Term store has some specific administrator roles: Term store admin, Group manager, Contributor and Owner. The Term store admin can manage the whole Term store, while Group managers and Contributors only can manage a Group and the term sets in them. An Owner is only responsible for one term set.

To assign a role, click on the level you want to assign a role for and edit the people properties shown in the main area. The higher levels can assign people to the lower levels.

16.4.4 Local Term Groups

A local Term group is created, managed and used within a site. You can reach it from the Site settings >Site administration >Term store management.

The global Term store is visible in the site too, and below it you can create Term groups with terms that should only be visible to users of the site.

To add a Term group, click on the link at the arrow in the image to the right.

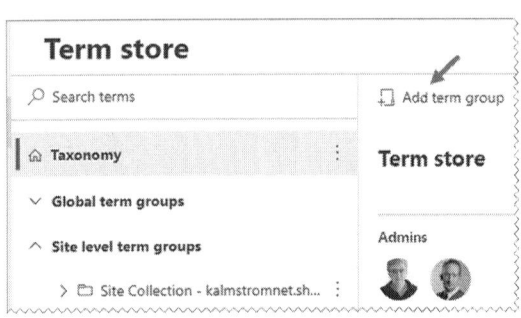

After that, you can create and manage term sets and terms in the local Term group in the same way as described above for the global Term store.

322

16.4.5 Enterprise Keywords

An "Enterprise Keywords" column is a column of the type Managed Metadata that is connected to a single, non-hierarchical Term set called "Keywords" under the 'System' group in the tenant's Term store. It is added to apps in a specific way, see below.

The "Keywords" Term set is a folksonomy – a collection of terms that have been added to Enterprise Keywords columns in the whole tenant.

Any user with Edit permission on a SharePoint app that has an "Enterprise Keywords" column can add keywords to the column, and they will then be added to the folksonomy and available across the organization.

If you need to edit the keywords, for example to remove inappropriate or wrongly spelled words, like in the image below, you can edit term in the "Keywords" Term set in the Term store.

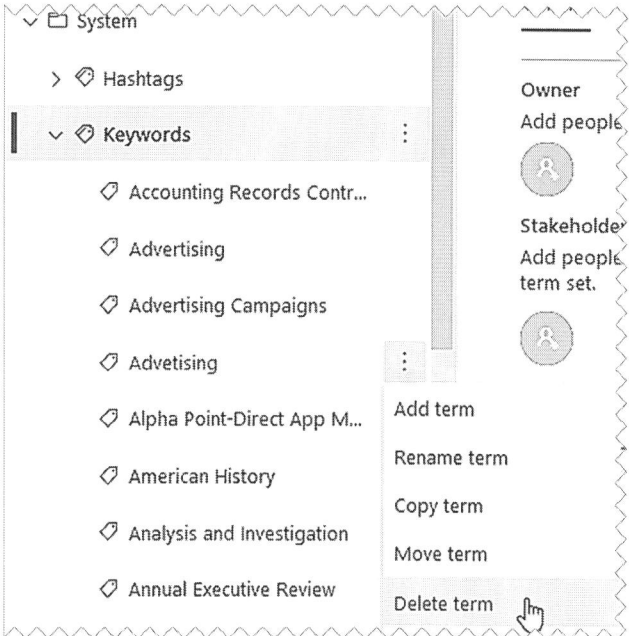

16.4.5.1 Add an Enterprise Keywords Column

When you want to add an "Enterprise Keywords" column to a SharePoint app, open the List settings and click on 'Enterprise Metadata and Keywords Settings' under Permissions and Management.

When the page opens, check the box for Enterprise Keywords.

Enterprise Keywords

☑ Add an Enterprise Keywords column to this list and enable Keyword synchronization

Click OK, and an "Enterprise Keywords" column will be added to the app.

323

The "Enterprise Keywords" column is not automatically added to the default view, but I would recommend that you edit the view and add it. To be useful, this column should be visible in at least the default view. You can also rename the column if necessary.

When the "Enterprise Keywords" column is added to the view, you can also open the app in grid view mode and enter keywords there.

16.4.5.2 Tag with Enterprise Keywords

When you create or edit an item that has an "Enterprise Keywords" column, you will have keyword suggestions as soon as you start writing in the "Enterprise Keywords" column. These suggestions come from the whole Term store.

You can also see in which Term set the term is stored, which will make it easier to select the right term.

If no suggestion is good enough, you can add your own keyword. It will then be added to the Keywords Term set.

Demo:

https://www.kalmstrom.com/Tips/SharePoint-Online-Course/Categorization-Enterprise-Keywords.htm

16.4.5.3 Remove the Enterprise Keywords column.

To add the "Enterprise Keywords" column, you just need to check a box in the app settings, as described above. You cannot remove the column by unchecking the same box. Of course, you can remove the column from any view, but the column will still be visible in the properties.

To remove the "Enterprise Keywords" column from a SharePoint app, you must do like with other columns; *refer to* 7.11.2.1, Delete a List Column.

When the column has been deleted, the "Keywords" Term set is still left in the Term store and can be used in other apps. If you want to remove them totally, you must delete the Term set.

Demo:

https://www.kalmstrom.com/Tips/SharePoint-Online-Course/Categorization-Remove-Keywords.htm

16.4.6 *Custom Managed Metadata Column*

If you want a more controlled tagging, or if you create a column where a limited number of options should be possible, you can create a Choice column. That works well for few options, but if the options are many, or if you want to control them centrally for the whole tenant, a custom Managed Metadata column is a better alternative.

When you use a custom Managed Metadata column, you first add the choices users should select from to a term set in the Term store. Then you connect the column to that term set.

The column you use for the keywords can be called anything, but it must be of the Managed Metadata type. I recommend that you create it as a site column, so that you can reuse it.

A Managed Metadata column must be created and edited in the List settings. Select 'More ...' if you create the column from the modern interface.

16.4.6.1 Connect to a Term Set

To connect a column to a term set and use the keywords stored there for tagging, create a column of the Managed Metadata type and give it any name.

In the Create Column dialog you can then connect the column to one of your term sets.

Now all keywords that are added to this Term set will be displayed as suggestions to users. By default, users can add their own keywords, but that is only possible if the Term set is open in the Term store settings, *see* above.

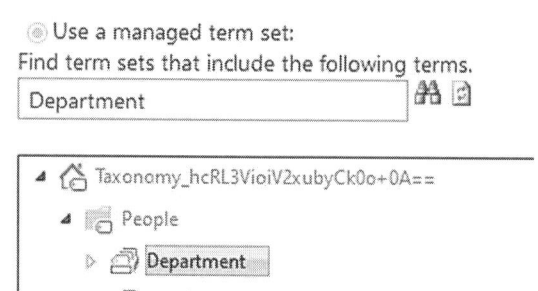

You can always open an existing Managed Metadata column from the List settings to change which Term set the column should be connected to. If you do that, you probably want to change the name of the column too.

16.4.6.2 Tag a Custom Managed Metadata Field

When users create or edit an item with a Managed Metadata column, they will see a Term store icon in the right part of the column field. The image to the right is from the modern experience. The classic interface has a double icon.

When users click on the icon in the **modern** interface, a right pane will open where they can select among all the terms in the connected term set. When terms have sub terms, these are also displayed and possible to select.

325

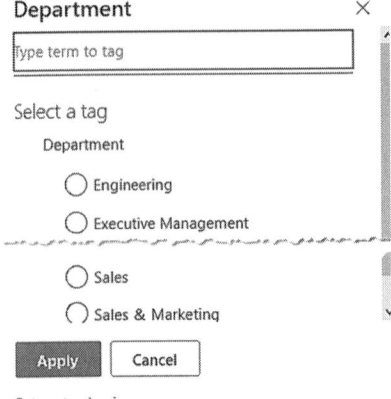

The **classic** experience work in a similar way, but it opens a dialog instead of a right pane.

Demo:

https://www.kalmstrom.com/Tips/SharePoint-Online-Course/Categorization-Term-Store-Start.htm

16.5 Page Categorization

SharePoint site pages are stored in the "Site Pages" library, as described in chapter 13, and in that library, you can add new columns to categorize the pages. Users will benefit from these columns in searches.

16.5.1 Add Property Column

To add a column that stores page properties, open the "Site Pages" library and create a new column. This is done in the same way as when you create a list column in a document library.

The properties column can be of any type. A choice column is often suitable to categorize site pages, but you can also create a Managed Metadata column as described in the section above – or any other column that suits your pages.

You can filter the columns and create views for the "Site Pages" library, just as you can do in other SharePoint libraries.

16.5.1.1 Properties in Modern Pages

If you want to display the values in one or more "Site pages" columns in a page, there is a special web part for it: Page properties. Edit the web part and add the column(s) you wish to display. The page value for that column will be shown in the page. When a page does not have a value in the field that should be display, the web part will be collapsed.

Use the Highlighted content or News web part to display pages or other content with specified properties. You can combine multiple filters to narrow down the options.

If you select to show content from the "Site Pages" library in the current site, you can display tiles with multiple pages on another page. When users click on a tile, the corresponding tile will open.

The image below shows how a Highlighted content web part is edited to show only pages that are categorized with "Helpdesk".

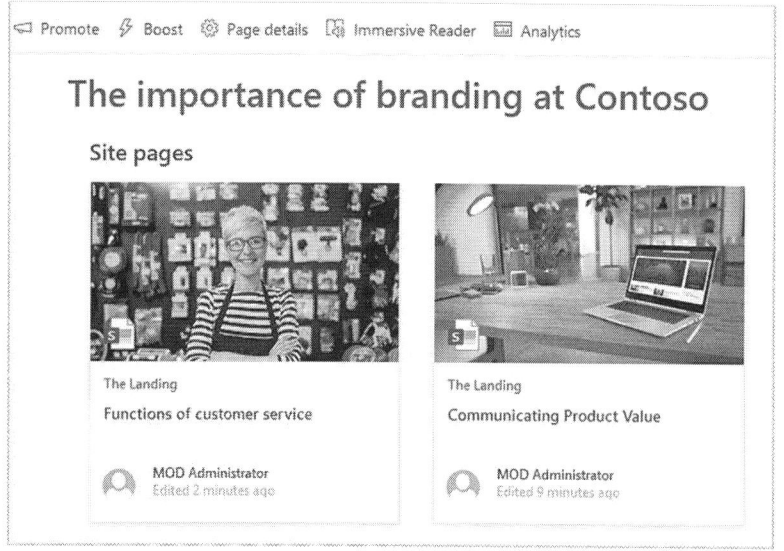

16.5.2 *Edit Page Properties*

Once the property column has been added to the "Site Pages" library, the values can of course be edited for all pages in the library.

All pages also give users a possibility to view and edit the page properties in the page itself.

The properties of **modern** pages are reached via the 'Page details' control in the command bar. When the page is in Edit mode, the properties can be modified.

To see or edit the page properties of a **classic** page, open the PAGE tab in the ribbon and click on 'Edit Properties'.

A dialog will open in read or edit mode, depending on choice. Filter by Page Properties.

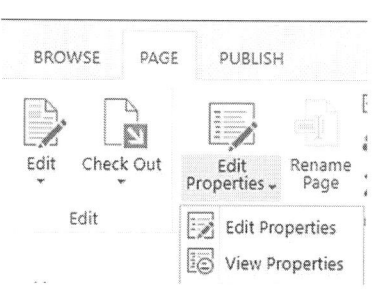

16.6 Managed Properties

When you want SharePoint to search only among content with specific properties, you can use Managed Properties. These are written before the search term, with a colon as separator.

Example: to find files with the word "consumer" in the file name, you should write Filename:consumer in the search box. Note that there must not be any space between the property and the term!

When you enter the search term like this, you are telling the search engine to give you all files with the word "consumer" in the filename. (By default, if you do not supply a managed property, you are searching all content.)

When you want to search for a name or another term that has two parts, use quotation marks around that term to indicate that it should be considered as one term: author:"Lisa Morrison".

You can even use the operators AND and OR. The operators must be written in capitals.

author:"Lisa Morrison" OR author:"Robert Smith"

Which managed properties are the most relevant ones depends on how you are using SharePoint, but the Body, Title, Author and FileType managed properties are often very useful.

16.6.1 Automatic Managed Properties Creation

When you create **site columns**, SharePoint will create managed properties from the column names if you use columns of the type:

- Single line of text
- Choice
- Managed Metadata
- Date and Time
- Number
- Currency
- Yes/No

For example, if you create a Single line of text column named "Street", you can use "street" as a managed property and search for street:avenue. That will give you all the street names that include the word "avenue".

16.6.2 Find Managed Properties

You can find and learn new managed properties from the Site settings of any site. Click on 'Schema' under the Search heading to see all the tenant's managed properties.

All managed properties are not searchable, but you can use those who are marked with Search, like AccountName and AnchorText in the image below.

Property Name	Type	Multi	Query	Search	Retrieve	Refine	Sort	Safe	Mapped Crawled Properties
AADObjectID	Text	-	Query	-	Retrieve	-	Sort	Safe	People:msOnline-ObjectId
AboutMe	Text	-	Query	-	Retrieve	-	-	Safe	People:AboutMe, ows_Notes
Account	Text	-	Query	-	Retrieve	-	-	Safe	ows_Name
AccountName	Text	-	Query	Search	Retrieve	-	-	Safe	People:AccountName
AnalyticsPath	Text	-	Query	-	Retrieve	-	-	Safe	
AnchorText	Text	-	-	Search	-	-	-	Safe	Basic:28

The search schema determines how content is collected and retrieved from the search index. Click on a managed property to modify it.

Demos:

https://kalmstrom.com/Tips/SharePoint-Online-Course/SharePoint-Search-Managed-Properties.htm

16.7 Summary

In this chapter, I have given some tips on how you can categorize content in SharePoint apps, to make it easier to find. You have learned categorization methods like rating and required and default column values.

A bit more complicated, but very rewarding in the long run, is to use the column type Manage Metadata. I have shown some different ways to take advantage of this column type, and I have explained how to reach the Term Store and manage keywords centrally there.

We have also seen how pages can be categorized in the "Site Pages" library and how you can edit page properties directly in classic and modern pages.

Finally, you have learned some about how managed properties can be used in searches.

Now we will go over to something else: links. Ever since we started using the internet, everyone knows what a link is, and in next chapter you will learn how to find and use links in SharePoint.

17 LINKS

Links are the foundation of everything on the web. A link, also called hyperlink or shortcut, is usually a reference to another specific web page, section, document, image or sound.

To create a link, you often need to know the web address, or URL, to the content you want to link to.

In SharePoint, the mouse cursor sometimes transforms into a hand when you hover over linked text or images. When you hover over clickable text, the link will often be highlighted or underlined.

In this chapter you will learn:

- Where to find the URL to a SharePoint item
- How links can be added, edited and used in SharePoint Online
- Different ways to add links that point to pages, apps and images
- How to write and use wiki links
- How to add captions and make a link open in a new window
- How to create promoted links
- How to create a Links app and add links to it.

17.1 GET THE URL

To copy a URL, you can select it in the browser's address field, right-click and select Copy. You can do this for any URL, and for SharePoint apps and pages it works well.

When you need a link to a SharePoint site or item there are better options.

17.1.1 Item Link

When you copy the URL to a list item or library file as described in chapter 15, Sharing, you will also have the possibility to set permission for the shared link. *Refer to* 15.3.3, Share with a Link.

17.1.2 Site Link

The easiest way to get the correct link to a site, is to right-click on the SharePoint banner or site logo in the top left corner of any page in the site you want to open.

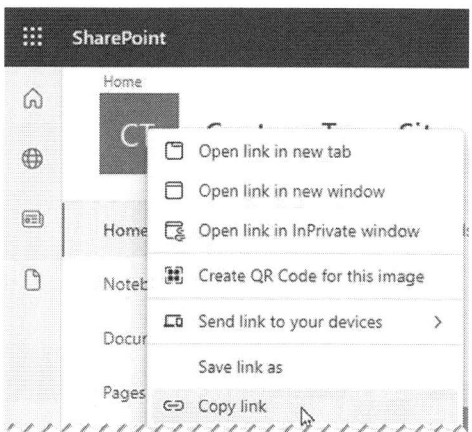

When you select 'Copy link', you will get the correct URL for the site. It is often shorter than the URL in the address field, which also may include the specific page.

17.2 ADD LINKS TO A PAGE

Links can be added to pages in many ways. The classic pages give a few more options than the modern pages, especially when it comes to linking images. Pages must always be in edit mode when links are added.

17.2.1 Add Links to a Modern Page

Modern pages have two web parts dedicated to links, Links and Quick Links. It is also possible to add links in some other web parts, like the Hero, Button, Call to action and Sites web parts, and to link text in the Text web part.

17.2.1.1 The Link Web Part

In the Link web part, you can paste any link directly into the web part. If available, a preview of the item you link to will be displayed. You can only add one link to each Link web part.

17.2.1.2 The Quick Links Web Part

The Quick Links web part is more of a "pin" tool for multiple links.

Click on '+ Add links' in the web part, and the Location pane will open. When you have added the link, you can add a custom image and an alternate text.

Select the web part and click on the Edit web part pen icon to select layout. The screenshot in 17.5, Views Landing Page below, shows a page where the Quick Links web part has been used with the Tile layout and auto-selected link images.

331

17.2.1.3 The Highlighted Content Web Part

In the Highlighted content web part, there is a possibility to show only links.

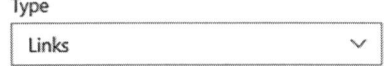

17.2.1.4 The Sites Web Part

In the Sites web part, links are shown as tiles in a modern SharePoint page. Each tile has linked info about popular and the current user's recently reached content on the site.

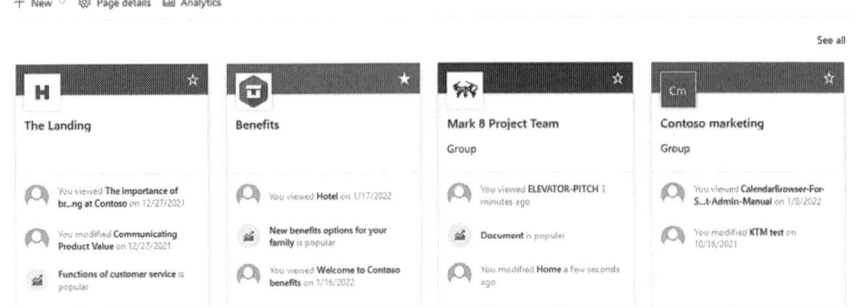

The Sites web part can only show links to sites within the tenant.

The image to the right shows the Site web part's Edit pane in a hub site, which gives some more options than other sites.

There are two automatic options: to show all sites in the hub or to show frequent sites for the current user.

You can also choose the 'Select sites' radio button. That gives you a possibility to search for sites.

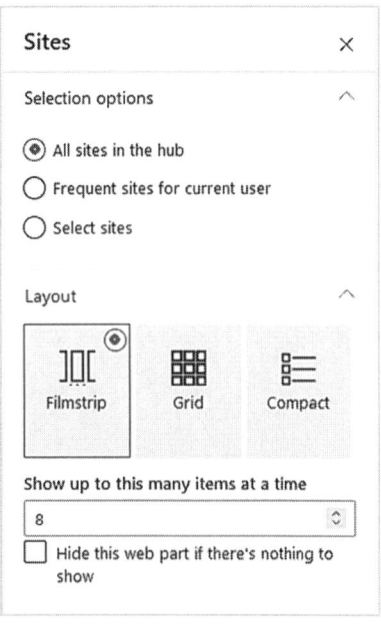

Site name suggestions will be added below the search field, and when you check a box, a tile with a link to the site will be added to the page. Then you can add another site in the same way.

An additional alternative for the 'Select sites' option, is to select sites among associated, frequent and recent sites.

17.2.2 Add Links to a Classic Page

When you want to add links to classic pages in classic sites, you have two options: 'From SharePoint' and 'From Address'.
Both are found under the ribbon INSERT tab.

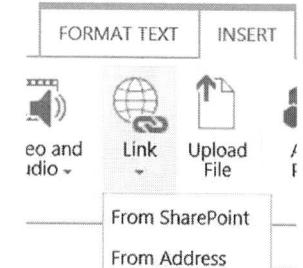

Place the mouse cursor where you want to add a link or select the text or image you want to add a link to. The click on the 'Link' button in the ribbon and select the link option you want to use.

Use the 'From Address' link option, when you want to add a link to a page that is outside the site or even outside your tenant.

When you select 'From Address', a dialog will open where you can enter a URL. If you have selected a text, it will be filled out under Text to display. Otherwise, you can enter an anchor text to be displayed. You can also try the link before you click OK.

When you create a wiki page in a modern Team site, you will only have the 'From Address' option, but you can of course use it for links from SharePoint too.

Use the 'From SharePoint' link option, when you want to select a page, document or item in the same site. When you select 'From SharePoint', a new page will open where you can pick the location to link to.

17.2.2.1 Link Options

When you place click on the new link, a LINK tab will be displayed. Here you can add a description that will be shown in a pop-up window when users hover the mouse cursor over the link.

Check the box for 'Display icon' if you have linked to an Office file and want the file type to be indicated with an icon. For other file types, you will just have a white icon of no interest.

333

Under the LINK tab you can also set the link location to open in a new tab and remove the link. When you remove the link this way, the display text or image that you have linked will still be visible on the page.

17.3 ADD LINKS IN APPS

SharePoint Online apps have a specific column type for links, but if rich text is allowed, users can also add links in Multiple lines of text fields.

17.3.1 The Hyperlink Column

To make it possible to add links to app items, you can create a Hyperlink column from a modern app interface. In classic apps, or if you create the column from the List settings, the same column type is called 'Hyperlink or Picture'. ⦿ Hyperlink or Picture

When you add a link to a Hyperlink/Hyperlink or Picture column, the link source will open in a new tab in the browser when someone clicks on it.

In Standard view mode, enter the URL and display text in the Properties pane (modern) or dialog (classic).

In Grid view mode, a dialog opens when you click in a cell in the **modern** interface. Here, you can add the URL and a display text.

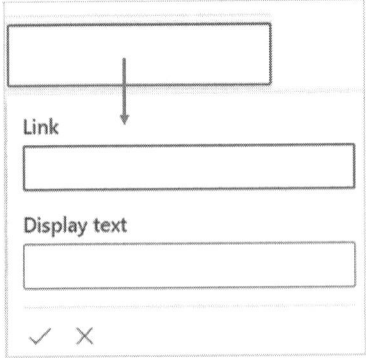

In the **classic** interface, you should instead click on a link icon to open the dialog.

17.3.2 The Multi-Line Column

You can add links in list columns of the type Multiple lines of text, if enhanced rich text is enabled in the column settings, *refer to* 8.8.1. Note that only list apps have this option in the Multiple lines of text column.

When you add a link to a Multiple lines of text field in the **modern** experience, you can enter a link in the text field, and it will become clickable.

However, if you want to use an anchor text, you must open the ellipsis to the right in the tool bar and select 'Add or edit hyperlink'. Then you can add a URL and a display text in the dialog that opens.

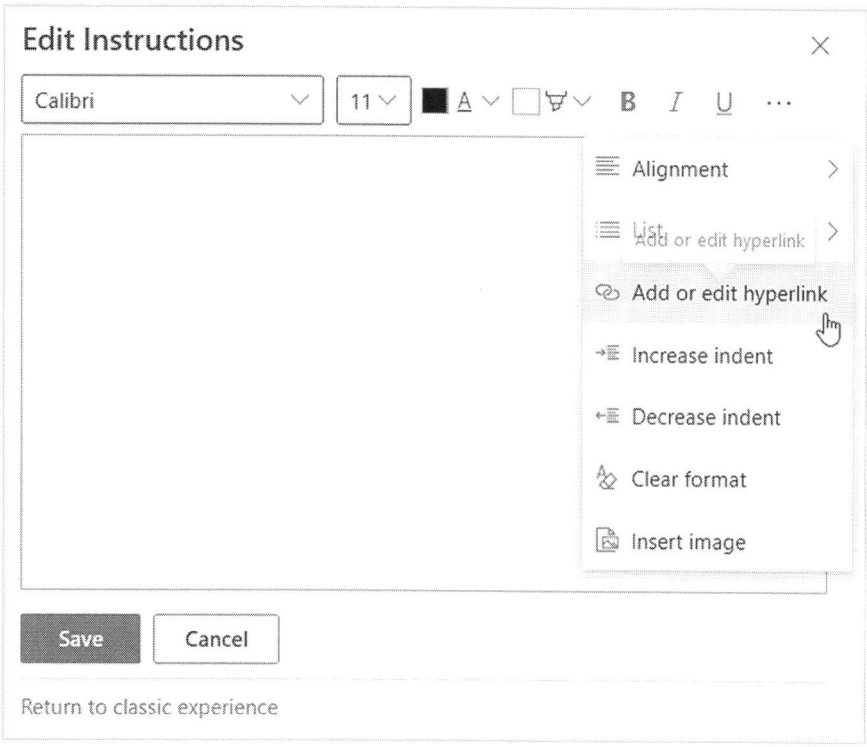

There are currently no other options, and the link does *not* open in a new tab. Therefore, it is better to switch to the classic interface, if possible, to add the link. There, you will have the same link options as when you add links to a classic page, *see* above.

When you add a link to a Multiple lines of text field in the **classic** experience, you should not paste the link directly into the field. Instead, use the 'Link' button under the Insert tab in the ribbon.

When you have added the link, click in it, and you will have the same link options as when you edit a classic page.

17.4 LINK AN IMAGE IN A PAGE

In **modern** pages, you can add a link to an image that is added to the Image web part. When you have added the image, edit the web part and enter the link in the right pane.

335

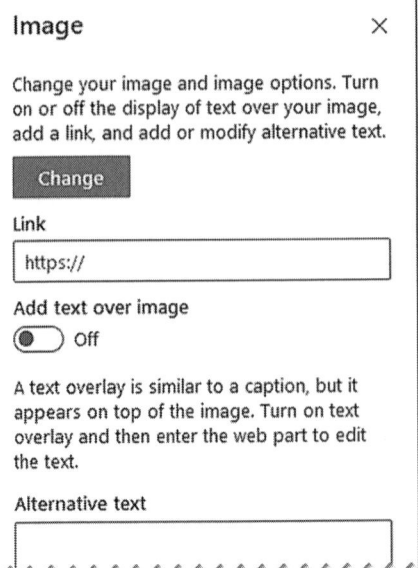

If you add a picture to a **classic** SharePoint page, you can link the image just like you link text. Click on the image instead of in the text, and you will have all the link options.

Demo:

https://kalmstrom.com/Tips/SharePoint-Online-Course/Links-From-Images.htm

17.5 Views Landing Page

SharePoint apps have the limitation of displaying only one (modern) or three (classic) views right on the page. To reach the other views, you must open a dropdown.

If you want to give users an overview of all views, you can create a landing page that is displayed when users open the app. You can of course also add more data than just the view links to this page.

The landing page is created in two steps, whether you do in in a modern or classic page:

1. Create the page with links to the views. The view URLs are copied from the app address field and pasted into the landing page, so keep the list open in another tab so that you quickly can move between the app and the landing page you are creating.
2. The app link in the Site navigation should of course point to the Views landing page and not directly to the app. Edit the navigation as described in chapter 11 to replace the link.

Also *refer to* 23.4, Landing Pages, where we expand the landing page with a list and then add a dynamic Excel chart to the page.

17.5.1   *Modern Views Landing Page*

For a modern page, I recommend the Quick links web part, but a Text web part can also work. It is not possible to link an image in the Text web part, but if you only want links the Text web part will work well.

The image below shows a modern page where the Quick Links web part has been used with the Tiles layout.

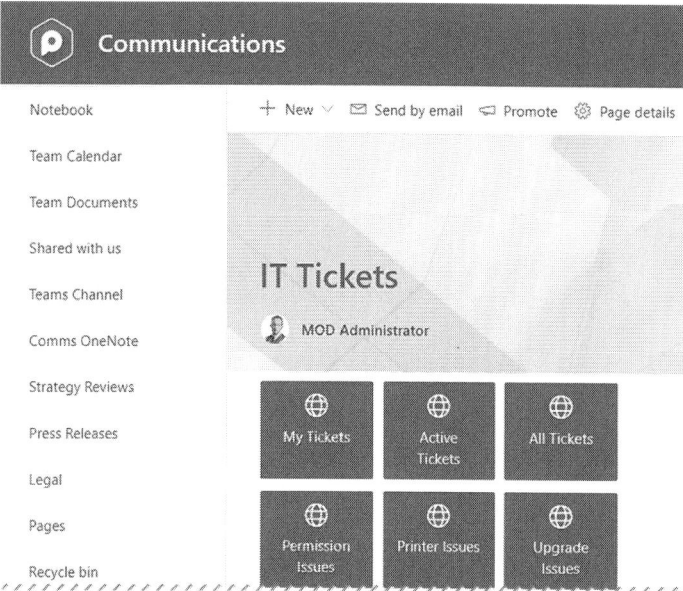

1. Add the Quick Links web part to a modern page in edit mode.
2. Edit the web part and select layout.
3. Click on '+ Add links' in the web part to open the Location pane. Select 'From a link'.
4. Copy the URL for one of the views from the list's address field and paste it in the main area of the Location pane.
5. A right pane opens with various options for the link, for example a custom image for each link. (In the image above, all tiles have the same background.)
6. Repeat step 5 for each link and Publish the page.

17.5.2   *Classic Views Landing Page*

This description is for a wiki page. For a web part page, first add the Content Editor web part and then add the links in the same way as for the wiki page.

1. Under the Insert tab, select the 'From Address' link option.
2. Write a display text in the dialog and paste the view URL.
3. Repeat step 2-4 for each view.

You can also add images to the page and link them to the various views.

Demos:

https://kalmstrom.com/Tips/SharePoint-Online-Course/View-Combining.htm

https://www.kalmstrom.com//Tips/SharePoint-Online-Course/View-Landing.htm

17.6 WIKI LINKING

Wiki links can be added to classic wiki pages in edit mode and help you achieve things that are difficult to manage in other ways. With wiki links, you can for example link from one page to another page that has not yet been created.

Wiki links only work within a site. This means that you can link to pages, apps and even to a certain view or item in the site, but you cannot use a wiki link for content in another site or outside SharePoint.

The wiki link syntax must be typed in, and the links must start and end with double square brackets, [[…]]. When you type the first two brackets on a SharePoint wiki page, you will be shown a list of the site's pages, apps and views. Select one of the options, and the closing brackets will be added automatically.

You can also type in the syntax instead of selecting, for example if you want to link to a non-existing page. Then you must add the closing brackets manually too.

17.6.1 Wiki Link and Create a Wiki Page

When using wiki links, you can first create the link and then create the page you have linked to:

1. When the wiki page is in edit mode, type the name of the new page surrounded by double square brackets, for example [[Sales]].
2. Save the page you are working on, and the link will be displayed with a dotted underline, to show that the page does not exist yet.
3. Click on the link, and you will be asked if you want to create the page.

Add a page ×

The page 'Sales' does not exist. Do you want to create it?
Find it at https://m365x446726.sharepoint.com/sites/ci/SitePages/Sales.aspx

Create   Cancel

4. Click on 'Create', and the new wiki page will open in edit mode, so that you can customize it.

5. When you return to the page where you created the link, it will no longer be underlined, and the link will take you to the page you just created.

17.6.2 *Wiki Link to an App*

When you link to an existing app, you can use the select option instead of typing the syntax within the double brackets.

1. When the page is in edit mode, type the two brackets.
2. Click on List:

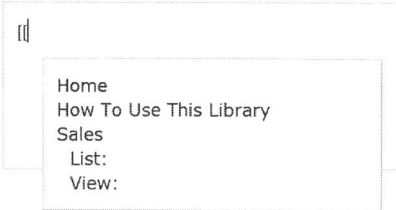

3. Now all apps will be displayed, and you can click on the list or library you want to link to.
4. The two end brackets are added automatically.

[[List:KTM Tasks/]]

5. Save the page, and the link will be shown with the list name as display text.

17.6.3 *Wiki Link to a View*

To create a wiki link that points directly to a view, you must perform some more steps when you have selected the app.

1. When the page is in edit mode, type the two brackets.
2. Click on View.
3. All apps are displayed. Click on the app that has the view you want to link to. Now the link is completed – but it still only points to the app.
4. Remove the two end brackets.
5. Press the Ctrl key + the space key. Now the views of that list will be displayed, and you can select the view you want to link to.
6. When you save the page, the link will be shown with the view name as display text.

[[View:Documents/

All Documents
Manuals
Slideshows

Demo:

https://kalmstrom.com/Tips/SharePoint-Online-Course/HelpDesk-Landing-Page.htm

339

17.6.4 Wiki Link to an Item

When you want to link to a specific item in a list or library, the process is nearly the same as when you link to a view.

1. When the page is in edit mode, type the two brackets,
2. Click on List.
3. All apps are displayed. Click on the app that has the item you want to link to. Now the link is completed – but it still only points to the app.
4. Remove the two end brackets.
5. Press the Ctrl key + the space key. Now the items of that list will be displayed, and you can select the item you want to link to.
6. If there are many items in the list, you will first be asked to start typing to have choice. In the image below I have written an s, and then all items that begin with an s are displayed so that I can select one of them.

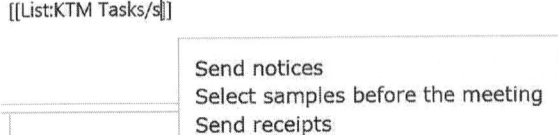

7. When SharePoint creates the link, the ID number of the item is added as the actual location for the link. After that comes a pipe (vertical bar) and then the display text, which is the title of the item.

[[List:KTM Tasks/6|Send notices]]

8. When you save the link, the item title or file name will be shown as display text for the link.

17.6.5 Manipulate Display Text

As we have seen in the section above, the wiki link to an item uses the item ID and then adds the item name after a pipe (|) to get the link to show the item name as display text.

Pipe + display name can be used in all wiki links:

1. Create the wiki link as described in one of the sections above.
2. Type a pipe + the word(s) you want to use as display text before the two square brackets at the end.
3. Save the page, and the text after the pipe will be shown as display text.

Demo:

https://kalmstrom.com/Tips/SharePoint-Online-Course/Wiki-Pages.htm

17.7 CREATE A LINKS APP

A nice way of adding links to SharePoint is to add them to an app that is designed to display links. The Links app is such an app, and it can have both the classic and the modern interface. A Links app can also be added to a page.

Links

(By default, it is not possible to create a Picture library app in a Communication site. *Refer to* 7.5.1.1, Apps in Communication Sites, if you want to have that possibility.)

Create the links app by opening the 365 Settings icon and selecting 'Add an app'. Then search for the Links app.

To add links to the links app, click on '+ New' in the command bar and select 'Item' (modern) or 'new link' (classic).

Enter the address in the URL field and write a description that gives a suitable display text. The Notes text will be shown in a separate column, *see* the image above.

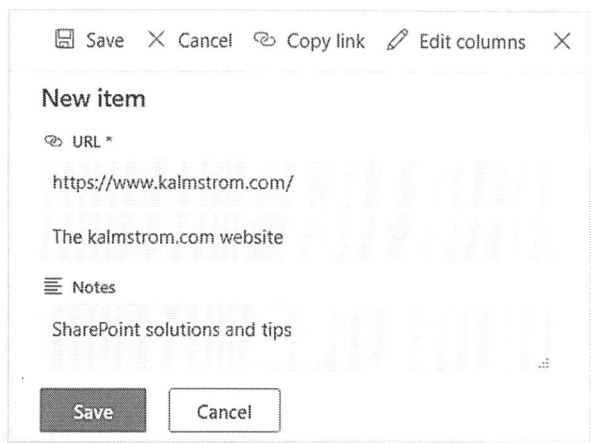

Demo:

https://kalmstrom.com/Tips/SharePoint-Online-Course/Links-List-App.htm

17.7.1 Add a Links App to a Page

The Links app can be added to the List web part in a **modern** page in the same site:

1. Add the List web part to the page.
2. Select the Links app from the lists that are displayed in the web part.
3. When you edit the List web part, you will have various options on what to show on the page.

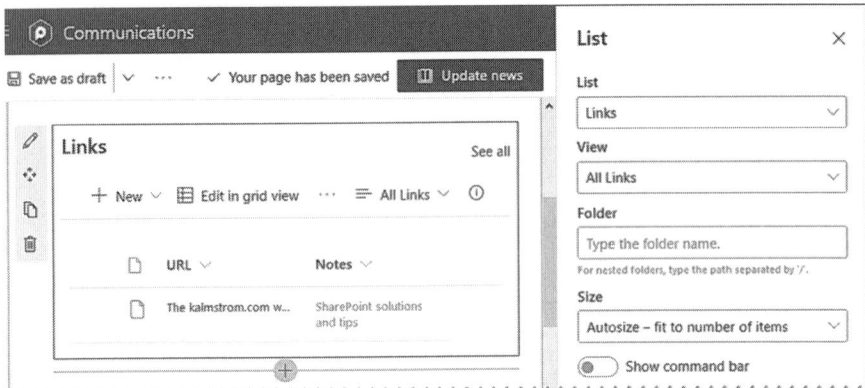

When you edit a **classic** page, you will find the Links app among the app parts or among the web parts in the App category. Select it and click on 'Add', and you will have the same information as in the Links app displayed on the page.

17.8 PROMOTED LINKS

When you create a classic Team site, the homepage has links in the shape of moving tiles. These links are called promoted links. You can create such tile links yourself by using the Promoted links app.

The image below shows two tiles in an embedded Promoted links app. One has a background image, and one is without an image. The title is always visible, but the description is only displayed when you move the mouse cursor over the tile.

342

17.8.1 *Create a Promoted Links App*

Use the command 'Add an app' to create a Promoted Links app.

Follow these steps to add tiles to the app:

1. Open the Promoted Links app.
2. Click on '+ New' in the command bar (modern) or 'new item' (classic). (In the classic interface you must first click on the link to the 'All Promoted Links' view.)

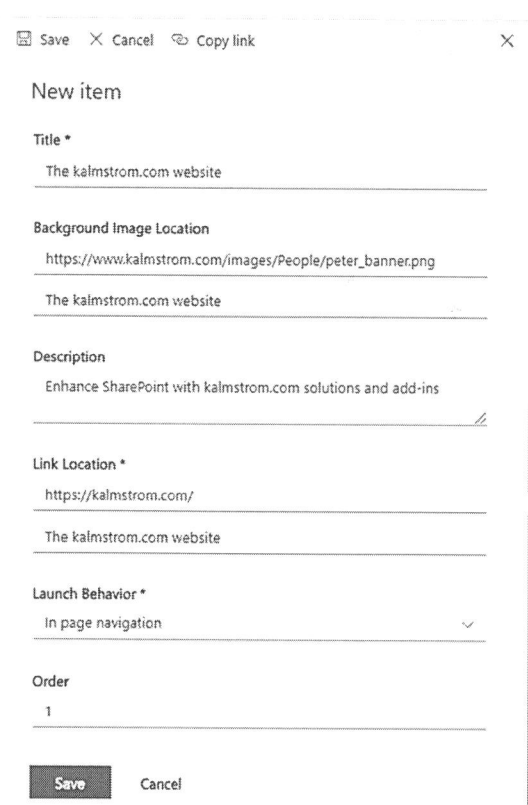

Promoted Links

3. Enter a link to a background image, a target link and a description.
4. You should also set the sequence order of the tile and select if the link location should open in the same page, in a new tab or in a dialog.
5. Click on Save when the form is filled out.
6. Repeat step 2-5 for each tile.

343

17.8.1.1 Promoted Links Images

You don't need to add images to the promoted links, but if you want to do that, any image can be used. The size will be 150x150px, so if you use a bigger image, it will be compressed. Avoid using a smaller image, as it will give bad quality. (It is only possible to change the size of the promoted link tiles by using code.)

17.8.2 *Add Promoted Links to a Page*

When you have created a promoted links app, you can add it in a modern List web part or as a classic app part on a SharePoint page. This is done in the same way as with the Links app, *see* above.

Demo:

https://kalmstrom.com/Tips/SharePoint-Online-Course/Promoted-Links.htm

17.9 SUMMARY

As the SharePoint site grows, it becomes increasingly important to have a good navigation. In this Links chapter, I have introduced promoted links, wiki links and links apps in addition to the more well-known kinds of hyperlinks. I have also shown how to add captions, how to make a link open in a new window and how you can create a views landing page.

In the next chapter, we will look at different ways to add images to SharePoint.

18 PICTURES

Images can be added to SharePoint from different sources. They can be edited in various ways, and they can also be linked, as we saw in the previous chapter.

When you upload an image to a library it will be stored there, but images that are uploaded directly to a page or a list app will by default be stored in the Site Assets library. This library is created automatically when a new site is created.

In this chapter, I will introduce picture libraries and explain how you can add pictures to pages. I will also show two ways to create and add so called hotspot images – images that have different links in different areas of the image.

At first, I will however introduce the modern Image column and tell you about two new features for images that are uploaded to a SharePoint or OneDrive library.

18.1   THE MODERN IMAGE COLUMN

The modern experience has an Image column type that lets you display thumbnails of pictures that you upload from your computer to the app.

The image below shows thumbnails in an Image column named Icon in the default List view mode. In list apps, you can use the Gallery layout to get bigger images.

Products ☆

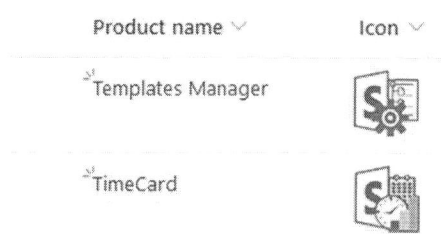

The images in the Image column are just thumbnails, and currently you cannot click on them to see the full image. Use the Hyperlink column instead, if you want users to be able to reach the full image.

The images are added in the item properties. If you just upload an image to a library via the 'Upload' button, no thumbnail will be shown in the Image column.

18.2 Library Image Options

This section describes two new features that have not yet been released when the book is published. I have not found any documentation on how these features will work with the classic interface, and as I don't yet have the features, I have not been able to check them.

18.2.1 *Image Tags*

When you upload an image to a SharePoint app, a new column called "Image Tags" will be created.

If an image contains keywords when it is uploaded, those tags will be added to the "Image Tags" column, and if possible, some basic tags will also be added. The automatically generated tags are reanalyzed every time the image is updated, so these tags might be removed and new tags added.

Users can add and remove tags as they wish. The only limit is that the "Image Tags" column cannot contain more than 255 characters for each item. Tags that users add manually will never be removed.

As the keywords in the "Image Tags" column are searchable, I recommend that you make use of this new feature once it is implemented. Note that you might need to edit the view to see the new "Image Tags" column in the library interface.

18.2.2 *Image Filters*

Microsoft plans to add a feature that lets users add image filters to uploaded photos. With these filters, you can change the color and light settings of the image.

Initially the image filters can only be added to JPEG and JPG files, but the PNG file format will be supported later.

18.3 Picture Library

Instead of using the default Site Assets library to store images that should be used in a SharePoint site, you can create a picture library. You may very well create several picture libraries, to categorize the images.

Picture Library

The benefit of using a picture library is that it by default will have two extra views, in additional to the standard library views:

- The Thumbnails view, which shows thumbnails of all pictures.
- The Slides view, where you can move between different pictures like in a slideshow.

To create a Picture Library, use the command 'Add an app' under the 365 Settings icon and search for the Picture Library template. (By default, it is not possible to create a Picture library app in a Communication site. *Refer to* 7.5.1.1, Apps in Communication Sites, if you want to have that possibility.)

An important picture library benefit is that you can add the library to a web part in a page and show pictures in a slideshow on that page, see below.

18.4 ADD IMAGES TO PAGES

Images make SharePoint pages more interesting, and sometimes an image can be more explanatory than text. The images can be fetched to the page from multiple sources, but you should consider how to do with updates.

When you add an image that you have no control over, for example from an external website, it will no longer be shown on your SharePoint page when it is removed from the original site. If the image is updated on the original site, it will be updated on your site too.

To have full control over the image, download it and add it to the page from your computer. Then it will be saved to SharePoint, and you don't risk losing it on the page. But this of course means that your picture will not be updated when the original picture is updated!

Be careful to only use creative commons or images that are free to share and use, when you take images from a website that you don't control. Both Google and Bing Image search allow you to filter by license.

18.4.1 *Modern Page Picture Options*

The modern Hero and Highlighted content web parts can have both images and other content, but Microsoft also offers two modern web parts that are solely intended for images: Image and Image gallery. When images are added to one of these web parts, users can see the images, but they cannot do anything with them.

If you want to give users a possibility to work with the images, you can instead add the images to a library and use the Document library web part.

18.4.1.1 The Image Web Part

The Image web part is intended for one picture only. When you add the web part to a page, the right pane will open so that you can select the image source.

Another option is to open the page in edit mode and drag an image to the place where you want it. The image will automatically be added to an Image web part.

When you have added the image, a toolbox will be displayed above it so that you can work with the image. From left to right, you can:

- Resize the image by dragging in the handles that appear when you click on the icon.
- Crop the image.
- Crop with aspect ratios.

- Align the image.

- Reset the image to the state it was when you last saved it.
- Save the change to the image. This icon might also be placed below the resize icon.

When you click on the edit icon to the left of the web part, you can add a text overlay to the image. You can also add a link and an alternative text, *refer to* 17.4.

18.4.1.2 The Image Gallery Web Part

If you want to add multiple images in the same web part, you can use the Image gallery web part. Here you can display selected images or show images dynamically from a document library.

In the Image gallery web part, you cannot resize or crop images, but you can choose between Brick, Tile and Carousel layout.

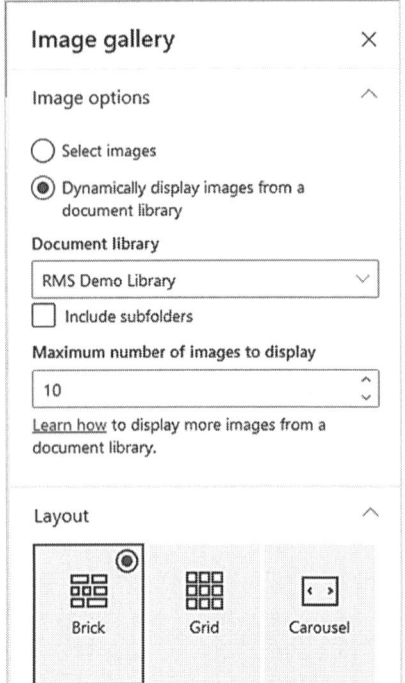

The Carousel layout shows the images in a slideshow. Currently users need to cycle through the images with arrows on the sides, but in the future, Microsoft will add a possibility to set automatic cycling through images.

I suggest that you first add the images to the web part and then try different layouts with them. Generally, the Image gallery works best if the images are of similar size.

Dynamic:
When you want to show the images dynamically, select one of the source options in the dropdown and set the maximum number of images to display.

Select:
If you want to select the images yourself, click on the 'Add images'

348

button in the web part. This opens the Location pane with source options.

It is also possible to drag the images to the web part, but in this case, you need to add the web part first. (If you drag multiple images to a page without an Image gallery web part, they will be placed in one Image web part each.)

In the Tile layout, you can choose an aspect ratio (1:1, 16:9, or 4:3) for the images and drag and drop the images within the web part to reorder them.

Click on each image to show the edit and remove icons. When you click on the edit icon for each image, you can add image titles, captions and alternate texts. Links are currently not supported in the Image gallery web part.

18.4.1.3 Picture Library in Document Library Web Part

It is not (yet) possible to dynamically display images from a Picture library in the Image gallery web part. You can however add a picture library to the Document library web part, because the picture library will show up among the library options when you have added the web part.

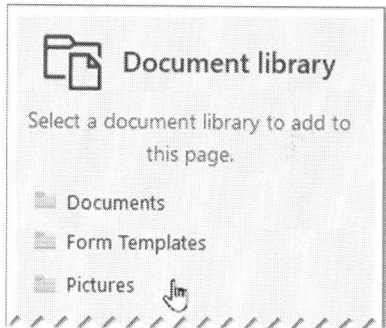

Adding the Picture library to a Document library web part is a good option when you want to give users a possibility to work with the images, like downloading them and seeing their properties.

18.4.2 *Classic Page Picture Options*

In classic sites, images can be added directly to SharePoint wiki pages from three different kinds of sources: Computer, Address and SharePoint. Modern sites with a wiki page only have the options Computer and Address.

You can find the Picture button under the INSERT tab.

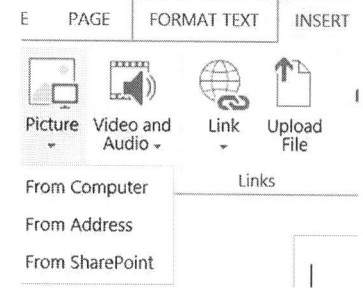

When you select the 'From Computer' option to add a picture, a copy of your file will be uploaded to a SharePoint library in the site.

In the Upload Image dialog, you can select a destination library where you want to place your picture. The default option is the 'Site Assets' library, but if you have created a picture library you may want to choose it instead.

When you select 'From Address' you can enter the URL any picture, and when you add an image 'From SharePoint', it means "from this SharePoint site". With this option, you can pick the image without needing a URL.

349

18.4.2.1 Picture Display

When you select a picture on a wiki page in edit mode, the IMAGE tab will be displayed. Here, you can modify how the image is displayed in several ways.

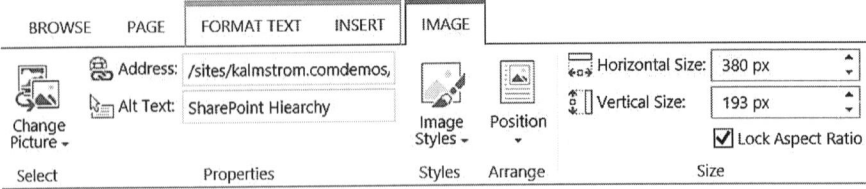

From left to right you can:

- Change Picture. This button gives the same options as the Picture button under the INSERT tab.
- See the path to the image.
- Enter and change an alternative text.
- Set image borders in various styles.
- Set the relative position of the image. (If you want to give the image an absolute position, I recommend that you first insert a table, *refer to* 13.5.1.2, Add a Table, and then insert the image in a cell.)
- Change the size and lock the aspect ratio while doing so.

Demos:

https://kalmstrom.com/Tips/SharePoint-Online-Course/Add-an-Image-from-the-Computer.htm

https://kalmstrom.com/Tips/SharePoint-Online-Course/Adding-an-Image-from-Address.htm

https://kalmstrom.com/Tips/SharePoint-Online-Course/Adding-an-Image-from-SharePoint.htm

18.4.3 *Classic Picture Web Parts*

When you insert a picture web part in a classic page and add your images there, you will have additional options.

18.4.3.1 The Picture Library Slideshow Web Part

If you want to show all the images in a picture library, you can add it in the Picture Library Slideshow web part. It shows the images one by one, either with controls for manual selection or with a timer that switches images automatically.

A limitation of the Picture Library Slideshow web part is that the picture library must be stored in the same site as the page where you insert the web part.

1. Add the Picture Library Slideshow web part from the Media and Content category to the page.
2. Edit the web part and select which picture library should be used and how the images should be displayed.
3. Click OK and save the page.

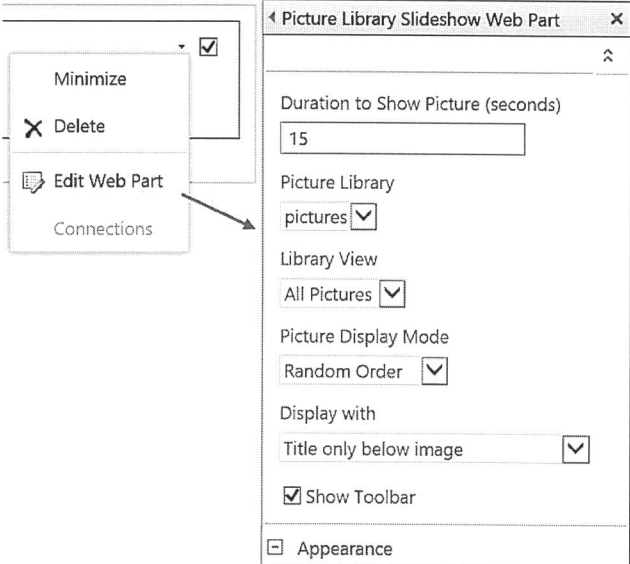

Demo: https://kalmstrom.com/Tips/SharePoint-Online-Course/Picture-Library-Slideshow-Web-Part.htm

18.4.3.2   The Image Viewer Web Part

In SharePoint versions before 2010, the Image Viewer Web Part was the only way to add a picture to a SharePoint page. Nowadays this web part is not so commonly used, but it is still there and possible to use for single images.

1. Add the Image Viewer web part from the Media and Content category to a classic page.
2. Edit the web part and type or paste the image URL in the 'Image Link' field. The picture will be displayed on the page.
3. Make other changes you prefer and then click OK and save the page.

Demo:

https://kalmstrom.com/Tips/SharePoint-Online-Course/Image-Viewer-Web-Part.htm

351

18.5 HOTSPOT IMAGE

Images with clickable regions are often called HTML maps, image maps or hotspot images. Such pictures with areas linked to different destinations can be created in Excel or PowerPoint. The creation is out of scope for this book, but you can see the process in the demos I refer to in this section.

The PowerPoint option is the easiest one, and the file can be added to modern as well as classic SharePoint pages with the file's embed code.

The Excel option gives a cleaner picture, but it can only be added to classic pages.

In both options, you must first save or upload the file to the SharePoint site where you want to add the picture.

The Excel image can be updated automatically from the computer to SharePoint. For the PowerPoint file you must save a new image to SharePoint.

18.5.1 Add a PowerPoint File to a Page

When you have saved a .pptx file to a SharePoint library, you can add it to a page. The links will work, but unfortunately you cannot get rid of the slideshow banner at the bottom when you use a PowerPoint file.

In a **modern** page, add the file to the modern File Viewer web part. You can also use the classic interface to copy the Embed Information of the file, *refer to* 9.2.4, Other Unique Features, and paste it in the Embed web part.

In a **classic** page, copy the Embed Information of the file and paste it in the page by INSERT >Embed Code.

Demo:

https://kalmstrom.com/Tips/SharePoint-Online-Course/Clickable-Links-PowerPoint.htm

18.5.2 Add an Excel image to a Classic Page

When you have created an Excel image, it should be added to the classic Content Editor web part in the Media and Content category.

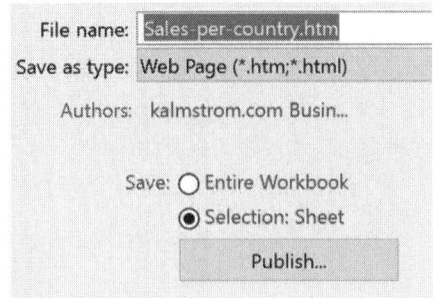

1. Save the image sheet as a web page to the site where you want to show it.

    Click on Save as >More options and select the Web Page file type. At 'Save' select the option 'Selection Sheet'.

2. Click on 'Publish...' and check the box to allow 'AutoRepublish every time this workbook is saved'.

3. Save the file as an .xlsx file to your computer, so that you can continue working with it, and select the radio button for 'Enable the AutoRepublish feature'.

4. Open the SharePoint page in edit mode and insert the Content Editor web part from the Media and Content category.

5. Edit the web part and set the URL to the .htm file you saved from Excel to SharePoint.

6. Make any other changes you prefer before you apply and save the page.

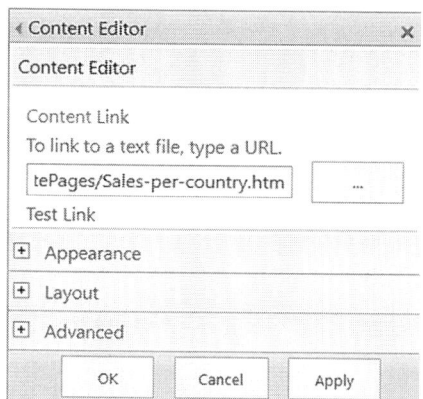

Now, each time you change something in the file on your computer and save it, the SharePoint image will be updated automatically.

Demo:

https://www.kalmstrom.com/Tips/SharePoint-Online-Course/Clickable-Links-Excel.htm

18.6 SUMMARY

In the Pictures chapter you have learned about the Picture library and how to add pictures to modern and classic SharePoint pages. I have also shown some ways to add hotspot images to SharePoint pages and introduced some upcoming features that will enhance the use of images in SharePoint libraries.

We have already talked a lot about web parts and page customization, but in next chapter I will give more information about that subject. I will explain how you can connect two web parts to each other on a page, so that the content in one of them depends on a selection in the other web part.

19 CONNECT WEB PARTS

SharePoint web parts are very useful, and you have already learned how to take advantage of different kinds of web parts in modern and classic site pages. In this chapter, we will go into more advanced use of web parts.

We will look at how two web parts can be connected on a page. By connecting web parts, you can give users an interactive and dynamic experience. This can be done in both modern and classic site pages.

It is often best to use the two columns layout for connected web parts, so that users don't need to scroll unnecessarily to see the result of their selection.

If you get problems with the connections described below, check if one of the apps has a datasheet/grid view as the default view. That can create problems, so try with a standard view instead.

19.1 WEB PART CONNECTION IN MODERN PAGES

When you connect two web parts in a modern page, you must add both web parts to the page first. Then you can make the connection by selecting the appropriate values.

When users select an item to show content in a connected web part, they must select by clicking in the ring to the left of the item. If they click on the first column, the document or list item will open in a new tab.

Modern web parts that allow connecting are:

- Document library – filters a document library based on a selection in another list or library
- List – filters a list based on a selection in another list or library
- Embed – connects to a list and shows the selected video or location
- File viewer – connects to a document library and shows the selected file
- List properties – connects to a list and shows the selected item

Note: when you want to make a connection between two web parts, you might get suggestions that don't work – for example a list suggestion when you use the File viewer web part (which only works with document libraries).

19.1.1 Dynamic Filtering

The modern List and Library web parts can filter one app based on a selection made in another app. For this, you should apply Dynamic filtering in the web part you want to filter.

In the example below, the Employees list has been filtered to only show staff in the West department – that is, the department of the item that is selected in the Departments list.

For this scenario, use two List web parts, and enable Dynamic filtering in the web part where you have added the list you want to filter.

Select the list in the other List web part and also select the corresponding columns in both web parts.

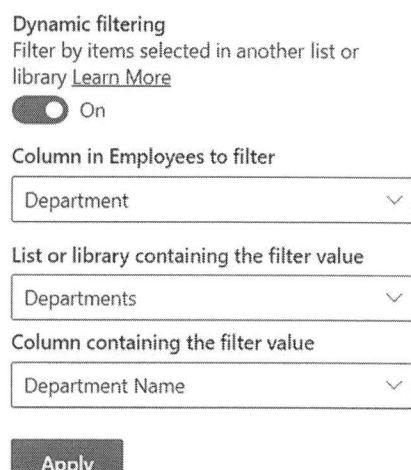

Dynamic filtering can be used with multiple items too. You can for example select two items in the Departments list, so that staff belonging to these two departments will be displayed in the Employees list.

19.1.2   Connect to Source

The modern Embed, List properties and File viewer web parts can connect to another web part and display content depending on what has been selected in that web part.

Connect via the 'Connect to source' command under the ellipsis in the top right corner of the web part's Edit pane.

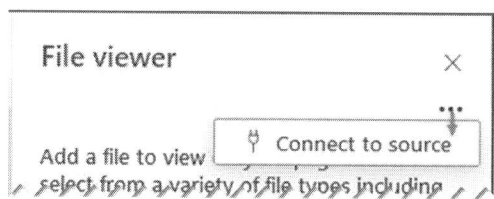

19.1.2.1 File Viewer Example

In the image below, I have used a File viewer web part. It is connected to a Document library web part that shows a Picture library. When users select any item in the Picture library, it will be displayed in the File viewer web part.

Here, a .png file is selected in the Document library web part to the left, and the image is shown in the File viewer to the right.

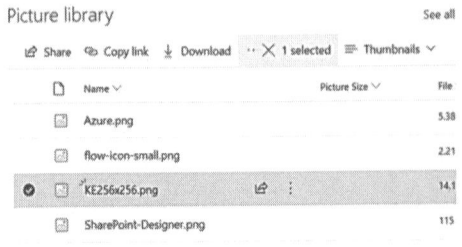 

1. Add the Document library web part to the page and select the library you want to display.
2. Add the File viewer web part.
3. Cancel the file selection.
4. Edit the File viewer web part.
5. Open the ellipsis in the top right corner of the right pane and select 'Connect to source'.
6. Select the library you added to the Document library web part.

In the same way, you can connect a List properties web part to a List web part and display items in the List properties web part based on what the user selects in the List web part.

19.1.2.2 Embed Examples

When you use the Embed web part, you must have a list that has a column with a value that is also contained in the link or embed code for each item. To make the connection work, you need to replace the item specific value with a variable.

A variable has an opening bracket, a $ and a closing bracket after the name. For example, https://www.youtube.com/watch?v=[$VideoID].

In my first example, I will connect an Embed web part to a list app that contains links to YouTube videos. The list must have a column for the video IDs, here called VideoID.

(The name of the ID column cannot be just "ID", as a column for the item ID is auto-created and already exists, and it cannot have a space as it will be included in a variable. You can of course make the name in the interface more user friendly, as I have done in the image below. *Refer to* 4.4.1, *Naming New Content*.)

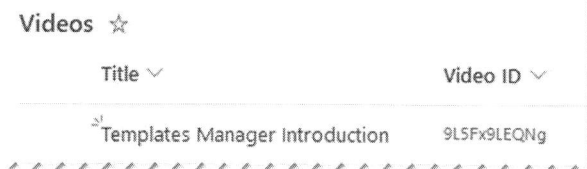

The video ID is the part of the video link that comes after the "v=". For example, in https://www.youtube.com/watch?v=9L5Fx9LEQNg, the video ID is 9L5Fx9LEQNg.

On YouTube, you can click on the Share button below the video to get a link to the video.

1. Add the List web part to the page and select the list with the video IDs.
2. Add an Embed web part to the page.
3. Click on the edit button on the left side of the Embed web part.
4. Click on the ellipsis and then on 'Connect to source'.
5. Select the video list.
6. Copy the link to one of the videos.
7. Paste the link in the Embed web part, 'Web site address or embed code'.
8. Remove the individual video ID after v=.
9. After v=, type a variable with the name of the list column that contains the IDs.

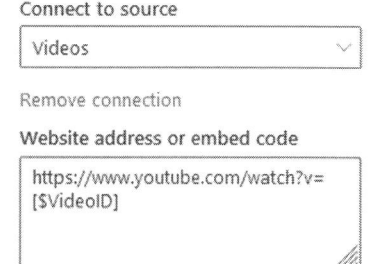

Now, when the page is published, users can select a video in the List web part, and that video will be shown in the Embed web part.

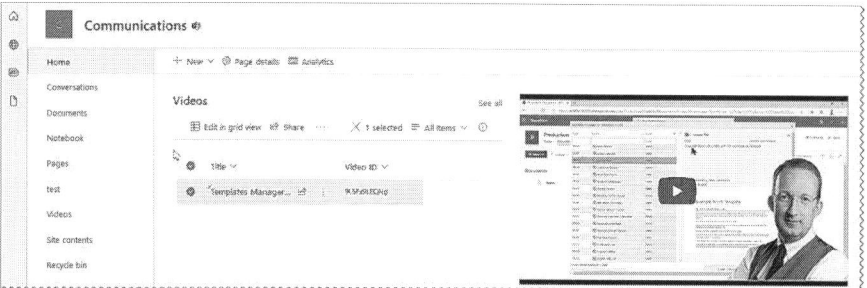

In the same way, you can let users select a location in a list with two columns called "Latitude" and "Longitude" and let the Embed web part show the location on a map from Bing. To do this, the values for both latitude and longitude must be replaced in the embed code for one of the items, but otherwise the process is the same as described above.

It might be easier to work in the Notepad to modify the embed code and then paste the embed code with the variables into the Embed web part.

Use https://www.bing.com/maps/ to get the coordinates for each location. They are found at the bottom of the left pane that opens when you search. Under the ellipsis above the map, you can find a link to the embed code.

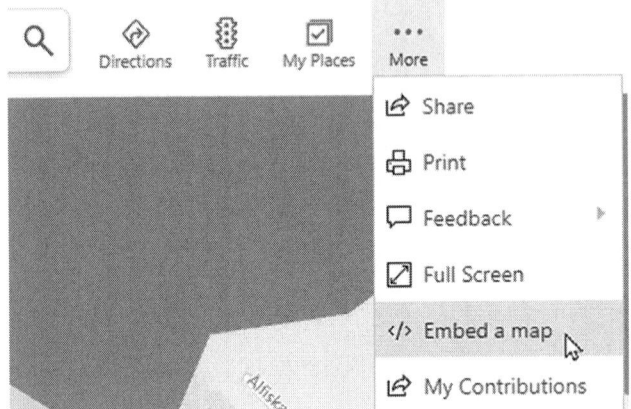

Copy the iframe part of the embed code for one of the locations and paste it in Notepad. Replace the coordinates with the variables [$Latitude] and [$Longitude] and paste them into the Embed web part.

Here is an example on how the finished code looks in the Embed web part:

```
<iframe width="500" height="400" frameborder="0" src="https://www.bing.com/maps/embed?h=400&w=500&cp=[$Latitude]~[$Longitude]&lvl=16&typ=d&sty=r&src=SHELL&FORM=MBEDV8" scrolling="no"></iframe>
```

19.2 WEB PART CONNECTION IN CLASSIC PAGES

In classic pages it is possible to connect two web parts, so that specified content from one web part is displayed in another web part on the same page.

To connect a web part to another web part, you must have the Edit pane open in the first web part. Otherwise. you will not get the connect option when you click on the edit arrow in the top right corner of the web part.

In this section, I will use country information from a "Customers" list app as an example of how connected web parts can be useful. The list has a "Country" column, and I will show three different ways to let users select or click on a country and see all customers in the list that are tagged with that country.

19.2.1 Choice Filter Web Part

When you edit the Choice Filter web part, it has a field similar to a list choice field, where you can enter the options you want to filter by. If you already have these data in a list column, it is easy to copy them and paste them into the Choice Filter web part.

The Choice Filter web part is not available when you create the classic page in a modern site. If you are on a modern site, use a modern page instead, *see* above.

When you add a Customers web part on a page where you also add a Choice Filter web part, users can click on the icon to the right of the search box in the Choice Filter web part to see the choices.

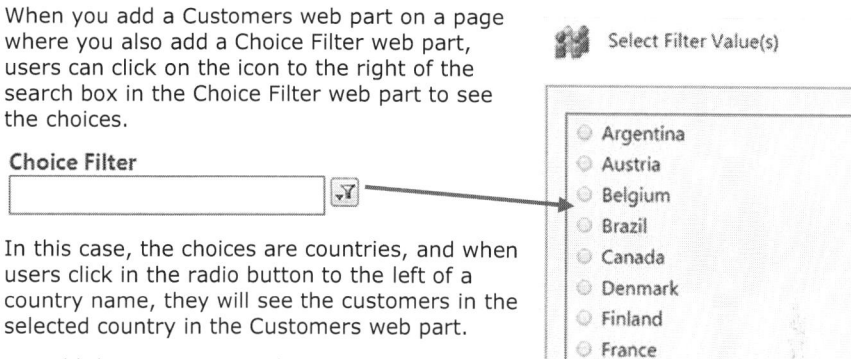

In this case, the choices are countries, and when users click in the radio button to the left of a country name, they will see the customers in the selected country in the Customers web part.

1. Add the Customers web part to the page.
2. Place the mouse cursor outside the Customers web part on the page and add the Choice Filter web part from the Filters category.
3. Edit the Customers web part and enter your choice alternatives in the right pane, in this case all the countries. You can very well copy and paste them into the web part.

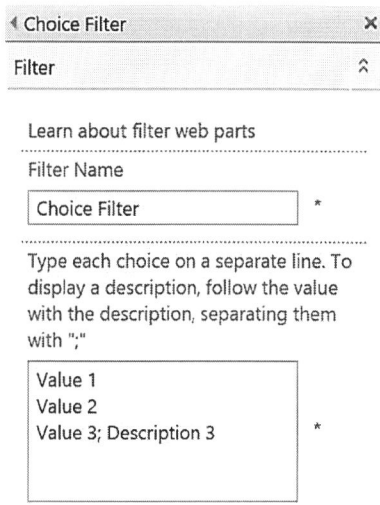

4. Click on 'Apply' at the bottom of the Edit pane.
5. Expand the edit accordion in the top right corner of the Choice Filter web part and select Connections >Send Filter Values To >Customers.

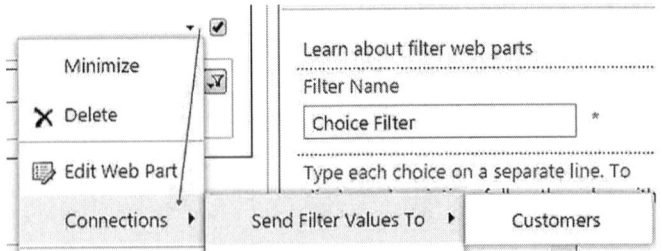

6. In the pop-up window, select 'Get Filter Values From'. (Allow pop-ups if the pop-up window does not open).
7. Click on 'Configure' and select the 'Country' Choice Filter.

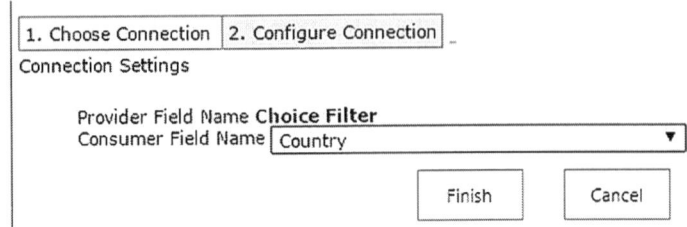

8. Click on 'Finish' and save the page.

Demo:

https://kalmstrom.com/Tips/SharePoint-Online-Course/Connect-Web-Parts-Choice.htm

19.2.2 Click to Filter with Connected List Web Parts

Instead of using the Choice Filter web part, as described above, you can connect the "Customers" list to a "Countries" list by adding them as two separate web parts on the same page.

This method reminds very much of the dynamic filtering in modern pages, and it can be used on classic pages in modern as well as classic Team sites. The result lets users click on an icon to the left of a country to see all customers from that country.

To use this method, you must first create a separate list that contains all the country names from the "Customers" list. You must also allow pop-up windows.

1. Add the "Countries" and the "Customers" lists as web parts on the page.
2. Edit the Countries web part (but don't do anything in the right pane).
3. Expand the edit accordion in the top right corner of the Countries web part and select Connections >Send Row of Data To >Customers.
4. In the pop-up dialog, select 'Get Filter Values From'.
5. Click on 'Configure Connection'.
6. Connect the 'Country' field in the Provider to the 'Country' field in the Consumer.

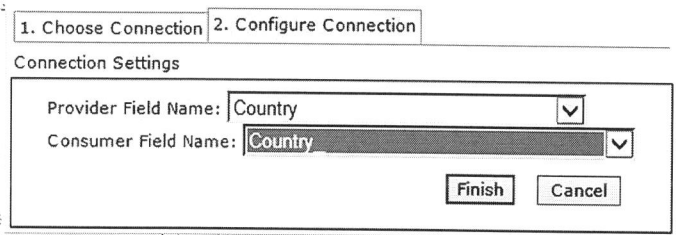

7. Click on 'Finish' and save the page.

This method is quicker to use than the "Choice Filter", at least for the alternatives on top of the list, because no extra dialog must be opened. But if the list is long, users will have to scroll – first down to find their country and then up again to see the customers. The solution in the next section might work better if you have customers in many countries.

Demo:

https://www.kalmstrom.com/Tips/SharePoint-Online-Course/Connect-Web-Parts-Click-To-Filter.htm

19.2.3 *Show Connected List Data in Display Form*

In this connection example we will use the same two lists as in the section above, but we will create a new kind of connection. We will not connect the lists on a page.

Instead, we will enhance the Display form of the "Countries" list, so that all customers from that country in the "Customers" list are displayed in the form when you open an item in the "Countries" list.

This method can be used with classic pages in a classic as well as a modern Team site. The 'Form Web Parts' control is inactive in the modern Team site, but you can open one of the items in the "Countries" list instead to get the Display Form.

The "Countries" list must use the classic interface for the customers to show, and pop-ups must be allowed in the browser for the connection creation.

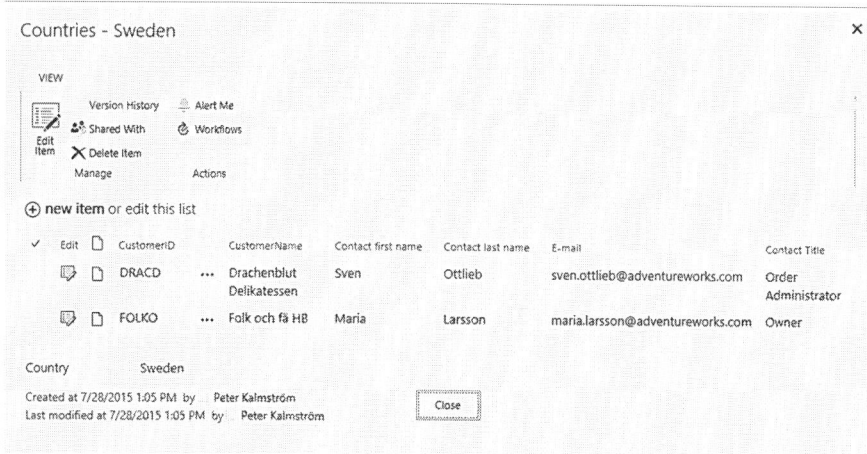

361

The list item Display form is a web part page, so you can very well enhance it to show data from another list by connecting web parts.

1. In the "Countries" list, using the classic interface, open the ribbon LIST tab and click on 'Form Web Parts'. Select 'Default Display Form' and its web part page will open in edit mode.
2. OR
3. Open one of the items in the "Countries" list. Click on the 365 Settings icon and select 'Edit page' to open the web part page in edit mode.
4. Click on the link 'Add a Web Part' and select the Customers web part. Click on Add.
5. Open the accordion in the top right corner of the Countries web part and select Connections.
6. Select 'Provide Row To' and then "Customers".

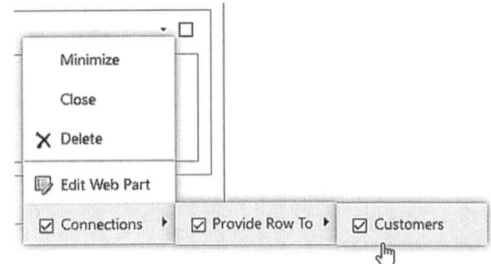

7. In then pop-up dialog, select 'Get Filter Values From' and click on 'Configure'.
8. Connect the "Country" field in the Provider to the "Country" field in the Consumer.
9. Click on 'Finish' and 'Stop Editing'.

Now users can click on a country in the "Countries" list, and when the item opens, they will see all customers from that country.

Demo:

https://www.kalmstrom.com/Tips/SharePoint-Online-Course/Connect-Web-Parts-Display-Form.htm

19.3 SUMMARY

In this chapter, we have seen how you can connect two web parts on a modern or classic page, so that specified content from one web part is displayed in another web part on the same page.

We have seen what possibilities the Connect to source and Dynamic filtering features in modern web parts can give.

I have also shown three different examples on connecting classic web parts. You have learned how to connect the Choice Filter web part to a list web part and how to connect two list web parts to each other.

In the next chapter, I will introduce three different surveys that can be reached from SharePoint. A survey can be used for all kinds of questions, from simple lunch meeting setups to advanced questionnaires about work processes.

20 Surveys

SharePoint offers three different options when you want to create survey questions that colleagues or even people outside the organization can answer.

Use a survey when you want to know people's opinion about things. You can also use a SharePoint survey when you want to measure knowledge but not show the correct answers or give points for them.

Among the three kinds of questionnaires that can be reached from SharePoint Online, the Survey app has been there for a long time. The Excel survey and the Excel form are newer additions.

In this chapter, we will have look at all three survey options. They can be used in different types of sites:

- Forms for Excel can be used in OneDrive and in modern and classic Team sites that are connected to a Microsoft 365 group.
- The Excel survey can be used in Communication sites. External sharing with anyone must be allowed.
- Survey apps can be used in all Team sites, with or without a Microsoft 365 Group.

20.1 Forms for Excel

A link to a simplified edition of the 365 service Forms for Excel can be found under the '+ New' command in the default OneDrive for Business library. Document libraries in modern and classic Group Team sites also have this 'Forms for Excel' link.

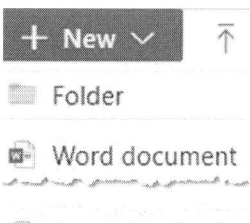

The full Forms app, which is included in the 365 subscription and can be reached from the App launcher, gives a possibility to create quizzes where you can show correct answers and give points. Such quizzes cannot be created in the SharePoint Forms edition.

When you click on the 'Forms for Excel' link in SharePoint, the Forms site at https://forms.office.com/ opens in a new tab. Here, you can add questions under the 'Questions' tab and see the answers under 'Responses' tab.

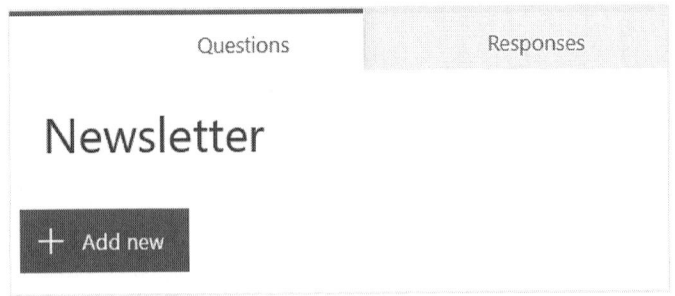

20.1.1 Create a Form

Click on the 'Add new' button on the Forms site to start creating questions. You will have several options on how people should answer them.

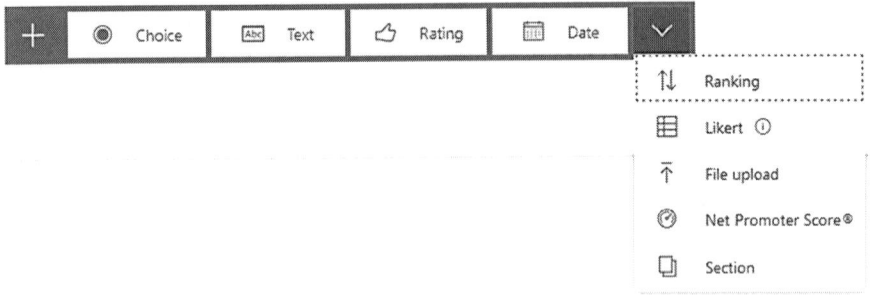

- For the 'Text' option, the answers must be typed in, but you can restrict them to be a number and even limit the number span.
- The 'Likert' option is easy to answer, because here the respondents just need to rate how much they think a statement is right or wrong.
- The 'Rating' option, just as the default 'Choice' and the 'Net Promoter Score' options, are also easy for respondents to fill out. They only need to select an option.
- When you select 'File upload', respondents can upload files to a new folder that will be created in SharePoint. The uploading person's name and file details will be recorded in SharePoint.
- With the 'Section' control, you can categorize the questions in a long survey, so that they will be easier for respondents to overview. Sections are especially useful when you want to branch the questions, *see* below.

When the first question has been finished, click on 'Add new' again to continue with the next one. The form is saved automatically.

20.1.1.1 Edit

Click on a question to edit it. In the top right corner of each question in edit mode, you can find icons for copying and deleting the question and for moving the question up and down in the form.

364

20.1.1.2 Branching

When the form is in edit mode, you can find an ellipsis in the bottom right corner of each question. One of the options is to add branching. (Some question types have more options under the ellipsis than subtitle and branching.)

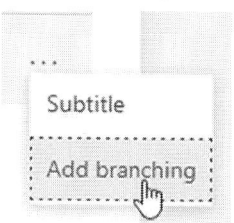

With branching, questions will have an option to continue in a specific way: to the next question, to another question or to the end of the form.

That way, you can follow up with questions that only apply to certain answers and/or let respondents skip questions that are not relevant to them.

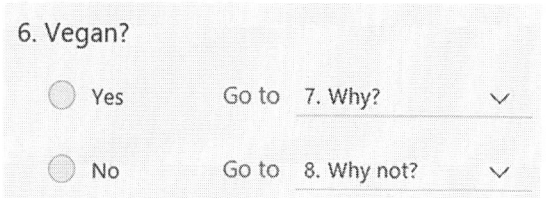

20.1.2 *Share the Form*

Click on the 'Share' button in the right part of the top command bar to share the form. Select one of the four options and copy the link/embed code if needed. These are the options:

- Copy a link and paste it in a shared area, for example a chat.
- Download a QR-code and paste it where your intended audience can scan it, for example with a mobile device.
- Copy the embed code and embed the form into a blog, a SharePoint page or other web page.
- Send a link in an e-mail by selecting the fourth option. This opens an e-mail with the link and some explaining, editable text. The first time you use this option, you must specify from what e-mail account the e-mail should be sent.

365

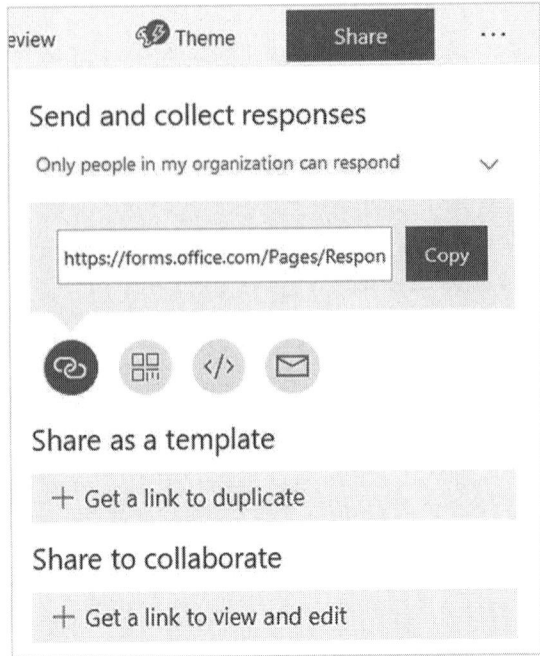

In the Share pane, you can also share the form to people who are not supposed to answer it:

- Get a template link. All receivers of this link can use the form as a template. Responses are not included.
- Get a collaboration link. Receivers of this link can work with the form, for example add or remove questions, see the responses and share the form with others.

  By default, all users with a 365 work or school account can view and edit using this collaboration link, but you can restrict the permission to people within the tenant or even specific people.

20.1.3   Check Form Results

To see the answers as they come in, open the 'Responses' tab on the Forms site and see statistics.

For more elaborate analysis you can open the results in Excel directly from the 'Responses' tab.

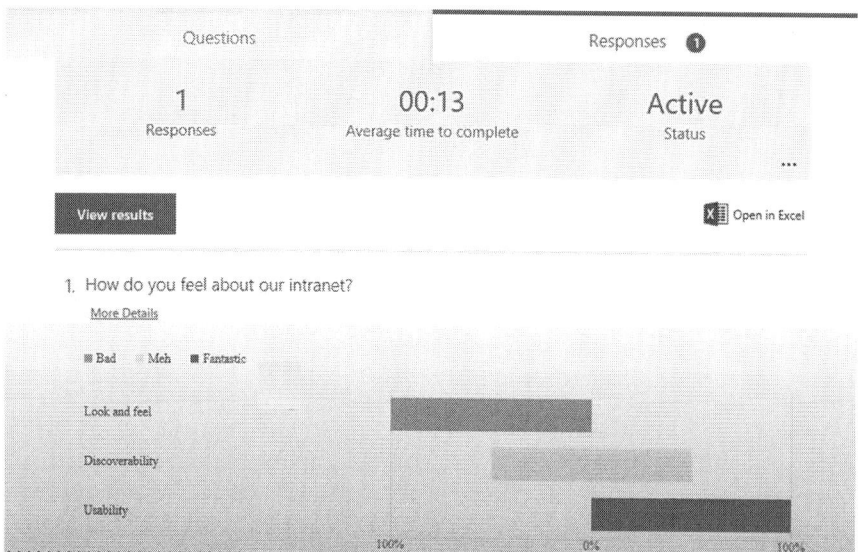

20.1.4 Form Options

The Form settings are found under the ellipsis in the top right corner of the Form page. Here, you can also find some more commands.

20.1.4.1 Settings

The image below shows the default settings. The non-default options include a start and end date for the form and an e-mail notification of each response.

You can also set the questions to be shown in random order for each respondent (shuffle questions).

For multi-page forms, you can show the respondents a progress bar that indicates how much of the form has been answered.

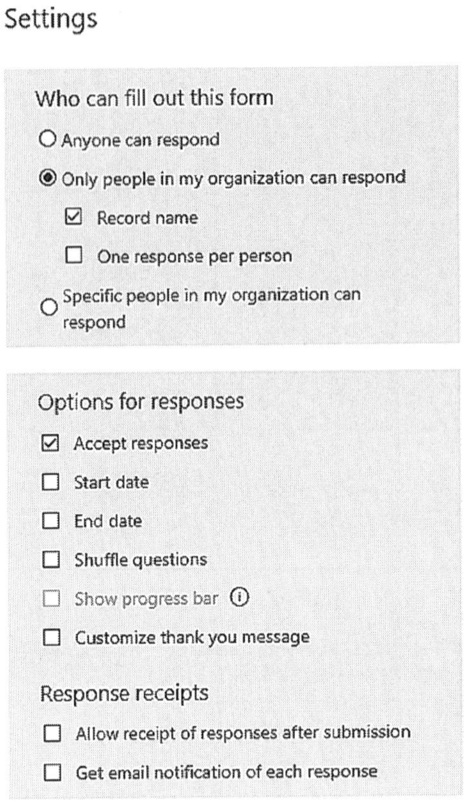

Settings

Who can fill out this form
- ○ Anyone can respond
- ● Only people in my organization can respond
    - ☑ Record name
    - ☐ One response per person
- ○ Specific people in my organization can respond

Options for responses
- ☑ Accept responses
- ☐ Start date
- ☐ End date
- ☐ Shuffle questions
- ☐ Show progress bar ⓘ
- ☐ Customize thank you message

Response receipts
- ☐ Allow receipt of responses after submission
- ☐ Get email notification of each response

20.1.4.2   Multilingual

The Multilingual link lets you translate the questions. Each user will see the questions in his/her default language.

When you click on 'More Details' at each question under the Responses tab, you can see how each language group has responded.

20.1.4.3   Print

Under the ellipsis, form owners can print the form for respondents who is unable to complete the form online.

20.1.5   *Forms Admin Settings*

In the Microsoft 365 Admin center >Settings >Org settings >Microsoft Forms, administrators can turn off the default permission to share forms and results with users outside the organization.

When an external setting option is turned off, only people within organization will have access to that option, and only when they are signed in.

The image below shows the default settings, where everything is allowed. Phishing protection is also enabled by default.

> **Microsoft Forms**
>
> Create surveys, quizzes, and polls, and easily see results as they come in. Learn how to create a form.
>
> **External sharing**
>
> Control how people in your org can collaborate on forms with people outside your org.
>
> ☑ Send a link to the form and collect responses
>
> ☑ Share to collaborate on the form layout and structure
>
> ☑ Share the form as a template that can be duplicated
>
> ☑ Share form result summary
>
> **Record names of people in your org**
>
> By default, your forms will capture the names of people in your org who fill them out. This setting can be changed on individual forms.
>
> ☑ Record names by default
>
> **Allow YouTube and Bing**
>
> ☑ Include Bing search, YouTube videos
>
> Allow users in your organization to add images from Bing and YouTube videos to Forms. Note: If unchecked, previously added images from Bing will remain, but any previously added YouTube videos will be converted into a YouTube link that will launch outside of Forms.
>
> **Phishing protection**
>
> Help protect against personal data loss of a compromised account.
>
> ☑ Add internal phishing protection

Demo:

https://www.kalmstrom.com/Tips/Office-365-Course/Forms.htm

(This demo shows the full Forms edition.)

20.2 EXCEL SURVEY

The Excel survey can be used in Team sites without a group, as well as in Communication sites. A drawback is that external sharing with anyone must enabled in the site, and of course also in the tenant.

20.2.1 Create an Excel Survey

When the most allowing sharing option is enabled in the tenant and in the site, the Excel survey option is shown when you create a new item in a document library.

When you have given the survey a name and clicked on 'Create', an 'Edit Survey' dialog will open in Excel Online. Enter a title and a description for the survey and start adding your questions.

Each question is edited in a pane where you can enter your question (and subtitle if needed) and select a response type. You can also set a default answer and decide that an answer is required.

The various response types remind of SharePoint column types. The Paragraph Text option corresponds to a Multiple lines of text column and gives a bigger field to enter the response.

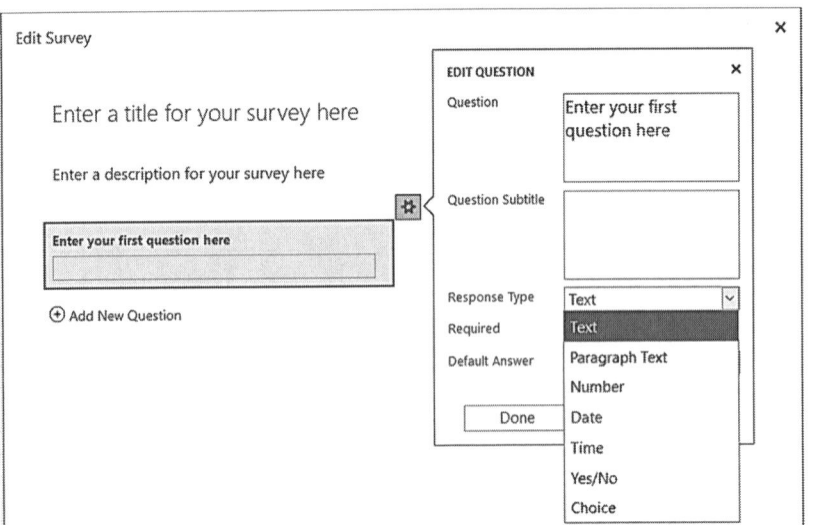

In the image below, you can see an example on a simple prompt to sign up for a newsletter. The 'Type of products' field will be answered by selection. The other fields will be filled out by the responder.

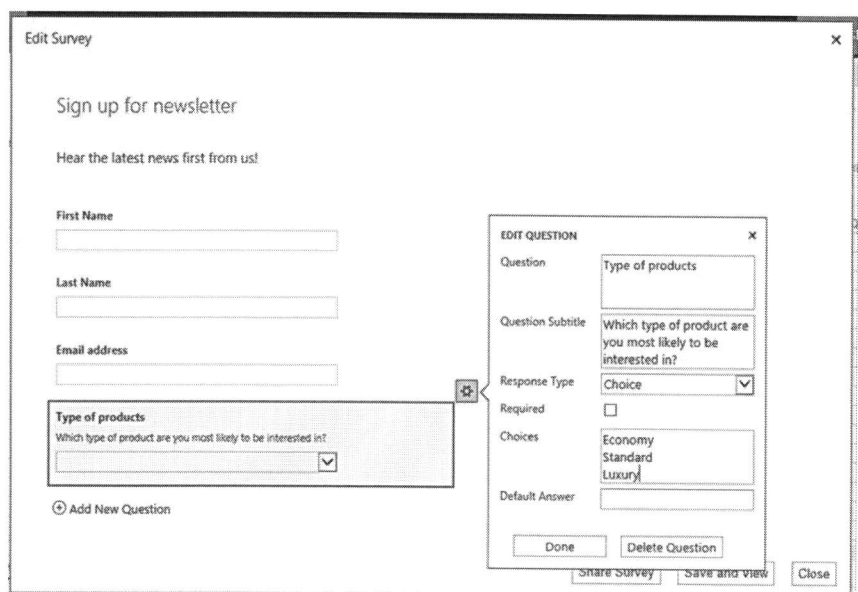

20.2.2 Share an Excel Survey

To share the survey, click on 'Share Survey' at the bottom of the Edit Survey dialog.

You can also click on the 'Survey' button under the Insert tab in the Excel ribbon and select 'Share Survey'.

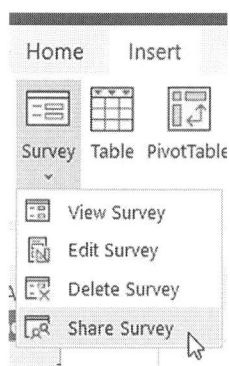

Now you will have a link to the survey. Share the link by pasting it on a website or in an e-mail or chat.

This dialog is also where you can stop sharing the survey.

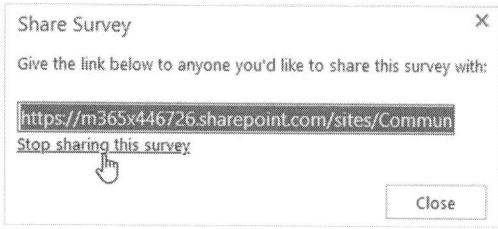

371

People who click on the link you have shared, will be directed to the survey and can fill out or select their answers.

Below is the newsletter survey created above as it looks when shared.

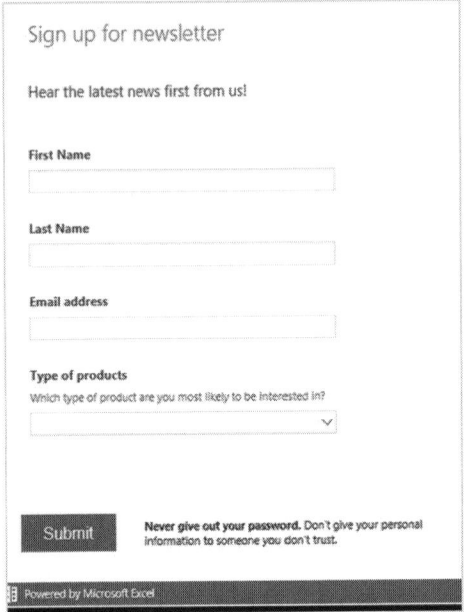

20.2.3 See Excel Survey Results

As soon as a respondent has submitted an answer, it will be visible in Excel Online.

To edit the spreadsheet in Excel, and for example create a pivot table or chart from it, you must stop sharing the survey.

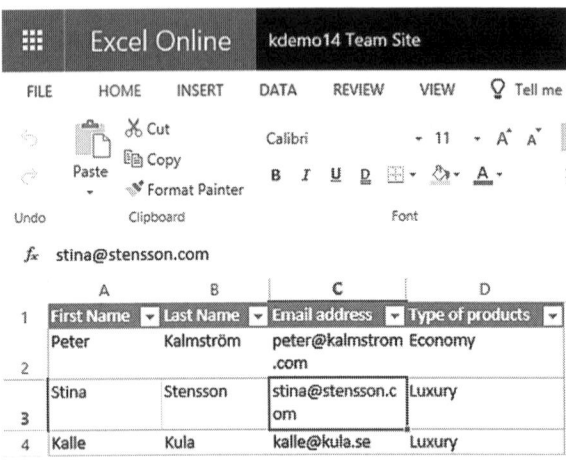

Demo:

https://www.kalmstrom.com/Tips/SharePoint-Online-Course/Excel-Survey.htm

20.3 SURVEY APP

The Survey app has its own interface, which is neither modern nor classic but rather a "before classic". Thus, it cannot be used in Communication sites.

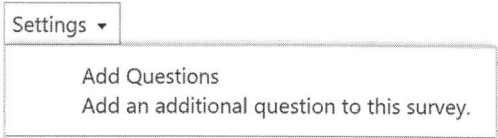

20.3.1   *Create a Survey App*

A Survey app is created with the 'Add an app' command, and when it has been created you can add your questions to it.

There are several response options to choose from, depending on what type of response you want to collect. Among the most common response types are Rating Scale, Number and Choice with a dropdown menu or radio buttons.

Survey

1. When you have added the Survey app to a site and opened it, expand the Settings accordion and select 'Add Questions'.

    Settings ▾
    > Add Questions
    > Add an additional question to this survey.

2. A new page will open that resembles the Create a Column page. Select question type and enter choices if necessary.

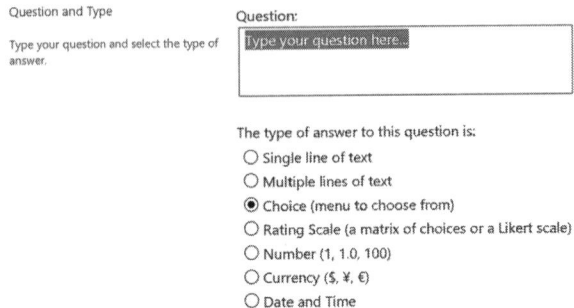

3. When you have added the first question, click on 'Next Question' and repeat the process. Click on 'Finish' when all questions are added.

20.3.1.1 Survey Branching Logic

Some answers need a follow up question while other answers don't, and for that you can use the Branching Logic. Each question has a Branching Logic option, where you can decide which should be the next question depending on the answer.

After you have entered your questions, open the question(s) that should have branching.

Under Jump To you can select the correct question to come next for those answers that should not have all questions.

Possible Choices	Jump To
Every day	No Branching
Now and then	No Branching
Never	What should be the name of our next bicycle

20.3.2 Respond to a Survey App

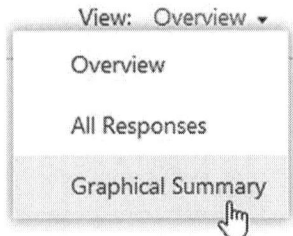

When the Survey app has been setup, users can click on the 'Respond to this Survey' link in the app and answer the questions.

20.3.3 See Survey Results

Once answers to a Survey app have been submitted, you will see a graphical summary of the responses via the View dropdown in the top right corner of the Survey dashboard.

You can also export the survey results to a spreadsheet, like Excel. This is done' under 'Actions'.

374

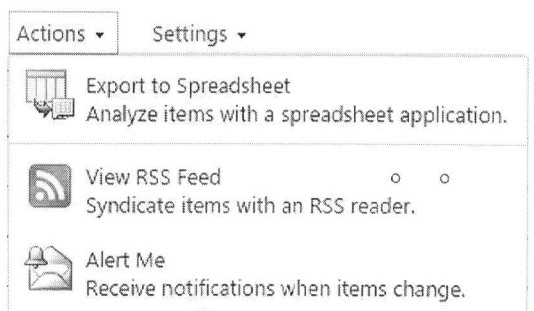

By default, all users who can respond to the survey also can see the results of it. However, under Survey Settings >Advanced Settings, you can set the Read access, so that each user only sees their own responses.

Item-level Permissions

Specify which responses users can read and edit.

Note: Users with the Cancel Checkout permission can read and edit all responses. Learn about managing permission settings.

Read access: Specify which responses users are allowed to read

○ Read all responses
◉ Read responses that were created by the user

Create and Edit access: Specify which responses users are allowed to create and edit

○ Create and edit all responses
◉ Create responses and edit responses that were created by the user
○ None

When you have exported the results to an Excel spreadsheet, you can just refresh the sheet to have new responses included. From the Excel sheet you can create graphical representations of the survey answers.

Demo:

https://www.kalmstrom.com//Tips/SharePoint-Online-Course/Survey-setting-responding-and-using.htm

20.4 SUMMARY

Microsoft/Office 365 offers three survey options, and in this chapter, we have seen how they can be reached from within SharePoint. You now understand how to use and share such surveys and how to analyze the results when the answers come in. You also know how to add branching to a survey when that is possible.

Now we will go over to something different: When you have been trying apps with the modern interface, you have probably already seen that there is a 'Power Apps' button in the library command bar and an 'Integrate' button in list apps. In the next chapter, we will see what you can do with them.

375

21 POWER APPS

Power Apps is an Office 365 app that is often used with SharePoint list apps, as the service makes it possible to create user friendly list and form interfaces that work for computers as well as for mobile devices.

With Power Apps, IT professionals can create powerapps for both mobile and desktop devices and distribute them to users within their organization. Users with Edit permission and a Power Apps license can even create their own apps, because it is not very difficult.

A powerapp is owned by the user who created it, so I recommend that you create a special user account for powerapps. This account can be available to a group of people or to the whole organization.

When you click on the Power Apps icon under the App launcher, you will be directed to the Power Apps Portal at https://make.powerapps.com/. Powerapps can be created from other data sources than SharePoint, for example from Excel files and data bases, and if you want to do that, you should start the creation here.

Under 'Apps' in the site's left menu, you can reach all apps that you own, whether you started the creation on the Power Apps site or in SharePoint.

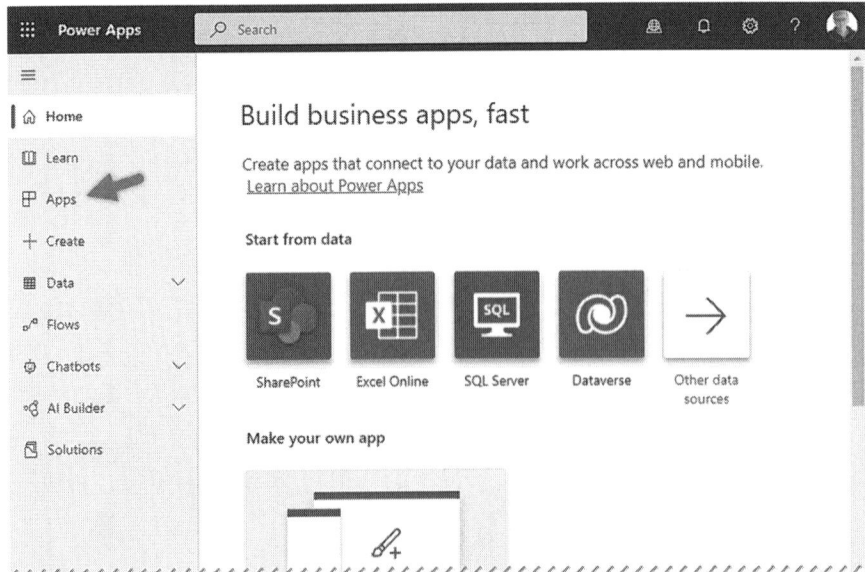

In this chapter, we will focus on what you can do with Power Apps when you start from SharePoint. I first give some general information about the Power Apps studio, where forms and powerapps are created. After that, I will show how an app form can be customized in Power Apps and how you can create a powerapp from a SharePoint list.

Most of the features I show in the form customization section are applicable to the powerapp customization too, so study the form section even if you are only interested in the powerapp!

21.1 POWER APPS IN SHAREPOINT

From a user perspective, a powerapp can be regarded as a touch screen adapted list view, where users can see and edit the data in the SharePoint list that the powerapp is connected to. Such a powerapp can be created directly from the list that it should display, via the 'Integrate' button in the modern command bar.

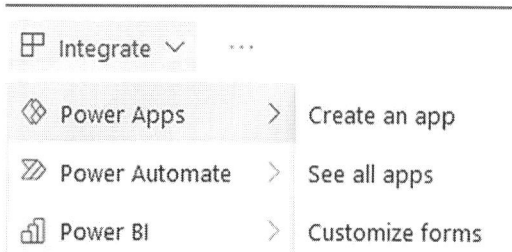

SharePoint library apps with the modern interface have a Power Apps button in the command bar. It is however not possible to create new powerapps directly from a library.

In addition to the powerapp creation, Power Apps gives a possibility to customize the item form. That can be done in both list apps and libraries.

In both lists and libraries, you can also reach the powerapps you own or are allowed to edit. 'See all apps' will open the 'Apps' page in the Power Apps site.

21.2 THE POWER APPS STUDIO

Powerapps and forms are edited on a canvas in the Power Apps Studio. You can either work in the Power Apps Studio web application at https://create.powerapps.com/studio/ or use the Power Apps Studio desktop application. They have similar interfaces.

When you open a powerapp in the Power Apps Studio, you will see panes to the left and right and a workspace with the form or app in the middle. The properties of the first item in the app are displayed when you create a powerapp or form from SharePoint.

377

Far to the left, there is a toolbar with various icons. The Tree view icon, which is selected by default, shows two tabs in the left pane: Screens and Components. The Screens tab shows a tree view of screens and cards, while the Components tab only shows something if you have added extra components to the powerapp.

The other icons let you:

1. edit the powerapp with commands also available from the top menu
2. add another data source
3. add media
4. monitor activity and test the powerapp.

The back arrow in the top left corner takes you to the Power Apps Portal if you are creating a powerapp and back to the SharePoint list if you create a form.

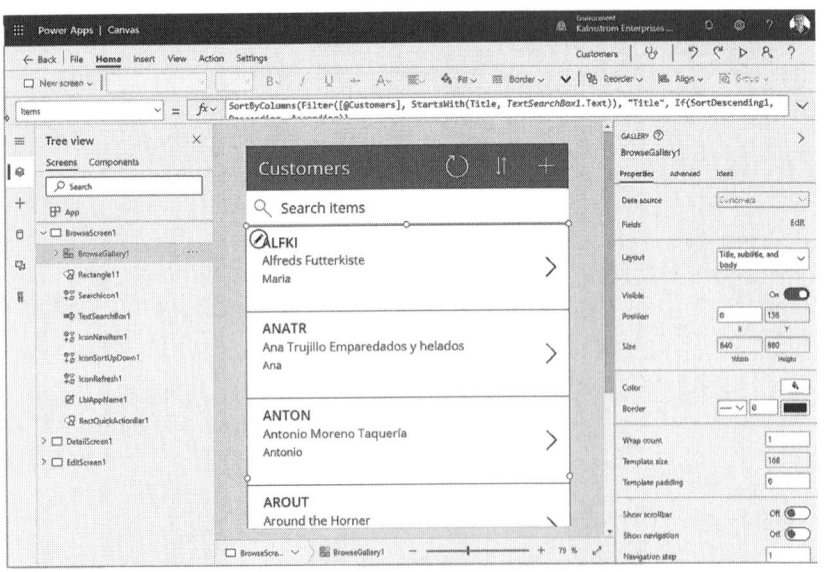

The form or app can be resized with Ctrl + the plus or minus key or by the slider below the workspace.

Above the panes and the workspace, the canvas has a command bar, for changes in look and behavior, and a formula bar that shows the value for the selected property. The value can be a number, a string of text or a formula, just like in Excel.

Each field in the powerapp or form is represented by a card in Power Apps, and all the cards are listed to the left of the workspace. The cards can be reordered with drag and drop.

An ellipsis at each card gives options on what to do with the card. The options depend on what kind of field the card represents.

378

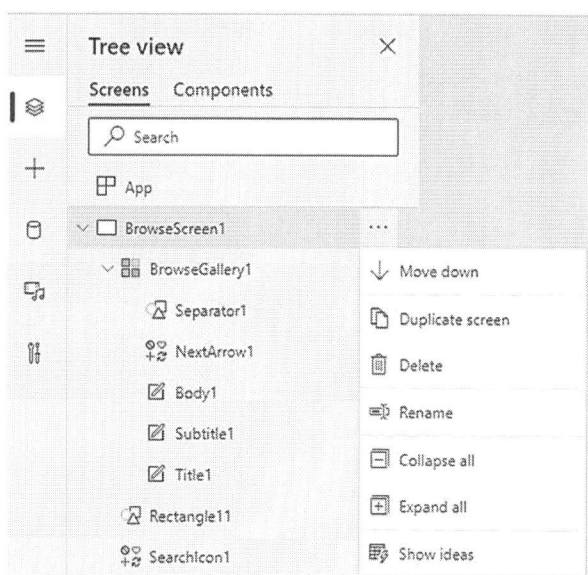

The pane to the right in PowerApps Studio has different content depending on which card is selected in the workspace or in the left menu. Here you can change which fields will be displayed, in which order they should come, how they should look and much more.

21.2.1   Preview, Save and Publish

When you have made changes to the app or form, you can try it by clicking on the Play button to the right in the command bar.

You can also try the app or form directly on the canvas, by holding down the Alt key.

Click on File >Save, to save the app or form when you have previewed it and are satisfied, or when you want to stop working with it temporarily.

Click on File >Publish, to publish a powerapp and make it possible to share.

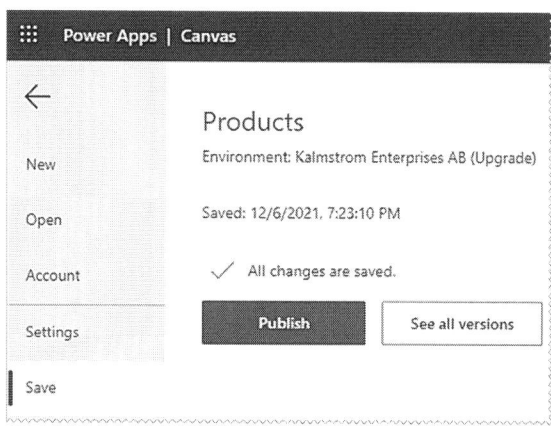

When you have customized an app form, the button text is instead 'Publish to SharePoint' and it publishes the form to all users of the app.

From this area, you can also reach and work with all versions of the form or powerapp.

379

21.3 CUSTOMIZE A LIST FORM IN POWER APPS

SharePoint forms can be customized in different ways. In this section, I will explain how to customize a SharePoint list or library form in the Power Apps Studio.

The option 'Customize forms' under the Power Apps button in the modern command bar, creates a special kind of powerapp that is only used with SharePoint. It is not displayed in the App launcher.

When the modified form has been published to SharePoint, it will automatically replace the default form in new as well as existing items. The custom form will be displayed in both app experiences.

You can switch back to the original form in the List settings >General settings >Form settings. When you have set the list to use the default form again, a delete link will be displayed below the Power Apps form option.

Form Options

Use Microsoft PowerApps to customize the forms for this list. You can modify the form layout, add pictures and formatted text, add custom data validation, create additional views, and add rules.

◉ Use the default SharePoint form

○ Use a custom form created in PowerApps (requires new list experience)
   Modify form in PowerApps
   See versions and usage
   Delete custom form

Note that text "requires new list experience" in the custom form setting only applies to the creation of the custom form. Once the form is published, it will be displayed in the classic interface too.

21.3.1 Why Customize a Form?

Why customize app forms at all, in the first place? Isn't it enough that you can add and remove or hide columns and put them in any order you want? Yes, those features are certainly useful, and we should absolutely take advantage of them, but they don't solve all form issues.

One of the reasons for form customization is to avoid unnecessary scrolling. In most SharePoint forms the fields are just put below each other, even if the value should be something short and maybe only requires a number or a choice of yes and no. Such fields can very well be placed side by side instead. Or, you might want to have more space in the description field, to avoid scrolling there.

21.3.2 Example Form

I use a "Customers" list in this example, and as you see from the image to the right below, the default form is very long and requires scrolling.

To make the form quicker to fill out, and to give a better overview, I first used the Power Apps command 'Customize forms' in the "Customers" list. That gave me an automatically created form that I needed to modify to make it work well.

These are the changes I made to the auto-created form:

- Added the fields that were missing in the automatically created app.
- Shortened the column names in the form, so that there is more space.
- Edited the fields so that they are shown in rows with two fields in each row.
- Hid the State field from the view.
- Removed the field boxes for the fields that are filled out automatically.

The image below shows how the form looks after these modifications.

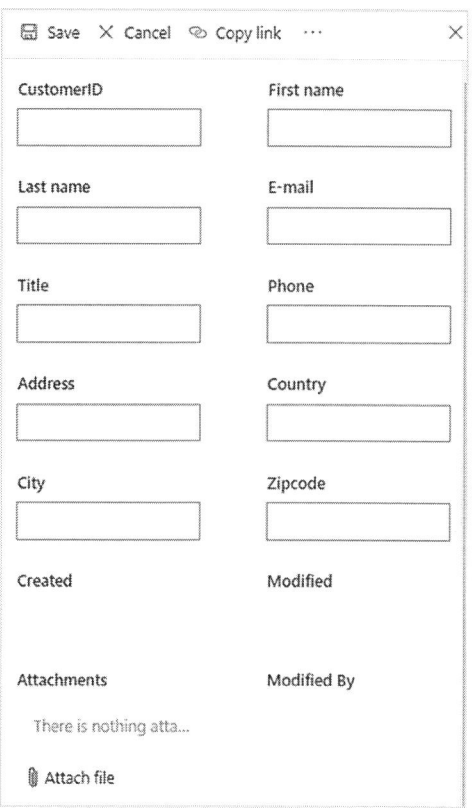

21.3.3 Modifications

The command 'Customize forms' opens the current form in the Power Apps Studio, where Power Apps generates a single-screen form app. This app can be modified in several ways.

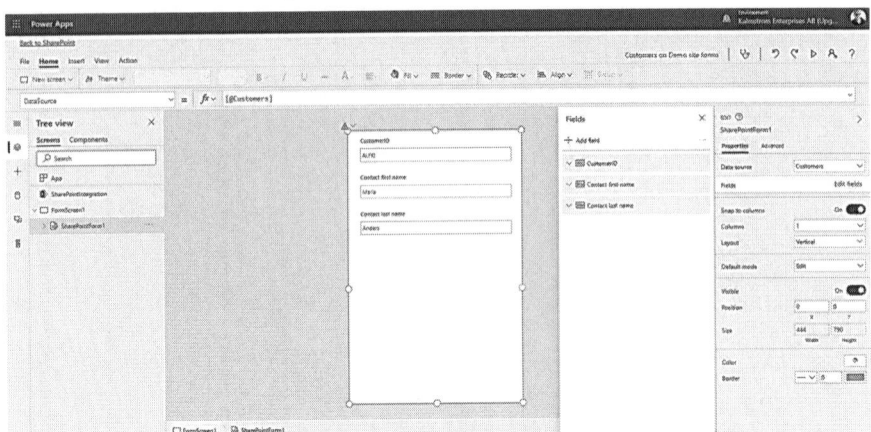

21.3.3.1 Edit the Form

When the new app opens, the level SharePointForm1, is selected to the left, so that the properties of the whole form are displayed and can be modified.

The right Edit pane gives multiple customization possibilities. When you click on some of the properties in the right Edit pane, the formula bar opens with the current data so that you can make changes. Other changes can be made directly in the Edit pane.

The cards can have the display name and the field displayed vertically (like two rows) or horizontally (display name + field), and they can be shown below each other or in two or more columns. I will keep the vertical layout but change into two columns.

The 'Snap to columns' setting in the image to the right, gives a form that is easy to overview, as there are two columns instead of the default one. When the vertical card layout is selected, the column names are displayed above the fields. (A horizontal layout would not be practical together with two columns, as there would be very little space for each title and field!)

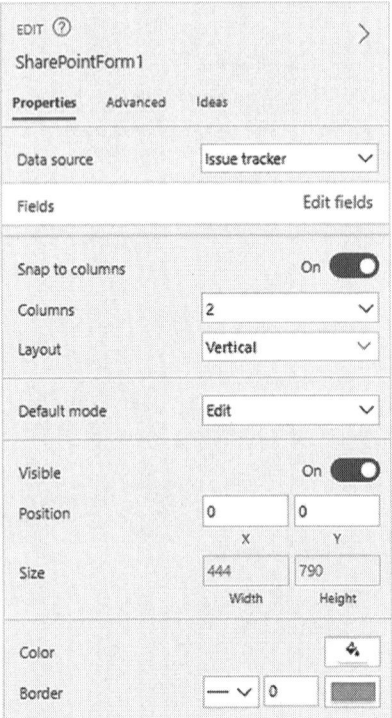

382

Turn off 'Snap to columns' if you want to size the fields manually according to the space needed, instead of having them equally distributed.

The Fields pane is also displayed when the app form first opens in Power Apps. Here, you can modify the control type for each field and see additional information. Open the Fields pane anytime by clicking on 'Edit fields' in the Edit pane.

Each field can be expanded to show information about the field. When you hover the mouse cursor over a field in the Fields pane, an ellipsis will be visible. Click on the ellipsis to remove a field or move it up or down.

In the Fields pane, you can also add any fields that were not included in the auto-created app. All the app fields will be displayed when you click on the plus sign, so that you can check the boxes for the ones you want.

21.3.3.2 Edit Fields

When you select a card in the left pane or in the form in the workspace, you can make changes to that card in the right pane. You can change its color and size, add a border and more.

Maybe you don't want to display all the fields in the form? In that case you can easily hide a field by toggle the Visible control in the right pane to Off.

Some cards might be locked for editing, but you can unlock each locked card by right-clicking on the card and selecting to unlock.

Cards can also be unlocked under the Advanced tab in the card's Edit pane. Then open the Properties tab again make your modifications.

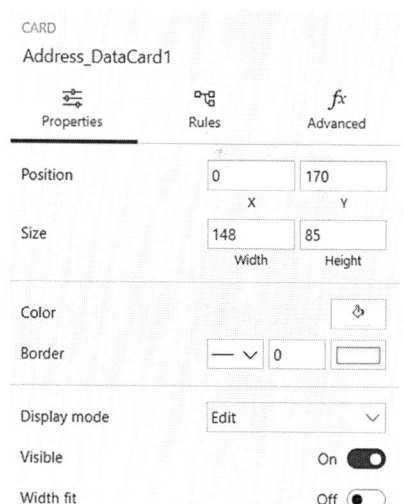

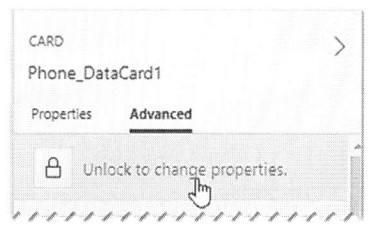

383

Sometimes you want to make a field read only, so that users cannot edit it. This is suitable for example if the field data is fetched from outside the SharePoint list. Select the 'View' option to make the field read only.

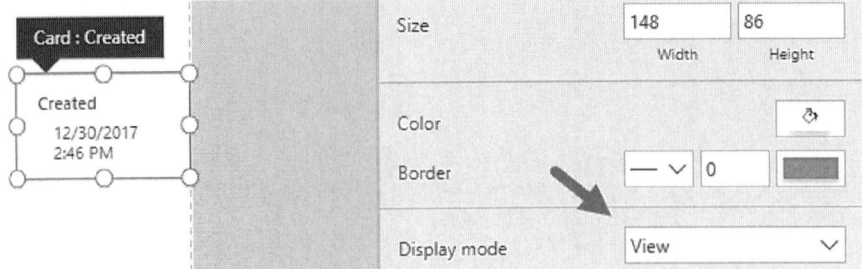

To change the display name for a field, select the card and open the Advanced tab in the Edit pane. Click in the DisplayName field to edit the text.

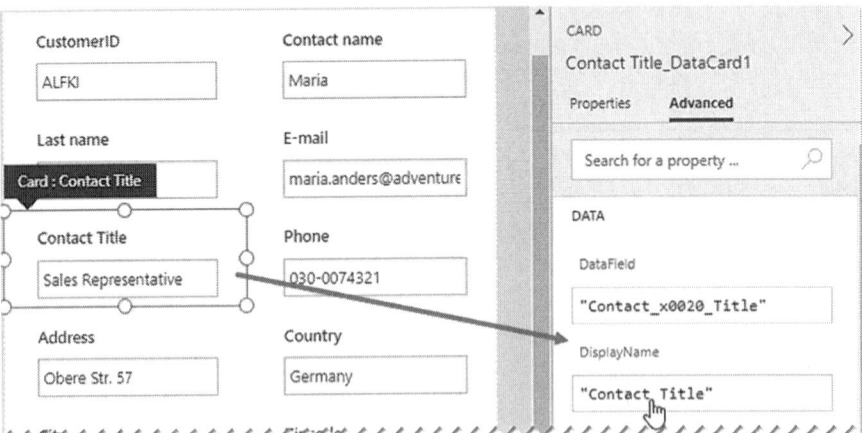

Demo:

https://www.kalmstrom.com/Tips/Office-365-Course/Customize-Form-Power Apps.htm

21.4 CREATE A POWERAPP FROM A SHAREPOINT LIST

When you select 'Create an app' in the Power Apps dropdown, a pane will open to the right. Here you should enter a name for the new app.

Click on 'Create', and the powerapp will be created from the data in the list where you clicked on the button. It will open in the Power Apps Studio.

The Power Apps Studio canvas that opens when a new powerapp has been created reminds of the form page, but there are three screens to select in the left pane: BrowseScreen, DesignScreen and EditScreen.

For a simple app with just a few columns, the powerapp works reasonably well without modification.

For a more complex list, the design of the automatically created powerapp might be less optimal. You can however make the app more useful and appealing by customizing it.

You can for example change which fields are displayed and in which order they are shown in the same way as when you customize a form.

21.4.1   Change the General Layout

Select 'BrowseGallery1' in the left menu tree view to change the general layout of the app. Now can change color, enable scrollbar and navigation and more in the left pane.

Click on the 'Layout' dropdown under the 'Properties' tab to select layout.

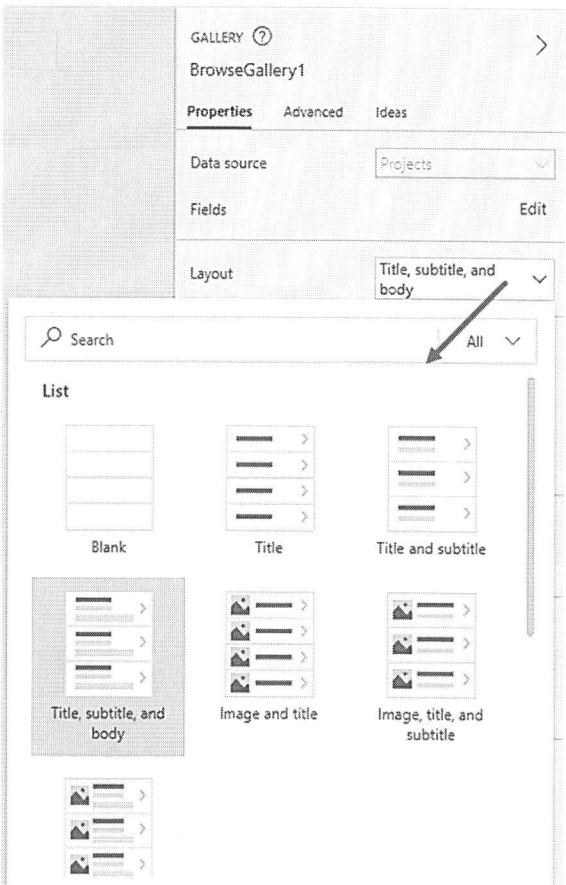

21.4.1.1   Hide a Field

As the app is meant to be used in mobile devices, you don't want to have too many fields to scroll among. I recommend that you hide the cards and not delete them, in case you want to use them later.

To hide a field, so that it is not displayed in the app, select the card and set the 'Visible' control under the 'Properties' tab in the right pane to 'Off', as explained in the list form section.

21.4.1.2 Change what is Displayed

The Browse screen in a mobile app only shows a little bit of each item, so the most informative fields should be displayed first. Maybe the auto-created powerapp does not show the data that is most important to show in an app? In that case, you can change that manually.

Select a control, which might be empty, and change the text in the function field. In the image below, the first field card is empty because it shows a non-existing ComplianceAssetId.

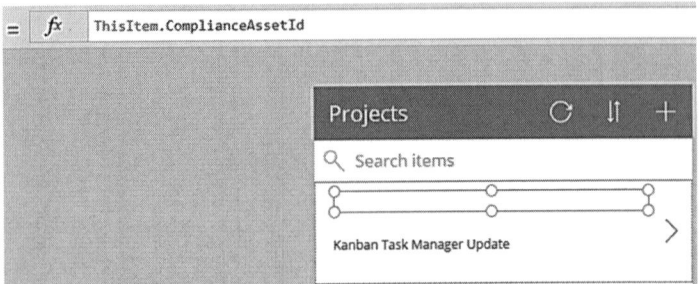

Normally you want the title here, and if you write Title after the dot instead, the card will show the title.

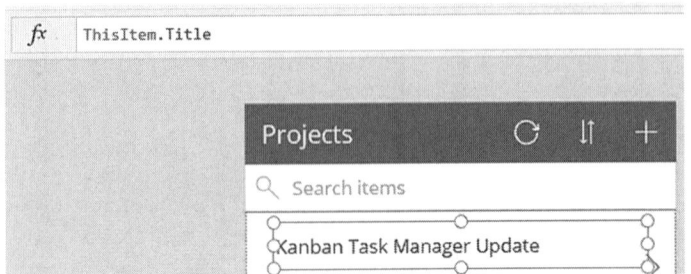

When you start typing, you will have suggestions on parameters to add to ThisItem.

The function can also be edited under the 'Advanced' tab in the right pane.

Another way to change what is displayed, is to first select the Browse gallery in the left pane, to open its right pane, and then click on 'Edit' at 'Fields' to open the Data pane.

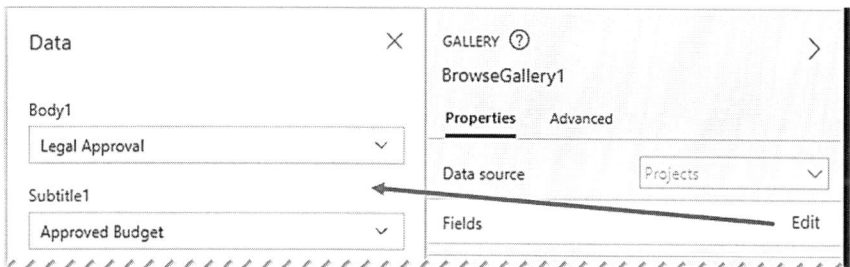

Select first the field you want to change on the dashboard and then another field than the current one from its dropdown.

21.4.2 Add a Field

If you want to add an extra field on the Browse screen, select the first card in the Browse screen and click on 'Label' under the Insert tab. Change what 'ThisItem' should display, in the way that is described above, and drag the new field to the place where you want it to be displayed in the cards on the Browse screen.

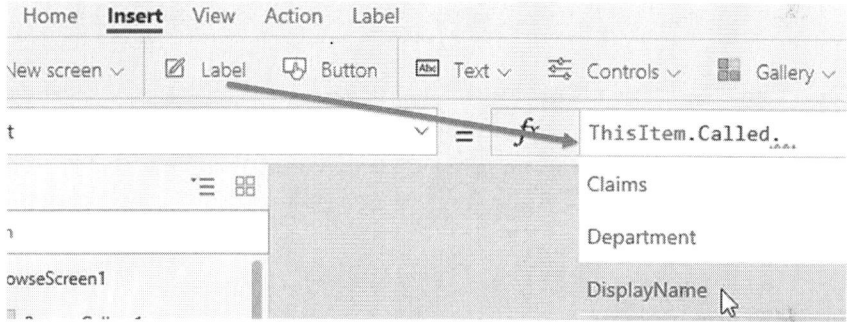

You can also edit the display text in the field under the Advanced tab in the right Edit pane.

21.4.3 Change Text Color

To change the text color in a specific field, select the text where you want to add another color. Then select the property you want to change in the top left dropdown, in this case 'Color'.

The default color is shown as RGBA, but if you don't have the code you can start typing a color and get suggestions on nuances.

| Color | = | fx ∨ | RGBA(0, 0, 0, 1) |

21.4.3.1 Conditional Formatting

To take the color modification a step further, you can add conditional formatting, so that the text only changes color when a specific column has a specific value.

In the image below, I have entered a condition instead of the default color. It says that the color should be green when the value of the Legal Approval column is 'Approved'.

If(ThisItem.'Legal Approval'="Approved",Green)

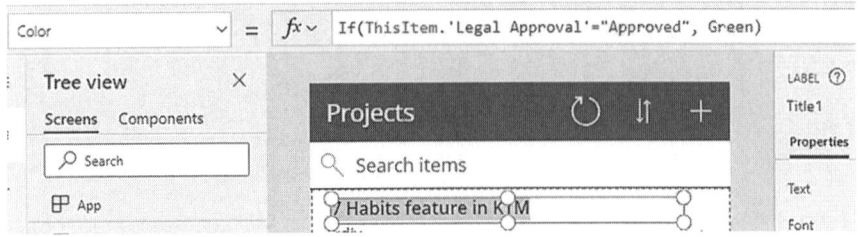

Build the function like this:

1. Enter If and select If from the dropdown. Now a start parenthesis will be added.
2. Start typing This and select ThisItem.
3. Add a dot after ThisItem.
4. Start typing the column name and select the correct option.
5. Add an equal sign and a quotation mark.
6. Start typing the value and select the correct option.
7. End the quotation.
8. Add a comma.
9. Start typing the color and select the correct option.
10. Finish the parenthesis.

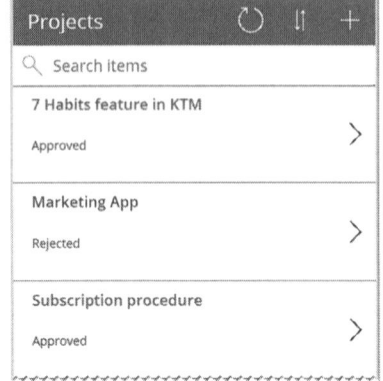

Now title texts are green for approved projects.

21.4.4   Share a PowerApp

To share a powerapp from the Power Apps Studio, use the 'Share' button under 'Files'. This button will be visible when you have saved and published the powerapp.

In the Power Apps Portal, open the 'Apps' page and select 'Share' under the ellipsis at the powerapp you want to share.

The 'Share' command will open a right pane, where you can add the names or e-mail addresses of the people or groups that you want to share your app with and select among the suggestions that will come up.

Make sure that the people you share the app with have access to the data you have used.

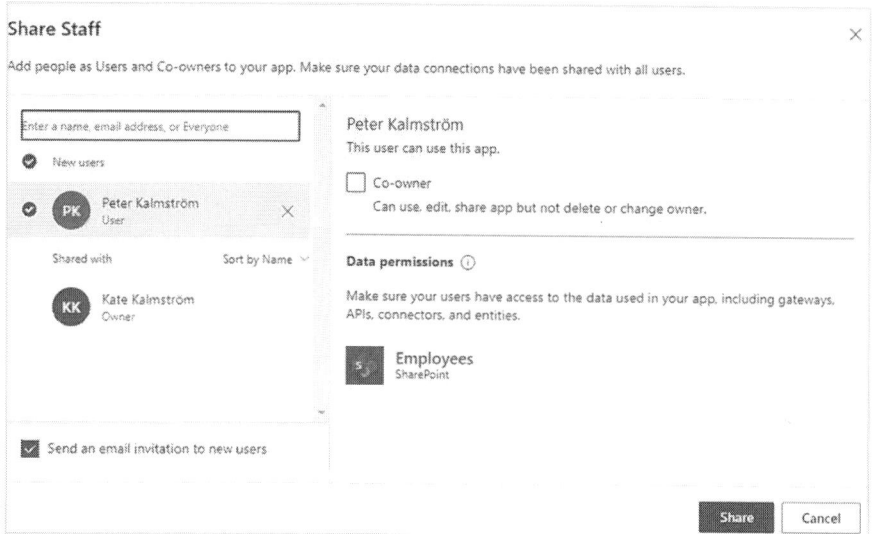

For some data sources, read permissions are given automatically when an app is shared. In other cases, the app creator must share the data source, or the user must take steps to connect to the data source.

The creator of the powerapp is its owner, but you can give the people or groups you share it with co-owner permission. Co-owners can run and customize the app and share it, but they cannot delete the powerapp or change its owner.

By default, an e-mail with a link to the new app is sent to people with whom you have shared the PowerApp. When you have invited people to edit, the e-mail will also have a link that opens the powerapp in Power Apps Studio.

Users can run the app by clicking on the link in the invitation e-mail. If that is done on a mobile device, the powerapp opens in Power Apps Mobile. If a user clicks on the link on a desktop computer, the app opens in a browser.

You can also find all powerapps that you share among the apps under the App launcher or among 'All apps'.

21.4.4.1 Publish Changes

When you want to propagate changes to a shared app, you must first publish it again with the 'Publish this version' button under the 'Files' tab.

Be aware that any changes you make to a shared app will flow through to the people you shared it with as soon as you have published your changes. This is good when you enhance the app, but if you remove or significantly change features, it may have a negative impact on other users.

21.4.5 *Use a Powerapp*

Power Apps has a web player, a mobile player and a Windows desktop player. When you use a powerapp, all your changes will be saved back to the data source, and vice versa.

21.4.5.1 Power Apps Mobile

When you have Power Apps installed on a smartphone or tablet, you will have the new powerapp among the other apps in your device. You can download Power Apps Mobile from the App Store or Google Play.

Power Apps running on a mobile can take advantage of the location and camera of the device, but you must give your consent to that before you use the app.

21.4.5.2 Add to a Page

A powerapp can be added to a modern page with the Microsoft Power Apps web part. For that, you need a link or an ID, which you can find in the Power Apps Portal.

1. Open the Power Apps button in a SharePoint app and select 'See all apps' or go directly to the Power Apps Portal and open 'Apps'.
2. Click on the ellipsis at the powerapp you want to add to the page and select 'Details'.
3. Now you can see both the URL and the ID on the page that opens.

Demo:

https://www.kalmstrom.com/Tips/Office-365-Course/First-Powerapp.htm

21.5 POWER APPS ADMIN CENTER

You can reach the Power Apps Admin center via the Settings icon in the Power Apps Portal and Studio and from the Microsoft 365 Admin center >All admin centers >Power Apps.

The Power Platform Admin center will open in a new tab, and here, administrators can study Power Apps statistics, create environments and set security policies.

21.6 SUMMARY

In this chapter, I have introduced Power Apps, a service that makes it possible to customize list forms and create apps that show list data in a mobile and touch friendly interface.

I have shown some examples on what you can do, and I hope my descriptions will act as a starting point for your own powerapps creation and form customization.

I have also explained how to share a powerapp and what to think about when you share such apps.

SharePoint may be used together with more Microsoft services than Power Apps. In the next chapter, we will have a look at more options. Power Apps can only be reached from the modern experience, but some of the options we will look at next is the other way around: you need to switch to the classic interface to use them.

22 CONNECT AND EXPORT SHAREPOINT DATA

In this chapter, I will show several different ways to connect and synchronize SharePoint apps with Outlook, Excel and Access.

Excel and Access can be used independently of app interface and app type, while the Outlook connections only can be made in the classic interface and for certain list types.

I will explain how the result of the connection is different for connections to Excel compared to Outlook and Access, and I will make a comparison between Excel and SharePoint.

I will also give some examples on how Access can be used with SharePoint, and I will describe how to show content from Excel in a web part.

22.1 CONNECT SHAREPOINT AND OUTLOOK

The classic Calendar, Tasks and Contacts list types, created via 'Add an app', have a lot of semi-hidden functionality that allows them to synchronize with the personal desktop edition of Outlook. You need to use the **classic** interface to make the connection.

Connect to Outlook

1. In the list that you want to connect to Outlook, click on the 'Connect to Outlook' button under the LIST/CALENDAR tab.
2. Click on the 'Open link' button.

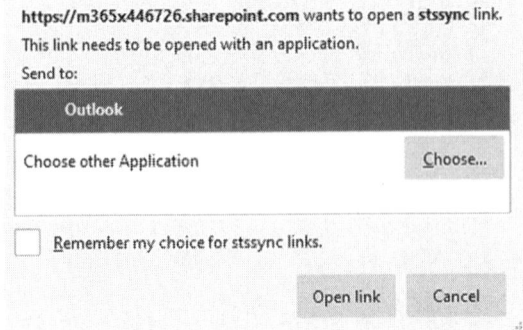

3. Click 'Yes' to the warning message.

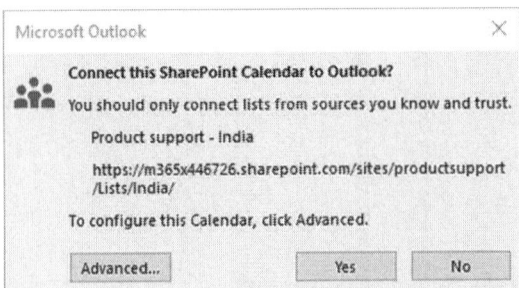

4. Enter your password if you are asked to do that.

The Outlook desktop app normally stores its data in the Exchange Server mailbox, but the connected SharePoint data (appointments, contacts, tasks and files) is stored in SharePoint.

You can work with the SharePoint items in Outlook even if you are off-line. As soon as you are connected to SharePoint again, they will be synchronized with SharePoint.

There is also an Outlook export button in the classic library interface, but the synchronization does not work well, and the files will become read-only. If you need files to be available offline, I suggest that you instead sync the library with OneDrive, *refer to* 12.2.3, OneDrive for Business Sync.

22.1.1 Synch Calendar, Contacts and Tasks with Outlook

When you add a SharePoint list built on the classic Calendar, Contacts or Tasks template to your local Outlook, these lists will be shown as separate folders in Outlook. Here, I will show the calendar. Contacts and Tasks lists work in the same way, but they are added to your personal Contacts and Tasks.

In the image to the right, from the Outlook calendar view, the calendar named "Calendar" is a personal calendar. The calendar called 'HR – HR Events' is the SharePoint calendar. The two parts of the name are the name of the site (HR) and the name of the calendar within that site (HR Events).

When the boxes for both lists are checked, they will be displayed side by side. Uncheck one of the boxes if you want to see only one calendar.

If you show the calendars side by side, you can drag and drop or copy and paste items from one app to the other.

When apps are synchronized with Outlook, they are also displayed under the heading SharePoint Lists in the Outlook Folders view. (To open the Folders view, click on the ellipses at the bottom left in the desktop edition. In Outlook on the web, click on the left pane toggle at the top left if you cannot see the Folders.)

22.1.1.1 Calendar Benefits in Outlook

Outlook has more calendar features than SharePoint has, so it is often useful to connect the SharePoint team calendar to your personal Outlook.

In Outlook, you can categorize the SharePoint calendar events with colors, just as you do with your personal calendar, but these colors are not displayed in SharePoint.

Demos:

https://www.kalmstrom.com//Tips/SharePoint-Online-Course/Outlook-Sync-Calendars.htm

https://www.kalmstrom.com//Tips/SharePoint-Online-Course/Outlook-Sync-Contacts.htm

393

https://www.kalmstrom.com/Tips/SharePoint-Online-Course/Sync-SharePoint-Tasks-List-with-Outlook.htm

22.1.2   Remove a Synchronized List from Outlook

If you no longer have a 365 license, or you don't want to have a synchronized SharePoint list in your Outlook for some other reason, right-click on the list in Outlook and select 'Delete Folder'.

The data will not be deleted in SharePoint. You are only removing the connection between SharePoint and Outlook.

Demo:

https://www.kalmstrom.com/Tips/SharePoint-Online-Course/Remove-Synched-SharePoint-List-from-Outlook.htm

22.1.3   Import an Outlook Calendar to SharePoint

You can import calendar info from an Outlook calendar to a new SharePoint calendar by using the Connect to Outlook feature.

1. Create a classic SharePoint Calendar app via 'Add an app'.
2. Connect the new calendar to Outlook, as described above.
3. In Outlook, change the view for the Outlook calendar you want to import from into List view.

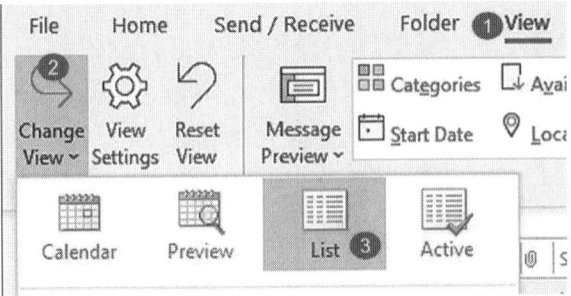

4. Select all the items in the original Outlook calendar with Ctrl+A and copy them with Crtl+C.
5. Open the SharePoint calendar, still in Outlook, and change the view into List.
6. Paste all the items into the SharePoint calendar with Ctrl+V.

You can even use this method to get a calendar ICS file from another place, for example a website, into SharePoint. Use Outlook as an intermediate step, so that you first import the external calendar to Outlook and then copy the items to the synchronized SharePoint calendar in Outlook, as described above.

Demo:

https://www.kalmstrom.com/Tips/SharePoint-Online-Course/Copy-Events-from-Calendar-or-ics-File.htm

22.2 Connect SharePoint and Excel

SharePoint apps and Excel tables have many similarities – but also important differences.

Even if Microsoft Excel was not originally created for data sharing, it is often used that way. SharePoint, on the other hand, was designed for collaboration from the beginning, and therefore, SharePoint has advantages that make it more suitable for data sharing than Excel:

- Editing.
  A SharePoint app does not get locked when someone is editing it. An Excel file on a file server is locked, so that no one else can access it until the editing is finished and the new version of the file has been saved.

- Version history.
  In SharePoint it is easier to track changes in rows or cells, and SharePoint can show and restore earlier versions of each row in an app. Excel does not have a versioning feature, so to have several versions of a file you must give them different names – and even if you do that, you have to manually find out the differences between the two files.

- Alerts.
  SharePoint apps have an Alert feature, so that you can have an automatic e-mail each time a list item has been changed. You can also create more advanced notifications using a flow or workflow, *refer to* chapter 24, SharePoint Automation. Excel does not have this possibility without extensive coding.

- Independence.
  In a SharePoint app, each item is independent from the others, so that you can edit and lock each row (=item) and set independent row permissions. That is not possible in Excel.

SharePoint also has some problems that you should be aware of:

- Portability.
  A SharePoint app cannot be transferred as easily as an Excel file. (This might also be a benefit! It is not always an advantage that you easily can share an Excel file.)

- Re-training and moving costs.
  If you already have your data in Excel, it will take some time to move it to SharePoint. It is always easier to let people work as they have always done!

- The 5000 items limit.
  Currently SharePoint Online apps have a limitation of 5000 items in a view. Therefore, you should split up the data if it will give more than 5000 items. (Another option is to upload the Excel files to SharePoint and share them that way.)

- It is often easier to clean and modify the data in Excel than in SharePoint.

The conclusion is that SharePoint is much better when it comes to sharing, so data that should be shared should be kept in SharePoint.

On the other hand, Excel has excellent calculation, analysis and visualization features. The good thing is that you can use these Excel features on your SharePoint data too. In this section I will explain how this is done.

In the methods described in this section, you need to make any changes in SharePoint to have them reflected in Excel. It does not work the other way around.

Click on the 'Refresh All' button under the Data tab in Excel to bring a fresh copy of the SharePoint app to Excel.

Excel does not give you an error message if you try to edit the data in Excel, but your input will not be visible in SharePoint, and when you refresh the table, it will be overwritten with any changes in SharePoint.

Note: I have already described how a new SharePoint list can be created from an Excel file in the Microsoft Lists app, *refer to* 8.3.2.2, From Excel. That method gives a totally separate list with *no connection to Excel*, so it is not included here.

Demo:

https://www.kalmstrom.com/Tips/SharePoint-Online-Course/Excel-vs-SP.htm

22.2.1   Export a SharePoint App to Excel

The SharePoint export feature saves the app's current view to Excel, so that you can take advantage of the analysis, calculation and visualization features where Excel shines.

When you click on the 'Export' button in modern list apps, Windows gives two options for the export: Excel Workbook and CSV. On Macs, only the Export to CSV option is available, but CSV files can also be opened in Excel.

In the classic ribbon and in library apps, the button is called 'Export to Excel', and there is no CSV option.

Different browsers give different options, so I have put parentheses around steps that are not needed in all browsers.

1. In the SharePoint app, click on the 'Export' button in the command bar and select Excel workbook (modern). Or click on the 'Export to Excel' button under the ribbon LIST tab (classic).
2. Download the file to your computer or open it directly.
3. Click on 'Enable' on the warning message.
4. (Log in to 365 again.)
5. (Select how you want to view the data in Excel. The default option, Table, is often the most useful. If there is no choice, the list opens as a table.)

All the columns of the SharePoint view that you export will be included and visible in Excel. When you export a library app, the "Name" column will show links to the files.

You will also have two extra columns, "Item Type" and "Path", which you might want to hide in Excel. However, if you have exported a library that contains folders, the folder structure does not appear in the Excel table. In that case, the "Item Type "and "Path" columns are useful, as you can filter and sort the data based on type and location.

Demo:

https://www.kalmstrom.com/Tips/SharePoint-Online-Course/HelpDesk-Totals-ExcelExport.htm

22.2.1.1   Analyze SharePoint Data in Excel

When you have worked with a SharePoint app for a while, you probably want to study the data in it. By exporting the app to Excel, you can both analyze the data and visualize it in charts.

1. Click anywhere in the Excel table and then on 'PivotTable' under the Insert tab.
2. Select what data you want to view in the Pivot table. The default option is the table you clicked in.

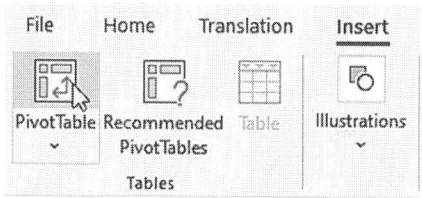

3. Drag and drop the fields you want to work with to some of the Pivot areas.
4. To create a chart, click in the Pivot table to open the PivotTable Analyze tab.

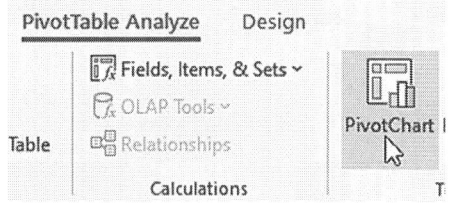

5. Click on the PivotChart button.
6. Select the chart type and design you prefer, to visualize the data from the SharePoint list.

Demo:

https://kalmstrom.com/Tips/SharePoint-Online-Course/HelpDesk-PivotTable-Chart.htm

In my book *Excel 2016 from Scratch*, you can learn much more about Excel. My focus is on calculation and visualization, from basics to advanced, and I give links to more than 60 online articles with video demonstrations and downloadable exercises: https://www.kalmstrom.com/Education/Excel-2016.htm

With the kalmstrom.com product *Pivot Explorer*, you can analyze data directly in a SharePoint list app, without exporting it to Excel first: https://www.kalmstrom.com/products/Pivot-Explorer/.

22.2.2 Direct Export from Excel to SharePoint

Exporting Excel data to SharePoint gives many sharing advantages. The transfer can be done in two ways, and the major question is how much functionality and control you need.

The easiest way to move items from Excel to SharePoint is to export an Excel table to a SharePoint list by using the 'Export Table to SharePoint List' button in Excel.

For more influence over the result, you might want to take the extra trouble and use Access as an intermediary. *Refer to* 22.3.4, Export an Excel Table to a SharePoint List via Access to learn about that option.

The direct export method is quick, but it has some serious drawbacks compared to the Access method:

- A new SharePoint list will be created for your data. Excel cannot push data into an existing list.
- The columns created in the new list will be list columns, not site columns.
- When you have exported the Excel data to SharePoint, it can only be updated in SharePoint.
- You cannot change the order of columns or exclude columns from the export/import. The range or table will be transferred just as it is.

There are also other problems with a direct transferring of data between Excel and SharePoint, but they can be helped by a "clean up" of the SharePoint list, see below.

This is the process for a direct data export from Excel to SharePoint:

1. Copy the URL to the SharePoint site where you want the new list to be created. Note that you should only copy the site URL, *refer to* 17.1.2, Site Link.
2. In Excel, format the data as a table if it is not already done.
3. Click on the 'Export' button under the Table Design tab and choose 'Export Table to SharePoint List'.

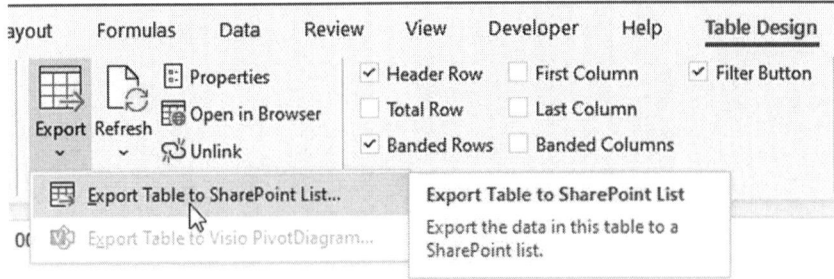

4. Paste the URL you copied in the 'Address' field in the dialog that opens.
5. Check the box for read-only connection.
6. Write the name you wish to use for the SharePoint list that will be created. You may also add a description for it. Click on 'Next.'
7. In the new dialog that opens, you can see the different list columns that will be created. It is not possible to change anything here, so if the list looks wrong you must go back and make changes in the Excel table. Click on 'Finish' when the data looks as it should.

Now a new SharePoint list app will be created in the site you gave the URL to, and the data from the Excel table will be added to that list.

When the process is finished, you will get a message dialog with a link to the new list.

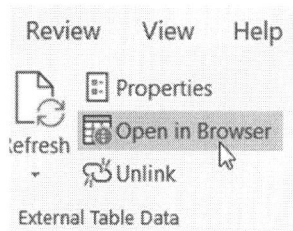

You can also open the list from Excel by clicking on the new 'Open in Browser' button.

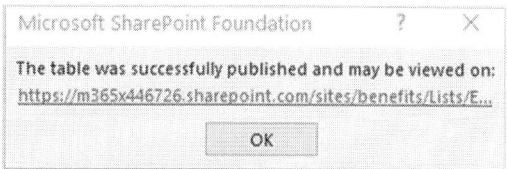

Demos:

https://kalmstrom.com/Tips/SharePoint-Online-Course/Export-Excel.htm

https://www.kalmstrom.com/Tips/SharePoint-Online-Course/Problems.htm

22.2.2.1 Enhance a SharePoint List Created from Excel Export

The SharePoint list that is created when an Excel table is directly exported to SharePoint does not take advantage of all available SharePoint features. Here are some tips on how you can make the new list app better adapted to SharePoint:

- At export, the default view of the new list is grid view, but having the grid as default view creates problems if you want to display the list in a web part or automate a process with the list. Therefore, you might want to create a new standard list view and make that the default view.
- Make the view cleaner by not showing all columns.
- Create more views to show the data from different perspectives.

- Add the list to the Site navigation.

Demo:

https://www.kalmstrom.com/Tips/SharePoint-Online-Course/Clean.htm

22.2.3 Display Excel Data in a Web Part

When you store an Excel file in a SharePoint library, you can display all or just a part of the workbook in a web part. This is possible in modern as well as classic pages, but the classic web part gives more options for the user interaction with the Excel content.

The Excel file can be stored anywhere in the tenant, but make sure that users have permission to access the file. When you upload a file from your computer, it will by default be placed in the site's "Site Assets" library.

22.2.3.1 Show Excel Data in a Modern Page

In a modern page, you can use the File Viewer web part, *refer to* 13.7.1.1. File Viewer, to display an Excel workbook or part thereo.

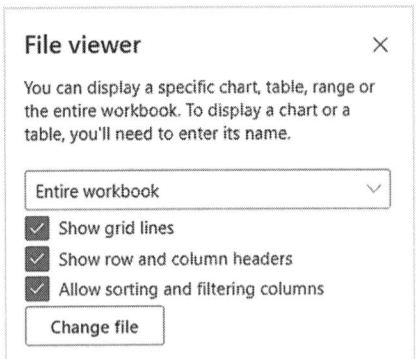

Edit the web part, if you want to show something else than the whole workbook or change the default settings for grid lines, headers, sorting and filtering.

22.2.3.2 Show Excel Data in a Classic Page

The Excel Web Access web part can only be used in classic pages, but it gives a lot of options for the user interaction with the Excel data.

Unfortunately, the Excel Web Access web part is only available in the SharePoint Enterprise Plans E3 and E5. If you have that and still cannot find the web part, make sure that 'Enterprise Site Collection Features' is activated under Site settings >Site collection features and in Site settings >Manage site features in the root site.

Here I will just go through the most basic: how to define which workbook and which part of that workbook should be displayed in SharePoint.

1. Open the page where you want to add content from Excel in edit mode and add the Excel Web Access web part from the Business Data category.
2. Edit the web part: enter the URL to the Excel file in the 'Workbook' field or click on the 'Browse' button to the right of the field and find the Excel file.

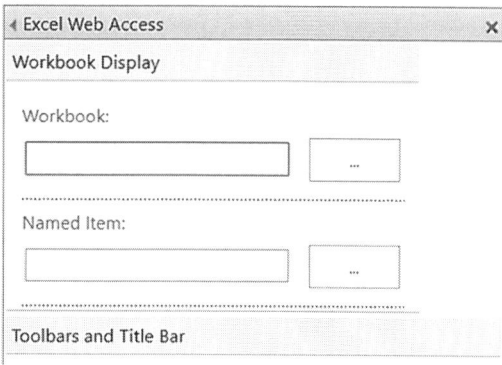

3. If you want to show the whole workbook, click on 'Apply' and then save the page.
4. If you want to show only part of the workbook, select that part in Excel and give it a name. Then add the name in the 'Named Item' field in the web part pane before you apply and save the page.

Demo:

https://www.kalmstrom.com/Tips/SharePoint-Online-Course/Excel-Web-Access.htm

22.3 CONNECT SHAREPOINT AND ACCESS

When you open a SharePoint app in Access, you can take advantage of Access features like 'Find' and 'Replace', and you can copy and paste more easily in Access than in the SharePoint grid/datasheet view mode.

Both list and library apps can be opened and managed in Access. When you open a library, the files will be replaced by links that open the files.

Access is also a suitable intermediary to connect platforms that cannot be directly connected. You can, for example, work with SharePoint lists from different tenants or connect an SQL Server database to SharePoint via Access.

When you use Access as an intermediate platform for export of an Excel table to a SharePoint list, you will have more influence over the connection than if you make the kind of direct export I described above.

In this section, I will first explain how the synchronization between SharePoint and Access works and how you can open a SharePoint app in Access. Then I will give a few examples on what you can achieve when you use Access as an intermediary to get data in to or out of SharePoint.

22.3.1 *SharePoint-Access Synchronization*

When you open a SharePoint app in Access, the app and the resulting Access table are synchronized. You can make changes in Access, as well as in SharePoint.

When you enter data in the Access table, it is saved to the SharePoint app as soon as you move to another row. When you enter data in the SharePoint app, the linked Access table will be updated next time it is opened or refreshed.

22.3.2 Open a SharePoint App in Access

There is an Access button in the classic app interface, but in most cases, it is best to connect SharePoint to Access from within Access:

1. In Access, create a blank database.
2. A table will be created automatically. Now you can choose between two methods:
   - Click on 'New Data Source' under the 'External Data' tab and select 'From Online Services' >SharePoint List.

   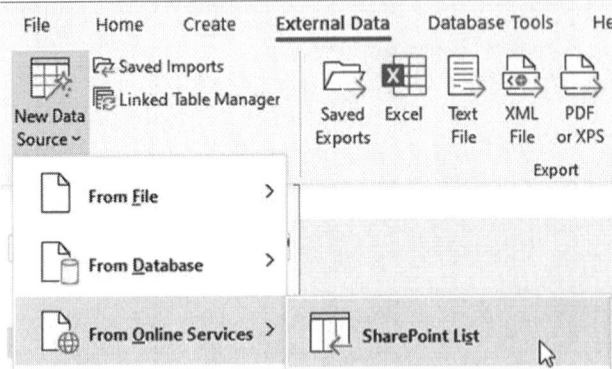

   - Right-click on the automatically created table and select 'Import' and then 'SharePoint List'.

   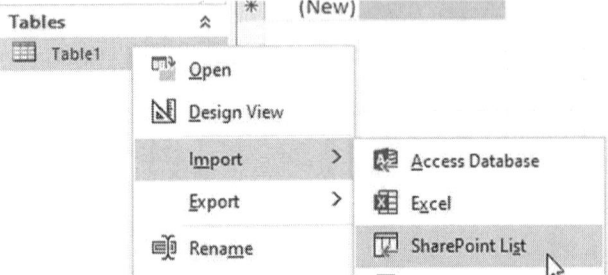

3. In both cases, a dialog opens where you can select, paste or type the path to the site that has the list you want to open in Access.

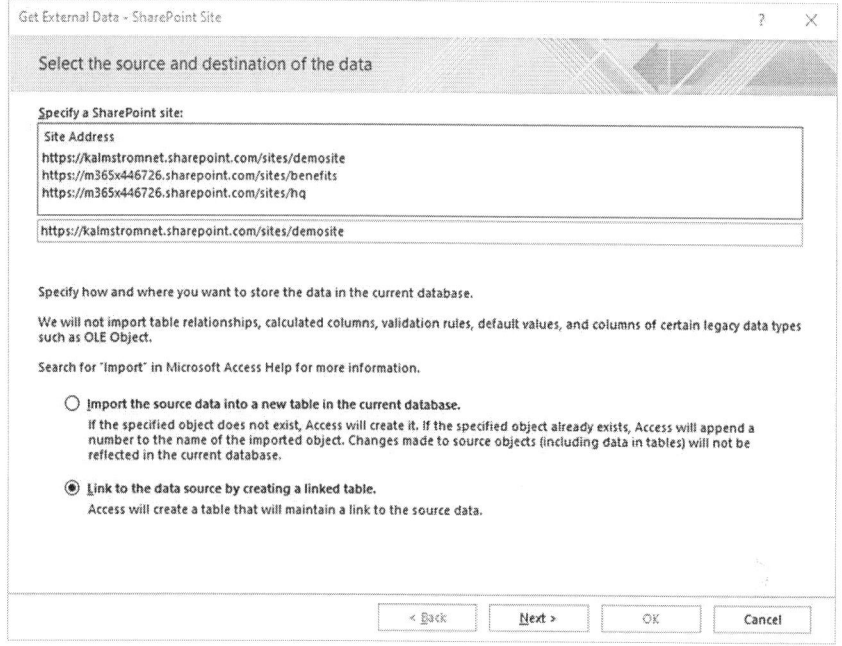

4. Select the linked table option and click Next.

   This selection controls where the data is going to be stored. When you import, the data will be stored in in the Access file and no connection to SharePoint will be maintained. When you link, only the connection is stored in the Access file and every data update is immediately saved to the SharePoint list.

5. Now all apps in the site will be displayed. Check the box for the app you want to use and click OK. A new table with the same name as the app will be created.

   You can also select multiple apps. Each of them will be connected as a separate linked table.

6. Drag the list table to the main area to work with it.

22.3.2.1 User Info

The "UserInfo" list is a hidden SharePoint list that becomes visible when you link Access to SharePoint. When you connect an app that has a People or Group type column, Access creates a linked UserInfo table from the "UserInfo" list as well, even if you don't check the box for it.

If you don't need the "Userinfo" table, you can always right-click on the table and hide it.

403

22.3.3 Edit Multiple List Items

When you open the list in Access and drag the table into the main area, you can copy and paste more quickly than in SharePoint. In Access, you can also:

- Use the Access Replace feature (under the Home tab) to edit multiple items that should be changed in the same way.

- Run an Access Query. When you have a SharePoint list open in Access and want to change multiple items in the same way, the quickest method is to run a query. With this method, you can even replace two different values with one other value.

    a. Click on the 'Query Design' button under the Create tab in the ribbon.
    b. Drag the list table to the query area.
    c. Click on the 'Update' button under the Design tab.
    d. In the grid area, select the field you want to update.
    e. Fill out the update value (= the new value).
    f. Fill out the criteria (= the current value(s)).

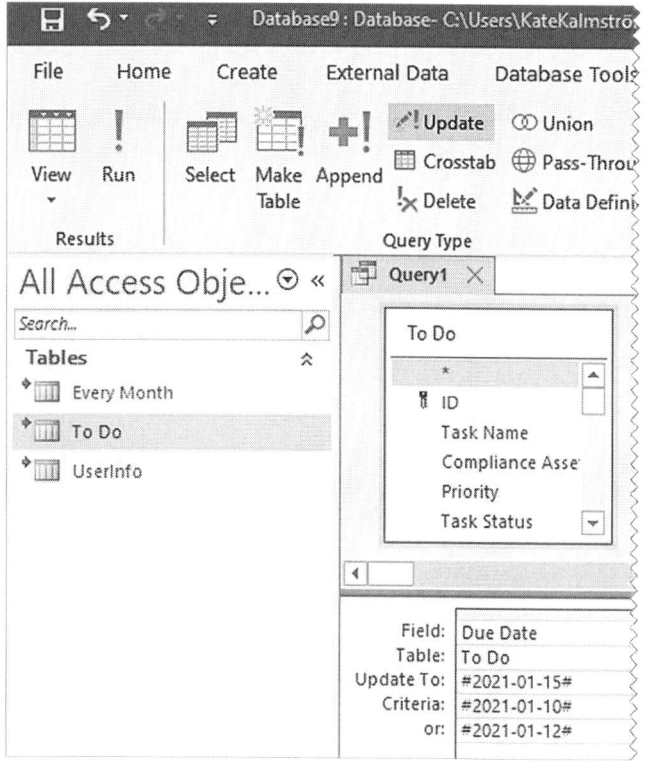

g. Click on the 'Run' button under the Design tab in the ribbon and click OK to the warning messages. Now the values will be replaced quickly.

Demo:

https://www.kalmstrom.com/Tips/SharePoint-Online-Course/HelpDesk-Edit-Multiple-Items.htm

22.3.4   Export an Excel Table to a SharePoint List via Access

Above I have described how to send Excel data to SharePoint with the export button in Excel. This is a quick method, but as I mentioned it has some drawbacks.

The Access method is more complicated than the direct method, but it gives you better control over how data is added to the SharePoint list:

- You can decide which Excel columns you want to include in the SharePoint list.
- You can decide how data should be distributed.
- You can use an existing list with site columns for the import of Excel data.
- Changes can be made in both Access and SharePoint.

With the Access method, you import both a SharePoint list and an Excel datasheet to Access, where they are shown as database tables.

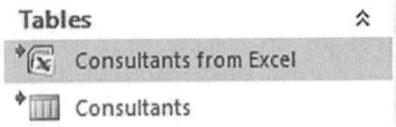

Then you can create a query that copies the data you want to use from the Excel table to the SharePoint table.

1. Import the SharePoint list to Access, as described above.
2. Import the Excel file in the same way and select the option 'Link to the data source by creating a linked table'.
3. Check the box for headings if your Excel table has headings.
4. Give a name to the new, linked table with your Excel data.
5. In Access, click on the 'Query Design' button under the Create tab.

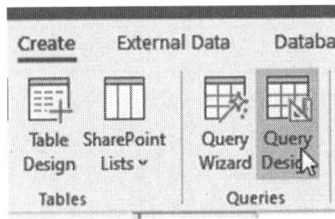

6. Drag the Excel table from the left menu into the Query field.
7. Under the Design tab, click on the 'Append' button.

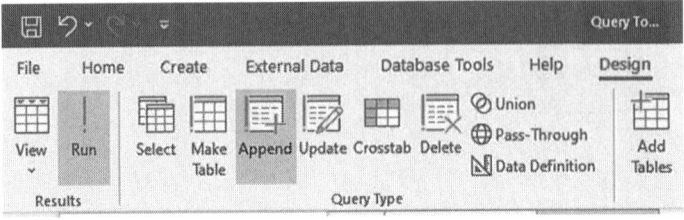

8. Select to append to the SharePoint list you have opened in Access, and click OK.
9. In the Excel table in the 'Query' field, double click on the names of the columns you want to include in the SharePoint list. They will then be displayed in the grid below, so that you can append them to columns in the SharePoint list. You may also drag and drop the Excel column names to the grid.
10. Append the Excel columns to the corresponding columns in the SharePoint list.

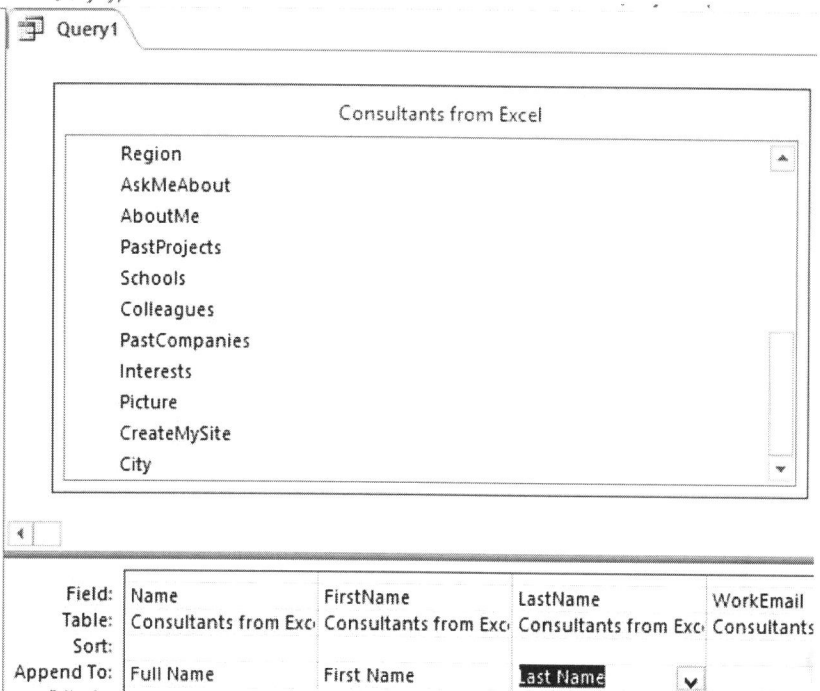

11. Save the query and give it a more suitable name than the default one.

12. Run the query by clicking on the 'Run' button under the Design tab.

When you go back to the SharePoint list and refresh the page, you can see the Excel data distributed in the columns in the way you mapped it in Access.

This method of using Access to get data into SharePoint works very well with other data sources too, not only Excel data sources. *Refer to* 22.3.6, Import Data from SQL to SharePoint, to see an example.

Demo:

https://www.kalmstrom.com/Tips/SharePoint-Online-Course/Import-Access.htm

22.3.5 Recurring Tasks

In this section, I will give another example of how you can use an Access query to update a SharePoint app. The starting point is a table in Excel. This table shows tasks that must be done repeatedly each month, and it has info about tasks, assigned people and due dates in columns called "What", "Who" and "Day of Month".

SharePoint has no simple way to handle recurring tasks, but you can still make it easy to both remember recurring tasks and to verify that the tasks have been done.

The trick is to let an Access query update a "To Do" Tasks list in SharePoint. Then you can let SharePoint Alerts remind the responsible people about the tasks, and when the task is done the responsible person can set the task to completed.

22.3.5.1 Export to SharePoint

The first step is to make a direct export of Excel data to SharePoint, so that you get the recurring tasks data into a SharePoint list app. Here I will call that list "Every Month".

22.3.5.2 Create a To Do List

When you have the Excel data in SharePoint, create a new app on the Tasks list template. Here I will call this list "To-Do". Now, you *could* copy and paste the "What" and "Who" data from the "Every Month" list into the "To Do" list by using the grid view mode in both lists.

However, the Due date column cannot be copied as easily as the other columns – you must copy and paste recurring tasks for every month.

A better solution is to let Microsoft Access handle the update with a query. Then you will just have to run the query for each month to get all data into the SharePoint "To Do" list – including the due dates.

22.3.5.3 Update the To Do list with an Access Query

Here I will give the steps to create a query that takes data from the SharePoint lists "Every Month", (imported from Excel) and "UserInfo" and appends it to a new SharePoint "To Do" list.

The "What" field in the "Every Month" list can be directly appended to the Task name field in the "To Do" list, but the "Who" field cannot be directly appended to the "Assigned To" field. Instead, we need to use the "UserInfo" table.

1. In Access, import the "Every Month" and "To Do" lists from SharePoint in the way that is described above. Now two new tables with the same names and content as the lists will be created in the database. A "UserInfo" table will also be created, and this time we will use that table.
2. Under the Create tab, click on the 'Query Design' button.
3. Drag the "Every Month" table from the left menu into the Query field.
4. Drag the "What" field to the Design grid at the bottom.
5. Click on the 'Append' button under the Design tab and select to append to the "To Do" list.
6. In the Design grid, append the "What" field in the "Every Month" table to "Task Name" in the "To Do" table.
7. Click on the 'Add Tables' button under the Design tab to open a right pane.
8. Select the "UserInfo" table and click on the 'Add Selected Tables' button at the bottom of the pane.

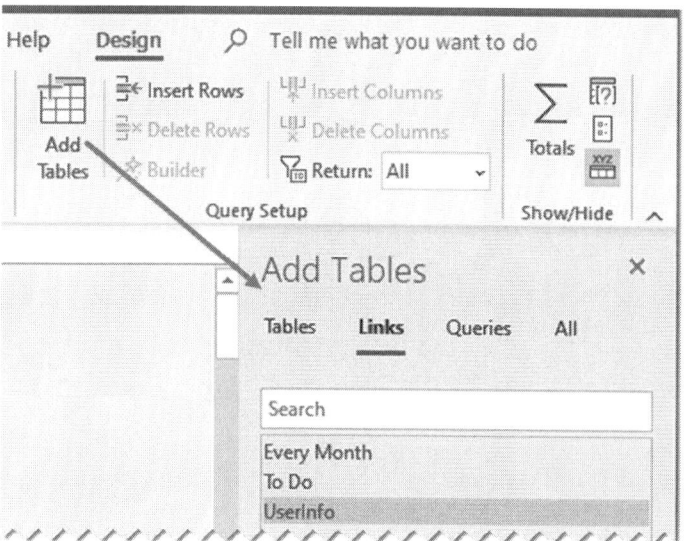

9. Append the "ID" field in the "UserInfo" table to the "Assigned To" field.

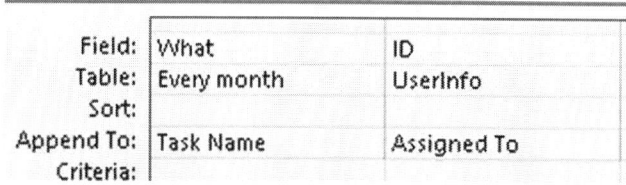

10. To have the Due Date info into the "To Do" table, select the "Every Month" table in the left pane and click on the 'Parameters' button under the Design tab.
11. Enter the two parameters Year and Month. Both should be Integers.
12. Put the mouse cursor in the cell to the right of the ID cell in the Design grid.
13. Click on the 'Builder' button under the Design tab to create an expression for the selected cell.
14. Select Functions >Built-in Functions >Date/Time >Date Serial.
15. Double-click on 'Date Serial' to display the expression.
16. Still in the Builder, select the query. Select 'year' in the expression and then double-click on the parameter 'Year'. Then select 'month' in the expression and double-click on the 'Month' parameter to get the parameters into in the expression.

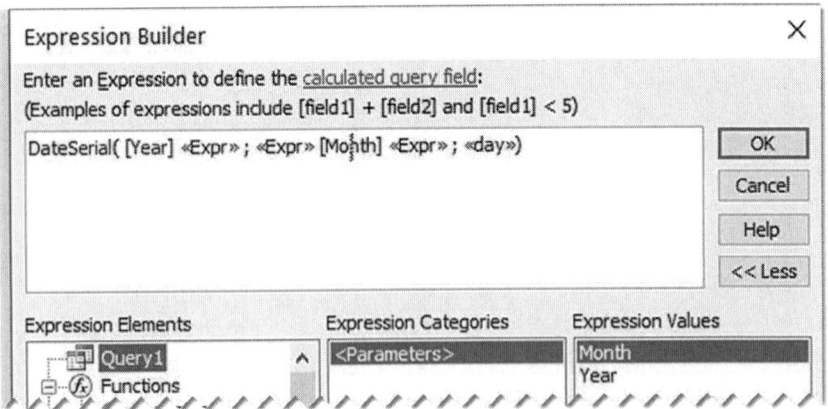

17. Select 'day' in the expression. Then, select the "Every Month" table and the "Day of Month" field. Double-click on 'Value' and then OK.

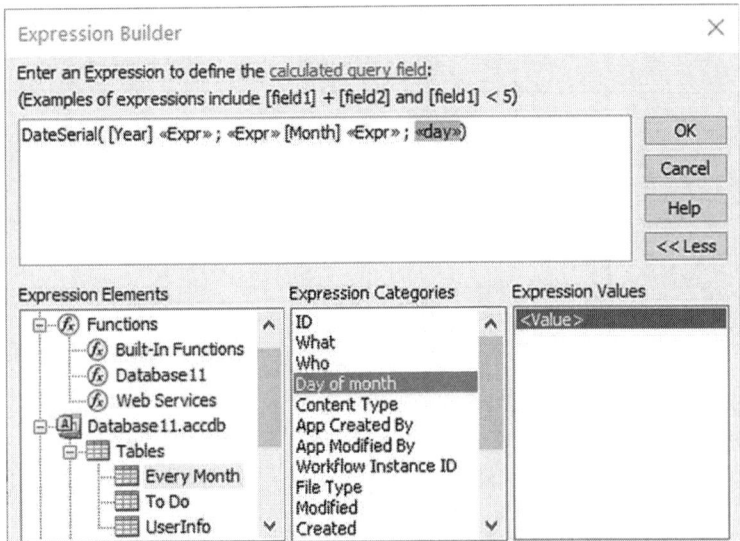

18. Click OK, and the expression you have built will be filled out in the third Design grid column, where you put the mouse cursor.
19. Change the text "Expr1" into "Due" and append to the Due Date field.

Field:	What	ID	Due: DateSerial([Year],
Table:	Every month	UserInfo	
Sort:			
Append To:	Task Name	Assigned To	Due Date

20. Save the query and give it a more suitable name than the default one.
21. Click on the 'Run' button under the Design tab to run the query. You will now be asked to enter values for the parameters Year and Month. Use numbers for both.

410

22. Run the query for every month and year, to have the SharePoint "To Do" list updated with all the recurring tasks.

Demo:

https://kalmstrom.com/Tips/SharePoint-Online-Course/Recurring-Tasks.htm

22.3.6 Import Data from SQL to SharePoint

When you want to input data from an SQL Server database to a SharePoint list, you cannot do that directly. Instead, you can open both the SQL Server database table and the SharePoint list in Access and create a query that copies data from the SQL Server to SharePoint.

Here I will describe how to add data from a "Contacts" SQL database table to a SharePoint Online "Contacts" list.

1. In SharePoint, create a list app on the Contacts template. Here, I will call it "Contacts".
2. Add and remove columns as you prefer.
3. Import the "Contacts" list to Access.
4. Under the External tab in the ribbon, select New data Source >From Other Sources >ODBC Database.
5. In the window that opens, check the radio button 'Link to the data source by creating a linked table' and click OK.
6. In the Select Data Source dialog, click on 'New' to create a new data source, and select SQL Server.

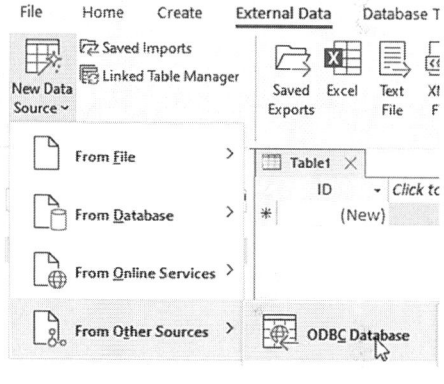

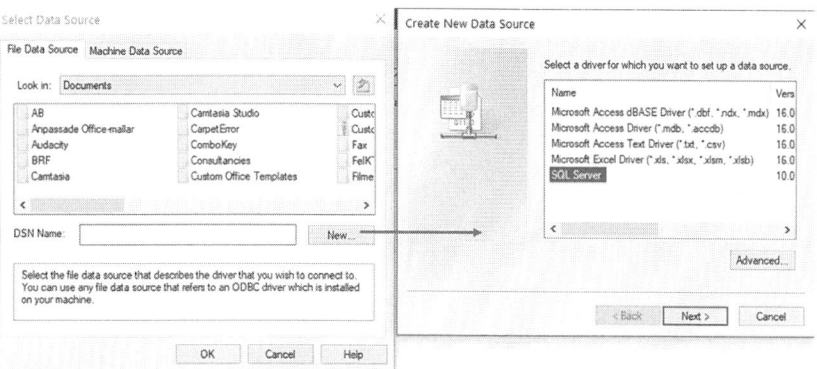

7. Click on 'Next' and type in or browse to the data source.
8. Click 'Next' and 'Finish'.

9. In the wizard, fill out or select your data and change the default database to pick up the new data source.
10. When you are back in the Select Data Source dialog again, select the new data source and link it to the Access table.
11. Select the appropriate id SQL column as the Unique Record. Usually, it is the first column.

Now we have two connections in Access, with SQL and with SharePoint, and we can connect the SQL contacts database to the SharePoint contacts list.

To do that, we will create a query that selects data from the SQL database table and appends it to the SharePoint list. This is done in the same way as in the examples above.

1. Click on the 'Query Design' button under the Create tab and select the SQL database table.
2. Click on the 'Append' button under the Design tab to append data from the SQL Server database to the SharePoint list.
3. Select how the data from the SQL database table should be added to the SharePoint list.

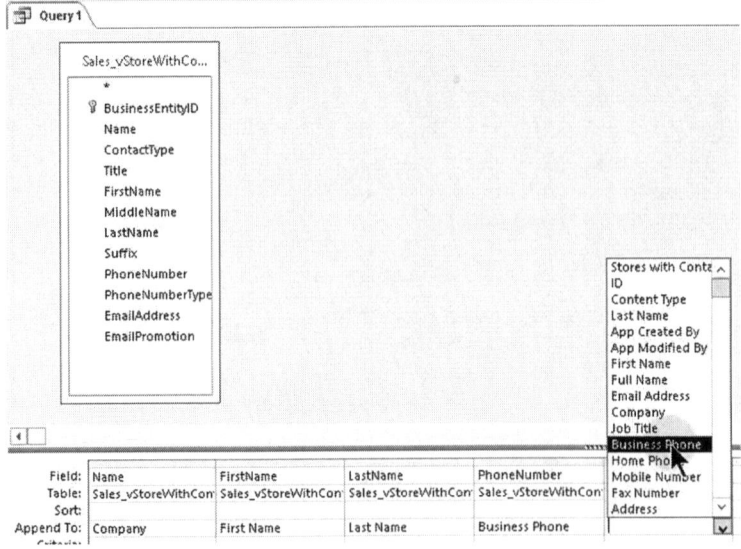

4. Click on the 'View' button under the Design tab to view the result.
5. If everything looks good, click on the 'Save' icon and give the query a more suitable name.
6. Run the query. Now the SQL Server data will be imported to the SharePoint list.

Demo:

https://kalmstrom.com/Tips/SharePoint-Online-Course/Import-data-from-SQL-to-SharePoint-online.htm

22.3.6.1 Update Imported SQL Data

If you continue to update the information on the SQL Server, you need a way to keep imported data up to date in the SharePoint list too. You can do this by creating an additional query that deletes the old data from the SharePoint list.

If you do that, you will have two queries: the add query, which adds the SQL Server data to Access and appends it to the SharePoint list, and the delete query. If you run first the delete query and then the add query, the data will be updated in SharePoint.

If you create a macro that runs the two queries in sequence and a 'Run' button in Access, you can update the SharePoint list even more quickly when data has been changed in the SQL Server database table.

Create a delete query:

1. Click on the 'Query Design' button and drag the SharePoint "Contacts" table into the query design area. Make sure that the * sign is selected, to remove all data from the list.
2. Click on the 'Delete' button under the 'Design' tab to create a delete query.
3. Save and name the query.
4. Run the query to test that it removes the SQL Server data from the SharePoint list and click OK to the warnings.

A macro is a way to automate a task that you perform repeatedly or on a regular basis. It consists of a series of commands and actions that can be stored and run when you need to perform the task.

Here is how you create a macro that runs the two queries mentioned above in sequence, first the delete query and then the add query.

1. Click on the 'Macro' button to the right under the Design tab.

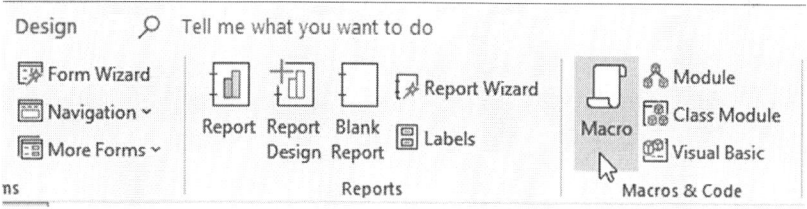

2. In the 'Add New Action' dropdown, select the action 'Open Query' and the query that deletes data.
3. Select the action 'Open Query' again and now select the query that adds the updated contacts to SharePoint.

413

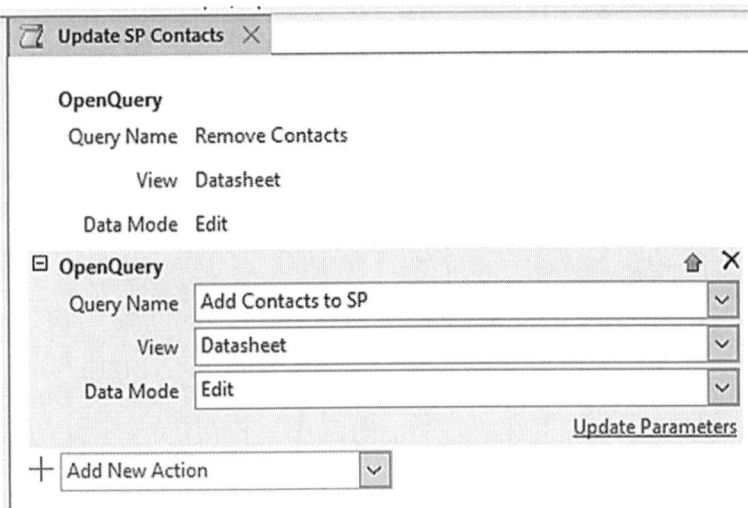

4. Select the action 'Close the database' from the dropdown.
5. Save and name the macro.

To further simplify the update, you can add a 'Run' button that runs the macro. The image to the right shows such a button with the default Access macro image.

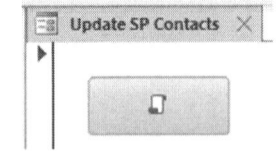

(Remove the macro from the design area before you create the button, to make the 'Blank Form' button active.)

6. Click on the 'Blank Form' button under the Create tab.

7. Click on the button icon under the Design tab and then in the form design area. A button and a wizard dialog will open in the design area.
8. Select the action Miscellaneous >Run Macro.

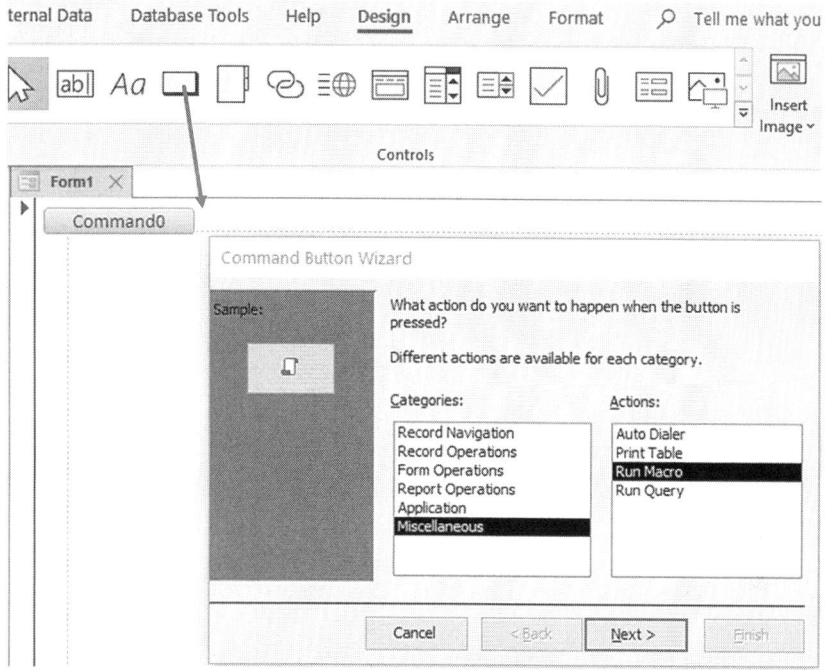

9. Select the new macro you just created.
10. Give the button a text or a picture and click on Next.

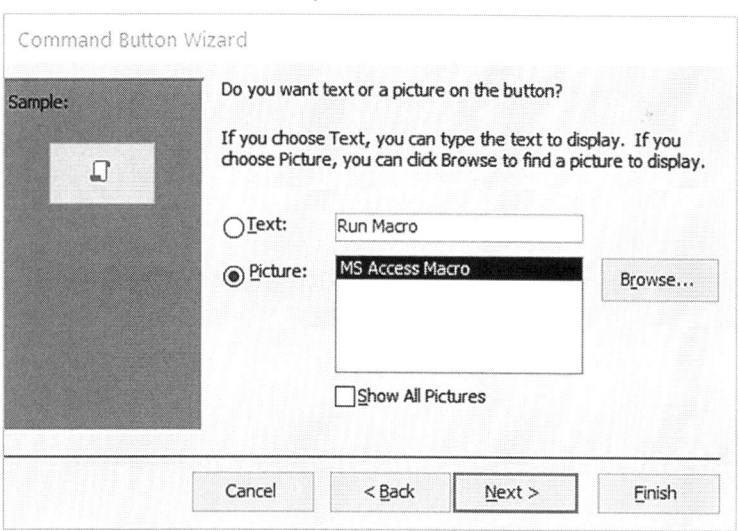

11. Give the button a name before you finish.
12. Save and name the form.
13. Click on 'Options 'under the File tab, and select the new form as Display Form for the Current Database.

14. To test, close Access and open it again. Then click on the button to run the query.

Demo:

https://www.kalmstrom.com/Tips/SharePoint-Online-Course/Update-Imported-SQL-Data.htm

22.4 SUMMARY

In this chapter we have seen how SharePoint app data can be used with Outlook, Excel and Access. I have also mentioned how SharePoint Tasks lists can be used with Microsoft Project Professional.

After showing how to create connections between SharePoint and other platforms, I have given examples on more advanced use of Access as an intermediary when exporting data from Excel and from an SQL Server database table to a SharePoint list.

23 Issue Tracking Tips

SharePoint list templates for tasks and issues are useful for helpdesk and support groups, and they are suitable for incident management, issue tracking and other shared tasks. In this section I will give some tips on how you can handle and enhance such list templates.

My intention is not to give a recipe on the perfect helpdesk list. Instead, I want to point to these various options, so that you can make the modifications that best suit each team:

- Comparison of the three templates
- Suggestions for a helpdesk list
- Data entry and edit button
- Landing page with views, issues list and Excel chart

23.1 List templates

SharePoint provides three list templates that can be used as helpdesk lists and often can replace each other: the modern Issue tracker and the classic Tasks and Issue Tracking. All have their benefits and drawbacks, and there are some differences you should be aware of when you decide which list template to use:

- When this is written, the Tasks list only have the classic user interface, so there is no way to switch to the modern experience. This also means that the Tasks list cannot be embedded in a modern page with the List web part.

    Lists that build on the Issue tracker and Issue Tracking templates can have the modern interface as well as the classic, and they can be used with all modern web parts that interact with lists.

- Only the Tasks list has a timeline.
- If you use the Issue tracker or Issue Tracking list templates, you cannot synchronize the list with Outlook and Project.
- Only Tasks list items have a 'Show more' link in the open form, but there is no way to decide what should be hidden when you open the list form.

    The other two lists show all fields in the item as soon as you open it.

- The Tasks list has a 'Start Date' column, the Issue tracker has a "Date reported" column and the Issue Tracking has no similar column. All three have a "Created" column, but it is not visible in the default views.
- The Tasks list has a "Completed" column with the options 'Yes' and 'No'. It is calculated, so that the "Completed" column is automatically set to 'Yes' when the "% Complete" value is '100' and vice versa.
- The Tasks and Issue Tracking lists have a setting that sends an e-mail to the assigned when an item is created or changed. The Issue tracker list has no such setting.

- The Tasks and Issue tracker lists have a possibility to set general Item-level Permissions at List settings >Advanced settings. The Issue Tracking list has no such possibility.

Item-level Permissions
Specify which items users can read and edit.

Note: Users with the Cancel Checkout permission can read and edit all items. Learn about managing permission settings.

Read access: Specify which items users are allowed to read
- ◉ Read all items
- ○ Read items that were created by the user

Create and Edit access: Specify which items users are allowed to create and edit
- ◉ Create and edit all items
- ○ Create items and edit items that were created by the user
- ○ None

- The Issue tracker list is created in Microsoft Lists, while the other two templates are found at Add an app >classic experience.
- Only the Issue tracker list can by default be created in Communication sites, *refer to* 7.5.1.1, Apps in Communication Sites.

Issue tracker	Tasks	Issue Tracking
classic and modern	classic	classic and modern
-	timeline	-
-	Calculated column	
-	simple initial form	-
-	Sync with Outlook/Project	-
-	Auto-email to assigned	Auto-email to assigned
item-level permissions	item-level permissions	-
Communication site	-	-

There are more differences between the templates than the ones I mentioned above, but they concern views and columns. The Tasks list has 7 built-in views, the Issue tracker has 4 and the Issue Tracking has 3, and the default columns are different in the three templates.

It is easy to add and delete columns and views, so I would recommend that you disregard those differences when you choose which of the list templates to use. Instead, consider which you will need most of the features listed in the table above.

Demo:

https://www.kalmstrom.com/Tips/SharePoint-Online-Course/Tasks-Issues.htm

23.1.1 Multiple Assignees

Multiple selection is allowed for the "Assigned To" column in the Tasks list. However, to allow multiple selections can create problems in several scenarios, for example when you want to group the "Assigned To" column by assigned in a view. If you use the Tasks list template, I therefore advise you to open the List settings and change that setting.

Allow multiple selections:
○ Yes ● No

If the same group of people often need to be responsible for a task, create a Security group for them instead, *refer to* 14.3, Security Groups. Then you can assign tasks to that group.

You can also create an additional column for stakeholders or other additional people you want to assign a task to.

23.2 CREATE A HELPDESK LIST

Here are some suggestions on how you can modify the default SharePoint templates for tasks and issues to make them suitable for a support team:

- Delete any default columns that you will not need.
- Add new columns for additional important metadata, for example "Minutes Worked" if you want to keep track of time spent on each task.
- In an Issue Tracking list, change the "Category" options names into something that suits your team better than 1, 2, 3.
- In the Tasks and Issue Tracking lists, click Yes to 'Send e-mail when ownership is assigned' under List settings >Advanced, if you don't intend to create an alert flow or workflow (which is the only option for the Issue tracker list).
- Create a "Data Entry" view that is displayed in the Grid view mode.
- The modern experience has an 'Edit' button in the command bar, but for the **classic** experience you can save users a few clicks if you add an 'Edit' button to the standard view mode. Go into the List settings and open the view to edit it. Check the Display checkbox for 'Edit (link to edit item)'.   ☑ Edit (link to edit item) 1

Demo:

https://www.kalmstrom.com/Tips/SharePoint-Online-Course/HelpDesk-Creation.htm

23.2.1 Data Entry View

In some situations, there are many users who create new items, for example to report an issue, but fewer people who handle them. In such cases, it is suitable to give a simpler entry form to the people who report and leave the more complicated form to the people who work with the issue.

That is the thought behind the simpler initial item form in the Tasks list, but it is even easier to fill out the new items in the Grid/Quick Edit mode.

When you have a Data Entry view, users are directed to a grid view when they create a new item. Of course, they might as well click on 'edit this list' or 'Quick Edit', but in a Data Entry view you can also remove columns and only keep those that are important when a user creates a new item.

You can for example remove the ID and the status columns. The ID is not important when the item is first added to the list, and at that time the issue or task is always New/Active/Not started – the default value.

In the **modern** interface, it is easy to create such a view:

1. Edit the list in grid view.
2. Use the column dropdown >Column settings to hide all columns that should not be included in the Data Entry view.
3. Open the View selector and select 'Save view as'.
4. Give the new view a name and click on 'Save'.

In the **classic** interface, you need to create a new view and select the Datasheet, as described in 7.9.5, Classic "New View" Options.

23.2.1.1 Hide Previous Items

If you don't want to show any previously created items in the Data Entry view, you can filter the view to only show items where the ID is 0. There are no such items, so you will not see any of the other items. The view will only show an empty grid row to fill out.

1. Open the List settings and click on your Data Entry view to modify it.
2. At 'Filter', set the view to show only items where the ID column is equal to zero.

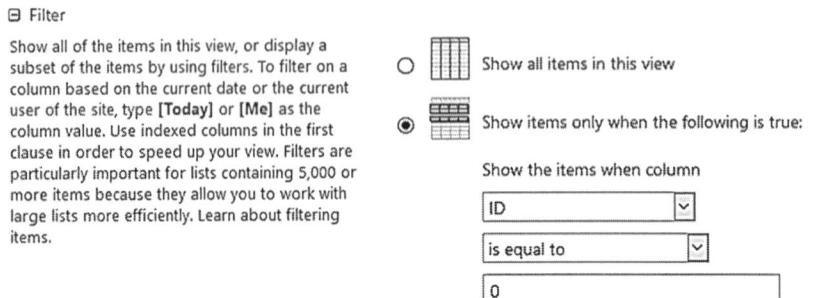

In chapter 25, Content Types, I explain how you can create a content type form and a workflow that switches to the full form the second time the item opens.

Demo:

https://www.kalmstrom.com/Tips/SharePoint-Online-Course/HelpDesk-Data-Entry-View.htm

23.3 MY TASKS VIEW

It is often convenient to let each user only see his/her own issues or tasks. In this view, the "Assigned to" column should be hidden, as it will always show the name of the current user. Most often users only want to see the items they need to work with, so they don't want this view to show completed tasks.

The Issue tracker list has no such view, but as it can use the **modern** interface it is very easy for each user to create it.

1. Filter the "Status" column to only show items with the value New or In Progress.
2. Filter the "Assign to" column to only show @Me.
3. Open the View selector and select 'Save view as'.
4. Give the new view a name and click on 'Save'.
5. In the "Assigned to" column, open the Column settings and hide the column.

When you create a new Tasks or Issue Tracking list, a "My Tasks" or "My Issues" view will be created automatically, but by default, these views show *all* tasks, even if completed tasks are crossed over in the Tasks list. Therefore, it is preferable to add another filter to the view.

For the Issue Tracking list, you can use the modern interface and filter the Status column in the My Issues view before you save it as another view.

In the **classic** interface, you need to go via the List settings:

1. Click on the "My Tasks"/"My Issues" view to open it.
2. Scroll down to 'Filter' and add a second filter after the "Assigned To" filter.
3. For the **Tasks** list, select the column 'Completed' and set it to 'is not equal to' 'Yes'. (This is a more secure option than "is equal to' 'No'.)
4. For the **Issue Tracking** list, select the column 'Issue Status' and set it to 'is equal to' 'Active'. (You must type Active).
5. Even more secure, is to set two filters for 'Issue Status': 'is not equal to' 'Resolved' and 'is not equal to 'Closed'.

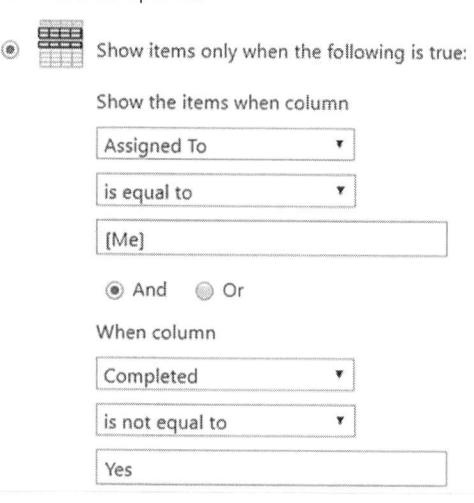

421

23.3.1 Embed My Tasks/My Issues

You can add a web part that shows each user his/her tasks to a page that is often visited, for example a site's homepage. This is easy and works well when there is just a single list to show.

When a user has tasks/issues in multiple lists, it becomes more complicated, and the result is not as good as for a single list. For the Issue tracker list, multiple lists do not give an acceptable result at all.

23.3.1.1 Single List

If tasks are created in just one site, you can use the **modern** List web part to add an Issue tracker or Issue tracking list to a modern page. When you have added the web part, it will show a selection of list apps from the site, and you can just click a list to add it to the page.

When the list has been added, edit the web part and select the "My" view in the right pane.

When you have published the page, users can work with and create new items. They open in a new tab with the classic item form, not in a right pane.

Tasks lists are not displayed in the List web part, so to embed a Tasks list in a modern page, you need to use the Highlighted content web part instead, see Multiple Lists below.

Issue tracker, Tasks and Issue Tracking lists can all be added as app parts in a **classic** page. Edit the web part and select the view as for the modern web part.

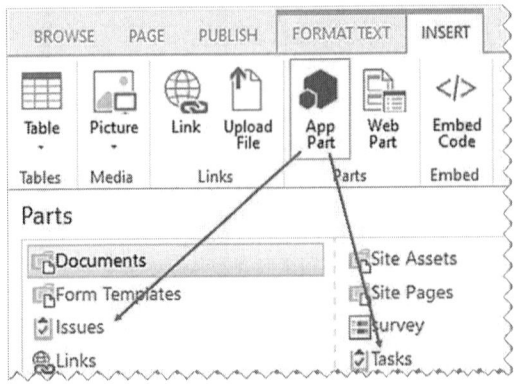

23.3.1.2 Multiple Lists

The modern Highlighted content web part and the classic Content Search web part can display items of a specific content type from all sites, so they can show the current user's tasks independently of which site the tasks were created in.

Note however that the Issue tracker list template has the general content type for list apps: Item (not Task or Issue). The Item content type cannot be selected in the Highlighted content web part at all. In the Content Search web part, the Item can be selected, but the result will not be good. There are probably many apps built on the Item content type in the tenant, so there would not be a choice of just Issue tracker items.

For just viewing My Tasks/Issues, from multiple Tasks or Issue Tracking lists, the Highlighted content and Content Search web parts work well. They are however not as good as the modern List web part or classic app part when it comes to editing. There is no command bar, so you need to open the task/issue to do something with it.

Another problem with these web parts is that they do not open the task/issue in a new tab. When you have edited the item and close it again, the original list will open. The user must go back in the browser a couple of steps to reach the page again.

Unfortunately, there is currently no other no-code solution to show tasks/issues from multiple sources on a SharePoint page.

On a **modern** page, add the Highlighted content web part.

1. Edit the web part and keep the default 'Filter' radio button selected.
2. At 'Source', select if you want to get lists from all sites or specific sites.
3. At 'Type', select Tasks or Issues.
4. In the 'Filter 'dropdown, select Managed property.
5. Start writing Assigned To in the 'Find a managed property' field. When 'Managed property name' becomes active, select AssignedTo.
6. Keep 'Equals' and set the search value to [Me].

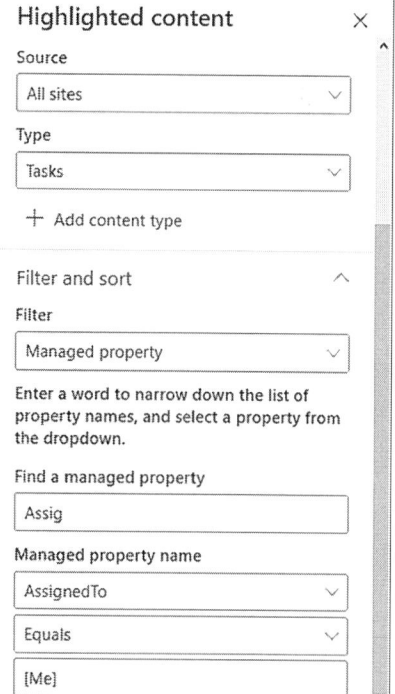

In a **classic** page, use the Content Search web part from the Content Rollup category.

1. Edit the web part and click on the 'Change query' button.
2. In the Query Builder, select 'Items matching a content type'. Do not restrict by app. Restrict the content type to the Task or Issue type.

![Build Your Query screenshot showing Basics tab with Select a query, Restrict by app, Restrict by tag, and Restrict by content type set to Task]

3. Switch to Advanced Mode.
4. At Property Filter, select 'AssignedTo'.
5. At Contains, select 'The name of the user who runs the query'.

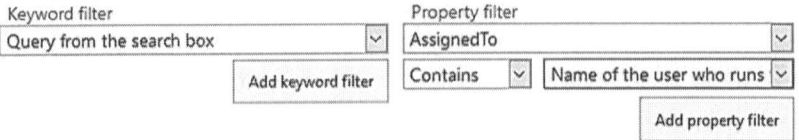

6. Click on 'Add property filter'.
7. At Property Filter, select 'Status'.
8. For the Task content type, select 'Not equals' and type the manual value 'Completed'.
9. For the Issue content type, select Equals' and type the manual value 'Active'.
10. Click on 'Add property filter' again and then OK.
11. Click OK to the web part right pane and save the page.
12. Make any other web part settings you prefer, apply and save the page

Demo:

https://www.kalmstrom.com/Tips/SPSearch-My-Open-Tasks.htm

Another way to collect tasks from several sites in a collection in a classic page, is to use the Content Query Web Part, *refer to* 27.4.

23.4 LANDING PAGES

In section 17.5. we created a simple views landing page for a list app. Such a page can be enhanced is several ways, and below I give suggestions on how you can add a list or a chart to a page with view links.

A good layout for both suggestions is a wide column combined with one that is narrower for the links. You may of course also combine the suggestions and for example put the chart in a new section below the section with the list and links.

23.4.1 *Landing Page with Tasks*

A Views landing page can have a web part that shows the list items in the default view, for example "My Tasks", on the same page as the links to other views in the original app.

In the **modern** interface, use a One-third right section and add a List or Highlighted content web part to the wide column. Edit the web part as described above and add the links in a Text or Quick links web part, as described in 17.6.1, Modern Views Landing Page.

A landing page with the list in the default view is especially useful for **classic** pages, because when you add an app as an app part to a classic page, there is no possibility to change view from the app part.

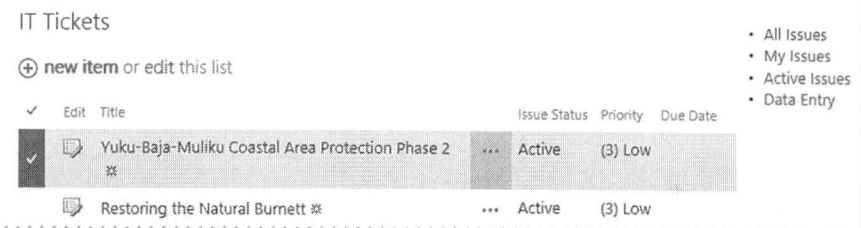

1. With the page in Edit mode, click on the 'Text Layout' button under the ribbon FORMAT TEXT tab and select the layout One column with sidebar.
2. Move the view links to the sidebar by copy and paste.
3. Add your list App part to the column.
4. Edit the web part. Under 'Selected View', select the list view you want to show by default and click on 'Apply'. Save the page.
5. Now the default view is displayed in the web part, and you can work with the list items as usual. The only limitation is that you must select an item to see the LIST and ITEM tabs in the ribbon.

Demo:

https://kalmstrom.com/Tips/SharePoint-Online-Course/HelpDesk-Landing-Page-Webpart.htm

23.4.2 Landing Page with Chart

We can enhance a Views landing page with a chart that visualizes the data in the list. (If the chart size does not fit the SharePoint page, you can change it in Excel. Save and refresh the SharePoint page, to check if it looks better.)

Look back at section 22.2, Connect SharePoint and Excel, if you don't remember how to make the connections in the steps below.

1. Export the SharePoint list to Excel.
2. Create a chart that visualizes the list data.
3. Note the chart name, which can be found to the left of the function field (by default Chart 1, 2 and so on).
4. Save the Excel file with the chart to a library in the SharePoint site that contains the list.

Use the File viewer web part to insert the Excel chart in a **modern** page. Upload the Excel file with the chart that you want to display and then select the chart when you edit the web part.

To insert an Excel chart in a **classic** page, you need to use the Excel Web Access web part in the Business Data category, which is available in the Enterprise Plans of SharePoint Online. You also need to use a Team site without a group, modern or classic.

If you have an Enterprise plan and still cannot see the Business Data category and the Excel Web Access web part, check that the SharePoint Server Enterprise Site Collection features are activated under Site settings >Site collection features. It is activated by default in the classic but not in the modern Team site.

1. Copy the path to the Excel file.
2. Open the SharePoint page in edit mode and place the mouse cursor in the column where you want to add the chart.
3. Add the Excel Web Access web part.
4. Edit the web part and click on the ellipsis to select the Excel file.
5. Type the name of the chart you want to show in the web part.
6. Uncheck the box for All Workbook interactivity and make other settings to customize the web part before you click OK.
7. Save the page.

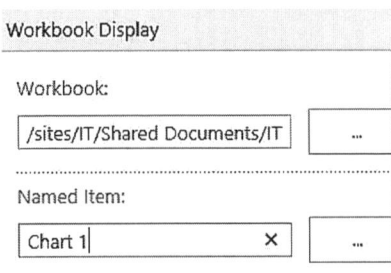

426

Demos:

https://kalmstrom.com/Tips/SharePoint-Online-Course/Excel-Modern-Page.htm

https://kalmstrom.com/Tips/SharePoint-Online-Course/HelpDesk-Landing-Page-Chart.htm

23.4.2.1 Refresh an Excel Chart on a SharePoint Page

When an Excel chart is added to a SharePoint page in the way described above, the chart will be updated automatically if you edit the Excel file in Excel Online, or if you open the file in the Excel desktop app and save the changes to SharePoint.

The chart will *not* be updated automatically when SharePoint list data behind the chart is changed. Instead, you must open Excel and refresh the chart. This can be done in two ways:

- Click on the 'Refresh' button under the 'PivotChart Analyze' tab and select Refresh All.
- Click on the 'Refresh All' button under the Data tab.

Demo:

https://kalmstrom.com/Tips/SharePoint-Online-Course/HelpDesk-Chart-Update-Overview.htm

23.4.2.2 VBS Script that Updates an Excel Chart on a SharePoint Page

If you don't want to update Excel manually, by refresh, you can add a scheduled task with a script that updates the Excel chart automatically when there are changes in the SharePoint list. This is the script when the URL to the Excel file that has the chart is https://kalmstromdemo2.sharepoint.com/sites/IT/SharedDocuments/ITTicketsSummary.xlsx:

Set xl = CreateObject("Excel.Application")

set wb = xl.WorkBooks.open("https://kalmstromdemo2.sharepoint.com/sites/IT/SharedDocuments/ITTicketsSummary.xlsx")

xl.DisplayAlerts = False

WScript.Sleep 1000

wb.RefreshAll

wb.Save

wb.Close

xl.Quit

Save the log in information in your browser, so that the script can work automatically.

To run the script, use the Windows Task Scheduler.

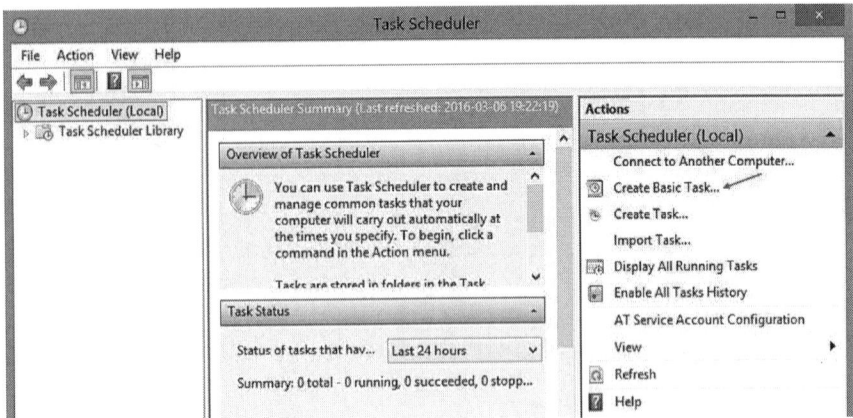

1. Open the Task Scheduler.
2. Create a basic task, give it a name and click on Next.
3. Set how often the task should be run and click on Next.
4. Set when the task should start running and click on Next.
5. Select the option 'Start a program' and click on Next.
6. Browse to the VBS file and click on Next.
7. Check the box for 'Open the Properties Dialog for this task when I click Finish' and click on Finish.
8. Under the Triggers tab, select the Daily task and click on the Edit... button. Set the task to be repeated with the interval you prefer and click OK.
9. Click OK to the Properties Dialog.
10. Select the new task and enable the All Tasks history if you want to have a log over what is happening.
11. Right-click on the new task and select Run.

When you have updated the Excel file, refresh the page that have the chart to see your changes.

Demo:

https://kalmstrom.com/Tips/SharePoint-Online-Course/HelpDesk-Update-Excel-Chart-Script.htm

Note that if you have Excel as part of Microsoft 365 Apps license, you must log in to Excel once a month anyway, to make sure the subscription is updated. This is not necessary with a regular Office license.

23.5 Summary

Most organizations use SharePoint lists for different kinds of issue tracking. In this chapter, I have explained the differences between the three most common list apps used for cooperation around such tasks and given suggestions on various ways to enhance them.

I have also described how to create a My Tasks view and embed it in a classic or modern page and how to build a landing page with view links, list items and an Excel chart that visualizes the list data.

In the next chapter, I will introduce flows and workflows. These are important for making SharePoint processes more exact and efficient. I have written separate books about both flows and workflows, and they of course contain much more information than we have room for in this book.

24 SHAREPOINT AUTOMATION

SharePoint flows and workflows can be used in all kinds of SharePoint apps to automate time consuming processes. They are often used for notification sending, but they can also calculate time, archive items and perform many other tasks that would have been tedious and time consuming – or not performed at all – without a flow/workflow.

The principle of all flows and workflows is that you select conditions to be met and actions to be taken when these conditions are met. A predefined trigger decides when the flow or workflow should run.

Here I will first give an overview over how flows and workflows are created in general and then show a few examples. I hope this chapter will make you understand the flow/workflow possibilities and encourage you to explore them and create your own automation applications. For more information about flows and workflows, and how they can be used with SharePoint, *refer to* my books *SharePoint Flows from Scratch* and *SharePoint Workflows from Scratch*.

This chapter will cover:

- The general principle behind flows and workflows
- Some differences between a flow and a workflow
- How built-in flows can be used for approvals and alerts in modern SharePoint apps and pages

At the end of the chapter, I will give two exercises with a flow and a workflow that you can create yourself, to compare and try the two automation methods. These are simple automation examples, and both the flow and the workflow achieve the same thing.

24.1 WHY AUTOMATE?

Most organizations have processes that need to be performed in a specific way and order, but when processes are performed manually, you can never be sure that everything is done 100% correctly. Therefore, the best way to make sure that such processes are correct and quick, is to automate them.

Another benefit of automation is that flows and workflows make it easy to track processes. They can log and document what has been done, something that is often requested by the management and sometimes even by law. Such tasks are often tedious and boring to perform manually, and they sometimes tend to be performed insufficiently or not at all.

Demo: https://www.kalmstrom.com/Tips/SharePoint-Flows/Flow-Why-Automate.htm

24.2 COMPONENTS

A flow/workflow is built with three components: trigger, condition(s) and action(s). You create the flow/workflow by combining these components in a way that gives the result you require. A trigger and at least one action must always be present, but the condition is optional.

- The trigger decides in general when the flow/workflow should be run.
- An action make things happen. You are creating a flow/workflow because you want an action to be performed, for example an e-mail to be sent.
- A condition controls under which condition an action should be executed within a flow/workflow. For example, an e-mail about a new task should only be sent **if** the task priority is high. The word "if" in the previous statement is very important and in many programming languages this conditional control is called an "if statement".

24.3 FLOW VERSUS WORKFLOW

Workflows are the traditional way of automating SharePoint processes, and they are most often created in and limited to one SharePoint site.

Microsoft Power Automate is a more modern 365 service, and the workflows created with Power Automate are often called flows.

While workflows are mostly limited to SharePoint, flows can be used extensively for many cloud-based services, called connectors, and several connectors are often combined in one flow.

Microsoft wants Power Automate to be a no-code, rapid application development environment, and as such it has certain limitations. However, given that you have a possibility to call a REST service from a flow, Power Automate has high potential.

There are however still things that can only be done with a workflow, and to have the best flexibility, I recommend that you learn to create both flows and workflows. The examples I give below, will hopefully show the differences but also the similarities.

For examples on what can easily be done with one of the platforms but not with the other, *refer to* 25.10.2, Workflow that Switches Content Type and 30.3, Scheduled Review Alert Flow.

24.3.1 *Storage*

While workflows are stored in SharePoint and accessible for all with enough permission, flows are owned by the users who created them. This might be good for personal flows, but it creates issues if a user who has created flows for the organization leaves his/her position.

Therefore, any organization that decides to automate things with flows, should make sure that flows are not limited to one person's user account.

The most secure method is to create a dedicated account that is used for all flows that automate business processes within the organization. However, the number of flow-runs that are allowed each month is counted per account, not per tenant. If the organization uses many flows that run often, a better solution might be to make sure that all business flows have multiple owners.

24.3.2 Changes in SharePoint

If you change a name in a SharePoint app, it affects any automation tied to the app in different ways depending on if a workflow or a flow is used.

SharePoint workflows will continue to run even if you change the name of an app or a column that is used in the workflow.

When you change an app or column name that is included in a flow, you must change the name in the flow too, otherwise, the flow will stop working. The more mission-critical a flow is, the more serious this issue becomes.

24.4 POWER AUTOMATE BUILT-IN FLOWS

Power Automate has its own 'Automate' button in the command bar of apps with the **modern** interface. It gives some options to use built-in SharePoint flows that are very easy to create.

The 'Automate' button in library apps lets users:

- Create a new custom flow from a template.
- Reach the Power Automate site to manage the flows they have already created and to create new flows from scratch; *see* below.
- Configure built-in approval flows for the app.

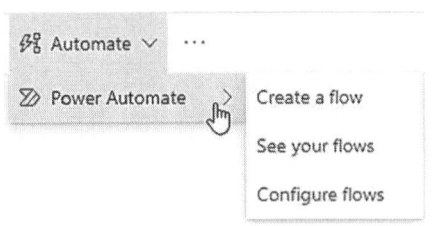

In list apps, the same options are found under the 'Integrate' button. List apps may also have an 'Automate' button that gives a possibility to create rules and/or simple reminder flows. Microsoft plans to add the same features to library apps.

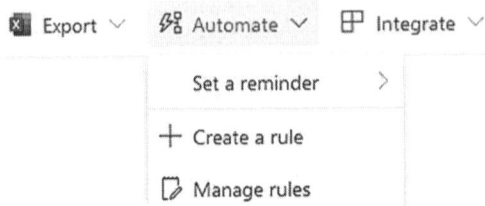

24.4.1 Create a Rule

When you open the 'Automate' dropdown in a list app with the **modern** interface, you can either create a new rule for the list or manage existing rules. These options are displayed when no item is selected and when one item is selected, but the rules are for the list, not for the item.

The 'Create a rule' command opens a dialog where you can select to create a flow that sends an e-mail when a column or a column value changes or when an item is created or deleted. You can create up to 15 such rules.

Create a rule

Create rules to take action when data changes in this list. Choose a condition that triggers the rule and the action that the rule will take. Learn more

Notify someone when

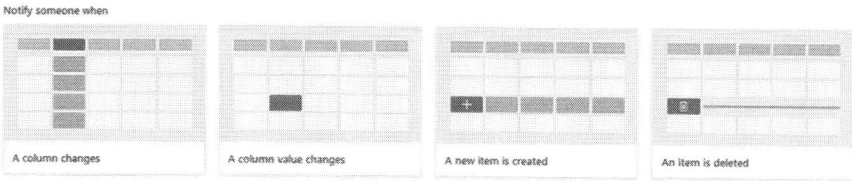

| A column changes | A column value changes | A new item is created | An item is deleted |

The flows are created in a way that reminds of workflow creation in SharePoint Designer, *see* below, even if it is much simplified. For each rule, you are asked to specify to where the e-mail should be sent.

When a new item is created

send email to Enter a name or email address .

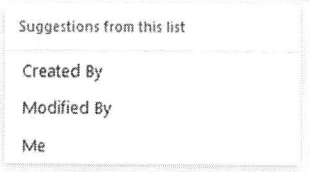

For the column and column value rules, you need to select a column from the current list, in addition to the e-mail receiver. Rules based on a multi-line text columns are not supported.

The image below shows the second rule option: when a column value changes, where I also need to specify 'is' or 'is not' and the column value.

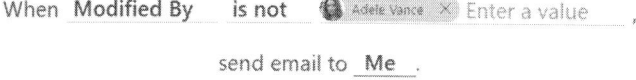

send email to Me .

When you have created the rule, the 'Manage rules' dialog will open, and the new rule will be turned on. When you click on the rule it will open so that you can edit or delete it.

When this is written, it is only possible to create rules in list apps, but Microsoft plans to add the same features to library apps. These flows are not displayed in the Power Automate site.

24.4.2 *Reminder*

When an app has the modern interface and a Date and Time column, it gets a built-in flow that sends an e-mail reminder any number of days in advance of a specific date. It is possible to set multiple reminders for the same app and column, but users can only set reminders for themselves.

Enable the reminder under Automate >Set a reminder >the Date and Time column you want to use.

433

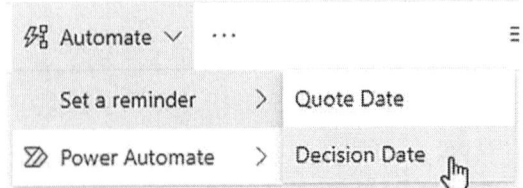

A right pane with flow information will open. Here, you can sign in if needed, but in most cases, you are already signed in to the services that are used in the flow.

A green check means that you are signed in. A plus sign indicates that you need to sign in.

When you have clicked on 'Continue', you can give the flow a name and decide how many days before the date in each item that you want to receive a reminder by e-mail.

This reminder flow can be seen and edited in the Power Automate site, under 'My flows'.

It is also on the 'My flows' page that users can remove the reminder. When this is written, the reminder cannot be removed from within the app.

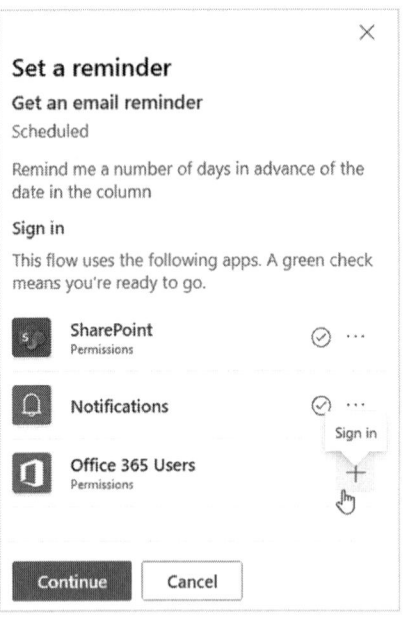

24.4.3 Require Association Approval

Hub site owners can create an approval flow, so that sites cannot be associated with the hub site until after approval:

1. In the hub site, click on the 365 Settings icon and select 'Hub site settings'.
2. A right pane will open, where you can enable 'Require approval for associated sites to join'. When that toggle is on, a 'Create' button will be visible.
3. Click on the 'Create' button, enter the person(s) who should approve and click on 'Create flow'.

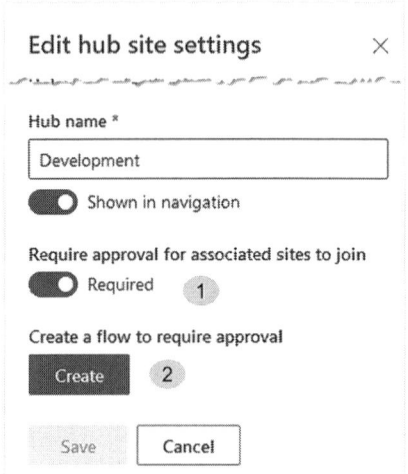

434

Now an approval flow will be created, and the Edit hub settings pane will have two links to the Power Automate site, where flows and approvals can be managed.

In the image to the right, an approval flow has been created.

The 'Request to join a SharePoint hub site' links opens the flow on the 'My flows' page in the Power Automate site.

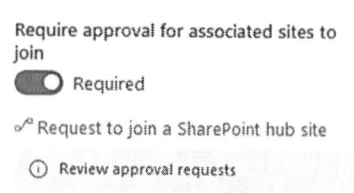

The 'Review approval requests' link opens the 'Approvals' page in the Power Automate site.

24.4.4 Approve/Reject App Items

New or changed business documents must often be approved by someone else than the author, and that process can be managed in many ways. The easiest way is to use one of SharePoint's built-in flows for requesting and giving approval on new app items.

In libraries, it is the document that gets approved. In list apps, it is the whole item.

Click on Power Automate >Configure flows to open a right pane, where you can set approvals on and off.

By default, the approvals feature is set to On, and the option Request sign-off is selected. Disable approvals if you want to turn off the possibility to send Request Sign-off messages.

The Request sign-off option can only be set this way, and it can only be used with the modern app interface.

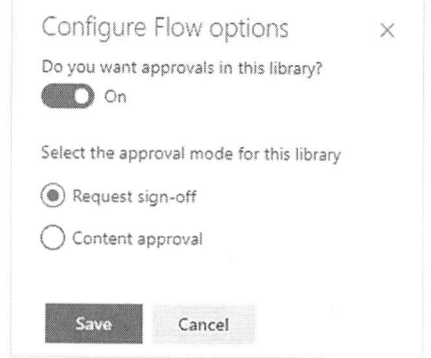

The other option, Content approval, can be set via the List settings too, and it can be used with the classic interface as well.

These two flows are hidden and cannot be edited in the Power Automate site >My flows.

When you use these built-in flows, the approval is not registered as a modification of the item in the version history. This means that there is no easy way to see who made the approval. For some business scenarios that information is required or very important, and in such cases, you need to use a more elaborate flow or workflow for the approval process.

24.4.4.1 Request Sign-off

When approvals with request sign-off is used in an app, there is no mandatory approval process. Instead, it is up to each author to ask for feedback on a new or updated list item or library file, by running an approval flow.

The request sign-off option is displayed under 'Automate' when an item has been selected and if the feature has not been turned off.

When a user requests sign-off, a right pane will open. Here, the user can see information about connectors and permissions, and connect if necessary. Normally the user just needs to click on 'Create flow'.

When the user clicks on the 'Create flow' button, another right pane will open with fields for approver and a message. If more than one approver is added, anyone of them can approve the request.

When the flow is run, it sends an e-mail to the approver(s). When Microsoft Teams is used, there might also be a message under the Activity button in Teams.

All messages have a link to the file or item and buttons for approval and rejection, and there is also room for a comment that is sent to the requester.

The first time someone requests sign-off, a 'Sign-off status' column is added to the app. This is a standard SharePoint text column. It works like any other text column and can be reached and edited from the List settings.

The value of the 'Sign-off status' column is blank for items where no request sign-off flow has been used.

The value is Pending when an item is sent for approval, and then Approved or Rejected. The item can be seen by all users, whichever status it has.

24.4.4.2 Content Approval

The Content approval option can be enabled in the modern Configure flows right pane and in the List settings >Versioning settings. The List settings is the only option for the classic interface.

Content Approval
Specify whether new items or changes to existing items should remain in a draft state until they have been approved. Learn about requiring approval.
Require content approval for submitted items?
● Yes ○ No

When the Content approval option is selected, *all* new items must be approved, and the approver marks the approval or rejection in the app. No e-mail is sent.

436

The **modern** interface has the 'Approve/Reject' dialog under the item ellipsis >More >Approve/Reject.

The **classic** interface has the 'Approve/Reject' option in the ribbon, when a pending item is selected, and under the item ellipsis >Advanced >Approve/Reject.

An advantage with this type of approval is that you can easily set the app to hide the new item from everyone but the creator and the approver until it has been approved. This is done in the List settings >Versioning settings.

Who should see draft items in this document library?
- Any user who can read items
- Only users who can edit items
- Only users who can approve items (and the author of the item)

24.4.5 Approve/Reject Pages

The "Site Pages" library has its own built-in approval flow. In many respects, the Page approval flow reminds of the Sign-off request flow. There are however important differences:

- The Page approval flow will apply to *all* pages in the library, also classic pages.
- The Page approval flow can be seen and edited on the Power Automate site >My flows.
- The new or modified page can be hidden from other users than the approver and creator until it has been approved.

New and modified **modern** pages can be approved or rejected in the library, on the page, on the Power Automate site and in e-mails sent by the flow.

Classic pages can only be approved/rejected in the "Site Pages" library.

24.4.5.1 Configure the Flow

The **modern** "Site Pages" library interface in SharePoint Online has an 'Automate' button in the command bar, where site owners can configure the page approval flow.

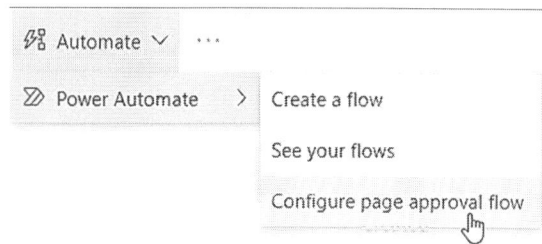

When you click on 'Configure page approval flow', a right pane for the flow configuration will open.

1. Click on 'Create flow'.
2. A new pane with connectors information will open. Log in if necessary.

437

3. Click on 'Continue'.
4. Give the flow a name and add approvers. These must have at least edit permission over the site. By default, anyone of these approvers can approve.
5. Click on 'Create'.

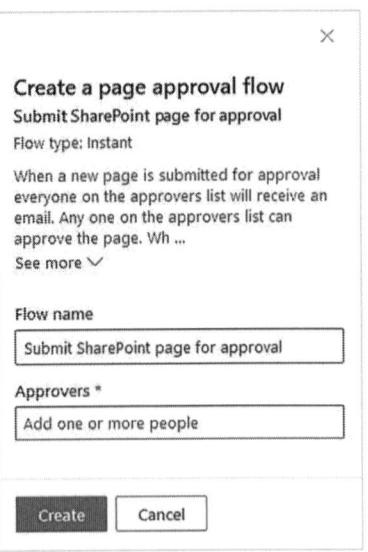

Now the approval flow will be created automatically, and a new 'Approval Status' column will be added to the "Site Pages" library.

It is possible to add multiple flows, for different approvers. If another flow is created, no additional status column will be added. All flows in the "Site Pages" library will use the same column.

24.4.5.2 Process

Even if the page approval flow works on all new or modified pages in the library, the process is different for modern and classic pages, and it works considerably better for modern pages.

When an approval flow has been created in the "Site Pages" library, no pages can be published until they are approved, but the approval submission is not sent automatically.

On **modern** pages, the 'Publish' button on the page is replaced by a 'Submit for approval' button, and the page author must enter a message in the right pane before submitting the page for approval.

When there is more than one flow, the person who submits the page for approval will have a selection under the 'Submit for approval' button.

In classic pages, there is no possibility to select approval flow.

The page can also be submitted for approval in the "Site pages" library, and this is the only option for classic pages. Hover over the ellipsis at the page and then on the link 'Submit for approval now'.

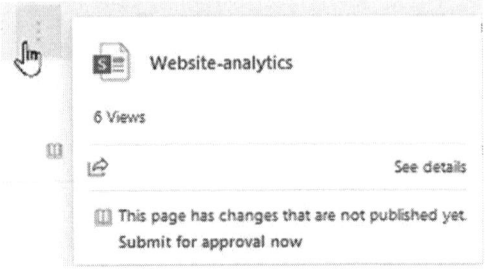

The page can also be sent for approval from 'More' under the page ellipsis.

The page will be published automatically once it has been approved.

438

When the page approval flow has been configured in the modern interface of the "Site Pages" library, it works for **classic** wiki pages too, and for web part pages if you select to save them in the "Site Pages" library.

However, no e-mail is sent, and the page author must send the approval request from the "Site Pages" library. The approver must open the "Site Pages" library in the classic interface and publish the page under the FILES tab. Pages can also be published under the page ellipsis >Advanced.

24.4.5.3 Turn Off Page Approval

In the "Site Pages" Library settings >Versioning settings, you can set the approval to 'No', to stop requesting approvals at page creation. You can also turn off or delete the page approval flow on the 'My Flows' page on the Power Automate site.

24.4.5.4 Edit a Page Approval Flow

The page approval can be edited in two ways.

- In the library settings >Versioning settings you can decide who should be allowed to see the page before it has been approved. Any user is default, but it might not be the best option for you.
- The flow will show up under 'My flows' on the Power Automate site, *see* below, and it can be modified there. You can for example, edit the approvers or change the Approval type.

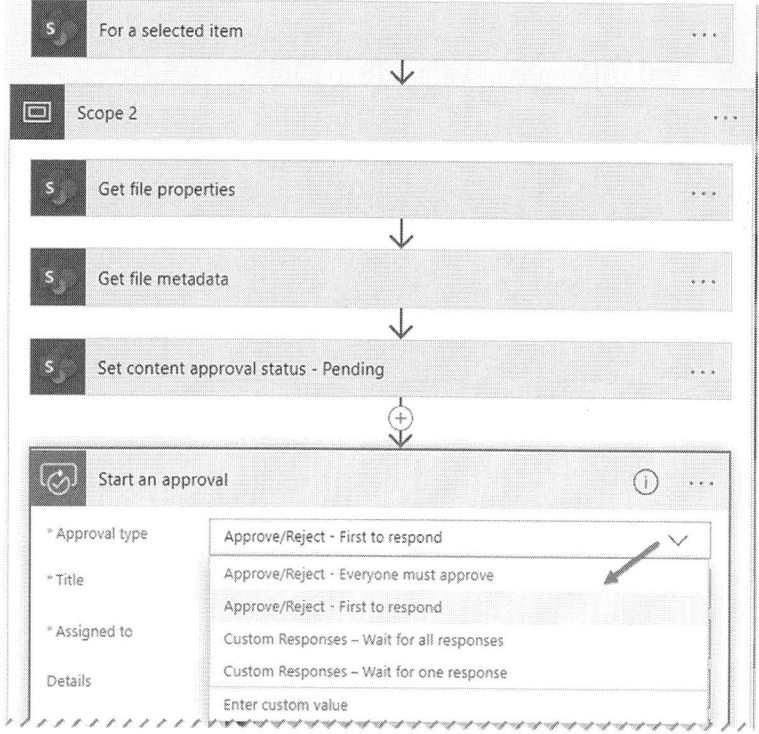

24.5 POWER AUTOMATE CUSTOM FLOWS

Custom flows are built and managed in the Power Automate site at https://flow.microsoft.com. If you select 'See my flows' from the modern command bar in a SharePoint app, you will be directed to the 'My flows' page in that site. Here, you can see a list of all your flows and manage them in various ways, like edit, delete and turn flows on or off.

When you click on the Power Automate tile in the 365 App Launcher, you will be directed to the homepage of the same site.

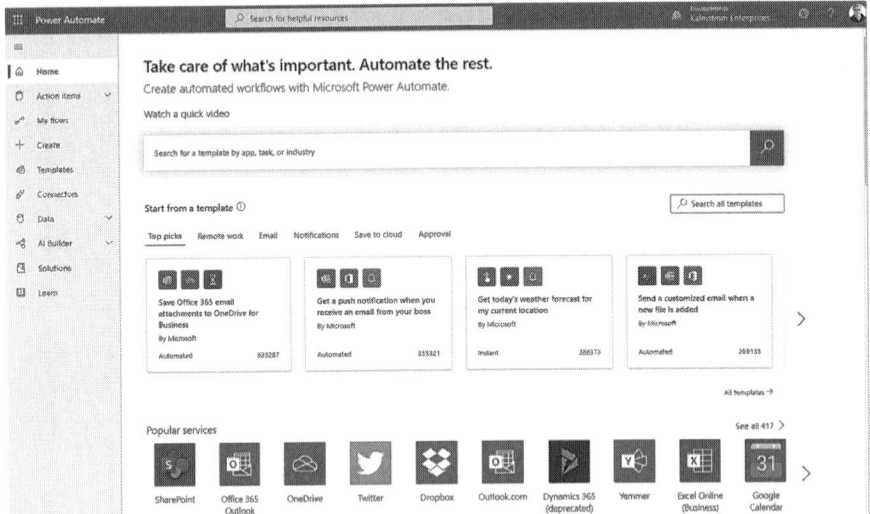

When you create a flow, you can either start with a template or start from scratch (called "blank" in Power Automate).

There are many predefined templates to choose from, and you can reach all of them from the Power Automate homepage. When you select the template for the flow, you also select the trigger. Therefore, what you do in the creation is to define parameters for the trigger and set condition(s) and action(s).

The templates that include SharePoint can also be reached from all SharePoint apps with the modern interface, but as soon as you have selected a template you will be directed to the Power Automate site.

When this is written, you cannot start from blank from the SharePoint command bar. Instead, you must go to the Power Automate site >My flows. The first step in a blank flow creation is to set the flow trigger.

24.5.1 Flow Editor

Flows are built in a Flow Editor with boxes where you select the right triggers, actions and conditions and parameters for them. The image above, in the section "Edit a Page Approval Flow", shows such boxes in the Flow Editor.

440

The steps in the Flow Editor vary with each flow. When you use a template, the actions and conditions are often pre-defined. They can of course be changed, and you often need to add your parameters. If you start from blank, you can add actions and conditions as you prefer.

24.5.2   Create a Flow from SharePoint

Click on Power Automate >Create a flow in the command bar, to create a flow directly from a SharePoint app with the modern interface.

A right pane will open, where you can select a template for the flow. The choice of templates is of course limited to templates where SharePoint is one of the connectors.

Select a template, and you will be directed to the Power Automate site to continue building your flow there.

If you cannot find a suitable template, click on 'Show more' and then 'See more templates'. That will take you to the Power Automate site.

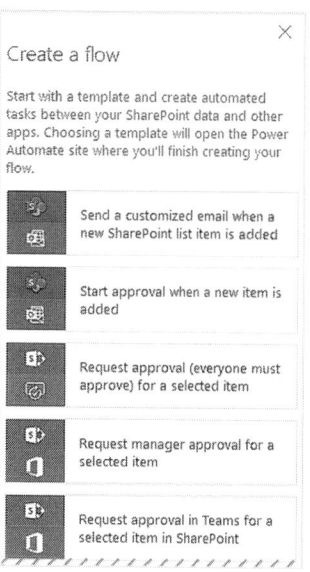

24.5.3   Create a Flow from Blank

I often create my flows from blank instead of from a template, as I find that it gives better control over the flow.

When you use a template, the connector(s) and trigger are always chosen for you, but with a blank flow you must start with selecting a suitable connector and trigger.

Start building your blank flow on the 'My flows' page in the Power Automate site. Select 'New flow' and then one of the "from blank" options.

The Automated option gives flows that run automatically when triggered, while the Instant option gives flows that are run manually. The Scheduled option is intended for flows that should be run with specific intervals.

When you have selected one of the "from blank" options under 'New flow', a dialog will open. Here you can give the flow a name, and for the automated and instant flows you can select a trigger. If you cannot find the trigger you want to use, click on 'Skip'.

441

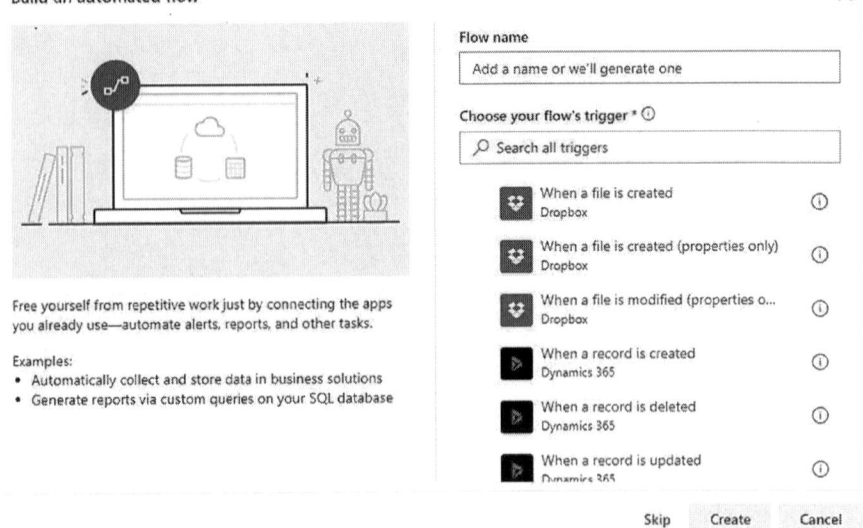

The scheduled flow gives another dialog, where you can set the start date and frequency for the flow.

When you click on 'Create', the Flow Editor will open so that you can continue building your flow.

If you click on 'Skip', you must first select connector and a trigger for the flow. Click on a connector icon to see all available triggers for that connector.

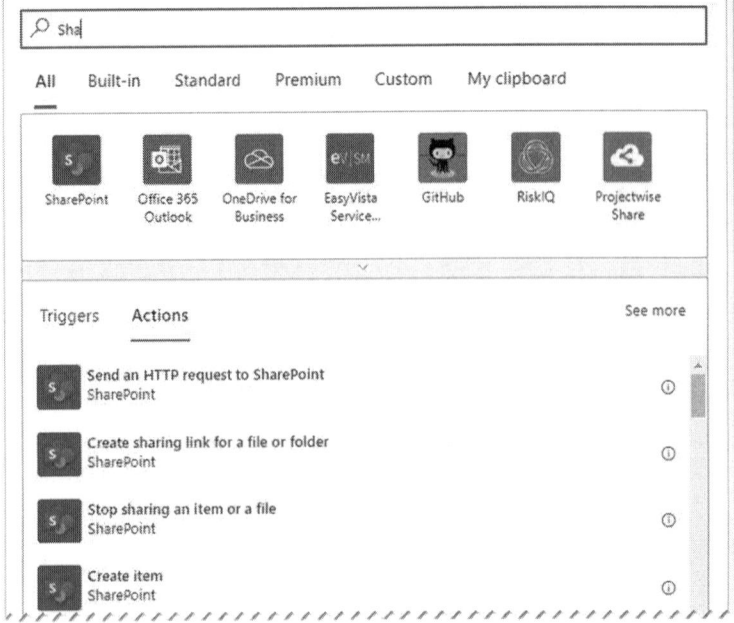

You can also directly search for a trigger or choose one of the suggestions below the connector icons.

When you have selected the trigger you want to use, the Flow Editor will open, and you can continue building the flow.

24.5.4 Finalize the Flow

When you have finished creating a flow, you should always test it by performing the trigger action. That way you can make sure it runs and gives the result you wished to achieve when you created it. Save the flow by clicking on the 'Save' button below your last step or at the top right.

The Flow checker usually has a red warning if something is wrong in the flow syntax. Click on the button to see an explanation. If the flow has a syntax error, it is not possible to save and test it.

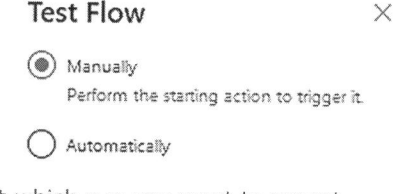

If there is no warning message, you can directly click on the 'Test' button and then 'Save and Test'.

For new flows, only the 'Manually' test option is valid.

The option 'Automatically' can be used when you need to repeat the testing. That way, you don't have to perform the trigger action (for example create a new test item) for each test run. Select which run you want to repeat.

In the left corner above the Flow Editor, Power Automate will give you a hint what to do to test the flow.

ⓘ To see it work now, modify a list item in the SharePoint folder you selected.

24.5.5 Flow Activity

On the Activity page, you can see runs, failures and notifications for all your flows. You can reach the Activity page from the Power Automate Settings icon.

Under the Settings icon there are also links to the Power Automate Admin center and to settings for region and language.

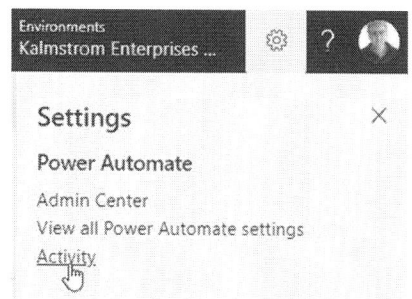

443

24.5.6 Dynamic Content

When you add dynamic content in flow fields, the content in actions changes depending on what happened in the services used in the flow, for example in a SharePoint app. Dynamic content can be selected from a list that is displayed to the right when you click in a flow field.

The dynamic content is fetched from the trigger and from the previous actions in the flow. In the image below, the mouse cursor is placed in a 'Start Date' field, so the date options 'Modified' and 'Created' are suggested as dynamic content for that field.

When the screen is narrow, the dynamic content is instead displayed below the field. Sometimes, you might need to click on the 'Add dynamic content' link below a field to display the dynamic content list.

Search, or click on 'See more' above the suggestions, if you cannot find the dynamic content you are looking for.

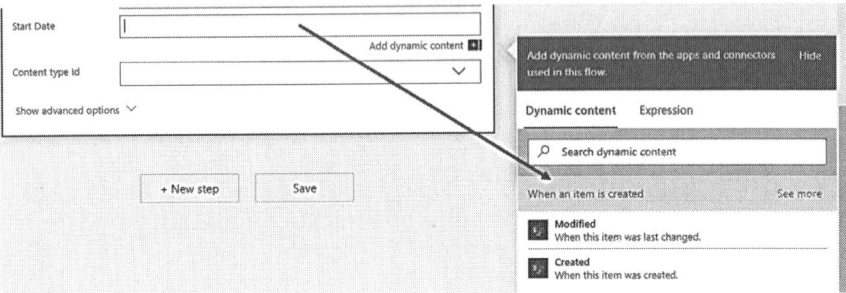

24.5.7 Custom Value

When you create a flow, you must specify the site and app for each step in the flow. Often, you can select both, but sometimes you need to type in the data. When you do that, you must also select your value as a custom value.

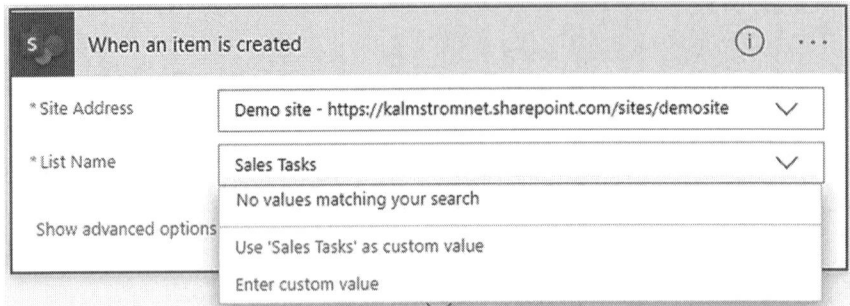

You can either type the name and then select 'Use [NAME] as custom value' or scroll to the bottom of the list first and select 'Enter custom value'.

Sites are mostly possible to select, but with apps it happens in two cases that you need to select a custom value:

- Only lists that can use a modern interface will show up in the 'List Name' dropdowns in Power Automate. If you use a list based on for example the Tasks template, you need add the list name as a custom value.
- In the exercise below, we use the trigger 'SharePoint - when an item is created'. That trigger is primarily intended for list apps, but it gives the dynamic content 'ID', as opposed to the "when a file is created" actions. Therefore, I often use an "item" trigger even if the flow runs in a document library.

    In such cases, the document library name will not be displayed in the editor dropdown for 'List Name'. Instead, you must add the library name as a custom value.

24.6 EXPORT AND IMPORT FLOWS

A flow can be exported as a .zip package and imported and re-used as a template. That way, you don't have to start from scratch with a new flow. Instead, you can just change those flow settings that should be different.

24.6.1 Export a Flow

When you export a flow from the Power Automate site, you download it to your computer in compressed format.

1. Under 'My flows', click on the ellipsis at the flow you want to export and select 'Export'.

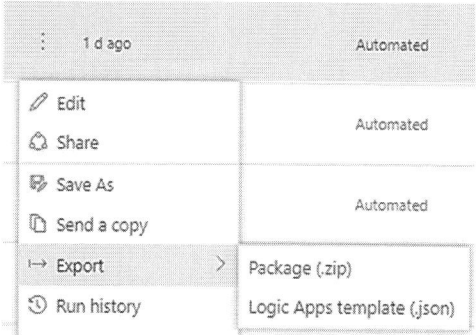

2. Select file format: 'Package (.zip)'. (The .json option gives a logic app than can be imported for example to Microsoft Azure.)

3. Give the package a name and click on 'Export'. Select to download the package to your computer if that does not happen automatically.

24.6.2 Import a Flow

When you have received a flow package, you can import it to your 'My flows' page.

1. Click 'Import' in the 'My flows' command bar.

2. Upload the flow .zip package you want to import.
3. When the file has been uploaded, a new page will open.

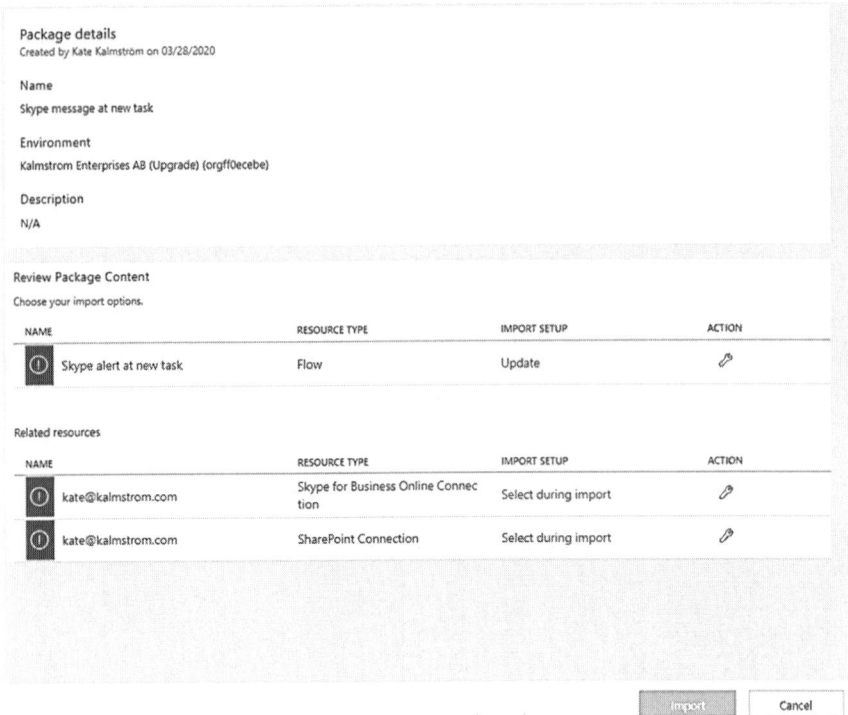

4. Click on the 'ACTION' icon under 'Review Package Content'. An Import Setup pane will open to the right.
5. Select to create a new flow from the imported one.
6. Give the new flow another name than the original flow and save.

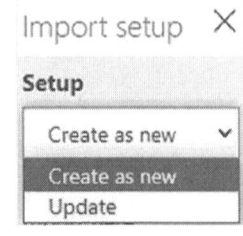

7. Click on ACTION under Related resources' to establish the required flow connector(s). Either create new connections or click on the existing ones before you save.
8. Click on 'Import'.
9. Now the new flow will be created, and you can open it directly from the Import page. It is also added under 'My flows'.

The imported flow still has all the settings from the original flow, so you should edit the new flow and make any changes needed so that it works as you wish.

The imported flow is turned off by default, so before you test it you need to turn it on under My flows >the flow's ellipsis.

24.7 WORKFLOWS

Workflows are created in SharePoint Designer 2013, *refer to* chapter 10. The most commonly used workflow designer is the text-based one, where you can find buttons for condition and action in the ribbon.

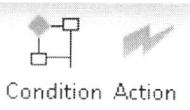
Condition Action

When you have clicked on one of these buttons, you will have this kind of links for the Condition and Action:

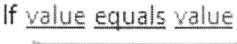 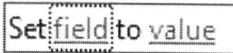

Click on the links to select or type the parameters your workflow should use.

There is also a Visual Designer view for SharePoint 2013 workflows, where you can create workflows by dragging shapes to a design surface.

24.7.1 Start Creating a List Workflow

The most common workflow, the list workflow, is only intended to be used on the items in one app. (Note that SharePoint Designer 2013 talks about lists and libraries and doesn't use the word "app" anywhere: I will continue to use "app" here for consistency.)

List Workflow ▾

1. Open the site that has the app you want to create a workflow for, *refer to* 10.2, Open a Site in SharePoint Designer.
2. Select the site homepage in the left menu.
3. Click on the 'List Workflow' button in the ribbon, to create a new workflow.
4. Select the app you want to use.
5. Give the workflow a name and a description. Keep the default SharePoint 2013 workflow. 2010 workflows are no longer supported in SharePoint Online.

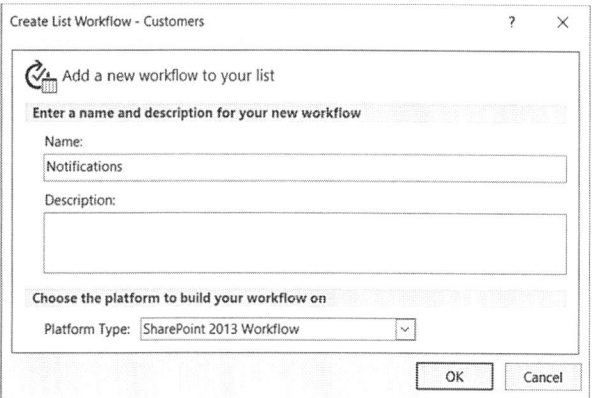

447

When you click OK, the summary page will have a new tab with the name of the workflow, and two new pages have been created: the Edit Workflow page and the Workflow Settings page.

The image below shows the tabs when creating a "Set Title" workflow in the Sales site.

Switch between the two workflow pages with the thumbnail links under the tab, or use the buttons Edit Workflow and Workflow Settings in the ribbon.

Edit Workflow   Workflow Settings

Before you start building the workflow, open the Workflow Settings page and set when the workflow should be started.

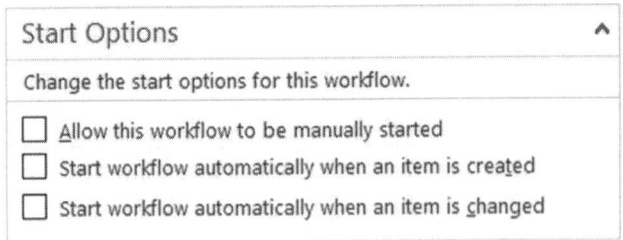

I would recommend that you make sure the boxes are checked, because the checking does not always stick in the box.

24.7.2 Dynamic Content

When you add dynamic content to a workflow, the content in actions changes depending on what happens in the SharePoint app that the workflow is associated with.

In *SharePoint Designer*, dynamic content is called "lookup" content, and it is added via 'Add or Change Lookup' buttons. What is shown as suggestions in the dropdowns depends on the action and the app content.

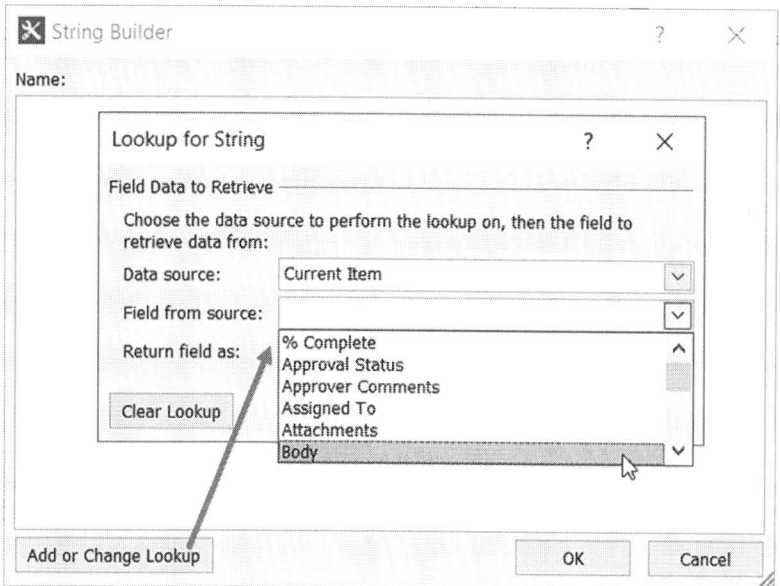

24.7.3 Finalize the Workflow

When you have created a list workflow, you must publish it. In the same ribbon group as the Publish button, you can also find buttons to save the workflow (to continue working with it later) and to check the workflow for errors.

Even if you have checked the workflow for errors, you should also perform the trigger and see if the action is performed as intended.

24.7.4 The Workflows Page

You can see details on running and completed workflows if you right-click on the ellipsis at an app item and select More/Advanced and then Workflow.

Modern interface:

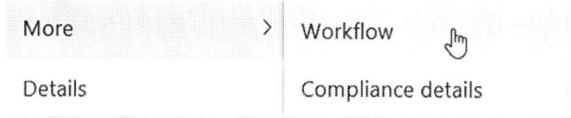

Classic interface:

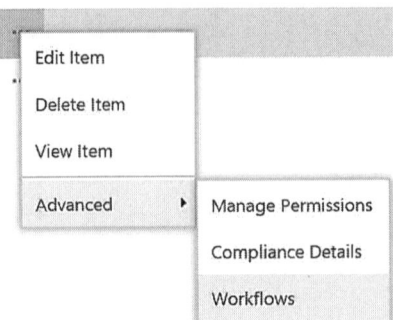

If you cannot check a workflow directly, because it is activated by a timer, you can select the workflow in the Workflows page and click on the Start button to run the workflow manually.

24.8 EXERCISE: SET TITLES

In two exercises, I will show how to automate updates of title fields in SharePoint libraries. Good document titles are important if you want to get relevant results from searches, but for many organizations it is a problem that titles in SharePoint document libraries are either missing or not accurate.

Therefore, I will suggest a flow and workflow that update file properties and set the title to the same as the file name when the "Title" field is empty. It is not an ideal solution, but the document name is most often more relevant than an empty title.

I use a "Procedures" SharePoint document library for these exercises. To be able to check the flow/workflow smoothly, I suggest that you make the "Title" column visible in the "All items" view. When the flow or workflow runs as it should, you can hide the "Title" column again.

24.8.1 Set Titles Flow

Below, I will give an example on how to create a simple flow that updates the "Title" column in a new or modified item in a SharePoint document library. Before the update, the flow looks if the "Title" field is empty.

We use dynamic content in several places in this flow, and in some cases, you will have two options: content from the trigger and content from the action. In other flows, the source of the dynamic content may be crucial, but here, it does not matter which one you choose – the result will be the same.

24.8.1.1 Actions

To set the title to be the same as the file name, we must get the column values, or properties, of the new or modified file. When we have that, we will know the file name, and we can set the flow to perform an update of the "Title" column.

We will use the action 'SharePoint – Get file properties' to fetch column values from the new or modified item. Each item is identified with its ID.

When the values have been fetched by the first action, we will add a 'SharePoint – Update file properties' action to update the "Title" value in the item, so that it becomes the same as the item's "Name" value.

24.8.1.2 Condition

As we don't want to change any existing "Title" values, we will add a condition after the trigger. This condition limits the flow, so that the actions are only executed when the condition is met.

A condition is set in three fields, where your selection in the middle field decides the relation between the two other fields.

A condition can be either true (If yes) or false (If no), and you can build different scenarios depending on the condition compliance. Often only the 'If yes' option is used, as no action is required when the condition is not met. That is the case in this example flow.

We will set the condition to be true when the "Title" value of the item that triggered the flow is equal to 'null', which means that the field has no value.

The image below shows the finished flow. You can see the expanded 'Get file properties' action in the steps below.

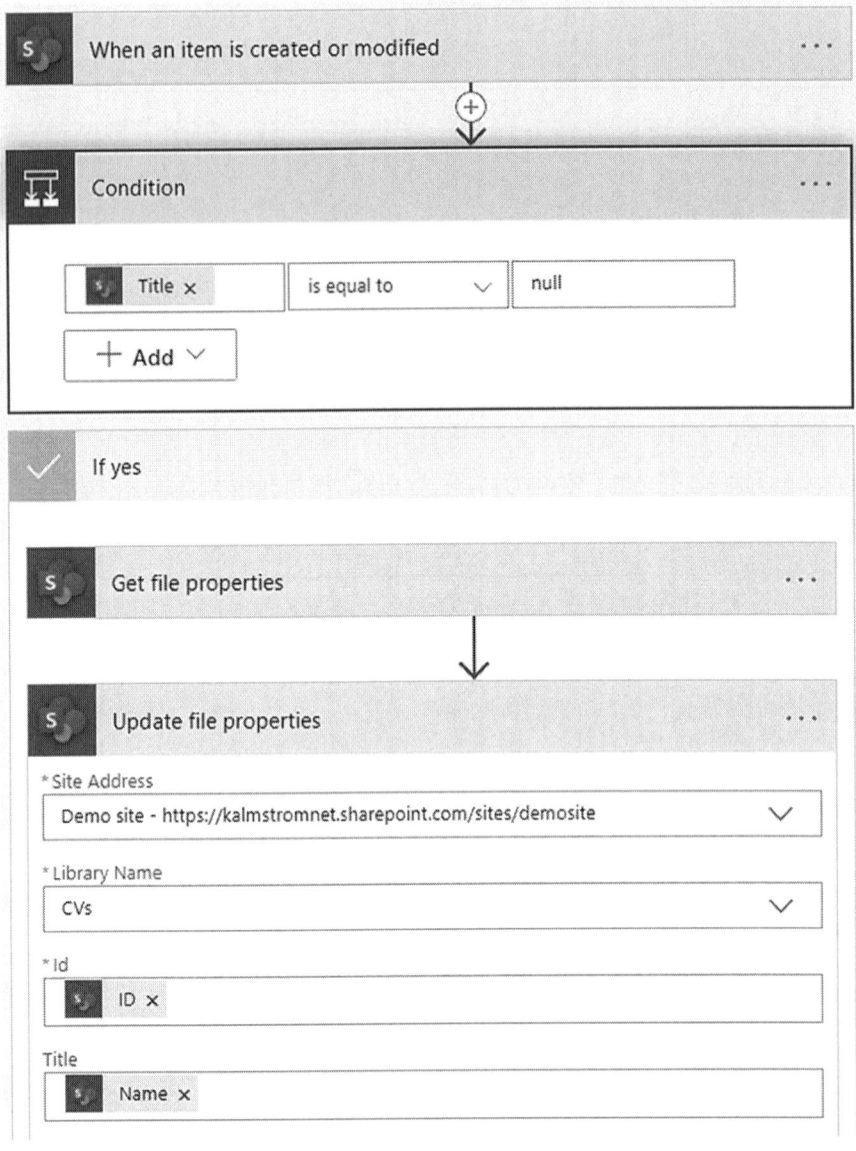

24.8.1.3   Steps

This flow is triggered when an item in a SharePoint document library is created or modified. If the item's "Title" field is empty, the flow fetches the item's properties, reads the file name, and adds the same value to the item's "Title" field.

1. Create an blank automated cloud flow and give it a name.
2. Select the trigger 'SharePoint - when an item is created or modified'.

3. Click on 'Create'.
4. Enter your site name and library name.
5. Click on 'New step'.
6. Add a Condition:
   a. In the left Condition field, add the dynamic content in the Title field of the item that triggered the flow.
   b. Keep the default 'is equal to' in the middle field.
   c. Type null in the right field.
7. Add the action 'SharePoint – Get file properties'.
   a. Enter your site name and library name.
   b. In the 'Id' field, add the dynamic content 'ID' from the trigger.

8. Click on 'New step'.
9. Add the action 'SharePoint – Update file properties'.
   a. Enter your site name and library name.
   b. In the 'Id' field, add the dynamic content 'ID'.
   c. In the 'Title' field, add the dynamic content 'Name'.
10. Save and test the flow.

Demo:

https://www.kalmstrom.com/Tips/SharePoint-Flows/Flow-Update-Title.htm

24.8.2 Set Titles Workflow

The image to the right shows a finished workflow that sets the "Title" value to the same as the "Name" value if the "Title" field is empty. As you see, it looks much simpler than the flow!

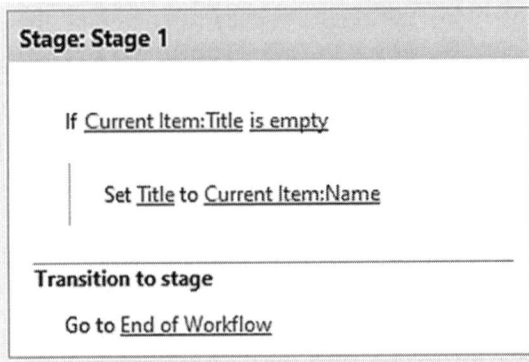

24.8.2.1 Steps

1. Open the site that has the list you want to use in SharePoint Designer.
2. Create a list workflow for the library you want to use.
3. Click on the 'Workflow Settings' button in the ribbon and set the workflow to start automatically when an item is created or modified.
4. Click on the 'Edit the workflow' link.
5. Click on 'Transition to stage' at tbe bottom of the Stage 1 box.
6. Type 'go' and press Enter.
7. Click on stage and select 'End of Workflow'.
8. Click in the 'Stage 1' box.
9. Click on the 'Condition' button in the ribbon and select 'If any value equals value':
   a. Click on the first value and open the Function Builder.
   b. Keep Current Item and set the field to 'Title'.

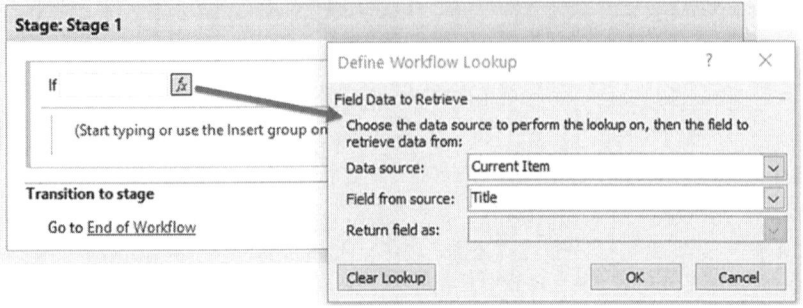

   c. Click on equals and select 'is empty' from the dropdown.
10. Click in the box below the condition box.
11. Click on 'Action' in the ribbon and select 'Set Field in Current Item':
    a. Click on field and select 'Title' from the dropdown.

b. Click on <u>value</u> and open the Function Builder.

c. Keep Current Item and set the field to 'Name'.

12. Check, publish and test the workflow.

Demo:

https://kalmstrom.com/Tips/SharePoint-Workflows/Title-List-Workflow.htm
(The demo shows how to set the title when it is not the same as the name.)

24.9 SUMMARY

After studying this chapter, I hope you have a general idea of how different kinds of flows and workflows are created and can be used.

We have looked at Power Automate, Microsoft's modern alternative to the classic SharePoint workflows. I have described some important differences between the two automation methods and shown the basics in both flow and workflow creation and management.

I have also explained how the SharePoint built-in flows are configured. Finally, I have given two exercises for you to try. I hope they gave you a good overview over how it is to work with the two automation tools.

You can find more automation descriptions in later chapters: 25.11.1.1, Workflow that Switches Content Type, and 30.3, Review Flow.

In the next chapter, I will introduce an important feature that is necessary to understand for more advanced use of SharePoint: the content types.

25 CONTENT TYPES

One of the best ways to make sure that apps in a SharePoint tenant or site will contain the desired content and are managed in a consistent way, is to use content types. A content type is a template for a specific type of item, like a task, a contact item or a library item. The content type has the metadata columns and settings that is needed for every item of that kind.

By default, SharePoint includes many predefined content types, such as Document, Item or Announcement, because all content in SharePoint is created from a content type. You can (and probably should) also create your own content types.

In this chapter, I will describe how to create a custom content type that can be used by the whole tenant and how to create a content type for a site.

I will also explain how a content type can be associated with an app and how you can create a template that gives the values of the metadata columns in printed documents.

Finally, I will introduce the built-in Document Set content type, which automatically creates multiple documents based on specified templates for each new library item. We will also create a custom Task Entry content type.

25.1 CONTENT TYPE EXAMPLE

When your company often sends quotations, you can create a special content type for quotations and add it to a document library. Such a content type would include a template for the quotation document and metadata columns like client company, contact person and PO number. It can also have settings for retention, *see* below in 25.4.3.2, Policies – Retention and More.

When you add such a content type to a document library, people who use that library can select the Quotation content type from the 'New' dropdown each time they want to create a new quotation. That way, all quotations will use the same template for the file as well as the metadata and settings.

Instead of just adding the content type to a document library, you can create a document library that is solely intended for quotations and remove the default content type (which is called Document) from that library. Then all new items will use the Quotation content type.

25.2 SITE AND LIST CONTENT TYPES

Content types are sometimes called site content types and sometimes list content types. Which term you use depends on how the content type is used.

- A content type is called a site content type when it is created or modified. The site content types can be managed in the SharePoint Admin center and in each site's Site settings, and they are grouped in categories.

- When you add a site content type to an app, it is called a list content type. A list content type can be customized for its specific app, and these customizations will not be added to the site content type.

25.2.1 Use Custom Columns with a Content Type

If you make changes to the columns in a custom content type, they will be overwritten in your app if the content type is updated. Therefore, it is better to add new columns in an app than to modify the content type columns, if you need specific metadata.

When you add new columns, the app will be like in the content type design, except for the new columns you have added. If the content type is updated, the columns you have added will be kept as they are.

You might need to allow editing in the content type settings of the app where you want to add columns.

1. In the List settings, click on the link to the content type that the app is using.
2. Click on the 'Advanced settings' link.
3. At 'Should this content type be read only?' select 'No'.

Demo:

https://kalmstrom.com/Tips/SharePoint-Online-Course/SharePoint-Meetings-Flexibility.htm

25.3 THE CONTENT TYPE GALLERY/HUB

Content types can be created in the SharePoint Admin center >Content type gallery, which connects to a classic site called Content Type Hub. Technically, the Content type gallery is just a user interface showing the content types from the Content Type Hub. When you create and publish content types in the SharePoint Admin center (or directly the Content Type Hub site), they become available for the whole tenant, and you don't need to create content types for each site. This gives reusability and consistency of information across the tenant.

Even if you create and manage your content types in the SharePoint Admin center, you might need to open the Content Type Hub site for advanced settings and editing and to test the content type before you publish it.

The Content Type Hub site is not listed in the SharePoint Admin center under Active sites. Instead, it can be reached from the Site settings of any root site in the tenant. Click on 'Content type publishing' under the Site Collection Administration heading. On the page that opens, you can find a link to the Content Type Hub.

Taxonomy_hcRL3VioiV2xubyCk0o+0A==
https://m365x446726.sharepoint.com/sites/contentTypeHub/_layouts/15/mngctype.aspx

Of course, you can also just type in the address, since it will always be the main URL to your SharePoint tenant followed by "/sites/contentTypeHub/". The rest of the link above points to the Manage Content Types page within that site.

25.4 CREATE A CONTENT TYPE FOR THE TENANT

When you create a custom content type, you always start from an existing content type. The new content type inherits all the attributes of its parent content type, for example document template, columns and settings. As the new content type is created, you can change any of these attributes, and you often want to add more columns.

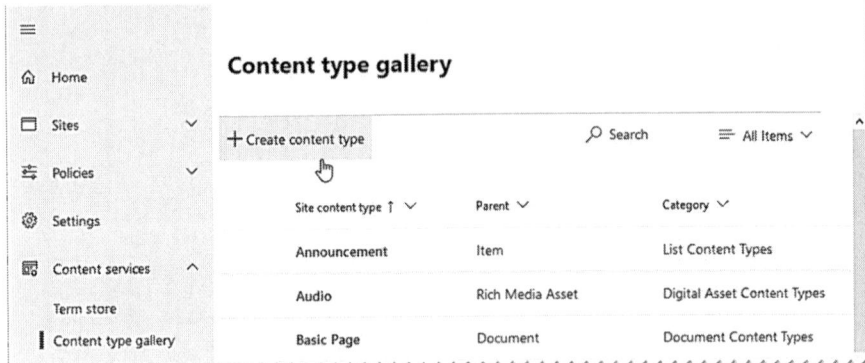

1. Click on '+ Create content type' in the Content type gallery, to open the right Create content type pane.
2. Enter a content type name and a description.
3. Add your content type to an existing or new category.
4. Select first category and then content type for the Parent content type you wish to build your custom content type on.
5. Click on 'Create', and your content type will be added to the list of content types in the Content Type Gallery.
6.

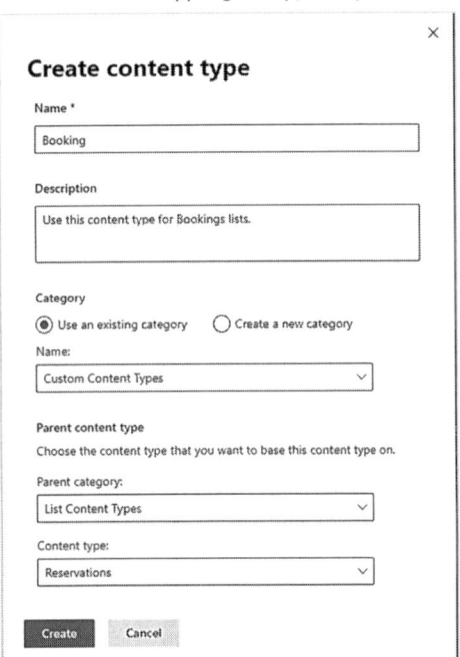

458

25.4.1 Add Site Columns to a Content Type

When you have created the content type, you should modify the site columns. The Content Type Gallery has no "Created" column to sort the content types by, but you can filter by category and/or parent content type and then sort the names alphabetically to find your new content type. Click on the name of the new content type to open it.

As you have built your custom content type on top of a predefined content type, some predefined properties for that content type are kept, as the "Name" and "Title" columns from the Document content type.

Now you can add more columns to the content type. You can either create a new site column or use an existing one. In both cases, a right pane will open where you can add details for the new column.

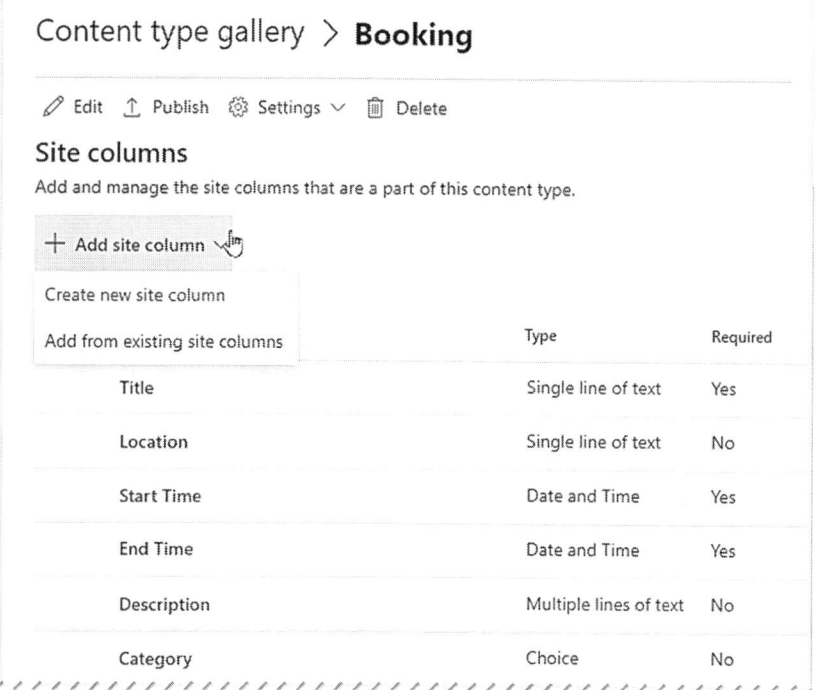

25.4.2 Edit Site Column

Open the ellipsis to the right of the column name to edit a column, or select the column and use the buttons that become visible in the command bar.

459

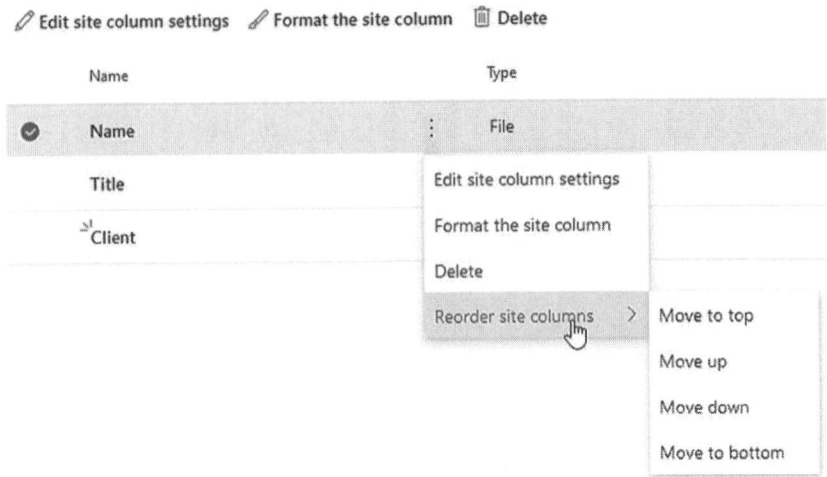

The column settings are edited in a right pane. Here, you can hide a column from the form or set it to be required. Check the box for update if you want all content types that inherit from this one to be updated with your modification.

The same checkbox is available when you add an existing site column to the content type. If you have modified an existing content type, you should think twice before you enable update of inheriting content types! The existing content type might already be in use in the tenant, and in that case your modification can create problems.

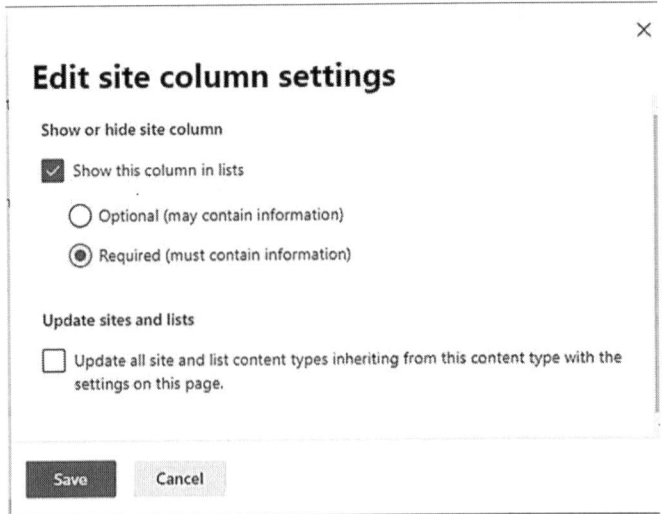

You can also change the column order and delete a column. Note however that all columns cannot be deleted, for example the Title column.

('Format the site column' under the column ellipsis is for addition of JSON code and out of scope for this book.)

25.5 EDIT CONTENT TYPE SETTINGS

Click on the Settings icon in the top command bar to change the content type settings. In the 'Advanced Settings' pane, you can change the default edit permission for the content type if necessary. Here is also a checkbox for updates of inheriting content types.

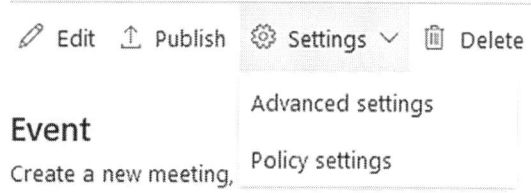

25.5.1 Associate a Template with a Content Type

When your content type builds on the Document content type, you can associate a custom file template with the content type under the Advanced settings. Enter the path to an existing template or upload a template from your computer.

Word, Excel and PowerPoint files can be added to a content type. As always in SharePoint, it does not have to be a real template file. Any document with the correct content and layout will do. *Refer to* 25.7, Document Template with Metadata, on how to create a template that has the content type property fields in the document body.

25.5.2 Policy Settings

When you select 'Policy settings' under the content type settings, a page in the Content Type Hub will open in a new tab. Here, you can make settings for retention, auditing, barcodes and labels, and you can also add an administrative description and a policy statement.

When you check one of the boxes, you will have options to continue.

461

Site Content Types ▸ Edit Policy

Name and Administrative Description
The name and administrative description are shown to list managers when configuring policies on a list or content type.

Name:
[Meeting]

Administrative Description:
[   ]

Policy Statement
The policy statement is displayed to end users when they open items subject to this policy. The policy statement can explain which policies apply to the content or indicate any special handling or information that users need to be aware of.

Policy Statement:
[   ]

Retention
Schedule how content is managed and disposed by specifying a sequence of retention stages. If you specify multiple stages, each stage will occur one after the other in the order they appear on this page.

☑ Enable Retention

Specify how to manage retention:
　　Items will not expire until a stage is added.
　　Add a retention stage...

Note: If the Library and Folder Based Retention feature is active, list administrators can override content type policies with their own retention schedules. To prevent this, deactivate the feature on the site collection.

Auditing
Specify the events that should be audited for documents and items subject to this policy.

☐ Enable Auditing

Barcodes
Assigns a barcode to each document or item. Optionally, Microsoft Office applications can require users to insert these barcodes into documents.

☐ Enable Barcodes

Labels
You can add a label to a document to ensure that important information about the document is included

☐ Enable Labels

25.5.2.1 Retention Settings

The 'Enable Retention' box in the Policy settings gives a link, 'Add a retention stage', that opens a dialog. Here, you can decide how long items entered in an app that uses this content type should be retained.

Note that items that should be retained still can be deleted from an app. They will then be moved to the site's automatically created Preservation Hold Library, which can be found in the Site contents and is only visible to the site owner.

You can also decide what should happen to the item when it no longer should be kept in the app.

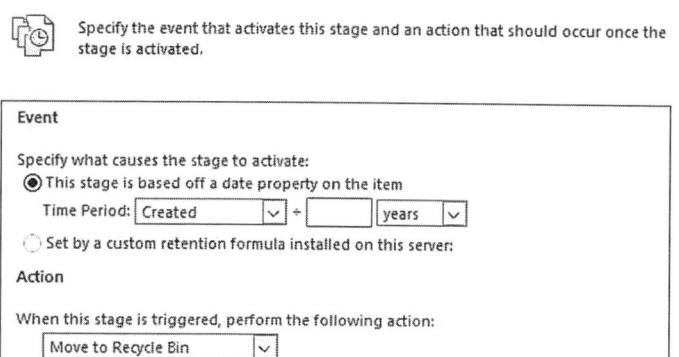

25.6 TEST A CONTENT TYPE

Before you publish a content type, you should check how it works. You can try it in the Content Type Hub site, because here, the content type works without publishing. The publishing is just a method to propagate the content type to the other sites in the tenant.

The Content Type Hub is a classic site, and here you can add the content type to an app and try it. *Refer to* 25.5. below to learn how to add a new content type to an app.

25.7 PUBLISH AND UNPUBLISH A CONTENT TYPE

When a new content type has been created, it must be published to be available in other sites than the Content Type Hub. And if a change has been made, the content type must be republished. The publication can take an hour or even more to be finished, but it is often quicker than that.

To publish from the SharePoint Admin center, open the content type in the Content type gallery and click on the 'Publish' button in the command bar. A right pane will open where the 'Publish' option is checked, and you only need to click on 'Save'.

When the content type has been published, the default option in the right pane will switch to 'Republish'.

The Publish right pane also has an 'Unpublish' option. Select this option, if you don't want the content type to be available anymore but not want to delete it.

If you have been editing or testing the content type in the Content Type Hub, it might be more convenient to publish it there:

1. Under Site settings >Site content types, click on the content type you want to publish to open it.

463

2. Click on 'Manage publishing for this content type'.
3. Select your option from the new page that opens. It has the same three options as the gallery right pane.

25.8 Add a Content Type to an App

When you have created a custom content type, you need to add it to the app(s) where you want to use it. If you don't want to give users a selection, you also need to remove the default content type.

If you remove the default content type, all new items in the app will be based on the content type you added. This means that they will all have the same columns and settings, and thereby the same kind of metadata information.

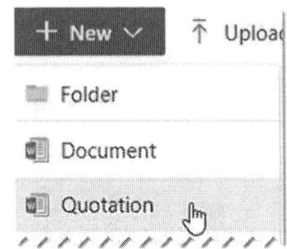

If you don't remove the default content type, users can select the custom content type when needed.

You might find it useful to add several content types to an app, but my preference is usually to create new apps for each content type. There are exceptions, though, and I describe one such case in chapter 30 below.

25.8.1 Allow Management of Content Types

Before you can add a content type to the app, you need to allow multiple content types in the app:

1. Open the List settings and click on 'Advanced settings' in the General Settings section.
2. Select the 'Yes' option under 'Allow management of content types' and click OK.

Settings ▸ Advanced Settings

Content Types
Specify whether to allow the management of content types on this document library. Each content type will appear on the new button and can have a unique set of columns, workflows and other behaviors.

Allow management of content types?
◉ Yes ○ No

3. Now you will see a new 'Content Type' heading in the List settings.

25.8.2 Classic Method

The classic way to add content type to an app can be used for all content types, sites and interfaces:

1. Under the 'Content Type' heading in the Site settings, click on 'Add from existing site content types'.

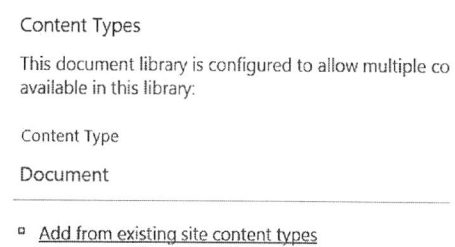

2. Select the category and content type you want to use. Click Add and then OK.

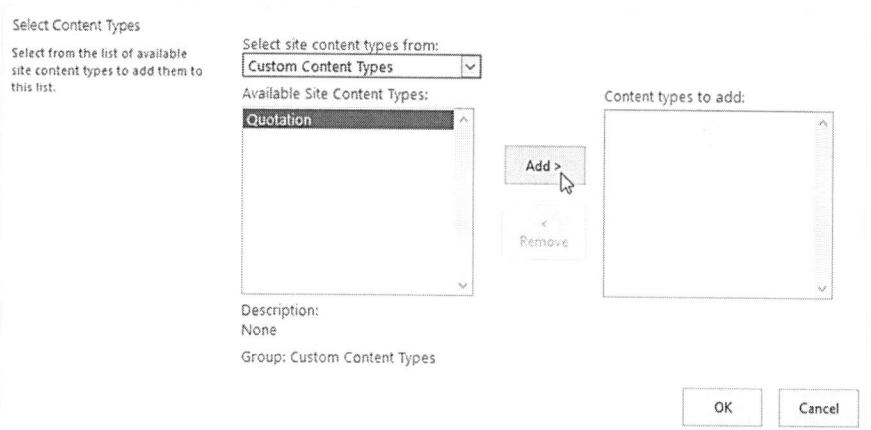

Now the content type is associated with the app, but when you look at the default view, you cannot see the content type columns there. They are not automatically added to any view, so you need to add them by editing the view. You probably also need to create some new views.

25.8.3   Modern Option

When management of content types has been allowed in an app, the modern app interface gives an option to add the content type directly from the user interface, under '+ Add column'.

In the Add Content Type page, select 'Choose content type' and then the content type you want to add. Now you will see details about the selected content type. Select 'Apply' to finish.

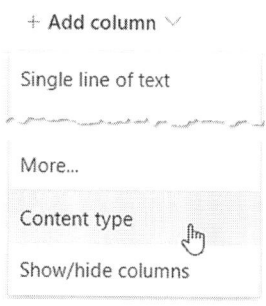

This modern experience method is currently only available for custom content types. Use the classic method if you want to view or add an out-of-box content type.

465

25.8.4 Delete Default Content Type

Even if you have added a custom content type to an app, the default content type is still there and gives a possibility to create other kind of items. I would recommend that you remove the default content type from the app. If you do that, all new items will be of the same kind, as there is no other option.

In the Content Types section of the List settings, click on the content type you want to remove and then on the link 'Delete this content type'. T(he content type will only be removed from this app. You will always have the possibility to add it again.)

Demo:

https://kalmstrom.com/Tips/SharePoint-Online-Course/Content-Types-Use.htm

25.9 CREATE A CONTENT TYPE FOR A SITE

To see all content types that are available for the site, open the Site settings from the root site and click on 'Site content types' under Web Designer Galleries. You will be directed to the site's Content type gallery, where you can see a list of all the content types that can be used in the site, whether they were created in the SharePoint Admin center/Content Type Hub or in the current site.

The site Content type gallery reminds very much about the Content type gallery in the SharePoint admin center, but the content types you create here will only be available for the site and any subsites.

The process to create a content type for a site is the same as when you create a content type in the SharePoint Admin center. You can associate a template with the Document content type created from a site, just as you can do when you create the content type from the SharePoint Admin center, and if you so wish, you can use the same category for your custom content types as when you create from the Admin center.

In the top right corner of the Content type gallery page there is a link to the classic experience, which gives a few more options. If you for example need to set retention rules for the content type, you need to use the classic experience. The Document Set content type, see below, also requires use of the classic page.

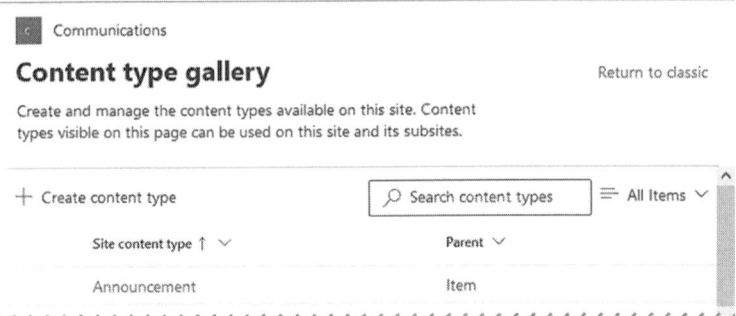

When you create a content type for a site, there is no publication. You only need to add the content type to one or more apps. You can try the content type in a test app before you add it to the app(s) where you want to use it.

Any changes in the content type are normally propagated to all apps in that site and in any subsites where the content type is used.

25.10 Document Template with Metadata Columns

When you have added a custom content type to a library app, the metadata entered in the columns can be displayed in the SharePoint app interface.

However, the metadata columns can only be seen and set in the Word document if you open its properties, and they will not be included if you print the document.

To include the values of the metadata columns in a printed document, you need to create a template which has the content type fields in a table in the document body. The column values for each item will be added to the document automatically when you add them to the library item – and when they are filled out in the document, they will be added to the library item.

Quote Date	2/26/2017
Decision Date	2/24/2017
Value	[Value]
Decision	3. Declined

Create a template by creating a Word document that you associate with your content type:

1. Using the content type you want to add the template to and create a new Word document. It opens in Word Online by default.
2. Switch to the desktop application.
3. Insert a table with two columns and as many rows as you have columns in the content type.
4. Enter the column names in the left column cells.
5. Place the mouse cursor in the first row of the right column. Under the Insert tab in the ribbon, click on the Quick Parts icon and select Document Property and then the column name.

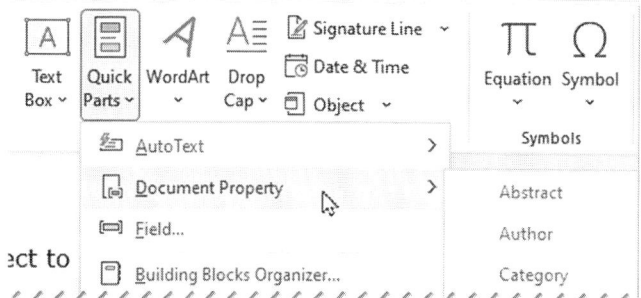

6. Repeat step 5 for each row and select the other columns.
7. Save the document as a .docx or .dotx file to your computer.

Now you can connect the Word document to your content type, to be used as a template for new library items, as described above. You should also open the Library settings >Advanced settings and set documents to open in the client application.

You can of course use all other Word features in your template and make it compliant with your company graphic profile as needed.

Demos:

https://kalmstrom.com/Tips/SharePoint-Online-Course/Content-Types-Template.htm

25.11 THE DOCUMENT SET CONTENT TYPE

When you work with projects within an organization, you usually need to create a set of documents for each project. Templates are often used for such documents, to make them consistent.

With a Document Set content type, you can have project documents created and named automatically from your specified templates when you create a new project item. All the documents needed for a project are found in that project item.

If you plan to use folders for project documents or similar, I recommend that you study document sets first. Using document sets is a better option than folders in many ways.

Another way to avoid folders, is of course to use one library for each project. In my opinion, the document sets give a better overview, and separate libraries do not give you the automatic creation and name giving of documents that document sets do.

The Document Set content type works in both the classic and the modern library interface and in modern as well as classic sites. When this is written, the Document Set content type can only be created on site level.

While simpler content types like Document and Item becomes visible in sites soon after they have been created in the SharePoint Admin center, the Document Set content type can take several hours. Document sets created in sites are quickly available.

In **modern** sites, Document Set content types cannot be selected until you have activated the feature. (In classic sites the feature is activated by default.) This is done under Site settings > Site Collection Administration >Site collection features.

25.11.1 *Use A Document Set in a Library*

When a user creates a new project item in a library and uses a document set content type, the specified set of documents will be created automatically.

The content writer can just open each document and start writing, instead of creating and naming multiple new documents.

In the image from a modern library below, the default content type is kept, but all options except the standard Word document are hidden. The Document Set content type has been added as an option.

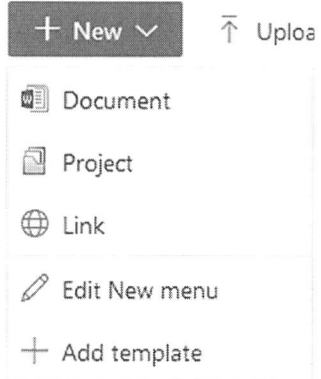

In the image from a classic library below, the default content type has been removed and folders are not allowed.

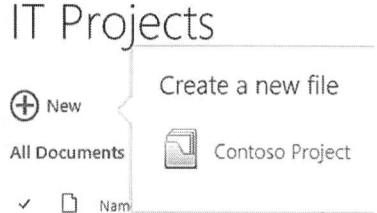

25.11.2 The Document Set Files

When a new document set item has been created in a library, it has a specific icon in the library list. After creation, the document set opens so that you can reach the included file templates and set metadata.

You can add any templates to the document set, but in the image of the open "Support system" document set below, the specified documents are an Excel cost break-down, a PowerPoint executive overview and a Word specification.

By default, the auto-created documents are named with the name of the project item (Support system) + the name of the template.

Support system

View All Properties
Edit Properties

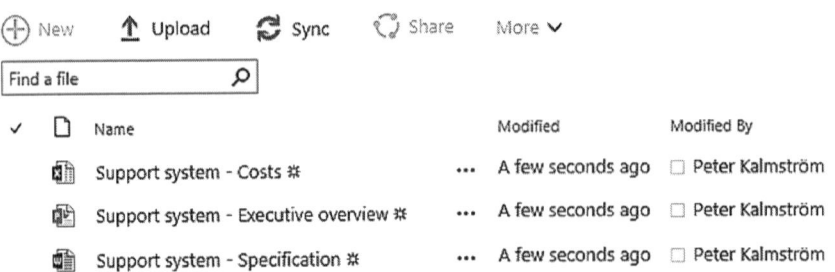

The image above comes from the **classic** library interface, that has a heading, called welcome page. The image shows the default look.

The welcome page is a web part that can be edited, by editing the page. You can also create a welcome page for all instances in the Content Type Hub on the page where you add the files to the document set, *see* below.

The **modern** interface has no such welcome page. It just shows the files, and the open Information pane.

25.11.3 Create a Document Set Content Type

Create a custom content type built on the Document Set parent for the site in the same way as described for other content types above. Start with the Parent category Document Set Content Types and the content type Document.

Document Set content types can be created from the SharePoint Admin center, the Content Type Hub or from the Site settings, but currently, the file templates can only be added from the site where the content type should be used.

25.11.3.1 Add Files to the Document Set

Use the classic experience to add the templates to the content type.

1. Open Site settings >Site content types.
2. Click on 'Return to classic'.
3. Click on the name of the Document Set content type to open it.
4. Click on the link 'Document Set settings'.

470

5. At Default Content, add links to the templates you want to use in this document set.

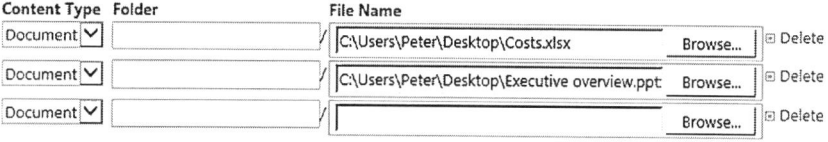

Now you only need to add the Document Set content type to a library, as described above in 25.8, Add a Content Type to an App.

Demos:

https://kalmstrom.com/Tips/SharePoint-Online-Course/Document-Set-Content-Type.htm

https://kalmstrom.com/Tips/SharePoint-Online-Course/Document-Set-Use.htm

25.12 Content Types in the Highlighted Content Web Part

The modern Highlighted Content web part gives a possibility to show content that is associated to one or more content types.

However, custom content types are *not* included among the options you can choose. Neither is the very common Item content type. Hopefully, Microsoft will add more content types in the future.

The image to the right shows the current options, and it has not changed for a couple of years As you see, there are some content types to choose from, even if Item and custom content types are missing.

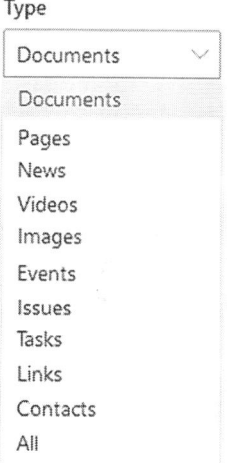

25.13 Data Entry Content Type

In chapter 23, we created a Data Entry view for users who wanted to report an issue. Another option for data entry is to create a content type form for the first creation of an item.

Just as with the view, you can hide fields in the Data Entry form that in are not important when users create a new item. When you have added the Entry Form content type to a list, you should set it as the first content type.

In the modern experience Users will have a choice when they create a new item. In the classic experience, users will have the first content type when they create a new item.

When users edit an item, there is a dropdown for content type above the other fields in both experiences. Here, they can select the elaborate content type, with all the columns.

Content Type | Task Entry Form ▼
             | Task Entry Form
Task Name * | Task

The switch to the more elaborate form can also be done automatically with a workflow, *see* below.

25.13.1 *Create a Data Entry Content Type*

Here I will assume that the Data Entry content type will be used in a list for tasks or issues. Tasks lists use the Task content type, while the content type is Issue in Issue Tracking lists and Item in Issue tracker lists. It is of course possible to build on another parent and content type too.

1. Create a new content type, in the site or in the SharePoint Admin center. Select the parent content type to be fetched from List Content Types and then select Task, Issue or Item.
2. Hide columns that are not necessary in an entry form.
3. Associate the content type with an app where you want to use the new form. order
4. Under Content Types in the List settings, click on the link 'Change new button and default content type'.

   ▫ Add from existing site content types

   ▫ <u>Change new button order and default content type</u>

   Columns

5. Set the new content type as number one.

25.13.2 *Workflow that Switches Content Type*

If you want a different form to be shown automatically when an item is opened after creation, you can let the full form stay as default and let a workflow show the Entry form when the item is first created.

This workflow only runs when an item is created. Therefore, the default content type will be used when an existing item is opened.

```
Stage: Stage 1

    Set Content Type ID to Task Entry Form
    Transition to stage
        Go to End of Workflow
```

Flows do not work as well with content types as workflows, so it is not possible to use a flow for this automation in the same easy way.

1. Open the site in SharePoint Designer and create a list workflow for the app you want to use.
2. Click on the 'Workflow Settings' icon in the ribbon and select 'Start workflow automatically when an item is created'.
3. Click on the 'Edit the workflow' link.
4. At Transition to stage, end the workflow by entering 'go to End of Workflow'.
5. Click in Stage 1 and select the Action 'Set Field in Current Item'.
6. Click on field and select 'Content Type ID' from the dropdown.
7. Click on value and from the dropdown, select the value to the content type that should be used when an item is created.
8. Publish and check the workflow.

Demos:

https://kalmstrom.com/Tips/SharePoint-Online-Course/SharePoint-Forms-Content-Types.htm

25.14 SUMMARY

After studying this chapter, I hope that you understand how content types are used and feel inspired to create your own content types for lists and libraries.

You have learned to create a content type and associate it with an app, and you can also connect a document template to a content type.

In this chapter, I have also introduced the Document Set content type and described how you can create a Data Entry form content type to be used when an item is first created.

You will find more information about content types in the two last chapters in this book, but in the next chapter, I will describe how you can add CSS and JavaScript code to classic SharePoint pages.

26 CSS, JAVASCRIPT AND RSS IN CLASSIC PAGES

In this chapter, we will see how you can use the **classic** Content Editor web part to add CSS and JavaScript to a page. I will also introduce the classic RSS Viewer web part, which helps you add an RSS feed to your SharePoint site.

The techniques described in this chapter can only be used in classic pages. Modern SharePoint pages have a Code snippet web part, but it is only used to display code. It does not do anything - the code is not executed.

To customize modern pages with code, you need to build or install a client-side web part app. After uploading it to the tenant's App Catalog, it can be available to modern pages in all sites or activated in each site as needed.

CSS is a language that describes how HTML (or XML) elements must be rendered, for example in a web page. The look of your SharePoint site is decided by CSS code in the background. JavaScript is a programming language for web pages.

How to write CSS and JavaScript is far out of scope for this book, which is mainly no-code, but here I will show how you can do if you have a snippet of code that you want to use on a classic SharePoint page.

I will describe how you can add code to make small changes in a site page. There are three ways to do it, but you cannot do it by directly pasting your CSS or JavaScript code into a page's HTML source. It will look fine until you save the page, but when you do that, your code will disappear. You must use the Script Editor or the Content Editor.

If you want to modify an object on the page but don't know the name for it, press the F12 key to show the browser's developer tools.

26.1.1 Script Editor

You can paste CSS or JavaScript code to the minimal Script Editor web part in the Media and Content category.

In wiki pages, you can also use the Embed Code button under the INSERT tab, which inserts the Script Editor web part in the page.

Embed Code

Embed

26.1.2 Content Editor Source

The Content Editor web part, in the Media and Content category, can be used to add code to a page. When you have added the Content Editor web part to the page, the CSS or JavaScript code can be pasted into the web part HTML source:

1. Add the Content Editor web part to the page.
2. Click on the Edit Source button under the FORMAT TEXT tab in the ribbon.
3. Paste your code in the HTML source.
4. Apply and save the page.

Edit Source

Demos:

https://www.kalmstrom.com/Tips/SharePoint-Online-Course/Content-Editor-CSS.htm

https://www.kalmstrom.com/Tips/SharePoint-Online-Course/Content-Editor-JavaScript.htm

26.1.2.1 Content Editor Link

In my opinion, the best method for adding CSS or JavaScript code to a page, is to create a separate .css, .txt, .js or .htm file with the code. Upload it to the Site Assets library and add a link to the file in the Content Editor web part.

This method is good if you often change the CSS code, because you can make the change directly in the file. Another advantage is that you can use the same file in multiple pages.

1. Add the code to a file and upload it to the Site Assets library.
2. Add the Content Editor web part to the page.
3. Edit the web part and type the path to the CSS or JavaScript file in the Content Link field.
4. Apply and save the page

Demos:

https://www.kalmstrom.com/Tips/SharePoint-Online-Course/Content-Editor-CSS-Link.htm

https://www.kalmstrom.com/Tips/SharePoint-Online-Course/Content-Editor-JavaScript-Link.htm

If you want to change the CSS for a site and not just for a page, *refer to* 27.4.1, Link to an Alternate CSS File.

26.1.3 The RSS Viewer Web Part

Use the RSS Viewer web part when you want to show content on a SharePoint page from any site that has an RSS feed. When you have added the web part and entered the link to the Atom page of the site you want to display in the web part, it will be updated automatically.

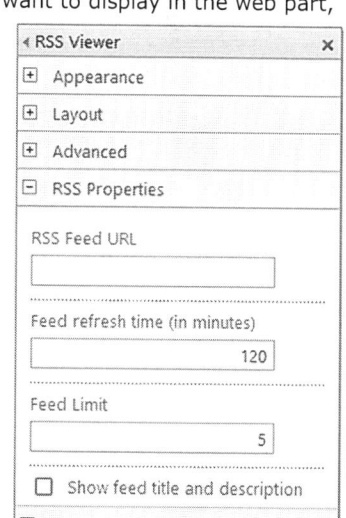

1. In the site that you want to display in SharePoint, click on the 'Atom' subscription button and copy the URL to the page that opens.
2. Open a SharePoint wiki or web part page where you want to add RSS content in edit mode.
3. Add the RSS Viewer web part from the Content Rollup category.
4. Edit the web part and paste the URL in the 'RSS Feed URL' field in the web part pane.
5. Define settings for how often the RSS feed should be updated and how many items should be shown on the page.
6. (To avoid having the title 'RSS Viewer' on

475

the web part, expand the Appearance section and set the Chrome Type to 'None'.)

7. Click on 'Apply' and save the page.

Demo:

https://www.kalmstrom.com/Tips/SharePoint-Online-Course/RSS-Viewer.htm

26.2 SUMMARY

In this short chapter, we have looked at the various possibilities to add CSS and JavaScript to a classic SharePoint page. We have also seen how the RSS Viewer web part can enhance a SharePoint page.

Now I will describe how you can enhance SharePoint by activating the SharePoint Server Publishing Infrastructure.

27 SHAREPOINT SERVER PUBLISHING INFRASTRUCTURE

As we have seen earlier in this book, SharePoint Online has various features that are not enabled by default. One of them is the SharePoint Server Publishing Infrastructure, that is available in modern and classic Team sites.

Note: currently there is an entry for SharePoint Server Publishing Infrastructure in Communication sites too, but when you try to activate it you will get an error message. Hopefully, Microsoft has fixed that issue when you are reading this book!

When the SharePoint Server Publishing Infrastructure has been activated, several new features become available in the site. Some of them are immediately obvious, while others are visible only through the links in the Site settings page or in galleries or libraries.

In this chapter, we will have a look at some features that require activation of the SharePoint Server Publishing Infrastructure. You will learn how the options in the Look and Feel group in the Site settings become different after activation and what possibilities the new options give. I will also introduce the classic Content Query web part.

When you have activated the SharePoint Server Publishing Infrastructure for a site, you can also activate the SharePoint Server Publishing feature for that site and any subsite. This feature gives you more powerful layout options, and we will look at them in the last sections of this chapter.

27.1 ACTIVATE THE PUBLISHING INFRASTRUCTURE

Activate the SharePoint Server Publishing Infrastructure at Site settings >Site Collection Administration >Site collection features. The activation might take a few minutes.

When you have activated the SharePoint Server Publishing Infrastructure, the site will have new features, and the navigation settings will also be changed.

Demo:

https://kalmstrom.com/Tips/SharePoint-Online-Course/Publishing-Infrastructure-Activate.htm

27.2 NAVIGATION CHANGES WITH PUBLISHING INFRASTRUCTURE

When the SharePoint Server Publishing Infrastructure has been activated for a site collection, the Look and Feel group in the Site settings has become different.

The image to the right comes from a classic site. The modern Team site does not have the 'Title, description and logo' setting here but under Site information.

Look and Feel
Design Manager
Title, description, and logo
Device Channels
Navigation Elements
Change the look
Import Design Package
Navigation

The links to the Site navigation and Top link bar are now replaced with a 'Navigation' link, which give more options than before:

- The navigation areas are called Current and Global Navigation instead of Site navigation and Top link bar.
- You must enable 'Show subsites' in the Navigation Settings to display links to subsites. Even if you select 'Use the top link bar from the parent site' when you create a new subsite, the link will not be shown until you enable 'Show subsites'.
- The image below shows the default setting for the Global Navigation. The Current Navigation has similar settings.

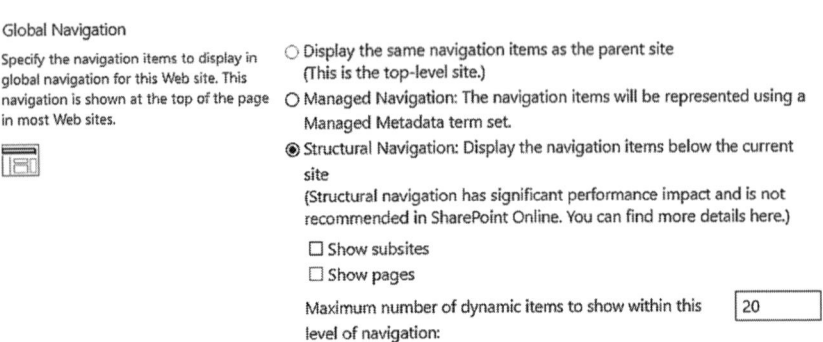

The default Structural Navigation is easy to maintain, security trimmed and updates automatically when content has been changed.

If you instead enable Managed Navigation, you can add a term set for the navigation.

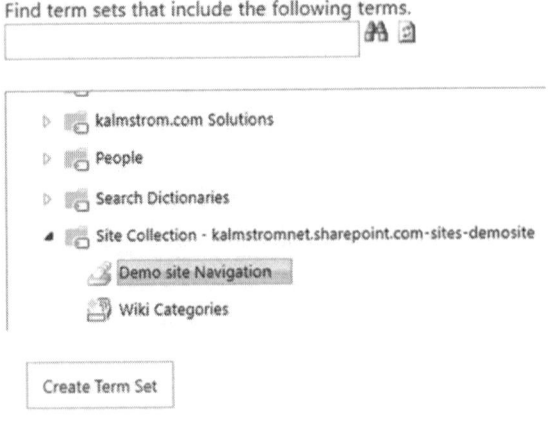

Open the Term Store Management Tool to edit term sets.

Microsoft warns that both these options might influence the SharePoint Online performance. I have not noticed any problem, but you should be aware of the possibility so that you can disable the SharePoint Server Publishing Infrastructure if necessary.

- A bit down on the Navigation Settings page, you can find the entry 'Structural Navigation: Editing and Sorting'. Here you can add headings and links, delete links or move them up and down in the navigation.

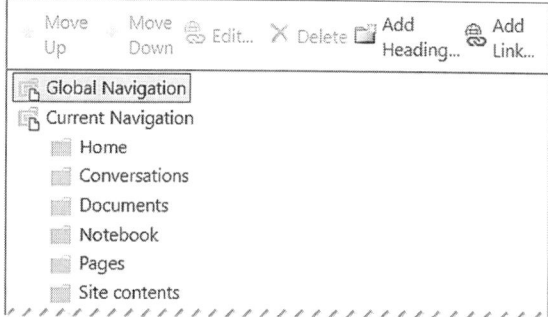

- When the SharePoint Server Publishing Infrastructure is activated, you can use the Navigation page to create a mega menu in classic sites more easily that with drag and drop.
- When you click on 'Add Link...' 'in the top right corner of the Structural Navigation: Editing and Sorting' box, you will have more advanced options than before. You can, for example, set links to open in a new window.

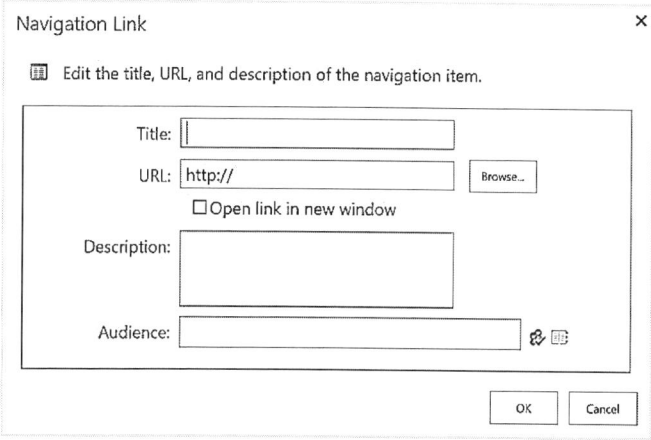

Demos:

https://www.kalmstrom.com/Tips/SharePoint-Online-Course/Publishing-Infrastructure-Navigation-Changes.htm

https://www.kalmstrom.com/Tips/SharePoint-Online-Course/Publishing-Infrastructure-Mega-Menu.htm

27.3 SHAREPOINT SERVER PUBLISHING

Once the SharePoint Server Publishing Infrastructure feature has been activated, you can activate the SharePoint Server Publishing feature for the site. This is done in the Site Settings >Site Actions >Manage site features. The activation only takes a few seconds.

Enable the SharePoint Server Publishing feature for sites where you want to have more layout options than those I have shown in earlier chapters. The image to the right below comes from a modern site.

The SharePoint Server Publishing gives you access to the Master page. Here you can specify a master page for the site and use an alternate CSS URL for the entire site.

Under 'Page layouts and site templates', you can define a set of templates that can be published to an intranet or Internet site so that they can be used in other sites.

Another SharePoint Server Publishing feature is the Image Renditions, which lets you define different image formats.

Look and Feel
Design Manager
Master page
Page layouts and site templates
Welcome Page
Device Channels
Navigation Elements
Change the look
Import Design Package
Navigation
Image Renditions

27.4 THE CONTENT QUERY WEB PART

The Content Query web part is available for classic pages when the SharePoint Server Publishing Infrastructure feature has been activated. You can find it in the Content Rollup web part category.

The Content Query reminds of the Content Search web part that I have used in several earlier examples, but there is an important difference in how the search is performed: The Content Search can search the index of the entire tenant, while the Content Query only can search the site (default) or specified sites in the site collection.

There is a certain delay before the index is updated, so you will not see your changes right away when you let the Content Search web part search the whole index. With the Content Query web part any changes are shown more quickly, and therefore the Content Query is suitable for content that is often modified, like tasks and issues.

The Content Query is a bit easier to configure than the Content Search, as you don't have to build a query. You can find all options in the Content Query web part properties.

Here is an example of how you can use the Content Query web part to collect tasks from subsites within the same site collection and show them on a page.

1. Open a classic page in edit mode and add the Content Query web part from the Content Rollup category.
2. Edit the web part and expand the Query accordion.
3. Add site URLs, if you want to restrict the search to certain sites in the collection.
4. Select list and content type to show items from.
5. Expand the Presentation accordion and remove the text in the Link textbox under 'Fields to display'. (If you don't do that, you will have an error message.)
6. Under Presentation you can also group and sort the displayed items, set the number of columns and make other settings.
7. Expand the Appearance accordion and enter a suitable web part title.
8. Make any other web part settings you prefer before you apply the changes and save and publish the page.

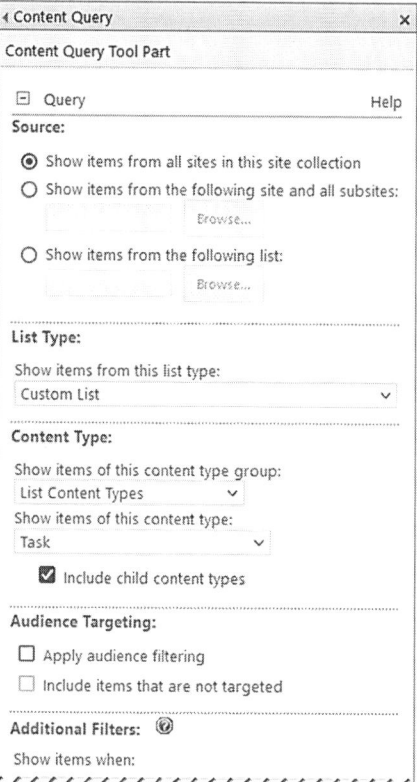

Demo:

https://www.kalmstrom.com/Tips/SharePoint-Online-Course/Publishing-Infrastructure-Content-Query.htm

27.4.1 Link to an Alternate CSS File

When the SharePoint Server Publishing Infrastructure feature and the SharePoint Server Publishing feature is activated, you can use an alternate CSS file for that site. Add the alternate CSS file in the Master Page settings:

1. Upload the CSS file to the Site Assets or to another location on your SharePoint site.
2. In the Site settings, click on 'Master page' under 'Look and Feel'.
3. Expand 'Alternate CSS URL'.
4. Select the 'Specify a CSS file' option and browse to the location where you uploaded your CSS file.
5. Before you click OK, check the box for subsite inheritance if you want subsites to use the CSS file.

Alternate CSS URL

Typically, Master Pages define CSS styles for your site. If you would like to apply a separate CSS style sheet independent of your master page, specify it here.

Choose the first option to inherit these settings from the parent site. Choose the second option to rely only on the styles defined in master pages. Choose the third option to apply a separate CSS style sheet.

○ Inherit Alternate CSS URL from parent of this site
○ Use default styles and any CSS files associated with your Master Page
● Specify a CSS file to be used by this site and all sites that inherit from it:

All Channels [   ] Browse...

☑ Reset all subsites to inherit this alternate CSS URL

Demo:

https://www.kalmstrom.com/Tips/SharePoint-Online-Course/Publishing-Infrastructure-Alternate-CSS-URL.htm

27.4.2 Publishing Pages

When SharePoint Server Publishing is activated, you can create pages of the Publishing type. These are classic pages that resembles wiki pages, but they have more layout and image options.

While other site pages are stored in the "Site Pages" library, the Publishing pages are stored in a separate "Pages" library that you can reach from the Site contents. Under the '+ New' button in the "Pages" library, you can find a selection of publishing pages.

Note that the Publishing pages can only be created from the "Pages" library.

You can create other kinds of pages even if SharePoint Server Publishing has been enabled for the site. When you add a page from the settings icon in the 365 navigation bar, it will still be a modern page, and if you want to create wiki or web part pages, you can do that from the "Site pages" library as usual.

Demo:

https://kalmstrom.com/Tips/SharePoint-Online-Course/Publishing-Infrastructure-Server-Publishing.htm

27.4.2.1 Image Renditions

Image Renditions is one of the new features you get when the SharePoint Server Publishing feature has been activated. When you create a new Publishing page and insert an image, multiple renditions of the image will be created.

Click on the 'Pick Rendition' button under the IMAGE tab to see the options. The image below shows the default options.

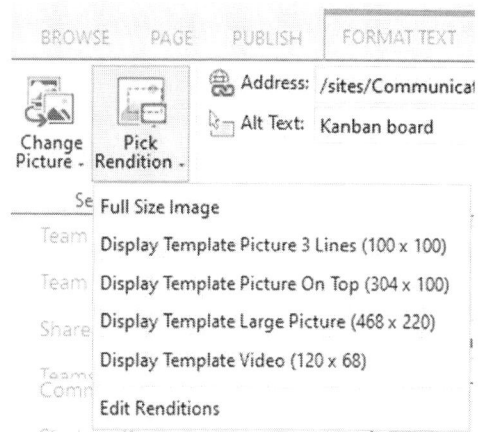

The wiki page picture options are present in Publishing pages too, and you insert an image in the same way, under the INSERT tab. When you upload an image from your computer, you will have a chance to add metadata to your image.

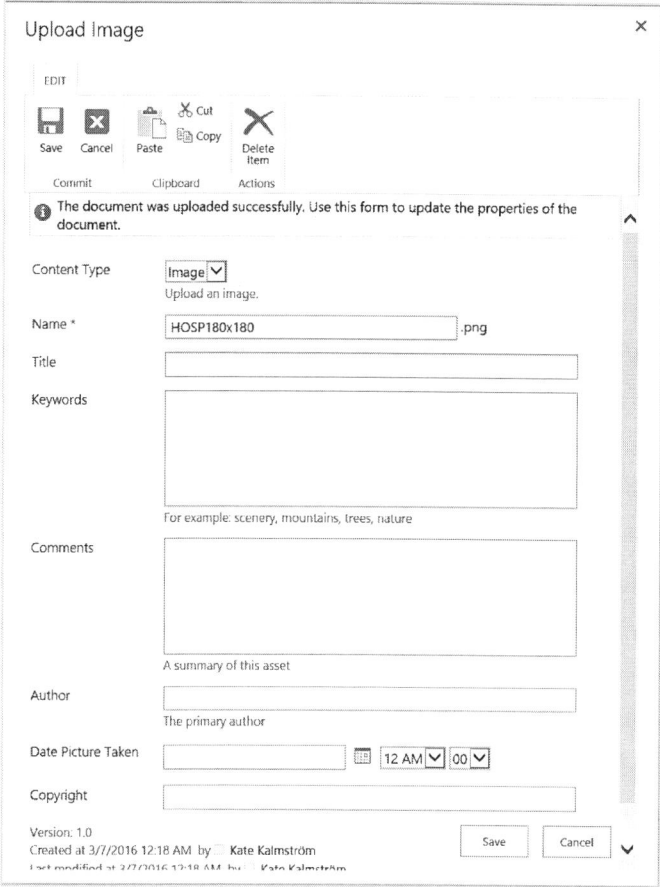

483

When you have clicked on Save, the renditions will be created, and you can select which format you want to use for your image.

If you select 'Edit Renditions', you can see all renditions of the image.

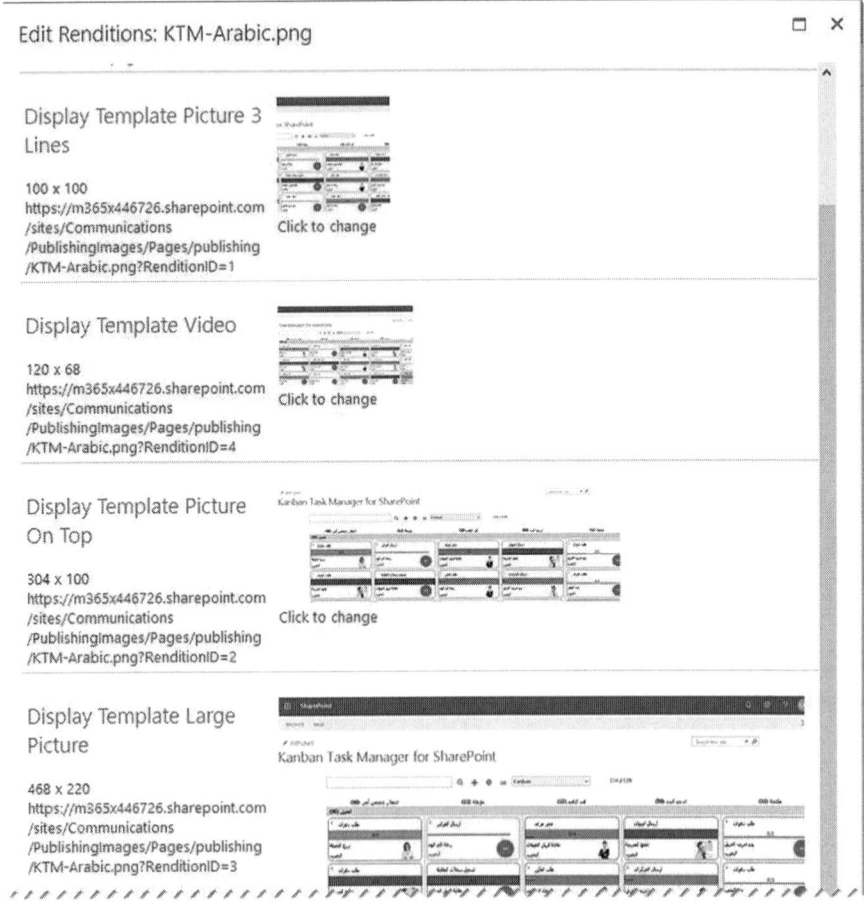

Click on the 'Click to change' link at the size you want to edit and drag the handles to the portion of the image you want to use.

You can add your own rendition sizes in the Site settings >Look and Feel >Image Renditions. Click on the 'Add new item' link, give the new rendition a name and specify its width and height in pixels.

Demo:

https://www.kalmstrom.com/Tips/SharePoint-Online-Course/Publishing-Infrastructure-Image-Renditions.htm

27.5 Summary

In the chapter about SharePoint Server Publishing Infrastructure, we have looked at the changes this feature gives in the Site settings 'Look and Feel' group and at the new navigation options they give.

You have also learned how to use the Content Query web part, and you have seen how the activation of SharePoint Server Publishing can give a site more layout options for pages and images.

In the next chapter, I will explain how you can use Excel or Access to create example data for SharePoint testing.

28 CREATE EXAMPLE DATA

When you are trying different solutions and scenarios for SharePoint apps, it is helpful to use example data. In this chapter I will show how to create example data for a SharePoint list in Microsoft Excel and Access.

28.1 COPY AND PASTE EXAMPLE DATA FROM EXCEL

When you don't have too many items in the list, it works well to paste values you have created in Excel into the SharePoint grid view mode. In this example, I will add 100 example data to a Number column called "Hours Worked". To create the example data, I will use the Excel RAND function.

1. If necessary, edit the SharePoint view in the List settings, so that the item limit includes all the rows you want to use. This way you can open the list in grid view and easily paste example data you create in Excel into the "Hours Worked" column.
2. Open a new Excel spreadsheet.
3. Enter a RAND function in the function field to generate 100 random numbers: =int(RAND()*100)
4. Drag the cell down to copy the formula to as many cells as you need for the items in the SharePoint list column.
5. Copy the Excel data and paste it into the SharePoint "Hours Worked" column.

If you have a long SharePoint list, it is safer to open it in Access and paste the values into the "Hours Worked" column there, as Access is more stable.

Demo:

https://www.kalmstrom.com/Tips/SharePoint-Online-Course/HelpDesk-Hours-Worked.htm

28.2 CREATE EXAMPLE DATA IN ACCESS

To create more complex example data, you can open the app in Access, *refer to* 22.3.2, and let a query combine values from various columns.

Here, I will use example data for a "Tasks" list as an example. Multiple selections must not be allowed in the "Assigned To" column.

1. Import the "Tasks" list to Access as a linked table. As it has a People or Group type column, we will also have a "User Info" table.
2. Create a new table. It will open automatically in the design area. Give it the name "Priorities".
3. Name the column "Priority'.

4. Enter the priority values under 'Priority'. (The ID values will be set automatically.)

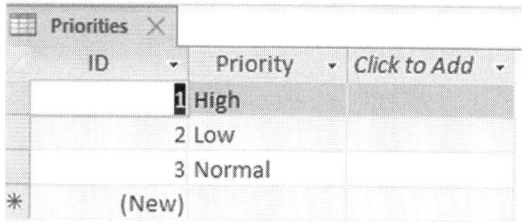

5. Create another table named "Titles" with the column 'Title'. Add some titles to the column.
6. Click on the 'Query Wizard' button under the Create tab in the ribbon. Keep the default 'Simple Query Wizard' option. Click OK.
7. Select first the table and then the columns that you want to include in the query. In this case, it is the Title and Priority we created but also the ID and theWork email from the "User info" table.

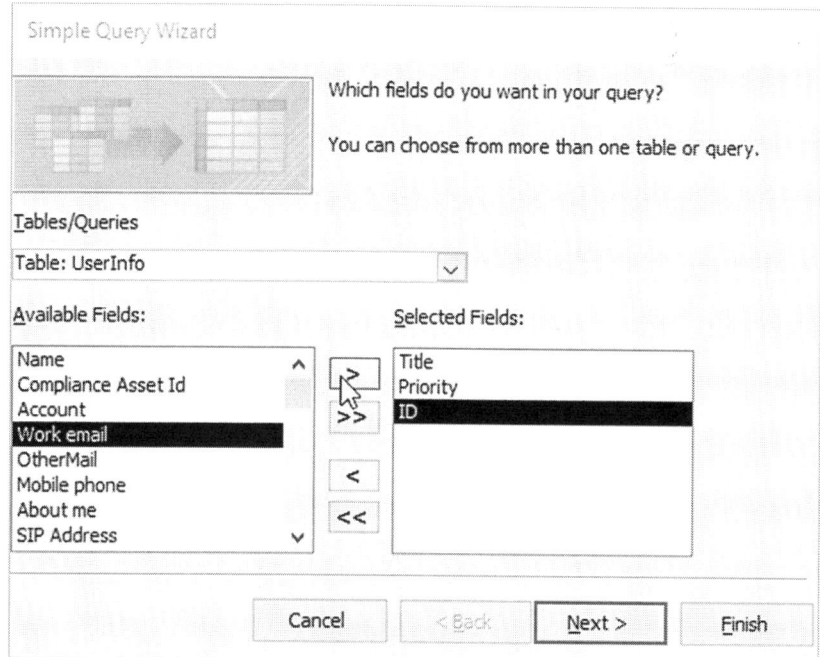

8. Click OK to the Relationships message and close the 'Relationship' tab.
9. Click on the 'Query Design' button under the Create tab in the ribbon.
10. Select the All tab in the right pane that opens and drag the tables you want to use to the query design area.
11. Double-click on the four column names we want to use, to add them to the grid area.

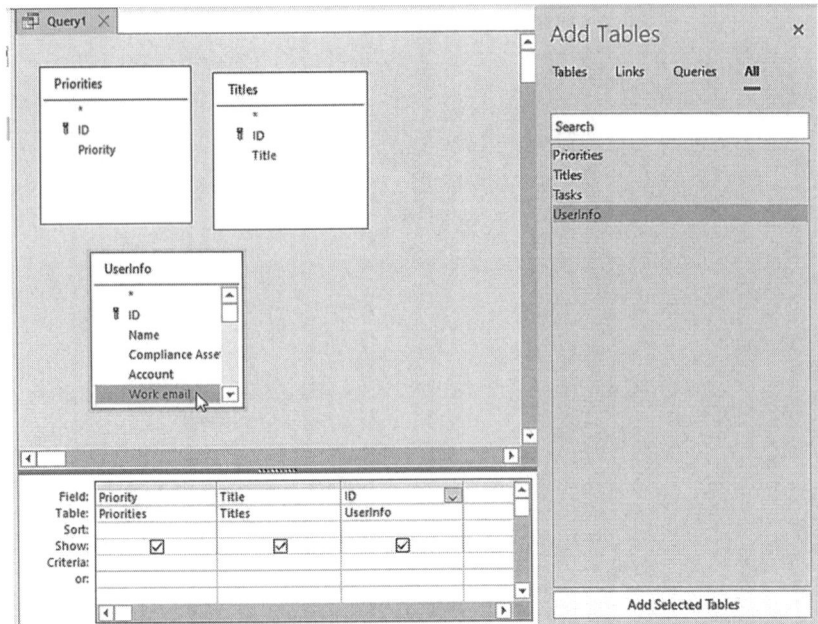

12. Add the parameter 'Is Not Null' to the 'Work email' column, in case there are any blank rows that you want to get rid of. You can also add 'And Not' + any e-mail address you don't want to use in the example date.

13. Click on the 'Run' button under the 'Design' tab in the ribbon to get all possible combinations of the included columns.

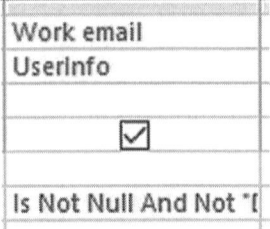

14. If needed, click on View >Design View to adjust the query so that you get reasonable values. Then run the query again.

15. Click on the 'Append' button under the ribbon 'Design' tab.

16. From the dropdown in the Append dialog, select the SharePoint list where you want to have the example data. Click OK.

17. In the grid area, append the query columns to suitable columns in the SharePoint list if needed.

18. Click on the 'Run' button under the ribbon 'Design' tab.

Now when you refresh the SharePoint list, you will see the new items created by the Access query there.

Demo:

https://kalmstrom.com/Tips/SharePoint-Online-Course/HelpDesk-ExampleData-Access.htm

28.3 SUMMARY

It is often important to try out different scenarios in SharePoint before you go out in production, and in such cases, it is useful to create example data. In this short chapter, have given tips on how such example data can be created in Excel and Access.

Now, we are getting close to the end of this book. I will just give you two chapters more, and in those I will show how business processes can be enhanced by using the techniques you have learned by studying *SharePoint Online from Scratch*.

We will start with a solution for Meetings management within an organization. It includes creation of a content type, but now I will not give you the creation steps. Go back to chapter 25 if you have forgotten how to create content types.

29 MEETING NOTES AND ACTION POINTS

In this chapter, we will repeat and expand techniques that we have gone through earlier. I will show how you can combine what you have learned, to create a SharePoint solution that automates the management of meetings, meeting notes and meeting decisions in general.

I hope my suggestions will inspire you to try something similar for your organization. By now, you should have the knowledge to modify the solution given in this chapter, so that it suits your environment perfectly!

The solution has a "Meetings" list for all meetings. Each meeting will be entered as a new item in this list. The list is associated with a content type called Meeting.

The Meeting content type has a Hyperlink column, which is intended for links to an "Action points" list. There is one such list for each meeting. One person will be assigned to creating an "Action points" list before each meeting, so the creation of this list must be a quick task.

The building of this system involves several steps:

- What to consider?
- Create a content type for the "Meetings" list.
- Create a content type for the "Action Points" list.
- Add the new content types to the lists.
- Manage changes in the content types.
- Create list templates.
- Copy templates to other site collections.
- Create a meetings overview page.
- Use list specific columns with content types.
- Display "My Action Points" on a page.

29.1 CONSIDERATIONS

Before you start creating a SharePoint solution for meetings management, you should consider your organization's information strategy.

- What do you want to store?
- How many mandatory fields are necessary? In general, you should try to keep them at a minimum!
- How should data be categorized?
- How to best find information?
- Which permissions are needed? Some meeting notes will need strict permissions, others can be open to all users. How to manage that in the best way?

- For how long should we store the meeting notes? How can the retention time be set?
- Should the meeting notes be stored in lists or libraries? Lists are more powerful in general, but if it must be easy to print the meeting notes, you need to use libraries.

Demo:

https://www.kalmstrom.com/Tips/SharePoint-Online-Course/SharePoint-Meetings-Intro.htm

29.2 CREATE CONTENT TYPES

For this meeting management example, I create two content types in the SharePoint Admin center: a "Meeting" content type and an "Action Point" content type.

29.2.1 Meeting Content Type

We start with creating a Meeting content type for the "Meetings" list.

1. Create a Meeting content type. It should inherit from the regular Item content type in the List Content Types category.

2. When the new content type has been created, we can start customizing it. As we have built this content type on the Item, there is only one column, the "Title" (besides the created by, modified at and similar auto generated columns).

3. I suggest a "Description" column from the existing site columns, for information about the meeting before it is held. As this is an existing site column, it is already indexed and included in searches.

    If you want rich text in the column, you should create a new site column instead and enable rich text there.

4. Maybe you also have an existing "Department" column of the Managed Metadata type, connected to a "Departments" term store.

    If not, I would recommend that you create a new "Department" Managed Metadata site column and connect it to a term set in the tenant's Term Store, before you add the (now existing) "Department" column to the "Meeting" content type.

5. For the rest of the columns, you may have to create new site columns:
    a. Meeting notes – Multiple lines of text. Under 'More options', turn on 'Append changes to existing text'. This column should be used for notes during and after the meeting.
    b. Chairperson – Person or Group
    c. Internal Attendees – Person or Group, allow multiple choices
    d. External Attendees – Multiple lines of text, plain text
    e. Action Points – Hyperlink

6. Test the content type.
7. Publish the content type if you have created it for the tenant.

Demo:

https://kalmstrom.com/Tips/SharePoint-Online-Course/SharePoint-Meetings-Content-Type-Item.htm (shows creation from the Content Type Hub)

29.2.1.1 Set Retention on the Meeting Content Type

Meeting information should not be kept forever, so you can add retention to them.

1. Open the Meeting content type settings and select 'Policy settings'. An 'Edit Policy' page in the Content Type Hub will open in a new tab.
2. Check the box at 'Enable retention'.
3. Click on the link 'Add a retention stage...'
4. In the dialog that opens, set how long the item should be kept in the list.
5. Select what to do with the item when it no longer should be kept.

29.2.2 Action Point Content Type

In the Content Type Gallery, you should also create a content type from the List Content Types group for the "Action Points" lists:

- Item will give you a list with just a Title column, so you need to add at least Assigned to and Due date.
- Issue and Task will give so many columns that you probably want to remove some of them.

Demo:

https://kalmstrom.com/Tips/SharePoint-Online-Course/SharePoint-Meetings-Content-Type-Task.htm

29.3 CREATE APPS AND ADD CONTENT TYPES

When the content types have been published, it is time to create apps for meetings and action points and associate them with the new content types.

29.3.1 Meetings List

In my suggestion, one common "Meetings" list is used for all meetings – or all meetings within a department or similar, and each meeting is entered as an item.

1. Create a new blank list. Call it "Meetings" and make your preferred changes to it.
2. Allow management of content types under List Settings >Advanced settings.

3. In the new Content Type group in the List settings, click on the link 'Add from existing site content types' and add the Meeting content type.
4. Remove the default content type.
5. Create views.

Demo:

https://kalmstrom.com/Tips/SharePoint-Online-Course/SharePoint-Meetings-Content-Type-Use.htm

29.3.2 Action Points List

The "Action Points" list must be created for each meeting. For the creation and content type modification, you can follow the steps for the "Meetings" list above but select the Action Point content type.

However, if you have built on the Task content type, you must create a list from the Tasks template instead of a blank list and add the Action Point content type to it. Otherwise, you will not have the unique Tasks features.

29.3.2.1 Use "Action Points" as a Template

To make it easier for the people who are responsible for creating the "Action Points" lists, you should create views and in other ways modify the list so that it becomes as you want it. Then you can give permission to the responsible people to create a new list from it via Microsoft Lists.

That way the responsible people can either just 'Add an app' and select the "Meeting Action Points" template or create a new list from the Site content and select to create it from the "Action Points" list.

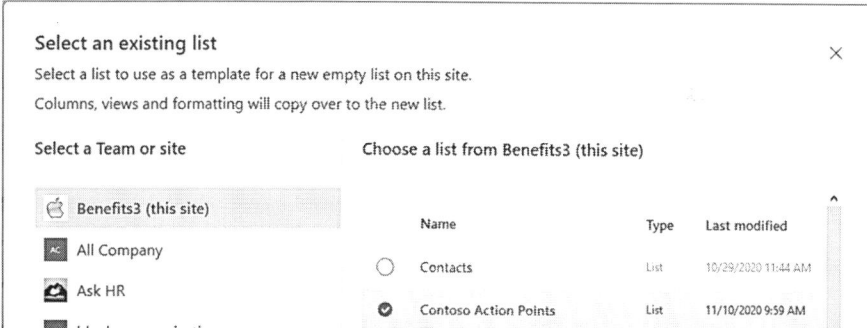

If you have used a classic site and the Task content type, you can instead save the list as a template. Tasks lists are not displayed in Microsoft Lists, so to create a copy of the list you need to use the template option, which is only available in classic sites. *Refer to* 7.14.2, Save as Template.

Demo:

https://kalmstrom.com/Tips/SharePoint-Online-Course/SharePoint-Meetings-Action-Points.htm

29.4 Create a Meetings Overview Page

It is convenient to have a page that gives an overview of all company meetings. If you only want to include meetings from one list, you can use the modern List web part or add the list as an app part in a classic page.

When the meetings are stored in different pages, we cannot use a modern page. The Highlighted content web part can show content from all sites, but custom content types are not yet displayed in the list of content types to be selected.

You can still collect meetings from multiple sites in the Highlighted content web part if you use a keyword in the title for each meeting item that is not used elsewhere.

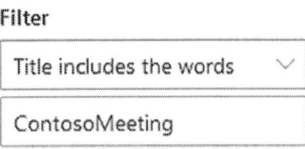

In a **classic** page, it is possible to show content from multiple sites with the Content Search web part.

1. In a classic page, insert the Content Search web part and edit it.
2. In the Query Builder, select 'Items matching a content type' and don't restrict by app. Restrict the search to the Meeting content type.
3. Switch to Advanced Mode and click on SORTING, to sort the meetings. When you sort them after creation date, the most recent meetings will be displayed on top.

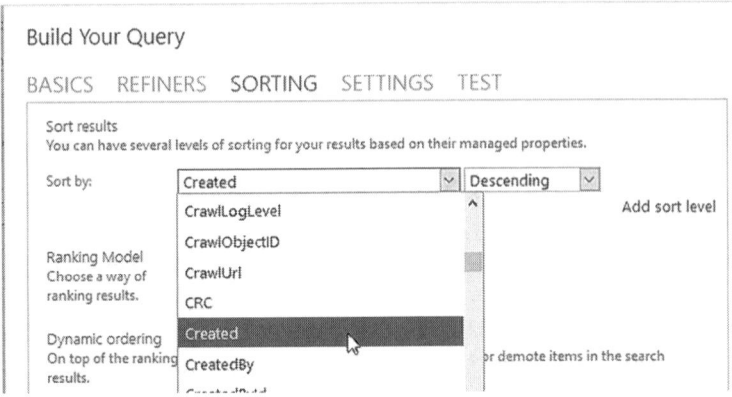

4. Make other changes to the web part, like how many items should be shown, how many rows and what should be mapped to the rows.

29.5 Summary

I hope the building of the meeting management system I suggest in this chapter has given a deeper understanding of content types and other SharePoint features.

In the last chapter, we will have a look at another business solution, this time for rental agreements. Here, I will give the steps for a flow that sends a reminder about contract renewal. This flow runs on a schedule, so you will learn something new in the last chapter too!

494

30 RENTAL AGREEMENTS

This chapter has rental agreements as the starting point. Such contracts must be stored in a way that gives a good overview over what the organization is renting, and renewals must be taken care of in due time.

My intention is not to give a recipe on how to create the perfect application for rental agreements management. Instead, I want to point to various options that might be useful when you handle similar information sharing situations in your own organization.

We will create a Rental Agreement content type with suitable site columns and associate it with a list app. Then we can create the same type of list in other sites via the 'Add an app' command or by using Microsoft Lists.

We will also automate the renewal reminders with a flow that sends a reminder to the person who is responsible for the renewal.

30.1 CREATE A CONTENT TYPE

The first step when building a rental agreements solution, is to create a content type for the rental agreement items.

The content type should be based on the List Content Types and the Item. That will give you a list with just a "Title" column, which you can rename to "Location Name" when the content type is used in a list. (You cannot rename the column when you create a content type. That would rename all "Title" columns in all content types in the tenant!)

I suggest the following columns: (My comments about new or existing site columns are based on which site columns most organizations have or not have already, so don't take them too literally.)

- Square Meters (of the location that is being rented): a new site column of the Number type.
- Start Date (for the rental agreement): an existing site column.
- End Date (for the rental agreement): an existing site column.
- Department (that is renting the location): an existing site column.
- Renewal Date: a new site column of the Date and Time type. Set the internal column name to, "RenewalDate", because it should be used in a query when we build a flow. *Refer to* 7.13, Internal Name.
- Responsible Person: a new site column of the Person or Group type.

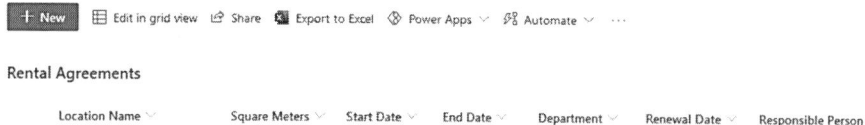

When the content type has been created, create a custom "Rental Agreements" list app and associate it to the Rental Agreement content type.

I suggest that you also add an edit button in the views if you are using the classic experience.

Demos:

https://www.kalmstrom.com/Tips/SharePoint-Online-Course/Rental-Agreements-Content-Type.htm (This demo shows creation in a site, but you can of course create the content type in the SharePoint Admin center too.)

https://www.kalmstrom.com/Tips/SharePoint-Online-Course/Rental-Agreements-Content-Type-Use.htm

30.2 "Rental Agreements" Template

You can of course have all the rental agreements in one list, but if you have multiple lists, you can set different permissions on them, and users will not be burdened by many items in one list.

When you have created a "Rental Agreements" custom list and added the views and settings you prefer, it is easy to create new lists for other kinds of contracts or agreements from it.

You can either create new lists from the "Rental Agreements" list via Microsoft Lists or save the app as a template in a classic site.

Demo:

https://www.kalmstrom.com/Tips/SharePoint-Online-Course/Rental-Agreements-Template.htm

30.3 Scheduled Review Alert Flow

When you have many rental agreements, it is useful to let a flow send an e-mail to the responsible person when it is time to review the agreement and either renew or cancel it. (Since Microsoft stopped supporting SharePoint 2010 workflows in SharePoint Online, there is no easy way to create a similar workflow in SharePoint Designer.)

As we saw earlier, Microsoft has given a built-in reminder flow for modern SharePoint apps that contains a column of the type Date and Time, but it only sends a reminder to the person who created the flow. This flow is suitable if all rental contracts have the same responsible person.

With multiple responsible persons, it is still possible to use the built-in reminder flow, if all responsible people create their own flows. That is however an insecure way.

Here, I will explain how you can create a flow that works for all people who are added as responsible for a rental contract in a "Rental Agreements" list. We will use an expression that sets the reminder date to seven days before the contract's expiry date.

The flow is set to run every day. It searches the "Renewal Date" value of each rental agreement for items that will expire in 7 days. When such a rental agreement is found, the flow will generate an e-mail to the responsible person.

The flow should send the reminder seven days before each rental agreement's end date. To find those contracts, we will use the flow action 'Get items' with a filter query. In this query, we need to use the internal column name "RenewalDate".

The query picks items where the value of the "Renewal Date" column is equal to seven days after today. We will use an expression for the "seven days after today" parameter.

30.3.1   Steps

In this flow, we will use a 'Get items' action with a filter query to find the contracts that expire in seven days. In the steps below, I give the formula for the query.

1. On the Power Automate site >My flows, create a flow of the type 'Scheduled cloud flow'.
2. Give the flow a name and set the 'interval' to '1' and the 'Frequency' to 'Day'. You can also set a start time.

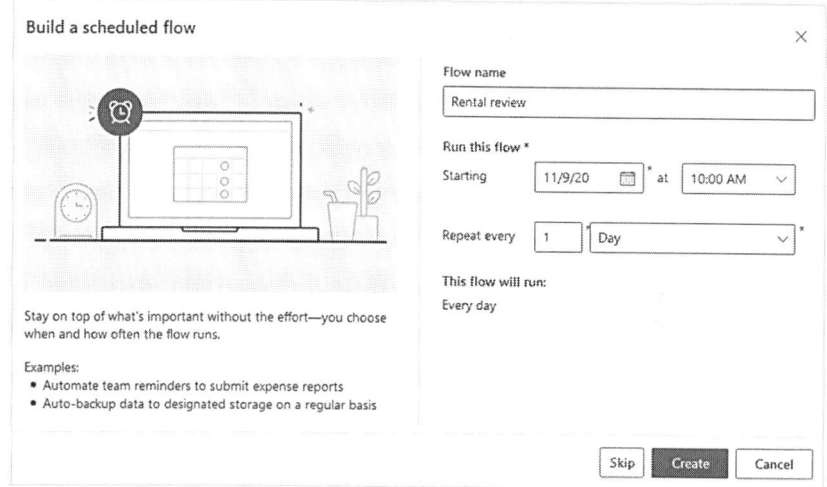

3. Click on 'Create', and the Flow Editor will open with the Recurrence trigger.
4. Click on 'New step' and add the action 'SharePoint - Get items'.
   a. Select or type the site and the "Rental Agreements" list.
   b. Open the advanced options.
   c. At 'Filter Query', enter the internal name for the "Renewal Date" column + eq. Add an apostrophe (') to start building a string.
   d. Open the Expression tab to build an expression for the rest of the field:

497

i. In the function field, start writing "format" and then select 'formatDateTime'.
ii. Add a parenthesis for input and start writing "add" inside it. Select 'addDays'.
iii. Add another parenthesis and start writing "utc" inside it. Select 'utcNow'. That will also add a new parenthesis to the function.
iv. After the new, empty parenthesis, enter a comma and 7 (for seven days) inside the addDays parenthesis.
v. Before the last parenthesis, add a comma and a string. Enter the date format, by ISO standard yyyy-MM-dd, inside the single quotes.

You should now have this expression:
FormatDateTime(addDays(utcNow(),7),'yyy-MM-dd').

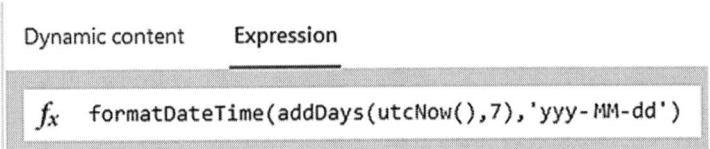

e. Place the cursor after the start of string apostrophe in the 'Filter Query' field and click on 'OK' under the expression.
f. Add an end of string apostrophe in the 'Filter Query' field.

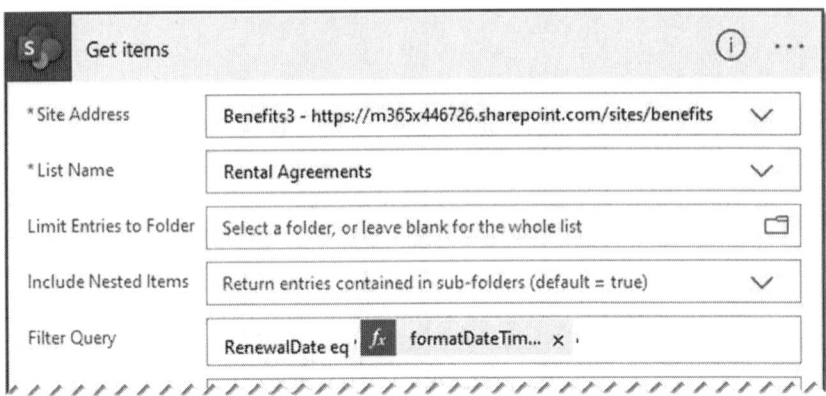

5. Click on 'New step'.
6. Add an 'Apply to each' action.
7. Add the dynamic content 'value' from the 'Get items' action to the output field.
8. Click on 'New step'.
9. Add the action 'Office 365 Outlook - Send an email (V2)'
    a. In the 'To' field, enter the dynamic content 'Responsible Person Email' from the 'Get items' action.

b. For the e-mail subject, type some general text and add the Title of the rented object as dynamic content. (You might find your custom name "Location Name" in the list of dynamic content instead of "Title".)
c. Insert a link in the 'Body' field:
   i. Switch to HTML view.
   ii. Instead of the default <br>, enter <a href="[the dynamic content 'Link to Item']">See Rental Agreement</a>.

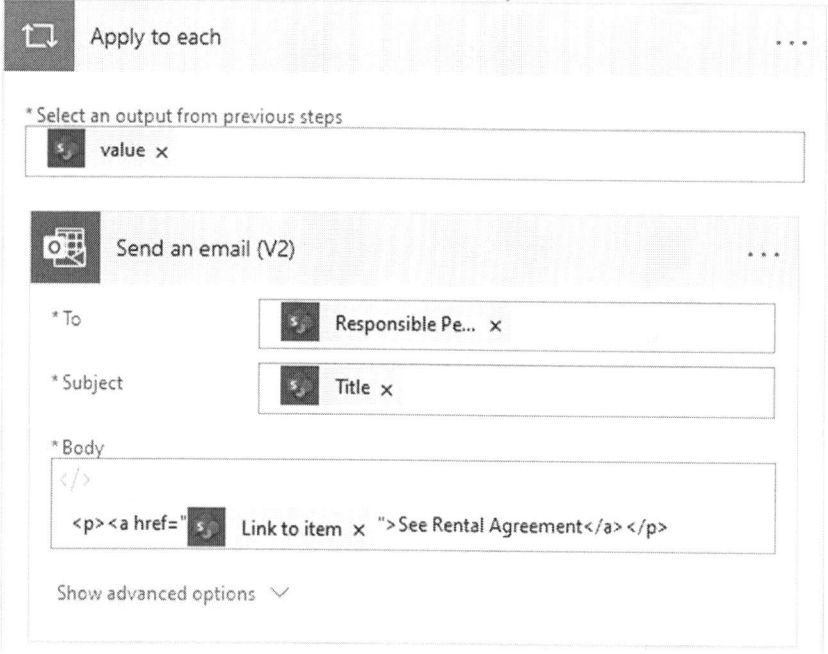

10. Click on 'Save'.
11. Click on 'Test' in the top right corner.
12. Select 'I'll perform the trigger action' and then 'Test'.
13. Add a test item that has its Renewal day 7 days from today in the Rental Agreements list.
14. Click on 'Run flow' in the Flow Editor right pane.
15. Check that the e-mail is sent to the person you added as responsible in the list and that the subject is correct and the link to the item works.

Demo:

https://www.kalmstrom.com/Tips/SharePoint-Flows/Flow-Contract-Reminder.htm (The demo shows a library, so another action is used to fetch the items. Otherwise, the steps are similar.)

30.4 SUMMARY

In this chapter, we have looked at how SharePoint can be used to facilitate the management of rental agreements. We have created a rental agreement content type that you can associate to multiple lists.

I have also suggested a way to automate the renewal reminders with a flow.

This was the last chapter, and as you have come all this way, I hope you have found my book interesting and useful. You should now be ready to continue exploring SharePoint Online on your own, with the help of more advanced books and online information.

Good luck!

Peter

31 ABOUT THE AUTHORS

Peter Kalmstrom is the CEO and Systems Designer of the Swedish family business Kalmstrom Enterprises AB, well known for the software brand *kalmstrom.com Business Solutions*. Peter has 19 Microsoft certifications, among them several for SharePoint, and he is a certified Microsoft Trainer.

Peter begun developing his kalmstrom.com products around the turn of the millennium, but for a period of five years he also worked as a Skype product manager. In 2010 he left Skype, and since then he has been focusing on developing standard and custom SharePoint solutions.

Peter has published eight more books, all available from Amazon:

- Excel 2016 from Scratch
- Microsoft Teams from Scratch
- Office 365 from Scratch
- PowerShell for SharePoint from Scratch
- SharePoint Flows from Scratch
- SharePoint Online Exercises
- SharePoint Online Essentials
- SharePoint Workflows from Scratch

Peter divides his time between Sweden and Spain. He has three children, and apart from his keen interest in development and new technologies, he likes to sing and act. Peter is also a dedicated vegan and animal rights activist.

Kate Kalmström is Peter's mother and a former teacher, author of schoolbooks and translator. Nowadays she only works in the family business and assists Peter with his books.

32 INDEX

@

@mention · 177

+

+ Add column · 126
+ Add template' · 205
+ New · 173, 174, 191, 192
+ New list · 169

3

365 app web part · 249
365 navigation bar · 28
365 search box · 29
365 Settings icon · 30
365 theme · 30
365 trial · 23

A

Access control · 59
access issue · 271
access request · 294
Access requests · 70
Access-SharePoint sync · 401
action · 431
activate SharePoint Server Publishing Infrastructure · 477
Active sites · 59, 66
Activity tab · 68
Add a column · 126
add a group of users · 38
Add a page · 241
add a single user · 36
Add an app · 118
add app link in Site navigation · 211
add content · 54
add content to modern web part · 248
add content type to app · 464
add CSS or JavaScript to page · 475

add Excel image to page · 352
Add from existing site columns · 128
add link to app · 334
Add members button · 292
add Microsoft 365 Group to classic site · 89
add modern web part · 248
Add or Change Lookup · 448
Add page to navigation · 305
add powerapp field · 387
add powerapp to page · 390
Add shortcut to OneDrive · 188
add site columns · 459
add table to wiki page · 263
add user accounts · 36
add users with PowerShell · 39
add web part to form · 267
add web part to web part page · 265
Admin centers · 42
Admin sharing settings · 287
Admin tile · 28, 33
administrator roles · 40
Advanced permission settings · 280
Alert Me · 151
all activity · 176
All apps icon · 28
Allow access requests · 294
Allow management of content types · 464
alternate CSS file · 481
Always keep · 228
anonymous users · 307
Anyone with the link · 299
app · 22, 50
app bar · 78
App Catalog · 61
app display modes · 121
app ellipsis · 29
app filtering · 133
app interface, classic and modern · 113
App Launcher · 28
app part · 240, 422
app settings · 116
app template · 158
app templates · 120
Append Changes to Existing Text · 179
Apply a site template · 79
Apply label to items in this list or library · 160
approval flow, associated sites · 434

approval flow, items · 435
approval flow, pages · 437
assign admin role · 40
assign translators · 80
associate hub sites · 105
associate template with content type · 461, 466
Associate with a hub · 103
associated sites · 101
Attach · 304
audience targeting · 309
Audience targeting settings · 310
Audit · 42
authenticated users · 307
auto-apply label · 45
Automate · 114
Automate button · 437
automation principle · 430
Azure Active Directory · 46
Azure AD · 46

B

Billing · 25
Blank list · 169
block download · 300
Board view · 144
branching · 365, 374
break inheritance · 284
BrowseGallery · 385
BrowseScreen · 384
built-in flows · 432
Button web part · 249

C

Calculated column · 129
calculated value · 316
Calendar app · 182
calendar app part · 267
calendar view · 145
Calendar view · 144, 147
calendar views · 182
Calendars Overlay · 184
Call to action web part · 249
CamelCase · 55
categorize items · 313
change field display name · 384

Change how members can share · 293
Change the look · 74
Change the look pane · 77
Change the order of links · 218
check and publish workflow · 449
Check in · 314
check out · 237
check out a file · 202
check out wiki page · 238
Check Permission · 280
Choice column · 130
Choice Filter web part · 359
classic app templates · 118
classic compatibility, Communication sites · 79
classic compatibility, modern Team sites · 84
classic experience · 51
classic homepage · 87
classic list experience · 166
classic Team site · 86, 100
clear filter · 134
Code snippet web part · 474
collaborating on a document in Word Online · 199
column · 112, 123
column character limits · 132
column settings · 135, 460
column types · 129
command bar · 114
comment icon · 175
comments · 176
Comments, page · 246
Communication site · 79, 96
Community site · 107
compare file versions · 157
Compliance center · 42
condition · 431, 451
conditional formatting · 136, 388
Configure page approval flow · 437
connect SharePoint team calendar to Outlook · 393
Connect to new Microsoft 365 Group · 89
Connect to source · 355
connect to term set · 325
connect web parts · 354
connect Windows 10 to 365 · 26
Content approval · 436
Content Editor web part · 266, 267, 337, 474
Content Query web part · 480

503

Content Search web part · 272, 422, 423, 494
Content services · 60, 318
Content Type Hub · 457, 463
content type Policy settings · 461
Content type publishing · 457
content type settings · 461
content types · 128, 456
Contents tab · 71
copy files · 203
Copy link · 302
Copy of this page · 241
Copy to · 189, 204, 239
copy URL · 330
create a file in a library · 192
Create a flow · 441
create a list from an existing list · 171
create a list from Excel · 170
create a new Office file · 193
Create a powerapp · 384
create app · 118
Create column · 124
Create column button · 126
Create Column page · 124
create content type · 458
create example data in Access · 486
create example data in Excel · 486
create flow from blank · 441
create new item · 174
create new sites and apps within OneDrive · 229
Create new view · 141, 144
create page · 240
create rule · 432
create Security group · 278
Create shared library · 97, 223
create site · 94, 98, 104
create site column · 129
create site from hub · 104
create subsite · 106
Create View · 142, 146
create wiki page · 240
Current navigation · 211
custom app · 121
custom file template · 461
custom permission level · 281
custom SharePoint group · 283
custom value · 444
customize a powerapp · 385
Customize forms · 380
customize wiki page · 262

D

Data bars · 136
Data Entry content type · 472
Data Entry view · 420
Data sources tab · 34
Date and Time column · 131
DateTimePicker · 131
declare record · 161
default app experience · 115
default app view · 141
default apps · 95
default column type · 124
default column value · 315
default file name · 193
default sharing permission · 299
default site permission · 274
Defender center · 42
delete app · 155
Delete button · 153
delete column · 153
delete item version · 157
delete link · 218
delete list column · 154
delete multiple items · 152
delete one item · 152
delete site · 108
delete site column · 154
delete view · 154
Deleted sites · 66
Delve · 32
DesignScreen · 384
disable creation of modern sites · 60
disable default permissions · 59
disable modern pages · 242
disable Spaces · 259
disable subsite creation · 108
Divider web part · 249
document libraries, why? · 186
Document library web part · 250, 356
document open behavior · 198
Document Set content type · 468
drag files to SharePoint · 196
dynamic content, flow · 444
dynamic content, workflow · 448
Dynamic filtering · 354

E

E3 · 23
edit app form · 140
edit button · 419
edit classic web part · 265
Edit Column page · 135
Edit columns · 140
Edit current view · 142
Edit Event · 183
Edit fields · 383
edit hub navigation · 217
edit links · 218
edit list column · 135
edit modern page · 244
edit multiple items · 404
edit navigation · 214
Edit New menu · 205
edit page approval · 439
edit page properties · 327
edit permissions · 298
edit Renditions · 484
edit site column · 138
edit site name · 68
Edit Source · 263
edit view · 143
Edit View page · 143
edit web part page · 265
Edit web part pane · 266
edit wiki page · 261
Edit Workflow button · 448
EditScreen · 384
Embed Code · 271
Embed Code button · 474
embed file · 271
Embed Information · 190
Embed My Tasks/Issues · 422
Embed web part · 271, 355, 356, 358
enable targeting · 311
enable the append feature · 180
enhance SharePoint List created from Excel export · 399
enhanced rich text · 178, 334
Enterprise Keywords · 318
Enterprise Keywords column · 323
Events app · 95
Events web part · 250
Excel survey · 370
Excel Web Access web part · 400, 426
Expand content · 219
expanded search · 53

export Excel table to SharePoint · 398
export Excel table to SharePoint via Access · 405
export flow · 445
Export to CSV · 396
Export to Excel · 396
expression · 497
external guest · 292, 307
external sharing · 69, 306
external sharing settings · 288

F

file editing by multiple users · 199
File plan · 43
file tile · 189
File viewer web part · 249, 269, 270, 355, 356, 400, 426
Files On-Demand · 227
filter multiple columns · 133
filter query · 497
find managed properties · 328
flow Activity page · 443
flow and workflow storage · 431
Flow checker · 443
Flow Editor · 440
Flows versus Workflows · 431
focus mode · 219
Focus on content · 219
folder · 111, 313
folksonomy · 323
follow site · 95, 222
footer · 77, 80
form · 113
Form library · 95
Form settings · 367
Form Web Parts · 361
format column · 136
Format current view · 142
Format dates · 136
format text in wiki page · 262
Forms Admin Settings · 368
Forms for Excel · 363
Forms survey · 193
From blank · 174
From Excel · 170
From existing list · 171
From template · 171
funnel icon · 133

G

Gallery view · 144, 145
Gantt view · 147
Get a link · 303
Get Started tiles · 87
Get started web part · 264
Global administrator · 25, 40
Global navigation · 87, 93, 213
Global reader · 40
global search · 54
Grid · 122
group resources · 84
Group Team site · 84
Group Team site with full Web Designer Galleries · 89
grouped view · 148
guest access · 307

H

Heading 1 text · 255
helpdesk list · 419
Hero web part · 251
hide folder option · 202
hide link · 218
hide navigation · 219
hide page comments · 246
hide powerapp field · 386
Highlighted content web part · 252, 272, 327, 332, 422, 471, 494
Home site · 93
Home site navigation · 93
homepage · 65
hotspot image · 352
HTML map · 352
hub association · 105
Hub button · 102
hub family · 101
hub navigation · 103, 213
hub permission setting · 105
hub site · 101
hub site navigation · 214
hyperlink · 330
Hyperlink column · 334
Hyperlink or Picture column · 334

I

Image gallery web part · 348
image map · 352
image renditions · 482
Image Viewer web part · 351
Image web part · 249, 335, 347
import calendar to SharePoint · 394
import flow · 445
import multiple users · 38
import SQL data to SharePoint · 411
In Place Records Management · 162
include metadata in document · 467
Information pane · 67, 115
inherit links · 213
inheritance · 274
Inside look · 190
install SharePoint Designer · 207
Integrate · 166
internal name · 55, 158
Issue tracker list · 181, 417
Issue Tracking list · 181, 417
item · 112
item limit · 113
item link · 330
Items with sync issues · 173

K

Keywords term set · 323

L

Label · 216
labels · 43
landing page · 425
Language settings · 80
library folders · 201
Library Record Declaration Settings · 163
library settings · 116
library specific commands · 187
library synchronization · 225
Library web part · 354
likes rating · 317
link expiration date · 300
link headings · 219
link image · 335, 336
link item · 192

link password · 300
linked table · 403
LinkedIn sharing · 47
Links app · 341
links hierarchy · 218
links in wiki pages · 333
Links web part · 331
list apps · 165
list column · 124, 126
list columns with content type · **457**
list content type · 457
List properties web part · 355, 356
list settings · 116
list templates · 171
List Templates gallery · 159
List web part · 250, 342, 354, 356, 422, 494
list workflow · 447
Lists desktop app · 172
local search · 54
local Term group · 322
Locally available · 228
Location list column · 127
Location menu · 248
Look and Feel · 214
lookup · 448
Lookup column · 132

M

make app view default · 148
make field read only · 384
make homepage · 239
Manage access · 297
manage members · 295
manage Microsoft 365 Group · 296
Manage roles · 41
Manage site features · 75
Managed Metadata · 318, 325
Managed Navigation · 478
Managed Properties · 328
mandatory field · 314
manual records declaration · 163
manual sync · 226
mega menu · 77, 479
metadata · 112, 123
Microsoft 365 · 22
Microsoft 365 Admin center · 33
Microsoft 365 Group · 84
Microsoft Lists · 167

Microsoft Search · 52
Microsoft Teams · 86
Migration · 60
modern and classic app experience · 52
modern and classic sites · 51
modern compatibility, classic team sites · 88
modern experience · 51
modern interface · 51
modern link web parts · 331
modern list experience · 165
modern page · 241
modern page command bar · 76
modern page sections · 246
modern picture options · 349
modern Team site · 84
modern Team site without a group · 86
modern Team site without a Microsoft 365 group · 99
modern web parts · 249
modify form fields · 383
Modify this View · 142
Modify View · 143
More features · 60
move documents to folder · 201
Move to · 189
multi-line column · 177
Multiple lines of text · 177, 334
My apps · 119
My feed · 253
My files · 223
My Issues · 421
My lists · 168
My Office profile · 31
My profile · 32
My Tasks · 421
My Tasks/Issues · 423

N

Name column · 186, 191
navigation · 211
navigation hierarchy · 218
navigation in edit mode · 215
new calendar events · 183
New Document · 192
New Event · 183
new experience · 51
new folder · 201
New Heading · 218

new list item · 174
New Navigation Link · 218
new subsite · 107
News link · 259
News posts · 258
News site · 94
News web part · 257, 327
Notebook · 91

O

Office 365 · 22
Office Online editions · 199
office.com homepage · 27
OneDrive for Business · 222
OneDrive settings · 228, 232
OneDrive usage · 232
OneNote · 91
Online-only · 228
open a file/folder · 188
open behavior · 198
open Office file · 188
open SharePoint app in Access · 402
open site in SharePoint Designer · 208
Org settings tab · 34
Organization chart web part · 253
Organization profile tab · 35
Oslo theme · 75
Other options · 99
Outlook Folders view · 393

P

Page details · 235, 255, 327
Page diagnostics · 268
page properties · 235
Page properties web part · 326
page templates · 242
page URL · 234
pages instead of documents · 272
paste CSS or JavaScript code · 474
permission levels · 275, 281
permission sync with associated sites · 104
Permissions pane · 295
Permissions tab · 69
personal view · 141
Picture library · 346, 356
Picture library Slideshow web part · 350

Pin a thumbnail · 188
Pivot table · 397
PivotChart · 397
plan · 85
Planner · 85
Policies · 42
Policies tab · 69
portal · 79
Post as News on this site · 305
Power Apps · 114, 376
Power Apps Admin center · 390
Power Apps button · 377
Power Apps Mobile · 390
Power Apps Studio · 377
Power Automate site · 440
Power BI · 166
powerapp · 376
powerapp layout · 385
powerapp owner · 389
powerapp text color · 387
private site · 97
profile picture · 31
Promote · 305
promote page · 256
promoted links · 342
Promoted Links app · 343
promoted links images · 344
propagate powerapp changes · 390
Properties · 112, 189, 302
public site · 97
public view · 141
Publish · 244
publish content type · **463**
publish label · 45
publish powerapp · 379
Publishing pages · 482

Q

questionnaires · 363
Quick Access · 223
quick actions pane · 114
Quick Edit · 122
Quick launch · 211
Quick links web part · 331, 337
Quotation content type · 456

R

rating · 316
reach powerapps · 389
Recent lists · 168
recurring tasks · 407
Recycle bin · 70
Refresh All · 396
refresh Excel chart on SharePoint page · 427
regional settings · 30
register as hub site · 101, 102
Release options · 35
reminder flow · 433
remove default content type · 466
remove Enterprise Keywords column · 324
rename a column · 137
rename file or folder · 189, 197
replace the Home icon · 94
Republish · 244
request sign-off · 435
require check out · 237
required column values · 314
resolve conflict · 173
restore a root site · 109
restore a subsite · 109
restore content · 155
restore earlier versions · 155
Restore file version · 157
restore item version · 157
restore OneDrive · 230
restrict external sharing for site · 69
retention label · 44
retention stage · 462
review alert flow · 497
revoke guest user access · 288
revoke link · 303
ribbon · 87
rich text in multi-line fields · 178
root site · 65
Root site · 92
RSS Viewer web part · 475

S

save app as template · 159
save file to SharePoint · 195
save for later · 222
save page as a template · 243
save site as template · 88
save wiki page · 264
Schedule site launch · 81
scheduled flow · 496
scheduled publishing · 238
scheduling tool · 81
Schema · 328
Script Editor web part · 474
Search & intelligence · 34
search crawler · 52, 112
search index · 52, 112
search verticals · 53
Seattle theme · 75
second-stage recycle bin · 70, 155
Security center · 42
Security group · 81, 277
see Version history · 155
select a label · 160
select multiple files · 194
selective sync · 230
send link · 302
set default app view · 142
Set Titles flow · 450
Set Titles workflow · 453
Setup tab · 41
share a site · 289
Share button · 290, 298
share Excel survey · 371
share information · 54
share OneDrive files · 224
share powerapp · 388
Share site button · 292
Shared with · 291, 300
SharePoint Admin center · 57
SharePoint Admin center experiences · 57
SharePoint Admin center left menu · 58
SharePoint Apps · 50
SharePoint automation · 430
SharePoint Designer · 207, 447
SharePoint Designer summary page · 209
SharePoint Designer, create list · 209
SharePoint Designer, import files or folders · 209
SharePoint group · 275
SharePoint hierarchy · 49
SharePoint Online start page · 95, 221
SharePoint permissions · 274
SharePoint Search · 52
SharePoint Server Publishing · 479
SharePoint Server Publishing Infrastructure · 477
Sharing column · 224

sharing policies · 287
short link · 296
shortcut · 330
show app in Site navigation · 120
show Excel data in web part · 400
sign in · 25
Sign-off status · 436
Single sign-on · 27
site · 64, 65
Site Admin · 76, 275
Site Assets" library · 248
site collection · 65
Site Collection Administration · 75
Site collection features · 75
site column · 124, 128
site content type · 456
Site content types · 466
Site contents · 69
site details · 71
Site information · 73
Site information link · 73
site Information pane · 67
site link · 330
Site Member · 76, 275
Site navigation · 64, 211
Site Owner · 76, 275
Site Pages library · 235
Site permissions · 291
site settings · 49
Site settings link · 72
Site settings page · 73
site statistics · 70
site template · 78
site types · 64
Site usage · 75
Site Visitor · 76, 275
SitePages folder · 248
Sites web part · 332
Snap to columns · 383
sort column · 134
Space page · 259
Spacer web part · 254
Standard view mode · 121, 123
star rating · 317
stop following site · 222
Stop inheriting · 213
stop page approvals · 439
stop site sharing · 283
Structural Navigation · 478
Styles library · 95, 262
sub link · 218
subscription plans · 23

subsite · 106
subsite link in the parent site · 212
Subsites tab · 71
Survey app · 373
Survey app Settings · 375
survey options · 363
switch app interface · 115
switch to original form · 380
sync issues · 227
sync settings · 227
synchronize with desktop Outlook · 392

T

tag Managed Metadata · 326
tagging · 318
Targeted release · 36
Tasks and Issues alerts · 181
Tasks list · 180, 417
Taxonomy · 319
team calendar · 182
Team Collaboration Lists · 121
template · 78, 205
tenant · 23
tenant name · 24
tenant Root site · 92
term set · 320
Term store · 318
term store group · 319
Term store settings · 320
test flow · 443
Text web part · 254
timeline · 180
Title · 175, 191, 200
title area · 245
Top link bar · 87, 213
Totals · 149
Track view · 66
translate pages and news · 80
trial account · 25
trigger · 431
try powerapp · 379
turned off page creation · 241

U

unique subsite permissions · 107, 285
unregister as hub site · 102

Upload button · 194
upload file template · 205
upload files · 194
use existing list as template · 158
use powerapp · 390
user management · 36
user templates · 37
UserInfo list · 403

V

values · 112
VBS script that updates Excel chart on SharePoint page · 427
Version history · 155, 238
Verticals · 34
view · 140
View account · 31
view list item · 175
View selector · 66, 141, 142
View Type page · 146
Views landing page · 336
Views landing page with chart · 426
Views landing page with tasks · 425
views, Active sites · 66

W

waves · 81

web browser · 22
Web Designer Galleries · 89
web part · 239
web part page · 264
why automate · 430
wiki link display text · 340
wiki link page creation · 338
wiki link syntax · 338
wiki link to app · 339
wiki link to item · 340
wiki link to view · 339
wiki links · 338
wiki page · 261
wiki page image display · 350
wiki page image options · 349
wiki page link options · 333
Work progress tracker · 181
Workflow Settings · 448
workflow that switches content type · 473
Workflows page · 449

Y

Yammer · 305
Your Apps · 120
YouTube videos · 356

Printed in Great Britain
by Amazon

87038236R00289